Rick Steves'

ENGLAND

2010

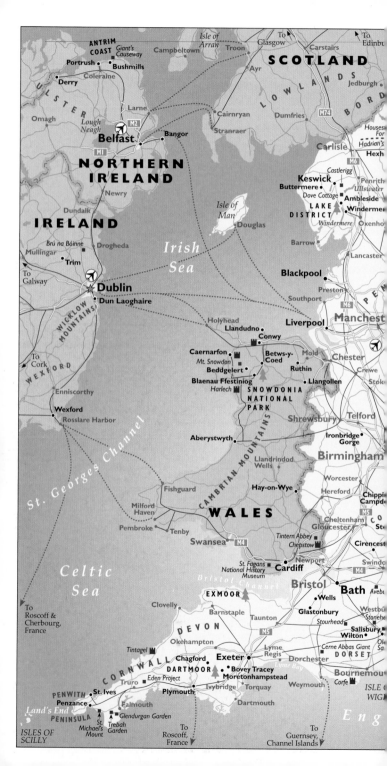

Berwick-upon-Tweed
Holy Island
Bamburgh Castle
Alnwick
Newcastle-upon-Tyne
amish useum
Durham
Middlesbrough
Staithes
Grosmont
Whitby
Robin Hood's Bay
YORK-SHIRE DALES
NORTH YORK MOORS
Rievaulx Abbey
Goathland
Thirsk
Hutton-le-Hole
Pickering
ES
Castle Howard
Eden Camp
Scarborough
York
Bridlington
eeds
Doncaster
Kingston-upon-Hull
Sheffield
M1
Grimsby
North Sea
MIDLANDS
Lincoln
Newark
Skegness
erby
Nottingham
Boston
The Wash
ENGLAND
Cromer
eicester
Stamford
Peter-borough
King's Lynn
Norwich
To Esbjerg, Denmark
Coventry
Warwick
Northampton
Ely
Cambridge
E A S T
Great Yarmouth
tratford
O L D S
Moreton
M1
Luton
Stansted
A N G L I A
Ipswich
To Amsterdam, Netherlands
enheim lace
M40
Oxford
Hertford
M11
Harwich
Colchester
To Hoek van Holland, Netherlands
Didcot
Reading
Windsor
Heathrow
London
City
Greenwich
Southend-on-Sea
M3
Winchester
Gatwick
Southampton
Portsmouth
Arundel
ewport
Fishbourne Roman Palace
Newhaven
M23
M20
M2
Whitstable
Ramsgate
K E N T
Canterbury
Ashford
White Cliffs of Dover
Dover
Folkestone
Sissinghurst Gardens
Rye
Battle
Hastings
Brighton
Pevensey
Alfriston
Eastbourne
Beachy Head
Ostende
Bruges
Dunkerque
Calais
Channel Tunnel
Boulogne
BELGIUM
E40
E17
FRANCE
Lille
E42
s h   *Channel*
To Cherbourg, France
To Ouistreham, France
To Dieppe, France
A16
To Paris
A26
To Paris
To Brussels

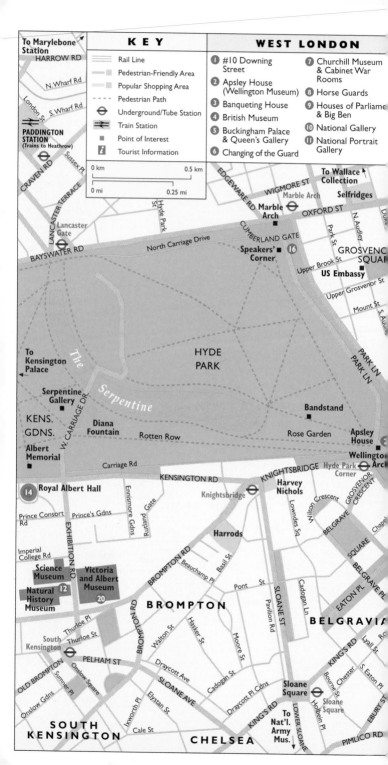

KEY

≡≡≡	Rail Line
▨	Pedestrian-Friendly Area
▨	Popular Shopping Area
- - - -	Pedestrian Path
⊖	Underground/Tube Station
⇄	Train Station
■	Point of Interest
i	Tourist Information

0 km ————— 0.5 km
0 mi ————— 0.25 mi

WEST LONDON

1. #10 Downing Street
2. Apsley House (Wellington Museum)
3. Banqueting House
4. British Museum
5. Buckingham Palace & Queen's Gallery
6. Changing of the Guard
7. Churchill Museum & Cabinet War Rooms
8. Horse Guards
9. Houses of Parliament & Big Ben
10. National Gallery
11. National Portrait Gallery

To Marylebone Station

HARROW RD
N. Wharf Rd
London St.
S. Wharf Rd
PADDINGTON STATION
(Trains to Heathrow)
CRAVEN RD
Sussex Pl.
Lancaster Terrace
Lancaster Gate
BAYSWATER RD
Sussex St.
Hyde Park St.

EDGEWARE RD
WIGMORE ST
Marble Arch
Marble Arch ⊖
OXFORD ST
To Wallace Collection
Selfridges
N. Audley St.
Dunc
Park St.
CUMBERLAND GATE
North Carriage Drive
Speakers' Corner ■ 16
Upper Brook St.
GROSVENC SQUAR
US Embassy
Upper Grosvenor St.
Mount St.
S. Au

To Kensington Palace

The Serpentine

HYDE PARK

PARK LN
PARK LN

Serpentine Gallery ■
KENS. GDNS.
Diana Fountain ■
W. CARRIAGE DR.
Rotten Row
Bandstand ■
Rose Garden
Apsley House ■
Wellington Arch ⊖

Albert Memorial ■
Carriage Rd
KENSINGTON RD
KNIGHTSBRIDGE
Hyde Park ⊖ Corner

14 **Royal Albert Hall**
Prince Consort Rd
Prince's Gdns
EXHIBITION RD
Rutland Gate
Ennismore Gdns
Knightsbridge ⊖
Harvey Nichols
Wilton Crescent
Lowndes Sq.
GROSVENOR CRESCENT
BELGRAVE CRESCENT
Chapel

Imperial College Rd
Science Museum 12
Natural History Museum
Victoria and Albert Museum 20
BROMPTON RD
Beauchamp Pl.
Basil St.
Harrods
Pont St.
BROMPTON
Walton St.
Hasker St.
Moore St.
Cadogan Ln.
SLOANE ST
SQUARE
Pavilion Rd
EATON PL
BELGRAVE PL
BELGRAVIA

Thurloe Pl.
South Kensington ⊖
Thurloe St.
PELHAM ST
Onslow Square
Draycott Ave
SLOANE AVE
Cadogan St.
Draycott Pl Cdns
KING'S RD
Lyall St.
S. Eaton Pl
Chester
Bourne St.
EBURY ST

OLD BROMPTON
Sumner Pl.
Onslow Gdns
Ixworth Pl.
Elysan St.
Cale St
Ilsworth Pl.
SOUTH KENSINGTON
CHELSEA
Sloane Square ⊖
Sloane Square
Holbein Pl
To Nat'l. Army Mus.
LOWER SLOANE
Chester
Holbein Pl
PIMLICO RD

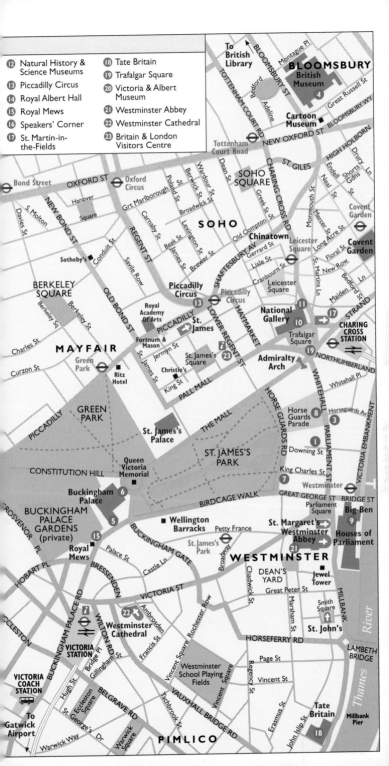

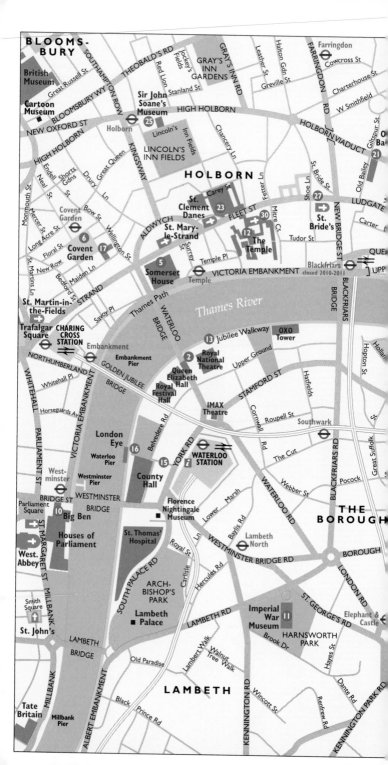

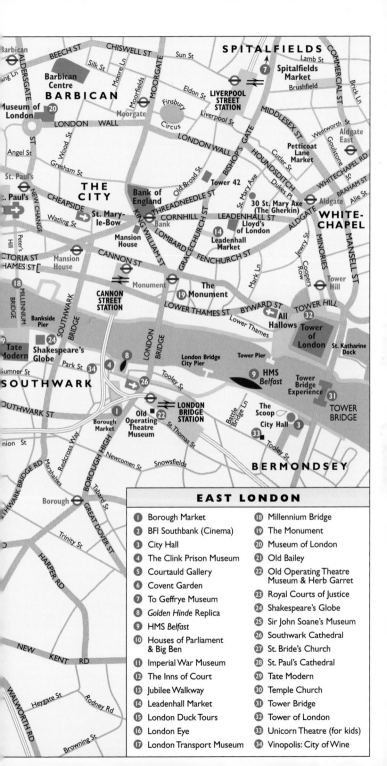

EAST LONDON

1. Borough Market
2. BFI Southbank (Cinema)
3. City Hall
4. The Clink Prison Museum
5. Courtauld Gallery
6. Covent Garden
7. To Geffrye Museum
8. *Golden Hinde* Replica
9. HMS *Belfast*
10. Houses of Parliament & Big Ben
11. Imperial War Museum
12. The Inns of Court
13. Jubilee Walkway
14. Leadenhall Market
15. London Duck Tours
16. London Eye
17. London Transport Museum
18. Millennium Bridge
19. The Monument
20. Museum of London
21. Old Bailey
22. Old Operating Theatre Museum & Herb Garret
23. Royal Courts of Justice
24. Shakespeare's Globe
25. Sir John Soane's Museum
26. Southwark Cathedral
27. St. Bride's Church
28. St. Paul's Cathedral
29. Tate Modern
30. Temple Church
31. Tower Bridge
32. Tower of London
33. Unicorn Theatre (for kids)
34. Vinopolis: City of Wine

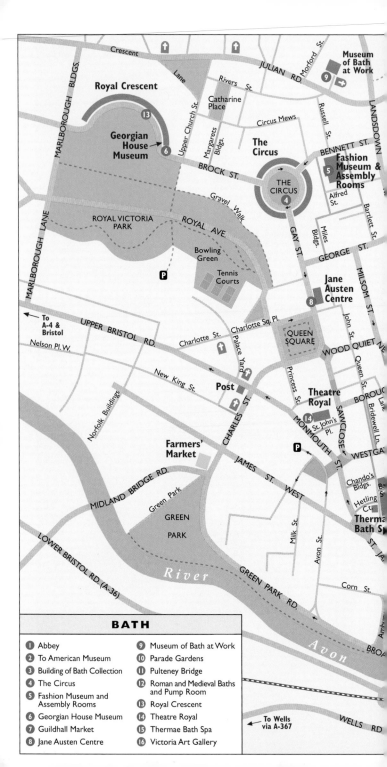

BATH

- ❶ Abbey
- ❷ To American Museum
- ❸ Building of Bath Collection
- ❹ The Circus
- ❺ Fashion Museum and Assembly Rooms
- ❻ Georgian House Museum
- ❼ Guildhall Market
- ❽ Jane Austen Centre
- ❾ Museum of Bath at Work
- ❿ Parade Gardens
- ⓫ Pulteney Bridge
- ⓬ Roman and Medieval Baths and Pump Room
- ⓭ Royal Crescent
- ⓮ Theatre Royal
- ⓯ Thermae Bath Spa
- ⓰ Victoria Art Gallery

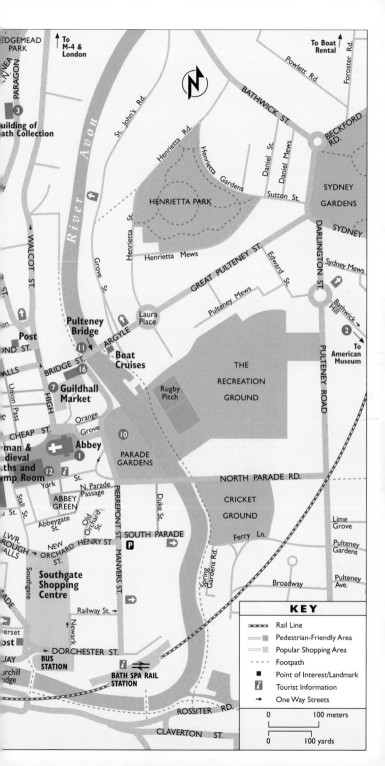

Rick Steves'

ENGLAND

AVALON
TRAVEL

CONTENTS

British History and Culture   578

Top Destinations in England

INTRODUCTION

From the grandeur and bustle of London, to a pastoral country-side that inspired Shakespeare, to some of the quaintest towns you'll ever experience, England delights. Stand in a desolate field and ponder an ancient stone circle. Strike up a conversation just to hear the Queen's English. Bite into a scone smothered with clotted cream, sip a cup of tea, and wave your pinky as if it's a Union Jack.

This book breaks England into its top big-city, small-town, and rural destinations. It gives you all the information and opinions necessary to wring the maximum value out of your limited time and money in each of these locations.

Note that this book covers only England, which occupies the southern two-thirds of the island of Great Britain. If you want to visit Wales and Scotland too, pick up a copy of *Rick Steves' Great Britain* instead.

Experiencing English culture, people, and natural wonders economically and hassle-free has been my goal for three decades of traveling, tour guiding, and travel writing. With this new edition, I pass on to you the lessons I've learned, updated for your trip in 2010.

While including the predictable biggies (such as Big Ben, Stratford-upon-Avon, and Stonehenge), the book also mixes in a healthy dose of Back Door intimacy (windswept Roman lookouts, angelic boys' choirs, and nearly edible Cotswold villages). I've been selective. For example, there are plenty of great countryside palaces; I recommend just the best—Blenheim.

The best is, of course, only my opinion. But after spending half my adult life researching Europe, I've developed a sixth sense for what travelers enjoy. The places featured in this book will knock your spots off.

INTRODUCTION

About This Book

Rick Steves' England 2010 is a personal tour guide in your pocket. The book is organized by destinations, each one a mini-vacation on its own—filled with exciting sights, strollable neighborhoods, homey and affordable places to stay, and memorable places to eat. I update this book every year in person, but even with annual updates, things change. For the latest, visit www.ricksteves.com /update, and for reports and experiences—good and bad—from fellow travelers, check www.ricksteves.com/feedback.

In the following chapters, you'll find these sections:

Planning Your Time suggests a schedule with thoughts on how best to use your limited time.

Orientation includes specifics on public transportation, helpful hints, local tour options, easy-to-read maps, and tourist information (abbreviated **TI** in this book).

Sights, described in detail, are rated:

▲▲▲—Don't miss.

▲▲—Try hard to see.

▲—Worthwhile if you can make it.

No rating—Worth knowing about.

Self-Guided Walks take you through interesting neighborhoods, with a personal tour guide in hand.

Sleeping describes my favorite hotels, from good-value deals to cushy splurges.

Eating serves up a range of options, from inexpensive pubs to fancy restaurants.

Connections outlines your options for traveling to destinations by train, bus, and plane. In car-friendly regions, I've included route tips for drivers.

British History and Culture is a quick overview of Britain, past and present.

The **appendix** is a traveler's tool kit, with telephone tips, useful phone numbers, transportation basics (on trains, buses, car rentals, driving, and flights), recommended books and films, a festival list, climate chart, handy packing checklist, a hotel reservation form, and a fun British–Yankee dictionary.

Browse through this book and select your favorite sights. Then have a brilliant trip! Traveling like a temporary local, you'll get the absolute most out of every mile, minute, and dollar. I'm happy that you'll be visiting places I know and love, and meeting my favorite English people.

Major Holidays and Weekends

Popular places are even busier on weekends, especially sunny weekends, which are sufficient cause for an impromptu holiday in this soggy corner of Europe. Three-day weekends can make towns, trains, buses, roads, and hotels even more crowded. Book your accommodations well in advance for these times.

A few national holidays jam things up, especially Bank Holiday Mondays. Mark these dates in red on your travel calendar: New Year's Day, Good Friday through Easter Monday (April 2–5 in 2010), the Bank Holidays that occur on the first and last Mondays in May (May 3 and 31 in 2010) and the last Monday in August (Aug 30), Christmas, and December 26 (Boxing Day). For more information, see "Holidays and Festivals" in the appendix.

Many businesses, as well as many museums, close on Good Friday, Easter, and New Year's Day. On Christmas, virtually everything closes down, even the Tube in London (taxi rates are high). Museums are also generally closed December 24 and 26; smaller shops are usually closed December 26.

Planning

This section will help you get started on planning your trip—with advice on trip costs, when to go, and what you should know before you take off.

Travel Smart

Your trip to England is like a complex play—easier to follow and to really appreciate on a second viewing. While no one does the same trip twice to gain that advantage, reading this book in its entirety before your trip accomplishes much the same thing.

Design an itinerary that enables you to visit sights at the best possible times. Note the holidays, festivals, colorful market days, and days when sights are closed. Sundays have the same pros and cons as they do for travelers in the US (special events, limited hours, banks and many shops closed, limited public transportation, no rush hours). Saturdays are virtually weekdays with earlier closing hours and no rush hour (though transportation connections outside London can be less frequent than on weekdays). Sights normally closed on Monday are often open on Bank Holiday Mondays.

Be sure to mix intense and relaxed periods in your itinerary. To maximize rootedness, minimize one-night stands. It's worth a long drive after dinner to be settled into a town for two nights. B&Bs are also more likely to give a better price to someone staying more than one night.

England at a Glance

▲▲▲**London** Thriving metropolis packed with world-class museums, monuments, churches, parks, palaces, theaters, pubs, Beefeaters, telephone boxes, double-decker buses, and all things British.

▲▲**Greenwich, Windsor, and Cambridge** Easy side-trips from London: Famous observatory at the maritime center of Greenwich, the Queen's palace at Windsor, and England's best university town, Cambridge.

▲**Canterbury** Pleasant pilgrimage town with England's top church.

▲**Dover and Southeast England** The imposing Dover Castle, famous White Cliffs, lush Sissinghurst Gardens, hill town of Rye, and historic site of the Battle of Hastings.

▲**Brighton** Flamboyant beach resort on England's south coast, near the rolling hills of South Downs Way and the chalky cliffs at Beachy Head.

▲**Portsmouth** Newly rejuvenated shipbuilding city with top nautical sights at the Historic Dockyard, plus Roman ruins and stately Arundel Castle nearby.

▲**Dartmoor** Mysterious, desolate, moor-cloaked national park with wild ponies, hiking paths, and an ancient stone circle.

▲**Cornwall** Feisty peninsula littered with prehistoric ruins, plus the seaside resort towns of Penzance and St. Ives, King Arthur's supposed Tintagel Castle, the tip of England at Land's End, and other offbeat sights.

▲▲▲**Bath** Genteel Georgian showcase city, built around the remains of an ancient Roman bath.

▲▲**Near Bath** England's mysterious heart, including the prehistoric-meets–New Age hill at Glastonbury, spine-tingling stone circles at Stonehenge and Avebury, enjoyable cathedral towns of Wells and Salisbury, and delightful Dorset countryside.

▲**Oxford** Stately university town with Blenheim Palace—one of England's best—on its doorstep.

▲▲**The Cotswolds** Remarkably quaint villages—including the cozy market town Chipping Campden, popular hamlet Stow-on-the-Wold, and handy transit hub Moreton-in-Marsh—scattered over a hilly countryside.

▲**Stratford-upon-Avon** Shakespeare's hometown and top venue for seeing his plays performed, plus the medieval Warwick Castle and Coventry's inspiring cathedral.

▲**Ironbridge Gorge** Birthplace of the Industrial Revolution, with sights and museums that tell the earth-changing story.

▲**Blackpool and Liverpool** England's tackiest, most fun-loving beach resort at Blackpool, and the increasingly rejuvenated port city (and Beatles hometown) of Liverpool.

▲▲**The Lake District** Idyllic lakes-and-hills landscape, with enjoyable hikes and joyrides, time-passed valleys, William Wordsworth and Beatrix Potter sights, and the charming home-base town of Keswick.

▲▲▲**York** Walled medieval town with grand Gothic cathedral, excellent museums (Viking, Victorian, Railway), and atmospheric old center.

▲**North Yorkshire** Smattering of ruined abbeys, desolate moors, seaside towns (including bustling Whitby and tiny Staithes), and other sights near York.

▲**Durham and Northeast England** Youthful working-class town with magnificent cathedral, plus nearby: an open-air museum, the Roman remains of Hadrian's Wall, Holy Island, and Bamburgh Castle.

INTRODUCTION

Every trip (and every traveler) needs at least a few slack days (for picnics, laundry, people-watching, and so on). Pace yourself. Assume you will return.

Reread this book as you travel, and visit local TIs. Upon arrival in a new town, lay the groundwork for a smooth departure; write down (or print out from an online source) the schedule for the train or bus that you'll take when you depart. Drivers can study the best driving route to their next destination.

While traveling, take advantage of the Internet and phones to make your trip run smoothly. By going online (at Internet cafés or your hotel) and making phone calls, you can get tourist information, learn the latest on sights (special events, tour schedules, etc.), book tickets and tours, make reservations, reconfirm hotels, research transportation connections, and keep in touch with loved ones.

Connect with the culture. Set up your own quest for the best pub, cathedral, or chocolate bar. Enjoy the friendliness of your English hosts. Slow down and be open to unexpected experiences. You speak the language—use it! Ask questions—most locals are eager to point you in their idea of the right direction. Keep a notepad in your pocket for organizing your thoughts. Wear your money belt, and learn the local currency and how to estimate prices in dollars. Those who expect to travel smart, do.

Trip Costs

Five components make up your trip costs: airfare, surface transportation, room and board, sightseeing and entertainment, and shopping and miscellany.

Airfare: A basic round-trip US-to-London flight costs $600–1,200, depending on where you fly from and when (cheaper in winter). If your trip extends beyond England, consider saving time and money by flying "open jaw" (into one city and out of another; for instance, into London and out of Amsterdam).

Surface Transportation: For a three-week whirlwind trip of all my recommended English destinations, allow $550 per person for public transportation (train pass, key buses, and Tube fare in London) or $750 per person for car rental (based on two people sharing a three-week rental), including parking, gas, and insurance. Leasing is worth considering for trips of two and a half weeks or more. Car rental and leases are cheapest when arranged from the US. Train passes are normally available only outside of Europe (although you can buy a bus pass in England). You may save money by simply buying tickets as you go (see "Transportation" in the appendix).

Room and Board: You can thrive in England on $115 per day per person for room and board (less in villages). A $115-per-day budget allows an average of $15 for lunch, $30 for dinner, $5 for snacks, and $65 for lodging (based on two people splitting a $130 double room that includes breakfast). Students and tightwads can do it on $60 ($35 for hostel bed, $25 for groceries).

Sightseeing and Entertainment: Figure on paying roughly $10–30 apiece for the major sights that charge admission (Stonehenge-$11, Shakespeare's Birthplace in Stratford-$19, Westminster Abbey-$19, Tower of London-$27), $7 for minor ones (climbing church towers), $12 for guided walks, and $20 for bus tours and splurge experiences. For information on various sightseeing passes, see page 19.

Fortunately, many of the best sights in London are free, including the British Museum, National Gallery, National Portrait Gallery, Tate Britain, Tate Modern, Victoria & Albert Museum, and the British Library (though most request donations). An overall average of $30 a day works in most cities (allow $50 for London). Don't skimp here. After all, this category is the driving force behind your trip—you came to sightsee, enjoy, and experience England.

Shopping and Miscellany: Figure roughly $2 per postcard, $3 for tea or an ice-cream cone, and $6 per pint of beer. Shopping can vary in cost from nearly nothing to a small fortune. Good budget travelers find that this category has little to do with assembling a trip full of lifelong and wonderful memories.

Sightseeing Priorities
Depending on the length of your trip, and taking geographic proximity into account, the following are my recommended priorities.

3 days:	London
5 days, add:	Bath and nearby sights (take a minibus tour or choose among Stonehenge, Avebury, Wells, Glastonbury, and Salisbury)
7 days, add:	Cotswolds
9 days, add:	York
11 days, add:	Lake District
14 days, add:	Durham, Stratford, Warwick
17 days, add:	Ironbridge Gorge, Blackpool
21 days, add:	Cornwall, Dartmoor
24 days, add:	Choose two of the following—Cambridge, Oxford, Portsmouth, Brighton, Canterbury, and Dover

This list includes virtually everything on "England's Best Three-Week Trip by Car" itinerary and map on pages 8 and 9.

Your itinerary will depend on your interests. Nature-lovers will likely put the lovely Lake District and the more remote Dartmoor nearer the top of their list, while engineers are drawn

England's Best Three-Week Trip by Car

Day	Plan	Sleep in
1	Arrive in London, bus to Bath	Bath
2	Bath	Bath
3	Pick up car, Avebury, Wells, Glastonbury	Bath
4	Early drive to Cornwall	Penzance
5	Cornwall	Penzance
6	Dartmoor	Salisbury
7	Salisbury, Portsmouth	Salisbury
8	Oxford, Blenheim	Chipping Campden
9	Explore the Cotswolds	Chipping Campden
10	Stratford, Warwick, Coventry	Ironbridge Gorge
11	Ironbridge Gorge	Blackpool
12	Liverpool, Blackpool	Blackpool
13	South Lake District	Keswick area
14	North Lake District	Keswick area
15	Hadrian's Wall and Durham, to York, turn in car	York
16	York	York
17	Early train to London	London
18	London	London
19	London	London
20	Canterbury, Dover	London
21	Brighton, Greenwich, Windsor, Cambridge (choose one)	London
22	Whew!	

While this three-week itinerary is designed to be done by car, it can be done by train and bus or, better yet, with a BritRail & Drive Pass (best car days: Cornwall/Dartmoor, Cotswolds, and Lake District); for more on the pass, see page 606. For three weeks without a car, I'd cut back on the recommended sights with the most frustrating public transportation (Cornwall, Dartmoor, and

like a magnet to Ironbridge Gorge. Coastal Blackpool offers amusement-park fun, refreshing for families and those who've had enough of museums. Literary fans like Cambridge, Oxford, Stratford, and the South Lake District.

When to Go

In England, July and August are peak season—my favorite time—with very long days, the best weather, and the busiest schedule of tourist fun.

Prices and crowds don't go up during peak times as dramati-

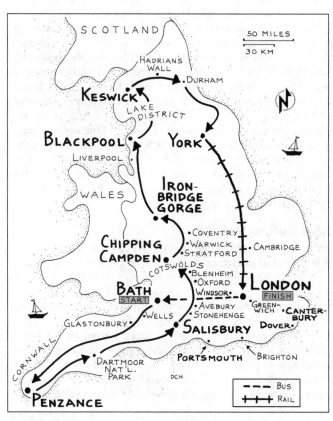

Ironbridge Gorge). Lacing together the cities by train is very slick, and buses get you where the trains don't go. With more time, everything is workable without a car.

cally in England as they do in much of Europe, except for holidays and festivals (see "Major Holidays and Weekends" sidebar, earlier). Still, travel during "shoulder season" (May, early June, Sept, and early Oct) is easier and can be a bit less expensive. Shoulder-season travelers usually enjoy smaller crowds, decent weather, the full range of sights and tourist fun spots, and the ability to grab a room almost whenever and wherever they like—often at a flexible price. Winter travelers find absolutely no crowds and soft room prices, but shorter sightseeing hours and reliably bad weather. Some attractions are open only on weekends or are closed entirely in the winter (Nov–

Feb). The weather can be cold and dreary, and nightfall draws the shades on sightseeing well before dinnertime. While rural charm falls with the leaves, city sightseeing is fine in the winter.

Plan for rain no matter when you go. Just keep traveling and take full advantage of bright spells. The weather can change several times in a day, but rarely is it extreme. As the locals say, "There is no bad weather, only inappropriate clothing." Bring a jacket and dress in layers. Temperatures below 32°F cause headlines, and days that break 80°F—while increasingly frequent in recent years—are still rare in England. July and August are not much better than shoulder months. May and June can be lovely anywhere in England. (For more information, see the climate chart in the appendix.) While sunshine may be rare, summer days are very long. The midsummer sun is up from 6:30 until 22:30. It's not uncommon to have a gray day, eat dinner, and enjoy hours of sunshine afterward.

Know Before You Go

Your trip is more likely to go smoothly if you plan ahead. Check this list of things to arrange while you're still at home.

You need a **passport**—but no visa or shots—to travel in Great Britain. You may be denied entry into certain European countries if your passport is due to expire within three to six months of your ticketed date of return. Get it renewed if you'll be cutting it close. It can take up to six weeks to get or renew a passport (for more on passports, see www.travel.state.gov). Pack a photocopy of your passport in your luggage in case the original is lost or stolen.

Book your rooms well in advance if you'll be traveling during peak season and any major **holidays** (see "Major Holidays and Weekends" sidebar, earlier).

Most people fly into London and remain there for a few days. Instead, consider a gentler **small-town start** in Bath (the ideal jet-lag pillow), and let London be the finale at the end of your trip. You'll be more rested and ready to tackle England's greatest city. Heathrow Airport has direct bus connections to Bath and other cities. (Bristol Airport is also near Bath.)

If you'll be in London or Stratford and want to **see a play,** check theater schedules ahead of time. For simplicity, I book plays while in England, but if there's something you have to see, consider buying tickets before you go. For the current schedule of London plays and musicals, visit www.officiallondontheatre.co.uk or check the American magazine *Variety.* Even though Stratford's major Shakespeare theaters are closed for renovation for much of 2010, the town will host productions by the Bard all year (see www.rsc .org.uk for details). Note that if it's just Shakespeare you're after— with or without Stratford—you can see his plays in London, too.

Where Do I Find Information On...?

Credit Card Theft	See page 15.
Packing Light	See the packing list on page 627.
Phoning	See "Telephones" on page 594.
Language	See page 629.
Making Hotel Reservations	See page 27.
Tipping	See page 15.
Tourist Information Offices	See page 593.
Updates to This Book	See www.ricksteves.com/update.

To attend the free **Ceremony of the Keys** in the Tower of London, write for tickets (see page 98). At **Stonehenge,** anyone can see the stones from behind the rope line, but if you want to go inside the stone circle, you'll need advance reservations.

If you're interested in **travel insurance,** do your homework before you buy. Compare the cost of the insurance to the likelihood of your using it and your potential loss if something goes wrong. For details on the many kinds of travel insurance, see www.ricksteves.com/plan/tips/insurance.htm.

Call your **debit- and credit-card companies** to let them know the countries you'll be visiting, so that they won't deny your international charges. Confirm what your daily withdrawal limit is; consider asking to have it raised so you can take out more cash at each ATM stop. Ask about international transaction fees.

If you'll be **renting a car** in Great Britain, bring your driver's license. Confirm pick-up hours—many car-rental offices close Saturday afternoon and all day Sunday.

If traveling to continental Europe on the **Eurostar** train, consider ordering a ticket in advance (or buy it in Britain); for details, see page 165.

Because **airline carry-on restrictions** are always changing, visit the Transportation Security Administration's website (www.tsa.gov/travelers) for an up-to-date list of what you can bring on the plane with you, and what you have to check. Remember to arrive with plenty of time to get through security. Some airlines may restrict you to only one carry-on (no extras like a purse or daypack); check Britain's website for the latest (www.dft.gov.uk).

Practicalities

Emergency Telephone Numbers: Dial 999 for police or medical emergencies.

Time: In British schedules—and in this book—you'll use the

INTRODUCTION

24-hour clock. It's the same through 12:00 noon, then keep going: 13:00, 14:00, and so on. For anything over 12, subtract 12 and add p.m. (14:00 is 2:00 p.m.).

Britain, which is one hour earlier than most of continental Europe, is five/eight hours ahead of the East/West coasts of the US. The exceptions are the beginning and end of Daylight Saving Time: Britain and Europe "spring forward" the last Sunday in March (two weeks after most of North America), and "fall back" the last Sunday in October (one week before North America). For a handy online time converter, try www.timeanddate.com/worldclock.

Business Hours: In England, most stores are open Monday through Saturday from roughly 10:00 to 17:00. In London, stores stay open later on Wednesday or Thursday (until 19:00 or 20:00), depending on the neighborhood. On Sunday, when some stores are closed, street markets in London are lively with shoppers.

Watt's Up? Britain's electrical system is different from North America's in two ways: the shape of the plug (three square prongs—not the two round prongs used in continental Europe) and the voltage of the current (220 volts instead of 110 volts). For your North American plug to work in Britain, you'll need a three-prong adapter plug, sold inexpensively at travel stores in the US, and in British airports and drugstores. As for the voltage, most newer electronics or travel appliances (such as hair dryers, laptops, and battery chargers) automatically convert the voltage—if you see a range of voltages printed on the item or its plug (such as "110–220"), it'll work in Great Britain and Europe. Otherwise, you can buy a converter separately in the US (about $20).

Discounts: While discounts (called "concessions" or "concs" in Britain) aren't listed in this book, many English sights offer discounts for seniors (loosely defined as those who are retired or willing to call themselves a senior), youths (ages 8–18), students, groups of 10 or more, and families. Always ask. To get a student or teacher ID card, visit www.isic.org or www.statravel.com.

News: British papers cover global events, and Americans can also peruse the *International Herald Tribune* (published almost daily throughout Europe and online at www.iht.com). Other newsy sites are http://news.bbc.co.uk and www.europeantimes.com. Every Tuesday, the European editions of *Time* and *Newsweek* hit the stands with articles of particular interest to travelers in Europe. Sports addicts can get their daily fix online or from *USA Today*. Many hotels have the BBC (of course) and CNN television channels.

Money

This section offers advice on getting cash, using credit and debit cards, dealing with lost or stolen cards, and tipping.

Cash from ATMs

Throughout Britain, cash machines (ATMs) are the standard way for travelers to get local currency. Bring plastic—credit and/or debit cards. It's smart to bring two cards, in case one gets demagnetized or eaten by a temperamental machine. As an emergency backup, bring several hundred dollars in hard cash (in $20 bills rather than hard-to-exchange $100 bills).

Avoid using currency exchange booths (lousy rates and/or outrageous fees); if you have currency to exchange, take it to a bank. Don't use traveler's checks—they're a waste of time (long waits at banks) and a waste of money in fees.

You'll find cash machines all over Britain, always open and providing quick transactions. To withdraw money, you'll need a debit card (ideally with a Visa or MasterCard logo for maximum usability), plus a PIN code. Know your PIN code in numbers; there are only numbers—no letters—on European keypads.

Before you go, verify with your bank that your cards will work overseas, and alert them that you'll be making withdrawals in Europe; otherwise, the bank may not approve transactions if it perceives unusual spending patterns. (Your credit-card company may do the same thing—let them know your travel plans, too.) Also ask about international transaction fees; see "Credit and Debit Cards," below.

When using a cash machine, try to take out large sums of money to reduce your per-transaction bank fees. If the machine refuses your request, try again and select a smaller amount (some cash machines limit the amount you can withdraw—don't take it personally). If that doesn't work, try a different machine.

Even in jolly olde England, you'll need to keep your cash safe. Use a money belt—a pouch with a strap that you buckle around your waist like a belt, and wear under your clothes. Thieves target tourists. A money belt provides peace of mind, allowing you to carry lots of cash safely. Don't waste time every few days tracking down a cash machine—withdraw a week's worth of money, stuff it in your money belt, and travel!

Credit and Debit Cards

Visa and MasterCard are more commonly accepted than American Express. Just like at home, credit and debit cards work easily at larger hotels, restaurants, and shops, but smaller businesses prefer payment in local currency (in small bills—break large bills at a

INTRODUCTION

Exchange Rate

I list prices in pounds (£) throughout this book.

1 British pound (£1) = about $1.60

While the euro (€) is now the currency of most of Europe, Britain is sticking with its pound sterling. The British pound (£), also called a "quid," is broken into 100 pence (p). Pence means "cents." You'll find coins ranging from 1p to £2 and bills from £5 to £50. Fake pound coins are easy to spot (real coins have an inscription on their outside rims; the fakes look like tree bark).

London is so expensive that some travelers try to kid themselves that pounds are dollars. But when they get home, that £1,000-pound Visa bill isn't asking for $1,000...it wants $1,600. (To get the latest rate and print a cheat sheet, see www.oanda.com.)

bank or larger store). If receipts show your credit-card number, don't toss these thoughtlessly.

Fees: Credit and debit cards—whether used for purchases or ATM withdrawals—often charge additional, tacked-on "international transaction" fees of up to 3 percent plus $5 per transaction. Note that if you use a credit card for ATM transactions, it's technically a "cash advance" rather than a "withdrawal"—and subject to an additional cash-advance fee.

To avoid unpleasant surprises, call your bank or credit-card company before your trip to ask about these fees. Ask your bank if it has agreements with any British bank for lower withdrawal fees. If the fees are too high, consider getting a card just for your trip: Capital One (www.capitalone.com) and most credit unions have low to no international transaction fees.

If merchants offer to convert your purchase price into dollars (called dynamic currency conversion, or "DCC"), refuse this "service." You'll pay even more in fees for the expensive convenience of seeing your charge in dollars.

Dealing with "Chip and PIN": Some parts of Europe (especially Britain, Ireland, France, the Netherlands, and Scandinavia) are adopting a "chip and PIN" system for their credit and debit cards. These "smartcards" come with an embedded microchip, and cardholders enter a PIN code instead of signing a receipt. In most cases, you can still use your credit or debit card at the cashier and sign the receipt the old-fashioned way. But a few merchants might insist on the PIN code—making it helpful for you to know the PIN code for your credit card (ask your credit-card company). Some newer, automated pay-at-the-pump gas stations or ticket machines can no longer read the magnetic strip on American credit cards at all. But even in these situations, there's usually a cashier nearby who can take your credit or debit card and make it work.

Damage Control for Lost Cards

If you lose your credit, debit, or ATM card, you can stop people from using it by reporting the loss immediately to the respective global customer-assistance centers. Call these 24-hour US numbers collect: Visa (410/581-9994), MasterCard (636/722-7111), and American Express (623/492-8427). Diner's Club has offices in Britain (0870-1900-011) and the US (702/797-5532, call collect).

At a minimum, you'll need to know the name of the financial institution that issued you the card, along with the type of card (classic, platinum, or whatever). Providing the following information will allow for a quicker cancellation of your missing card: full card number, whether you are the primary or secondary cardholder, the cardholder's name exactly as printed on the card, billing address, home phone number, circumstances of the loss or theft, and identification verification (your birth date, your mother's maiden name, or your Social Security number—memorize this, don't carry a copy). If you are the secondary cardholder, you'll also need to provide the primary cardholder's identification-verification details. You can generally receive a temporary card within two or three business days in Europe.

If you promptly report your card lost or stolen, you typically won't be responsible for any unauthorized transactions on your account, although many banks charge a liability fee of $50.

Tipping

Tipping in Britain isn't as automatic and generous as it is in the US, but for special service, tips are appreciated, if not expected. As in the US, the proper amount depends on your resources, tipping philosophy, and the circumstances, but some general guidelines apply.

Restaurants: At a pub or restaurant with waitstaff, check the menu or your bill to see if the service is included; if not, tip about 10 percent. At pubs where you order at the counter, you don't have to tip. (Regular customers ordering a round sometimes say, "Add one for yourself" as a tip for drinks ordered at the bar—but this isn't expected.)

Taxis: To tip the cabbie, round up. For a typical ride, round up to a maximum of 10 percent (to pay a £4.50 fare, give £5; for a £28 fare, give £30). If the cabbie hauls your bags and zips you to the airport to help you catch your flight, you might want to toss in a little more. But if you feel like you're being driven in circles or otherwise ripped off, skip the tip.

Special Services: It's thoughtful to tip a pound to someone who shows you a special sight and who is paid in no other way. Tour guides at public sights often hold out their hands for tips after they give their spiel; if I've already paid for the tour, I don't tip extra unless they've really impressed me. At hotels, porters expect about 50p for each bag they carry (another reason to pack light). Leaving the maid a pound at the end of your stay is a nice touch. In general, if someone in the service industry does a super job for you, a tip of a pound or two is appropriate, but not required.

When in doubt, ask. If you're not sure whether (or how much) to tip for a service, ask your hotelier or the TI; they'll fill you in on how it's done on their turf.

Getting a VAT Refund

Wrapped into the purchase price of your British souvenirs is a Value-Added Tax (VAT) of about 17.5 percent. If you purchase more than £20 (about $32) worth of goods at a store that participates in the VAT-refund scheme, you're entitled to get most of that tax back. Getting your refund is usually straightforward and, if you buy a substantial amount of souvenirs, well worth the hassle. If you're lucky, the merchant will subtract the tax when you make your purchase. (This is more likely to occur if the store ships the goods to your home.) Otherwise, you'll need to:

Get the paperwork. Have the merchant completely fill out the necessary refund document, called a "Tax-Free Shopping Cheque." You'll have to present your passport at the store.

Get your stamp at the border or airport. Process your cheque(s) at your last stop in the EU (e.g., at the airport) with the customs agent who deals with VAT refunds. It's best to keep your purchases in your carry-on for viewing, but if they're too large or dangerous (such as knives) to carry on, track down the proper customs agent to inspect them before you check your bag. You're not supposed to use your purchased goods before you leave. If you show up at customs wearing your new Wellingtons, officials might look the other way—or deny you a refund.

Collect your refund. You'll need to return your stamped document to the retailer or its representative. Many merchants work with a service, such as Global Refund (www.globalrefund.com) or Premier Tax Free (www.premiertaxfree.com), which have offices at major airports, ports, or border crossings. These services, which extract a 4 percent fee, can refund your money immediately in your currency of choice or credit your card (within two billing cycles). If the retailer handles VAT refunds directly, it's up to you to contact the merchant for your refund. You can mail the documents from home, or more quickly from your point of departure (using a stamped, addressed envelope you've prepared or one that's been provided by the merchant). You'll then have to wait—it could take months.

Customs for American Shoppers

You are allowed to take home $800 worth of items per person duty-free, once every 30 days. The next $1,000 is taxed at a flat 3 percent. After that, you pay the individual item's duty rate. You can also bring in duty-free a liter of alcohol (slightly more than a standard-size bottle of wine; you must be at least 21), 200 cigarettes, and up to 100 non-Cuban cigars. You may take home vacuum-packed cheeses; dried herbs, spices, or mushrooms; and canned fruits or vegetables, including jams and vegetable spreads. Baked goods, candy, chocolate, oil, vinegar, mustard, and honey are OK. Fresh fruits or vegetables are not. Meats, even if canned, are generally not allowed. Remember that you'll need to carefully pack any bottles of wine and other liquid-containing items in your checked luggage, due to limits on liquids in carry-ons. To check customs rules and duty rates before you go, visit www.cbp.gov, and click on "Travel," then "Know Before You Go."

Sightseeing

Sightseeing can be hard work. Use these tips to make your visits to England's finest sights meaningful, fun, efficient, and painless.

Plan Ahead

Set up an itinerary that allows you to fit in all your must-see sights. For a one-stop look at opening hours in the bigger cities, see the "At a Glance" sidebars throughout this book. Most sights keep stable hours, but you can easily confirm the latest by checking their website or asking at the local TI.

Don't put off visiting a must-see sight—you never know when a place will close unexpectedly for a holiday, strike, or restoration. If you'll be visiting during a holiday, find out if a particular sight will be open by phoning ahead or visiting its website.

To get the most out of the self-guided walks and sight descriptions in this book, read them before you visit.

When possible, visit major sights in the morning (when your energy is best) and save other activities for the afternoon. Hit the museum highlights first, then go back to other things if you have the stamina and time.

Going at the right time can also help you avoid crowds. This book offers tips on specific sights. Try visiting very early, at lunch, or very late. Evening visits are usually peaceful, with fewer crowds. For specifics on London at night, see "London for Early Birds and Night Owls" on page 82.

Get It Right

Americans tend to use "England," "Britain," and "UK" interchangeably, but they're not the same:

- **England** is in the southeast part of Britain. All of the places in this book are part of England.
- **Britain** is the name of the island.
- **Great Britain** is the political union of England, Scotland, and Wales.
- The **United Kingdom** adds Northern Ireland.
- The **British Isles** (not a political entity) also includes the independent Republic of Ireland.
- The **British Commonwealth** is a loose association of possessions and former colonies (including Canada, Australia, and India) that profess at least symbolic loyalty to the Crown.

At Sights

All sights have rules, and if you know about them in advance, they're no big deal.

At churches—which often offer interesting art (usually free) and a cool, welcome seat—a modest dress code (no bare shoulders or shorts) is encouraged.

Some important sights have metal detectors or conduct bag searches that will slow your entry. Major museums and sights require you to check daypacks and coats. They'll be kept safely. If you have something you can't bear to part with, stash it in a pocket or purse. To avoid checking a small backpack, carry it under your arm like a purse as you enter. From a guard's point of view, a backpack is generally a problem while a purse is not.

Photography is sometimes banned at major sights. Look for signs or ask. If cameras are allowed, video cameras are as well, but flashes or tripods are usually not. Flashes damage oil paintings and distract others in the room. Even without a flash, a handheld camera will take a decent picture (or buy postcards or posters at the museum bookstore).

Museums have special exhibits in addition to their permanent collection. Some exhibits are included in the entry price; others come at an extra cost (which you may have to pay even if you don't want to see the exhibit).

Many sights rent audioguides, which offer excellent recorded descriptions (about £3.50). If you bring along your own pair of headphones and a Y-jack, you can sometimes share one audioguide with your travel partner and save money. Guided tours are most likely to occur during peak season (usually between £3 and £8 and widely ranging in quality).

Expect changes—artwork can be on tour, on loan, out sick, or shifted at the whim of the curator. To adapt, pick up any available free floor plans as you enter. Ask the museum staff if you can't find a particular piece.

Major sights often have an on-site café or cafeteria (usually a good place to rest and have a snack or light meal). The WCs at many sights are free and clean.

Many places sell postcards that highlight their attractions. Before you leave, scan the postcards and thumb through the biggest guidebook (or skim its index) to be sure you haven't overlooked something that you'd like to see.

Most sights stop admitting people 30–60 minutes before closing time, and some rooms close early (often 45 minutes before the actual closing time). Guards usher people out, so don't save the best for last.

Every sight or museum offers more than what is covered in this book. Use the information in this book as an introduction—not the final word.

Sightseeing Pass and Memberships

Many sights in England are covered by the Great British Heritage Pass or these memberships: English Heritage or National Trust. If you're a whirlwind sightseer, seriously consider the Great British Heritage Pass, which covers the most sights.

The Great British Heritage Pass: The best deal for busy travelers, this pass covers all of the major English Heritage and National Trust sights, plus many others (including several major attractions in Scotland, Wales, and Northern Ireland). Covering about 600 historic sights, this pass is good for a certain number of consecutive days (2009 prices: £32 for 4 days, £45 for 7 days, £60 for 15 days, £80 for 30 days; £72/£99/£135/£180 family pass also available for up to 2 adults and 3 kids ages 5–15, though note that kids already get discounts at sights; for more information and the latest prices, call 0870-242-9988 or see www.britishheritagepass .com). You can buy this pass online (£6.50 extra for shipping) or at various tourist information centers in Britain; for example, in London, this pass is sold by the Britain and London Visitors Centre on Lower Regent Street.

Memberships: Many sights in England are managed by either the English Heritage or the National Trust (the sights don't overlap). Both organizations sell annual memberships that allow free or discounted entry to the sights they supervise; the English Heritage also sells passes. You can join the National Trust or English Heritage online (see websites on next page), or at just about any of their sights.

Membership in **English Heritage** includes free entry to more than 400 sights in England, and half-price admission to about 100 more sights in Scotland and Wales (2009 prices: £43 for one person, £75 for two people, good for one year; discounts for students, couples, and seniors; children under 19 free, toll tel. 0870-333-1182, www.english-heritage.org.uk/membership). For most travelers, their Overseas Visitor Pass is a better choice than the pricier one-year membership (Visitor Pass: £20/7 days, £24/14 days, discounts for couples and families, www.english-heritage.org.uk/ovp).

Membership in the **National Trust** is best suited for garden-and-estate enthusiasts, ideally those traveling by car. It covers more than 300 historic houses, manors, and gardens throughout Great Britain (£48 for one year, student and couple discounts, children under 5 free, www.nationaltrust.org.uk).

The Bottom Line: These deals can save a busy sightseer money...but only if you choose carefully. Make a list of the sights you plan to see, check which sights are covered (visit the websites listed above), and then add up the total if you paid individual admissions to the covered sights. Compare the total to the cost of the pass or membership. Keep in mind that an advantage to any of these deals is that you'll feel free to dip into lesser sights that normally wouldn't merit paying admission.

Fine Points: If you have children and you're all avid sight-seers, consider the Great British Heritage family pass; otherwise don't get a pass or membership for them, because they get in free or cheap at most sights. Similarly, people over 60 also get "concessions" (discounted prices) at many English sights (and can get a senior discount on an English Heritage membership). If you're traveling by car and can get to the more remote sights, you're more likely to get your money's worth out of a pass or membership, especially during peak season (Easter–Oct). If you're traveling off-season (Nov–Easter) when many of the sights are closed, these deals are a lesser value.

Sleeping

I favor accommodations (and restaurants) handy to your sight-seeing activities. Rather than list hotels scattered throughout a city, I choose two or three favorite neighborhoods and recommend the best accommodations values in each, from $30 bunk beds to fancy-for-my-book $300 doubles. Outside of pricey London you can expect to find good doubles for $80–160, including cooked breakfasts and tax. (For specifics on London, see page 126.)

I look for places that are friendly; clean; a good value; located in a central, safe, quiet neighborhood; and not mentioned in other guidebooks. I'm more impressed by a handy location and a fun-loving philosophy than hair dryers and shoeshine machines.

For tips on making reservations, see page 27.

I've described my recommended accommodations using a Sleep Code (see sidebar on next page). Prices listed are for one-night stays in peak season, include a hearty breakfast (unless otherwise noted), and assume you're booking directly and not through a TI.

You should find prices listed in this book to be good through 2010 (except during major holidays and festivals—see page 622). Prices can soften off-season, for stays of two nights or longer, or for payment in cash rather than credit card. Always mention that you found the place through this book—many of the accommodations listed offer special deals to our readers.

Official "rack rates" (the highest rates a hotel charges) can be misleading, since they often omit cheaper oddball rooms and special clearance deals. (Some fancy £120 rooms can rent for a third off if you arrive late on a slow day and ask for a deal.) With all the economic uncertainty these days, many hotels will likely be discounting deeply to snare what customers they can. Try to avoid paying rack rates. If you email several places and ask for their best prices, you'll find some eager to discount and others more passive. This can save you big bucks—with prices potentially far below those listed in this guidebook.

When establishing prices with a hotelier or B&B owner, confirm if the charge is per person or per room (if a price is too good to be true, it's probably per person). Because many places in England charge per person, small groups often pay the same for a single and a double as they would for a triple. In this book, however, room prices are listed per room, not per person.

Many places listed have three floors of rooms and steep stairs; expect good exercise and be happy you packed light. Elevators are rare except in the larger hotels. If you're concerned about stairs, call and ask about ground-floor rooms or pay for a hotel with a lift (elevator).

Learn the terminology: An "en suite" room has a bathroom (toilet and shower/tub) actually inside the room; a room with a "private bathroom" can mean that the bathroom is all yours, but it's across the hall; and a "standard" room has access to a bathroom down the hall that's shared with other rooms. Figuring there's little difference between "en suite" and "private" rooms, some places charge the same for both. If you want your own bathroom inside

Sleep Code

(£1 = about $1.60, country code: 44)

To help you easily sort through these listings, I've divided the rooms into three categories, based on the price for a double room with bath:

$$$ **Higher Priced**
$$ **Moderately Priced**
$ **Lower Priced**

To give maximum information in a minimum of space, I use the following code to describe accommodations. Prices in this book are listed per room, not per person. When a price range is given for a type of room (such as "Db-£80-120"), it means the price fluctuates with the season, size of room, or length of stay.

S = Single room, or price for one person in a double.

D = Double or twin room. (I specify double- and twin-bed rooms only if they are priced differently, or if a place has only one or the other. When reserving, you should specify.)

T = Three-person room (often a double bed with a single).

Q = Four-person room (adding an extra child's bed to a T is usually cheaper).

b = Private bathroom with toilet and shower or tub.

s = Private shower or tub only. (The toilet is down the hall.)

According to this code, a couple staying at a "Db-£80" hotel would pay a total of £80 (about $130) per night for a room with a private toilet and shower (or tub). Unless otherwise noted, credit cards are accepted and breakfast is included.

If I mention "Internet access" in a listing, there's a public terminal in the lobby for guests to use. If I include "Wi-Fi," you can generally access it in your room (usually for free), but only if you have your own laptop.

the room, request "en suite."

If money's tight, ask for a standard room. You'll almost always have a sink in your room. And, as more rooms go "en suite," the hallway bathroom is shared with fewer standard rooms.

"Twin" means two single beds, and "double" means one double bed (in my listings, I list all two-person rooms as "doubles"). If you will take either one, let them know, or you might be needlessly turned away. Most hotels offer family deals, which means that parents with young children can easily get a room with an extra child's bed or a discount for larger rooms. Call to negotiate the price. Teenage kids are generally charged as adults. Kids under five almost always sleep free.

Note that to be called a "hotel," a place technically must have certain amenities, including a 24-hour reception (though this rule is loosely applied). A place called "townhouse" or "house" (such as "London House") is like a big B&B or a small family-run hotel—with fewer amenities but more character than a "hotel."

England has a rating system for hotels and B&Bs. These diamonds and stars are supposed to imply quality, but I find that they mean only that the place sporting these symbols is paying dues to the tourist board. Rating systems often have little to do with value.

If you're traveling beyond my recommended destinations, you'll find accommodations where you need them. Any town with tourists has a TI that books rooms or can give you a list and point you in the right direction. In the absence of a TI, ask people on the street or in pubs or restaurants for help. Online, visit www .smoothhound.co.uk, which offers a range of accommodations for towns throughout the UK (searchable by town, airport, hotel name, or price range).

Types of Accommodations
B&Bs
Compared to hotels, bed-and-breakfast places give you double the cultural intimacy for half the price. While you may lose some of the conveniences of a hotel—such as lounges, in-room phones, daily bed-sheet changes, and credit-card payments—I happily make the trade-off for the lower rates and personal touches. If you have a reasonable but limited budget, skip hotels and go the B&B way.

In 2010, you'll generally pay £25–50 (about $40–80) per person for a double room in a B&B in England. Lately the big impersonal chain hotels are offering rooms cheaper than the mom-and-pop places (but without breakfast); see "Big, Cheap, Modern Hotels" later in this section. When considering the price of a B&B or small hotel, remember you're getting two breakfasts (up to a £25 value) for each double room.

B&Bs range from large guest houses with 15–20 rooms to small homes renting out a spare bedroom, but they typically have six rooms or fewer. The philosophy of the management determines the character of a place more than its size and facilities offered. I avoid places run as a business by absentee owners. My top listings are run by people who enjoy welcoming the world to their breakfast table.

B&Bs come with their own etiquette and quirks. Keep in mind that B&B owners are at the whim of their guests—if you're getting up early, so are they; and if you check in late, they'll wait

Smoke-Free Great Britain

Great Britain's public places are now smoke-free. Hotels, B&Bs, and restaurants are required to be non-smoking (though hoteliers are permitted to designate specific rooms for smokers). In the "Sleeping" sections of each chapter, I've listed the rare instance where a hotel has smoking rooms—but for the most part, the smoke truly is clearing in Britain.

up for you. Be considerate. It's polite to call ahead to confirm your reservation the day before and give them a rough estimate of your arrival time. This allows them to plan their day and run errands before or after you arrive...and it also allows them to give you specific directions for driving or walking to their place.

A few tips: B&B proprietors are selective as to whom they invite in for the night. At some B&Bs, children are not welcome. Risky-looking people (two or more single men are often assumed to be potential troublemakers) find many places suddenly full. If you'll be staying for more than one night, you are a "desirable." In popular weekend-getaway spots, you're unlikely to find a place to take you for Saturday night only. If my listings are full, ask for guidance. Mentioning this book can help. Owners usually work together and can call up an ally to land you a bed.

B&Bs serve a hearty fried breakfast (for more about B&B breakfasts, see "Eating," later in this chapter). You'll figure out quickly which parts of the "fry" you like and don't like. Your hosts prefer to know this up front, rather than serve you the whole shebang and have to throw out uneaten food. Because your B&B owner is also the cook, there's usually a limited time span when breakfast is served (typically about an hour—make sure you know when it is). It's an unwritten rule that guests shouldn't show up at the very end of the breakfast period and expect a full cooked breakfast—instead, aim to arrive at least 10 minutes before breakfast ends. If you do arrive late (or if you need to leave before breakfast is served), most B&B hosts are happy to let you help yourself to cereal, fruit, and coffee; ask politely if it's possible.

B&Bs are not hotels: If you want to ruin your relationship with your hostess, treat her like a hotel clerk. Americans often assume they'll get new towels each day. The English don't, and neither will you. Hang them up to dry and reuse.

Be aware of luggage etiquette. A large bag in a compact older building can easily turn even the most graceful of us into a bull in an English china shop. If you've got a backpack, don't wear it indoors. If your host offers to carry your bag upstairs, accept—they're adept at maneuvering luggage up tiny staircases without damaging their walls and banisters. Finally, use your room's luggage racks—putting bags on empty beds can dirty and scuff nice comforters. Treat these lovingly maintained homes as you would a friend's house.

In almost every B&B, you'll encounter unusual bathroom fixtures. The "pump toilet" has a flushing handle that doesn't kick in unless you push it just right: too hard or too soft, and it won't go. Be decisive but not ruthless. There's also the "dial-a-shower," an electronic box under the shower head where you'll turn a dial to select the heat of the water, and (sometimes with a separate dial or button) turn on or shut off the flow of water. If you can't find the switch to turn on the shower, it may be just outside the bathroom.

Rooms in most B&Bs come with a hot-water pot, cups, tea bags, and coffee packets (if you prefer decaf, buy a jar at a grocery before leaving home, and dump into a baggie for easy packing). Electrical outlets have switches that turn the current on or off; if your electrical appliance isn't working, flip the switch.

Most B&Bs come with thin walls and doors. This can make for a noisy night, especially with people walking down the hall to use the bathroom. If you're a light sleeper, bring earplugs. And please be quiet in the halls and in your rooms (talk softly, and keep the TV volume low). Those of us getting up early will thank you for it.

Your B&B bedroom probably won't include a phone. In the mobile-phone age, street phone booths can be few and far between. Some B&B owners will allow you to use their phone (with an international phone card), but many are disinclined to let you ring up charges. That's because most British people pay for each local call (whether from a fixed line or a mobile phone), and rates are expensive. Therefore, to be polite, ask to use their phone only in an emergency—and offer to use an international calling card or to pay for the call. If you plan to be staying in B&Bs and making frequent calls, consider buying a British mobile phone (see page 598). And if you're bringing your laptop, look for places with Wi-Fi (noted in my hotel listings).

Many B&B owners are also pet owners. And, while pets are rarely allowed into guest rooms, and B&B proprietors are typically very tidy, those with pet allergies might be bothered. I've tried to list which B&Bs have pets, but if you're allergic, ask about pets when you reserve.

Big, Cheap, Modern Hotels

Hotel chains—popular with budget tour groups—offer predictably comfortable, no-frills accommodations at reasonable prices. These hotels are popping up in big cities in England. Some are located near the train station, on major arterials, or outside the city center. What you lose in charm, you gain in savings.

These hotels are ideal for families, offering simple, clean, and modern rooms for up to four people (two adults/two children) for £60–90, depending on the location. Note that couples or families (up to four) pay the same price for a room. Most rooms have a double bed, single bed, five-foot trundle bed, private shower, WC, and TV. Hotels usually have an attached restaurant, good security, an elevator, and a 24-hour staffed reception desk. Breakfast is always extra. Of course, they're as cozy as a Motel 6, but many travelers love them. You can book over the phone (or online) with a credit card, then pay when you check in. When you check out, just drop off the key, Lee.

If you choose to stay in these hotels, book through their websites, as they are often the easiest way to make reservations, and will generally net you a discount. The biggies are Travelodge (reservations tel. 0870-085-0950, www.travelodge.co.uk) and Premier Travel Inn (reservations tel. 0870-242-8000, www.premierinn.com). The Irish chain Jurys Inn also has some hotels in England (book online at www.jurys.com).

Couples could also consider Holiday Inn Express, spreading throughout England. These are like a Holiday Inn Lite, with cheaper prices and no restaurant. Many of their hotels allow only two per room, but some take up to four (doubles cost about £60–100, make sure Express is part of the name or you'll pay more for a regular Holiday Inn, reservations tel. 0871-423-4896, www.hiexpress.co.uk).

More Hotel Deals Online: For recommendations for online hotel deals in London, as well as using auction-type sites, see page 126.

Hostels

If you're traveling alone, hosteling is the best way to conquer hotel loneliness. Hostels are also a tremendous source of local and budget travel information. You'll pay an average of £20 for a bed and £3 for breakfast. Anyone of any age can hostel in England. While there are no membership concerns for private hostels, International Youth Hostel Federation (IYHF) hostels require membership. Those without cards simply buy one-night guest memberships for £3.

England has hundreds of hostels of all shapes and sizes. Choose your hostel selectively. Hostels can be historic castles or depressing tenements, serene and comfy or overrun by noisy school groups. Unfortunately, many of the IYHF hostels have become overpriced and, in general, I no longer recommend them. The only time I do is if you're on a very tight budget, want to cook your own meals, or are traveling with a group that likes to sleep on bunk beds in big rooms. But many of the informal private hostels are more fun, easygoing, and cheaper. These alternatives to the IYHF hostels are more common than ever, and allow you to enjoy the benefits of hosteling. Good listings are plentiful at Hostels of Europe (www.hostelseurope.com) and Hostels.com. You can also book online for many hostels (for London: www.hostellondon .com, for England: www.yha.org.uk).

Phoning

To make international calls to England to line up hotel reservations, you'll need to know its country code: 44. To call from the US or Canada, dial 011-44-local number (drop the initial 0 from the local number). If calling England from another European country, dial 00-44-local number (without its initial zero). For more information on telephoning, see "Communicating" in the appendix.

Making Reservations

Given the quality of the places I've found for this book, I'd recommend that you reserve your rooms in advance, particularly if you'll be traveling during peak season. Book several weeks ahead, or as soon as you've pinned down your travel dates. Note that some national holidays jam things up and merit your making reservations far in advance (see "Major Holidays and Weekends" sidebar on page 3). Just like at home, holidays that fall on a Monday, Thursday, or Friday can turn the weekend into a long holiday, so book the entire weekend well in advance.

Requesting a Reservation: To make a reservation, contact hotels directly by email, phone, or fax. Email is the clearest and most economical way to make a reservation. Or you can go straight to the hotel website; many have secure online reservation forms and can instantly inform you of availability and any special deals. But be sure you use the hotel's official site and not a booking agency's site—otherwise you may pay higher rates than you should. If phoning from the US, be mindful of time zones (see page 11).

The hotelier wants to know these key pieces of information (also included in the sample request form on page 628):
- number and type of rooms
- number of nights
- date of arrival
- date of departure
- any special needs (e.g., bathroom in the room or down the hall, twin beds vs. double bed, air-conditioning, quiet, view, ground floor, etc.)

When you request a room, use the European style for writing dates: day/month/year. For example, a two-night stay in July would be "2 nights, 16/07/10 to 18/07/10." Consider in advance how long you'll stay; don't just assume you can tack on extra days once you arrive.

If you don't get a reply to your email or fax, it usually means the hotel is already fully booked (but you can try sending the message again, or call to follow up).

Confirming a Reservation: If the hotel's response includes its room availability and rates, it's not a confirmation. You must tell them that you want that room at the given rate. Many hoteliers will request your credit-card number for a one-night deposit to hold the room. While you can email your credit-card information (I do), it's safer to share that personal info via phone call, fax, two successive emails, or secure online reservation form (if the hotel has one on its website).

Canceling a Reservation: If you must cancel your reservation, it's courteous to do so with as much advance notice as possible—at least three days. Simply make a quick phone call or send an email. Family-run hotels and B&Bs lose money if they turn away customers while holding a room for someone who doesn't show up. Understandably, many hotels bill no-shows for one night.

Hotels in larger cities such as London sometimes have strict cancellation policies. For example, you might lose a deposit if you cancel within two weeks of your reserved stay, or you might be billed for the entire visit if you leave early. Ask about cancellation policies before you book.

If canceling via email, request confirmation that your cancellation was received to avoid being billed accidentally.

Reconfirming Your Reservation: Always call to reconfirm your room reservation a day or two in advance from the road. Smaller hotels and B&Bs appreciate knowing your time of arrival. If you'll be arriving after 17:00, be sure to let your hotelier know. On the small chance that a hotel loses track of your reservation, bring along a hard copy of their emailed or faxed confirmation. Don't have the TI reconfirm rooms for you; they'll take a commission.

Reserving Rooms as You Travel: If you enjoy having a flexible itinerary, you can make reservations as you travel, calling hotels or B&Bs a few days to a week before your visit. If you prefer the flexibility of traveling without any reservations at all, you'll have greater success snaring rooms if you arrive at your destination early in the day. When you anticipate crowds (weekends are worst), call hotels at about 9:00 on the day you plan to arrive, when the hotel clerk knows who'll be checking out and just which rooms will be available.

Most TIs in Britain can book you a room in their town, and also often in nearby towns. They generally charge a £4 fee, and you'll pay a 10 percent "deposit" at the TI and the rest at the B&B

(meaning that you pay extra and the B&B loses money, as the TI keeps the "deposit"). While this can be useful in a pinch, it's a better deal for everyone (except the TIs) to book direct, using the listings in this book.

Eating

England's reputation for miserable food is now dated, and the British cuisine scene is lively, trendy, and pleasantly surprising. (Unfortunately, it's also very expensive.) Even the basic, traditional pub grub has gone "up market," with "gastropubs" serving fresh vegetables rather than soggy fries and mushy peas.

All English eateries are now smoke-free. Restaurants and pubs that sell food are non-smoking indoors; establishments keep their smokers contented by allowing them to light up in doorways and on outdoor patios.

The Great English Breakfast

The traditional "fry," often included in the cost of your room, is famous as a hearty way to start the day. Also known as a "heart attack on a plate," the breakfast is especially feast-like if you've just come from the land of the skimpy continental breakfast across the Channel.

The standard fry gets off to a healthy start with juice and cereal or porridge. (Try Weetabix, a soggy English cousin of shredded wheat and perhaps the most

absorbent material known to humankind.) Next, with tea or coffee, you get a heated plate with a fried egg, Canadian-style bacon or sausage, a grilled tomato, sautéed mushrooms, and baked beans. Toast comes on edge on a rack (to cool quickly and crisply) with butter and marmalade or jam. Try kippers (herring fillets smoked in an oak fire). This protein-stuffed meal is great for stamina, and tides many travelers over until dinner. To avoid wasting food, remember to order only what you'll eat. There's nothing wrong with skipping the fry—few Brits actually start their day with this heavy breakfast. Many progressive B&B owners offer vegetarian, organic, or other creative variations on the traditional breakfast.

These days, the best coffee is served in a *cafetière* (also called a "French press"). When your coffee has steeped as long as you like, plunge down the filter and pour. To revitalize your brew, pump the plunger again.

Tips on Budget Eating

You have plenty of inexpensive choices: pub grub, daily specials, ethnic restaurants, cafeterias, fast food, picnics, fish-and-chips, greasy-spoon cafés, pizza, and more.

Portions are huge and, with locals feeling the pinch of their recession, **sharing plates** is generally just fine. Ordering two drinks, a soup or side salad, and splitting a £10 meat pie can make a fine and filling meal. On a limited budget, I'd share a main course in a more expensive place for a nicer eating experience. Plus, if you split a meal, the price is cut in half—and you might lose a little weight.

Pub grub is the most atmospheric budget option. You'll usually get fresh, tasty buffets under ancient timbers, with hearty lunches and dinners priced at £6–10 (see "Pub Grub and Beer," later).

Classier restaurants have some affordable deals. Lunch is usually cheaper than dinner; a top-end, £25-for-dinner-type restaurant often serves the same quality two-course lunch deals for £10. Look for early-bird dinner specials, allowing you to eat well and affordably (generally two courses-£17, three courses-£20), but early (about 17:30–19:00, last order by 19:00).

Ethnic restaurants from all over the world add spice to England's cuisine scene. Eating Indian or Chinese is cheap (even cheaper if you take it out). Middle Eastern stands sell gyro sandwiches, falafel, and *shwarmas* (lamb in pita bread). An Indian samosa (greasy, flaky meat-and-vegetable pie) costs £2, can be microwaved, and makes a very cheap, if small, meal. (For more, see "Indian Food," later in this section.) You'll find all-you-can-eat Chinese and Thai places serving £6 meals and offering £3.50 take-away boxes. While you can't "split" a buffet, you can split a take-away box. Stuff one full and you and your partner can eat in a park for less than £2 each—making the Chinese take-away box England's cheapest hot meal.

Most large **museums** (and some historic **churches**) have handy, moderately priced cafeterias.

Fast food places, both American and British, are everywhere.

Cheap chain restaurants, such as steak houses and pizza places, serve no-nonsense food in a family-friendly setting (steak-house meals about £10; all-you-can-stomach pizza about £5). For specific chains to keep an eye out for, see "Good Chain Restaurants," on the next page.

Picnicking saves time and money. Fine park benches and polite pigeons abound in most neighborhoods. You can easily get prepared food to go (e.g., see "Ethnic restaurants," above). Munch a relaxed "meal on wheels" picnic during your open-top bus tour or river cruise to save 30 precious minutes for sightseeing.

Bakeries sell yogurt, cartons of "semi-skimmed" milk,

Sounds Bad, Tastes Good

The English have a knack for making food sound funny. Here are a few examples:

Toad in the Hole: Sausage dipped in batter and fried
Bubble and Squeak: Leftovers, usually potatoes, veggies, and meat, all fried up together
Bap: Small roll
Treacle: Golden syrup, similar to light molasses

---

pastries, and pasties (PASS-teez). Pasties are "savory" (not sweet) meat pies that originated in the Cornish mining country; they had big crust handles so miners with filthy hands could eat them and toss the crust (see sidebar on page 289).

Good **sandwich shops** and corner **grocery stores** are a hit with local workers eating on the run. Try boxes of orange juice

(pure, by the liter), fresh bread, tasty English cheese, meat, a tube of Colman's English mustard, local eatin' apples, bananas, small tomatoes, a small tub of yogurt (drinkable), trail mix, nuts, plain or chocolate-covered digestive biscuits, and any local specialties. At **open-air markets** and **super-markets,** you can get produce in small quantities (3 tomatoes and 2 bananas cost me £1). Supermarkets often have good deli sections, even offering Indian dishes, and sometimes salad bars. Decent packaged sandwiches (£3) are sold everywhere.

Good Chain Restaurants

I know, I know—you're going to Britain to enjoy characteristic little hole-in-the-wall pubs, so mass-produced food is the furthest thing from your mind. But several excellent chains with branches across the UK can be a nice break from pub grub. I've recommended these restaurants throughout this book, but if you see a location that I haven't listed...go for it.

Wagamama is a mod noodle bar serving up reliably delicious pan-Asian dishes, usually with long shared tables and busy servers toting high-tech handheld ordering computers (typically £6–12 main dishes).

At **Yo! Sushi,** freshly prepared sushi dishes trundle past on a conveyor belt. Color-coded plates tell you how much each dish costs (£1.75–5), and a picture-filled menu explains what you're eating. Just help yourself.

Marks & Spencer Simply Food, an offshoot of the department-store chain, is a picnicker's and budget traveler's dream come true. They have a wide range of tasty, high-quality prepared salads, sandwiches, and more, all ready to take away (no seating, but plasticware is provided). Most Marks & Spencer (M&S) department stores have a grocery store in the basement—with the same delicious packaged items as in the Simply Food outlets—and sometimes an inexpensive Café Revive on the top floor. Sainsbury's supermarkets also feature surprisingly good prepared food; Tesco is a distant third.

Ask and **Pizza Express** restaurants serve quality pasta and pizza in a pleasant, sit-down atmosphere that's family-friendly.

On the High Street of most English cities, you'll find an array of healthier-than-expected fast food. **Pret à Manger** and **Eat** offer inexpensive and generally good sandwiches and salads to go.

Afternoon Tea

People of leisure punctuate their day with an "afternoon cream tea" at a tearoom. You'll get a pot of tea, small finger foods (like cucumber sandwiches), homemade scones, jam, and thick clotted cream. A lighter "cream tea" gets you tea and a scone or two. Tearooms, which often serve appealing light meals, are usually open for lunch and close at about 17:00, just before dinner. For more on this most English of traditions, see "Taking Tea in London" on page 152.

Pub Grub and Beer

Pubs are a basic part of the British social scene, and, whether you're a teetotaler or a beer-guzzler, they should be a part of your travel here. "Pub" is short for "public house." It's an extended living room where, if you don't mind the stickiness, you can feel the pulse of England.

Smart travelers use the pubs to eat, drink, get out of the rain, watch the latest sporting event, and make new friends. Unfortunately, many city pubs have been afflicted with an excess of brass, ferns, and video games. Most traditional atmospheric pubs are in the countryside and in smaller towns.

Pub grub gets better each year. In London, it offers the best indoor eating value. For £6–10, you'll get a basic, budget, hot lunch or dinner in friendly surroundings. The *Good Pub Guide,* published annually by the British Consumers Union, is excellent (www.thegoodpubguide.co.uk). Pubs that are attached to restaurants, advertise their food, and are crowded with locals are more likely to have fresh food and a chef than to be the kind of pub that sells only lousy microwaved snacks.

Pubs generally serve traditional dishes, such as fish-and-chips, vegetables, "bangers and mash" (sausages and mashed potatoes),

roast beef with Yorkshire pudding (batter-baked in the oven), and assorted meat pies, such as steak-and-kidney pie or shepherd's pie (stewed lamb topped with mashed potatoes). Side dishes include salads (sometimes even a nice self-serve salad bar), vegetables, and—invariably—"chips" (French fries). "Crisps" are potato chips. A "jacket potato" (baked potato stuffed with fillings of your choice) can almost be a meal in itself. A "ploughman's lunch" is a modern "traditional English meal" of bread, cheese, and sweet pickles that nearly every tourist tries...once. These days, you'll likely find more Italian pasta, curried dishes, and quiche on the menu than traditional fare.

Meals are usually served from 12:00 to 14:00 and from 18:00 to 20:00, not throughout the day. There's usually no table service. Order at the bar, then take a seat and they'll bring the food when it's ready (or sometimes you pick it up at the bar). Pay at the bar (sometimes when you order, sometimes after you eat). Don't tip unless it's a place with full table service. Servings are hearty, service is quick, and you'll rarely spend more than £10. (If you're on a tight budget, consider sharing a meal—note the size of portions around you before ordering.) A beer or cider adds another couple of pounds. (Free tap water is always available.) Because pubs make more money selling drinks than food, many stop cooking fairly early.

The English take great pride in their **beer.** They think that drinking beer cold and carbonated, as Americans do, ruins the taste. Most pubs will have lagers (cold, refreshing, American-style beer), ales (amber-colored, cellar-temperature beer), bitters (hop-flavored ale, perhaps the most typical British beer), and stouts (dark and somewhat bitter, like Guinness). At pubs, long-handled pulls are used to pull the traditional, rich-flavored "real ales" up from the cellar. These are the connoisseur's favorites: fermented naturally, varying from sweet to bitter, often with a hoppy or nutty flavor. Notice the fun names. Short-hand pulls at the bar mean colder, fizzier, mass-produced, and less interesting keg beers. Mild beers are sweeter, with a creamy malt flavoring. Irish cream ale is a smooth, sweet experience. Try the draft cider (sweet or dry)...carefully.

Order your beer at the bar and pay as you go, with no need to tip. An average beer costs £3. Part of the experience is standing before a line of "hand pulls," or taps, and wondering which beer to choose.

Drinks are served by the pint (20-ounce imperial size) or the half-pint. (It's almost feminine for a man to order just a half; I order mine with quiche.) Proper English ladies like a shandy—half beer and half 7-Up.

Besides beer, many pubs actually have a good selection of wines by the glass, a fully stocked bar for the gentleman's "G and T" (gin and tonic), and the increasingly popular bottles of alcohol-plus-sugar (such as Bacardi Breezers) for the younger, working-class set. Pimm's is a refreshing and fruity summer cocktail, traditionally popular during Wimbledon. It's an upper-class drink—a rough bloke might insult a pub by claiming it sells more Pimm's than beer. Teetotalers can order from a wide variety of soft drinks. Children are served food and soft drinks in pubs, but you must be 18 to order a beer.

Pub hours vary. Pubs generally serve beer Monday–Saturday 11:00–23:00 and Sunday 12:00–22:30, though many are open later, particularly on Friday and Saturday. As it nears closing time, you'll hear shouts of "Last orders." Then comes the 10-minute warning bell. Finally, they'll call "Time!" to pick up your glass, finished or not, when the pub closes.

A cup of darts is free for the asking. People go to a public house to be social. They want to talk. Get vocal with a local. This is easiest at the bar, where people assume you're in the mood to talk (rather than at a table, where you're allowed a bit of privacy). The pub is the next best thing to having relatives in town. Cheers!

Indian Food

Eating Indian food is "going local" in cosmopolitan, multiethnic England. You'll find recommended Indian restaurants in most English cities, and even in small towns. Take the opportunity to sample food from Britain's former colony. Indian cuisine is as varied as the country itself, featuring more exotic spices than British or American cuisine—some hot, some sweet. Indian food is very vegetarian-friendly, offering many dishes to choose from on any given menu.

For a simple meal that costs about £10–12, order one dish with rice and *naan* (Indian bread that can be ordered plain, with garlic, or other ways). Many restaurants offer a fixed-price combination meal that offers more variety, and is simpler and cheaper than ordering à la carte. For about £20, you can make a mix-and-match platter out of several sharable dishes, including *dal* (lentil soup) as a starter; one or two meat or vegetable dishes with sauce (for example, chicken curry, chicken *tikka masala* in a creamy tomato sauce, grilled fish tandoori, chickpea *chana masala*, or the spicy *vindaloo* dish); *raita* (a cooling yogurt that's added to spicy dishes); rice; *naan;* and an Indian beer (wine and Indian food don't really mix) or chai (a cardamom- and cinnamon-spiced tea).

British Chocolate

My chocoholic readers are enthusiastic about British choco-
lates. Like other dairy products, chocolate seems richer and
creamier here than it does in the US, so even the basics like
Kit Kat and Twix have a different taste. Some favorites include
Cadbury Gold bars (filled with liquid caramel), Cadbury
Crunchie bars, Nestlé's Lion bars (layered wafers covered in
caramel and chocolate), Cadbury's Boost bars (a shortcake
biscuit with caramel in milk chocolate), Cadbury Flake bars
(crumbly folds of melt-in-your-mouth chocolate), and Galaxy
chocolate bars (especially the ones with hazelnuts). Thornton
shops (in larger train stations) sell a box of sweets called the
Continental Assortment, which comes with a tasting guide.
The highlight is the mocha white-chocolate truffle. British
M&Ms, called Smarties, are better than American ones. At
ice-cream vans, look for the beloved traditional "99p"—a
vanilla soft-serve cone with a small Flake bar stuck right into
the middle.

Desserts (Sweets)

To the British, the traditional word for dessert is "pudding,"
although it's also referred to as "sweets" these days. Sponge cake,
cream, fruitcake, and meringue are key players.

Trifle is the best-known British concoction, consisting of
sponge cake soaked in brandy or sherry (or orange juice for children), then covered with jam and/or fruit and custard cream.
Whipped cream can sometimes put the final touch on this "light"
treat.

Castle puddings are sponge puddings cooked in small molds
and topped with Golden Syrup (a popular brand and a cross
between honey and maple syrup). Bread and butter pudding consists of slices of French bread baked with milk, cream, eggs, and
raisins (similar to the American preparation), served warm with
cold cream. Hasty pudding, supposedly the invention of people
in a hurry to avoid the bailiff, is made from stale bread with dried
fruit and milk. Queen of puddings is a breadcrumb pudding
topped with warm jam, meringue, and cream. Treacle pudding
is a popular steamed pudding whose "sponge" mixture combines
flour, suet (animal fat), butter, sugar, and milk. Christmas pudding (also called plum pudding) is a dense mixture with dried and
candied fruit served with brandy butter or hard sauce. Sticky toffee
pudding is a moist cake made with dates, warmed up and drizzled
with toffee sauce, and served with ice cream or cream. Banoffee pie
is the delicious British answer to banana cream pie.

The English version of custard is a smooth, yellow liquid.

How Was Your Trip?

Were your travels fun, smooth, and meaningful? If you'd like to share your tips, concerns, and discoveries, please fill out the survey at www.ricksteves.com/feedback. I value your feedback. Thanks in advance—it helps a lot.

Cream tops most everything custard does not. There's single cream for coffee. Double cream is really thick. Whipped cream is familiar, and clotted cream is the consistency of whipped butter.

Fool is a dessert with sweetened pureed fruit (such as rhubarb, gooseberries, or black currants) mixed with cream or custard and chilled. Elderflower is a popular flavoring for sorbet.

Scones are tops, and many inns and restaurants have their secret recipes. Whether made with fruit or topped with clotted cream, scones take the cake.

Traveling as a Temporary Local

We travel all the way to Europe to enjoy differences—to become temporary locals. You'll experience frustrations. Certain truths that we find "God-given" or "self-evident," such as cold beer, ice in drinks, bottomless cups of coffee, hot showers, and bigger being better, are suddenly not so true. One of the benefits of travel is the eye-opening realization that there are logical, civil, and even better alternatives.

Americans are enjoying a surge in popularity in Europe these days. But if there is a negative aspect to the image the English have of Americans, it's that we are big, loud, aggressive, impolite, rich, superficially friendly, and a bit naive.

The English (and Europeans in general) place a high value on speaking quietly in restaurants and on trains. Listen while on the bus or in a restaurant—the place can be packed, but the decibel level is low. Try to adjust your volume accordingly to show respect for their culture.

While the English look bemusedly at some of our Yankee excesses—and worriedly at others—they nearly always afford us individual travelers all the warmth we deserve. Judging from all the happy feedback I receive from travelers who have used this book, it's safe to assume you'll enjoy a great, affordable vacation—with the finesse of an independent, experienced traveler.

Thanks, and have a brilliant holiday!

Back Door Travel Philosophy
From Rick Steves' Europe Through the Back Door

Travel is intensified living—maximum thrills per minute and one of the last great sources of legal adventure. Travel is freedom. It's recess, and we need it.

Experiencing the real Europe requires catching it by surprise, going casual..."Through the Back Door."

Affording travel is a matter of priorities. (Make do with the old car.) You can travel—simply, safely, and comfortably—anywhere in Europe for $120 a day plus transportation costs (allow more for bigger cities). In many ways, spending more money only builds a thicker wall between you and what you came to see. Europe is a cultural carnival, and, time after time, you'll find that its best acts are free and the best seats are the cheap ones.

A tight budget forces you to travel close to the ground, meeting and communicating with the people, not relying on service with a purchased smile. Never sacrifice sleep, nutrition, safety, or cleanliness in the name of budget. Simply enjoy the local-style alternatives to expensive hotels and restaurants.

Connecting with people carbonates your experience. Extroverts have more fun. If your trip is low on magic moments, kick yourself and make things happen. If you don't enjoy a place, maybe you don't know enough about it. Seek the truth. Recognize tourist traps. Give a culture the benefit of your open mind. See things as different but not better or worse. Any culture has much to share.

Of course, travel, like the world, is a series of hills and valleys. Be fanatically positive and militantly optimistic. If something's not to your liking, change your liking.

Travel can make you a happier American as well as a citizen of the world. Our Earth is home to six and a half billion equally important people. It's humbling to travel and find that people don't have the "American Dream"—they have their own dreams. Europeans like us, but, with all due respect, they wouldn't trade passports.

Thoughtful travel engages us with the world. In tough economic times, it reminds us what is truly important. By broadening perspectives, travel teaches new ways to measure quality of life.

Globe-trotting destroys ethnocentricity, helping you understand and appreciate different cultures. Rather than fear the diversity on this planet, celebrate it. Among your prized souvenirs will be the strands of different cultures you choose to knit into your own character. The world is a cultural yarn shop, and Back Door travelers are weaving the ultimate tapestry. Join in!

ENGLAND

ENGLAND

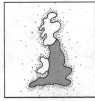

England (pop. 50 million) is a hilly country the size of Louisiana (50,346 square miles) located in the lower two-thirds of the isle of Britain. Scotland is to the north and the English Channel to the south, with the North Sea to the east and Wales (and the Irish Sea) to the west. Fed by ocean air from the southwest, the climate is mild, with a chance of cloudy, rainy weather almost any day of the year.

England has an economy that can stand alongside many much larger nations. It boasts high-tech industries (software, chemicals, aviation), international banking, and textile manufacturing, and is a major exporter of beef. While farms and villages remain, England is now an urban, industrial, and post-industrial colossus.

England was traditionally very class-conscious, with the wealthy landed aristocracy, the middle-class tradesmen, and the lower-class farmers and factory workers. While social stratification is fading with the new global economy, regional differences remain strong. Locals can often identify where someone is from by their dialect or local accent—Geordie, Cockney, or Queen's English.

One thing that sets England apart from its fellow UK countries (Scotland, Wales, Northern Ireland) is its ethnic makeup. Traditionally, those countries had Celtic roots, while the English mixed in Saxon and Norman blood. In the 20th century, England welcomed many Scots, Welsh, and Irish as low-wage workers. More recently, it's become home to immigrants from former colonies of its worldwide empire—

particularly from India/Pakistan/Bangladesh, the Caribbean, and Africa—and to many workers from poorer EU countries in Eastern Europe. These days it's not a given that every "English" person speaks English. Nearly one in three citizens does not profess the Christian faith. As the world becomes interconnected by communications technology, it's possible for many immigrants to physically inhabit the country while remaining closely linked to their home culture—rather than truly assimilating into England.

This is the current English paradox. England—the birthplace and center of the extended worldwide family of English-speakers—is losing its traditional Englishness. Where Scotland, Wales, and Northern Ireland have cultural movements to preserve their local languages and customs, England does not. Politically, there is no "English" party in the UK Parliament. In fact, Scotland, Wales, and Northern Ireland now have their own parliaments to decide local issues; England must depend on the decisions of the UK government at large. Except for the occasional display of an English flag at a soccer match (the red St. George's cross on a white background), many English people don't really think of themselves as "English"—more as "Brits," a part of the wider UK.

Today, England tries to preserve its rich past as it races forward as a leading global player. There are still hints of its legacy of farms, villages, Victorian lamplighters, and upper-crust dandies. But it's also a jostling world of unemployed factory workers, investment bankers, soccer matches, and faux-Tudor suburbs. Modern England is a culturally diverse land in transition. Catch it while you can.

LONDON

London is more than 600 square miles of urban jungle. With eight million people—who don't all speak English—it's a world in itself and a barrage on all the senses. On my first visit I felt extremely small.

London is more than its museums and landmarks. It's a living, breathing, thriving organism...a coral reef of humanity. The city has changed dramatically in recent years, and many visitors are surprised to find how "un-English" it is. White people are now a minority in major parts of the city that once symbolized white imperialism. Arabs have nearly bought out the area north of Hyde Park. Chinese take-outs outnumber fish-and-chips shops. Eastern Europeans pull pints in British pubs. Many hotels are run by people with foreign accents (who hire English chambermaids), while outlying suburbs are home to huge communities of Indians and Pakistanis. London is a city of eight million separate dreams, inhabiting a place that tolerates and encourages them. With the English Channel Tunnel making travel between Britain and the Continent easier than ever, many locals see even more holes in their bastion of Britishness. London is learning—sometimes fitfully—to live as a microcosm of its formerly vast empire. In anticipation of the 2012 Olympic Games, London is busy spiffing up the place, especially its rapidly developing Olympic Park in East London.

With just a few days here, you'll get no more than a quick splash in this teeming human tidal pool. But with a good orientation, you'll find London manageable and fun. You'll get a sampling of the city's top sights, history, and cultural entertainment, and a good look at its ever-changing human face.

Blow through the city on the open deck of a double-decker orientation tour bus, and take a pinch-me-I'm-in-London walk through the West End. Ogle the crown jewels at the Tower of London, hear the chimes of Big Ben, and see the Houses of Parliament in action. Cruise the Thames River, and take a spin on the London Eye. Hobnob with the tombstones in Westminster Abbey, and visit with Leonardo, Botticelli, and Rembrandt in the National Gallery. Enjoy Shakespeare in a replica of the Globe Theatre, then marvel at a glitzy, fun musical at a modern-day theater. Whisper across the dome of St. Paul's Cathedral, then rummage through our civilization's attic at the British Museum. And sip your tea with pinky raised and clotted cream dribbling down your scone.

Planning Your Time

The sights of London alone could easily fill a trip to England. It's a great one-week getaway. On a three-week tour of England, I'd give it three busy days. You won't be able to see everything, so don't try. You'll keep coming back to London. After dozens of visits, I still enjoy a healthy list of excuses to return. If you're flying in, consider starting your trip in Bath and making London your English finale. Especially if you hope to enjoy a play or concert, a night or two of jet lag is bad news.

Here's a suggested schedule:

Day 1: 9:00–Tower of London (crown jewels first, then Beefeater tour, then White Tower); 12:30–Munch a sandwich on the Thames while cruising from the Tower to Westminster Bridge; 14:00–Tour Westminster Abbey; 15:30–Follow the self-guided Westminster Walk. When you're finished, you could return to the Houses of Parliament and pop in to see the House of Commons in action.

Day 2: 9:00–Take a double-decker hop-on, hop-off London sightseeing bus tour (start at Victoria Street and hop off for the Changing of the Guard); 11:30–Buckingham Palace (guards change most days, but worth confirming); 13:00–Covent Garden for lunch, shopping, and people-watching; 14:30–Tour the British Museum. Have a pub dinner before a play, concert, or evening walking tour.

Day 3: Choose among these remaining London highlights: Tour British Library, Imperial War Museum, the two Tates (Tate Modern on the South Bank for modern art, Tate Britain on the North Bank for British art), St. Paul's Cathedral, or the Museum of London; take a spin on the London Eye or a cruise to Kew or Greenwich; enjoy a Shakespearean play at Shakespeare's Globe; do some serious shopping at one of London's elegant department stores or open-air markets; or take another historic walking tour.

Orientation to London

(area code: 020)

To grasp London more comfortably, see it as the old town in the city center without the modern, congested sprawl. The Thames River runs roughly west to east through the city, with most of the visitor's sights on the North Bank. Mentally, maybe even physically with scissors, trim down your map to include only the area between the Tower of London (to the east), Hyde Park (west), Regent's Park (north), and the South Bank (south). This is roughly the area bordered by the Tube's Circle Line. This four-mile stretch between the Tower and Hyde Park (about a 90-min walk) looks like a milk bottle on its side (see map on next page), and holds 80 percent of the sights mentioned in this chapter.

Sprawling London becomes much more manageable if you think of it as a collection of neighborhoods:

Central London: This area contains Westminster and what Londoners call the West End. The **Westminster** district includes Big Ben, Parliament, Westminster Abbey, and Buckingham Palace—the grand government buildings from which Britain is ruled. Trafalgar Square, London's gathering place, has major museums. The **West End** is the center of London's cultural life, with bustling squares: Piccadilly Circus and Leicester Square host cinemas, tourist traps, and nighttime glitz. Soho and Covent Garden are thriving people-zones with theaters, restaurants, pubs, and boutiques.

North London: Neighborhoods in this part of town, such as Bloomsbury, Fitzrovia, and Marylebone, contain major sights such as the British Museum and the overhyped Madame Tussauds Waxworks. Nearby, along busy Euston Road, is the British Library plus a trio of train stations, including St. Pancras International, the Eurostar launchpad for Paris.

The City: "The City," today's modern financial district, was a walled town in Roman times. Gleaming skyscrapers are interspersed with historical landmarks such as St. Paul's Cathedral, legal sights (Old Bailey), and the Museum of London. The Tower of London and Tower Bridge lie just outside The City's eastern border.

The South Bank: The South Bank of the Thames River offers major sights (Tate Modern, Shakespeare's Globe, London Eye) linked by a riverside walkway. Pedestrian bridges connect the South Bank with The City and Trafalgar Square.

West London: This huge area contains neighborhoods such as Mayfair, Belgravia, Chelsea, South Kensington, and Notting Hill. It's home to London's wealthy, and has many trendy shops and enticing restaurants. Here you'll find a range of museums (Victoria

London's Neighborhoods

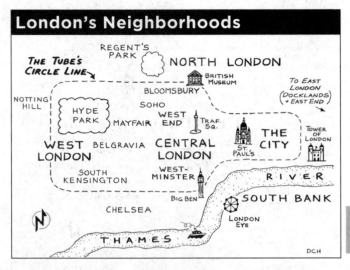

and Albert Museum, Kensington Palace, Tate Britain, and more), recommended hotels, lively Victoria Station, and the vast green expanses of Hyde Park and Kensington Gardens.

East London: London's version of Manhattan—the Docklands—has sprung up far to the east around Canary Wharf. Energized by big businesses and gearing up to host parts of the 2012 Olympics, the Docklands show you London at its most modern. Historic Greenwich lies just south of the Docklands/Canary Wharf area, across the Thames.

Tourist Information

The **Britain and London Visitors Centre,** just a block off Piccadilly Circus, is the best tourist information service in town (June–Sept Mon–Fri 9:30–18:30, Sat 9:00–17:00, Sun 10:00–16:00; Oct–May Mon–Fri 9:30–18:00, Sat–Sun 10:00–16:00; 1 Lower Regent Street, tel. 020/8846-9000, toll tel. 0870-156-6366, www .visitbritain.com, www.visitlondon.com).

This TI has many different departments. It's a great one-stop-shopping place to get tourist information, buy advance tickets to big sights, buy sightseeing passes, arrange coach tours, buy theater tickets, plan travel beyond London, and even book trains to the Continent. Bring your itinerary and a checklist of questions.

Entering the lobby, check out the various departments and get in the right line for what you need. At the Tourist Information desk handling both London and Britain inquiries, pick up various free publications: the *London Planner* (a great free monthly that lists all the sights, events, and hours), walking tours info, a theater guide, London bus map, and the Thames River Services brochure.

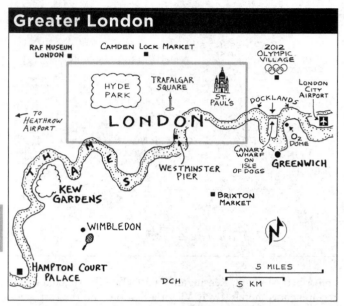

Greater London

RAF MUSEUM LONDON
CAMDEN LOCK MARKET
2012 OLYMPIC VILLAGE
HYDE PARK
TRAFALGAR SQUARE
ST. PAUL'S
LONDON CITY AIRPORT
DOCKLANDS
TO HEATHROW AIRPORT
LONDON
O₂ DOME
CANARY WHARF ON ISLE OF DOGS
WESTMINSTER PIER
GREENWICH
THAMES
KEW GARDENS
BRIXTON MARKET
WIMBLEDON
N
HAMPTON COURT PALACE
DCH
5 MILES
5 KM

LONDON

The staff sells a good £1 map and all the various sightseeing deals, including the London Pass (described on the next page) and the Great British Heritage Pass and English Heritage membership (both described on page 19).

The Entertainment and Tickets desk sells tickets to plays (20 percent booking fee). The Hotels and Travel desk sells long-distance bus tickets and passes, train tickets (convenient for reservations), and Fast Track tickets to some of London's attractions. The Fast Track tickets, which allow you to skip the queue at the sights at no extra cost, are worthwhile for places that sometimes have long ticket lines, such as the Tower of London, the London Eye, and Madame Tussauds Waxworks. (If you'll be going to the Waxworks, buy tickets here, since—at £20—they're cheaper than at the sight itself.)

The Visitors Centre reserves hotel rooms, but you can avoid their £5 booking fee by contacting hotels on your own. A Rail Europe section books the Eurostar and train travel or train passes on the Continent.

Upstairs, there are even more brochures, Internet access (£1/20 min), and comfy chairs where you can read or get organized. If you visit only one TI, make it this one, the Britain and London Visitors Centre. Unfortunately, London's many Tourist Information Centres (which represent themselves as TIs at major train and bus stations and airports) are now simply businesses selling advertising space to companies with fliers to distribute.

The **London Pass** is only worth considering if you're a whirlwind sightseer (£39/1 day, £52/2 days, £63/3 days, £87/6 days, includes 160-page guidebook, toll tel. 0870-242-9988, www.londonpass.com). It covers plenty of sights that cost £11–17, including the Tower of London, St. Paul's Cathedral, Shakespeare's Globe, Cabinet War Rooms, Kensington Palace, Windsor Palace, and Kew Gardens. But if you saw just these sights without the pass, you'd pay about £90, roughly the cost of a six-day London Pass. Note that busy sightseers can make a short pass work for a longer trip by seeing only covered sights during the validity of the pass, and touring London's many free sights before or after the pass' validity period. Think through your sightseeing plans carefully before you buy.

Arrival in London

By Train: London has nine major train stations, all connected by the Tube (subway). All have ATMs, and many of the larger stations also have shops, fast food, exchange offices, and luggage storage. From any station, you can ride the Tube or taxi to your hotel. For more info on train travel, see page 602 and www.nationalrail.co.uk.

By Bus: The bus ("coach") station is one block southwest of Victoria Station, where you can take the Tube. For more info on bus travel, see www.nationalexpress.com.

By Plane: London has five airports. Most tourists arrive at Heathrow or Gatwick airports, although flights from elsewhere in Europe may land at Stansted, Luton, or London City airports. For specifics on getting from London's airports to downtown London, see "London Connections" on page 156.

Helpful Hints

Theft Alert: The Artful Dodger is alive and well in London. Be on guard, particularly on public transportation and in places crowded with tourists. Tourists, considered naive and rich, are targeted. More than 7,500 purses are stolen annually at Covent Garden alone. Wear your money belt.

Pedestrian Safety: Cars drive on the left side of the road, so before crossing a street, I always look right, look left, then look right again just to be sure. Many crosswalks are even painted with instructions, reminding foreign guests to "Look right" or "Look left."

Medical Problems: Local hospitals have good-quality 24-hour emergency care centers where any tourist who needs help can drop in and, after a wait, be seen by a doctor. Your hotel has details. St. Thomas' Hospital, immediately across the river from Big Ben, has a fine reputation.

Affording London's Sights

London is, in many ways, Europe's most expensive city, with the dubious distinction of having some of the world's most expensive admission prices. Fortunately, many of its best sights are free.

Free Museums: Many of the city's biggest and best museums won't cost you a dime. Free sights include the British Museum, British Library, National Gallery, National Portrait Gallery, Tate Britain, Tate Modern, Wallace Collection, Imperial War Museum, Victoria and Albert Museum, Natural History Museum, Science Museum, National Army Museum, Sir John Soane's Museum, the Museum of London, the Geffrye, and, on the outskirts of town, the Royal Air Force Museum London.

Several museums, such as the British Museum, request a donation of a few pounds, but whether you contribute or not is up to you. If I spend money for an audioguide, I feel fine about not otherwise donating. If that makes you uncomfortable, donate.

Free Churches: Smaller churches let worshippers (and tourists) in free, although they may ask for a donation. The big sightseeing churches—Westminster Abbey and St. Paul's—charge steep admission fees, but offer free evensong services daily. Westminster Abbey offers free organ recitals most Sundays at 17:45.

Other Freebies: There are plenty of free performances, such as lunch concerts at St. Martin-in-the-Fields (see page 77) and summertime movies at The Scoop amphitheatre near City Hall (Tube: London Bridge, schedule at www.morelondon.com—click on "The Scoop"). For other freebies, check out www.freelondon-listings.co.uk. There's no charge to enjoy the pageantry of the Changing of the Guard, rants at Speaker's Corner in Hyde Park, displays at Harrods, and the people-watching scene at Covent Garden. It's free to view the legal action at Old Bailey and the legislature at work in the Houses of Parliament. And you can get into a bit of the Tower of London by attending Sunday services in the Tower's chapel (chapel access only).

Sightseeing Deals: If you buy a paper Travelcard or rail ticket at a National Rail station (such as Paddington or Victoria), you may be eligible for two-for-one discounts at many popular sights, such as the Tower of London, Westminster Abbey, and Madame Tussauds Waxworks. Get details and print out vouchers at www.daysoutguide.co.uk, or look for brochures with coupons at major train stations.

Festivals: For one week in February and another in September, fashionistas descend on the city for **London Fashion Week.** The famous **Chelsea Flower Show** blossoms May 25–29 in 2010 (book tickets ahead for this popular event at www.rhs.org.uk/chelsea). During the annual **Trooping the Colour** on June 13, there are military bands and pageantry, and the Queen's birthday parade. Tennis fans pack the stands at the

Good-Value Tours: The £7–9 city walking tours with professional guides are one of the best deals going. And with the free Royal London walking tour (see page 61), you always get at least your money's worth. Hop-on, hop-off big-bus tours (£15–25), while expensive, provide a great overview, and include free boat tours as well as city walks. A one-hour Thames ride to Greenwich costs £8.40 one-way, but generally comes with an entertaining commentary. A three-hour bicycle tour is about £16–19.

Pricey...But Worth It?: Big-ticket sights worth their admission fees are Kew Gardens (£13), Shakespeare's Globe (£10.50), and the Cabinet War Rooms, with its fine Churchill Museum (£13). The London Eye has become a London must-see (£17).

While Kensington Palace (£12.50) and Hampton Court Palace (£14) are expensive, they are well-presented and a reasonable value if you have a real interest in royal history. The queen charges big time to open her palace to the public: Buckingham Palace (£16.50, Aug–Sept only) and her art gallery and carriage museum (adjacent to the palace, about £8 each, £14.50 for both) are expensive but interesting. Madame Tussauds Waxworks is pricey but still fun and popular (£25, £20 if purchased at TI, drops to £16 after 17:00 if booked on Waxworks' website). The Vinopolis wine museum provides a way to get a buzz and call it museum-going (from £25, includes five small glasses of wine).

Many smaller museums cost only around £5. My favorites include the Courtauld Gallery (free on Mon until 14:00) and the Wellington Museum at Apsley House (£5.70).

Not Worth It: Gimmicky, overpriced, bad-value enterprises include the London Dungeon (£20) and the Dalí Universe (great location next to the popular London Eye, but for £14.50, skip it).

Theater: Compared with Broadway's prices, London theatre is a bargain. Seek out the freestanding "tkts" booth at Leicester Square to get discounts from 25–50 percent (though not necessarily for the hottest shows; see page 121). A £5 "groundling" ticket for a play at Shakespeare's Globe is the best theater deal in town (see page 122). Tickets to the Open Air Theatre at north London's Regent's Park start at £10 (see page 123).

London doesn't come cheap. But with its many free museums and affordable plays, this cosmopolitan, cultured city offers days of sightseeing thrills without requiring you to pinch your pennies (or your pounds).

Wimbledon Tennis Championship June 21–July 4 in 2010 (www.wimbledon.org), and partygoers head for the **Notting Hill Carnival** August 29–30 in 2010.

Winter: London dazzles year-round, so consider visiting in winter, when airfares and hotel rates are generally cheaper and there are fewer tourists. For ideas on what to do, see the "Winter Activities in London" article at www.ricksteves.com/winteracts.

Internet Access: The **easyInternetcafé** chain offers dozens of computers per store (generally daily 8:00–22:00, £3/30 min). You'll find branches at Trafalgar Square (456 Strand), Bayswater (Queensway, second floor of Whiteley's Shopping Centre), Oxford Street (#358, opposite Bond Street Tube station), and Kensington High Street (#160–166). Your hotelier can direct you to the nearest Internet café.

Travel Bookstores: Located in Covent Garden, **Stanfords Travel Bookstore** is good and stocks current editions of my books (Mon, Wed, and Fri 9:00–19:30, Tue 9:30–19:30, Thu 9:00–20:00, Sat 10:00–20:00, Sun 12:00–18:00, 12–14 Long Acre, Tube: Covent Garden, tel. 020/7836-1321, www.stanfords .co.uk).

Two impressive **Waterstone's** bookstores have the biggest collection of travel guides in town: on Piccadilly (Mon–Sat 9:00–22:00, Sun 11:30–18:00, 203 Piccadilly, tel. 020/7851-2400) and on Trafalgar Square (Mon–Sat 9:30–21:00, Sun 12:00–18:00, Costa Café on second floor, tel. 020/7839-4411).

Baggage Storage: Train stations have replaced their lockers with more secure baggage-storage counters, known as "left luggage." Each bag must go through a scanner (just like at the airport), so lines can be slow. Expect long waits in the morning to check in (up to 45 min) and in the afternoon to pick up (each item–£8/24 hours, most stations daily 7:00–22:00). You can also store bags at the airports (similar rates and hours, www.excess-baggage.com). If leaving London and returning later, you may be able to leave a box or bag at your hotel for free—assuming you'll be staying there again.

Getting Around London

To travel smart in a city this size, you must get comfortable with public transportation. London's excellent taxis, buses, and subway (Tube) system make a private car unnecessary. An £8 congestion charge levied on any private car entering the city center has been effective in cutting down traffic jam delays and bolstering London's public transit. The revenue raised subsidizes the buses, which are now cheaper, more frequent, and even more user-friendly than before. Today, the vast majority of vehicles in the city center are buses, taxis, and service trucks. (Drivers can find out more information on the congestion charge at www.cclondon.com.)

Public-Transit Passes: Oyster Cards and Travelcards

London has the most expensive public transit in the world—you will definitely save money on your Tube and bus rides using a multi-ride pass. There are two options: plastic Oyster cards and paper Travelcards (details online at www.tfl.gov.uk, click on "Tickets").

Oyster Cards

An Oyster card (a plastic card embedded with a computer chip) is the standard, smart way to economically ride the Tube, buses, and

Docklands Light Railway (DLR). You prepay an amount, and fares are automatically deducted each time you use your card. On each type of transport, you simply touch the card to the yellow card reader at the turnstile/entrance, it flashes green, and you've paid your fare. (You'll need the card to exit the Tube and DLR turnstiles, but not to exit buses.)

With an Oyster card, you'll pay only £1.80–2.40 per ride on the Tube (in Zones 1–6 off-peak) instead of £4-4.50 per ride with a full-fare ticket. For the bus, it's £1.20 versus £2. A price cap guarantees you'll never pay more than the One-Day Travelcard price within a 24-hour period (see "One-Day Travelcard," described later). An Oyster card is worth considering if you'll be in London for even a few days, and it is especially handy if you're not sure you'll ride enough each day to justify a Travelcard.

You can buy Oyster cards at any Tube station ticket window. With the standard **pay-as-you-go Oyster card,** you load up your Oyster with as much credit you want (there's no minimum, but start with at least £10). When your balance gets low, you simply pay more money (at a ticket window or machine) to keep riding. To see how much credit remains on your card, swipe it at any automatic ticket machine. You can also see a record of all your travels (and what you paid). Try it. Pay-as-you-go Oyster balances never expire (though they need reactivating at a ticket window every two years); you can use the card whenever you're in London, or lend it to someone else. The only downside, and it's minor, is that you pay a £3 one-time refundable deposit for the card itself (you can turn in your card for the £3 refund at any ticket window, but allow 20 minutes for the process).

The **Seven-Day Oyster card** is another good possibility to consider, even for a visit as short as four days. Technically a seven-day Travelcard (see below), this odd hybrid is generally issued on a plastic Oyster card. The least expensive version is £25.80 and covers unlimited, peak-time travel through Zones 1 and 2 (no deposit required, cards covering more zones are also available).

Travelcards

A paper Travelcard works like a traditional ticket: You buy it at any Tube station ticket window or machine, then feed it into a turnstile (and retrieve it) to enter and exit the Tube. On a bus, just show it to the driver when you get on. If you take at least two rides a day, a Travelcard is a better deal than buying individual tickets. Like the Oyster

card, Travelcards are valid on the Tube, buses, and Docklands Light Railway. Before you buy a card, estimate where you'll be going; there's a card for Zones 1 and 2, and another for Zones 1–6 (which includes Heathrow Airport).

The **One-Day Travelcard** gives you unlimited travel for a day; cheaper off-peak versions are good for travel after 9:30 on weekdays and anytime on weekends (**Zones 1–2:** £7.20, off-peak version £5.60; **Zones 1–6:** £14.80, off-peak version £7.50).

Which Pass to Buy?

Trying to decide between an Oyster and a Travelcard? Here's what I recommend:

- For one to two days, get a One-Day Travelcard each day.
- For three consecutive days, buy a pay-as-you-go Oyster card.
- For four consecutive days, choose a Seven-Day Oyster card (£25.80) or a pay-as-you-go Oyster card. Or you could buy a One-Day Travelcard each day (total £22.40–28.80 in Zones 1–2).
- For five or more days in a row, a Seven-Day Oyster card is usually your best bet. But if you aren't sure if you'll ride enough each day to justify the expense, get the pay-as-you-go Oyster card instead.
- If your trip involves travel to Heathrow Airport, depending on the time of day you travel, you may be better off just paying £4.50 for a full-fare ticket to or from Heathrow, and buying a Zones 1–2 Travelcard for the rest of your time in London.

Other Discounts

Groups of 10 or more adults can travel all day on the Tube for £3.70 each (but not on buses). Kids 11–17 pay £1 when part of a group of 10.

Families: A paying adult can take up to four kids (aged 10 and under) for free on the Tube and Docklands Light Railway all day, every day. In the Tube, use the manual gate, rather than the turnstiles, to be waved in. Families with older kids can consider the "Zip" card: Kids ages 11–15 travel for £1 on the Tube and for free on buses. Apply online, and pick up the card in London (takes 3 weeks; requires £5 deposit and digital photo, see www.tfl .gov.uk).

River Cruises: A Travelcard or a Seven-Day Oyster card gives you a 33 percent discount on most Thames cruises (see "Cruises" on page 65).

Sightseeing Deal: Buy a paper Travelcard or rail ticket at a National Rail station and you may qualify for two-for-one discounts at many popular sights (look for brochures with coupons at major train stations or print out vouchers at www.daysoutguide .co.uk).

By Tube

London's subway system (called the Tube or Underground, but never "subway," which refers to a pedestrian underpass) is one of this planet's great people-movers and often the fastest long-distance transport in town (runs Mon–Sat about 5:00–24:00, Sun about 7:00–23:00).

Start by studying a Tube map (free at any station). Each line has a name (such as Circle, Northern, or Bakerloo) and two directions (indicated by the end-of-the-line

stops). Find the line that will take you to your destination, and figure out roughly what direction (north, south, east, or west) you'll need to go to get there.

You can use paper tickets, Travelcards, or an Oyster card to pay for your journey. At the Tube station, feed your paper ticket or Travelcard into the turnstile, reclaim it, and hang on to it—you'll need it to get through the turnstile at the end of your journey. If using a plastic Oyster card, touch the card to the yellow card reader when you enter and exit the station.

Find your train by following signs to your line and the (general) direction it's headed (such as Central Line: east). Since some tracks are shared by several lines, double-check before boarding a train: First, make sure your destination is one of the stops listed on the sign at the platform. Also, check the electronic signboards that announce which train is next, and make sure the destination (the end-of-the-line stop) is the one you want. Some trains, particularly on the Circle and District lines, split off for other directions, but each train has its final destination marked above its windshield.

Trains run roughly every 3–10 minutes. If one train is absolutely packed and you notice another to the same destination is coming in three minutes, wait to avoid the sardine experience. The system can be fraught with construction delays and breakdowns, so pay attention to signs and announcements explaining necessary detours (the Circle Line is notorious for problems). Rush hours (8:00–10:00 and 16:00–19:00) can be packed and sweaty. Bring something to do to make your waiting time productive. If you get confused, ask for advice from a local, a blue-vested staff person, or at the information window located before the turnstile entry.

Remember that you can't leave the system without feeding your ticket or Travelcard to the turnstile or touching your Oyster card to an electronic reader. If you have a single-trip paper ticket, the turnstile will eat your now-expired ticket; if it's a Travelcard, it will spit out your still-valid card. Save walking time by choosing the best street exit—check the maps on the walls or ask any station personnel. For Tube and bus information, visit www.tfl.gov.uk (and check out the journey planner).

Any ride in Zones 1–6 (the center of town all the way out to Heathrow Airport) costs a steep £4.50 for adults paying cash. If you plan to ride the Tube and buses more than twice in one day, you'll save money by getting a Travelcard (or for visits of four days or more, an Oyster card is a good choice).

If you do buy a single Tube ticket, you can avoid ticket-window lines in stations by using the coin-op machines; practice on the punchboard to see how the system works (hit "Adult Single" and your destination). These tickets are valid only on the day of purchase.

Tube Etiquette
- When waiting at the platform, get out of the way of those exiting the train. Board only after everyone is off.
- Avoid using the hinged seats near the doors of some trains when the car is jammed; they take up valuable standing space.
- In a crowded train, try not to block the exit. If you're blocking the door when the train stops, step out of the car and to the side, let others off, then get back on.
- Talk softly in the cars. Listen to how quietly Londoners communicate and follow their lead.
- On escalators, stand on the right and pass on the left (even though Brits do the opposite behind the wheel). But note that in some passageways or stairways, you might be directed to walk on the left (same as car direction).
- When leaving a station, it's polite to hold the door for the person behind you.

- Flash photos are not allowed on the Tube or in any of the stations because they can affect the drivers' vision.
- Discreet eating and drinking are fine (nothing smelly); drinking alcohol and smoking are not.

By Bus

If you figure out the bus system, you'll swing like Tarzan through the urban jungle of London. Pick up a free bus map at a TI, transport office, or some major museums; it will list the bus routes best for sightseeing (also see "Handy Bus Routes" sidebar, later).

The first step in mastering the bus system is learning how to decipher the bus-stop signs. Find a bus stop and study the signs mounted on the pole next to the stop. You'll see a chart listing (alphabetically) the destinations served by buses that pick up at this spot or nearby; the names of the buses; and alphabet letters that identify exactly where the buses pick up. After locating your destination, remember or write down the bus name and bus stop letter. Next, refer to the neighborhood map (also on the pole) to find your bus stop. Just match your letter with a stop on the map. Make your way to that stop—you'll know it's yours because it will have the same letter on its pole—and wait for the bus with the right name to arrive. Some fancy stops have electric boards indicating the minutes until the next bus arrives; but remember to check the name on the bus before you hop on. Crack the code and you're good to go.

On almost all buses, you'll pay at a machine at the bus stop (no change given), then show your ticket or pass as you board. You can also use Travelcards and Oyster cards (see page 51). If you're using an Oyster card, touch it to the electronic card reader as you board; no need to do so when you hop off. On "Heritage Routes" #9 and #15 (which use older double-decker buses), you still pay a conductor; take a seat, and he or she will come around to collect your fare or verify your pass.

Any bus ride in downtown London costs £2 for those paying cash; £1.20 if using an Oyster card. If you're staying longer, consider the £16.60 Seven-Day bus pass. If you have a Travelcard or Oyster card, save your feet and get in the habit of hopping buses for quick little straight shots, even just to get to a Tube stop. During bump-and-grind rush hours (8:00–10:00 and 16:00–19:00), you'll usually go faster by Tube.

By Taxi

London is the best taxi town in Europe. Big, black, carefully regulated cabs are everywhere. (While historically known as "black cabs," some of London's official taxis are now covered with wildly colored ads.)

Handy Bus Routes

Since London instituted a congestion charge for cars, the public bus system has gotten faster, easier, and cheaper than ever. Tube-oriented travelers need to get over their tunnel vision, learn the bus system, and get around fast and easy. The best views are upstairs on a double-decker.

Here are some of the most useful routes:

Route #9: Knightsbridge (Harrods) to Hyde Park Corner to Piccadilly Circus to Trafalgar Square. This is one of two "Heritage Routes" using old-style double-decker buses.

Routes #11 and #24: Victoria Station to Westminster Abbey to

LONDON

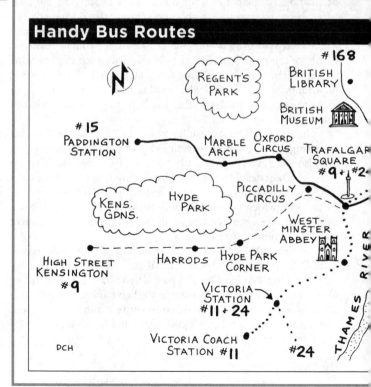

Handy Bus Routes

#168 BRITISH LIBRARY

REGENT'S PARK

BRITISH MUSEUM

#15 PADDINGTON STATION

MARBLE ARCH OXFORD CIRCUS TRAFALGAR SQUARE #9 + #2

PICCADILLY CIRCUS

KENS. GDNS. HYDE PARK

WEST-MINSTER ABBEY

HIGH STREET KENSINGTON #9

HARRODS HYDE PARK CORNER

VICTORIA STATION #11 + 24

VICTORIA COACH STATION #11

#24

THAMES RIVER

DCH

Trafalgar Square (#11 continues to St. Paul's and Liverpool Street Station).

Route #RV1: Tower of London to Tower Bridge to Tate Modern/Shakespeare's Globe to London Eye/Waterloo Station/County Hall Travel Inn accommodations to Aldwych to Covent Garden (a scenic South Bank joyride).

Route #15: Paddington Station to Oxford Circus to Regent Street/TI to Piccadilly Circus to Trafalgar Square to Fleet Street to St. Paul's to Tower of London. This is the other "Heritage Route" that uses old-style double-decker buses.

Route #168: Waterloo Station/London Eye to Covent Garden and then near British Museum and British Library.

In addition, several buses (including #6, #13, #15, #23, #139, and #159) make the corridor run from Trafalgar, Piccadilly Circus, and Oxford Circus to Marble Arch. Check the bus stop closest to your hotel—it might be convenient to your sightseeing plans.

LONDON

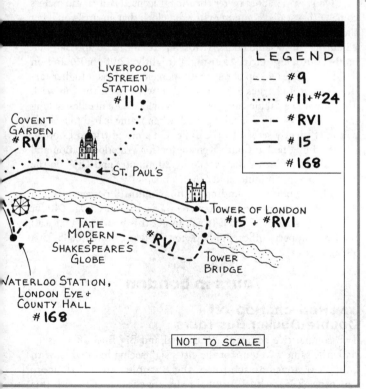

I've never met a crabby cabbie in London. They love to talk, and they know every nook and cranny in town. I ride in one each day just to get my London questions answered (drivers must pass a rigorous test on "The Knowledge" of London geography to earn their license). Rides start at £2.20. Connecting downtown sights is quick and easy, and will cost you about £6–8 (for example, St. Paul's to the Tower of London). For a short ride, three adults in a cab generally travel at close to Tube prices, and groups of four or five adults should taxi everywhere. Telephoning a cab will get you one in a few minutes (toll tel. 0871-871-8710; £2 surcharge, plus extra fee to book ahead by credit card), but it's generally not necessary; hailing a cab is easy and costs less. If a cab's top light is on, just wave it down. Drivers flash lights when they see you wave. They have a tight turning radius, so you can hail cabs going in either direction. If waving doesn't work, ask someone where you can find a taxi stand.

Don't worry about meter cheating. Licensed British cab meters come with a sealed computer chip and clock that ensures you'll get the regular tariff #1 most of the time (Mon–Fri 6:00–20:00), tariff #2 during "unsociable hours" (Mon–Fri 20:00–22:00 and Sat–Sun 6:00–22:00), and tariff #3 at night (nightly 22:00–6:00) and on holidays. (Rates go up about 15–20 percent with each higher tariff.) All extra charges are explained in writing on the cab wall. The only way a cabbie can cheat you is by taking a needlessly long route. Another pitfall is taking a cab when traffic is bad to a destination efficiently served by the Tube. On a recent trip to London, I hopped in a taxi at South Kensington for Waterloo Station and hit bad traffic. Rather than spending 20 minutes and £2–4 on the Tube, I spent 40 minutes and £16 in a taxi.

Tip a cabbie by rounding up (maximum 10 percent). If you drink too much and ride in a taxi, be warned: Taxis charge £40 for "soiling" (a.k.a., pub puke). If you forget this book in a taxi, call the Lost Property office and hope for the best (toll tel. 0845-330-9882).

Tours in London

▲▲▲Hop-on, Hop-off Double-Decker Bus Tours

Two competitive companies (Original and Big Bus) offer essentially the same two tours of the city's sightseeing highlights, with almost 30 stops on each route. Big Bus tours are a little more expensive (£25), while Original tours are cheaper (£21 with this book) and nearly as good.

These two-hour, once-over-lightly bus tours drive by all the famous sights, providing a stress-free way to get your bearings and

see the biggies. They stop at a core group of sights regardless of which overview tour you're on: Piccadilly Circus, Trafalgar Square, Big Ben, St. Paul's, the Tower of London, Marble Arch, Victoria Station, and elsewhere. With a good guide and nice weather, sit back and enjoy the entire two hours. Narration is important—so hop on and hop off to see the sights or to change guides (if yours is more boring than entertaining).

Each company offers at least one route with live (English-only) guides, and a second (sometimes slightly different route) comes with tape-recorded, dial-a-language narration. In addition to the overview tours, both Original and Big Bus include river cruises and three walking tours.

Pick up a map from any flier rack or from one of the countless salespeople, and study the complex system. Note: If you start at Victoria Station at 9:00, you'll finish near Buckingham Palace in time to see the Changing of the Guard at 11:30; ask your driver for the best place to hop off. Sunday morning—when the traffic is light and many museums are closed—is a fine time for a tour. Unless you're using the bus tour mainly for hop-on, hop-off transportation, consider saving money by taking a night tour (described later).

Buses run about every 10–15 minutes in summer, every 20 minutes in winter, and operate daily. They start at about 8:00 and run until early evening in summer, until late afternoon in winter. The last full loop usually leaves Victoria Station at about 17:00 (confirm by checking the schedule or asking the driver).

You can buy tickets from drivers or from staff at street kiosks (credit cards accepted at kiosks at major stops such as Victoria, ticket good for 24 hours).

Original London Sightseeing Bus Tour: For a live guide on the city highlights tour, look for a yellow triangle on the front of the bus. A red triangle means a longer, tape-recorded multilingual tour that includes Madame Tussauds—avoid it, unless you have kids who'd enjoy the entertaining recorded kids' tour. A blue triangle connects far-flung museums, while green, black, and purple triangle routes link major train stations to the central routes. All routes are covered by the same ticket. Keep it simple and just take the city highlights tour (£24, £21 after £3 discount with this book, limit two discounts per book, they'll rip off the corner of this page—raise bloody hell if the staff or driver won't honor this discount, also online deals, info center at 17 Cockspur Street, tel.

020/8877-1722, www.theoriginaltour.com). Your ticket includes a City Cruises "River Red Rover" all-day river cruise ticket (normally £11.50; for details see "Cruises: To Greenwich," page 65), as well as three free 90-minute walking tours.

Big Bus London Tours: For £25 (£20 online if you pick a specific date; requires printer), you get the same basic overview tours: Red buses come with a live guide, while the blue route has a recorded narration and a longer path around Hyde Park. Your ticket includes three silly one-hour London walks, as well as river cruises on the Thames (similar to "Rover" ticket mentioned above; cruises operated by City Cruises). These pricier tours tend to have better, more dynamic guides than Original, and more departures as well—meaning shorter waits for those hopping on and off (daily 8:30–18:00, winter until 16:30, info center at 48 Buckingham Palace Road, tel. 020/7233-9533, www.bigbustours.com).

At Night: The **London by Night Sightseeing Tour** offers a two-hour circuit, but after hours, with no extras (e.g., walks, river cruises), and at a lower price. While the narration can be pretty lame, the views at twilight are grand—though note that it stays light until late on summer nights (£15, £11 online, drivers take cash only; May–late Sept departs 19:30, 20:30, and 21:30 from Victoria Station, Jan–April and late Sept–late Dec departs 19:30 only, no tours between Christmas and New Year; Taxi Road, at front of station near end of Wilton Road; or board at any stop, such as Paddington Station, Marble Arch, Trafalgar Square, London Eye, or Tower of London; tel. 020/8545-6109, www.london-by-night .net). For a memorable and economical evening, munch a scenic picnic dinner on the top deck. There are plenty of take-away options in the train stations and near the various stops.

▲▲Walking Tours

Several times a day, top-notch local guides lead (sometimes big) groups through specific slices of London's past. Look for brochures at TIs or ask at hotels, although the latter usually push higher-priced bus tours. *Time Out*, the weekly entertainment guide (£3 at newsstands) lists some, but not all, scheduled walks. Check with the various tour companies by phone or online to get their full picture.

To take a walking tour, you simply show up at the announced location and pay the guide. Then enjoy two chatty hours of Dickens, Harry Potter, the Plague, Shakespeare, Legal London, the Beatles, or whatever is on the agenda.

London Walks: This leading company lists its extensive daily schedule in a beefy, plain *London Walks* brochure. Pick it up at St. Martin-in-the-Fields on Trafalgar Square, or access it on their website. Their two-hour walks cost £7 (cash only, walks offered year-round—even Christmas, private tours for groups-£100, tel. 020/7624-3978, for a recorded listing of today's walks call 020/7624-9255, www.walks.com). They also run Explorer day trips, a good option for those with limited time and transportation (£12 plus £10–40 for transportation and any admission costs, cash only, trips change most days: Stonehenge/Salisbury, Oxford/Cotswolds, Cambridge, Bath, and so on; fewer trips offered in winter).

Sandemans New London Tours: This company employs English-speaking students to give three-hour London tours. The fast-moving, youthful tours are light, irreverent, entertaining, and fun. Best of all, one of their tours—Royal London—is free (daily at 11:00, meet at Wellington Arch, Tube: Hyde Park Corner, Exit 2; they push for tips at the end and cross-promote their evening pub crawl). Their other tours include Old City (£9, daily at 10:00, meet at sundial opposite the Tower Hill Tube station exit); Grim Reapers (£9, daily at 14:00, also meets at Tower Hill Tube sundial); and a Pub Crawl (£12, Tue–Sat at 19:30, meet at Belushi's at 9 Russell Street, Tube: Covent Garden). Look for the guides in their red T-shirts (www.newlondon-tours.com).

The Beatles: Fans of the Fab Four can take one of three Beatles walks (London Walks, above, has two that run 5/week; Big Bus, above, includes a daily walk with their bus tour). For a photo op, go to Abbey Road and walk the famous crosswalk (at intersection with Grove End Road, Tube: St. John's Wood). The Beatles Store is at 231 Baker Street (daily 10:00–18:30, next to Sherlock Holmes Museum, Tube: Baker Street, tel. 020/7935-4464, www.beatlesstorelondon.co.uk).

Jack the Ripper: Each walking tour company seems to make most of its money with "haunted" and Jack the Ripper tours. Many guides are historians and would rather not lead these lightweight tours—but tourists pay more for gore (the ridiculously juvenile London Dungeon is one of the city's top sights). You'll find plenty of Ripper tours, but for a little twist, you might consider the scary walk given by Ripping Yarns, guided by Yeoman Warders of the Tower of London (£7, pay at end, 2.5 hours, nightly at 18:45 at Tower Hill Tube station, no tours between Christmas and New Year, mobile 07813-559-301, www.jack-the-ripper-tours.com).

Local Guides—Standard rates for London's registered "Blue Badge" guides usually run about £120 for four hours, and £190 or more for nine hours (tel. 020/7780-4060, www.touristguides.org.uk, www.blue-badge.org.uk).

Consider Sean Kelleher (£120/half-day, £200/day, also conducts tours about the history of transportation in London, tel. 020/8673-1624, mobile 07764-612-770, seankelleher@btinternet.com) or Britt Lonsdale (£150/half-day, £220/day, great with families, tel.

Daily Reminder

Sunday: The Tower of London and British Museum are both especially crowded today. The Speakers' Corner in Hyde Park rants from early afternoon until early evening. These places are closed: Banqueting House, Sir John Soane's Museum, and legal sights (Houses of Parliament, City Hall, and Old Bailey; the neighborhood called The City is dead). Westminster Abbey and St. Paul's are open during the day for worship but closed to sightseers. Many stores are closed, and some minor sights don't open until noon. The Camden Lock, Spitalfields, Greenwich, and Petticoat Lane street markets flourish, but Portobello Road and Brixton are closed. Except for the Globe, theaters are quiet, as most actors take today off.

Monday: Virtually all sights are open except for Apsley House, Sir John Soane's Museum, Vinopolis, and a few others. The Courtauld Gallery is free until 14:00. The Houses of Parliament are usually open until 22:30. The Portobello Road market is sparse.

Tuesday: Virtually all sights are open, except for Vinopolis and Apsley House. The British Library is open until 20:00. On the first Tuesday of the month, Sir John Soane's Museum is also open 18:00–21:00. The Houses of Parliament are usually open until 22:30.

Wednesday: Virtually all sights are open, except for Vinopolis. Westminster Abbey is open until 19:00.

020/7386-9907, mobile 07813-278-077, brittl@btinternet.com).

Drivers: Robina Brown leads small group tours in her Toyota Previa minivan (with car £270/half-day, £410–600/day; without car £120/half-day, £200/day; prices vary by destination, tel. 020/7228-2238, www.driverguidetours.com, robina@driverguide tours.com). Janine Barton provides a similar driver-and-guide tour and similar prices (tel. 020/7402-4600, http://seeitinstyle .synthasite.com, jbsiis@aol.com). Robina's and Janine's services are particularly helpful for travelers with disabilities who want to see more of London.

London Duck Tours

A bright-yellow amphibious WWII-vintage vehicle (the model that landed troops on Normandy's beaches on D-Day) takes a gang of 30 tourists past some famous sights on land—Big Ben, Trafalgar Square, Piccadilly Circus—then splashes into the Thames for a cruise. All in all, it's good fun at a rather steep price. The live guide works hard, and it's kid-friendly to the point of goofiness (£20, 2/ hr, daily 10:00–17:00, 75 min—45 min on land and 30 min in the

Thursday: All sights are open, plus evening hours at the British Museum (selected galleries until 20:30), National Portrait Gallery (until 21:00), and Vinopolis (until 22:00).

Friday: All sights are open, plus evening hours at the British Museum (selected galleries until 20:30), National Gallery (until 21:00), National Portrait Gallery (until 21:00), Vinopolis (until 22:00), Victoria and Albert Museum (until 22:00), and Tate Modern (until 22:00). The Houses of Parliament close early today (15:00). Best street market today: Spitalfields.

Saturday: Most sights are open except legal ones (Old Bailey, City Hall, Houses of Parliament; skip The City). Vinopolis is open until 22:00, and the Tate Modern until 22:00. Best street markets: Portobello, Camden Lock, Greenwich.

Notes: The St. Martin-in-the-Fields church offers **concerts** at lunchtime (free, Mon, Tue, and Fri at 13:00) and in the evening (jazz: £5-8, Wed at 20:00; classical: £6-25, at 19:30 Thu-Sat, sometimes Tue). **Evensong** occurs daily at St. Paul's (Mon-Sat at 17:00 and Sun at 15:15), Westminster Abbey (Mon-Fri at 17:00—may be spoken on Wed, Sat-Sun at 15:00), and Southwark Cathedral (weekdays at 17:30, Sat at 16:00, Sun at 15:00, no service on Wed or alternate Mon). **London by Night Sightseeing Tour** buses leave from Victoria Station every evening (19:30-21:30, only at 19:30 in winter). The **London Eye** spins nightly (until 20:00-21:30, depending on the season). See also the "London for Early Birds and Night Owls" sidebar on page 82.

LONDON

river, £2.50 online booking fee, these book up in advance, departs from Chicheley Street—you'll see the big, ugly vehicle parked 100 yards behind the London Eye, Tube: Waterloo or Westminster, tel. 020/7928-3132, www.londonducktours.co.uk).

Bike Tours

London, like Paris, is committed to making more bike paths, and many of its best sights can be laced together with a pleasant pedal through its parks.

London Bicycle Tour Company: Three tours covering London are offered daily from their base at Gabriel's Wharf on the south bank of the Thames. Sunday is the best, as there is less car traffic (Central Tour—£16, April–Oct daily at 10:30, 6 miles, 2.5 hours, includes Westminster, Covent Garden, and St. Paul's; West Tour—£19, April–Oct Sat–Sun at 12:00, Nov–March only on Sun, 9 miles, 3.5 hours, includes Westminster, Hyde Park, Buckingham Palace, and Covent Garden; East Tour—£19, April–Oct Sat–Sun at 14:00, Nov–March only on Sat, 9 miles, 3.5 hours, includes south side of the river to Tower Bridge, then The City to the East

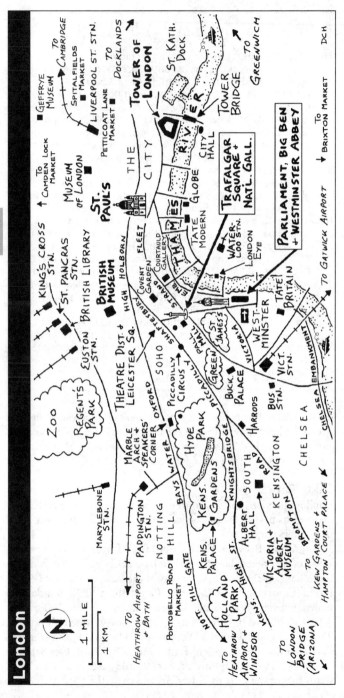

London

End). They also rent bikes (office open daily 10:00–18:00, west of Blackfriars Bridge on the South Bank, 1a Gabriel's Wharf, tel. 020/7928-6838, www.londonbicycle.com).

Fat Tire Bike Tours: Daily bike tours cover the highlights of downtown London. The spiel is light and irreverent rather than scholarly, but the price is right. This is a fun way to see the sights and enjoy the city on two wheels (£16, daily June–Aug at 11:00 and 15:30, March–May and Sept–Nov at 11:00, Dec–Feb by reservation only, covers 7 miles in 4 hours, pay when you show up—no reservations needed except for kids' bikes or in winter, Queensway Tube station, mobile 078-8233-8779, www.fattire biketourslondon.com).

▲▲Cruises

Boat tours with entertaining commentaries sail regularly from many points along the Thames. It's a bit confusing, since several companies offer essentially the same trip. Your basic options are to use the boats to go downstream to the Tower and Greenwich, upstream to Kew Gardens and Hampton Court, or just enjoy a round-trip scenic tour cruise. Most people depart from the Westminster Pier (at the base of Westminster Bridge across the street from Big Ben). You can catch many of the same boats (with less waiting) from Waterloo Pier at the London Eye across the river. For pleasure and efficiency, consider combining a one-way cruise (to Kew Gardens, Greenwich, or wherever) with a Tube or train ride back.

Buy boat tickets at the small ticket offices on the docks. While individual Tube and bus tickets don't work on the boats, a Travelcard or Seven-Day Oyster card can snare you a 33 percent discount on most cruises (just show the card when you pay for the cruise, not valid with pay-as-you-go Oyster cards). Children and seniors get discounts. You can purchase drinks and scant, pricey snacks on board. Clever budget travelers pack a picnic and munch while they cruise.

Here are some of the most popular cruise options:

To the Tower of London: City Cruises boats sail 30 minutes to the Tower from Westminster Pier (£6.90 one-way, £8.70 round-trip, one-way included with Big Bus London tour; covered by £11.50 "River Red Rover" ticket that includes Greenwich; daily April–Oct roughly 10:00–21:00, until 18:00 in winter, every 20 min).

To Greenwich: Two companies—City Cruises and the Thames River Services—head to Greenwich from Westminster Pier. The cruises are usually narrated by the captain, with most commentary given on the way to Greenwich. The companies' prices are the same, though **City Cruises** offers a few more alternatives (£8.40 one-way, £11 round-trip; or get their £11.50 all-day, hop-on,

Thames Boat Piers

While Westminster Pier is the most popular, it's not the only dock in town. Consider all the options:

Westminster Pier, at the base of Big Ben, offers round-trip sightseeing cruises and lots of departures in both directions.

Waterloo Pier, at the base of the London Eye, is a good, less-crowded alternative to Westminster, with many of the same cruise options.

Embankment Pier is near Covent Garden, Trafalgar Square, and Cleopatra's Needle (the obelisk on the Thames). You can take a round-trip cruise from here, or catch a boat to the Tower of London and Greenwich.

Tower Pier is at the Tower of London. Boats sail west to Westminster Pier or east to Greenwich.

Bankside Pier (near Tate Modern and Shakespeare's Globe) and **Millbank Pier** (near Tate Britain) are connected to each other by the Tate Boat ferry service.

hop-off "River Red Rover" ticket to have the option of getting off at the London Eye and Tower of London—included with Original London bus tour; daily April–Oct generally 10:00–17:00, less off-season, about every 40 min, 75 min to Greenwich; also departs for Greenwich from the pier at the Tower of London for less: £6.90 one-way, £8.70 round-trip, 30 min; tel. 020/7740-0400, www.citycruises.com). The **Thames River Services** goes to Greenwich from Westminster Pier a bit more frequently and a little quicker (£8.40 one-way, £11 round-trip, April–Oct 10:00–16:00, July–Aug until 17:00, daily 2/hr; Nov–March shorter hours and runs every 40 min; 1 hour to Greenwich, tel. 020/7930-4097, www.thamesriverservices.co.uk).

To Kew Gardens: Boats run by the Westminster Passenger Services Association leave for Kew Gardens from Westminster Pier (£11 one-way, £17 round-trip, cash only, 4/day, April–Oct daily 10:30–14:00, 90 min, narrated for 45 min, tel. 020/7930-2062, www.wpsa.co.uk). Some boats continue on to **Hampton Court Palace** for an additional £3 (and 90 min). Because of the river current, you'll sometimes save 30 minutes cruising from Hampton Court back into town (depends on the tide).

Round-Trip Cruises: The London Eye operates its own "River Cruise," offering a 40-minute live-guided circular tour from Waterloo Pier (£12, reservations recommended, departures daily generally at :45 past the hour, April–Oct 10:45–18:45, Nov–March 11:45–16:45, closed mid-Jan–mid-Feb, toll tel. 0870-500-0600, www.londoneye.com).

From Tate to Tate: The Tate Boat service for art-lovers connects the Tate Modern and Tate Britain via a sleek, 220-seat catamaran (£5 one-way or £12 for a day ticket, discounted with Travelcard, buy ticket at gallery desk or on board, runs daily every 40 min, from Tate Modern 10:10–16:50, from Tate Britain 10:30–17:10, 18-min trip, tel. 020/7887-8888, www.tate.org.uk).

On Regent's Canal: Consider exploring London's canals by taking a cruise on historic Regent's Canal in north London. The good ship *Jenny Wren* offers 90-minute guided canal boat cruises from Walker's Quay in Camden Town through scenic Regent's Park to Little Venice (£8.50, Aug daily at 10:30, 12:30, 14:30 and 16:30, April–July and Sept–Oct daily at 12:30 and 14:30, Sat–Sun also at 16:30; Walker's Quay, 250 Camden High Street, 3-min walk from Tube: Camden Town; tel. 020/7485-4433, www.walkersquay.com). While in Camden Town, stop by the popular, punky Camden Lock Market to browse through trendy arts and crafts (daily 10:00–18:00, busiest on weekends, a block from Walker's Quay, www.camdenlock.net).

Self-Guided Walk

Westminster Walk

Just about every visitor to London strolls along historic Whitehall from Big Ben to Trafalgar Square. This quick nine-stop walk gives meaning to that touristy ramble. Under London's modern traffic and big-city bustle lie 2,000 fascinating years of history. You'll get a whirlwind tour as well as a practical orientation to London.

Start halfway across **Westminster Bridge (❶)** for that "Wow, I'm really in London!" feeling. Get a close-up view of the **Houses of Parliament** and **Big Ben** (floodlit at night). Downstream, you'll see the **London Eye.** Down the stairs to Westminster Pier are boats to the Tower of London and Greenwich (downstream) or Kew Gardens (upstream).

En route to Parliament Square, you'll pass a **statue of Boadicea (❷)**, the Celtic queen defeated by Roman invaders in A.D. 60.

For fun, call home from a pay phone near Big Ben at about three minutes before the hour, to let your loved one hear the bell ring. You'll find four red phone booths lining the north side of **Parliament Square (❸)** along Great George Street.

Wave hello to Churchill in Parliament Square. To his right is **Westminster Abbey** with its two stubby, elegant towers.

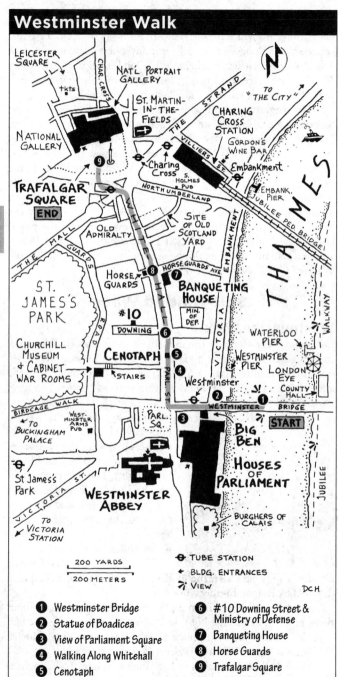

Westminster Walk

LEICESTER SQUARE

tkts

NAT'L PORTRAIT GALLERY

ST. MARTIN-IN-THE-FIELDS

CHAR. CROSS

THE STRAND

TO "THE CITY"

CHARING CROSS STATION

GORDON'S WINE BAR

VILLIERS ST.

NATIONAL GALLERY

Charing Cross

S. HOLMES PUB

Embankment

EMBANK. PIER

THAMES

JUBILEE PED. BRIDGE

TRAFALGAR SQUARE
END

NORTHUMBERLAND

OLD ADMIRALTY

SITE OF OLD SCOTLAND YARD

THE MALL

GUARDS

ROAD

ST. JAMES'S PARK

Horse Guards

HORSE GUARDS AVE.

BANQUETING HOUSE

WHITEHALL

VICTORIA EMBANKMENT

CHURCHILL MUSEUM & CABINET WAR ROOMS

#10 DOWNING

MIN. OF DEF.

WATERLOO PIER

Cenotaph

STAIRS

PARL. ST.

Westminster

WESTMINSTER PIER

LONDON EYE

COUNTY HALL

BIRDCAGE WALK

WEST-MINSTER ARMS PUB

PARL. SQ.

WESTMINSTER BRIDGE

START

TO BUCKINGHAM PALACE

St James's Park

BIG BEN

HOUSES OF PARLIAMENT

VICTORIA ST.

WESTMINSTER ABBEY

WALKWAY

JUBILEE

TO VICTORIA STATION

BURGHERS OF CALAIS

200 YARDS
200 METERS

⊖ TUBE STATION
← BLDG. ENTRANCES
🏃 VIEW

DCH

1 Westminster Bridge
2 Statue of Boadicea
3 View of Parliament Square
4 Walking Along Whitehall
5 Cenotaph

6 #10 Downing Street & Ministry of Defense
7 Banqueting House
8 Horse Guards
9 Trafalgar Square

LONDON

Head north up Parliament Street, which turns into **Whitehall** (❹), and walk toward Trafalgar Square. You'll see the thought-provoking **Cenotaph** (❺) in the middle of the street, reminding passersby of Britain's many war dead. To visit the Churchill Museum and Cabinet War Rooms (see page 74), take a left before the Cenotaph, on King Charles Street.

Continuing on Whitehall, stop at the barricaded and guarded **#10 Downing Street** (❻) to see the British "White House," home of the prime minister. Break the bobby's boredom and ask him a question.

Nearing Trafalgar Square, look for the 17th-century **Banqueting House** across the street (❼) and the **Horse Guards** (❽)

behind the gated fence (Changing of the Horse Guards Mon–Sat at 11:00, Sun at 10:00, dismounting ceremony daily at 16:00).

The column topped by Lord Nelson marks **Trafalgar Square** (❾). The stately domed building on the far side of the square is the **National Gallery** (free), which has a classy café upstairs in the Sainsbury wing. To the right of the National Gallery is **St. Martin-in-the-Fields Church** and its Café in the Crypt.

To get to Piccadilly from Trafalgar Square, walk up Cockspur Street to Haymarket, then take a short left on Coventry Street to colorful **Piccadilly Circus.**

Near Piccadilly you'll find the **Britain and London Visitors Centre** (on Lower Regent Street) and piles of theaters. **Leicester Square** (with its half-price "tkts" booth for plays, see page 121) thrives just a few blocks away. Walk through seedy **Soho** (north of Shaftesbury Avenue) for its fun pubs (consider my recommended Soho "Food Is Fun" Three-Course Dinner Crawl on page 149). From Piccadilly or Oxford Circus, you can take a taxi, bus, or the Tube home.

Sights in London

Central London
Westminster
▲▲▲**Westminster Abbey**—The greatest church in the English-speaking world, Westminster Abbey is the place where England's kings and queens have been crowned and buried since 1066. A thousand years of English history—3,000 tombs, the remains of 29 kings and queens, and hundreds of memorials to poets, politicians, and warriors—lie within its stained-glass splendor and under its

stone slabs. Like a stony refugee camp huddled outside St. Peter's Pearly Gates, this place has many stories to tell. The steep admission includes an excellent audioguide, worthwhile if you have the time and interest. To experience the church more vividly, take a live tour, or attend evensong or an organ concert (see below). You can even have a sandwich or bowl of soup in the cloister...but you can't take photos.

Two tiny **museums** ring the cloisters: the Chapter House (where the monks held daily meetings, notable for its fine architecture, stained glass, and faded but well-described medieval art), and the Abbey Museum (which tells of the abbey's history, royal coronations, and burials). Look into the impressively realistic eyes of Henry VII's funeral effigy (one of a fascinating series of wax-and-wood statues that, for three centuries, graced royal coffins during funeral processions).

Cost: £15, £30 family ticket for three, includes cloisters, audioguide, and Abbey Museum.

Hours and Information: Abbey open Mon–Fri 9:30–16:30, Wed until 19:00; Sat 9:30–14:30, last entry one hour before closing, closed Sun to sightseers but open for services; Abbey Museum open daily 10:30–16:00; cloisters open daily 8:00–18:00; £3 90-min guided tours, 5/day in summer; Tube: Westminster or St. James's Park. Info desk tel. 020/7222-5152 or 020/7654-4834, www.westminster-abbey.org.

Avoiding Crowds: The main entrance, on the Parliament Square side, often has a sizable line; visit early, during lunch, or late to avoid tourist hordes. Midmornings are most crowded, while weekdays after 14:30 are less congested; come then and stay for the 17:00 evensong.

Music: The church hosts **evensong** performances daily, sung every night but Wednesday, when it is spoken (Mon–Fri at 17:00; Sat–Sun at 15:00). A free 30-minute **organ recital** is usually held on Sunday at 17:45.

▲▲**Houses of Parliament (Palace of Westminster)**—This Neo-Gothic icon of London, the royal residence from 1042–1547, is now the meeting place of the legislative branch of government. The Houses of Parliament are located in what was once the Palace of Westminster—long the palace of England's medieval kings—until it was largely destroyed by fire in 1834. The palace was rebuilt in the Victorian Gothic style (a move away from Neoclassicism back to England's Christian and medieval heritage, true to the

Romantic Age) and completed in 1860.

Tourists are welcome to view debates in either the bickering House of Commons or the genteel House of Lords. You're only allowed inside when Parliament is in session, indicated by a flag flying atop the Victoria Tower at the south end of the building (generally Mondays through Thursdays, plus some Fridays). While the actual debates are generally quite dull, it is a thrill to be inside and see the British government in action.

Cost and Hours: Free, both Houses usually open Mon–Tue 14:30–22:30, Wed–Thu 11:30–17:50, Fri 9:30–15:00, closed Sat–Sun, generally less action and no lines after 18:00, Tube: Westminster. Tel. 020/7219-4272; see www.parliament.uk for schedule. The House of Lords has more pageantry, shorter lines, and less interesting debates (tel. 020/7219-3107 for schedule, and visit www.parliamentlive.tv for a preview).

Visiting the Houses of Parliament (HOP): Enter the venerable HOP midway along the west side of the building (across the street from Westminster Abbey) through the Visitor Entrance (with the tourist ramp, next to the St. Stephen's Entrance—if lost, ask a guard). As you enter, you'll be asked if you want to visit the House of Commons or the House of Lords. Inquire about the wait—an hour or two is not unusual. If there's a long line for the House of Commons and you just want a quick look inside the grand halls of this grand building, start with the House of Lords. Once inside you can switch if you like.

Just past security, you enter the vast and historic **Westminster Hall,** which survived the 1834 fire. The hall was built in the 11th century, and its famous self-supporting hammer-beam roof was added in 1397. Racks of brochures here explain how the British government works, and plaques describe the hall. The Jubilee Café, open to the public, has live video feeds showing exactly what's going on in each house. Just seeing the café video is a fun experience (and can help you decide which house—if either—you'd actually like to see). Walking through the hall and up the stairs, you'll enter the busy world of government with all its high-powered goings-on.

Houses of Parliament Summer Recess Tours: Though Parliament is in recess during much of August and September, you can get a behind-the-scenes peek at the royal chambers of both houses with a tour (£13, 75 min, tours generally Tue–Thu, times vary so confirm in advance; book ahead through Keith Prowse ticket agency—toll tel. 0870-906-3773, www.keithprowse.com, no booking fee).

The **Jewel Tower,** across the street from the Parliament building's St. Stephen's Gate, is a rare remnant of the old Palace of Westminster used by kings until Henry VIII. The crude stone tower (1365–66) was a guard tower in the palace wall, overlooking

London at a Glance

▲▲▲**Westminster Abbey** Britain's finest church and the site of royal coronations and burials since 1066. **Hours:** Mon–Fri 9:30–16:30, Wed until 19:00; Sat 9:30–14:30, closed Sun to sightseers except for worship. See page 69.

▲▲▲**Churchill Museum and Cabinet War Rooms** Underground WWII headquarters of Churchill's war effort. **Hours:** Daily 9:30–18:00. See page 74.

▲▲▲**National Gallery** Remarkable collection of European paintings (1250–1900), including Leonardo, Botticelli, Velázquez, Rembrandt, Turner, Van Gogh, and the Impressionists. **Hours:** Daily 10:00–18:00, Fri until 21:00. See page 76.

▲▲▲**British Museum** The world's greatest collection of artifacts of Western civilization, including the Rosetta Stone and the Parthenon's Elgin Marbles. **Hours:** Daily 10:00–17:30, Thu–Fri until 20:30 but only a few galleries open after 17:30. See page 87.

▲▲▲**British Library** Impressive collection of the most important literary treasures of the Western world. **Hours:** Mon–Fri 9:30–18:00, Tue until 20:00, Sat 9:30–17:00, Sun 11:00–17:00. See page 89.

▲▲▲**St. Paul's Cathedral** The main cathedral of the Anglican Church, designed by Christopher Wren, with a climbable dome and daily evensong services. **Hours:** Mon–Sat 8:30–16:30, closed Sun except for worship. See page 93.

▲▲▲**Tower of London** Historic castle, palace, and prison, today housing the crown jewels and a witty band of Beefeaters. **Hours:** March–Oct Tue–Sat 9:00–17:30, Sun–Mon 10:00–17:30; Nov–Feb Tue–Sat 9:00–16:30, Sun–Mon 10:00–16:30. See page 96.

▲▲**London Eye** Enormous observation wheel, dominating—and offering commanding views over—London's skyline. **Hours:** Daily June–Sept 10:00–21:00, July–Aug until 21:30, Oct–May until 20:00. See page 101.

▲▲**Tate Modern** Works by Monet, Matisse, Dalí, Picasso, and Warhol displayed in a converted powerhouse. **Hours:** Daily 10:00–18:00, Fri–Sat until 22:00. See page 103.

▲▲**Houses of Parliament** London's famous Neo-Gothic landmark, topped by Big Ben and occupied by the Houses of Lords and Commons. **Hours** (both Houses): Generally Mon–Tue 14:30–22:30, Wed–Thu 11:30–17:50, Fri 9:30–15:00, closed Sat–Sun. See page 70.

▲▲**National Portrait Gallery** A *Who's Who* of British history, featuring portraits of this nation's most important historical figures. **Hours:** Daily 10:00–18:00, Thu–Fri until 21:00. See page 77.

▲▲**Victoria and Albert Museum** The best collection of decorative arts anywhere. **Hours:** Daily 10:00–17:45, Fri until 22:00. See page 110.

▲▲**Imperial War Museum** Examines the military history of the bloody 20th century. **Hours:** Daily 10:00–18:00. See page 101.

▲▲**Shakespeare's Globe** Timbered, thatch-roofed reconstruction of the Bard's original wooden "O." **Hours:** Theater complex, museum, and actor-led tours generally daily May–Sept 9:00–17:00, Oct–April 10:00–17:00; in summer, morning theater tours only. Plays are also held here. See page 103.

▲▲**Tate Britain** Collection of British painting from the 16th century through modern times, including works by William Blake, the Pre-Raphaelites, and J. M. W. Turner. **Hours:** Daily 10:00–17:50, first Fri of the month until 21:40. See page 107.

▲**Courtauld Gallery** Fine collection of paintings filling one wing of the Somerset House, a grand 18th-century palace. **Hours:** Daily 10:00–18:00. See page 83.

▲**Buckingham Palace** Britain's royal residence with the famous Changing of the Guard. **Hours:** Palace—Aug–Sept only, daily 9:45–18:00; Guard—May–July daily at 11:30, Aug–April every other day. See page 83.

▲**Old Operating Theatre Museum** 19th-century hall where surgeons performed amputations for an audience of aspiring med students. **Hours:** Daily 10:30–17:00. See page 106.

a moat. It contains a fine little exhibit on Parliament and the tower. Next to the tower (and free) is a quiet courtyard with picnic-friendly benches (£3, daily March–Oct 10:00–17:00, Nov–Feb 10:00–16:00, tel. 020/7222-2219).

Big Ben, the clock tower (315 feet high), is named for its 13-ton bell, Ben. The light above the clock is lit when the House of Commons is sitting. The face of the clock is huge—you can actually see the minute hand moving. For a good view of it, walk halfway over Westminster Bridge.

▲▲▲**Churchill Museum and Cabinet War Rooms**—This is a fascinating walk through the underground headquarters of the British government's fight against the Nazis in the darkest days of the Battle for Britain. The 27-room nerve center of the British war effort was used from 1939 to 1945. Churchill's room, the map room, and other rooms are just as they were in 1945. For all the

blood, sweat, toil, and tears details, pick up the excellent, essential, and included audioguide at the entry and follow the 60-minute tour; be patient—it's well worth it.

Don't bypass the Churchill Museum (entrance is a half-dozen rooms into the exhibit), which shows the man behind the famous cigar, bowler hat, and V-for-victory sign—allow an hour for that museum alone. It shows his wit, irascibility, work ethic, American ties, writing talents, and drinking habits. A long touch-the-screen timeline lets you zero in on events in his life from birth (November 30, 1874) to his appointment as prime minister in 1940. It's all the more amazing considering that, in the 1930s, the man who would become my vote for greatest statesman of the 20th century was considered a washed-up loony ranting about the growing threat of fascism.

Cost, Hours, Location: £13, daily 9:30–18:00, last entry one hour before closing; on King Charles Street, 200 yards off Whitehall, follow the signs, Tube: Westminster. Tel. 020/7930-6961, www.iwm.org.uk. The museum's gift shop is great for anyone nostalgic for the 1940s.

Nearby: If you're hungry, get your rations at the Switch Room café (in the museum) or, for a nearby pub lunch, try the Westminster Arms (food served downstairs, on Storey's Gate, a couple of blocks south of Cabinet War Rooms).

Horse Guards—The Horse Guards change daily at 11:00 (10:00 on Sun), and there's a colorful dismounting ceremony daily at

16:00. The rest of the day, they just stand there—terrible for video cameras (on Whitehall, between Trafalgar Square and #10 Downing Street, Tube: Westminster, www.changing-the-guard .com). Buckingham Palace pageantry is canceled when it rains, but the horse guards change regardless of the weather.

▲**Banqueting House**—England's first Renaissance building was designed by Inigo Jones in about 1620. It's one of the few

London landmarks spared by the 1698 fire and the only surviving part of the original Palace of Whitehall. Don't miss its Rubens ceiling, which, at Charles I's request, drove home the doctrine of the legitimacy of the divine right of kings.

In 1649—divine right ignored—Charles I was beheaded on the balcony of this building by order of a Cromwellian Parliament. Admission includes a restful 20-minute audiovisual history, which shows the place in banqueting action; a 30-minute audioguide— interesting only to history buffs; and a look at the exquisite banqueting hall.

Cost, Hours, Location: £4.80, includes audioguide, Mon– Sat 10:00–17:00, closed Sun, last entry at 16:30, subject to closure for government functions, aristocratic WC, immediately across Whitehall from the Horse Guards, Tube: Westminster. Tel. 020/3166-6154 or 020/3166-6155, www.hrp.org.uk. Just up the street is Trafalgar Square.

On Trafalgar Square

▲▲**Trafalgar Square**—London's recently renovated central square, the climax of most marches and demonstrations, is a

thrilling place to simply hang out. Lord Nelson stands atop his 185-foot-tall fluted granite column, gazing out toward Trafalgar, where he lost his life but defeated the French fleet. Part of this 1842 memorial is made from his victims' melted- down cannons. He's surrounded by spraying fountains, giant

lions, hordes of people, and—until recently—even more pigeons. A former London mayor decided that London's "flying rats" were a public nuisance and evicted Trafalgar Square's venerable seed salesmen (Tube: Charing Cross).

Trafalgar Square

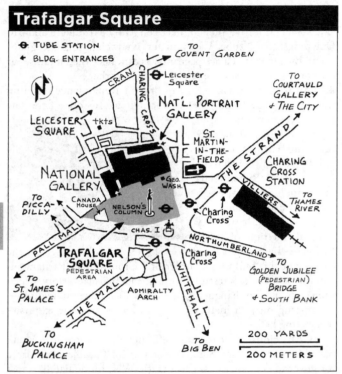

- ⊖ TUBE STATION
- ← BLDG. ENTRANCES

TO COVENT GARDEN

⊖ Leicester Square

NAT'L. PORTRAIT GALLERY

LEICESTER SQUARE

tkts

CRAN

CHARING CROSS

ST. MARTIN-IN-THE-FIELDS

TO COURTAULD GALLERY & THE CITY

THE STRAND

CHARING CROSS STATION

NATIONAL GALLERY

GEO. WASH.

VILLIERS

TO PICCA-DILLY

Canada House

NELSON'S COLUMN

Charing Cross

TO THAMES RIVER

PALL MALL

CHAS. I

NORTHUMBERLAND

TRAFALGAR SQUARE
PEDESTRIAN AREA

Charing Cross

TO GOLDEN JUBILEE (PEDESTRIAN) BRIDGE & SOUTH BANK

TO ST. JAMES'S PALACE

THE MALL

ADMIRALTY ARCH

WHITEHALL

200 YARDS

200 METERS

TO BUCKINGHAM PALACE

TO BIG BEN

▲▲▲National Gallery—Displaying Britain's top collection of European paintings from 1250–1900—including works by Leonardo, Botticelli, Velázquez, Rembrandt, Turner, Van Gogh, and the Impressionists—this is one of Europe's great galleries.

While the collection is huge, following the route suggested on the highlights map (see pages 78–79) will give you my best quick visit. The audioguide tour (suggested £3.50 donation) is one of the finest I've used in Europe.

Cost, Hours, Location: Free, but suggested donation of £1–2; daily 10:00–18:00, Fri until 21:00; last entry to special exhibits 45 min before closing, free one-hour overview tours daily at 11:30 and 14:30; no photography, on Trafalgar Square, Tube: Charing Cross or Leicester Square. Recorded info tel. 020/7747-2885, switchboard tel. 020/7839-3321, www.national gallery.org.uk. The excellent-but-pricey museum restaurant called the National Dining Rooms is a good spot to split afternoon tea (see page 152). Two cheaper eateries, also in the museum, are located near the Getty Entrance: the National Café (with both a casual sandwich/soup/salad/pastry area and a table-service restaurant) and the Espresso Bar (sandwiches, soft couches, and ArtStart computers).

▲▲**National Portrait Gallery**—Put off by halls of 19th-century characters who meant nothing to me, I used to call this "as interesting as someone else's yearbook." But a selective walk through this 500-year-long Who's Who of British history is quick and free, and puts faces on the story of England. The collection is well-described, not huge, and in historical sequence, from the 16th century on the second floor to today's royal family on the ground floor.

Some highlights: Henry VIII and wives; portraits of the "Virgin Queen" Elizabeth I, Sir Francis Drake, and Sir Walter Raleigh; the only real-life portrait of William Shakespeare; Oliver Cromwell and Charles I with his head on; portraits by Gainsborough and Reynolds; the Romantics (William Blake, Lord Byron, William Wordsworth, and company); Queen Victoria and her era; and the present royal family, including the late Princess Diana.

Cost, Hours, Location: Free, but suggested donation of £3; daily 10:00–18:00, Thu–Fri until 21:00, last entry to special exhibits 45 min before closing, excellent themed audioguides—£2 suggested donation; entry 100 yards off Trafalgar Square, around corner from National Gallery, opposite Church of St. Martin-in-the-Fields; Tube: Charing Cross or Leicester Square. Tel. 020/7306-0055, recorded info tel. 020/7312-2463, www.npg.org.uk.

The elegant Portrait Restaurant on the top floor is pricey but has a fine view of Trafalgar Square (£15–20 entrées, reservations smart, tel. 020/7312-2490). The Portrait Café in the basement (take the lift down) is cheaper and offers sandwiches, salads, and pastries.

▲**St. Martin-in-the-Fields**—The church, built in the 1720s with a Gothic spire atop a Greek-type temple, is an oasis of peace on the wild and noisy Trafalgar Square. St. Martin cared for the poor. "In the fields" was where the first church stood on this spot (in the 13th century), between Westminster and The City. Stepping inside, you still feel a compassion for the needs of the people in this neighborhood—the church serves the homeless and houses a Chinese community center. The modern east window—with grillwork bent into the shape of a warped cross—was installed in 2008 to replace one damaged in World War II.

A new freestanding glass pavilion to the left of the church serves as the entrance to the church's underground areas. There you'll find the concert ticket office, a gift shop, a brass-rubbing

LONDON

National Gallery Highlights

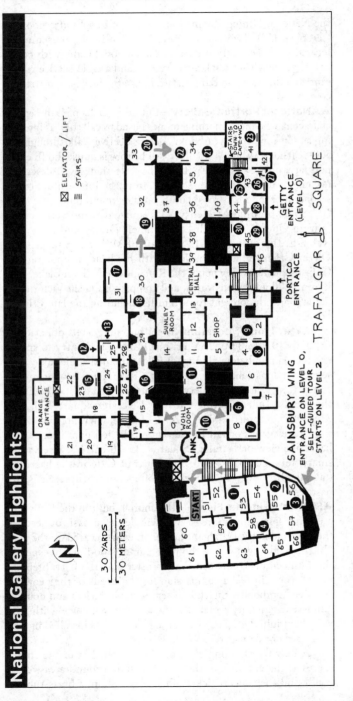

MEDIEVAL & EARLY RENAISSANCE
1. ANONYMOUS – The Wilton Diptych
2. UCCELLO – Battle of San Romano
3. VAN EYCK – The Arnolfini Marriage

ITALIAN RENAISSANCE
4. BOTTICELLI – Venus and Mars
5. CRIVELLI – The Annunciation, with Saint Emidius

HIGH RENAISSANCE
6. MICHELANGELO – Entombment
7. RAPHAEL – Pope Julius II
8. HOLBEIN – The Ambassadors
9. DA VINCI – The Virgin of the Rocks; Virgin and Child with St. Anne and St. John the Baptist

VENETIAN RENAISSANCE
10. TINTORETTO – The Origin of the Milky Way
11. TITIAN – Bacchus and Ariadne

NORTHERN PROTESTANT ART
12. VERMEER – A Young Woman
13. "A Peepshow"
14. REMBRANDT – Belshazzar's Feast
15. REMBRANDT – Self-Portrait

BAROQUE & ROCOCO
16. RUBENS – The Judgment of Paris
17. VAN DYCK – Equestrian Portrait of Charles I
18. VELÁZQUEZ – The Rokeby Venus
19. CARAVAGGIO – The Supper at Emmaus
20. BOUCHER – Pan and Syrinx

BRITISH
21. CONSTABLE – The Hay Wain
22. TURNER – The Fighting Téméraire
23. DELAROCHE – The Execution of Lady Jane Grey

IMPRESSIONISM & BEYOND
24. MONET – Gare St. Lazare
25. MONET – The Water-Lily Pond
26. MANET – Corner of a Café-Concert (a.k.a. The Waitress)
27. RENOIR – Boating on the Seine
28. SEURAT – Bathers at Asnières
29. VAN GOGH – Sunflowers
30. CÉZANNE – Bathers

LONDON

center, and the fine support-the-church Café in the Crypt (described on page 143).

Cost, Hours, Location: Church entry free, donations welcome, audioguide available, open daily, Tube: Charing Cross. Tel. 020/7766-1100, www2.stmartin-in-the-fields.org.

Music: The church is famous for its concerts. Consider a free lunchtime concert (Mon, Tue, and Fri at 13:00), an evening concert (£6–25, at 19:30 Thu–Sat and on some Tue), or live jazz in the church's café (£5–8, Wed at 20:00). See the church's website for the concert schedule.

West End and Nearby

To explore this area during dinner, take my recommended Soho "Food Is Fun" Three-Course Dinner Crawl, and munch your way from Covent Garden to Soho (see page 149).

▲▲**Piccadilly Circus**—London's most touristy square got its name from the fancy ruffled shirts—*picadils*—made in the neighborhood long ago. Today, the square (Tube: Piccadilly), while pretty grotty, is surrounded by fascinating streets swimming with youth on the rampage. Look no further than the gargantuan **Ripley's Believe-It-Or-Not Museum** to capture the gimmicky flavor of today's Piccadilly. For overstimulation in a grimy mall that smells like teen spirit, drop by the extremely trashy **Trocadero Center** for its Funland arcade games, nine-screen cinema, and 10-lane bowling alley (admission to Trocadero is free; individual attractions cost £2–10; located between Piccadilly and Leicester Squares on Coventry Street, Tube: Piccadilly Circus). Chinatown, to the east, swelled when the former British colony of Hong Kong was returned to China in 1997, but is now threatened by developers. Nearby Shaftesbury Avenue and Leicester Square teem with fun-seekers, theaters, Chinese restaurants, and street singers.

Soho—North of Piccadilly, seedy Soho has become seriously trendy and is well worth a gawk. But Soho is also London's red light district (especially near Brewer and Berwick streets), where "friendly models" wait in tiny rooms up dreary stairways, and voluptuous con artists sell strip shows. Though venturing up a stairway to check out a model is interesting, anyone who goes into any one of the shows will be ripped off. Every time. Even a £5 show in a "licensed bar" comes with a £100 cover or minimum (as it's printed on the drink menu) and a "security man." You may accidentally buy a £200 bottle of bubbly. And suddenly, the door has no handle.

Telephone sex ads are hard to avoid these days in London. Phone booths are littered with racy fliers of busty ladies "new in town." Some travelers gather six or eight phone booths' worth of fliers and take them home for kinky wallpaper.

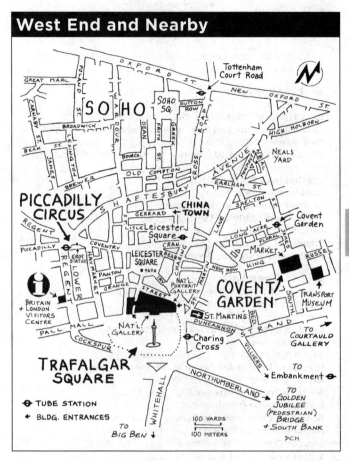

West End and Nearby

▲▲Covent Garden—The centerpiece of this boutique-ish shopping district is an iron-and-glass arcade. The opera house borders the square, and venerable theatres are nearby. The area is a people-watcher's delight, with cigarette eaters, Punch-and-Judy acts, food that's good for you (but not your wallet), trendy crafts, sweet whiffs of marijuana, two-tone hair (neither natural), and faces that could set off a metal detector (Tube: Covent Garden). For better Covent Garden lunch deals, walk a block or two away from the eye of this touristic hurricane (check out the places north of the Tube station along Endell and Neal streets).

▲London Transport Museum—This newly renovated museum is fun for kids and thought-provoking for adults. Whether you're cursing or marveling at the buses and Tube, the growth of Europe's third-biggest city (after Moscow and Istanbul) has been made possible by its public transit system. An elevator transports

LONDON

London for Early Birds and Night Owls

Most sightseeing in London is restricted to the hours between 10:00 and 18:00. Here are a few exceptions:

Sights Open Early
Every day several sights open at 9:30 or earlier.
Shakespeare's Globe: May–Sept daily at 9:00.
Churchill Museum and Cabinet War Rooms: Daily at 9:30.
Kew Gardens: Daily at 9:30.
Madame Tussauds Waxworks: Mon–Fri at 9:30, Sat–Sun at 9:00 (opens daily at 9:00 mid-July–Aug).
Westminster Cathedral: Daily at 7:00.
Buckingham Palace: Aug–Sept daily at 9:45.
St. Paul's Cathedral: Mon–Sat at 8:30.
Westminster Abbey: Mon–Sat at 9:30.
British Library: Mon–Sat at 9:30.
Tower of London: Tue–Sat at 9:00.
Houses of Parliament: Fri at 9:30.

Sights Open Late
Every night in London, at least one sight is open late, in addition to the London Eye. Here's the scoop from Monday through Sunday:
London Eye: July–Aug daily until 21:30, June and Sept until 21:00, otherwise until 20:00.
Vinopolis: Thu–Sat until 22:00, Sun until 18:00.
Houses of Parliament (when in session): Mon–Tue until 22:30.
British Library: Tue until 20:00.
Sir John Soane's Museum: First Tue of month until 21:00.
National Gallery: Fri until 21:00.
British Museum (some galleries): Thu–Fri until 20:30.
National Portrait Gallery: Thu–Fri until 21:00.
London Transport Museum: Some Fri until 21:00.
Victoria and Albert Museum: Fri until 22:00.
Tate Modern: Fri–Sat until 22:00.
Clink Prison Museum: Sat–Sun until 21:00 in summer.

you back to 1800, when horse-drawn vehicles ruled the road. London invented the notion of a public bus traveling a set route that anyone could board without a reservation. Next, you descend to the first floor and the world's first underground Metro system, which used steam-powered locomotives (the Circle Line, c. 1865). On the ground floor, horses and trains are quickly replaced by motorized vehicles (cars, taxis, double-decker buses, streetcars), resulting in 20th-century congestion. How to deal with it? In 2003, car drivers were slapped with a congestion charge. Today, a half-billion people ride the Tube every year. Learn how city planners hope to improve efficiency with better tracks and more coverage of the expanding East End. Finally, an exhibit lets you imagine four different scenarios for the year 2055 depending on the choices you make today. Will fresh strawberries in December destroy the planet?

Cost, Hours, Location: £10, includes optional £2 donation, Sat–Thu 10:00–18:00, Fri 11:00–18:00, some Fri until 21:00, last entry 45 min before closing, pleasant upstairs café with Covent Garden view, in southeast corner of Covent Garden courtyard, Tube: Covent Garden. Switchboard tel. 020/7379-6344 or recorded info tel. 020/7565-7299, www.ltmuseum.co.uk.

▲**Courtauld Gallery**—While less impressive than the National Gallery, this wonderful collection of paintings is still a joy. The gallery is part of the Courtauld Institute of Art, and the thoughtful description of each piece of art reminds visitors that the gallery is still used for teaching. You'll see medieval European paintings and works by Rubens, the Impressionists (Manet, Monet, and Degas), Post-Impressionists (such as Cézanne), and more. Besides the permanent collection, a quality selection of loaners and temporary exhibits is often included in the entry fee.

Cost, Hours, Location: £5, free Mon until 14:00, open daily 10:00–18:00, last entry at 17:30; downstairs cafeteria, lockers, and WC; bus #6, #9, #11, #13, #15, or #23 from Trafalgar Square; Tube: Temple or Covent Garden. Tel. 020/7848-1194 or 020/7848-2777, recorded info tel. 020/7848-2526, www.courtauld.ac.uk.

Somerset House: The Courtauld Gallery is located at Somerset House, a grand 18th-century civic palace that offers a

marvelous public space (housing temporary exhibits) and a riverside terrace with several eateries (between the Strand and the Thames). The palace once held the national registry that recorded Britain's births, marriages, and deaths: "...where they hatch 'em, match 'em, and dispatch 'em." Step into the courtyard to enjoy the fountain. Go ahead...walk through it. The 55 jets get playful twice an hour. In the winter, this becomes a popular ice-skating rink with a toasty café for viewing (www.somerset-house.org.uk).

Buckingham Palace

There are three palace sights that require admission: the State Rooms, Queen's Gallery, and Royal Mews. You can pay for each separately, or buy a combo-ticket. The combo-ticket for £29.50 admits you to all three sights; a cheaper version for £14.50 covers the Queen's Gallery and Royal Mews. Many tourists are more

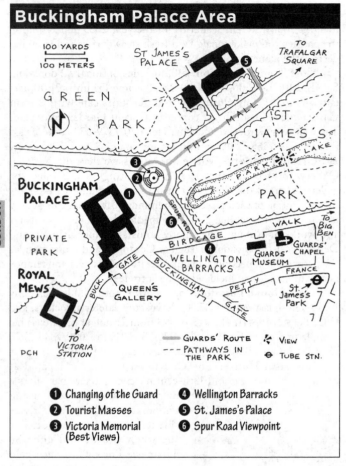

Buckingham Palace Area

100 YARDS
100 METERS

TO TRAFALGAR SQUARE

ST JAMES'S PALACE

GREEN PARK

THE MALL

ST. JAMES'S

LAKE

PARK

BUCKINGHAM PALACE

PRIVATE PARK

ROYAL MEWS

SPUR RD

BIRDCAGE WALK

WELLINGTON BARRACKS

GUARDS' MUSEUM

GUARDS' CHAPEL

TO BIG BEN

FRANCE

St. James's Park

BUCK GATE

QUEEN'S GALLERY

BUCKINGHAM GATE

PETTY

DCH

TO VICTORIA STATION

GUARDS' ROUTE
PATHWAYS IN THE PARK

VIEW
TUBE STN.

❶ Changing of the Guard
❷ Tourist Masses
❸ Victoria Memorial (Best Views)
❹ Wellington Barracks
❺ St. James's Palace
❻ Spur Road Viewpoint

interested in the Changing of the Guard, which costs nothing at all to view.

▲**State Rooms at Buckingham Palace**—This lavish home has been Britain's royal residence since 1837. When the queen's at home, the royal standard flies (a red, yellow, and blue flag); otherwise, the Union Jack flaps in the wind. Recently, the queen has opened her palace to the public—but only in August and September, when she's out of town.

Cost, Hours, Location: £16.50 for lavish State Rooms and throne room, includes audioguide, Aug–Sept only, daily 9:45–18:00, last admission 15:45; only 8,000 visitors a day by timed entry; come early to the Palace's Visitor Entrance (opens 9:15), or book ahead in person or by phone or online (£1.25 extra); Tube: Victoria. Tel. 020/7766-7300, www.royalcollection.org.uk.

▲**Queen's Gallery at Buckingham Palace**—Queen Elizabeth's personal collection of art is on display in a wing adjoining the Palace. Her 7,000 paintings make up the finest private art collection in the world, rivaling Europe's biggest national art galleries. It's actually a collection of collections, built on by each successive monarch since the 16th century. She rotates her paintings, enjoying some privately in her many palatial residences while sharing others with her subjects in public galleries in Edinburgh and London. Small, thoughtfully presented, and always exquisite displays fill the handful of rooms open to the public. As you're in "the most important building in London," security is tight. In addition to the permanent collection, you'll see temporary exhibits and a room full of the queen's personal jewelry. Compared to the crown jewels at the Tower, it may be Her Majesty's bottom drawer—but it's still a dazzling pile of diamonds. Temporary exhibits change about twice a year and are lovingly described by the included audioguide. While admission tickets come with an entry time, this is only enforced during rare days when crowds are a problem.

Cost, Hours, Location: £8.50, daily 10:00–17:30, last entry one hour before closing, Tube: Victoria. Tel. 020/7766-7301 but Her Majesty rarely answers. Men shouldn't miss the mahogany-trimmed urinals.

Royal Mews—Located to the left of Buckingham Palace, the queen's working stables, or "mews," are open to visitors. The visit is likely to be disappointing unless you follow the included guided tour, in which case it's thoroughly entertaining—especially if you're interested in horses and/or royalty. The 40-minute tours show off a few of the queen's 30 horses, a fancy car, and a bunch of old carriages, finishing with the Gold State Coach (c. 1760, 4 tons, 4 mph). Queen Victoria said absolutely no cars. When she died, in 1901, the mews got its first Daimler. Today, along with the hay-eating transport, the stable is home to five Rolls-Royce Phantoms, with one on display.

Cost, Hours, Location: £7.50, April–July and Oct Sat–Thu 11:00–16:00, Aug–Sept 10:00–17:00, last entry 45 min before closing, closed Fri and Nov–March, 2 tours/hr, Buckingham Palace Road, Tube: Victoria. Tel. 020/7766-7302.

▲▲**Changing of the Guard at Buckingham Palace**—The stone-faced, red-coated, bearskin-hatted guards change posts with much fanfare, in a 40-minute ceremony accompanied by a brass band. It happens at 11:30 daily from May through July, and every other day the rest of the year (no ceremony in very wet weather). The exact schedule is subject to change, so call 020/7766-7300 for the day's plan, or check www.changing-the-guard.com or www.royalcollection.org.uk (click on "Visit," then "Changing the Guard"). Then hop into a big black taxi and say, "Buck House, please" (a.k.a. Buckingham Palace).

Most tourists just show up and get lost in the crowds, but those who know the drill will enjoy the event more. The best place to see it is from on the circular Victoria Memorial in front of the Palace. More on that later, but here's the lowdown on what goes down:

It's just after 11:00, and the on-duty guards—actually working at nearby St. James's Palace—are ready to finish their shift. At 11:15, these tired guards, along with the band, head out to the Mall, and then take a right turn for Buckingham Palace. Meanwhile, their replacement guards—fresh for the day— gather at 11:00 at their Wellington Barracks, 500 yards east of the palace (on Birdcage Walk), for a review and inspection. At 11:30, they also head for Buckingham Palace. As both the tired and fresh guards converge on the palace, the Horse Guard enters the fray, marching down the Mall from the Horse Guard Barracks on Whitehall. At 11:45, it's a perfect storm of Red Coat pageantry, as all three groups converge. Everyone parades around, the guard changes (passing the regimental flag, or "color") with much shouting, the band plays a happy little concert, and then they march out. A few minutes later, fresh guards set up at St. James's Palace, the tired ones dress down at the barracks, and the tourists disperse.

So to recap, the event actually takes place in stages over the course of an hour, at several different locations. The main event is in the forecourt right in front of the Palace (between the Palace and the fence) from 11:30–12:00. To see it close up, you'll need to get here no later than 10:30 to get a place right next to the fence.

But there's equal pageantry elsewhere. Get out your map and strategize. You could see the guards mobilizing at Wellington Barracks or St. James's Palace (11:00–11:30). Or watch them parade with bands down The Mall and Spur Road (11:30). After the ceremony at Buckingham Palace is over (and many tourists have gotten bored and gone home), the parades march back along those same streets (12:10).

Pick one event and find a good, unobstructed place from which to view it. The key is to either get right up front along the road or fence, or find some raised elevation to stand or sit on—a balustrade or a curb—so you can see over people's heads. Don't come without a plan and end up milling around in the mobs and seeing nothing.

For the best overall view, stake out the high ground on the circular Victoria Memorial (come before 11:00 to get a place). From the Memorial, you have good views of the Palace as well as the arriving and departing parades along The Mall and Spur

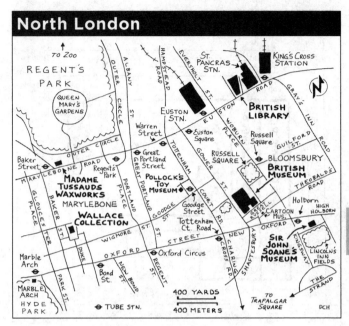

North London

TO ZOO

REGENT'S PARK

QUEEN MARY'S GARDENS

ALBANY ST.

OUTER CIRCLE

HAMPSTEAD ROAD

EVERSHOLT ST.

ST. PANCRAS STN.

KING'S CROSS STATION

GRAY'S INN ROAD

EUSTON ROAD

Warren Street

EUSTON STN.

EUSTON PLACE

WOBURN PLACE

BRITISH LIBRARY

N

Euston Square

Russell Square

GUILFORD ST.

RUSSELL SQUARE

BLOOMSBURY

Baker Street

OUTER CIRCLE

MARYLEBONE RD.

Regent's Park

Great Portland Street

TOTTENHAM

GOWER ST.

BRITISH MUSEUM

THEOBALD'S ROAD

MADAME TUSSAUDS WAXWORKS

GREAT PORTLAND ST.

PORTLAND PLACE

POLLOCK'S TOY MUSEUM

COURT RD.

Holborn

HIGH HOLBORN

MARYLEBONE

Goodge Street

CARTOON MUS.

WALLACE COLLECTION

GLOUCESTER PLACE

BAKER ST.

WIGMORE ST.

GOODGE ST.

Tottenham Ct. Road

NEW OXFORD

SHAFTESBURY

KINGSWAY

SIR JOHN SOANE'S MUSEUM

LINCOLN'S INN FIELDS

Marble Arch

OXFORD STREET

Oxford Circus

CHARING CROSS RD.

DUKE ST.

PARK ST.

NEW BOND ST.

REGENT ST.

Bond St.

MARBLE ARCH

HYDE PARK

400 YARDS

400 METERS

TO TRAFALGAR SQUARE

THE STRAND

⊖ TUBE STN.

DCH

Road. The actual changing of the guard in front of the Palace is a nonevent. It is interesting, however, to see just about every tourist in London gathered in one place at the same time. Afterward, stroll through nearby St. James's Park (Tube: Victoria, St. James's Park, or Green Park).

North London

▲▲▲**British Museum**—Simply put, this is the greatest chronicle of civilization...anywhere. A visit here is like taking a long hike through *Encyclopedia Britannica* National Park. While the vast British Museum wraps around its Great Court (the huge entrance

hall), the most popular sections of the museum fill the ground floor: Egyptian, Assyrian, and ancient Greek, with the famous Elgin Marbles from the Athenian Parthenon. The museum's stately Reading Room—famous as the place where Karl Marx hung out while formulating his ideas on communism and writing *Das Kapital*—sometimes hosts special exhibits. From the Great Court, doorways lead to all wings. Huge winged lions (which guarded an Assyrian palace 800 years before Christ) guard these great galleries. For a brief tour, connect these ancient dots:

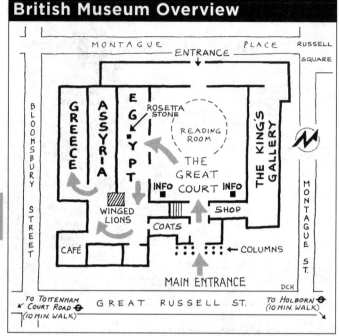

British Museum Overview

Start with the **Egyptian** section. Wander from the Rosetta Stone past the many statues. At the end of the hall, climb the stairs to mummy land.

Back at the winged lions, explore the dark, violent, and mysterious **Assyrian** rooms. The Nimrud Gallery is lined with royal propaganda reliefs and wounded lions (from the ninth century B.C.).

The most modern of the ancient art fills the **Greek** section. Find Room 11, behind the winged lions, and start your walk through Greek art history with the simple and primitive Cycladic fertility figures. Later, painted vases show a culture really into partying. The finale is the Elgin Marbles. The much-wrangled-over bits of the Athenian Parthenon (from about 450 B.C.) are even more impressive than they look. To best appreciate these ancient carvings, take the audioguide tour (see next page).

Be sure to venture upstairs to see artifacts from **Roman Britain** (Room 50) that surpass anything you'll see at Hadrian's Wall or elsewhere in Britain. Nearby, the Dark Age Britain exhibits offer a worthwhile peek at that bleak era; look for the Sutton Hoo Burial Ship artifacts from a seventh-century royal burial on the east coast of England (Room 41). A rare Michelangelo cartoon (preliminary sketch) is in Room 90.

Cost, Hours, Location: Museum free but a £3, $5, or €5 donation requested; temporary exhibits extra, daily 10:00–17:30, Thu–Fri until 20:30—but not all galleries open after 17:30, least crowded weekday late afternoons, Great Russell Street, Tube: Tottenham Court Road. Switchboard tel. 020/7323-8000, general info tel. 020/7323-8299, collection questions tel. 020/7323-8838, www.britishmuseum.org.

Tours: The 90-minute Highlights tours, led by licensed guides, are expensive but meaty, giving an introduction to the museum's masterpieces (£8, 90 min, daily at 10:30, 13:00, and 15:00). The free 30-minute eyeOpener tours focus on select rooms (daily 11:00–15:30, generally running every half-hour). There are three audioguide tours: Museum Highlights (90 min) and Parthenon Sculptures (60 min) are both substantial and cerebral, plus there's a fun Family Tour. The cost is £3.50 each or £5.50 for two tours (must leave photo ID).

▲▲▲**British Library**—Here, in just two rooms called "The Treasures of the British Library," are the literary gems of Western civilization, from early Bibles to the Magna Carta to Shakespeare's *Hamlet* to Lewis Carroll's *Alice's Adventures in Wonderland*. The map on the next page will help you find the highlights. You'll

see the Lindisfarne Gospels transcribed on an illuminated manuscript, as well as Beatles lyrics scrawled on the back of a greeting card. The British Empire built its greatest monuments out of paper, and it's with literature that England made her lasting contribution to civilization and the arts.

Cost, Hours, Location: Free but donations appreciated, temporary exhibits extra, Mon–Fri 9:30–18:00, Tue until 20:00, Sat 9:30–17:00, Sun 11:00–17:00; helpful free computers give you extra info; ground-floor café, self-service cafeteria upstairs; Tube: King's Cross–St. Pancras, walk a block west to 96 Euston Road; Euston Tube station is also close; bus #10, #30, #73, #91, #205, or #390. Library tel. 020-7412-7332, www.bl.uk.

▲**Wallace Collection**—Sir Richard Wallace's fine collection of 17th-century Dutch Masters, 18th-century French Rococo, medieval armor, and assorted aristocratic fancies fills the sumptuously furnished Hertford House on Manchester Square. From the rough and intimate Dutch life-scapes of Jan Steen to the pink-cheeked Rococo fantasies of François Boucher, a wander through this little-visited mansion makes you nostalgic for the days of empire.

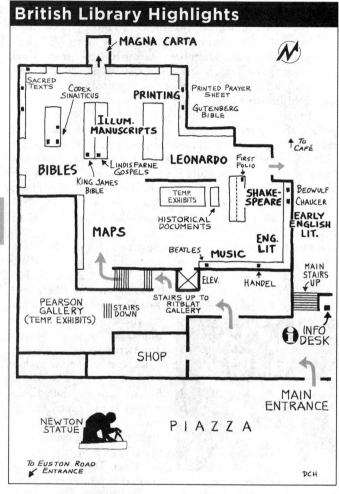

British Library Highlights

MAGNA CARTA

SACRED TEXTS

CODEX SINAITICUS

PRINTING

PRINTED PRAYER SHEET

GUTENBERG BIBLE

ILLUM. MANUSCRIPTS

TO CAFÉ

BIBLES

LINDISFARNE GOSPELS

LEONARDO

FIRST FOLIO

KING JAMES BIBLE

TEMP. EXHIBITS

SHAKE-SPEARE

BEOWULF

CHAUCER

HISTORICAL DOCUMENTS

MAPS

EARLY ENGLISH LIT.

ENG. LIT

BEATLES

MUSIC

MAIN STAIRS UP

ELEV.

HANDEL

PEARSON GALLERY (TEMP. EXHIBITS)

STAIRS DOWN

STAIRS UP TO RITBLAT GALLERY

INFO DESK

SHOP

MAIN ENTRANCE

NEWTON STATUE

PIAZZA

TO EUSTON ROAD ENTRANCE

DCH

LONDON

Cost, Hours, Location: Free, daily 10:00–17:00, £3 audio-guide, free guided tours or lectures almost daily—call to confirm times, just north of Oxford Street on Manchester Square, Tube: Bond Street. Tel. 020/7563-9500, www.wallacecollection.org.

▲**Madame Tussauds Waxworks**—This is gimmicky and expensive but dang good. The original Madame Tussaud did wax casts of heads lopped off during the French Revolution (such as Marie-Antoinette's). She took her show on the road and ended up in London in 1835. And now it's much easier to be featured. The gallery is one big photo op—a huge hit with the kind of travelers who skip the British Museum. After looking a hundred famous people in their glassy eyes and surviving a silly hall of horror, you'll board a Disney-

type ride and cruise through a kid-pleasing "Spirit of London" time trip. Your last stop is the auditorium for a 12-minute stage show (runs every 15 min). They've dumped anything really historical (except for what they claim is the blade that beheaded Marie-Antoinette), because "there's no money in it and we're a business." Now, it's all about squeezing Brad Pitt's bum, gambling with George Clooney, and partying with Beyoncé, Britney, and Bill Clinton. The unpopular Gordon Brown is the first prime minister in 150 years not to be immortalized in wax—but President Obama has already joined the club.

Cost, Hours, Location: £25 (£20 if purchased from TI), £37 combo-ticket with London Eye, cheaper for kids. Check the website for discounts on this pricey waxtravaganza. From 17:00 to closing, it's £16 if you buy online, £11 for kids (does not include London Eye). Children under 5 are always free. Open Mon–Fri 9:30–17:30, Sat–Sun 9:00–18:00, mid-July–Aug and school holidays daily 9:00–18:00; Marylebone Road, Tube: Baker Street. Toll tel. 08709-990-046, www.madametussauds.com.

Sir John Soane's Museum—Architects love this quirky place, along with fans of interior decor, eclectic knickknacks, and Back Door sights. Tour this furnished home on a bird-chirping square and see 19th-century chairs, lamps, and carpets, wood-paneled nooks and crannies, and stained-glass skylights. The townhouse is cluttered with Soane's (and his wife's) collection of ancient relics, curios, and famous paintings, including Hogarth's series on *The Rake's Progress* (read the fun plot) and several excellent Canalettos. In 1833, just before his death, Soane established his house as a museum, stipulating that it be kept as nearly as possible in the state he left it. If he visited today, he'd be entirely satisfied. You'll leave wishing you'd known the man.

Cost, Hours, Location: Free but donations much appreciated, Tue–Sat 10:00–17:00, last entry 30 min before closing, first Tue of the month also 18:00–21:00, closed Sun–Mon, long entry lines on Sat and first Tue, good £1 brochure, £5 guided tours Sat at 11:00, 13 Lincoln's Inn Fields, quarter-mile southeast of British Museum, Tube: Holborn. Tel. 020/7405-2107.

Cartoon Museum—This humble but interesting museum is located in the shadow of the British Museum. While its three rooms are filled with British cartoons unknown to most Americans, the satire of famous bigwigs and politicians—from Napoleon to Margaret Thatcher, the Queen, and Tony Blair—shows the power of parody to deliver social commentary. Upstairs, you'll see pages spanning from *Tarzan* to *Tank Girl, Andy Capp* to the British *Dennis the Menace*—interesting only to comic-book diehards.

Cost, Hours, Location: £5; Tue–Sat 10:30–17:30, Sun 12:00–17:30, closed Mon; 35 Little Russell Street—go one block south of the British Museum on Museum Street and make a right, Tube: Tottenham Court Road. Tel. 020/7580-8155, www.cartoon museum.org.

Pollock's Toy Museum—This rickety old house, with glass cases filled with toys and games lining its walls and halls, is a time-warp experience that brings back childhood memories to people who grew up without batteries or computer chips. Though the museum is small, you could spend a lot of time here, squinting at the fascinating toys and dolls that entertained the children of 19th- and early 20th-century England. The included information is great. The story of Theodore Roosevelt refusing to shoot a bear cub while on a hunting trip was celebrated in 1902 cartoons, resulting in a new, huggable toy: the Teddy Bear. It was popular for good reason—it could be manufactured during World War I without rationed products; it coincided with the new belief that soft toys were good for a child's development; it was an acceptable "doll for boys"; and it's *the* toy children keep long after they've grown up.

Cost, Hours, Location: £5, kids-£2, Mon–Sat 10:00–17:00, closed Sun, last entry 30 min before closing, 1 Scala Street, Tube: Goodge Street. Tel. 020/7636-3452, www.pollockstoymuseum .com. Call before you go to make sure it's open.

The City

When Londoners say "The City," they mean the one-square-mile business center in East London that 2,000 years ago was Roman Londinium. The outline of the Roman city walls can still be seen in the arc of roads from Blackfriars Bridge to Tower Bridge. Within The City are 23 churches designed by Sir Christopher Wren, mostly just ornamentation around St. Paul's Cathedral. Today, while home to only 5,000 residents, The City thrives with nearly 500,000 office workers coming and going daily. It's a fascinating district to wander on weekdays, but since almost nobody actually lives here, it's dull in the evenings and on Saturday and Sunday.

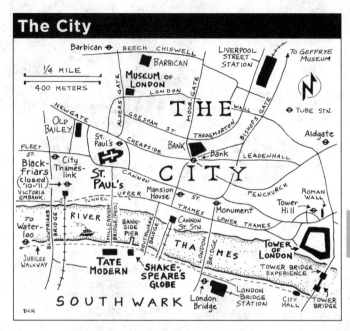

The City

Barbican

BEECH CHISWELL

BARBICAN

MUSEUM OF LONDON

LONDON

¼ MILE

400 METERS

NEWGATE

OLD BAILEY

ALDERS GATE

GRESHAM ST.

St. Paul's

CHEAPSIDE

MOOR GATE

THROGMORTON

WALL GATE

BISHOPS GATE

LIVERPOOL STREET STATION

TO GEFFRYE MUSEUM

TUBE STN.

Aldgate

FLEET ST.

Black-friars (closed '10-'11)

VICTORIA EMBANK.

City Thames-link

TUNNEL

ST. PAUL'S

CANNON

UPPER

BANK

Bank

Mansion House

ST.

THAMES

LEADENHALL

FENCHURCH

Monument

ROMAN WALL

Tower Hill

TO Water-loo

JUBILEE WALKWAY

BLACKFRIARS BRIDGE

RIVER

MILLENNIUM BRIDGE (PED.)

BANK-SIDE PIER

SOUTHWARK BRIDGE

LOWER THAMES

CANNON ST. STN.

LONDON BRIDGE

THAMES

TOWER OF LONDON

TOWER BRIDGE EXPERIENCE

TATE MODERN

SHAKE-SPEARE'S GLOBE

London Bridge

LONDON BRIDGE STATION

CITY HALL

TOWER BRIDGE

SOUTHWARK

DCH

THE CITY

LONDON

St. Paul's Cathedral and Nearby

▲▲▲**St. Paul's Cathedral**—Wren's most famous church is the great St. Paul's, its elaborate interior capped by a 365-foot dome.

Since World War II, St. Paul's has been Britain's symbol of resistance. Despite 57 nights of bombing, the Nazis failed to destroy the cathedral, thanks to the St. Paul's volunteer fire watchmen, who stayed on the dome.

St. Paul's is England's national church. There's been a church on this spot since 604. After the Great Fire of 1666 destroyed the old cathedral, Wren created a Baroque masterpiece. Even now, as skyscrapers encroach, the dome of St. Paul's rises majestically above the rooftops of the neighborhood.

Inside, this big church feels big. At 515 feet long and 250 feet wide, it's Europe's fourth-largest, after those in Rome (St. Peter's), Sevilla, and Milan. The spaciousness is accentuated by the relative lack of decoration. The simple, cream-colored ceiling and the clear glass in the windows light everything evenly.

There are many legends buried here: Horatio Nelson, who wore down Napoleon; the Duke of Wellington, who finished Napoleon off; and even Charles Cornwallis, who was finished off

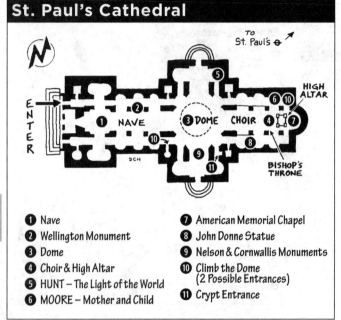

St. Paul's Cathedral

① Nave
② Wellington Monument
③ Dome
④ Choir & High Altar
⑤ HUNT – The Light of the World
⑥ MOORE – Mother and Child
⑦ American Memorial Chapel
⑧ John Donne Statue
⑨ Nelson & Cornwallis Monuments
⑩ Climb the Dome (2 Possible Entrances)
⑪ Crypt Entrance

by George Washington at Yorktown. Often the site of historic funerals (Queen Victoria and Winston Churchill), St. Paul's most famous ceremony was a wedding—when Prince Charles married Lady Diana Spencer in 1981.

During your visit, you can climb the dome for a great city view and have some fun in the Whispering Gallery. Whisper sweet nothings into the wall, and your partner (and anyone else) standing far away can hear you. For best effects, try whispering (not talking) with your mouth close to the wall, while your partner stands a few dozen yards away with his or her ear to the wall. The crypt (included with admission) is a world of historic bones and interesting cathedral models.

Cost, Hours, Location: £11, includes church entry and dome climb; Mon–Sat 8:30–16:30, last church entry 16:00, last dome entry 16:15, closed Sun except for worship, £3 tours and £4 audioguides, no photography allowed, cheery café and pricier restaurant in crypt, Tube: St. Paul's; bus #4, #11, #15, #23, #26, or #100. Don't head for St. Paul's Church near Covent Garden; your destination is St. Paul's Cathedral, in The City. Recorded info tel. 020/7246-8348, office tel. 020/7236-8350, www.stpauls.co.uk.

Music: The evensong services are free, but nonpaying visitors are not allowed to linger afterward (Mon–Sat at 17:00, Sun at 15:15, 40 min).

▲**Old Bailey**—To view the British legal system inaction—lawyers in little blonde wigs speaking legalese with a British accent—spend a few minutes in the visitors' gallery at the Old Bailey, called the "Central Criminal Court." Don't enter under the dome; signs point you to the two visitors' entrances.

Cost, Hours, Location: Free, generally Mon–Fri 10:00–13:00 & 14:00–17:00 depending on caseload, closed Sat–Sun, reduced hours in Aug; no kids under 14; no bags, mobile phones, cameras, or food, but small purses OK; Eddie at Bailey's Café across the street at #30 stores bags for £2; 2 blocks northwest of St. Paul's on Old Bailey Street, follow signs to public entrance, Tube: St. Paul's. Tel. 020/7248-3277.

▲**Museum of London**—London, a 2,000-year-old city, is so littered with ruins that when a London builder finds Roman antiquities, he simply documents the finds, moves the artifacts to a museum, and builds on. If you're asking, "Why did the Romans build their cities underground?" a trip to the creative and entertaining Museum of London is a must.

The museum features London's distinguished citizens through history—from Neanderthals to Romans to Elizabethans to Victorians to Mods to today. The museum's displays are chronological, spacious, and informative without being overwhelming. Scale models and costumes help you visualize everyday life in the city at different periods. There are enough whiz-bang multimedia displays (including the Plague and the Great Fire) to spice up otherwise humdrum artifacts. This regular stop for the local school kids gives the best overview of London history in town.

London's Story at the Museum of London: Here you can walk through London's history from prehistory to the present. First, zip quickly through a half a million years, when Britain morphed from peninsula to island, Neanderthals speared mammoths, and Stone Age humans huddled in crude huts on the South Bank of the Thames.

In 54 B.C., Julius Caesar invaded, and the Romans built "Londinium" on the North Bank. The settlement quickly became the hub of Britain and a river-trade town, complete with arenas, forums, baths, a bridge across the Thames, and a city wall. That wall—arcing from the present Tower of London to St. Paul's—defined the city's boundaries for the next 1,500 years. The Museum of London sits on the northwest perimeter of the city wall, and you can look out the windows to see a crumbling remnant along the street, now called "London Wall."

When Rome could no longer defend the city (A.D. 410), it fell to the Saxons (becoming "Lundenburg") and later, the Normans (in 1066), who built the Tower of London. Medieval London was devastated by the Black Death plague of 1348. As the city recovered and grew even bigger, it became clear to wannabe kings that whoever controlled London controlled Britain.

When Queen Elizabeth I brought peace to the land, London thrived as a capital of theaters (the Globe and Rose), arts, and ideas. Then, just when things were going so well, the city was disintegrated by the Great Fire of 1666, which left London a blank slate.

The exhibits covering 1666 to the present have been closed for years, but they're scheduled to reopen in spring 2010 with great fanfare. You'll see the opulence of rebuilt Georgian London in the Museum's prized possession—the Lord Mayor's Coach, a golden carriage pulled by six white horses that looks right out of Cinderella. Next, stroll through a multimedia "pleasure garden" and take a "Victorian Walk," experiencing what it was like to live in the world's greatest city.

Two world wars and the car changed 20th-century London into a concrete jungle. But it remained a cultural capital of elegance (see an Art Deco elevator from Selfridges) and a global trendsetter (Beatles-era memorabilia).

Finally, displays on the 21st century—including the terrorist bombings of July 7, 2005—weave contemporary London into the tapestry of history.

Cost, Hours, Location: Free, daily 10:00–18:00, until 21:00 first Thu of month, last entry 30 min before closing, Tube: Barbican or St. Paul's plus a five-minute walk, tel. 020/7814-5530, recorded info tel. 020/7001-9844, www.museumoflondon.org.uk.

Tower of London and Nearby

▲▲▲**Tower of London**—The Tower has served as a castle in wartime, a king's residence in peace time, and, most notoriously, as the prison and execution site of rebels. You can see the crown jewels, take a witty Beefeater tour, and ponder the executioner's block that dispensed with Anne Boleyn, Sir Thomas More, and troublesome heirs to the throne.

William I, still getting used to his new title of "the Conqueror," built the stone "White Tower" (1077–1097) to keep the

Londoners in line. The Tower also served as an effective lookout for seeing invaders coming up the Thames. His successors enlarged it to its present 18-acre size. Because of the security it provided, it has served over the centuries as the Royal Mint, the Royal Jewel House, and as a prison and execution site.

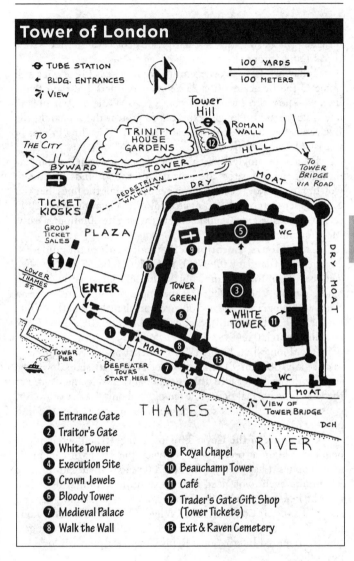

Tower of London

- ☩ TUBE STATION
- ← BLDG. ENTRANCES
- 𝕪 VIEW

100 YARDS
100 METERS

TO THE CITY

Tower Hill

TRINITY HOUSE GARDENS

ROMAN WALL

BYWARD ST. TOWER HILL

TO TOWER BRIDGE VIA ROAD

PEDESTRIAN WALKWAY

DRY MOAT

TICKET KIOSKS

GROUP TICKET SALES

PLAZA

LOWER THAMES ST.

ENTER

DRY MOAT

TOWER GREEN

WHITE TOWER

WC

TOWER PIER

MOAT

BEEFEATER TOURS START HERE

WC

MOAT

THAMES

VIEW OF TOWER BRIDGE

DCH

RIVER

1. Entrance Gate
2. Traitor's Gate
3. White Tower
4. Execution Site
5. Crown Jewels
6. Bloody Tower
7. Medieval Palace
8. Walk the Wall
9. Royal Chapel
10. Beauchamp Tower
11. Café
12. Trader's Gate Gift Shop (Tower Tickets)
13. Exit & Raven Cemetery

LONDON

The Tower's hard stone and glittering jewels represent the ultimate power of the monarch. The crown jewels include the world's largest cut diamond—the 530-carat Star of Africa—placed in the royal scepter. When Queen Elizabeth II opens Parliament, she checks out the Imperial State Crown with its 3,733 jewels, including Elizabeth I's pearl earrings.

You'll find more bloody history per square inch in this original tower of power than anywhere else in Britain, though the actual execution site (in the courtyard) looks just like a lawn. Not all prisoners died at the block—Richard III supposedly ordered two teenage princes strangled in their prison cells because they were a threat to his throne.

Today, while the Tower's military purpose is history, it's still home to the Beefeaters (the 25 Yeoman Warders and their families), who host three million visitors a year. While these men (and one woman) are no longer expected to protect the monarch, the Beefeaters have evolved into great entertainers, leading groups of tourists through the Tower.

For a refreshingly different Tower experience, come on Sunday mornings, when visitors are welcome on the grounds for free to worship in the Royal Chapel. You get in without the lines, but you can only see the chapel—no sightseeing (9:15 Communion or 11:00 service with fine choral music, meet at west gate 30 minutes early, dress for church).

Cost, Hours, Location: £17, family-£47; audioguide-£4; March–Oct Tue–Sat 9:00–17:30, Sun–Mon 10:00–17:30; Nov–Feb Tue–Sat 9:00–16:30, Sun–Mon 10:00–16:30; last entry 30 min before closing, the long but fast-moving ticket lines are worst on Sun, no photography allowed of jewels, in chapels, or in the White Tower; Tube: Tower Hill. Switchboard toll tel. 0844-482-7777, booking toll tel. 0844-482-7799.

Avoid long lines by buying your ticket online (www.hrp.org .uk), at any London TI, at the Trader's Gate gift shop down the steps from the Tower Hill Tube stop, or at the Welcome Centre to the left of the normal ticket line (credit card only). After your visit, consider taking the boat to Greenwich from here (see cruise info on page 65).

Ceremony of the Keys: This pageantry-filled ceremony is held every night at precisely 21:30, when the Tower of London is locked up (as it has been for the last 700 years). To attend this free 30-minute event, you need to request an invitation at least two months before your visit. For details, go to www.hrp.org.uk and select "Tower Of London," then "What's On" and "The Ceremony of the Keys." (Every year, some readers report that it's difficult getting the required International Reply Coupons from their local US post office.)

More Sights near the Tower—The best remaining bit of London's Roman Wall is just north of the Tower (at the Tower Hill Tube station). The iconic Tower Bridge (often mistakenly called London Bridge) has been freshly painted and is undergoing restoration. The hydraulically powered drawbridge was built in 1894 to accommodate the growing East End. While fully modern, its design was a retro Neo-Gothic look.

You can tour the bridge at the **Tower Bridge Experience,** with a history exhibit and a peek at the Victorian engine room that lifts the span (£6, family £14, daily 10:00–18:30 in summer, 9:30–18:00 in winter, last entry 30 min before closing, good view, poor value, enter at the northwest tower, tel. 020/7403-3761, Tube: Tower Hill, www.towerbridge.org.uk). The visit is most interesting when the drawbridge lifts to let ships pass, as it does a thousand times a year; for the bridge-lifting schedule, call 020/7940-3984.

The chic **St. Katharine Dock**, just east of Tower Bridge, has private yachts, mod shops, and the classic Dickens Inn, fun for a drink or pub lunch. Across the bridge is the South Bank, with the upscale Butlers Wharf area, City Hall, museums, and the Jubilee Walkway.

Northeast of The City

▲**Geffrye Museum**—This low-key but well-organized museum, in a building that was an 18th-century almshouse, is located north of Liverpool Street Station in the trendy Shoreditch area. Walk past a dozen English living rooms, furnished and decorated in styles from 1600 to 2000, then descend the circular stairs to see changing exhibits on home decor. In summer, explore the fragrant herb garden.

Cost, Hours, Location: Free, Tue–Sat 10:00–17:00, Sun 12:00–17:00, closed Mon, garden open April–Oct, 136 Kingsland Road, Shoreditch, Tube: Liverpool Street, then 10-min ride north on bus #149 or #242 north. If you're here after the new Hoxton Tube station opens in mid-2010, you can take the East London line directly to the museum. Tel. 020/7739-9893, www.geffrye -museum.org.uk.

South Bank

▲**Jubilee Walkway**—The South Bank is a thriving arts and cultural center tied together by this riverside path, a popular, pub-crawling pedestrian promenade

called the Jubilee Walkway. Stretching from Tower Bridge past Westminster Bridge, it offers grand views of the Houses of Parliament and St. Paul's. On a sunny day, this is the place to see London out strolling. The Walkway hugs the river except just east of London Bridge, where it cuts inland for a couple of blocks. Plans are underway to expand the path into a 60-mile "Greenway" encircling the city, scheduled to open in 2012 for the Olympic Games and Elizabeth's 60th year as queen (www.jubileewalkway.org.uk).

The South Bank

LONDON

The South Bank map showing: Tower of London, Tower Bridge, City Hall, H.M.S. Belfast, The Scoop, Unicorn Theatre, Tower Hill, Tower Pier, Southwark Cathedral, London Bridge Station, Old Operating Theatre Museum, London Bridge, Cannon St., Clink, "Golden Hinde", Vinopolis, Southwark St., Tooley St., High St., Borough, Marshalsea, Bankside Pier, Millennium Bridge, Shakespeare's Globe, Tate Modern, CITY, To St. Paul's, Thames R., Southwark, Imperial War Museum, Blackfriars Road, Jubilee Walkway, Upper Ground, BFI Southbank, Stamford, Southwark, Waterloo Station, Lambeth North, West. Road, Waterloo Pier, Embankment Pier, To Trafalgar Square, Jubilee Ped. Bridge, Belvedere, York Rd., County Hall, Dalí Universe, London Duck Tours, & Waterloo Pier, DCH, London Eye, Westminster Pier, West. Minster, Big Ben, Pedestrian Bridge, ½ Mile, 800 Meters, Tube Stn.

▲▲**London Eye**—This giant Ferris wheel, towering above London opposite Big Ben, is the world's highest observational

wheel and London's answer to the Eiffel Tower. While the experience is memorable, London doesn't have much of a skyline and the price is borderline outrageous. But whether you ride or not, the wheel is a sight to behold. Designed like a giant bicycle wheel, it's a pan-European undertaking: British steel and Dutch engineering, with Czech, German, French, and Italian mechanical parts. It's also very "green," running extremely efficiently and virtually silently. You start with a short "pre-flight" exhibit in the ticket hall, then step aboard. Twenty-five people ride in each of its 32 air-conditioned capsules for the 30-minute rotation. Each capsule has a bench, but most people stand. From the top of this 443-foot-high wheel—the highest public viewpoint in the city—even Big Ben looks small. You go around only once. Built to celebrate the new millennium, the Eye's original five-year lease has been extended, and it's becoming a permanent fixture on the London skyline. Thames boats come and go from here using the Waterloo Pier at the foot of the wheel.

Cost, Hours, Location: £17, or £37 combo-ticket with Madame Tussauds Waxworks, £10 extra buys a Fast Track ticket that lets you jump the queue, other packages available. Buy tickets there, in advance by calling 0870-500-0600, or save 10 percent by booking online at www.londoneye.com. Open daily July–Aug 10:00–21:30, June and Sept 10:00–21:00, Oct–May 10:00–20:00, closed Dec 25 and a few days in Jan for annual maintenance, Tube: Waterloo or Westminster.

By the Eye: The area next to the London Eye has developed a cotton-candy ambience of kitschy, kid-friendly attractions. There's an aquarium, a game arcade, and a new "Movieum" dedicated to movies filmed in London, from Harry Potter to Star Wars. I'd skip the overpriced Dalí Universe (£14.50) of mind-bending art by Salvador Dalí and Pablo Picasso.

▲▲**Imperial War Museum**—This impressive museum covers the wars of the last century—from WWI biplanes to the rise of fascism to Monty's Africa campaign tank to the Cold War, the Cuban Missile Crisis, the troubles in Northern Ireland, the wars in Iraq, and terrorism.

The core of the permanent collection, located downstairs, takes you step by step through World War I and World War II. Then you move on to conflicts since 1945. Most of the displays are

Crossing the Thames on Foot

You can cross the Thames on any of the bridges that carry car traffic over the river, but London's two pedestrian bridges are more fun. The Millennium Bridge connects the sedate St. Paul's Cathedral with the great Tate Modern. The Golden Jubilee Bridge, well-lit with a sleek, futuristic look, links bustling Trafalgar Square on the North Bank with the London Eye and Waterloo Station on the South Bank.

LONDON

low-tech—glass cases hold dummies in uniforms, weapons, newspaper clippings, ordinary objects from daily life—but have excellent explanations. Two multimedia experiences hammer home the horrors of war. The Trench Experience lets you walk through a dark, chaotic, smelly WWI trench. The Blitz Experience film assaults the senses with the noise and intensity of a WWII air raid on London. Also, the cinema shows a rotating selection of films.

In the entry hall are the large exhibits—including Montgomery's tank, several field guns, and dangling overhead, vintage planes. Imagine the awesome power of the 50-foot V-2 rocket, the kind the Nazis rained down on London, which could arrive silently and destroy a city block. Its direct descendant is the Polaris missile, capable of traveling nearly 3,000 miles in 20 minutes and obliterating an entire city.

Besides exhibits on the world wars, the museum has several other permanent sections. The "Secret War" peeks into the intrigues of espionage in World Wars I and II. The section on the Holocaust is one of the best on the subject anywhere, and there are always several temporary exhibitions that are top-notch.

War wonks will love the place, as will general history buffs who enjoy patiently reading displays. For the rest, there are enough multimedia exhibits and submarines for the kids to climb in to keep it interesting.

Rather than glorify war, the museum does its best to shine a light on the 100 million deaths of the 20th century. It shows everyday life for people back home and never neglects the powerful human side of one of humankind's most persistent traits.

Cost, Hours, Location: Free, daily 10:00–18:00, temporary exhibits extra, often guided tours on weekends—ask at info desk, £4 audioguide, Tube: Lambeth North or bus #12 or bus #159. Tel. 020/7416-5000, www.iwm.org.uk.

The museum is housed in what was the Royal Bethlam

Hospital. Also known as "the Bedlam asylum," the place was so wild it gave the world a new word for chaos. Back in Victorian times, locals—without reality shows and YouTube—paid admission to visit the asylum on weekends for entertainment.

▲▲**Tate Modern**—Dedicated in the spring of 2000, the striking museum across the river from St. Paul's opened the new century with art from the old one. Its powerhouse collection of Monet, Matisse, Dalí, Picasso, Warhol, and much more is displayed in a converted powerhouse. Of equal interest are the many temporary exhibits featuring cutting-edge art. Each year, the main hall features a different monumental installation by a prominent artist.

Cost, Hours, Location: Free but £3 donations appreciated, fee for special exhibitions, daily 10:00–18:00, Fri–Sat until 22:00—a good time to visit, last entry 45 min before closing, audioguide-£2, children's audioguide-£1; free guided tours at 11:00, 12:00, 14:00, and 15:00—confirm at info desk; view restaurant on top floor; cross the Millennium Bridge from St. Paul's; Tube: Southwark, London Bridge or Mansion House plus a 10–15 min walk; or connect by Tate Boat ferry from Tate Britain for £5 one-way, discounted with Travelcard. Switchboard tel. 020/7887-8888, recorded info tel. 020/7887-8008, www.tate.org.uk.

▲**Millennium Bridge**—The pedestrian bridge links St. Paul's Cathedral and the Tate Modern across the Thames. This is

London's first new bridge in a century. When it first opened, the $25 million bridge wiggled when people walked on it, so it promptly closed for an $8 million, 20-month stabilization; now it's stable and open again (free). Nicknamed the "blade of light" for its sleek minimalist design (370 yards long, four yards wide, stainless steel with teak planks), its clever aerodynamic handrails deflect wind over the heads of pedestrians.

▲▲**Shakespeare's Globe**—A replica of the original Globe Theatre has been built, half-timbered and thatched, as it was in Shakespeare's time. (This is the first thatched roof in London since they were outlawed after the Great Fire of 1666.) The Globe originally accommodated 2,200 seated and another 1,000 standing. Today, slightly smaller and

leaving space for reasonable aisles, the theater holds 800 seated and 600 groundlings. Its promoters brag that the theater melds "the three A's"—actors, audience, and architecture—with each contributing to the play. The working theater hosts authentic performances of Shakespeare's plays with actors in period costumes, modern interpretations of his works, and some works by other playwrights (generally all summer at 14:00 and 19:30—but confirm). For details on seeing a play, see page 122.

The complex has three parts: the theater itself, the box office, and the "Globe Exhibition" museum. The **Globe Exhibition** ticket (£10.50) includes both a tour of the theater and the museum. First, you browse on your own through displays of Elizabethan-era costumes, music, script-printing, and special effects. There are early folios and objects that were dug up on the site. A video and scale models help put Shakespearean theater within the context of the times. (The Globe opened one year after England mastered the seas by defeating the Spanish Armada. The debut play was Shakespeare's *Julius Caesar*.)

Next comes the tour of the theater—you must take the tour at the time stamped on your ticket, but you can come back to the museum afterward; tickets are good all day. The guide (usually an actor) leads you into the theater to see the stage and the different seating areas for the different classes of people. You take a seat and learn how the new Globe is similar to the old Globe (open-air performances, standing-room by the stage, no curtain) and how it's different (female actors today, lights for night performances, concrete floor). It's not a backstage tour—you don't see dressing rooms or costume shops or sit in on rehearsals, though you may see workers building sets for a new production. You mostly sit and listen. The guides are energetic, theatrical, and knowledgeable, bringing the Elizabethan period to life.

When performances are going on, you can't tour the theater. But you can see the museum, then tour the nearby (and less interesting) Rose Theatre instead.

Cost, Hours, Location: £10.50 includes museum and 60-min tour, £7.50 on Rose Theater days; tickets good all day; complex open daily 9:00–17:00; Exhibition and tours May–Sept 9:00–17:00—Globe tours offered mornings only in summer with Rose tours in afternoon, Oct–April daily 10:00–17:00—Globe tours run all day in winter; tours go every 15–30 min; on the South Bank directly across Thames over Southwark Bridge from St. Paul's, Tube: Mansion House or London Bridge plus a 10-min walk. Tel. 020/7902-1400 or 020/7902-1500, www.shakespeares-globe.org.

The Swan at the Globe café is open daily (11:00–1:00 in the morning, tel. 020/7928-9444).

Southwark

The next several sights are in Southwark, on the South Bank. The area stretching from the Tate Modern to London Bridge, known as Southwark (SUTH-uck), was for centuries the place Londoners would go to escape the rules and decency of the city and let their hair down. Bearbaiting, brothels, rollicking pubs, and theater—you name the dream, and it could be fulfilled just across the Thames. A run-down warehouse district through the 20th century, it's been gentrified with classy restaurants, office parks, pedestrian promenades, major sights (such as the Tate Modern and Shakespeare's Globe—described earlier), and this colorful collection of lesser sights. The area is easy on foot and a scenic—though circuitous—way to connect the Tower of London with St. Paul's.

Vinopolis: City of Wine—While it seems illogical to have a huge wine museum in beer-loving London, Vinopolis makes a good case. Built over a Roman wine store and filling the massive vaults of an old wine warehouse, the museum offers an excellent audioguide with a light yet earnest history of wine to accompany your sips of various mediocre reds and whites, ports, and champagnes. Allow some time, as the audioguide takes 90 minutes—and the sipping can slow things down pleasantly. This place is popular. Booking ahead for Friday and Saturday nights is a must.

Cost, Hours, Location: Various tour options range from £25 to £75 (save 20 percent by booking online at www.vinopolis .co.uk). Each includes about five wine tastes and an audioguide. Some packages also include whiskey (the new wine), other spirits, or a meal (Thu–Fri 12:00–22:00, Sat 11:00–22:00, Sun 12:00–18:00, closed Mon–Wed, last entry 2.5 hours before closing, between the Globe and Southwark Cathedral at 1 Bank End, Tube: London Bridge. Tel. 020/7940-8300 or toll tel. 0870-241-4040).

The Clink Prison Museum—Proudly the "original clink," this was, until 1780, where law-abiding citizens threw Southwark troublemakers. Today, it's a low-tech torture museum filling grotty old rooms with papier-mâché gore. Unfortunately, there's little that seriously deals with the fascinating problem of law and order in Southwark, where 18th-century Londoners went for a good time.

Cost, Hours, Location: Overpriced at £5, Mon–Fri 10:00–18:00, Sat–Sun until 21:00, 1 Clink Street, Tube: London Bridge. Tel. 020/7403-0900, www.clink.co.uk. Call before you come to make sure they're open.

***Golden Hinde* Replica**—This is a full-size replica of the 16th-century warship in which Sir Francis Drake circumnavigated the globe from 1577 to 1580. Commanding this ship, Drake earned the reputation as history's most successful pirate. The original is long gone, but this boat has logged more than 100,000 miles, including a voyage around the world. While the ship is fun to see, its interior is not worth touring.

Cost, Hours, Location: £7, Mon–Sat 10:00–17:30, Sun 10:30–17:00, may be closed if rented out for pirate birthday parties, school groups, or weddings, Tube: London Bridge. Tel. 020/7403-0123, www.goldenhinde.org.

Southwark Cathedral—While made a cathedral only in 1905, it's been the neighborhood church since the 13th century, and comes with some interesting history. The enthusiastic docents give impromptu tours if you ask.

Cost, Hours, Location: Free but £4 suggested donation, daily 10:00–18:00, last entry 30 min before closing, £2.50 audioguide, £2.50 guidebook, no photos without permission, Tube: London Bridge. Tel. 020/7367-6700, http://cathedral.southwark.anglican.org.

Music: The cathedral hosts evensong services (weekdays at 17:30, Sat at 16:00, Sun at 15:00, no service on Wed or alternate Mon).

▲**Old Operating Theatre Museum and Herb Garret**—Climb a tight and creaky wooden spiral staircase to a church attic, where you'll find a garret used to dry medicinal herbs, a fascinating exhibit on Victorian surgery, cases of well-described 19th-century medical paraphernalia, and a special look at "anesthesia, the defeat of pain." Then you stumble upon Britain's oldest operating theater, where limbs were sawed off way back in 1821.

Cost, Hours, Location: £5.60, daily 10:30–17:00, closed Dec 15–Jan 5, 9a St. Thomas Street, Tube: London Bridge. Tel. 020/7188-2679, www.thegarret.org.uk.

Near the Tower Bridge

HMS Belfast—"The last big-gun armored warship of World War II" clogs the Thames just upstream from the Tower Bridge. This huge vessel—now manned with wax sailors—thrills kids who always dreamed of sitting in a turret shooting off their imaginary guns. If you're into WWII warships, this is the ultimate. Otherwise, it's just lots of exercise with a nice view of Tower Bridge.

Cost, Hours, Location: £10.70, daily March–Oct 10:00–18:00, Nov–Feb 10:00–17:00, last entry one hour before closing, Tube: London Bridge. Tel. 020/7940-6300, www.hmsbelfast.iwm.org.uk.

City Hall—The glassy, egg-shaped building near the south end of Tower Bridge is London's City Hall, designed by Sir Norman Foster, the architect who worked on London's Millennium Bridge and Berlin's Reichstag. City Hall is where London's mayor works, the blonde, flamboyant, conservative, former journalist and author Boris Johnson. He consults here with the Assembly representatives of the city's 25 districts. An interior spiral ramp allows visitors to watch and hear the action below in the Assembly Chamber—ride the lift to the second floor (the highest visitors can go) and spiral down. On the lower ground floor is a large aerial photograph of London, an information desk, and a handy cafeteria. Next to City Hall is the outdoor amphitheatre called the Scoop.

Cost, Hours, Location: City Hall is open to visitors Mon–Fri 8:00–17:30, Tube: London Bridge station plus 10-min walk, or Tower Hill station plus 15-min walk. Tel. 020/7983-4000, www.london.gov.uk/gla/city_hall.

West London

▲▲**Tate Britain**—The world's best collection of British art, Tate Britain specializes in works from the 16th century through modern times. This is everyday art, with realistic paintings rooted in the people, landscape, and stories of the British Isles. You'll see Hogarth's stage sets, Gainsborough's ladies, Blake's angels, Constable's clouds, Turner's tempests, the swooning realism of the Pre-Raphaelites, and the camera-eye portraits of Hockney and Freud. What you won't see here are the fleshy goddesses, naked cherubs, and Madonna-and-child altarpieces so popular elsewhere in Europe. The largely Protestant English abhorred the "graven images" of the wealthy Catholic world.

The collection is constantly in motion but the basic layout stays the same: a roughly chronological walk through British paintings from 1500 to 1901 in the west half of the building, the 20th century in the east, and the swirling works of J. M. W. Turner in the adjoining Clore Gallery.

Cost, Hours, Location: Free, £2 donation requested, temporary exhibits extra, daily 10:00–17:50, first Fri of the month until 21:40, last entry 50 min before closing, fine and necessary £3.50 audioguide; free tours: Mon–Fri at 11:00 on art from 1500 to 1800, 12:00 on art from 1800 to 1900, 14:00 on Turner, and 15:00 on art from the 20th century; Sat–Sun tours at 12:00 and 15:00 on collection highlights; call to confirm schedule, kids' activities on weekends; no photography allowed without advance permission, café and restaurant; Tube: Pimlico, then 7-min walk; or arrive directly at museum by taking the Tate Boat ferry from Tate Modern; or take bus #87 from National Gallery or bus #88 from Oxford Circus. Recorded info tel. 020/7887-8008, switchboard tel. 020/7887-8888, www.tate.org.uk.

▲**Apsley House (Wellington Museum)**—Having beaten Napoleon at Waterloo, Arthur Wellesley, the First Duke of

West London

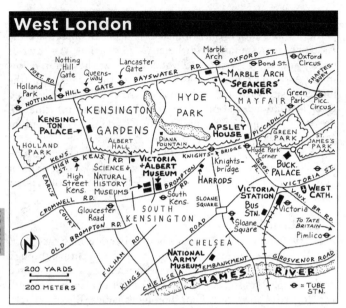

Wellington, was once the most famous man in Europe. He was given London's ultimate address, #1 London. His newly refurbished mansion offers a nice interior, a handful of world-class paintings, and a glimpse at the life of the great soldier and two-time prime minister. Those who know something about Wellington ahead of time will appreciate the place much more than those who don't, as there's scarce biographical background.

An 11-foot-tall marble statue of Napoleon, clad only in a fig leaf, greets you. Napoleon commissioned the sculptor Antonio Canova to make it for him but didn't like it, and after Napoleon's defeat, it was eventually sold to Wellington as a war trophy. It's one of several images Wellington acquired of his former foe to have in his home. The two great men were polar opposites—Napoleon the daring general and champion of revolution, Wellington the play-it-safe strategist and conservative politician—but they're forever linked in history.

The core of the collection is a dozen first-floor rooms decorated with fancy wallpaper, chandeliers, a few pieces of furniture, and wall-to-wall paintings from Wellington's collection. You'll see fancy dinnerware and precious objects given to the Irish-born general by the crowned heads of Europe, who were eternally grateful to him for saving their necks from the guillotine. The highlight is the large ballroom, the Waterloo Gallery, decorated with Van Dyck's *Charles I on Horseback* (over the main fireplace), Velázquez's earthy *The Water-Seller of Seville* (to the left of Van Dyck), Jan

Steen's playful *The Dissolute Household* (to the right), and a large portrait of Wellington by Goya (farther right).

Downstairs is a small gallery of Wellington memorabilia, including a pair of Wellington boots, which the duke popularized—Brits today still call rubber boots "wellies."

Cost, Hours, Location: £5.70, free on June 18—Waterloo Day, Wed–Sun 11:00–17:00 April–Oct, until 16:00 Nov–March, closed Mon–Tue, well-described by included audioguide which has sound bites from the current Duke of Wellington who still lives at Apsley, 20 yards from Hyde Park Corner Tube station. Tel. 020/7499-5676, www.english-heritage.org.uk. Hyde Park's pleasant and picnic-wonderful rose garden is nearby.

▲**Hyde Park and Speakers' Corner**—London's "Central Park,"

originally Henry VIII's hunting grounds, has more than 600 acres of lush greenery, the huge man-made Serpentine Lake, the royal Kensington Palace and Orangery, and the ornate neo-Gothic Albert Memorial across from the Royal Albert Hall. The western half of the park is known as Kensington Gardens. On Sundays from just after noon until early evening, Speakers' Corner offers soapbox oratory at its best (northeast corner of the park, Tube: Marble Arch). Characters climb their stepladders, wave their flags, pound emphatically on their sandwich boards, and share what they are convinced is their wisdom. Regulars have resident hecklers—who know their lines and are always ready with a verbal jab or barb. "The grass roots of democracy" is actually a holdover from when the gallows stood here and the criminal was allowed to say just about anything he wanted to before he swung. I dare you to raise your voice and gather a crowd—it's easy to do.

The **Princess Diana Memorial Fountain** honors the "People's Princess," who once lived in nearby Kensington Palace. The low-key circular stream, great for cooling off your feet on a hot day, is in the south central part of the park, near the Albert Memorial and Serpentine Gallery. (Don't be confused by signs

to the Diana, Princess of Wales Memorial Playground, in the northwest corner of the park.)

LONDON

▲▲**Victoria and Albert Museum**—The world's top collection of decorative arts (vases, stained glass, fine furniture, clothing, jewelry, carpets, and more) is a surprisingly interesting assortment of crafts from the West, as well as Asian and Islamic cultures. The V&A grew out of the Great Exhibition of 1851, that ultimate celebration of the Industrial Revolution. Now "art" could be brought to the masses through modern technology and mass production. The museum was founded on the idealistic Victorian notion that anyone can be continually improved by education and example. After much support from Queen Victoria and Prince Albert, the museum was renamed for the royal couple, and its present building was opened in 1909.

In 2004, the V&A received several grants for refurbishment projects to take place over the next 10 years. Changes so far include a new café, renovated sculpture gallery, and reopened Islamic room. The refurbished Medieval and Renaissance galleries reopen in late 2009. During this chaotic time, exhibits will likely be rearranged, so check with the information desk for current room closures, carry a copy of the museum's detailed map, and ask a nearby guard if you can't find one of the objects.

Many visitors start with the **British Galleries** (upstairs)—a one-way tour stretching through 400 years of high-class British lifestyles, almost a museum in itself.

In Room 46A are the plaster casts of **Trajan's Column,** a copy of Rome's 140-foot spiral relief telling the story of the conquest of Romania. (The V&A's casts are copies made for the benefit of 19th-century art students who couldn't afford a railpass.)

Room 46B, which has plaster casts of **Renaissance sculptures,** may be closed until 2010 (if so, you can peek down into it from the upper mezzanine). Compare Michelangelo's monumental *David* with Donatello's girlish *David,* and see Lorenzo Ghiberti's bronze Baptistery doors.

In Room 48A are **Raphael's "cartoons,"** seven of the full-size designs by Raphael that were used to produce tapestries for the Sistine Chapel (approximately 13' x 17', done in tempera on paper, now mounted on canvas). The cartoons were sent to factories in Brussels, cut into strips (see the lines), and placed on the looms. The scenes are the reverse of the final product—lots of left-handed saints.

The museum is large and gangly, with 150 rooms and more than 12 miles of corridors. While just wandering works well here, consider catching one of the free one-hour orientation tours or buying the fine £5 *V&A Guide Book*.

Cost, Hours, Location: Free, £3 donation requested, possible pricey fee for special exhibits, daily 10:00–17:45, Fri until 22:00; free 60-min tours daily on the half-hour from 10:30–15:30; Tube: South Kensington, a long tunnel leads directly from the Tube station to museum. Tel. 020/7942-2000, www.vam.ac.uk.

▲**Natural History Museum**—Across the street from Victoria and Albert, this mammoth museum is housed in a giant and wonderful Victorian, Neo-Romanesque building. Built in the 1870s specifically for the huge collection (50 million specimens), it has two halves: the Life Galleries (creepy-crawlies, human biology, "our place in evolution," and awesome dinosaurs) and the Earth Galleries (meteors, volcanoes, earthquakes, and so on). Exhibits are wonderfully explained, with lots of creative, interactive displays. Pop in, if only for the wild collection of dinosaurs and the roaring *Tyrannosaurus rex.*

Cost, Hours, Location: Free, fees for special exhibits, daily 10:00–17:50, last entry at 17:30, occasional tours, a long tunnel leads directly from South Kensington Tube station to museum. Tel. 020/7942-5000, www.nhm.ac.uk.

▲**Science Museum**—Next door to the Natural History Museum, this sprawling wonderland for curious minds is kid-perfect. It offers hands-on fun, from moonwalks to deep-sea exploration, with trendy technology exhibits, an IMAX theater (£8, kids-£6.25), and cool rotating themed exhibits, including "Cosmos and Culture: How Astronomy Has Shaped Our World," on display through 2010.

Cost, Hours, Location: Free entry, daily 10:00–18:00, Exhibition Road, Tube: South Kensington. Toll tel. 0870-870-4868, www.sciencemuseum.org.uk.

▲▲**Kensington Palace**—In 1689, King William and Queen Mary moved from Whitehall in central London to the more pristine and peaceful village of Kensington (now engulfed by London). Sir Christopher Wren renovated an existing house into Kensington Palace, which became the center of English court life until 1760, when the royal family moved into Buckingham Palace. Since then, lesser royals have bedded down in Kensington Palace. Princess Diana lived here from her 1981 marriage to Prince Charles until her death in 1997. Today, it's home to three of Charles' cousins and to employees of the royal family. The palace, while still functioning as a royal residence, also welcomes visitors with an impressive string of royal apartments and a few rooms of royal dresses. Enjoy a re-created royal tailor and dressmaker's workshop, the 17th-century splendor of the apartments of William and Mary, and the bed where Queen Victoria was born—fully clothed, it is said.

Cost, Hours, Location: £12.50, includes excellent audio-guide, daily 10:00–18:00, until 17:00 in winter, last entry one hour before closing, a 10-min hike through Kensington Gardens from either Queensway or High Street Kensington Tube station. Toll tel. 0870-751-5170 or 0844-482-7777, www.hrp.org.uk.

Nearby: Garden enthusiasts enjoy popping into the secluded Sunken Garden, 50 yards from the exit. Consider afternoon tea at the nearby Orangery (see page 152), built as a greenhouse for Queen Anne in 1704.

Victoria Station—From underneath this station's iron-and-glass canopy, trains depart for the south of England and Gatwick Airport. While Victoria Station is famous and a major Tube stop, few tourists actually take trains from here—most just come to take in the exciting bustle. It's a fun place to be just a "rock in a river" teeming with commuters and services. The station is surrounded by big red buses and taxis, travel agencies, and lousy eateries. It's next to the main bus station (National Express) and the best inexpensive lodgings in town.

Westminster Cathedral—This largest Catholic church in England, just a block from Victoria Station, is striking, but not very historic or important to visit. Opened in 1903, it has a brick neo-Byzantine flavor (surrounded by glassy office blocks). While it's definitely not Westminster Abbey, half the tourists wandering around inside seem to think it is. The highlight is the lift to the viewing gallery atop its 273-foot bell tower (£3 for the lift, tower open daily 9:30–12:30 & 13:00–17:00 in summer, Thu–Sat 9:00–17:00 in winter).

Cost, Hours, Location: Free entry, daily 7:00–19:00; 5-min walk from Victoria Station or take bus #11, #24, #148, #211, or #507 to museum's door; just off Victoria Street, Tube: Victoria, www.westminstercathedral.org.uk.

National Army Museum—This museum is not as awe-inspiring as the Imperial War Museum, but it's still fun, especially for kids who are into soldiers, armor, and guns. And while the Imperial War Museum is limited to wars of the 20th century, this tells the story of the British Army from 1415 through the Bosnian conflict and Iraq, with lots of Redcoat lore and a good look at Waterloo. Kids enjoy trying on a Cromwellian helmet, seeing the skeleton of Napoleon's horse, and peering out from a WWI trench through a working periscope.

Cost, Hours, Location: Free, daily 10:00–17:30, Royal Hospital Road, Chelsea, Tube: Sloane Square. Tel. 020/7730-0717 or 020/7881-2455, www.national-army-museum.ac.uk.

East London

The Docklands are easy to combine with an excursion to Greenwich; you can catch a boat (or the Tube) to Greenwich, then stop by the Docklands on the way back in the afternoon, when it's especially lively at the end of the workday.

▲▲**The Docklands**—Survey the skyline or notice the emergence of an entire new Tube network, and it becomes clear that London is shifting east. This vibrant city center will become even more important in the near future, as it will host several events during the 2012 Olympics. The heart of this new London is the Docklands, filling the Isle of Dogs—a peninsula created by a hairpin bend in the Thames—with gleaming skyscrapers springing out of a futuristic, modern art–filled people zone below.

By the late 1700s, 13,000 ships a year were loaded and unloaded in London, congesting the Thames. In 1802 the world's largest-of-its-kind harbor was built here in the Docklands, organizing shipping for the capital of the empire upon which the sun never set. When Britannia ruled the waves, the Isle of Dogs hosted the world's leading harbor. But with the advent of container shipping in the 1960s, London's shipping industry moved to deep-water ports. The Docklands became a derelict and dangerous wasteland—the perfect place to host a new and vibrant economic center. Over the past few decades, Britain's new Information Age industries—banking, finance, publishing, and media—have vacated downtown London and set up shop here.

Those 1802 West India warehouses survive, but rather than trading sugar and rum, today they house the Museum of London Docklands (described later) and a row of happening restaurants. And where sailors once drank grog while stevedores unloaded cargo, today thousands of office workers populate a forest of skyscrapers, towering high above the remnants of the Industrial Age. If you simply stroll around, you'll find this one of the most exciting hours of free entertainment London has to offer. This is today's London—there's not a tourist in sight.

The Tube and Docklands Light Railway stations themselves are awe-inspiring. Explore sprawling underground malls and delightfully peaceful, green parks with pedestrian bridges looping over the now-tranquil canals. Though you can't get up the skyscrapers, the ground-floor levels are welcoming with fun art. Photographers can't help but catch jumbo jets gliding past gleaming towers, goofy pose-with-me statues, and trendy pubs filled with trendier young professionals. Jubilee Park is an oasis of green in this Manhattan of Britain.

The Canary Wharf Tower (with its pyramid cap), once the tallest in Europe, remains the tallest in the UK—for now. Like its little sister skyscrapers, owned by HSBC (Hong Kong Shanghai Banking Corporation) and Citigroup, it's filled with big banks, finance, and media companies. The stubby building just to one side, occupied by an American bank, is a painfully truthful metaphor.

This pedestrian-friendly district is well-served by signs.

Follow them over the pedestrian bridge to the **Museum of London Docklands,** which tells the story of the world's leading 19th-century port (£5, daily 10:00–18:00, last entry 30 min before closing, West India Quay, Canary Wharf, tel. 020/7001-9844, www.museumin docklands.org.uk). Between the bridge and the museum is a line of fun, mod eateries (£10 main courses, huge variety of cuisines).

Getting There: Ride the Tube's Jubilee Line (just 15 min from Westminster, frequent departures) to its Canary Wharf stop, or take the Docklands Light Railway from Bank to Canary Wharf (this makes a good stop en route to or from Greenwich). At Canary Wharf, the Jubilee Line station and DLR station are a short walk apart.

Greater London

To locate the following sights, see the map on page 46.

▲▲**Kew Gardens**—For a fine riverside park and a palatial green-house jungle to swing through, take the Tube or the boat to every botanist's favorite escape, Kew Gardens.

While to most visitors the Royal Botanic Gardens of Kew are simply a delightful opportunity to wander among 33,000 different types of plants, to the hardworking organization that runs the gardens, it's a way to promote understanding and preservation of the botanical diversity of our planet. The Kew Tube station drops you in an herbal little business community, a two-block walk from Victoria Gate (the main garden entrance). Pick up a map brochure and check at the gate for a monthly listing of best blooms.

Garden lovers could spend days exploring Kew's 300 acres. For a quick visit, spend a fragrant hour wandering through three buildings: the **Palm House,** a humid Victorian world of iron, glass, and tropical plants built in 1844; a **Waterlily House** that Monet would swim for; and the **Princess of Wales Conservatory,** a modern greenhouse with many different climate zones growing countless cacti, bug-munching carnivorous plants, and more. The latest addition to the gardens is the **Rhizotron and Xstrata Treetop Walkway,** a 200-yard-long scenic steel walkway that puts you high in the canopy 60 feet above the ground.

Cost, Hours, Location: £13, discounted to £11 45 min before closing, kids under 17 free, £5 for Kew Palace only; April–Aug Mon–Fri 9:30–18:30, Sat–Sun 9:30–19:30; closes earlier Sept–March, last entry to gardens 30 min before closing, galleries and conservatories close at 17:30 in high season—earlier off-season, free 60-min walking tours daily at 11:00 and 14:00, £4 narrated floral 40-min hop-on, hop-off joyride on little tram departs on the hour from 11:00 from near Victoria Gate, Tube: Kew Gardens, boats run April–Oct between Kew Gardens and Westminster Pier—see page 66. Switchboard tel. 020/8332-5000, recorded info tel. 020/8332-5655, www.kew.org.

Nearby: For a sun-dappled lunch, walk 10 minutes from the Palm House to the Orangery (£6 hot meals, daily 10:00–17:30).

▲**Hampton Court Palace**—Fifteen miles up the Thames from downtown (£15 taxi ride from Kew Gardens) is the 500-year-

old palace of Henry VIII. Actually, it was the palace of his minister, Cardinal Wolsey. When Wolsey, a clever man, realized Henry VIII was experiencing a little palace envy, he gave the mansion to his king. The Tudor palace was also home to Elizabeth I and Charles I. Sections were updated by Christopher Wren

for William and Mary. The stately palace stands overlooking the Thames and includes some impressive Tudor rooms, including a Great Hall with a magnificent hammer-beam ceiling. The industrial-strength Tudor kitchen was capable of keeping 600 schmoozing courtiers thoroughly—if not well—fed. The sculpted garden features a rare Tudor tennis court and a popular maze.

The palace, fully restored after a 1986 fire, tries hard to please, but it doesn't quite sparkle. From the information center in the main courtyard pick up audioguides for self-guided tours of various wings of the palace (free). The Tudor kitchens, Henry VIII's apartments, and the King's apartments are most interesting. The Georgian rooms are pretty dull. The maze in the nearby garden is a curiosity some find fun (maze free with palace ticket, otherwise £3.50).

Cost and Hours: The palace costs £14, or £38 for families; daily April–Oct 10:00–18:00, Nov–March 10:00–16:30, last entry one hour earlier. Toll tel. 0870-751-5175, recorded info toll tel. 0870-752-7777, www.hrp.org.uk.

Getting There: The train (2/hr, 30 min) from London's Waterloo station drops you across the river from the palace (just walk across the bridge). Note that there are often discounts available for people riding the train from London to the palace. Check online or at the ticket office at Waterloo station for the latest offers.

Consider arriving at or departing from the palace by boat (connections with London's Westminster Pier, see page 66); it's a relaxing and scenic three-hour cruise past two locks and a fun new/old riverside mix.

Royal Air Force Museum London—A hit with aviation enthusiasts, this huge aerodrome and airfield contain planes from World War II's Battle of Britain up through the Gulf War. You can climb inside some of the planes, try your luck in a cockpit, and fly with the Red Arrows in a flight simulator.

Cost, Hours, Location: Free, daily 10:00–18:00, last entry 30 min earlier, café, shop, parking, Grahame Park Way, Tube: Colindale—top of Northern Line Edgware branch. Tel. 020/8205-2266, www.rafmuseum.org.uk.

Shopping in London

Harrods—Harrods is London's most famous and touristy department store. With more than four acres of retail space covering seven floors, it's a place where some shoppers could spend all day. (To me, it's still just a department store.) Big yet classy, Harrods has everything from elephants to toothbrushes (Mon–Sat 10:00–20:00, Sun 12:00–18:00, mandatory storage for big backpacks-£3, no shorts or flip-flops, on Brompton Road, Tube: Knightsbridge, tel. 020/7730-1234, www.harrods.com).

Sightseers should pick up the free Store Guide at any info post. Here's what I enjoy: On the ground floor, find the Food Halls, with their Edwardian tiled walls, creative and exuberant displays, and staff in period costumes—not quite like your local supermarket back home.

Descend to the lower ground floor and follow signs to the Egyptian Escalator (in the center of the store), where you'll find a memorial to Dodi Fayed and Princess Diana. Photos and flowers honor the late Princess and her lover, who both died in a car crash in Paris in 1997. Inside a small, clear pyramid, you can see a wine glass still dirty from their last dinner and the engagement ring that Dodi purchased the day before they died. True Di-hards can go back up one level to the ground floor and follow signs to Door #3 in Menswear. A huge (and more than a little creepy) bronze statue shows Di and Dodi releasing a symbolic albatross. It was commissioned  by Dodi Fayed's father, Mohamed Al Fayed, who owns Harrods.

Back in the center of the store, ride the Egyptian Escalator— lined with pharaoh-headed sconces, papyrus-plant lamps, and hieroglyphic balconies (Al Fayed is from Egypt)—to the fourth floor. From the escalator, make a U-turn left and head to the far corner of the store (toys) to find child-size luxury cars that actually work. A junior Jaguar or Mercedes will set you back about $13,000. The Mini Hummer H3 ($23,000) is as big as my car.

Also on the fourth floor is **The Georgian Restaurant,** where you can enjoy a fancy afternoon tea (see page 153). For non-tea drinkers, 27 other eateries are scattered throughout the store, including a sushi bar, kosher deli, pizzeria, classic pub, and—for the truly homesick—a Krispy Kreme.

Many of my readers report that Harrods is overpriced, snooty, and teeming with American and Japanese tourists. Still, it's the palace of department stores. The nearby Beauchamp Place is lined with classy and fascinating shops.

Harvey Nichols—Once Princess Diana's favorite, "Harvey Nick's" remains the department store du jour (Mon–Sat 10:00–20:00, Sun 12:00–18:00, near Harrods, 109–125 Knightsbridge, Tube: Knightsbridge, tel. 020/7235-5000, www.harveynichols .com). Want to pick up a little £20 scarf for the wife? You won't do it here, where they're more like £200. The store's fifth floor is a veritable food fest, with a gourmet grocery store, a fancy restaurant, a Yo! Sushi bar, and a lively café. Consider a take-away tray of sushi to eat on a bench in the Hyde Park rose garden two blocks away.

Toys—The biggest toy store in Britain is **Hamleys,** which in 2010 marks its 250th anniversary of delighting children. Seven floors buzz with 28,000 toys, managed by a staff of 200. Employees, some dressed in playful costumes, give demos of the latest gadgets. At the "Build-a-Bear Factory," kids can pick out a made-to-order teddy bear and watch while it's stuffed and sewn (Mon–Fri 10:00–20:00, Sat 9:00–20:00, Sun 12:00–18:00, 188–196 Regent Street, toll tel. 0870-333-2455, www.hamleys.com).

Street Markets—Antique buffs, people-watchers, and folks who brake for garage sales love London's street markets. There's good early-morning market activity somewhere any day of the week. Any London TI has a complete, up-to-date list. If you like to haggle, there are no holds barred in London's street markets. Warning: Markets attract two kinds of people—tourists and pickpockets.

The best markets are **Portobello Road** (Mon–Wed and Fri–Sat 8:00–18:30, Thu 8:00–13:00, sparse on Mon, closed Sun, Tube: Notting Hill Gate, near recommended B&Bs, tel. 020/7229-8354, www.portobelloroad.co.uk) and **Camden Lock Market** (daily 10:00–18:00, Tube: Camden Town, tel. 020/7284-2084, www .camdenlockmarket).

Famous Auctions—London's famous auctioneers welcome the curious public for viewing and bidding. You can preview estate catalogs or browse auction calendars online. To ask questions or set up an appointment, contact **Sotheby's** (Mon–Fri 9:00–16:30, closed Sat–Sun, café, 34–35 New Bond Street, Tube: Oxford Circus, tel. 020/7293-5000, www.sothebys.com) or **Christie's** (Mon–Fri 9:00–17:00, Sat–Sun usually 12:00–17:00 but weekend hours vary—call ahead, 8 King Street, Tube: Green Park, tel. 020/7839-9060, www.christies.com).

Entertainment in London

Theater (a.k.a. "Theatre")

London's theater rivals Broadway's in quality and usually beats it in price. Choose from 200 offerings—Shakespeare, musicals, comedy, thrillers, sex farces, cutting-edge fringe, revivals starring movie celebs, and more. London does it all well. I prefer big, glitzy—even bombastic—musicals over serious chamber dramas, simply because London can deliver the lights, sound, dancers, and multimedia spectacle I rarely get back home.

Most theaters, marked on tourist maps (also see map on next page), are found in the West End between Piccadilly and Covent Garden. Box offices, hotels, and TIs offer a handy free *London Theatre Guide* and *Entertainment Guide*. From home, it's easy to check www.officiallondontheatre.co.uk for the latest on what's currently playing in London.

Performances are nightly except Sunday, usually with one or two matinees a week (Shakespeare's Globe is the rare theater that does offer performances on Sun, May–Sept). Tickets range from about £11 to £55. Matinees are generally cheaper and rarely sell out.

To book a seat, simply call the theater box office directly, ask about seats and available dates, and buy a ticket with your credit card. You can call from the US as easily as from London. Arrive about 30 minutes before the show starts to pick up your ticket and to avoid lines.

For a booking fee, you can reserve online. Most theater websites link you to a preferred ticket vendor, usually www.ticketmaster.co.uk or www.seetickets.com. Keith Prowse Ticketing is also handy by phone or online (US tel. 800-669-8687, toll tel. 0844-209-0382, www.keithprowse.com).

While booking through an agency is quick and easy, prices are inflated by a standard 25 percent fee. Ticket agencies (whether in the US, at London's TIs, or scattered throughout the city) are scalpers with an address. If you're buying from an agency, look at the ticket carefully (your price should be no more than 30 percent over the printed face value; the 17.5 percent VAT is already included in the face value), and understand where you're sitting according to the floor plan (if your view is restricted, it will state this on the

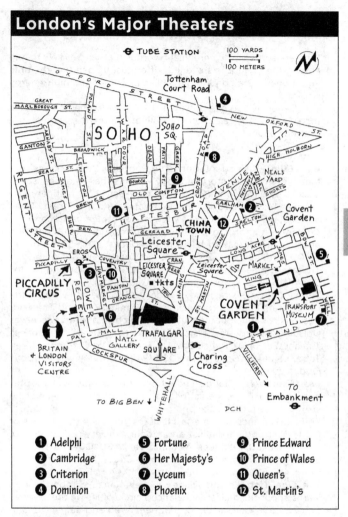

London's Major Theaters

⊖ TUBE STATION

100 YARDS
100 METERS

- ❶ Adelphi
- ❷ Cambridge
- ❸ Criterion
- ❹ Dominion
- ❺ Fortune
- ❻ Her Majesty's
- ❼ Lyceum
- ❽ Phoenix
- ❾ Prince Edward
- ❿ Prince of Wales
- ⓫ Queen's
- ⓬ St. Martin's

ticket; for floor plans of the various theaters, see www.theatre monkey.com). Agencies are worthwhile only if a show you've just got to see is sold out at the box office. They scarf up hot tickets, planning to make a killing after the show is sold out. US booking agencies get their tickets from another agency, adding even more to your expense by involving yet another middleman. Many tickets sold on the street are forgeries. Although some theaters have booking agencies handle their advance sales, you'll stand a good chance of saving money and avoiding the middleman by simply calling the box office directly to book your tickets (international phone calls are cheap, and credit cards make booking a snap).

What's On in the West End

Here are some of the perennial favorites that you're likely to find among the West End's evening offerings. If spending the time and money for a London play, I like a full-fledged high-energy musical.

Generally you can book tickets for free at the box office or for a £2-3 fee by telephone or online. See the theater map (on previous page) for locations.

Musicals

Billy Elliot—This adaptation of the popular British film is part family drama, part story of a boy who just has to dance, set to a score by Elton John (£17.50-50, Mon-Sat 19:30, matinees Thu and Sat 14:30, Victoria Palace Theatre, Victoria Street, Tube: Victoria, tel. 0870-895-5577, www.billyelliotthemusical.com).

Chicago—A chorus-girl-gone-bad forms a nightclub act with another murderess to bring in the bucks (£20-59, Mon-Thu 20:00, Fri 17:30 and 20:30, Sat 15:00 and 20:00, Cambridge Theatre, Earlham Street, Tube: Covent Garden, booking toll tel. 0844-412-4652, www.chicagothemusical.com).

Jersey Boys—This fast-moving, easy-to-follow show tracks the rough start and rise to stardom of Frankie Valli and The Four Seasons. It's light, but the music is so catchy that everyone leaves whistling the group's classics (£20-60, Mon-Sat 19:30, matinees Tue and Sat 14:30, Prince Edward Theatre, Old Compton Street, Tube: Leicester Square, tel. 0844-482-5151, www.jerseyboys london.com).

Les Misérables—Claude-Michel Schönberg's musical adaptation of Victor Hugo's epic follows the life of Jean Valjean as he struggles with the social and political realities of 19th-century France. This inspiring mega-hit takes you back to the days of France's struggle for a just and modern society (£12.50-52.50, Mon-Sat 19:30, matinees Wed and Sat 14:30, Queen's Theatre, Shaftesbury Avenue, Tube: Piccadilly Circus, box office toll tel. 0844-482-5160, www.lesmis.com).

The Lion King—In this Disney extravaganza, Simba the lion learns about the delicately balanced circle of life on the savanna (£30-59.50, Tue-Sat 19:30, matinees Wed and Sat 14:00, Sun

Theater Lingo: Stalls (ground floor), dress circle (first balcony), upper circle (second balcony), balcony (sky-high third balcony), slips (cheap seats on the fringes). Many cheap seats have a restricted view (behind a pillar).

Cheap Theater Tricks: Most theaters offer cheap returned tickets, standing-room, matinee, and senior or student standby deals. These "concessions" (discounted tickets) are indicated with a *conc* or *s* in the listings. Picking up a late return can get you a great seat at a cheap-seat price. If a show is "sold out," there's usually a

15:00, Lyceum Theatre, Wellington Street, Tube: Charing Cross or Covent Garden, booking toll tel. 0844-844-0005, theater info tel. 020/7420-8100, www.thelionking.co.uk).

Mamma Mia!—This energetic, spandex-and-platform-boots musical weaves together a slew of ABBA hits to tell the story of a bride in search of her real dad as her promiscuous mom plans her Greek Isle wedding. The production has the audience dancing by the time it reaches its happy ending (£19.50–58, Mon–Thu and Sat 19:30, Fri 20:30, matinees Fri 17:00 and Sat 15:00, Prince of Wales Theatre, Coventry Street, Tube: Piccadilly Circus, box office toll tel. 0844-482-5138, www.mamma-mia.com).

Phantom of the Opera—A mysterious masked man falls in love with a singer in this haunting Andrew Lloyd Webber musical about life beneath the stage of the Paris Opera (£20–55, Mon–Sat 19:30, matinees Tue and Sat 14:30, Her Majesty's Theatre, Haymarket, Tube: Piccadilly Circus or Leicester Square, US toll-free tel. 800-334-8457, London booking toll tel. 0844-412-2707, www.thephantomoftheopera.com).

We Will Rock You—Whether or not you're a Queen fan, this musical tribute (more to the band than to Freddie Mercury) is an understandably popular celebration of their work (£27.50–60, Mon–Sat at 19:30, matinee Sat 14:30, Dominion Theatre, Tottenham Court Road, Tube: Tottenham Court Road, Ticketmaster toll tel. 0844-847-1775, www.queenonline.com/wewillrockyou).

Thrillers

The Mousetrap—Agatha Christie's whodunit about a murder in a country house has continued to stump audiences since 1952 (£13.50–36, Mon–Sat 19:30, matinees Tue 15:00 and Sat 16:00, St. Martin's Theatre, West Street, Tube: Leicester Square, box office toll tel. 0844-499-1515, www.the-mousetrap.co.uk).

The Woman in Black—The chilling tale of a solicitor who is haunted by what he learns when he closes a reclusive woman's affairs (£13.50–39, Mon–Sat 20:00, matinees Tue 15:00 and Sat 16:00, Fortune Theatre, Russell Street, Tube: Covent Garden, box office toll tel. 0870-060-6626, www.thewomaninblack.com).

way to get a seat. Call the theater box office and ask how.

If you don't care where you sit, you can often buy the absolutely cheapest seats (those with an obstructed view or in the nosebleed section) at the box office; tickets generally cost less than £20. Many theaters are so small that there's hardly a bad seat. After the lights go down, scooting up is less than a capital offense. Shakespeare did it.

Half-Price "tkts" Booth: This famous ticket booth at **Leicester** (LESS-ter) **Square** sells discounted tickets for top-price seats to shows on the push list—but only on the day of the performance (generally £2.50 service charge per ticket, Mon–Sat 10:00–19:00, Sun 12:00–15:00, matinee tickets from noon, lines often form early, list of shows available online at www.tkts.co.uk). Most tickets are half-price; other shows are discounted 25 percent. Note that the real half-price booth (with its "tkts" name) is a freestanding kiosk at the edge of the garden in Leicester Square. Several dishonest outfits nearby advertise "official half-price tickets"; avoid these.

Here are some sample prices: A top-notch seat to *Chicago* costs £59 if you buy it directly from the theater; the same seat costs £32.50 at Leicester Square. The cheapest balcony seat is £20 through the theater. Half-price tickets can be a good deal, unless you want the cheapest seats or the hottest shows. But check the board; occasionally they sell cheap tickets to good shows. For example, a first-class seat to the long-running *Les Misérables* (which rarely sells out) costs £52.50 when you go through the theater ticket office, but you'll pay £30.50 at the "tkts" booth.

West End Theaters: The commercial (non-subsidized) theaters cluster around Soho (especially along Shaftesbury Avenue) and Covent Garden. With a centuries-old tradition of pleasing the masses, these present London theater at its glitziest. See the "What's On in the West End" sidebar.

Royal Shakespeare Company: If you'll ever enjoy Shakespeare, it'll be in Britain. The RSC performs at various theaters around London and in Stratford year-round. To get a schedule, contact the RSC (Royal Shakespeare Theatre, Stratford-upon-Avon, tel. 01789/403-444, www.rsc.org.uk).

Shakespeare's Globe: To see Shakespeare in a replica of the theater for which he wrote his plays, attend a play at the Globe. In this round, thatch-roofed, open-air theater the plays are performed much as Shakespeare intended—under the sky with no amplification.

The play's the thing from late April through October (usually Mon 19:30, Tue–Sat 14:00 and 19:30, Sun either 13:00 and/or 18:30, tickets can be sold out months in advance). You'll pay £5 to stand and £15–33 to sit, usually on a backless bench. Because only a few rows and the pricier Gentlemen's Rooms have seats with backs, £1 cushions and £3 add-on back rests are considered a good investment by many. Dress for the weather. The £5 "groundling" tickets—while open to rain—are most fun. Scurry in early to stake out a spot on the stage's edge, where the most interaction with the actors occurs. You're a crude peasant. You can lean your elbows on the stage, munch a picnic dinner (yes, you can bring in food), or walk around. I've never enjoyed Shakespeare as much as here, performed as it was meant to be in the "wooden O." If you can't get a ticket, consider waiting around. Plays can be long, and many groundlings leave before the end. Hang around outside and beg or buy a ticket from someone leaving early (groundlings are allowed to come and go).

For information on plays or £10.50 tours of the theater and museum (see page 103), contact the theater at tel. 020/7902-1400 or 020/7902-1500 (or see www.shakespeares-globe.org). To reserve tickets for plays, call or drop by the box office (Mon–Sat 10:00–18:00, Sun 10:00–17:00, stays open one hour later on performance days, New Globe Walk entrance, tel. 020/7401-9919). You can also reserve online (£2 booking fee per transaction). A few non-Shakespeare plays are also presented each year.

The theater is on the South Bank, directly across the Thames over the Millennium Bridge from St. Paul's Cathedral (Tube: Mansion House or London Bridge). The Globe is inconvenient for public transport, but the courtesy phone in the lobby gets a minicab in minutes. (These minicabs have set fees—e.g., £8 to South Kensington—but generally cost less than a metered cab and provide fine and honest service.) During theater season, there's a regular supply of black cabs outside the main foyer on New Globe Walk.

Outdoor Theater in Summer: Enjoy Shakespearean drama and other plays under the stars at the **Open Air Theatre,** in leafy Regent's Park in north London. Food is allowed: You can bring your own picnic; order à la carte from the theater menu; or preorder a £22.50 picnic supper from the theater at least one week in advance (tickets £10–50; season runs late May–mid-Sept, box office open April–late May Mon–Sat 10:00–18:00, closed Sun; late May–mid-Sept Mon–Sat 10:00–20:00, Sun 10:00–until start of play on performance days only; order tickets online after mid-Jan or by phone Mon–Sun 9:00–21:00; £1 booking fee by phone, no fee if ordering online or in person; toll tel. 0844-826-4242, www.openairtheatre.org; grounds open 1.5 hours prior to evening performances, one hour prior to 2:30 matinee, and 30 min prior to earlier matinees; 10-min walk north of Baker Street Tube, near Queen Mary's Gardens within Regent's Park; detailed directions and more info at www.openairtheatre.org).

Fringe Theatre: London's rougher evening-entertainment scene is thriving, filling pages in *Time Out.* Choose from a wide range of fringe theater and comedy acts (generally £5).

Classical Music
Concerts at Churches
For easy, cheap, or free concerts in historic churches, check the TIs' listings for **lunch concerts,** especially:

- St. Bride's Church, with free lunch concerts twice a week at 13:15 (generally Tue, Wed, or Fri—confirm by phone or online, church tel. 020/7427-0133, www.stbrides.com).

- St. James's at Piccadilly, with 50-minute concerts on Monday, Wednesday, and Friday at 13:10 (suggested donation £3, info tel. 020/7381-0441, www.st-james-piccadilly.org).
- St. Martin-in-the-Fields, offering free concerts on Monday, Tuesday, and Friday at 13:00 (suggested £3.50 donation, church tel. 020/7766-1100, www.smitf.org).

St. Martin-in-the-Fields also hosts fine **evening concerts** by candlelight (£6–25, at 19:30 Thu–Sat, sometimes Tue) and live jazz in its underground Café in the Crypt (£5–8, Wed at 20:00).

Evensong and Organ Recitals at Churches

Evensong services are held at several churches, including:

- St. Paul's Cathedral (Mon–Sat at 17:00, Sun at 15:15).
- Westminster Abbey (Mon–Tue and Thu–Fri at 17:00, Sat–Sun at 15:00; there's a service on Wed, but it's spoken, not sung).
- Southwark Cathedral (Mon–Tue and Thu–Fri at 17:30; Sat at 16:00, Sun at 15:00, no service on Wed or alternate Mon, tel. 020/7367-6700, www.southwark.anglican.org/cathedral).
- St. Bride's Church (Sun at 18:30, tel. 020/7427-0133, www.stbrides.com).

Free **organ recitals** are often held on Sunday at 17:45 in Westminster Abbey (30 min, tel. 020/7222-5152). Many other churches have free concerts; ask for the *London Organ Concerts Guide* at the TI.

Prom Concerts and Opera

For a fun classical event (mid-July–mid Sept), attend a **Prom Concert** (shortened from "Promenade Concert") during the annual festival at the Royal Albert Hall. Nightly concerts are offered at give-a-peasant-some-culture prices to "Promenaders"—those willing to stand throughout the performance (£5 standing-room spots sold at the door, £7 restricted-view seats, most £22–30 but depends on performance, Tube: South Kensington, tel. 020/7589-8212, www.bbc.co.uk/proms).

Some of the world's best **opera** is belted out at the prestigious Royal Opera House, near Covent Garden (box office tel. 020/7304-4000, www.roh.org.uk), and at the less-formal Sadler's Wells Theatre (Rosebery Avenue, Islington, Tube: Angel, info tel. 020/7863-8198, box office toll tel. 0844-412-4300, www.sadlerswells.com).

Evening Museum Visits

Many museums are open an evening or two during the week, offering fewer crowds. See a list on page 82.

Tours

Guided **walks** are offered several times a day. **London Walks** is the most established company. Daytime walks vary by theme: ancient London, museums, legal London, Dickens, Beatles, Jewish quarter, Christopher Wren, and so on. In the evening, expect a more limited choice: ghosts, Jack the Ripper, pubs, or literary-themed. Get the latest from their brochure or website, or call for a recorded listing of that day's walks. Show up at the listed time and place, pay the guide, and enjoy the two-hour tour (£7, cash only, tel. 020/7624-3978, recorded info 020/7624-9255, www.walks.com).

To see the city illuminated at night, consider a **bus** tour. A one-hour **London by Night Sightseeing Tour** leaves every evening from Victoria Station and other points (see page 60).

Summer Evenings Along the South Bank

If you're visiting London in summer, consider the South Bank.

Take a trip around the **London Eye** while the sun sets over the city (Ferris wheel spins until 21:00). Then cap your night with an evening walk along the pedestrian-only **Jubilee Walkway,** which runs east–west along the river. It's where Londoners go to escape the heat. This pleasant stretch of the walkway—lined with pubs and casual eateries—goes from the London Eye past Shakespeare's Globe to Tower Bridge (you can walk in either direction; see www .jubileewalkway.com for maps and Tube stops).

If you're in the mood for a movie, take in a flick at the **BFI Southbank,** located just across the river, alongside Waterloo Bridge. Run by the British Film Institute, the state-of-the-art theater shows mostly classic films, as well as art cinema (£8.60, £5 on Tue, Tube: Waterloo or Embankment, box office tel. 020/7928-3232, check www.bfi.org.uk for schedules).

Farther east along the South Bank is **The Scoop**—an outdoor amphitheater next to City Hall. It's a good spot for outdoor movies, concerts, dance, and theater productions throughout the summer—with Tower Bridge as a scenic backdrop. These events are free, nearly nightly, and family-friendly. For the latest event schedule, see www.morelondon.com and click on "The Scoop" (next to City Hall, Riverside, The Queen's Walkway, Tube: London Bridge).

Cruises

During the summer, boats sail as late as 21:00 between Westminster Pier (near Big Ben) and the Tower of London. (For details, see page 65.)

A handful of outfits run Thames River evening cruises with four-course meals and dancing. **London Showboat** offers the best value (£75, April–Oct Wed–Sun, Nov–March Thu–Sat, 3.5 hours, departs at 19:00 from Westminster Pier and returns by 22:30, reservations necessary, tel. 020/7740-0400, www.citycruises.com). Dinner cruises are also offered by **Bateaux London** (£65–120, tel. 020/7695-1800, www.bateauxlondon.com). For more on cruising, get the *River Thames Boat Services* brochure from a London TI.

Sleeping in London

London is perhaps Europe's most expensive city for rooms. Cheaper rooms are relatively dumpy. Don't expect £130 cheeriness in a £80 room. For £70, you'll get a double with breakfast in a safe, cramped, and dreary place with minimal service and the bathroom down the hall. For £90, you'll get a basic, clean, reasonably cheery double in a usually cramped, cracked-plaster building with a private bath, or a soulless but comfortable room without breakfast in a huge Motel 6–type place. My London splurges, at £150–260, are spacious, thoughtfully appointed places good for entertaining or romancing. Off-season, it's possible to save money by arriving late without a reservation and looking around. Competition softens prices, especially for multinight stays. Check hotel websites for special deals. All of Britain's accommodations are now non-smoking.

Hearty English or generous buffet breakfasts are included unless otherwise noted, and TVs are standard in rooms, but may come with only the traditional five British channels (no cable).

Looking for Hotel Deals Online

Given the high hotel prices and relatively weak dollar, consider using the Internet to help you score a hotel deal. Various websites list rooms in high-rise, three- and four-star business hotels. You'll give up the charm and warmth of a family-run establishment, and breakfast will probably not be included, but you might find the price is right.

Start by checking the websites of several chains to get an idea of typical rates and to check for online-only deals. Big London hotel chains include the following: Millennium/Copthorne (www.millenniumhotels.com), Thistle Hotels (www.thistle.com), InterContinental/Holiday Inn (www.ichotelsgroup.com), Radisson (www.radisson.com), Hilton (www.hilton.com), and Red Carnation (www.redcarnationhotels.com). For information on no-frills, Motel 6–type chains, see "Big, Good-Value, Modern Hotels," below.

Auction-type sites (such as www.priceline.com or www.hotwire.com) can be great for matching flexible travelers with empty hotel rooms, often at prices well below the hotel's normal rates.

Other favorite accommodation discount sites mentioned by my readers include www.londontown.com (an informative site

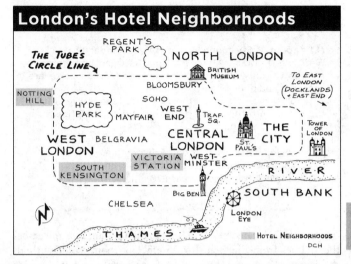

London's Hotel Neighborhoods

with a discount booking service), http://athomeinlondon.co.uk and www.londonbb.com (both list central B&Bs), www.lastminute .com, www.visitlondon.com, http://roomsnet.com, and www .eurocheapo.com. Read candid reviews of London hotels at www .tripadvisor.com. And check the "Graffiti Wall" at www.ricksteves .com for the latest tips and discoveries.

For a good overview on finding London hotel deals, go to www.smartertravel.com and click on "Travel Guides," then "London."

Big, Good-Value, Modern Hotels

These places—popular with budget tour groups—are well-run and offer elevators, 24-hour reception, and all the modern comforts in a no-nonsense, practical package. With the notable exception of my second listing, they are often located on busy streets in dreary train-station neighborhoods, so use common sense after dark and wear your money belt. The doubles for £90–100 are a great value for London. Midweek prices are generally higher than weekend rates. Breakfast is always extra. Online bookings are often the easiest way to make reservations, and will generally net you a discount.

$$ Jurys Inn Islington rents 200-plus compact, comfy rooms near King's Cross station (Db/Tb-£89–139, some discounted rooms available online, 2 adults and 2 kids under age 12 can share one room, 60 Pentonville Road, Tube: Angel, tel. 020/7282-5500, fax 020/7282-5511, www.jurysinns.com).

$$ Premier Inn London County Hall, literally down the hall from a $400-a-night Marriott Hotel, fills one end of London's massive former County Hall building. This family-friendly place

---

Sleep Code

(£1 = about $1.60, country code: 44, area code: 020)

S = Single, **D** = Double/Twin, **T** = Triple, **Q** = Quad, **b** = bathroom, **s** = shower only. Unless otherwise noted, credit cards are accepted and prices include breakfast.

To help you easily sort through these listings, I've divided the rooms into three categories, based on the price for a double room with bath:

$$$ Higher Priced—Most rooms £115 or more.

$$ Moderately Priced—Most rooms between £70-115.

$ Lower Priced—Most rooms £70 or less.

---

is wonderfully located near the base of the London Eye and across the Thames from Big Ben. Its 313 efficient rooms come with all the necessary comforts (Db-£109–119 for 2 adults and up to 2 kids under age 16, book in advance, no-show rooms released at 15:00, some easy-access rooms, 500 yards from Westminster Tube stop and Waterloo Station, Belvedere Road, central reservations toll tel. 0870-242-8000, reception desk toll tel. 0870-238-3300, easiest to book online at www.premierinn.com).

$$ Premier Inn London Southwark, with 59 rooms, is near Shakespeare's Globe on the South Bank (Db for up to 2 adults and 2 kids-£99–110, Bankside, 34 Park Street, toll tel. 0870-990-6402, www.premierinn.com).

$$ Premier Inn King's Cross–St. Pancras, with 276 rooms, is just east of King's Cross and St. Pancras stations (Db-£90–114, 26–30 York Way, toll tel. 0870-990-6414, www.premierinn.com).

Other **$$ Premier Inns** charging £87–114 per room include **London Euston** (big, blue, Lego-type building packed with vacationing families, on handy but noisy street at corner of Euston Road and Dukes Road, Tube: Euston, toll tel. 0870-238-3301), **London Kensington Earl's Court** (11 Knaresborough Place, Tube: Earl's Court or Gloucester Road, toll tel. 0870-238-3304), and **London Putney Bridge** (£79–89, farther out, 3 Putney Bridge Approach, Tube: Putney Bridge, toll tel. 0870-238-3302). Avoid the **Tower Bridge** location, which is an inconvenient, 15-minute walk from the nearest Tube stop. For any of these, call 0870-242-8000 or—the best option—book online at www.premierinn.com.

$$ Hotel Ibis London Euston St. Pancras, which feels a bit classier than a Premier Inn, rents 380 rooms on a quiet street a block behind and west of Euston Station (Db-£90–115, up to £150 during special events, no family rooms, 3 Cardington Street,

tel. 020/7388-7777 or 020/7304-7712, fax 020/7388-0001, www
.ibishotel.com, h0921@accor.com).

$$ Travelodge London Kings Cross is another typi-
cal chain hotel with lots of cookie-cutter rooms, just 200 yards
south of King's Cross Station (Db-£52–98, family rooms, can be
noisy, Grays Inn Road, toll tel. 0871-984-6256). Other convenient
Travelodge London locations are the nearby **Kings Cross Royal
Scot, Euston, Marylebone, Covent Garden, Liverpool Street,**
and **Farringdon.** For details on all Travelodge hotels, see www
.travelodge.co.uk.

Victoria Station Neighborhood (Belgravia)

The streets behind Victoria Station teem with little, moderately-
priced-for-London B&Bs. It's a safe, surprisingly tidy, and

decent area without a hint of the
trashy, touristy glitz of the streets
in front of the station. West of
the tracks is Belgravia, where the
prices are a bit higher and your
neighbors include Andrew Lloyd
Webber and Margaret Thatcher
(her policeman stands outside 73
Chester Square). Decent eateries
abound (see page 150).

All the recommended hotels
are within a five-minute walk of the Victoria Tube, bus, and
train stations. On hot summer nights, request a quiet back room.
Nearby is the 400-space Semley Place NCP **parking garage**
(£32/day, possible discounts with hotel voucher, just west of the
Victoria Coach Station at Buckingham Palace Road and Semley
Place, toll tel. 0845-050-7080, www.ncp.co.uk). The handy
Pimlico Launderette is about five blocks southwest of Warwick
Square (daily 8:00–19:00, self-service or full service, south of
Sutherland Street at 3 Westmoreland Terrace, tel. 020/7821-8692).
Launderette Centre is a block northeast of Warwick Square
(Mon–Fri 8:00–22:00, Sat–Sun until 19:00, about £7 wash and
dry, £11 full-service, 31 Churton Street, tel. 020/7828-6039).

$$$ Lime Tree Hotel, enthusiastically run by Charlotte and
Matt, comes with 28 spacious and thoughtfully decorated rooms
and a fun-loving breakfast room (Sb-£85–95, Db-£120–150,
Tb-£150–180, family room-£170–195, free Internet access and
Wi-Fi, small lounge opens into quiet garden, 135 Ebury Street,
tel. 020/7730-8191, www.limetreehotel.co.uk, info@limetreehotel
.co.uk, trusty Alan covers the night shift).

$$$ B+B Belgravia has done its best to make a tight-and-
tangled old guesthouse sleek and mod. While the rooms are small

Victoria Station Neighborhood

1. Lime Tree Hotel
2. B+B Belgravia
3. Elizabeth Hotel & Jubilee Hotel
4. Cartref House & Lynton Hotel B&Bs
5. Luna Simone Hotel
6. Morgan House
7. Winchester Hotel
8. Cherry Court Hotel
9. Bakers Hotel
10. easyHotel Victoria
11. Ebury Wine Bar
12. Jenny Lo's Tea House
13. To La Poule au Pot Rest.
14. Grumbles Restaurant
15. Chimes English Rest. & Cider Bar
16. The Jugged Hare Pub
17. Seafresh Fish Rest.
18. La Bottega Deli
19. St. George's Tavern
20. To The Duke of Wellington Pub
21. The Belgravia Pub
22. The Thomas Cubitt Pub
23. Grocery Stores (4)
24. Launderettes (2)
25. Bus Tours – Day (2)
26. Bus Tours – Night
27. Tube, Taxis & City Buses

and the management is absentee, the staff of young, mostly Eastern Europeans takes good care of guests, the coffee is always on in the lobby, and the location is unbeatable (Sb-£99, Db-£120, Db twin-£130, Tb-£150, Qb-£160, free Internet access and Wi-Fi, DVD library, loaner bikes, 64 Ebury Street, tel. 020/7259-8570, www.bb-belgravia.com, info@bb-belgravia.com).

$$$ Elizabeth Hotel is a stately old place overlooking Eccleston Square, with 37 well-worn, slightly overpriced rooms (Sb-£99, D-£99, small Db-£119, big Db-£129, Tb-£149, Qb-£159, Quint/b-£169, air-con-£9, Wi-Fi, 37 Eccleston Square, tel. 020/7828-6812, fax 020/7828-6814, www.elizabethhotel.com, info@elizabethhotel.com). The Elizabeth also rents apartments sleeping up to six (£259/night).

$$ Cartref House B&B offers rare charm on Ebury Street, with 10 delightful rooms and a warm welcome (Sb-£70, Db-£95, Tb-£126, Qb-£155, fans, free Wi-Fi, 129 Ebury Street, tel. 020/7730-6176, www.cartrefhouse.co.uk, info@cartrefhouse.co.uk).

$$ Lynton Hotel B&B is a well-worn place renting 12 inexpensive rooms with small prefab WCs. It's a fine value, exuberantly run by brothers Mark and Simon Connor (D-£80, Db-£90, these prices promised with this book in 2010, free Wi-Fi, 113 Ebury Street, tel. 020/7730-4032, www.lyntonhotel.co.uk, mark-and-simon@lyntonhotel.co.uk).

$$ Luna Simone Hotel rents 36 fresh and spacious rooms with modern bathrooms. It's a well-managed place, run for 40 years by twins Peter and Bernard and son Mark, and they still seem to enjoy their work (Sb-£70, Db-£100, Tb-£120, Qb-£150, these prices with cash and this book in 2010, free Internet access and Wi-Fi, corner of Charlwood Street and Belgrave Road at 47 Belgrave Road, handy bus #24 to Victoria Station and Trafalgar Square stops out front, tel. 020/7834-5897, www.lunasimonehotel.com, lunasimone@talk21.com).

$$ Morgan House rents 11 good rooms and is entertainingly run, with lots of travel tips and friendly chat from owner Rachel Joplin and her staff, Danilo and Fernanda (S-£52, D-£72, Db-£92, T-£92, family suites-£112–132 for 3–4 people, Wi-Fi, 120 Ebury Street, tel. 020/7730-2384, www.morganhouse.co.uk, morganhouse@btclick.com).

$$ Winchester Hotel has 19 small rooms and is an adequate value for the price (Db-£89–99, Tb-£115, Qb-£140, Internet access, 17 Belgrave Road, tel. 020/7828-2972, www.londonwinchesterhotel.co.uk, info@londonwinchesterhotel.co.uk). If you need a cab, call your own to avoid excessive fares. They also rent a few apartments around the corner (£125–230, see website for details).

$ Cherry Court Hotel, run by the friendly and industrious Patel family, rents 12 very small, basic, incense-scented rooms in a central location (Sb-£48, Db-£55, Tb-£80, Qb-£95, Quint/b-£110, these prices promised with this book through 2010, 5 percent fee to pay with credit card, fruit-basket breakfast in room, air-con, laundry, free Internet access and Wi-Fi, peaceful garden patio, 23 Hugh Street, tel. 020/7828-2840, fax 020/7828-0393, www.cherry courthotel.co.uk, info@cherrycourthotel.co.uk).

$ Jubilee Hotel is a well-run slumber mill with 24 tiny rooms and many tiny beds. It's a bit musty and its windows only open a few inches, but the price is right (S-£39, Sb-£59, tiny D-£59, tiny Db-£65, Db-£69, Tb-£89, Qb-£105, ask for the 5 percent Rick Steves discount when booking, pay Internet access and Wi-Fi, 31 Eccleston Square, tel. 020/7834-0845, www.jubileehotel.co.uk, stay@jubileehotel.co.uk, Bob Patel).

$ Bakers Hotel is a well-worn cheapie, with 10 tight rooms, but it's well-located and offers youth-hostel prices and a small breakfast (S-£30–35, D-£50–55, Db-£60–65, T-£60–65, Tb-£70–75, family room-£70–75, 126 Warwick Way, tel. 020/7834-0729, www.bakershotel.co.uk, reservations@bakershotel.co.uk, Amin Jamani).

$ easyHotel Victoria is a radical concept—offering what you need to sleep well and safe—and no more. Their 77 rooms fit the old floor plan, so some rooms are tiny windowless closets, while others are quite spacious. All rooms are well-ventilated and come with an efficient "bathroom pod"—just big enough to take care of business. Prices are the same for one person or two. You get two towels, soap and shampoo, and a clean bed—no breakfast, no fresh towels, and no daily cleaning. Rooms range from £25 to £65, depending on their size and when you book: "The earlier you book, the less you pay" (reserve only through website, 36 Belgrave Road, tel. 020/7834-1379, www.easyHotel.com, enquiries@victoria.easy Hotel.com). They also have branches at South Kensington, Earl's Court, Paddington, and Heathrow and Luton airports (see their website for details).

"South Kensington," She Said, Loosening His Cummerbund

To stay on a quiet street so classy it doesn't allow hotel signs, surrounded by trendy shops and colorful restaurants, call "South Ken" your London home. Shoppers like being a short walk from Harrods and the designer shops of King's Road and Chelsea. When I splurge, I splurge here. Sumner Place is just off Old Brompton Road, 200 yards from the handy South Kensington Tube station (on Circle Line, two stops from Victoria Station, direct Heathrow connection). The handy **launderette** is on the corner of Queensberry Place and Harrington Road (Mon–Fri 7:30–21:00, Sat 9:00–20:00, Sun 10:00–19:00, bring 50p and £1 coins).

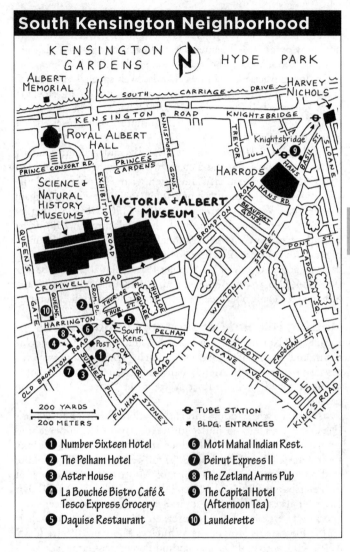

South Kensington Neighborhood

KENSINGTON GARDENS

HYDE PARK

ALBERT MEMORIAL

SOUTH CARRIAGE DRIVE

HARVEY NICHOLS

KENSINGTON ROAD

KNIGHTSBRIDGE

ROYAL ALBERT HALL

Knightsbridge

PRINCE CONSORT RD.

PRINCES GARDENS

ENNISMORE GDNS.

TREVOR

SLOANE ST.

BASIL ST.

HANS

HARRODS

SCIENCE & NATURAL HISTORY MUSEUMS

EXHIBITION ROAD

VICTORIA & ALBERT MUSEUM

HANS RD.

BEAUFORT GDNS.

ROAD

QUEEN'S GATE

BROMPTON

PONT ST.

CADOGAN PL.

CROMWELL ROAD

THURLOE PL.

THUR. ST.

THURLOE SQUARE

THURLOE ST.

WALTON STREET

❶ Number Sixteen Hotel
❷ The Pelham Hotel
❸ Aster House
❹ La Bouchée Bistro Café & Tesco Express Grocery
❺ Daquise Restaurant
❻ Moti Mahal Indian Rest.
❼ Beirut Express II
❽ The Zetland Arms Pub
❾ The Capital Hotel (Afternoon Tea)
❿ Launderette

HARRINGTON ROAD

QUEEN'S

South Kens.

PELHAM

PLACE

POST

ONSLOW SQ.

SUMNER PL.

DRAYCOTT

SLOANE AVE.

CADOGAN AVE.

OLD BROMPTON ROAD

FULHAM ROAD

SYDNEY

KING'S ROAD

200 YARDS
200 METERS

⊕ TUBE STATION
✦ BLDG. ENTRANCES

LONDON

$$$ Number Sixteen, for well-heeled travelers, packs over-the-top formality and class into its 42 rooms, plush lounges, and tranquil garden. It's in a labyrinthine building, with modern decor throughout—perfect for an urban honeymoon (Db-£200—but soft, ask for discounted "seasonal rates" especially in July–Aug—subject to availability, breakfast buffet in the garden-£17, elevator, 16 Sumner Place, tel. 020/7589-5232, fax 020/7584-8615, US tel. 800-553-6674, www.firmdalehotels.com, sixteen@firmdale.com).

$$$ The Pelham Hotel, a 52-room business-class hotel with a pricey mix of pretense and style, is not quite sure which investment company owns it. It's genteel, with low lighting and a pleasant drawing room among the many perks (Db-£180–260, breakfast extra, lower prices Aug and weekends, Web specials can include free breakfast, air-con, pay Internet access and Wi-Fi, elevator, gym, 15 Cromwell Place, tel. 020/7589-8288, fax 020/7584-8444, US tel. 1-888-757-5587, www.pelhamhotel.co.uk, reservations @pelhamhotel.co.uk).

$$$ Aster House, run by friendly and accommodating Simon and Leonie Tan, has a cheerful lobby, lounge, and breakfast room. Its rooms are comfy and quiet, with TV, phone, and air-conditioning. Enjoy breakfast or just lounge in the whisper-elegant Orangery, a Victorian greenhouse (Sb-£120, Db-£180, bigger Db-£225, 20 percent discount with this book through 2010 if you book three or more nights, additional 5 percent off for five or more nights with cash, check website for specials, VAT not included, pay Internet access and Wi-Fi, 3 Sumner Place, tel. 020/7581-5888, fax 020/7584-4925, www.asterhouse.com, asterhouse@btinternet.com). Simon and Leonie offer free loaner mobile phones to their guests.

Notting Hill and Bayswater Neighborhoods

Residential Notting Hill has quick bus and Tube access to downtown, and, for London, is very "homely" (Brit-speak for cozy). It's also peppered with trendy bars and restaurants, and is home to the famous Portobello Road Market (see "Street Markets," on page 117).

Popular with young international travelers, Bayswater's Queensway street is a multicultural festival of commerce and eateries. The neighborhood does its dirty clothes at **Galaxy Launderette** (£6 self-service, £8–10 full-service, daily 8:00–20:00, staff on hand with soap and coins, 65 Moscow Road, at corner of St. Petersburgh Place and Moscow Road, tel. 020/7229-7771). For **Internet access,** you'll find several stops along busy Queensway, and a self-serve bank of easyInternetcafé computer terminals is on the food circus level of the Whiteleys Shopping Centre (daily 8:30–24:00, corner of Queensway and Porchester Gardens).

Near Kensington Gardens Square

Several big old hotels line the quiet Kensington Gardens Square (not to be confused with the much bigger Kensington Gardens adjacent to Hyde Park), a block west of bustling Queensway, north of Bayswater Tube station. These hotels are quiet for central London.

$$$ Phoenix Hotel, a Best Western modernization of a 130-room hotel, offers American business-class comforts; large,

Notting Hill and Bayswater Neighborhoods

⊖ TUBE STN.

1/4 MILE

400 METERS

SUNDAY MARKET

PORTOBELLO

KENS. PK. RD.

Notting Hill Gate

LADBROKE ROAD

NOTTING HILL GATE

HILLSLEIGH

AUBREY

TO NORWEGIAN YWCA → 6

HOLLAND PARK WALK

HOLLAND PARK

DCH

PEMBRIDGE ROAD

DAWSON PL.

HEREFORD RD.

MOSCOW RD.

OSSINGTON ST.

PALACE CT.

KENSINGTON GARDENS SQUARE

GARWAY RD.

PRINCES SQ.

ST. PETERSBURGH PL.

PORCH.

ROAD

Bayswater

QUEENS GDNS.

Post

ROAD

Bayswater

WAY

Queensway

ROAD

BAYSWATER ROAD

PLAYGROUND

KENSINGTON GARDENS

BROAD WALK

KENSINGTON PALACE GDNS.

PALACE GREEN

KENS-INGTON PALACE

The Orangery → 15

KENSINGTON PALACE GARDENS

PALACE GARDENS TERR.

KENSINGTON CHURCH STREET

VIC. GATE ST.

KENSINGTON HIGH STREET

LUX. ST.

HILLGATE ST.

HILLGATE PLACE

KENS. PLACE

CAMPDEN ST.

CAMPDEN HILL ROAD

⊖ High Street Kensington

LONDON

1. Phoenix Hotel
2. Vancouver Studios & Princes Square Guest Accommodation
3. Kensington Gardens Hotel
4. Westland Hotel
5. London Vicarage Hotel
6. To Norwegian YWCA
7. Maggie Jones Restaurant
8. The Churchill Arms Pub & Thai Kitchens
9. The Prince Edward Pub
10. Café Diana
11. Royal China Restaurant
12. Whiteleys Mall (Food Court, Grocery, Internet)
13. Tesco Grocery
14. Spar Market
15. The Orangery (Afternoon Tea)
16. Launderette

plush public spaces; and big, fresh, modern-feeling rooms. Its prices—which range from fine value to rip-off—are determined by a greedy computer program, with huge variations according to expected demand. See their website and book online to save money (Db-£90–165, elevator, impersonal staff, 1–8 Kensington Gardens Square, tel. 020/7229-2494, fax 020/7727-1419, US tel. 800-528-1234, www.phoenixhotel.co.uk, info@phoenixhotel.co.uk).

$$$ **Vancouver Studios** offers 45 modern rooms with fully equipped kitchenettes (utensils, stove, microwave, and fridge) rather than breakfast (small Sb-£79, Db-£125, Tb-£170, extra bed-£15, 10 percent discount for weeklong stay or more, welcoming lounge and garden, near Kensington Gardens Square at 30 Prince's Square, tel. 020/7243-1270, fax 020/7221-8678, www.vancouverstudios.co.uk, info@vancouverstudios.co.uk).

$$ **Kensington Gardens Hotel** laces 17 pleasant rooms together in a tall, skinny building with lots of stairs and no elevator (Ss-£57, Sb-£64, Db-£86, Tb-£105; book by phone or email for these special Rick Steves prices, rather than through the pricier website; continental breakfast served at sister hotel next door, Wi-Fi, 9 Kensington Gardens Square, tel. 020/7221-7790, fax 020/7792-8612, www.kensingtongardenshotel.co.uk, info@kensingtongardenshotel.co.uk, Rowshanak).

$$ **Princes Square Guest Accommodation** is a big, impersonal 50-room place that's well-located, practical, and a good value, especially with its online discounts (Sb-£65–115, Db-£85–150, Tb-£110–175, elevator, 23–25 Princes Square, tel. 020/7229-9876, www.princessquarehotel.co.uk, info@princessquarehotel.co.uk).

Near Kensington Gardens

$$$ **Westland Hotel** is comfortable, convenient (5-min walk from Notting Hill neighborhood), and feels like a wood-paneled hunting lodge with a fine lounge. The rooms are spacious, recently refurbished, and quite plush. Their £130 doubles (less your 10 percent discount—see below) are the best value, but check their website for specials (Sb-£110, Db-£130, deluxe Db-£152, cavernous deluxe Db-£172, sprawling Tb-£165–193, gargantuan Qb-£186–220, Quint/b-£234, 10 percent discount with this book in 2010—claim upon booking or arrival; elevator, garage-£12/day, pay Wi-Fi, between Notting Hill Gate and Queensway Tube stations at 154 Bayswater Road, tel. 020/7229-9191, fax 020/7727-1054, www.westlandhotel.co.uk, reservations@westlandhotel.co.uk, Jim and Nora ably staff the front desk).

$$$ **London Vicarage Hotel** is family-run, understandably popular, and elegantly British in a quiet, classy neighborhood. It has 17 rooms furnished with taste and quality, a TV lounge, and facilities on each floor. Mandy and Monika maintain a homey

and caring atmosphere (S-£55, Sb-£93, D-£93, Db-£122, T-£117, Tb-£156, Q-£128, Qb-£172, 20 percent less in winter—check website, free Wi-Fi; 8-min walk from Notting Hill Gate and High Street Kensington Tube stations, near Kensington Palace at 10 Vicarage Gate; tel. 020/7229-4030, fax 020/7792-5989, www .londonvicaragehotel.com, vicaragehotel@btconnect.com).

Near Holland Park

$ Norwegian YWCA (Norsk K.F.U.K.)—where English is definitely a second language—is for women 30 and under only (and men 30 and under with Norwegian passports). Located on a quiet, stately street, it offers a study, a TV room, a piano lounge, and an open-face Norwegian ambience (goat cheese on Sundays!). They have mostly quads, so those willing to share with strangers are most likely to get a bed (July–Aug: Ss-£36, shared double-£35/bed, shared triple-£30/bed, shared quad-£26/bed, includes breakfast year-round plus sack lunch and dinner Sept–June, £20 key deposit required, pay Wi-Fi, 52 Holland Park, tel. 020/7727-9346 or 020/7727-9897, www.kfukhjemmet.org.uk, kontor@kfuk hjemmet.org.uk). With each visit, I wonder which is easier to get—a sex change or a Norwegian passport?

Other Neighborhoods

North of Marble Arch: **$$$ The 22 York Street B&B** offers a casual alternative in the city center, renting 10 stark, hardwood, comfortable rooms (Sb-£89, Db-£120, two-night minimum, Internet access and Wi-Fi, inviting lounge; from Baker Street Tube station, walk 2 blocks down Baker Street and take a right to 22 York Street; tel. 020/7224-2990, www.22yorkstreet.co.uk, mc@22yorkstreet .co.uk, energetically run by Liz and Michael Callis).

$$$ The Sumner Hotel, in a 19th-century Georgian townhouse, is located a few blocks north of Hyde Park and Oxford Street, a busy shopping destination. Decorated with fancy modern Italian furniture, this swanky place packs in all the extras (Db-£160–190, 20 percent discount with this book in 2010, extra bed-£30, free Wi-Fi, 54 Upper Berkeley Street just off Edgware Road, Tube: Marble Arch, tel. 020/7723-2244, fax 0870-705-8767, www .thesumner.com, hotel@thesumner.com, manager Peter).

Near Covent Garden: **$$$ Fielding Hotel,** located on a charming, quiet pedestrian street just two blocks east of Covent Garden, offers 24 no-frills rooms and a fine location (Db-£115–140, Db with sitting room-£160, pricier rooms are bigger with better bathrooms, no breakfast, no kids under 6, free Wi-Fi, 4 Broad Court, Bow Street, tel. 020/7836-8305, fax 020/7497-0064, www .thefieldinghotel.co.uk, reservations@the-fielding-hotel.co.uk, manager Graham Chapman).

Near Buckingham Palace: **$$ Vandon House Hotel,** run by Central College in Iowa, is packed with students most of the year, but rents its 32 rooms to travelers from late May through August at great prices. The rooms, while institutional, are comfy, and the location is excellent (S-£46, D-£70, Db-£90, Tb-£99, Qb-£119, only twin beds, elevator, Internet access and Wi-Fi; on a tiny road 3-min walk west of St. James's Park Tube station or 7-min walk from Victoria Station, near east end of Petty France Street at 1 Vandon Street; tel. 020/7799-6780, www.vandonhouse.com, info @vandonhouse.com).

Near Euston Station and the British Library: The **$$$ Methodist International Centre (MIC),** a modern, youthful, Christian hotel and conference center, fills its lower floors with international students and its top floor with travelers. The 28 rooms are modern and simple yet comfortable, with fine bathrooms, phones, and desks. The atmosphere is friendly, safe, clean, and controlled; it also has a spacious lounge and game room (annex S-£85, Sb-£140, deluxe Sb-£150, annex D-£95, Db-£155, deluxe Db-£175, Tb-£195; Sb-£95 and Db-£108 with £115 membership; 3-bedroom annex is great for families, check website for specials, elevator, Wi-Fi; on a quiet street a block west of Euston Station, 81–103 Euston Street—not Euston Road, Tube: Euston Station; tel. 020/7380-0001, www.micentre.com, reservations@micentre.com). From June through August, when the students are gone, they also rent simpler twin rooms (S or D-£50, includes one breakfast, extra breakfast-£12.50).

Hostels

$ London Central Youth Hostel is the flagship of London's hostels, with 300 beds and all the latest in security and comfortable efficiency. Families and travelers of any age will feel welcome in this wonderful facility. You'll pay the same price for any bed in a 4- to 8-bed single-sex dorm—with or without private bathroom—so try to grab one with a bathroom (£20–30 per bunk bed—fluctuates with demand, £3/night extra for non-members, breakfast-£4; includes sheets, towel and locker; families or groups welcome to book an entire room, free Wi-Fi, members' kitchen, laundry, book long in advance, between Oxford Street and Great Portland Street Tube stations at 104 Bolsover Street, toll tel. 0870-770-6144 or 0845-371-9154, www.yha.org.uk, london central@yha.org.uk).

$ St. Paul's Youth Hostel, near St. Paul's, is clean, modern, friendly, and well-run. Most of the 190 beds are in shared, single-sex bunk rooms (bed-£22–26 depending on number of beds in room and demand, twin D-£54–61, bunk-bed Q-£96, non-members pay

£3 extra, cheap meals, open 24 hours, 36 Carter Lane, Tube: St. Paul's, tel. 020/7236-4965 or toll tel. 0845-371-9012, www.yha.org .uk, stpauls@yha.org.uk).

$ A cluster of three **St. Christopher's Inn** hostels, south of the Thames near London Bridge, have cheap dorm beds (£20–25, 161–165 Borough High Street, Tube: Borough or London Bridge, tel. 020/7407-1856, www.st-christophers.co.uk).

Dorms

$ The **University of Westminster** opens its dorm rooms to travelers during summer break, from mid-June until late-September. Located in several high-rise buildings scattered around central London, the rooms—some with private bathrooms, others with shared bathrooms nearby—come with access to well-equipped kitchens and big lounges (S-£26–35, Sb-£35–55, D-£47–60, Db-£52–95, apartment Sb-£48–80, apartment Db-£58–90, weekly rates, tel. 020/7911-5181, www.wmin.ac.uk/comserv, unilet vacations@westminster.ac.uk).

$ **University College London** also has rooms for travelers, from mid-June until mid-September (S-£27–30, D-£55, breakfast extra, minimum 3-night stay, www.ucl.ac.uk/residences).

$ **Ace Hotel,** a budget hotel within four townhouses set in a residential neighborhood, has contemporary decor (£18–29 per bed in 3- to 8-bed dorms, bunk bed D-£53–57, bunk-bed Db-£57–61, Db with patio-£99, pay Internet access, lounge and garden, 16–22 Gunterstone Road, West Kensington, tel. 020/7602-6600, www .ace-hotel.co.uk, reception@ace-hotel.co.uk).

Heathrow and Gatwick Airports
At or near Heathrow Airport

It's so easy to get to Heathrow from central London, I see no reason to sleep there. But if you do, here are some options.

$$ **Yotel,** at the airport, has small sleep dens that offer a place to catch a quick nap (four hours-£37–64) or to stay overnight (tiny "standard cabin"—£59/8 hours, "premium cabin"—£82/8 hours; cabins sleep 1–2 people; price is per cabin not person, reserve online for free or by phone for small fee). Prices vary by day, week, and time of year, so check their website. All rooms are only slightly larger than a double bed, and have private bathrooms and free Internet access and Wi-Fi. Windowless rooms have oddly purplish lighting (Heathrow Terminal 4, tel. 020/7100-1100, www.yotel .com, customer@yotel.com).

$ **easyHotel** is your cheapest bet, with 53 podlike rooms on two floors (£25–45, no elevator, no breakfast, pay Internet access and Wi-Fi; Brick Field Lane, take local bus #140 from airport's

Central Bus Station or the £4 "Hotel Hoppa" shuttle bus #H8 or #H3 from Terminals 1, 2, or 3—runs 2–3/hr; on-demand shuttle available, tel. 020/8897-9237, www.easyhotel.com, enquiries @heathrow.easyhotel.com).

$$ Hotel Ibis London Heathrow is a chain hotel that offers predictable value (Db-£77, Db-£52 on Fri–Sun, check website for specials as low as £45, breakfast-£7, pay Internet access and Wi-Fi; 112–114 Bath Road, take local bus #105, #111, #140, #285, #423, or #555 from airport's Central Bus Station or #555 direct from Terminal 4, or the £4 "Hotel Hoppa" shuttle bus #H6 from Terminals 1, 2, or 3; tel. 020/8759-4888, fax 020/8564-7894, www .ibishotel.com, h0794@accor.com).

$$ Jurys Inn, another hotel chain, tempts tired travelers with 300-plus cookie-cutter rooms (Db-£85–105, check website for deals, breakfast extra; on Eastern Perimeter Road, Tube: Hatton Cross plus 5-min walk; take the £3.20 Tube one stop from Terminals 1, 2, or 3; or two stops from Terminals 4 or 5; or the £4 "Hotel Hoppa" shuttle bus #H9 from Terminals 1, 2, or 3; or buses #285, #482, #490, or #555; tel. 020/8266-4664, fax 020/8266-4665, www.jurysinns.com).

At or near Gatwick Airport

$$ Yotel, with small rooms, has a branch right at the airport (Gatwick South Terminal, see prices and contact info in Heathrow listing, above).

$$ Gatwick Airport Central Premier Inn rents cheap rooms 350 yards from the airport (Db-£75, £67 Fri–Sun, breakfast-£8, £2 shuttle bus from airport—must reserve in advance, Longbridge Way, North Terminal, toll tel. 0870-238-3305, frustrating phone tree, www.premierinn.com). Four more Premier Inns are within a five-mile radius from the airport.

$$ Barn Cottage, a converted 16th-century barn flanked by a tennis court and swimming pool, sits in the peaceful countryside, with a good pub just two blocks away. Its two wood-beamed rooms, antique furniture, and large garden makes you forget Gatwick is 10 minutes away (S-£55, D-£75, cash only, Church Road, Leigh, Reigate, Surrey, tel. 01306/611-347, warmly run by Pat and Mike Comer). Don't confuse this place with others of the same name; this Barn Cottage has no website. A taxi from Gatwick to here runs about £15; the Comers can take you back to the airport or train station for about £10.

$ Gatwick Airport Travelodge has budget rooms about a mile from the airport (Db-£39–57, breakfast extra, Wi-Fi, Church Road, Lowfield Heath, Crawley, £4 "Hotel Hoppa" shuttle bus from airport, toll tel. 0871-984-6031, www.travelodge .co.uk).

For Longer Stays

Staying a week or longer? Consider the advantages that come with renting a furnished apartment, or "flat," as the British say. Complete with a small, equipped kitchen and living room, this option can also sometimes work for families or groups on shorter visits. Among the many organizations ready to help, the following have been recommended by local guides and readers: www .perfectplaceslondon.co.uk, www.homefromhome.co.uk, www .london33.com, www.london-house.com, www.gowithit.co.uk, www.aplacelikehome.co.uk, and www.regentsuites.com.

Sometimes you can save money by renting directly from the apartment owner (check www.vrbo.com). Readers also report success using Craig's List (http://london.craigslist.co.uk; search within "holiday rentals").

Read the conditions of rental carefully and ask lots of questions. If a certain amenity is important to you (such as Wi-Fi or a washing machine in the unit), ask specifically about it and what to do if it stops working. Plot the location carefully (plug the address into http://maps.google.com), and remember to factor in travel time and costs from outlying neighborhoods to central London. Finally, it's a good idea to buy trip cancellation/interruption insurance, as many weekly rentals are nonrefundable.

Eating in London

In London, the sheer variety of foods—from every corner of its former empire and beyond—is astonishing. You'll be amazed at the number of hopping, happening new restaurants of all kinds.

If you want to dine (as opposed to eat), drop by a London newsstand to get a weekly entertainment guide or an annual restaurant guide (both have extensive restaurant listings). Visit www .london-eating.co.uk or www.squaremeal.co.uk for more options.

The thought of a £40 meal in Britain generally ruins my appetite, so my London dining is limited mostly to easygoing, fun, inexpensive alternatives. I've listed places by neighborhood—handy to your sightseeing or hotel. Considering how expensive London can be, if there's any good place to cut corners to stretch your budget, it's by eating cheaply.

Pub grub is the most atmospheric budget option. Many of London's 7,000 pubs serve fresh, tasty buffets under ancient timbers, with hearty lunches and dinners priced from £7-9.

Ethnic restaurants—especially Indian and Chinese—are popular, plentiful, and cheap. Most large museums (and many churches) have inexpensive, cheery cafeterias. Of course, picnicking is the fastest and cheapest way to go. Good grocery stores and sandwich shops, fine park benches, and polite pigeons abound in

Central London Eateries

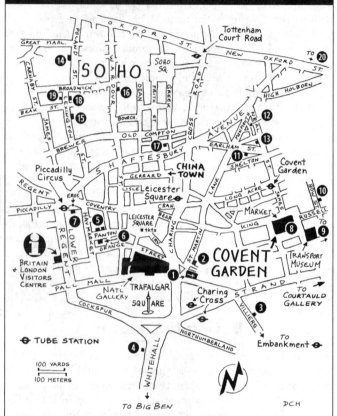

1. St. Martin-in-the-Fields Café in the Crypt
2. The Chandos Pub's Opera Room
3. Gordon's Wine Bar
4. The Lord Moon of the Mall Pub
5. Stockpot & Woodlands South Indian Vegetarian Restaurant
6. West End Kitchen
7. Criterion Restaurant
8. Just Falafs
9. To The Food Balcony, Joe Allen, Livebait & PJ's Bar and Grill
10. Ristorante Zizzi
11. Belgo Centraal
12. Neal's Yard Eateries
13. Food for Thought Café
14. Yo! Sushi
15. Wagamama Noodle Bar
16. Busaba Eathai Thai Rest. & Côte Restaurant
17. Y Ming Chinese Rest.
18. Andrew Edmunds Rest.
19. Mildred's Vegetarian Rest. & Fernandez & Wells
20. To The Princess Louise Pub

Britain's most expensive city.

London (and all of Britain) is now smoke-free, thanks to a recent smoking ban. Expect restaurants and pubs that sell food to be non-smoking indoors, with smokers occupying patios and doorways outside.

Central London

Near Trafalgar Square

These eateries are within about 100 yards of Trafalgar Square.

St. Martin-in-the-Fields Café in the Crypt is just right for a tasty meal on a monk's budget—maybe even on a monk's tomb. You'll dine sitting on somebody's gravestone in an ancient crypt. Their enticing buffet line is kept stocked all day, serving breakfast, lunch, and dinner (£6–8 cafeteria plates, Mon–Wed 8:00–20:00, Thu–Sat 8:00–21:00, Sun 11:00–18:00, profits go to the church, underneath Church of St. Martin-in-the-Fields on Trafalgar Square, Tube: Charing Cross, tel. 020/7766-1158 or 020/7766-1100). Wednesday evenings at 20:00 come with a live jazz band (£5–8 tickets). While here, check out the concert schedule for the busy church upstairs (or visit www.smitf.org).

The Chandos Pub's Opera Room floats amazingly apart from the tacky crush of tourism around Trafalgar Square. Look for it opposite the National Portrait Gallery (corner of William IV Street and St. Martin's Lane) and climb the stairs to the Opera Room. This is a fine Trafalgar rendezvous point and a wonderfully local pub. They serve traditional, plain-tasting £6–7 pub meals—meat pies are their specialty. The ground-floor pub is stuffed with regulars and offers snugs (private booths), the same menu, and more serious beer drinking (kitchen open daily 11:00–18:00, order and pay at the bar, 29 St. Martin's Lane, Tube: Leicester Square, tel. 020/7836-1401).

Gordon's Wine Bar, with a simple, steep staircase leading into a candlelit 15th-century wine cellar, is filled with dusty old bottles, faded British memorabilia, and local nine-to-fivers. At the "English rustic" buffet, choose a hot meal or cold meat dish with a salad, or a hearty (and splittable) plate of cheeses, bread, and pickles (£7.50). Then step up to the wine bar and consider the many varieties of wine and port available by the glass. This place is passionate about port. The low, carbon-crusted vaulting deeper in the back seems to intensify the Hogarth-painting atmosphere. Although it's crowded, you can normally corral two chairs and grab the corner of a table. On hot days, the crowd spills out onto a leafy back patio (arrive before 17:30 to get a seat, Mon–Sat 11:00–23:00, Sun 12:00–22:00, 2 blocks from Trafalgar Square, bottom of Villiers Street at #47, Tube: Embankment, tel. 020/7930-1408, manager Gerard Menan).

Pub Appreciation

The pub is the heart of the people's England, where all manner of folks have, for generations, found their respite from work and a home-away-from-home. England's classic pubs are national treasures, with great cultural value and rich history, not to mention good beer and grub.

The Golden Age for pub-building was in the late Victorian era (c. 1880–1905), when pubs were independently owned and land prices were high enough to make it worthwhile to invest in fixing up pubs. The politics were pro-pub as well: Conservatives, backed by Big Beer, were in, and temperance-minded Liberals were out.

Especially in class-conscious Victorian times, traditional pubs were divided into sections by elaborate screens (now mostly gone), allowing the wealthy to drink in a more refined setting, while commoners congregated on the pub's rougher side. These were really "public houses," featuring nooks (snugs) for groups and clubs to meet, friends and lovers to rendezvous, and families to get out of the house at night. Since many pub-goers were illiterate, pubs were simply named for the picture hung outside (e.g., The Crooked Stick, The Queen's Arms—meaning her coat of arms).

Historic pubs still dot the London cityscape. The only place to see the very oldest-style tavern in the "domestic tradition" is at **Ye Olde Cheshire Cheese,** which was rebuilt in 1667 from a 16th-century tavern (open daily, 145 Fleet Street, Tube: Temple or St. Paul's, Blackfriars station is nearest but is closed until 2011; tel. 020/7353-6170). Imagine this place in the pre-Victorian era: With no bar, drinkers gathered around the fireplaces, while tap boys shuttled tankards up from the cellar. (This was long before barroom taps were connected to casks in the cellar. Oh, and don't say "keg"—that's a gassy modern thing.)

Late Victorian pubs, such as the lovingly restored 1897 **Princess Louise** (open daily 12:00–23:00, 208 High Holborn, Tube: Holborn, tel. 020/7405-8816), are more common. These places are fancy, often coming with heavy embossed wallpaper ceilings, decorative tile work, fine-etched glass, ornate carved stillions (the big central hutch for storing bottles and glass), and even urinals equipped with a place to set your glass. London's best Art Nouveau pub is **The Black Friar** (c. 1900–1915), with fine carved capitals, lamp holders, and quirky phrases worked into the decor (open daily, Tube: Temple or St. Paul's, across from the Blackfriars Tube station—station closed until 2011—at 174 Queen Victoria Street, tel. 020/7236-5474).

The "former-bank pubs" represent a more modern trend in pub building. As banks increasingly go electronic, they're moving

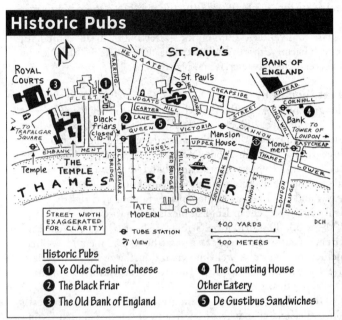

Historic Pubs

Historic Pubs

1️⃣ Ye Olde Cheshire Cheese

2️⃣ The Black Friar

3️⃣ The Old Bank of England

4️⃣ The Counting House

Other Eatery

5️⃣ De Gustibus Sandwiches

out of lavish, high-rent old buildings. Many of these former banks are being refitted as pubs with elegant bars and free-standing stillions, providing a fine centerpiece. Three such pubs are **The Old Bank of England** (closed Sat–Sun, 194 Fleet Street, Tube: Temple, tel. 020/7430-2255), **The Jugged Hare** (open daily, 172 Vauxhall Bridge Road, see map on page 130, Tube: Victoria, tel. 020/7828-1543, also see listing on page 151), and **The Counting House** (closed Sat–Sun, 50 Cornhill, Tube: Bank, tel. 020/7283-7123, also see listing on page 156).

Go pubbing in the evening for a lively time, or drop by during the quiet late morning (from 11:00), when the pub is empty and filled with memories. For more information, see Bob Steel's website, www.aletrails.com. Bob also offers London Heritage pub tours (about £50 per group for a leisurely half-day private walk).

The Lord Moon of the Mall pub has real ales on tap and good, cheap pub grub, including a two-meals-for-the-price-of-one deal (£8 Mon–Fri 14:00–22:00). The pub fills a great old former Barclays Bank building a block down Whitehall from Trafalgar Square (daily 9:00–22:00, no kids after 18:00, 16–18 Whitehall, Tube: Charing Cross or Embankment, tel. 020/7839-7701). Nearby are several cheap cafeterias and pizza joints.

Near Piccadilly

Hungry and broke in the theater district? Head for Panton Street (off Haymarket, 2 blocks southeast of Piccadilly Circus) where several hardworking little places compete, all seeming to offer a three-course meal for about £8.50. Peruse the entire block (vegetarian, Pizza Express, Moroccan, Thai, Chinese, and two famous eateries) before making your choice. **Stockpot** is a meat, potatoes, gravy, and mushy-peas kind of place, famous and rightly popular for its edible, cheap English meals (Mon–Sat 7:00–23:30, Sun 7:00–22:00, 38–40 Panton Street, cash only). The **West End Kitchen** (across the street at #5, same hours and menu) is a direct competitor that's also well-known and just as good. Vegetarians prefer the **Woodlands South Indian Vegetarian Restaurant** at #37 Panton Street.

The palatial **Criterion** offers grand-piano ambience beneath gilded tiles and chandeliers in a dreamy Byzantine church setting from 1880. It's right on Piccadilly Circus but a world away from the punk junk. The house wine is great, as is the food. After 19:00, the menu becomes really expensive. Anyone can drop in for coffee or a drink (£17–19 fixed-price meals, Mon–Sat 12:00–14:30 & 17:30–23:30, Sun 12:00–15:30 & 17:30–22:30, 224 Piccadilly, tel. 020/7930-0488).

The Wolseley is the grand 1920s showroom of a long-defunct British car. The last Wolseley drove out with the Great Depression, but today this old-time bistro bustles with formal waiters serving traditional Austrian and French dishes in an elegant black-marble-and-chandeliers setting fit for its location next to the Ritz. While the food can be unexceptional, prices are reasonable, and the presentation and setting are grand. Reservations are a must (£16.50 plates; cheaper soup, salad, and sandwich menu available; Mon–Fri 7:00–24:00, Sat 8:00–24:00, Sun 8:00–23:00, 160 Piccadilly, tel. 020/7499-6996). They're also popular for their fancy cream or afternoon tea (£9.75–19.75, served Sun–Fri 15:30–18:30, Sat 15:30–17:30).

Near Covent Garden

Covent Garden bustles with people and touristy eateries. While the area feels overrun, there are some good options.

Just Falafs is a healthy fast-food option in the chaos of Covent Garden. Located in the southeast corner, where rows of outdoor café tables line the tiny shop, they offer falafel sandwiches with yummy vegetarian-friendly extras (£4–6 sandwiches, daily until about 21:00, 27b Covent Gardens Square, tel. 020/7240-3838).

The Food Balcony, with great people-watching overlooking the Jubilee Market Piazza, is a sticky food circus of ethnic places serving £6 meals on disposable plates and wobbly plastic tables (closes at 18:30). A handy Wagamama Noodle Bar is around the corner on Tavistock Street (see description in next section).

Joe Allen, tucked in a basement a block away, serves modern international cuisine with both style and hubbub. Downstairs off a quiet street with candles and white tablecloths, it's comfortably spacious and popular with the theater crowd (meals for about £30, £15 two-course specials and £17 three-course specials 17:00–18:45, open Mon–Fri 8:00–24:45, Sat 11:30–24:45, Sun 11:30–23:45, piano music after 21:00, 13 Exeter Street, tel. 020/7836-0651).

Livebait Restaurant is an upscale fish-and-chips place with an elegant yet simple tiled interior. Their forte is fresh and well-prepared fish (£14–20 main courses, specials before 19:00, Mon–Sat 12:00–23:00, Sun 12:00–21:00, 21 Wellington Street, tel. 020/7836-7161).

Ristorante Zizzi is a fun, top-end Italian chain with a crisp contemporary atmosphere, an open pizza oven adding warmth and action, and a sharp local clientele (£7–10 pizzas, pastas, and salads; great chicken Caesar, daily 12:00–23:00, 20 Bow Street, tel. 020/7836-6101).

PJ's Bar and Grill, a tired diner that seems to be a hit with locals, serves decent "modern European" food. It's family-friendly, with more intimate seating in the back (£10–15 meals, Mon–Sat 12:00–24:00, Sun 11:30–16:00, 30 Wellington Street, 020/7240-7529).

Belgo Centraal serves hearty Belgian specialties in a vast, 400-seat underground lair. It's a seafood, chips, and beer emporium dressed up as a mod-monastic refectory—with noisy acoustics and waiters garbed as Trappist monks. The classy restaurant section is more comfortable and less rowdy, but usually requires reservations. It's often more fun just to grab a spot in the boisterous beer hall, with its tight, communal benches (no reservations accepted). The same menu and specials work on both sides. Belgians claim they eat as well as the French and as heartily as the Germans. Specialties include mussels, great-tasting fries, and a stunning array of dark, blonde, and fruity Belgian beers. Belgo actually makes Belgian things trendy—a formidable feat (£10–14 meals; Mon–Sat 12:00–23:00, Sun 12:00–22:30, Mon–Fri £5–6.30 "beat the clock" meal specials from 17:00–18:30—the time you order is the price you pay—including main dishes, fries, and beer; no meal-splitting after 18:30, and you must buy food with beer; daily £7.50 lunch special 12:00–17:00; 1 kid eats free for each parent ordering a regular entree; 1 block north of Covent Garden Tube station at intersection of Neal and Shelton streets, 50 Earlham Street, tel. 020/7813-2233).

Neal's Yard is *the* place for cheap, hip, and healthy eateries near Covent Garden. The neighborhood is a tabbouleh of fun, hippie-type cafés. One of the best is the vegetarian **Food for Thought,** packed with local health nuts (good £5 vegetarian meals, £7.50 dinner plates, Mon–Sat 12:00–20:30, Sun 12:00–17:00, 2 blocks north of Covent Garden Tube station, 31 Neal Street, near Neal's Yard, tel. 020/7836-0239).

Near Soho and Chinatown

London has a trendy scene that most Beefeater-seekers miss entirely. These restaurants are scattered throughout the hipster, gay, and strip-club district, teeming each evening with fun-seekers and theatergoers. Even if you plan to have dinner elsewhere, it's a treat just to wander around this lively area.

Beware of the extremely welcoming women standing outside the strip clubs (especially on Great Windmill Street). Enjoy the sales pitch—but only fools fall for the "£5 drink and show" lure. They don't get back out without emptying their wallet...literally.

Yo! Sushi is a futuristic Japanese-food-extravaganza experience. It's pricey—those plates add up fast. But it's a memorable experience, complete with thumping rock, Japanese cable TV, and a 195-foot-long conveyor belt—the world's longest sushi bar. For £1 you get unlimited green tea or water (from spigot at bar, with or without gas). Snag a bar stool and grab dishes as they rattle by (priced by color of dish; check the chart: £1.75–5 per dish, £1.75 for miso soup, daily 12:00–23:00, 2 blocks south of Oxford Street, where Lexington Street becomes Poland Street, 52 Poland Street, tel. 020/7287-0443). If you like Yo!, there are several locations around town, including a handy branch a block from the London Eye on Belvedere Road, as well as outlets within Selfridges, Harvey Nichols department stores, and Whiteleys Mall on Queensway.

Wagamama Noodle Bar is a noisy, pan-Asian, organic slurpathon. As you enter, check out the kitchen and listen to the roar of the basement, where benches rock with happy eaters. Everybody sucks. Stand against the wall to feel the energy of all this "positive eating." Portions are huge and splitting is allowed (£7–11 meals, Mon–Sat 11:30–23:00, Sun 12:00–22:00, crowded after 19:00, 10A Lexington Street, tel. 020/7292-0990 but no reservations taken). If you like this place, handy branches are all over town, including one near the British Museum (4 Streatham Street), Kensington

---

The Soho "Food Is Fun" Three-Course Dinner Crawl

For a multicultural, movable feast, consider enjoying a drink and eating (or splitting) one course at each of these places. Start around 17:30 to avoid lines, get in on early-bird specials, and find waiters willing to let you split a meal. Prices, while reasonable by London standards, add up. Servings are large enough to share. All are open nightly. Arrive at 17:30 at **Belgo Centraal** and split the early-bird dinner special: a kilo of mussels, fries, and dark Belgian beer. At **Yo! Sushi,** have beer or sake and a few dishes, then slurp your last course at **Wagamama Noodle Bar.** For a low-calorie dessert, people-watch at Leicester Square.

(26 High Street), in Harvey Nichols (109 Knightsbridge), Covent Garden (1 Tavistock Street), Leicester Square (14 Irving Street), Piccadilly Circus (8 Norris Street), Fleet Street (#109), and next to the Tower of London (Tower Place).

Busaba Eathai Thai Restaurant is a hit with locals for its snappy service, casual-yet-high-energy ambience, and good, inexpensive Thai cuisine. You'll sit around big, square communal 16-person hardwood tables or in two-person tables by the window—with everyone in the queue staring at your noodles. They don't take reservations, so arrive by 19:00 or line up (£7–10 meals, Mon–Thu 12:00–23:00, Fri–Sat 12:00–23:30, Sun 12:00–22:00, 106 Wardour Street, tel. 020/7255-8686). They have two other handy locations: at 22 Store Street, near the British Museum and Goodge Street Tube; and 8–13 Bird Street, just off Oxford Street and across from the Bond Street Tube.

Côte Restaurant is a contemporary French bistro chain, serving good-value French cuisine at the right prices (£9–13 mains, early dinner specials, Mon–Wed 8:00–23:00, Thu–Fri 8:00–24:00, Sat 10:00–24:00, Sun 10:00–22:30, 124–126 Wardour Street, tel. 020/7287-9280).

Y Ming Chinese Restaurant—across Shaftesbury Avenue from the ornate gates, clatter, and dim sum of Chinatown—has dressy European decor, serious but helpful service, and authentic Northern Chinese cooking (good £10 meal deal offered 12:00–18:00, £7–10 plates, open Mon–Sat 12:00–23:45, closed Sun, 35–36 Greek Street, tel. 020/7734-2721).

Andrew Edmunds Restaurant is a tiny, candlelit place where you'll want to hide your camera and guidebook and act as local as possible. This little place—with a jealous and loyal clientele—is the closest I've found to Parisian quality in a cozy restaurant in London. The modern European cooking and creative seasonal menu are worth the splurge (£25 meals, Mon–Sat 12:30–15:00 & 18:00–22:45, Sun 13:00–15:30 & 18:00–22:30, come early or call ahead, request ground floor rather than basement, 46 Lexington Street in Soho, tel. 020/7437-5708).

Mildred's Vegetarian Restaurant, across from Andrew Edmunds, has cheap prices, an enjoyable menu, and a plain-yet-pleasant interior filled with happy eaters (£7–9 meals, Mon–Sat 12:00–23:00, closed Sun, vegan options, 45 Lexington Street, tel. 020/7494-1634).

Fernandez & Wells is a delightfully simple little wine, cheese, and ham bar. Drop in and grab a stool as you belly up to the big wooden bar. Share a plate of top-quality cheeses and/or Spanish or French hams with fine bread and oil, while sipping a nice glass of wine and talking with Juan or Toby (Mon–Sat 11:00–22:00, Sun 12:00–19:00, quality sandwiches at lunch, wine/cheese/ham bar after 16:00, 43 Lexington Street, tel. 020/7734-1546).

West London
Near Victoria Station Accommodations
I've enjoyed eating at these places, a few blocks southwest of Victoria Station (see the map on page 130).

Ebury Wine Bar, filled with young professionals, provides a cut-above atmosphere, delicious £13–18 entrées, and a £15.50 two-course special at lunch and from 18:00–20:00. In the delightful back room, the fancy menu features modern European cuisine with a French accent; at the wine bar, find a cheaper bar menu that's better than your average pub grub. This is emphatically a "traditional wine bar," with no beers on tap (Mon–Sat 11:00–23:00, Sun 18:00–22:30, reserve after 20:00, at intersection of Ebury and Elizabeth streets, near bus station, 139 Ebury Street, tel. 020/7730-5447).

Jenny Lo's Tea House is a simple budget place serving up reliably tasty £7–8 eclectic Chinese-style meals to locals in the know. While the menu is small, everything is high quality. Jenny clearly learned from her father, Ken Lo, one of the most famous Cantonese chefs in Britain, whose fancy place is just around the corner (Mon–Sat 11:30–15:00 & 18:00–22:00, closed Sun, cash only, 14 Eccleston Street, tel. 020/7259-0399).

La Poule au Pot, ideal for a romantic splurge, offers a classy, candlelit ambience with well-dressed patrons and expensive but fine country-style French cuisine (£18.75 two-course lunch specials, £25 dinner plates, daily 12:30–14:30 & 18:45–23:00, Sun until 22:00, £50 for dinner with wine, leafy patio dining, reservations smart, end of Ebury Street at intersection with Pimlico Road, 231 Ebury Street, tel. 020/7730-7763).

Grumbles brags that it's been serving "good food and wine at non-scary prices since 1964." Offering a delicious mix of "modern eclectic French and traditional English," this unpretentious little place with cozy booths inside and four nice sidewalk tables is *the* spot to eat well in this otherwise workaday neighborhood (£8–16 plates, £11 early-bird specials 18:00–19:00, open Mon–Sat 12:00–14:30 & 18:00–22:45, Sun 12:00–22:30, reservations wise, half a block north of Belgrave Road at 35 Churton Street, tel. 020/7834-0149). Multitaskers take note: The self-service launderette down the street is open evenings.

Chimes English Restaurant and Cider Bar comes with a fresh, country farm ambience, serious ciders (rare in London), and very good, traditional English food. Experiment with the cider—it's legal here...just barely (£8–12 meals, £13 two-course specials, hearty salads, Mon–Sat 12:00–15:00 & 17:30–22:15, Sun 12:00–23:15, 26 Churton Street, tel. 020/7821-7456).

The Jugged Hare, a 10-minute walk from Victoria Station, is a pub in a lavish old bank building, its vaults replaced by tankards of beer and a fine kitchen. They have a fun, traditional menu with more fresh veggies than fries, and a plush and vivid pub scene good for a meal or just a drink (£8–10 meals, daily 12:00–21:30, 172 Vauxhall Bridge Road, tel. 020/7828-1543).

Seafresh Fish Restaurant is the neighborhood place for plaice—either take-out on the cheap or eat-in, enjoying a chrome-and-wood mod ambience with classic and creative fish-and-chips cuisine. Though Mario's father started this place in 1965, it feels like the chippie of the 21st century (meals-£5 to go, £6–13 to sit, Mon–Fri 12:00–15:00 & 17:00–22:30, Sat 12:00–22:30, closed Sun, 80–81 Wilton Road, tel. 020/7828-0747).

La Bottega is an Italian delicatessen that fits its upscale Belgravia neighborhood. It offers tasty, freshly cooked pastas (£5.50), lasagnas, and salads at its counter (lasagna and salad meal-£8), along with great sandwiches (£3) and a good coffee bar with pastries. While not cheap, it's fast (order at the counter), and the ingredients would please an Italian chef (Mon–Fri 8:00–18:30, Sat 9:00–18:00, closed Sun, on corner of Ebury and Eccleston streets, tel. 020/7730-2730). Grab your meal to go, or enjoy the good Belgravia life with locals, either sitting inside or on the sidewalk.

St. George's Tavern is *the* pub for a meal in this neighborhood. They serve dinner from the same fun menu in three zones: on the sidewalk to catch the sun and enjoy some people-watching, in the sloppy pub, and in a classier back dining room (£7–10 meals, proud of their sausages, Mon–Sat 10:00–22:00, Sun until 21:00, corner of Hugh Street and Belgrave Road, tel. 020/7630-1116).

Drinking Pubs That Serve Food: If you want to have a pub meal or just enjoy a drink surrounded by interesting local crowds,

Taking Tea in London

Once the sole province of genteel ladies in fancy hats, afternoon tea has become more democratic in the 21st century. While some tearooms—such as the £37-a-head tea service at the Ritz and the finicky Fortnum & Mason—still require a jacket and tie (and a big bank account), most welcome tourists in jeans and sneakers.

The cheapest "tea" on the menu is generally a "cream tea," while the most expensive is the "champagne tea." **Cream tea** is simply a pot of tea and a homemade scone or two with jam and thick clotted cream. **Afternoon tea** generally is a cream tea, plus a tier of three plates holding small finger foods (such as cucumber sandwiches) and an assortment of small pastries. **Champagne tea** includes all of the goodies, plus a glass of champagne. For maximum pinkie-waving taste per calorie, slice your scone thin like a miniature loaf of bread. **High tea** generally means a more substantial late afternoon or early evening meal, often served with meat or eggs and eaten at a "higher" (i.e., kitchen) table.

Tearooms, which often also serve appealing light meals, are usually open for lunch and close at about 17:00, just before dinner. At all the places listed below, it's perfectly acceptable to order one afternoon tea and one cream tea (at about £5) and split the afternoon-tea goodies. The fancier places, such as Harrods and The Capital Hotel, are happy to bring you seconds and thirds of your favorites, turning tea into an early dinner.

The Orangery at Kensington Palace serves four different varieties of tea meals, from the £12.50 "Orangery tea" to the £25 "Tregothnan tea," in its bright white hall near Princess Di's former residence. You can also order treats à la carte. The portions aren't huge, but who can argue with eating at a princess' house? (Tea served 15:00–18:00, no reservations taken; located on map on page 135, a 10-min walk through Kensington Gardens from either Queensway or High Street Kensington Tube stations to the orange brick building, about 20 yards from Kensington Palace; tel. 020/7938-1406, www.hrp.org.uk.)

The National Dining Rooms, a restaurant/café within the National Gallery on Trafalgar Square, is both classy and convenient. While the restaurant can book up in advance, you can generally waltz in for afternoon tea at the café. To play it safe, arrive in the early afternoon to reserve a tea time, then visit the National Gallery (page 76) before or after your appointed time (£4 cakes and tarts, £5.50 cream tea, £14.50 afternoon tea, tea served 15:00–17:00, located in Sainsbury Wing of National Gallery, Tube: Charing Cross or Leicester Square, tel. 020/7747-2525, www.thenationaldiningrooms.co.uk).

The Café at Sotheby's, located on the ground floor of the auction giant's headquarters, is manna for shoppers taking a break from fashionable New Bond Street. There are no windows—just a long leather bench, plenty of mirrors, and a dark-wood room where waiters serve sweet treats and the £5.50 mix-and-match Neal's Yard cheese plate to locals in the know

(£3 cakes and creams, £6.50 "small tea," £13.75 afternoon tea must be ordered 24 hours in advance—call 020/7293-5077, café open Mon–Fri only 9:30–11:30 & 12:00–16:45, afternoon tea served 15:00–16:45, 34–35 New Bond Street, Tube: Bond Street or Oxford Circus, www.sothebys.com/cafe/restaurant.html).

For a classier experience with an attentive waitstaff, try **The Capital Hotel,** a luxury hotel a half-block from Harrods. The Capital caters to weary shoppers with its intimate, linen-tablecloth tearoom. It's where the ladies-who-lunch meet to decide whether to buy that Versace gown they've had their eye on. Even so, casual clothes, kids, and sharing plates—with a £2.50 split-tea service charge—are all OK (£18.50 afternoon tea, daily 15:00–17:30, call to book ahead—especially on weekends, see map on page 133, 22 Basil Street, Tube: Knightsbridge, tel. 020/7589-5171).

Two famous department stores—Fortnum & Mason and Harrods—serve afternoon tea for sky-high prices. **Fortnum & Mason's St. James's Restaurant,** on the fourth floor, offers plush seats under the elegant tearoom's chandeliers. You'll get the standard three-tiered silver tea tray: finger sandwiches on the bottom, fresh scones with jam and clotted cream on the first floor, and decadent pastries and "tartlets" on the top floor, with unlimited tea. Consider it dinner (about £30–38, Mon–Sat 14:00–18:30, Sun 12:00–16:30, dress up a bit for this—no shorts, "children must be behaved," 181 Piccadilly, reserve in advance online or at toll tel. 0845-602-5694, www.fortnumandmason.com).

At **Harrods' Georgian Restaurant,** you (along with 200 of your closest friends) can enjoy a fancy tea under a skylight as a pianist tickles the keys of a Bösendorfer, the world's most expensive piano (£21 afternoon tea, includes finger sandwiches and pastries with free refills, served daily from 15:45, last order at 17:15, on Brompton Road, Tube: Knightsbridge, reservations tel. 020/7225-6800, store tel. 020/7730-1234, www.harrods.com).

If you want the teatime experience but are put off by the price, try the department stores on Oxford Street. **John Lewis** has a mod third-floor brasserie that serves a nice £10 afternoon-tea platter (on Oxford Street one block west of the Bond Street Tube station). **Selfridges'** afternoon tea, served after 15:00 in the Gallery Restaurant, is pricier at £16.50. Near the Ritz, consider the £9.75 cream tea or the £19.75 afternoon tea at **The Wolseley** (see listing on page 146).

Many museums and bookstores have cafés serving afternoon tea goodies à la carte, where you can put together a spread for less than £10; **Waterstone's** fifth-floor café and the **Victoria and Albert Museum** café are two of the best.

The modern **teapod,** on the South Bank, serves cream tea for £5 and afternoon tea for £10, along with sandwiches, soups, salads, and pastries (Mon–Fri 8:30–18:00, Sat 9:00–19:00, Sun 10:00–19:00, 31 Shad Thames, 200 yards from the Tower Bridge, tel. 020/7407-0000).

consider three pubs in the neighborhood, each with a distinct character: **The Duke of Wellington** is a classic neighborhood pub with forgettable grub, woodsy sidewalk seating, and an inviting interior (food served Mon–Sat 12:00–15:00 & 18:00–21:00, Sun 12:00–15:00 only, 63 Eaton Terrace, tel. 020/7730-1782). **The Belgravia Pub** is a sports bar with burgers, a stark interior, and a little outdoor garden (daily 12:00–21:30, corner of Ebury Street and South Eaton Place at 152 Ebury Street, tel. 020/7730-6040). **The Thomas Cubitt Pub,** packed with young professionals, is the neighborhood's trendy new "gastropub," great for a drink or pricey meals (44 Elizabeth Street, tel. 020/7730-6060).

Cheap Eats: For groceries, a handy **Marks & Spencer Simply Food** is inside Victoria Station (Mon–Sat 7:00–24:00, Sun 8:00–22:00), along with a **Sainsbury's Market** (daily 6:00–23:00, at rear entrance, on Eccleston Street; a second Sainsbury's is just north of the station on Victoria Street). A larger Sainsbury's is on Wilton Road near Warwick Way, a couple of blocks southeast of the station (daily 6:00–24:00). A string of good ethnic restaurants line Wilton Road (near the Seafresh Fish Restaurant, recommended earlier). For affordable if forgettable meals, try the row of cheap little eateries on Elizabeth Street.

Near Notting Hill and Bayswater Accommodations

The road called Queensway is a multiethnic food circus, lined with lively and inexpensive eateries. See the map on page 135.

Maggie Jones, a £40 splurge, is where Charles Dickens meets Ella Fitzgerald—exuberantly rustic and very English with a 1940s-jazz sound track. You'll get solid English cuisine, including huge plates of crunchy vegetables, served by a young and casual staff. It's pricey, but the portions are huge (especially the meat and fish pies—their specialty). You're welcome to save lots by splitting your main course. The candlelit upstairs is the most romantic, while the basement is kept lively with the kitchen, tight seating, and lots of action. If you eat well once in London, eat here—and do it quick, before it burns down (daily 12:30–14:30 & 18:30–23:00, reservations recommended, 6 Old Court Place, just east of Kensington Church Street, near High Street Kensington Tube stop, tel. 020/7937-6462).

The Churchill Arms pub and **Thai Kitchens** (same location) are local hangouts, with good beer and a thriving old-English ambience in front, and hearty £6 Thai plates in an enclosed patio in the back. You can eat the Thai food in the tropical hideaway or in the atmospheric pub section. The place is festooned with Churchill memorabilia and chamber pots (including one with Hitler's mug on it—hanging from the ceiling farthest from Thai Kitchen—sure to cure the constipation of any Brit during World

War II). Arrive by 18:00 or after 21:00 to avoid a line. During busy times, diners are limited to an hour at the table (daily 12:00–22:00, 119 Kensington Church Street, tel. 020/7792-1246).

The Prince Edward serves good grub in a quintessential pub setting (£7–10 meals, Mon–Sat 11:00–15:00 & 18:00–23:00, Sun 11:00–22:30, plush-pubby indoor seating or sidewalk tables, family-friendly, free Wi-Fi, 2 blocks north of Bayswater Road at the corner of Dawson Place and Hereford Road, 73 Prince's Square, tel. 020/7727-2221).

Café Diana is a healthy little eatery that serves sandwiches, salads, and Middle Eastern food. It's decorated—almost shrine-like—with photos of Princess Diana, who used to drop by for pita sandwiches (daily 8:00–23:00, 5 Wellington Terrace, on Bayswater Road, opposite Kensington Palace Garden Gates—where Di once lived, tel. 020/7792-9606).

Royal China Restaurant is filled with London's Chinese, who consider this one of the city's best eateries. It's dressed up in black, white, and gold, with candles, brisk waiters, and fine food (£7–11 dishes, daily 12:00–23:00, dim sum until 16:45, 13 Queensway, tel. 020/7221-2535).

Whiteleys Mall Food Court offers a fun selection of ethnic and fast-food chain eateries among Corinthian columns, and a multiscreen theater in a delightful mall (daily 9:00–23:00; options include Yo! Sushi, good salads at Café Rouge, pizza, Starbucks, and a coin-op Internet place; second floor, corner of Porchester Gardens and Queensway).

Supermarket: **Tesco** is a half-block from the Notting Hill Gate Tube stop (Mon–Sat 8:00–23:00, Sun 11:00–17:00, near intersection with Pembridge Road, 114–120 Notting Hill Gate). The smaller **Spar Market** is at 18 Queensway (Mon–Sat 7:00–24:00, Sun 9:00–24:00), and **Marks & Spencer** can be found in Whiteleys Mall (Mon–Sat 10:00–20:00, Sun 12:00–18:00).

Near South Kensington Accommodations

Popular eateries line Old Brompton Road and Thurloe Street (Tube: South Kensington), and a huge variety of cheap eateries are clumped around the Tube station. See the map on page 133.

The **Tesco Express** grocery store is handy for picnics (daily 7:00–24:00, 50–52 Old Brompton Road).

La Bouchée Bistro Café is a classy, hole-in-the-wall touch of France. This candlelit and woody bistro serves a two-course, £11.50 special weekdays at lunch and from 17:30–18:30, and £17 *plats du jour* all *jour* (daily 12:00–15:00 & 17:30–23:30, 56 Old Brompton Road, tel. 020/7589-1929).

Daquise, an authentic-feeling 1930s Polish time warp, is ideal if you're in the mood for kielbasa and kraut. It's likeably dreary—fast, cheap, family-run—and a much-appreciated part of the neighborhood (£10 meals, weekday lunch special, daily 12:00–23:00, 20 Thurloe Street, tel. 020/7589-6117).

Moti Mahal Indian Restaurant, with minimalist-yet-classy mod ambience and attentive service, serves delicious Indian and Bangladeshi cuisine. Chicken *jalfrezi* and butter chicken are the favorites (£10 dinners, Mon–Sat 11:30–14:30 & 17:30–23:00, Sun 12:00–23:30, 3 Glendower Place, tel. 020/7584-8428).

Beirut Express II has fresh, well-prepared Lebanese cuisine, with quick-serve barstools and take-away service in the front, and a sit-down restaurant in the back (65 Old Brompton Road, tel. 020/7591-0123).

The Zetland Arms serves good pub meals in a classic pub atmosphere on its noisy and congested ground floor, and in a more spacious and comfy upstairs—used only in the evenings. Large groups may find it too crowded after 18:00 (same menu throughout, £6–10 meals, food served daily 12:00–21:30, 2 Bute Street, tel. 020/7589-3813).

Elsewhere in London

Between St. Paul's and the Tower: The Counting House, formerly an elegant old bank, offers great £8–10 meals, nice homemade meat pies, fish, and fresh vegetables. The fun "nibbles menu" is available from 15:00–22:00 (Mon–Fri 11:00–23:00, closed Sat–Sun, gets really busy with the buttoned-down 9-to-5 crowd after 12:15, near Mansion House in The City, 50 Cornhill, tel. 020/7283-7123).

Near St. Paul's: De Gustibus Sandwiches is where a top-notch artisan bakery meets the public, offering fresh, you-design-it sandwiches, salads, and soups with simple seating or take-away picnic sacks (great parks nearby), just a block below St. Paul's (Mon–Fri 7:00–17:00, closed Sat–Sun, from church steps follow signs to youth hostel a block downhill, 53–55 Carter Lane, tel. 020/7236-0056; another outlet is inside the Borough Market in Southwark).

Near the British Library: Drummond Street (running just west of Euston Station) is famous in London for very cheap and good Indian vegetarian food. Consider **Chutneys** (124 Drummond, tel. 020/7388-0604) and **Ravi Shankar** (133–135 Drummond, tel. 020/7388-6458) for a good *thali* (both generally open daily until 21:30, later Fri–Sat).

London Connections

Airports

Phone numbers and websites for London's airports and major airlines are listed in the appendix. For accommodations at and near the major airports, see page 139.

Heathrow Airport

Heathrow Airport is one of the world's busiest airports. Think about it: 68 million passengers a year on 470,000 flights from 180 destinations riding 90 airlines, like some kind of global maypole dance. Read signs, and ask questions. For Heathrow's airport, flight, and transfer information, call the switchboard at 0870-000-0123 (www.heathrowairport.com).

Heathrow has five terminals: T-1 (mostly domestic and Irish flights, with some European); T-2 (mainly European flights; may close in 2010 for renovation); T-3 (flights from North and South America and Asia); T-4 (European and US flights; ongoing renovation may shuffle airlines); and T-5 (British Airways flights only). To travel between terminals, you can take the Heathrow Express and Connect trains (free), buses (free), or the Tube (requires a ticket).

It's critical to confirm which terminal your flight will use (check your plane ticket or call your airline in advance), because if it's T-4 or T-5, you'll need to allow extra time. Taxi drivers generally know which terminal you'll need, but bus drivers may not. If you're taking the Tube to the airport, note that some Piccadilly Line subway cars post which airlines are served by which terminals.

Each terminal has an airport information desk (generally daily 6:00–22:00), car-rental agencies, exchange bureaus, ATMs, a pharmacy, a **VAT refund desk** (tel. 020/8910-3682; you must present the VAT claim form from the retailer here to get your tax rebate on items purchased in Britain—see page 16 for details), and **baggage storage** (£8/item for 24 hours, hours vary by terminal but generally daily 5:30–23:00, www.left-baggage.co.uk). Get online 24 hours a day at Heathrow's **Internet access points** (at each terminal—T-4's is up on the mezzanine level) and with a laptop at pay-as-you-go wireless "hotspots"—including many hosted by T-Mobile—in its departure lounges. There's a **post office** on the first floor of T-2. Each terminal has cheap **eateries.**

Heathrow's small **"TI"** (tourist info shop), even though it's a for-profit business, is worth a visit to pick up free information: a simple map, the *London Planner,* and brochures (daily 6:30–22:00, 5-min walk from T-3 in Tube station, follow signs to Underground; bypass queue for transit info to reach window for London questions).

Getting to London from Heathrow Airport

You have several options for traveling the 14 miles between Heathrow Airport and downtown London. For one person on a budget, the Tube or bus is cheap but slow. To speed things up, though you'll spend a little more, combining the Heathrow Connect train with either a Tube or taxi ride (between Paddington

Station and your hotel) is nearly as fast and less than half the cost of taking a cab the whole way. For groups of four or more, a taxi is faster and easier, as well as cheaper. Some options are better than others for a specific terminal.

By Tube (Subway): For £4.50, the Tube takes you from any terminal to downtown London in 50–60 minutes on the Piccadilly Line (6/hr; depending on your destination, may require a transfer, buy ticket at the Tube station ticket window). Note that if you arrive at Terminal 4, you need to take the free Heathrow Connect train to the Heathrow Central terminal (from Terminal 5, take the free Heathrow Express train), which can add 20 minutes

to your trip (especially critical if your return plans involve getting back to these terminals). If you plan to use the Tube for transport in London, it may make sense to buy a Travelcard (Zones 1–6) or Oyster card at the Tube station ticket window at the airport. For information on these passes, see page 51.

If you're taking the Tube from downtown London to the airport, note that the Piccadilly Line trains don't stop at every terminal on every run. Trains either go to T-4, T-1, T-2, and T-3 (in that order); or T-1, T-2, T-3, and T-5 (so allow extra time if going to T-4 or T-5). Check before you board.

By Bus: Most buses depart from the outside common area called the Central Bus Station. It serves T-1, T-2, and T-3, and is a 5-minute walk from any of these terminals. To get to T-4 or T-5 from the Central Bus Station, go inside, go downstairs, and follow signs to take the Tube to your terminal (free, but runs only every 15–20 min to those terminals).

National Express has regular service from Heathrow's Central Bus Station to Victoria Coach Station in downtown London, near several of my recommended hotels. While slow, the bus is affordable and convenient for those staying near Victoria Station (£4, 1–3/hr, 45–75 min, toll tel. 0871-781-8181, calls 10p/min, www.nationalexpress.com).

By Train: Two different trains run between Heathrow Airport and London's Paddington Station. At Paddington Station, you're in the thick of the Tube system, with easy access to any of my recommended neighborhoods—Notting Hill Gate is just two Tube stops away. The **Heathrow Connect** train is the slightly slower, much cheaper option serving T-1, T-2, T-3, and T-4; you can get to T-5 if you transfer at T-1, T-2, or T-3 (£6.90 one-way, 2/hr, 25–28 min, toll tel. 0845-678-6975, www.heathrowconnect.com).

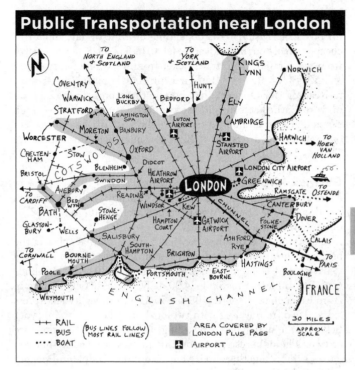

The **Heathrow Express** train is fast (15 min to downtown from T-1, T-2, and T-3; 21 min from T-5; not good for T-4) and runs more frequently (4/hr), but it's pricey (£16.50 "express class" one-way, £32 round-trip, ask about discount promos at ticket desk, kids under 16 ride half-price, under 5 ride free, buy ticket before you board or pay a £3 surcharge to buy it on the train, covered by BritRail pass, daily 5:10–23:25, toll tel. 0845-600-1515, www.heathrow express.co.uk). At the airport, you can use either the Heathrow Express or Heathrow Connect as a free transfer between terminals.

By Taxi: Taxis from the airport cost about £45–70 to west and central London (one hour). For four people traveling together, this can be a deal. Hotels can often line up a cab back to the airport for about £30–40. For the cheapest taxi to the airport, don't order one from your hotel. Simply flag down a few and ask them for their best "off-meter" rate.

Getting to Bath from Heathrow Airport

By Bus: Direct buses run daily from Heathrow to Bath (£19, 10/day direct, 2–3 hrs, more frequent but slower with transfer in London, toll tel. 0871-781-8181, 10p/min, www.nationalexpress.com). BritRail passholders may prefer the 2.5-hour Heathrow–Bath bus/

train connection via Reading (BritRail passholders just pay £15 for bus; otherwise £50–65 depending on time of day, about £10 cheaper when bought in advance; tel. 0118-957-9425, buy bus ticket from www.railair.com, train ticket from www.firstgreatwestern .co.uk). First catch the RailAir Link shuttle bus (2/hr, 45 min) to Reading (RED-ding), then hop on the express train (2/hr, 60 min) to Bath. Factoring in the connection in Reading—which can add at least an hour to the trip—the train is a less convenient option than the direct bus to Bath. For more bus information, see "By Bus," page 158.

Gatwick Airport

More and more flights land at Gatwick Airport, halfway between London and the South Coast (recorded airport info toll tel. 0870-000-2468).

Getting to London: Gatwick Express trains—clearly the best way into London from here—shuttle conveniently between Gatwick and London's Victoria Station (£16.90, £28.80 round-trip, 4/hr, 30 min, runs 5:00–24:00 daily, purchase tickets on train at no extra charge, toll tel. 0845-850-1530, www.gatwickexpress .com). If you're traveling with two or three other adults, buy your tickets at the station before boarding, and you'll travel for the price of two. The only restriction on this impressive deal is that you have to travel together. So if you see another couple in line, get organized and save 50 percent.

You can save a few pounds by taking Southern Railway's slower and less frequent shuttle between Gatwick's South Terminal and Victoria Station (£10.90, up to 4/hr, 45 min, toll tel. 0845-127-2920, www.southernrailway.com). A train also runs from Gatwick to St. Pancras International Station (£8.90, 8/hr, 60 min, www .firstcapitalconnect.co.uk), useful for travelers taking the Eurostar train (to Paris or Brussels) or staying in the King's Cross–St. Pancras neighborhood.

Getting to Bath: To get to Bath from Gatwick, you can catch a bus to Heathrow and take the bus to Bath from there (10/day, 4–5 hrs, £25 one-way, transfer at Heathrow Airport, www.national express.com—see above). By train, the best Gatwick–Bath connection involves a transfer in Reading (£45–60 one-way depending on time of day, £23 in advance, hourly, 2.5 hrs, www.firstgreat western.co.uk; avoid transfer in London, where you'll have to change stations).

London's Other Airports

Stansted Airport: If you're using Stansted (airport toll tel. 0870-0000-303, www.stanstedairport.com), you have several options for getting into or out of London. The National Express bus runs between the airport and downtown London's Victoria Coach Station (£8, £17 round-trip, 2–3/hr, 1.5 hrs, runs 24 hours a day, picks up and stops throughout London, toll tel. 0871-781-8181—calls 10p/min, www.nationalexpress.com). Or you can take the faster, pricier Stansted Express train (£18 one-way, £26.80 round-trip, connects to London's Tube system at Tottenham Hale and Liverpool Street, 4/hr, 45 min, 5:00–23:00, toll tel. 0845-850-0150, www.stanstedexpress.com). Stansted is expensive by cab; figure £99 one-way from central London.

Luton Airport: For Luton (airport tel. 01582/405-100, www.london-luton.co.uk), there are two choices into or out of London. The fastest way is to go by rail to London's St. Pancras International Station (£11.50 one-way, 1–5/hr, 25–45 min, check schedule to avoid the slower trains, toll tel. 0845-712-5678, www.eastmidlandstrains.co.uk); catch the 10-minute shuttle bus (£1) from outside the terminal to the Luton Airport Parkway train station. The Green Line express bus #757 runs to London's Victoria Station (£13 one-way, £14.50 round-trip, small discount for easyJet passengers who buy online, 2–4/hr, 1.25–1.5 hrs, 24 hours a day, toll tel. 0844-801-7261, www.greenline.co.uk). If you're sleeping at Luton, consider easyHotel (see listing on page 139).

London City Airport: There's a slim chance you might use London City Airport (tel. 020/7646-0088, www.londoncityairport.com). To get into London, take the Docklands Light Railway (DLR) to the Bank Tube station, which is one stop east of St. Paul's on the Central Line (£4 one-way, covered by Travelcard, £2.20–2.70 on Oyster card, 22 min, tel. 020/7222-1234, www.tfl.gov.uk/dlr).

Connecting London's Airports by Bus

More and more travelers are taking advantage of cheap flights out of London's smaller airports. The handy **National Express bus** runs between Heathrow, Gatwick, Stansted, and Luton airports—easier than having to cut through the center of London—although traffic can be bad and increase travel times (toll tel. 0871-781-8181, calls 10p/min, www.nationalexpress.com).

From Heathrow Airport to: Gatwick Airport (1–4/hr, 1.25–1.5 hrs, £19.50 one-way, £36.50 round-trip, allow at least three hours between flights), **Stansted Airport** (1–2/hr, 1.5–1.75 hrs, £22.50 one-way, £29.30 round-trip), **Luton Airport** (hourly, 1–1.5 hrs, £19.90 one-way, £24.50 round-trip).

Discounted Flights from London

London is one of Europe's cheapest places to fly into and out of. For information, see "Cheap Flights" on page 614.

Trains and Buses

Britain is covered by a myriad of rail systems (owned by different companies), which together are called National Rail. London, the country's major transportation hub, has a different train station for each region. There are nine main stations:

Euston—Serves northwest England, North Wales, and Scotland.

King's Cross—Serves northeast England and Scotland, including York and Edinburgh.

Liverpool Street—Serves east England, including Essex and Harwich.

London Bridge—Serves south England, including Brighton.

Marylebone—Serves southwest and central England, including Stratford-upon-Avon.

Paddington—Serves south and southwest England including Heathrow Airport, Windsor, Bath, South Wales, and the Cotswolds.

St. Pancras International—Serves north and south England, plus Eurostar to Paris or Brussels.

Victoria—Serves Gatwick Airport, Canterbury, Dover, and Brighton.

Waterloo—Serves southeast England, including Dover and Salisbury.

Any train station has schedule information, can make reservations, and can sell tickets for any destination. Most stations offer a baggage-storage service (£8/bag for 24 hours, look for *Left Luggage* signs); because of long security lines, it can take a while to check or pick up your bag (www.excess-baggage.com). For more details on the services available at each station, see www.nationalrail.co.uk/stations.

Buying Tickets: For general information, call 0845-748-4950 (or visit www.nationalrail.co.uk or www.eurostar.com; £5 booking fee for telephone reservations).

Railpasses: For train travel outside London, consider getting a BritRail pass. Options include passes that cover England as well as Scotland and Wales, England-only passes, England/Ireland passes, "London Plus" passes (good for travel in most of southeast England but not in London itself—see pass coverage on map on page 159), and BritRail & Drive passes (which offer you some rail days and some car-rental days). For specifics, contact your travel agent or see www.ricksteves.com/rail.

By Train
To Points West
From Paddington Station to: Bath (2/hr, 1.5 hrs; also consider a guided Evan Evans tour by bus—see page 164), **Oxford** (2–5/hr,

London's Train Stations

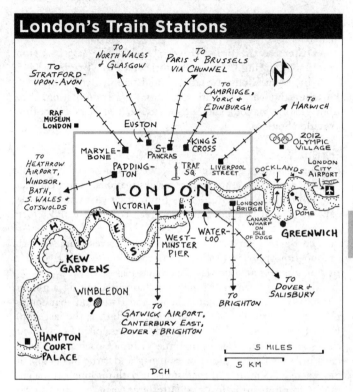

1 hr, possible transfer in Reading), **Penzance** (every 1–2 hours, 5–5.75 hrs, possible change in Plymouth), and **Cardiff** (2/hr, 2 hrs).

To Points North

From King's Cross Station: Trains run at least hourly, stopping in **York** (2 hrs), **Durham** (3 hrs), and **Edinburgh** (4.5 hrs). Trains to **Cambridge** also leave from here (2/hr, 1 hr).

From **Euston Station to: Conwy** (nearly hourly, 3.25–4 hrs, transfer in Chester or Crewe), **Liverpool** (hourly, 2 hrs, more with transfer), **Blackpool** (hourly, 3 hrs, transfer at Preston), **Keswick** (9/day, 3–3.5 hrs, transfer to bus at Penrith), **Glasgow** (1–2/hr, 4.5–5 hrs direct, some may leave from King's Cross Station).

From London's Other Stations

Trains run between London and **Canterbury,** leaving from Charing Cross Station and arriving in Canterbury West, as well as from London's Victoria Station and arriving in Canterbury East (2/hr, 1.5 hrs).

Direct trains leave for **Stratford-upon-Avon** from Marylebone

Station, located near the southwest corner of Regents Park (every 2 hrs, 2.25 hrs).

Other Destinations: Dover (1–2/hr, 1.75–2.25 hrs; from Waterloo, Charing Cross, or Victoria stations), **Brighton** (4–5/hr, 1 hr, from Victoria Station and London Bridge Station), **Portsmouth** (3/hr, 1.5–2 hrs, most from Waterloo Station, a few from Victoria Station), and **Salisbury** (1–2/hr, 1.5 hrs, direct from Waterloo Station).

By Bus

National Express' excellent bus service is considerably cheaper than the train, and a fine option for destinations within England (call toll tel. 0871-781-8181—calls 10p/min, or visit www.national express.com or the bus station a block southwest of Victoria Station).

To Bath: The National Express bus leaves from Victoria Station almost hourly (3.25–3.75 hrs, avoid those with layover in Bristol, sample fares one-way-£19, round-trip-£29).

To get to Bath via Stonehenge, consider taking a guided bus tour from London to Stonehenge and Bath, and abandoning the tour in Bath (be sure to confirm that Bath is the last stop). **Evan Evans'** tour is £69 and includes admissions (£44 without admissions). The tour leaves from the Victoria Coach station every morning at 8:45 (you can stow your bag under the bus), stops in Stonehenge (45 min), and then stops in Bath for lunch and a city tour before returning to London (offered year-round). You can book the tour at the Victoria Coach station or the Evan Evans office (258 Vauxhall Bridge Road, near Victoria Coach station, tel. 020/7950-1777, US tel. 866-382-6868, www.evanevans.co.uk, reservations@evanevanstours.co.uk). Golden Tours also runs a Stonehenge–Bath tour (£59, £39 without admissions, check website for seasonal tour days; departs from Fountain Square, located across from Victoria Coach Station, US tel. 800-548-7083, toll tel. 0844-880-6981, www.goldentours.co.uk, reservations@golden tours.co.uk).

To Other Destinations: Oxford (2–4/hr, 1.75–2.25 hrs), **Cambridge** (about hourly, 2–2.5 hrs), **Canterbury** (about hourly, 2–2.5 hrs), **Dover** (about hourly, 2.5–3.25 hrs), **Penzance** (6/day, 8.5–9 hrs, overnight available), **Cardiff** (every 1–2 hrs, 3.25 hrs), **Liverpool** (8/day direct, 5.25–6 hrs, overnight available), **Blackpool** (4/day direct, 6.25–7 hrs, overnight available), **York** (4/day direct, 4.75–5.25 hrs), **Durham** (4/day direct, 6–7.5 hrs), **Glasgow** (2/day direct, 8–9 hrs, train is a much better option), **Edinburgh** (2/day direct, 8.75–9.75 hrs, go via train instead).

To Dublin, Ireland: The bus/boat journey takes 9–10 hours (£35–43, 3/day, toll tel. 0871-781-8181, calls 10p/min, www.national

express.com). Consider a 75-minute Ryanair flight instead (www
.ryanair.com).

Crossing the Channel
By Eurostar Train

The fastest and most convenient way to get from Big Ben to the
Eiffel Tower is by rail. Eurostar, a joint service of the Belgian,
British, and French railways, is the speedy passenger train that
zips you (and up to 800 others in 18 sleek cars) from downtown
London to downtown Paris or Brussels (15/day, 2.5 hrs) faster and
more easily than flying. The actual tunnel crossing is a 20-min-
ute, silent, 100-mile-per-hour non-event. Your ears won't even
pop. Eurostar's monopoly expires at the beginning of 2010, and
Air France has already announced plans to start a competing
high-speed rail service between London and Paris in late autumn
of 2010.

Eurostar Fares

Channel fares are reasonable but complicated. Prices vary depending
on how far ahead you reserve, whether you can live with restrictions,
and whether you're eligible for
any discounts (children, youths,
seniors, round-trip travelers, and
railpass holders all qualify).

Fares can change without
notice, but typically a **one-way,
full-fare ticket** (with no restrictions on refundability) runs about
$425 first-class and $300 second-
class. **Cheaper seats** come with
more restrictions and can sell
out quickly (figure $80–160 for
second class, one-way). Those
traveling with a railpass that
covers France or Britain should
look first at the **passholder** fare

Eurostar Routes

ENGLAND
LONDON
EBBS-
FLEET
ASHFORD
CALAIS
FRETHUN
AMSTERDAM
NETH.
BELG.
LILLE
BRUSSELS
FRANCE
PARIS

50 MI
100 KM

—— EUROSTAR
--- CHANNEL TUNNEL
···· OTHER RAIL

(from $85–130 for second-class, one-way Eurostar trips). For more
details, visit www.ricksteves.com/rail/eurostar.htm.

Buying Eurostar Tickets

Since only the most expensive (full-fare) ticket is fully refundable,
don't reserve until you're sure of your plans. But if you wait too
long, the cheapest tickets will get bought up.

Once you're confident about the time and date of your crossing, you can check and book fares by phone or online in the US
and pay to have your ticket delivered to you in the US. (Order

online at www.ricksteves.com/rail/eurostar.htm, prices listed in dollars; order by phone at US tel. 800-EUROSTAR). Or you can order in Britain (toll tel. 08705-186-186, £5 booking fee by phone, www.eurostar.com, prices listed in pounds).

If you buy from a US company, you'll pay for ticket delivery in the US; if you book with the British company, you'll pick up your ticket at the train station. In continental Europe, you can buy your Eurostar ticket at any major train station in any country or at any travel agency that handles train tickets (expect a booking fee). In Britain, tickets can be issued only at the Eurostar office in St. Pancras International Station.

Remember that Britain's time zone is one hour earlier than France or Belgium. Times listed on tickets are local times (departure from London is British time, arrival in Paris is French time).

LONDON

Taking the Eurostar

Eurostar trains depart from and arrive at London's St. Pancras International Station. Check in at least 30 minutes in advance for your Eurostar trip. It's very similar to an airport check-in: You pass through airport-like security, show your passport to customs officials, and find a TV monitor to locate your departure gate. There are a few airport-like shops, newsstands, horrible snack bars, and cafés (bring food for the trip from elsewhere), pay-Internet terminals, and a currency-exchange booth with rates about the same as you'll find on the other end.

Crossing the Channel Without Eurostar

The old-fashioned ways of crossing the Channel are usually cheaper than Eurostar (taking the bus is cheapest). They're generally also twice as romantic, complicated, and time-consuming.

By Train and Boat

To Paris: You'll take a train from London to the port of Dover, then catch a ferry to Calais, France, before boarding another train for Paris. Trains go from London's Charing Cross, Waterloo, or Victoria stations to **Dover's** Priory station (1–2/hr, 1.75–2.25 hrs; bus or taxi from station to ferry dock). P&O Ferries sail from Dover to Calais; TGV trains run from Calais to Paris. You'll need to book your own train tickets to Dover and from Calais to Paris. The prices listed here are for the ferry only (from £25 one-way or £50 round-trip online, more at dock or by phone, book early for best fares; 22/day, 1.5 hrs, toll tel. 0871-664-5645, www.poferries.com).

To Amsterdam: Stena Line's Dutchflyer service combines train and ferry tickets between London and Amsterdam via the ports of **Harwich** and Hoek van Holland. Trains go from London's

Liverpool Street station to Harwich (hourly, 1.5 hrs). Stena Line ferries sail from Harwich to Hoek van Holland (7.5 hrs), where you can transfer to a train to Amsterdam or other Dutch cities (ferry—from £32, from £60 with cabin, book at least 2 weeks in advance for best price, 13 hrs total travel time, Dutchflyer toll tel. 0870-545-5455, www.stenaline.co.uk, Dutch train info at www .ns.nl).

For additional European ferry info, visit www.aferry.to. For UK train and bus info, go to www.traveline.org.uk.

By Tour

A tour company called Britain Shrinkers sells one- and two-day tours to Paris, Brussels, or Bruges, enabling you to side-trip to these cities from London for less than most train tickets alone. For example, you'll pay £99 for a one-day Paris "tour" (unescorted Mon–Sat day trip with Métro pass; tel. 207-713-1311 or www .britainshrinkers.com). This can be a particularly good option if you need to get to Paris from London on short notice, when only the costliest fares are available.

By Bus

You can take the bus from London direct to **Paris** (4/day, 8.25–9.75 hrs), **Brussels** (3–4/day, 7.75–9.25 hrs), or **Amsterdam** (4/day, 11.75–12.75 hrs) from Victoria Coach Station (via ferry or Chunnel, day or overnight). Sample prices to Paris for economy fares booked at least two days in advance: £25 one-way, £52 round-trip, book online early for best fares (toll tel. 0871-781-8181, calls 10p/min; visit www.eurolines.co.uk and look for "funfares").

By Plane

Check with budget airlines for inexpensive round-trip fares to Paris or Brussels (see "Cheap Flights" on page 614).

LONDON

GREENWICH, WINDSOR, AND CAMBRIDGE

Three of the best day-trip possibilities near London are Greenwich, Windsor, and Cambridge (listed from nearest to farthest). Greenwich is England's maritime capital; Windsor has a very famous castle; and Cambridge is easily England's best university town.

Getting Around

By Train: The British rail system uses London as a hub and normally offers same-day, round-trip fares that cost virtually the same as one-way fares. For day trips, these "cheap day return" tickets, available if you depart London after 9:30 on weekdays or anytime Sat–Sun, are best. You can save a little money (both one-way and round-trip) if you purchase advance tickets before 18:00 on the day before your trip.

By Train Tour: London Walks offers a variety of Explorer day trips year-round by train for about £12 plus transportation costs (pick up their walking-tour brochures at the TI or hotels, tel. 020/7624-3978, www.londonwalks.com; see listing on page 60).

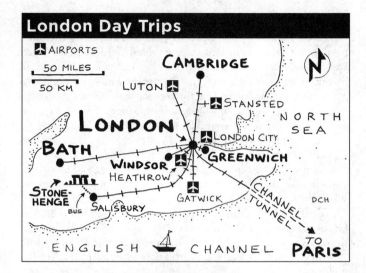

London Day Trips

GREENWICH

Greenwich

Tudor kings favored the palace at Greenwich (GREN-ich). Henry VIII was born here. Later kings commissioned Inigo Jones and Christopher Wren to beautify the town and palace. Yet in spite of Greenwich's architectural and royal treats, this is England's maritime capital, and visitors go for all things salty. While Greenwich's main attraction—the *Cutty Sark* clipper—is closed for restoration through 2010, the town is still worth a visit. It has the world's most famous observatory, stunning Baroque architecture, appealing markets, a fleet of nautical shops, and hordes of tourists. And where else can you set your watch with such accuracy?

Planning Your Time

Upon arrival, stroll past the *Cutty Sark* dry dock and walk the shoreline promenade. Enjoy a possible lunch or drink in the venerable Trafalgar Tavern, before heading up to the National Maritime Museum and then through the park to the Royal Observatory Greenwich.

Getting to Greenwich

It's a joy by boat, or a snap by Tube.

By Boat: From central London, cruise down the Thames from the piers at Westminster or the Tower of London (2/hr, about one hour; see page 65).

By Tube: Take the Tube to Bank and change to the Docklands Light Railway (DLR), which takes you right to Cutty Sark Station in central Greenwich (one stop before the main—but less central—Greenwich Station, 20 min, all in Zone 2, covered by any Tube pass). Some DLR trains terminate at Island Gardens (from which you can generally catch another train to Greenwich's Cutty Sark Station within a few minutes, though it may be more memorable to get out and walk under the river through the long Thames pedestrian tunnel). Many DLR trains terminate at Canary Wharf, so make sure you get on one that continues to Lewisham or Greenwich.

A fun way to return to London is to ride the DLR back to Canary Wharf and get off there to explore the Docklands area (London's Manhattan, most interesting at the end of the work-day, see page 113). When you're done exploring, hop on the speedy Jubilee line and zip back to Westminster in 15 minutes.

By Train: Mainline trains also go from London (Charing Cross, Cannon Street, Waterloo East, and London Bridge stations) several times an hour to Greenwich Station (10-min walk from the sights). While the train is fast and cheap, the Tube is preferable.

Orientation to Greenwich

(area code: 020)

Covered markets and outdoor stalls make weekends lively. Save time to browse the town. Wander beyond the touristy Church Street and Greenwich High Road to where flower stands spill into the side streets, and antique shops sell brass nautical knick-knacks. King William Walk, College Approach, Nelson Road, and Turnpin Lane are all worth a look. If you need pub grub, Greenwich has almost 100 pubs, with some boasting that they're mere milliseconds from the prime meridian.

Tourist Information

Until March 2010, the Greenwich TI is located across from Cutty Sark Station at 46 Greenwich Church Street. After that, you'll find it back within the Old Royal Naval College, inside the new Discover Greenwich Centre (just east of the closed-for-restoration *Cutty Sark* at 2 Cutty Sark Gardens, Pepys House). Regardless of the location, the hours and phone number are the same (daily 10:00–17:00, toll tel. 0870-608-2000, www.greenwichwhs.org.uk). Guided walks depart from the TI and cover the big sights (£6, daily at 12:15 and 14:15).

Helpful Hints

Markets: Thanks to its markets, Greenwich throbs with day-trip-pers on weekends. The **Greenwich Market** is an entertaining mini–Covent Garden, located between College Approach and Nelson Road (Wed 11:00–18:00, Thu–Fri 10:00–17:00,

Greenwich

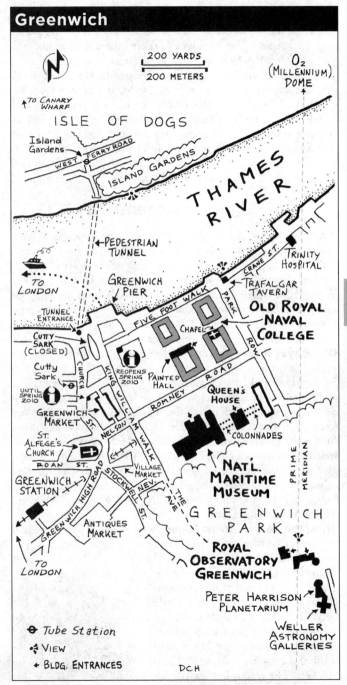

GREENWICH

200 YARDS
200 METERS

O₂ (MILLENNIUM) DOME

TO CANARY WHARF

ISLE OF DOGS

Island Gardens

WEST FERRY ROAD

ISLAND GARDENS

THAMES RIVER

PEDESTRIAN TUNNEL

TO LONDON

GREENWICH PIER

FIVE FOOT WALK

CRANE ST.

TRINITY HOSPITAL

TRAFALGAR TAVERN

PARK ROW

TUNNEL ENTRANCE

OLD ROYAL NAVAL COLLEGE

CHAPEL

CUTTY SARK (CLOSED)

CHURCH ST.

KING WILLIAM WALK

REOPENS SPRING 2010

PAINTED HALL

ROMNEY ROAD

Cutty Sark

UNTIL SPRING 2010

QUEEN'S HOUSE

GREENWICH MARKET

NELSON ST.

COLONNADES

ST. ALFEGE'S CHURCH

ROAN ST.

Village Market

NAT'L. MARITIME MUSEUM

PRIME MERIDIAN

GREENWICH STATION

STOCKWELL ST.

GREENWICH HIGH ROAD

THE AVE.

GREENWICH PARK

ANTIQUES MARKET

ROYAL OBSERVATORY GREENWICH

TO LONDON

PETER HARRISON PLANETARIUM

WELLER ASTRONOMY GALLERIES

⊖ Tube Station
❖ View
← Bldg. Entrances

DCH

Sat–Sun 10:00–17:30, Wed–Fri best for antiques, lots of crafts and food on weekends, tel. 020/7515-7153, www.greenwich market.net). The **Antiques Market** sells old odds and ends at high prices on Greenwich High Road, near the post office (Sat–Sun only 9:30–17:30). The **Village Market** has a little bit of everything—antiques, books, food, and flowers (Sat–Sun only 9:30–17:30, across Nelson Road from the Greenwich Market, enter from Stockwell Street or King William Walk).

Supermarket: If you're picnicking, visit the handy **Marks & Spencer Simply Food** across from the *Cutty Sark* dry dock (Mon–Sat 8:00–21:00, Sun 10:00–21:00, 55 Greenwich Church Street, tel. 020/7228-2545).

Sights in Greenwich

▲▲Cutty Sark—The Scottish-built *Cutty Sark* is closed for renovation until late 2010—call 020/8858-2698 or check www.cutty sark.org.uk for updates. She was the last of the great China tea clippers, and was the queen of the seas when first launched in 1869. With 32,000 square feet of sail, she could blow with the wind 300 miles in a day. You may be able to view some of the renovation from an observation window in the *Cutty Sark* gift shop adjacent to the dry dock (hours vary—call ahead).

Old Royal Naval College—Now that the Royal Navy has moved out, the public is invited in to see the college's elaborate Painted Hall and Chapel, grandly designed by Christopher Wren and completed by other architects in the 1700s. You'll also find fine descriptions and an altar painting by American Benjamin West (free, Mon–Sat 10:00–17:00, Sun 12:30–17:00, sometimes closed for private events, choral service Sun at 11:00 in chapel—all are welcome, in the two college buildings farthest from river). Guides give 90-minute tours covering the hall and chapel, along with three other places not open to the general public (£5, daily at 11:30 and 14:00, call ahead to check availability, tel. 020/8269-4799, www .oldroyalnavalcollege.org).

Stroll the Thames to Trafalgar Tavern—From the *Cutty Sark* dry dock, pass the pier and wander east along the Thames on Five Foot Walk (named for the width of the path) for grand views in front of the Old Royal Naval College (see above). Founded by William III as a naval hospital and designed by Wren, the college was split in two because Queen Mary didn't want the view from Queen's House blocked. The riverside view is good,

too, with the twin-domed towers of the college (one giving the time, the other the direction of the wind) framing Queen's House, and the Royal Observatory Greenwich crowning the hill beyond.

Continuing downstream, just past the college, you'll see the **Trafalgar Tavern.** Dickens knew the pub well, and he used it as the setting for the wedding breakfast in *Our Mutual Friend.* Built in 1837 in the Regency style to attract Londoners downriver, the tavern is popular with Londoners (and tourists) for its fine lunches. The upstairs Nelson Room is still used for weddings. Its formal moldings and elegant windows with balconies over the Thames are a step back in time (food served Mon–Sat 12:00–22:00, Sun 12:00–16:00, elegant ground-floor dining room as well as the more casual pub, Park Row, tel. 020/8858-2909).

From the pub, enjoy views of the former Millennium Dome a mile downstream. The Dome languished for almost a decade after its controversial construction and brief life as a millennial "world's fair" site. Plans for a casino and hotel project fell through, although it has come in handy as an emergency homeless shelter. It was finally bought by a developer a few years ago and rechristened "The O_2" in honor of the telecommunications company that paid for the naming rights. Currently, it hosts concerts and sporting events and will see action during the 2012 Summer Olympics. Whatever it's called, locals will no doubt continue to grumble about its original cost.

From the Trafalgar Tavern, you can walk the two long blocks up Park Row, and turn right into the park leading up to the Royal Observatory Greenwich.

Queen's House—This building, the first Palladian-style villa in Britain, was designed in 1616 by Inigo Jones for James I's wife, Anne of Denmark. All traces of the queen are long gone, and the Great Hall and Royal Apartments now serve as an art gallery for rotating exhibits from the National Maritime Museum. The Orangery is now home to the great J. M. W. Turner painting *Battle of Trafalgar.* His largest work (so big that a wall had to be opened to get it in here) and only royal commission, it is surrounded by Christ-like paintings of Admiral Horatio Nelson's death (free, daily 10:00–17:00, last entry 30 min before closing, tel. 020/8858-4422, recorded info tel. 020/8312-6565, www.nmm.ac.uk).

▲▲National Maritime Museum—Great for anyone remotely interested in the sea, this museum holds everything from a *Titanic* passenger's pocket watch and Captain Robert Scott's sun goggles (from his 1910 Antarctic expedition) to the uniform Admiral Nelson wore when he was killed at Trafalgar. Under a big glass roof—accompanied by the sound of creaking wooden ships and crashing waves—slick, modern displays depict lighthouse technology, a whaling cannon, and a Greenpeace "survival pod." Kids love the All Hands and Bridge galleries, where they can send secret messages by Morse code and operate a miniature dockside crane.

Note that some parts of the museum, such as the Nelson's Navy gallery, are closed for renovation until 2012 (free, daily 10:00–17:00, last entry 30 min before closing; look for family-oriented events posted at entrance—singing, treasure hunts, storytelling—particularly on weekends; toll tel. 0870-781-5168, www.nmm.ac.uk).

▲▲**Royal Observatory Greenwich**—Located on the prime meridian (0° longitude), the observatory is the point from which

all time is measured. However, the observatory's early work had nothing to do with coordinating the world's clocks to Greenwich Mean Time (GMT). The observatory was founded in 1675 by Charles II to find a way to determine longitude at sea. Today, the Greenwich time signal is linked with the BBC (which broadcasts the famous "pips" worldwide at the top of the hour).

Look above the observatory to see the orange Time Ball, also visible from the Thames, which drops daily at 13:00. (Nearby, outside the courtyard of the observatory, see how your foot measures up to the foot where the public standards of length are cast in bronze.)

In the courtyard, set your wristwatch to the digital clock showing GMT to a tenth of a second, and straddle the prime meridian.

Inside, check out the historic astronomical instruments and camera obscura. In the Time Galleries, see timepieces through the ages, including John Harrison's prizewinning marine chronometers that helped 18th-century sailors calculate longitude (the highlight for fans of Dava Sobel's book *Longitude*). The observatory is also home to the state-of-the-art, 120-seat Peter Harrison Planetarium, an education center, and the Weller Astronomy Galleries, where interactive displays allow you to guide a space mission and touch a 4.5-billion-year-old meteorite.

Cost and Hours: Free entry to observatory, planetarium shows-£6; observatory open daily 10:00–17:00, last entry 30 min before closing; courtyard open until 20:00; planetarium shows hourly Mon–Fri 13:00–16:00, Sat–Sun 11:00–16:00, fewer in winter, 30 min; tel. 020/8858-4422, www.nmm.ac.uk.

Observatory Grounds and Viewpoint: Before you leave the observatory grounds, enjoy the view from the overlook—the

symmetrical royal buildings, the Thames, the Docklands and its busy cranes (including the tallest building in the UK, Canary Wharf Tower, a.k.a. One Canada Square), the huge O_2 (Millennium) Dome, and the square-mile City of London, with its skyscrapers and the dome of St. Paul's Cathedral. At night (17:00–24:00), look for the green laser beam that the observatory projects into the sky (best viewed in winter), extending along the prime meridian for 15 miles.

Windsor

Windsor is a compact and easy walking town of about 30,000 people that originally grew up around the royal residence. In 1070, William the Conqueror continued his habit of kicking Saxons out of their various settlements, taking over what the locals called "Windlesora" (meaning "riverbank with a hoisting crane")— which later became "Windsor." William built the first fortified castle on a chalk hill above the Thames; later kings added on to his early designs, rebuilding and expanding the castle and surrounding gardens.

By setting up primary residence here, modern monarchs increased Windsor's popularity and prosperity—most notably, Queen Victoria, whose stern statue glares at you as you approach the castle. After her death, Victoria rejoined her beloved husband Albert in the Royal Mausoleum at Frogmore House, a mile south of the castle in a private section of the Home Park (house and mausoleum rarely open; check www.royalcollection.org.uk). The current queen considers Windsor her primary residence, and it's where she feels most at home. You can tell if Her Majesty is in residence by checking to see which flag is flying above the round tower: If it's the royal standard (a red, yellow, and blue flag) instead of the Union Jack, the queen is at home.

While 99 percent of visitors just come to see the castle and go, some enjoy spending the night. Windsor's charm is most evident when the tourists are gone. Consider overnighting here, since parking and access to Heathrow Airport are easy, day-tripping into London is feasible, and an evening at the horse races (on Mondays) is hoof-pounding, heart-thumping fun.

Getting to Windsor

By Train: Windsor has two train stations—Windsor & Eton Central (5-min walk to palace, TI inside) and Windsor & Eton Riverside (5-min walk to palace and TI). First Great Western trains run between London's Paddington Station and Windsor & Eton Central (2/hr, 35 min, change at Slough, £8 one-way standard class, £9–11 same-day return). South West Trains run between London's Waterloo Station and Windsor & Eton Riverside (2/hr, 1 hr, possible change at Staines, £8.50 one-way standard class, £9–15 same-day return; info toll tel. 0845-748-4950, www.national rail.co.uk).

If you're day-tripping into London from Windsor, ask at the train station about combining a same-day return train ticket with a One-Day Travelcard as one ticket (£12–21, lower price for travel after 9:30, covers rail transportation to and from London and doubles as an all-day Tube and bus pass in town, rail ticket may also qualify you for half-price London sightseeing discounts—ask or look for brochure at station, or go to www.daysoutguide .co.uk).

By Bus: Green Line buses #701 and #702 run from London's Victoria Colonnades (between the Victoria train and coach stations) to the Parish Church stop on Windsor's High Street, before continuing on to Legoland (£1–8.50 one-way, £9–12.50 round-trip, prices vary depending on time of day, 1–2/hr, 1.25 hours to Windsor, tel. 01344/782-222, www.rainbowfares.com).

By Car: Windsor is 20 miles from London, and just off Heathrow Airport's landing path. The town (and then the castle and Legoland) is well-signposted from the M4 motorway. It's a convenient first stop if you're arriving at and renting a car from Heathrow, and saving London until the end of your trip.

From Heathrow Airport: Buses #71 and #77 make the 45-minute trip between Terminal 5 and Windsor, dropping you in the center of town on Peascod Street (about £7, 1–2/hr, toll tel. 0871-200-2233, www.firstgroup.com). London black cabs can charge whatever they like from Heathrow to Windsor (and do); avoid them by calling a local cab company, such as Windsor Radio Cars (£20, tel. 01753/677-677).

Orientation to Windsor

(area code: 01753)

Windsor's pleasant pedestrian shopping zone litters the approach to its famous palace with fun temptations. You'll find most shops and restaurants around the castle on High and Thames streets, and down the pedestrian Peascod Street (PESS-cot), which runs perpendicular to High Street.

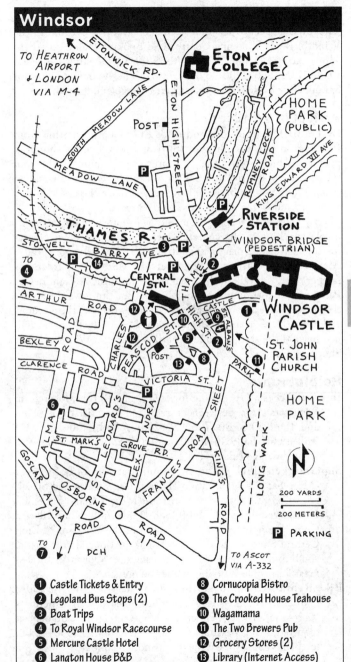

Windsor

TO HEATHROW AIRPORT & LONDON VIA M-4

ETONWICK RD.

ETON COLLEGE

HOME PARK (PUBLIC)

SOUTH MEADOW LANE

ETON HIGH STREET

POST

MEADOW LANE

ROMNEY LOCK ROAD

KING EDWARD VII AVE

RIVERSIDE STATION

THAMES R.

STOVELL

BARRY AVE.

WINDSOR BRIDGE (PEDESTRIAN)

TO ④

CENTRAL STN.

ARTHUR ROAD

THAMES

CASTLE HILL

HIGH ST.

ST. ALBANS

WINDSOR CASTLE

BEXLEY ROAD

CHARLES ROAD

PEASCOD ST.

POST

ST. JOHN PARISH CHURCH

CLARENCE ROAD

VICTORIA ST.

SHEET ROAD

HOME PARK

ST. LEONARD'S ROAD

ALMA ROAD

ST. MARK'S ROAD

GROVE RD.

ALEXANDRA RD.

FRANCES ROAD

KING'S ROAD

LONG WALK

GOSLAR

ALMA ROAD

OSBORNE ROAD

ROAD

TO ⑦

DCH

TO ASCOT VIA A-332

200 YARDS
200 METERS

P PARKING

WINDSOR

① Castle Tickets & Entry
② Legoland Bus Stops (2)
③ Boat Trips
④ To Royal Windsor Racecourse
⑤ Mercure Castle Hotel
⑥ Langton House B&B
⑦ To Park Farm B&B & Legoland
⑧ Cornucopia Bistro
⑨ The Crooked House Teahouse
⑩ Wagamama
⑪ The Two Brewers Pub
⑫ Grocery Stores (2)
⑬ Library (Internet Access)
⑭ Bike Rental

Tourist Information

The TI is adjacent to Windsor & Eton Central Station, in the Windsor Royal Shopping Centre's Old Booking Hall (April–Sept Mon–Sat 9:30–17:30, Sun 10:00–16:00; Oct–March Mon–Sat 10:00–17:00, Sun 10:00–16:00; tel. 01753/743-900, www.windsor .gov.uk). The TI sells discount tickets to Legoland for £34.

Arrival in Windsor

By Train: The train to Windsor & Eton Central Station from Paddington (via Slough) will spit you out in a shady shopping pavilion (which houses the TI), only a few minutes' walk from the castle. If you arrive at Windsor & Eton Riverside train station (from Waterloo, via Staines) instead, you'll see the castle as you exit—just follow the wall to the castle entrance.

By Car: Follow signs from the M4 motorway for pay-and-display parking in the center. River Street Car Park is closest to the castle, but pricey and often full. The cheaper, bigger Alexandra Car Park (near the riverside Alexandra Gardens) is farther west. To walk to the town center from the Alexandra Car Park, head east through the tour-bus parking lot toward the castle. At the souvenir shop, walk up the stairs (or take the elevator) and cross the overpass to the Windsor & Eton Central Station. Just beyond the station, you'll find the TI in the Windsor Royal Shopping Centre.

Helpful Hints

Internet Access: Get online for free at the **library,** located on Bachelors' Acre, between Peascod and Victoria streets (Mon and Thu 9:30–17:00, Tue 9:30–20:00, Wed 14:00–17:00, Fri 9:30–19:00, Sat 9:30–15:00, closed Sun, tel. 01753/743-940, www.rbwm.gov.uk).

Supermarkets: Pick up picnic supplies at **Marks & Spencer** (Mon–Sat 9:00–18:00, Sun 11:00–17:00, 130 Peascod Street, tel. 01753/852-266) or at **Waitrose** (Mon–Tue and Sat 8:30–19:00, Wed–Fri 8:30–20:00, Sun 11:00–17:00, King Edward Court Shopping Centre, just south of the Windsor & Eton Central Station, tel. 01753/860-565). Just outside the castle, you'll find long benches near the statue of Queen Victoria—great for people-watching while you munch.

Bike Rental: Extreme Motion, near the river in Alexandra Gardens, rents 21-speed mountain bikes as well as helmets (£12/4 hrs, £17/day, helmets-£1–1.50, £100 credit-card deposit required, bring passport as ID, summer daily 10:00–22:00, tel. 01753/830-220, www.extrememotion.com).

Sights in Windsor

▲▲Windsor Castle

Windsor Castle, the official home of England's royal family for

900 years, claims to be the largest and oldest occupied castle in the world. Thankfully, touring it is simple. You'll see immense grounds, lavish staterooms, a crowd-pleasing dollhouse, an art gallery, and the chapel.

Cost, Hours, Information: £15.50, family pass-£41, daily March–Oct 9:45–17:15, Nov–Feb

9:45–16:15, last entry 1.25 hours before closing, tel. 020/7766-7304, www.royalcollection.org.uk.

Tours: As you enter, ask about the warden's free 30-minute guided walks around the grounds (2/hr). They cover the grounds but not the castle, which is described well by the included audioguide (skip the official guidebook).

Other Activities: The **Changing of the Guard** takes place on alternate days at 11:00 (ceremonies begin a little earlier—get there by 10:45), except in very wet weather (and never on Sun). There's an **evensong** in the chapel nightly at 17:15—free for worshippers.

● Self-Guided Tour: Immediately upon entering, you pass through a simple modern building housing a **historical overview** of the castle. This excellent intro is worth a close look, since you're basically on your own after this. Inside, you'll find the motte (artificial mound) and bailey (fortified stockade around it) of William the Conqueror's castle. Dating from 1080, this was his first castle in England.

Follow the signs to the staterooms/gallery/dollhouse. **Queen Mary's Dollhouse**—a palace in miniature (1:12 scale, from 1924) and "the most famous dollhouse in the world"—often comes with the longest wait. If dollhouses aren't your cup of tea, you can skip that line and go immediately into the lavish **staterooms.** Strewn with history and the art of a long line of kings and queens, they're the best I've seen in Britain—and well-restored after the devastating 1992 fire. Take advantage of the talkative docents in each room, who are happy to answer your questions.

The adjacent gallery is a changing exhibit featuring the **royal art collection** (and some big names, such as Michelangelo and Leonardo). Signs direct you (downhill) to **St. George's Chapel.** Housing numerous royal tombs, it's a fine example of Perpendicular

Gothic, with classic fan vaulting spreading out from each pillar (dating from about 1500). The simple chapel containing the tombs of the current Queen's parents, King George VI and "Queen Mother" Elizabeth, and younger sister, Princess Margaret, is along the church's north aisle. Next door is the sumptuous 13th-century **Albert Memorial Chapel,** redecorated after the death of Prince Albert in 1861 and dedicated to his memory.

More Sights in Windsor

Legoland Windsor—Paradise for Legomaniacs under 12, this huge, kid-pleasing park has dozens of tame but fun rides (often with very long lines) scattered throughout its 150 acres. The impressive Miniland has 40 million Lego pieces glued together to create 800 tiny buildings and a mini-tour of Europe, while the Creation Centre boasts an 80 percent-scale Boeing 747 cockpit, made of two million bricks. Several of the more exciting rides

involve getting wet, so dress accordingly or buy a cheap disposable poncho in the gift shop. While you may be tempted to hop on the Hill Train at the entrance, it's faster and more convenient to walk down into the park. Food is available in the park, but you can save money by bringing a picnic.

Cost: Adults-£36, £32.40 in advance online, £34 at Windsor TI; children-£27, £24 online or from TI; free for ages 2 and under; optional £10/person "Q-Bot" ride-reservation gadget allows you to bypass lines; coin lockers-£1.

Hours: Mid-July–Aug daily 10:00–19:00, Sept–Oct and April–mid-July Thu–Mon only and closes 1–2 hours earlier, closed Nov–mid-March except around Christmas, call or check website for exact schedule.

Information: Toll tel. 0871-222-2001, www.legoland.co.uk.

Getting There: A £4.50 round-trip shuttle bus runs from opposite Windsor's Theatre Royal on Thames Street, and from the Parish Church stop on High Street (2/hr). If day-tripping from London, ask about rail/shuttle/park admission deals from Paddington or Waterloo train stations. For drivers, the park is on B3022 Windsor/Ascot road, two miles southwest of Windsor and 25 miles west of London. Legoland is clearly signposted from the M3, M4, and M25 motorways. Parking is easy and free.

Eton College—Across the bridge from Windsor Castle, you'll find many post-castle tourists filing toward the most famous "public" (the equivalent of our "private") high school in Britain. Eton was founded in 1440 by King Henry VI; today it educates about 1,300 boys (ages 13–18), who live on campus. Eton has molded the characters of 18 prime ministers, as well as members of the royal family, most recently princes William and Harry. The college is sparse on sights, but the public is allowed into the schoolyard, chapel, cloisters, and the Museum of Eton Life (£6, access only by one-hour guided tour at 14:00 and 15:15; tours available mid-April–Sept Wed and Fri–Sun, daily June–July; Oct–Nov Wed and Fri only; closed late Nov–mid-April and about once a month for special events, so call ahead, no photos in chapel, no food or drink allowed, tel. 01753/671-177, www .etoncollege.com).

Boat Trips—Cruise up and down the Thames River for relaxing views of the castle, the village of Eton, Eton College, and the Royal Windsor Racecourse. Relax onboard and nibble a picnic (£5, family pass-£12.50, 40 min; mid-Feb–Oct roughly 2/hr daily 10:00–17:00; Nov Sat–Sun hourly 10:00–16:00, closed Mon–Fri; closed Dec–mid-Feb; tel. 01753/851-900, www.frenchbrothers .co.uk). The same company also offers a longer, two-hour circular trip (£8, 1–2/day).

Horse Racing—The horses race near Windsor every Monday evening at the Royal Windsor Racecourse (£8–18 entry, off A308 between Windsor and Maidenhead, tel. 01753/498-400, www .windsor-racecourse.co.uk). The romantic way to get there is by a 10-minute shuttle boat (£5.50 round-trip, see "Boat Trips," above). The famous Ascot Racecourse (described below) is also nearby.

Near Windsor

Ascot Racecourse—Located seven miles southwest of Windsor and just north of the town of Ascot, this royally owned racecourse is one of the most famous horse-racing venues in the world. Originally opened in 1711, it is best known for June's five-day Royal Ascot race meeting, attended by the Queen and 299,999 of her loyal subjects. For many, the outlandish hats worn on Ladies Day (Thursday) are more interesting than the horses. Royal Ascot is usually the third week in June (June 15–19 in 2010), and the pricey tickets go on sale the preceding November (see website for details). In addition to Royal Ascot, the racecourse runs the ponies year-round—funny hats strictly optional (regular tickets generally £10–20, online discounts, children 16 and under free; parking-£5–7, more for special races; dress code enforced in some areas and on certain days, toll tel. 0870-727-1234, www.ascot .co.uk).

Sleep Code

(£1 = about $1.60, country code: 44, area code 01753)
S = Single, **D** = Double/Twin, **T** = Triple, **Q** = Quad, **b** = bathroom,
s = shower only. Unless otherwise noted, credit cards are
accepted.

To help you sort easily through these listings, I've divided
the rooms into three categories based on the price for a
standard double room with bath:

$$$ Higher Priced—Most rooms £100 or more.
$$ Moderately Priced—Most rooms between £60-100.
$ Lower Priced—Most rooms £60 or less.

Sleeping in Windsor

Most visitors stay in London and do Windsor as a day trip. But
here are a few suggestions for those staying the night.

$$$ Mercure Castle Hotel, with 108 business-class rooms, is
as central as can be, just down the street from Her Majesty's week-
end retreat (Db-£120–165, non-refundable online deals, break-
fast-£16, air-con, free Wi-Fi, 18 High Street, tel. 01753/851-577,
www.mercure.com, h6618@accor.com).

$$ Langton House B&B is a stately Victorian home with
three well-appointed rooms lovingly maintained by Paul and Sonja
Fogg (Sb-£70, Db-£90, Tb-£110, Qb-£130, 5 percent extra if paying by credit card, family-friendly, guest kitchen, free Internet
access and Wi-Fi, 46 Alma Road, tel. & fax 01753/858-299, www
.langtonhouse.co.uk, paul@langtonhouse.co.uk).

$$ Park Farm B&B, bright and cheery, is convenient for
drivers visiting Legoland (Sb-£65, Db-£85, Tb-£95, Qb-£105,
ask about family room with bunk beds, cash only—credit card
solely for reservations, free Wi-Fi, pay phone in entry, access
to shared fridge and microwave, free off-street parking, 1 mile
from Legoland on St. Leonards Road near Imperial Road, 5-min
bus ride or 1.25-mile walk to castle, £4 taxi ride from station,
tel. 01753/866-823, www.parkfarm.com, stay@parkfarm.com,
Caroline and Drew Youds).

Eating in Windsor

Cornucopia Bistro, a favorite with locals, is a welcoming little
place two minutes from the TI and castle, just beyond the tour-
ist crush. They serve tasty international dishes with everything
proudly made from scratch. The hardwood floors add a rustic

elegance (£11 two-course lunches, £10–14 dinner entrées, Tue–Sat 12:00–14:30 & 18:00–21:30, Sun 12:00–14:30, closed Mon, 6 High Street, tel. 01753/833-009).

The Crooked House is a touristy 17th-century timber-frame teahouse, serving fresh, hearty £8–10 lunches and cream teas in a tipsy interior or outdoors on its cobbled lane (Mon–Fri 10:30–18:00, Sat–Sun 10:00–19:00, 51 High Street, tel. 01753/857-534). The important-looking building next door is the Guildhall, which hosted the weddings of both Prince Charles (to Camilla) and Elton John (to David Furnish). It's also the home of the town's public WC.

Wagamama offers modern Asian food, mostly in the form of noodle soups. The setting is informal and communal, much like its London siblings (£7–10 main dishes, Mon–Sat 12:00–23:00, Sun 12:00–22:00, just off High Street, on the left as you face the entrance to Windsor Royal Shopping Centre, tel. 01753/833-105, www.wagamama.com).

The Two Brewers Pub, tucked away near the top of Windsor Great Park's Long Walk, serves meals in a cozy Old World atmosphere. Befriend the barman and he may point out a minor royal (open for drinks Mon–Sat 11:30–23:00, Sun 12:00–22:30; lunch served Mon–Sat 12:00–14:00, Sun 12:00–16:00; dinner served Mon–Thu 18:00–22:00, appetizers only Fri–Sat 18:30–21:30, no evening meal on Sun, reservations smart for meals, kids under 18 must sit outside, 34 Park Street, tel. 01753/855-426).

CAMBRIDGE

Cambridge

Cambridge, 60 miles north of London, is world-famous for its prestigious university. Wordsworth, Isaac Newton, Tennyson, Darwin, and Prince Charles are a few of its illustrious alumni. The

university dominates—and owns—most of Cambridge, a historic town of 100,000 people that's more pleasant than its rival, Oxford. Cambridge is the epitome of a university town, with busy bikers, stately residence halls, plenty of bookshops, and proud locals who can point out where DNA was originally modeled, the atom was first split, and electrons were initially discovered.

In medieval Europe, higher education was the domain of the Church, and was limited to ecclesiastical schools. Scholars lived in "halls" on campus. This academic community of residential halls, chapels, and lecture halls connected by peaceful garden courtyards survives today in the colleges that make up the universities of Cambridge and Oxford. By 1350 (Oxford is roughly 100 years older), Cambridge had eight colleges, each with a monastic-type courtyard and lodgings. Today, Cambridge has 31 colleges. While students' lives revolve around their independent colleges, the university organizes lectures, presents degrees, and promotes research.

Planning Your Time

Cambridge is worth most of a day, but not an overnight. Arrive in time for the 11:30 walking tour—an essential part of any visit— and spend the afternoon touring King's College Chapel and Fitzwilliam Museum (closed Mon except Bank Holidays), or simply enjoying the ambience of this stately old college town.

The university schedule has three terms: the Lent term from mid-January to mid-March, the Easter term from mid-April to mid-June, and the Michaelmas term from early October to early December. The colleges are closed to visitors during exams—in mid-April and late June—but King's College Chapel and the Trinity Library stay open, and the town is never sleepy.

Getting to Cambridge

By Train: It's an easy trip from London, about an hour away. Catch the train from London's King's Cross Station (2/hr, fast trains leave at :15 and :45 past the hour and run in each direction, 45 min, £19 one-way standard class, £20 same-day return after 9:30, operated by First Capital Connect, toll tel. 0845-748-4950, www.firstcapitalconnect.co.uk or www.nationalrail.co.uk).

By Bus: National Express coaches run from London's Victoria Coach Station to the Parkside stop in Cambridge (hourly, 2–3 hrs, £11.50, toll tel. 0871-781-8181).

Orientation to Cambridge

(area code: 01223)

Cambridge is congested but small. Everything is within a pleasant walk. There are two main streets, separated from the river by the most interesting colleges. The town center, brimming with tearooms, has a TI and a colorful open-air market (clothes and food Mon–Sat 9:30–16:00; arts, crafts, and food Sun 9:30–16:30; on Market Square).

Cambridge

NOTE: Many Roads are Pedestrian or Restricted

- ⬜ Other Colleges (Not All Shown)
- P Parking
- --- Paths
- Ⓑ Bus Stops

1 Michaelhouse Café
2 Café Carradines
3 The Eagle Pub
4 Marks & Spencer
5 Sainsbury's
6 Trinity Punt
7 Scudamore's Punts (2)

Tourist Information

An info kiosk on the train station platform dispenses free city maps and sells fancier ones. If it's closed, you can buy a map from a machine using a £1 coin, or get a free one from the nearby bike-rental shop (see "Helpful Hints," below). The official TI is well-signposted, just off Market Square. They book rooms for £5, and sell bus tickets and a £0.30 mini-guide/map (Mon–Fri 10:00–17:30, Sat 10:00–17:00, Easter–Sept also Sun 11:00–15:00—otherwise closed Sun, phones answered from 9:00, Wheeler Street, tel. 01223/464-732 or toll 0871-226-8006, room-booking tel. 01223/457-581, www.visitcambridge.org).

Arrival in Cambridge

By Train: To get to downtown Cambridge from the train station, take a 25-minute walk (any free map can help), a £5 taxi ride, or bus marked *Citi1*, *Citi3*, or *Citi7* (£1.30, every 5–10 min).

By Car: Drivers can follow signs from the M11 motorway to any of the handy and central short-stay parking lots. Or you can leave the car at one of five park-and-ride lots outside the city, then take the shuttle into town (free parking, £2.50 shuttle, buy ticket from machine or driver).

Helpful Hints

Festival: The **Cambridge Folk Festival** gets things humming and strumming (likely July 29–Aug 1 in 2010, www.cambridge folkfestival.co.uk).

Bike Rental: Station Cycles, located about a half-block to your right as you exit the station, rents bikes (£8/half-day, helmets-50p, £50–75 deposit, cash or credit card) and stores luggage (£3–4/bag depending on size; Mon–Fri 8:00–18:00, Wed until 19:00, Sat 9:00–17:00, Sun 10:00–16:00, tel. 01223/307-125, www.stationcycles.co.uk). They have a second location near the center of town (inside the Grand Arcade, on Corn Exchange Street near Wheeler, Mon–Fri 8:00–19:00, Wed until 20:00, Sat 9:00–19:00, Sun 10:00–18:00, tel. 01223/307-655).

Tours in Cambridge

▲▲**Walking Tour of the Colleges**—A walking tour is the best way to understand Cambridge's mix of "town and gown." The walks provide a good rundown of the historic and scenic highlights of the university, as well as some fun local gossip.

The TI offers **daily walking tours** (£10, 2 hrs, includes admission to King's College Chapel if it's open; July–Aug daily at 10:30, 11:30, 13:30, and 14:30, no 10:30 tour Sun; April–June and Sept daily at 11:30 and 13:30; Oct–March Mon–Sat at 11:30 and 13:30, Sun at 13:30; tel. 01223/457-574, www.visitcambridge.org). Drop by the TI (the departure point) one hour early to snare a spot. If you're visiting on a Sunday, call the day before to reserve a spot with your credit card and confirm departure time.

Private guides are also available through the TI (basic 1-hour tour–£3.50/person, £50 minimum; 90-min tour–£4/person, £58 minimum; 2-hour tour–£4.50/person, £65 minimum; does not include individual college entrance fees, tel. 01223/457-574, www .visitcambridge.org).

Walking and Punting Ghost Tour—If you're in Cambridge on the weekend, consider a £5 ghost walk Friday evenings at 18:00, or a spooky £16 trip on the River Cam followed by a walk most Saturdays at 20:00 (book ahead for both, tel. 01223/457-574, www .visitcambridge.org).

Bus Tours—City Sightseeing hop-on, hop-off bus tours are informative and cover the outskirts, including the American WWII Cemetery (£12, 80 min for full 21-stop circuit, departs every 20 min in summer, every 40 min in winter, first bus leaves train station at 10:06, last bus at 17:46, recorded commentary with some live English-language guides, can use credit card to buy tickets in their office in train station, tel. 01223/423-578, www.city-sightseeing.com). Walking tours go where the buses can't—right into the center.

Sights in Cambridge

▲▲**King's College Chapel**—Built from 1446 to 1515 by Henrys VI through VIII, England's best example of Perpendicular Gothic is the single most impressive building in town. Stand inside, look up, and marvel, as Christopher Wren did, at what was the largest single span of vaulted roof anywhere—2,000 tons of incredible fan vaulting. Wander through the Old Testament, with 26 stained-glass windows from the 16th century, the most Renaissance stained glass anywhere in one spot. The windows were removed to keep them safe during World War II, and then painstakingly replaced. Walk to the altar and admire Peter Paul Rubens' masterful *Adoration of the Magi* (£5, erratic hours depending on school schedule and events; during academic term usually Mon–Fri 9:30–15:30, Sat 9:30–15:15, Sun 13:15–14:15; during breaks—see "Planning Your Time," earlier— it's open Mon–Sat 9:30–16:30, Sun 10:00–17:00). When school's in session, you're welcome to enjoy an evensong service (Mon–Sat at 17:30, Sun at 15:30, tel. 01223/331-212, recorded info tel. 01223/331-155, www.kings.cam.ac.uk/chapel).

▲▲**Trinity College and Wren Library**—Nearly half of Cambridge's 83 Nobel Prize winners have come from this richest and biggest of the town's colleges, founded in 1546 by Henry VIII. Don't miss the 1695 Wren-designed library, with its wonderful carving and fascinating original manuscripts. There's a small fee to visit the campus (£2.50), but if you just want to see Wren Library (free), enter from the riverside entrance, located by the Garret Hostel Bridge. The Wren Library should remain open during a planned renovation that may close the grounds through July 2010 (otherwise campus open daily 10:00–17:00; library open Mon–Fri 12:00–14:00, Nov–mid-June also Sat 10:30–12:30, always closed Sun and during exams; only 15 people allowed in at a time, tel. 01223/338-400, www.trin.cam.ac.uk). Just outside the library entrance, Sir Isaac Newton, who spent 30 years at Trinity, clapped his hands and timed the echo to measure the speed of sound as it raced down the side of the cloister and back. In the library's 12 display cases (covered with cloth that you flip back), you'll see handwritten works by Sir Isaac Newton and John Milton, alongside A. A. Milne's original *Winnie the Pooh* (the real Christopher Robin attended Trinity College).

▲▲Fitzwilliam Museum—Britain's best museum of antiquities and art outside of London is the Fitzwilliam. Enjoy its wonderful paintings (Old Masters and a fine English section featuring Gainsborough, Reynolds, Hogarth, and others, plus works by all the famous Impressionists), old manuscripts, and Greek, Egyptian, and Mesopotamian collections. Watch your step—a visitor tripped a few years ago and accidentally smashed three 17th-century Chinese vases. Amazingly, the vases were restored and are now on display in Gallery 17...in a protective case (free, audio/videoguide-£3, Tue–Sat 10:00–17:00, Sun 12:00–17:00, closed Mon except Bank Holidays, no photos, Trumpington Street, tel. 01223/332-900, www.fitzmuseum.cam.ac.uk).

Museum of Classical Archaeology—While this museum—reopening in spring 2010 after a renovation—contains no originals, it offers a unique chance to see accurate copies (19th-century casts) of virtually every famous ancient Greek and Roman statue. More than 450 statues are on display (free, likely Mon–Fri 10:00–17:00, sometimes also Sat 10:00–13:00 during term, closed Sun, Sidgwick Avenue, tel. 01223/330-402, www.classics.cam.ac.uk/museum). The museum is a five-minute walk west of Silver Street Bridge; after crossing the bridge, continue straight until you reach a sign marked *Sidgwick Site*. The museum is in the long building on the corner to your right; the entrance is on the opposite side.

▲Punting on the Cam—For a little levity and probably more exercise than you really want, try hiring one of the traditional flat-bottom punts at the river and poling yourself up and down (or around and around, more likely) the lazy Cam. Once you get the

hang of it, it's a fine way to enjoy the scenic side of Cambridge. It's less crowded in late afternoon (and less embarrassing).

Two companies rent punts and offer tours. **Trinity Punt,** just north of Garret Hostel Bridge, is run by Trinity College students (£12/hr, £40 deposit, 45-min tours-£30/boat, can share ride and cost with up to 2 others, cash only, ask for quick and free lesson, Easter–mid-Oct Mon–Fri 11:00–17:30, Sat–Sun 10:00–17:30, return punts by 18:30, no rentals mid-Oct–Easter, tel. 01223/338-483). **Scudamore's** has two locations: Mill Lane, just south of the central Silver Street Bridge, and the less-convenient Quayside at Magdalene Bridge, at the north end of town (£16–18/hr, £80 deposit required—can use credit card, 45-min tours-£14/person, save £2 by buying at TI, open daily June–Aug 9:00–22:00, Sept–May at least 10:00–17:00, weather permitting, tel. 01223/359-750, www.scudamores.com).

Near Cambridge

Imperial War Museum Duxford—This former airfield, nine miles south of Cambridge, is nirvana for aviation fans and WWII buffs. Wander through seven exhibition halls housing 200 vintage aircraft (including Spitfires, B-17 Flying Fortresses, a Concorde, and a Blackbird), as well as military land vehicles and special displays on Normandy and the Battle of Britain. On many weekends, the museum holds special events, such as air shows (extra fee)—check the website for details (£16, show local bus ticket for discount, daily mid-March–late Oct 10:00–18:00, late Oct–mid-March 10:00–16:00, last entry one hour before closing, tel. 01223/835-000, http://duxford.iwm.org.uk).

Getting There: The museum is located off A505 in Duxford. From Cambridge, you can take the bus marked *Citi7* from the train station (45 min) or from Emmanuel Street's Stop A (55 min; bus runs 2/hr Mon–Sat, www.stagecoachbus.com/cambridge). On Sundays and Bank Holidays, catch the #132 bus, run by private bus operator Myalls, from the train station or the Drummer Street bus station (40 min, first bus at about 10:00, then every 2 hours until 18:00, tel. 01763/243-225).

Eating in Cambridge

While picnicking is scenic and saves money, the weather may not always cooperate. Here are a few ideas for fortifying yourself in central Cambridge.

The **Michaelhouse Café** is a heavenly respite from the crowds, tucked into the repurposed St. Michael's Church, just north of Great St. Mary's Church. At lunch, choose from salads, soups, and sandwiches, as well as a few hot dishes and a variety of tasty baked goods (£5–10 light meals, £4 "fill your plate" special available 14:30–15:00, open Mon–Sat 8:00–17:00, breakfast served 8:00–11:30, lunch served 11:30–15:00, hot drinks and baked goods available all the time, closed Sun, Trinity Street, tel. 01223/309-147).

Café Carradines is a cozy cafeteria that serves traditional British food at reasonable prices, including a Sunday roast lunch for £7 (Mon–Sat 8:00–17:00, Sun 10:00–16:00, down the stairs at 23 Market Street, tel. 01223/361-792).

The Eagle Pub, near the TI, is a good spot for a quick drink or a pub lunch. Look at the carefully preserved ceiling in its "Air Force Bar," signed by local airmen during World War II. Science fans can also celebrate the discovery of DNA—Francis Crick and James Watson first announced their findings here in 1953 (Mon–Sat 11:00–23:00, Sun 12:00–22:30, food served 12:00–14:30 & 17:00–21:30, pleasant patio, 8 Benet Street, tel. 01223/505-020).

Supermarkets: There's a **Marks & Spencer Simply Food** grocery at the train station and a larger store at 6 Sidney Street (Mon–Sat 9:00–18:00, Sun 11:00–17:00, tel. 01223/355-219). **Sainsbury's** supermarket, with slightly longer hours, is at 44 Sidney Street, on the corner of Green Street. A good picnic spot is Laundress Green, a grassy park on the river, at the end of Mill Lane near the Silver Street Bridge punts. There are no benches, so bring something to sit on. Remember, the college lawns are private property, so walking or picnicking on the grass is generally not allowed. When in doubt, ask at the college's entrance.

Cambridge Connections

From Cambridge by Train to: York (hourly, 2.5 hrs, transfer in Peterborough), **Oxford** (2/hr, 2.5 hrs, change in London involves Tube transfer between train stations), **London** (3/hr, 1 hr). Train info: Toll tel. 0845-748-4950, www.nationalrail.co.uk.

By Bus to: London (hourly, 2–3 hrs), **Heathrow Airport** (1–2/hr, 2–3 hrs). Bus info: Toll tel. 0871-781-8181, www.national express.com.

CANTERBURY

Canterbury is one of England's most important religious destinations. For centuries, it has welcomed hordes of pilgrims to its grand cathedral. While these days you'll probably see more iPods than Bibles in this college town, Canterbury's cathedral and medieval core still beckon with rich history and architectural splendor.

Pleasant, walkable Canterbury, like many cities in southern England, was originally founded by the pagan Romans. Then along came St. Augustine, sent by the pope to convert England's King Ethelbert of Kent to Christianity. Ethelbert (who had a Christian wife) joined the Church and allowed St. Augustine to set up a monastery on the edge of town. As Christianity became more established in England, Canterbury became its center, and the Archbishop of Canterbury emerged as one of the country's most powerful men.

The famous pilgrimages to Canterbury began in the 12th century, after the assassination of Archbishop Thomas Becket by followers of King Henry II (with whom Becket had been in a long fight). Becket was canonized as a martyr, rumors of miracles at the cathedral spread, and flocks of pilgrims showed up at its doorstep. Along the way, they'd stop off at inns and entertain each other with tales—sometimes bawdy and just for fun, sometimes devout and meaningful.

Today, much of the medieval city—heavily bombed during World War II—exists only in fragments. Miraculously, the cathedral and surrounding streets are fairly well-preserved. Thanks to its huge student population and thriving pedestrian-and-shopper-friendly zone in the center, Canterbury is an exceptionally livable and fun-to-visit town.

Planning Your Time

Because of its impressive cathedral, compact tourist zone, and relaxing break-from-a-big-city ambience, Canterbury is an ideal day trip from London. With more time, it merits an overnight. (You could even come straight from the airport to Canterbury and sleep here for two nights, with a day of sightseeing.) If visiting for a few hours, head straight for the cathedral, then spend the rest of your time strolling the town's pleasant pedestrian core, and maybe drop into some of Canterbury's other sights. Consider sticking around for an evensong in the cathedral (Mon–Fri at 17:30, Sat–Sun generally at 15:15).

Ambitious sightseers can fit both Canterbury and Dover (see next chapter) into a hectic one-day trip from London: Take an early train to Dover, taxi to Dover Castle, munch a picnic lunch on the train to Canterbury, tour Canterbury Cathedral, then enjoy the evensong and dinner in Canterbury before returning by train to London.

Orientation to Canterbury

(area code: 01227)

With about 45,000 people, Canterbury is big enough to be lively but small enough to be manageable. The center of town is enclosed by the old city walls, a ring road, and the Stour River to the west. High Street (also known as St. Peter's Street at one end and St. George's Street at the other) bisects the town center. During the day, the action is on High Street and in the knot of medieval lanes surrounding the cathedral. (At night, the city is quiet all around.) The center is walkable—it's only about 20 minutes on foot from one end to the other.

Tourist Information

The TI, in front of Christ Church Gate, assists modern-day pilgrims. Pick up the free Visitors Guide with a map (March–Oct Mon–Sat 9:30–17:00, July–Aug until 18:00, Sun 10:00–16:00; Nov–Feb Mon–Sat 10:00–16:00, closed Sun; 12–13 Sun Street, tel. 01227/378-100, www.canterbury.co.uk).

Combo-Ticket: The TI sells a "Canterbury Attractions Passport" that covers the cathedral, St. Augustine's Abbey, the Canterbury Tales audio-visual show, and either the Roman Museum or another lesser sight. It's a good deal only if you plan to see everything (£18.50, saves about £3.50, sold only at TI).

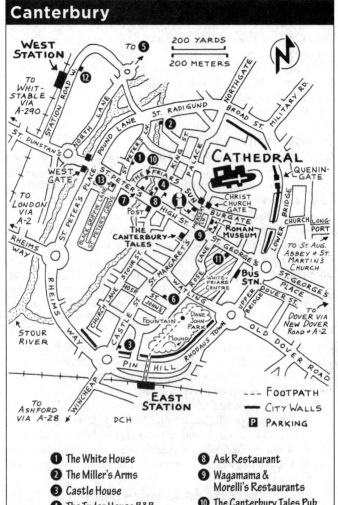

Canterbury

200 YARDS
200 METERS

- **1** The White House
- **2** The Miller's Arms
- **3** Castle House
- **4** The Tudor House B&B
- **5** To Harriet House & Bike Rental
- **6** St. John's Court Guest House
- **7** Old Weavers House Rest.
- **8** Ask Restaurant
- **9** Wagamama & Morelli's Restaurants
- **10** The Canterbury Tales Pub
- **11** Marks & Spencer (Supermarket)
- **12** Farmers Market
- **13** Pure Magick Shop (Internet Access)

- - - FOOTPATH
— CITY WALLS
P PARKING

Arrival in Canterbury

Canterbury's two train stations (East and West) flank the town center. Trains from London's Victoria Station arrive at Canterbury's East Station; trains from London's Charing Cross Station arrive at Canterbury's West Station. Each train station is about a 10-minute walk from downtown. The bus station is at the end of the High Street pedestrian area, inside the city walls just past the big Whitefriars shopping center.

Helpful Hints

Guided Walk: The **Canterbury Guild of Guides** offers a 1.5-hour walk departing from the TI (£5, April–Oct daily at 14:00, July–Aug also at 11:30, www.canterbury-walks.co.uk).

Internet Access: For patchouli-scented surfing, drop by the New Agey **Pure Magick** shop, which has three resident ghosts and two Internet terminals upstairs (£3/hr, Mon–Sat 10:00–17:00, Sun 11:00–15:00, on the main shopping drag at 43A St. Peter's Street, tel. 01227/780-000).

Shopping: A **Marks & Spencer** department store, with a supermarket at the back on the ground floor, is located near the end of High Street (Mon–Sat 9:00–19:00, Sun 11:00–17:00). Sprawling behind it is a vast shopping complex called **Whitefriars Centre** (most shops open Mon–Sat 9:00–17:30, Sun 11:00–16:00). A modest **farmers market** is held every day except Monday at The Goods Shed (Tue–Sat 9:00–19:00, Sun 10:00–16:00), just to the north of the West Station, adjacent to the parking lot.

Bike Rental: Downland Cycles rents and repairs bikes (£15/day, helmets-£3, up the street from the West Station in the Malthouse on St. Stephen's Road, tel. 01227/479-643, www.downland cycles.co.uk). For a pleasant daylong ride in the countryside, ask for a map of the Crab and Winkle Way, a popular biking trail from Canterbury to the charming fishing village of Whitstable.

Sights in Canterbury

▲▲▲Canterbury Cathedral

This grand landmark of piety, one of the most important churches in England, is the headquarters of the Anglican Church—in terms of church administration, it's something like the English Vatican. It's been a Christian site ever since St. Augustine, the cathedral's first archbishop, broke ground in 597. In the 12th century, the cathedral became world-famous because of an infamous act: the murder of its then-archbishop, Thomas Becket. Canterbury became a

prime destination for religious pilgrims, trumped in importance only by Rome and Santiago de Compostela, Spain. The dramatic real-life history of Canterbury Cathedral is the tale of two King Henrys (Henry II and Henry VIII), and of the martyred Becket.

Cost and Hours: £7.50, Easter–Oct Mon–Sat 9:00–17:30, Sun 12:30–14:00, slightly shorter hours Nov–Easter, last entry 30 min before closing, tel. 01227/762-862, www.canterbury-cathedral.org.

Tours and Information: Guides wearing golden sashes are posted throughout the cathedral to answer your questions. Guided £4.50 tours are offered Mon–Fri at 10:30, 12:00, and 14:30 (14:00 in winter); and Sat at 10:30, 12:00, and 13:30 (no tours Sun). At the shop inside the cathedral, you can rent a dry but informative £3.50 audioguide.

Evensong: The choral evensong is easy even for atheists. As you enter, they'll hand you a laminated placard telling you what to say for group responses, when to sit and stand, and when the music begins (free, Mon–Fri at 17:30, Sat–Sun at 15:15). Weekend schedules are subject to change, so it's smart to stop by or call to confirm (tel. 01227/762-862).

◉ Self-Guided Tour: Although you can take a guided tour or rent an audioguide, it's simple just to wander through on your own.

• *Begin your tour in the pedestrian shopping zone just outside the cathedral grounds, by the TI. Before going through the passageway, take a moment to appreciate the...*

Christ Church Gate: This highly decorated gate is the cathedral yard's main entrance. Find the royal seals and symbols on the gate, including the Tudor rose. This rose was the symbol of Henry VIII, who—shortly after the Christ Church Gate was built—divorced both his wife and the Vatican, establishing the Anglican Church.

• *Go through the gate (where you'll buy your ticket) and walk into the courtyard that surrounds this massive, impressive church. Examine the...*

Cathedral Exterior: Notice the cathedral's length, and how each section is distinctive. The church was already considered large in pre-pilgrim days, but in the 15th century, builders began another 100 years of construction (resulting in a patchwork effect that you'll notice in the interior).

• *Enter the church through the side door—the front doors of English cathedrals tend to be used only for special occasions—and pick up a map at the desk before you take a seat in the...*

Nave: The interior of the nave shows the inner workings of this sprawling, eclectic structure. Look around, and you'll see a church that's had many incarnations. Archaeological excavations in the early 1990s showed that the building's core is Roman. Through

Thomas Becket and Canterbury Cathedral

In the 12th century, Canterbury Cathedral had already been a Christian church for more than 500 years. The king at the time was Henry II (who rebuilt and expanded nearby Dover Castle, described in the next chapter). Henry was looking for a new archbishop, someone who would act as a yes-man and allow him to gain control of the Church (and its followers). He found a candidate in his drinking buddy and royal chancellor: Thomas Becket (also called Thomas à Becket). In 1162, the king's friend was consecrated as archbishop.

THE LIFE AND DEATH OF THOMAS BECKET

But Becket surprised the king, and maybe even himself. Inspired by his new position—and wanting to be a true religious leader to his mighty flock—he cleaned up his act, became dedicated to the religious tenets of the Church (dressing as a monk), and refused to bow to the king's wishes. As tensions grew, Henry wondered aloud, "Will no one rid me of this turbulent priest?" Four knights took his words seriously, and assassinated Becket during vespers in the cathedral. The act shocked the medieval world. King Henry later submitted to walking barefoot through town while being flogged by priests as an act of pious penitence.

Not long after Becket's death in 1170, word spread that miracles were occurring in the cathedral, prompting the pope to canonize Becket. Soon the pilgrims came, hoping some of Becket's steadfast goodness would rub off (and perhaps wanting, too, to see the world—just like travelers today).

CANTERBURY

the ages, new sections were added on, with the biggest growth during the 1400s, when the cathedral had to be expanded to hold all of its pilgrims.

While tourists still flock here, this is also a working church, the headquarters of the Anglican Church, and the seat of the Archbishop of Canterbury. The current archbishop, Rowan Williams, has made headlines with his liberal and accepting views on homosexuality and the ordination of women, as well as his concern about Britain's involvement in the Iraq War. He's been quoted as saying that creationism should not be taught in schools.

• *From here, we'll follow the route laid out by the map you picked up when you entered. Head up the left aisle. When you get to the quire*

(marked by a beautifully carved stone portal in the center of the nave),
go down the stairs to the left. On the landing is the...

Thomas Becket Memorial: This is where Thomas Becket
was martyred. You'll see a humble plaque and a wall sculpture of
lightning-rod arrows pointing to the
place where he died.

• *Continue down the stairs next to the*
memorial and enter the...

Crypt: Notice the heavy stone
arches. This lower section was started
by the Normans, who probably built
on top of St. Augustine's original
church. Cross over to the other (right)
side of the crypt. The small chapel
marked *Église Protestante Française*
celebrates a Mass in French every
Sunday at 15:00. This chapel has been
used for hundreds of years by French
(Huguenot) and Belgian (Walloon) Protestant communities, who
fled persecution in their home countries for the more welcoming
atmosphere in Protestant England.

• *Facing this chapel, turn right, walk to the end of the crypt, and climb*
up the stairs. At the landing, turn left to find...

St. Michael's Chapel: Also known as the Warrior's Chapel,
this was built by Lady Margaret Holland (d. 1439) to house family tombs. The chapel is also associated with the Royal East Kent
Regiment ("The Buffs"). Notice the bell on the wall to the left,
which once rang from the HMS *Canterbury,* a ship that waged
war against those disobedient colonists during the American
Revolution. Each day at 11:00, the bell is rung and a prayer is said
here to honor those who have lost their lives in battle.

• *Head up the stairs across from the tomb, and go through the ornate*
stone portal we passed earlier. This will bring you into the **quire,** *where*
the choir sings evensong. Walk toward the high altar, then turn left
through the gate and walk with the quire on your right to the far end of
the church (the apse). Behind the quire, you'll see a candle in the center of
the floor. This was the site of the...

Original Becket Shrine: Beginning in the 12th century,
hundreds of thousands of pilgrims came to this site to leave offerings. Imagine this site in the Dark Ages. You're surrounded by
humble, devout pilgrims who've trudged miles upon miles to reach
this spot. (Try to ignore the B.O.) Now that they've finally arrived,
they're hoping to soak up just a bit of the miraculous power that's
supposed to reside here.

Then came King Henry VIII, who broke away from the pope
so he could marry on his own terms. In 1538, he destroyed the

original altar (and lots more, including the original abbey on the edge of town). Dictatorial Henry VIII—no fan of a priest who would stand up to a king—had Thomas Becket's body removed from the cathedral. Legend says that Henry had Becket's body burned and the ashes scattered as part of his plan to drive religious pilgrims away from the site.

• Adjacent to the shrine, in the apse, is the...

Tomb of the Black Prince: This is the final resting place of the Black Prince, Edward of Woodstock (d. 1376). The Prince of Wales and the eldest son of Edward III, the Black Prince was famous for his cunning in battle and his chivalry—the original "knight in shining armor."

Our tour is finished. As you leave the cathedral, consider this: Even with all their power, wealth, and influence, two English kings were unable to successfully eradicate Thomas Becket's influence (if they had, the line to get into the cathedral would be shorter). A man of conscience—who once stood up to the most powerful ruler in England—continues to inspire visitors, even a thousand years after his death.

More Sights in the Old Town

▲**The Canterbury Tales**—If your visit to Canterbury gives you English Lit flashbacks, this corny audio-visual show offers a good review—or, if you're unfamiliar with Chaucer, it provides a decent introduction. Making use of creepy mannequins, primitive lighting effects, and medieval smells, it dramatizes five of the tales. More hokey than literary, the exhibit is useful as a CliffsNotes to Chaucer's masterpiece (£7.75, includes audioguide, daily 10:00–17:00, July–Aug from 9:30, Nov–Feb until 16:30, St. Margaret's Street, tel. 01227/479-227, www.canterburytales.org.uk).

Roman Museum—The colorful displays in this slight museum illustrate Canterbury's Roman origins and end with a view of sections of still-intact foundations and mosaics. Included are several shamelessly self-congratulatory exhibits celebrating the museum archaeologist...nice touch (£3, Mon–Sat 10:00–17:00, in summer also open Sun 13:30–17:00, last entry one hour before closing, two doors down from Gap store at Butchery Lane, tel. 01227/785-575, www.canterbury-museums.co.uk).

East of the Old Town

While historically significant, these two sights—about a 10-minute walk east of the Old Town walls—aren't worth the trek for most visitors.

St. Augustine's Abbey—These ruins of the original abbey—founded by the man himself, St. Augustine—sit right on the edge of town. At its height, the abbey was a hive of activity, with a large

The Canterbury Tales

*"Whan that Aprill, with his shoures soote /
The droghte of March hath perced to the roote..."*

So begins *The Canterbury Tales,* one of the earliest and most influential works of English literature. In the late 14th century, author and diplomat Geoffrey Chaucer (c. 1343–1400) was so inspired by the cross-section of humanity undertaking the pilgrimage to Canterbury that he penned a collection of 24 tales told by fictional travelers. *The Canterbury Tales* is arguably the oldest surviving travelogue, and the greatest work written in the Middle English vernacular—a bold move at a time when Latin and French were the literary languages of choice. (Because Middle English is essentially a different language—see the first two lines, above—the work is most often read today in present-day English translation.)

Chaucer demonstrates an impressive range of themes and genres within these tales, ranging from tragedy to romance to humor. *The Canterbury Tales* is a microcosm of human experience, featuring yarns spun by people from diverse walks of life: knight, miller, cook, lawyer, wife, merchant, squire, physician, monk, nun. Despite their obvious differences, all of these travelers were drawn together by a shared faith and the desire to experience the power of the shrine of Thomas Becket...and by a mutual appreciation for a good story.

church, cloister, and a cluster of service buildings for the monks. In the 16th century, King Henry VIII grew jealous of the wealth and influence held by England's monks, so he closed down the monasteries, retired the monks, and sold off the land and buildings. The abbey's buildings were converted to houses, while the large church was slowly dismantled and used as a building-material quarry for projects in the area.

Today, the site is dull even compared to other ruined abbeys. A modest museum sets up your visit. Outside, the foundations and some fragments of the original structures are still visible in a grassy field, and the uninspired audioguide struggles to bring the site to life. Pace the square of the cloister and imagine yourself as a monk in the early days of Christianity in England (£4.10, includes audioguide; April–June Wed–Sun 10:00–17:00, closed Mon–Tue; July–Aug daily 10:00–18:00; Sept–March Sat–Sun 11:00–16:00, closed Mon–Fri; tel. 01227/767-345).

St. Martin's Church—Set in the center of an old, slanted graveyard, humble little St. Martin's has the honor of being the oldest parish church in England. In continual use since 650, it sits on the foundations of a Roman temple, and features an elegant

Norman-era baptismal font to the right of the entrance (generally open Tue, Thu, and Sat 11:00–15:00; tel. 01227/462-686 or 01227/768-072). Because the church is run by volunteers, it has very sporadic hours, so call to confirm. To find the church, continue on the busy road 100 yards past the abbey, and turn down the first real road to the left (North Holmes Road); you'll see the churchyard's wooden entry gate from the main road.

Sleeping in Canterbury

Canterbury is a pleasant college town with lots of shops, restaurants, and pubs, making it a fine home base. There are relatively few options within the old walls, but I've listed my favorites. The roads heading out of town, particularly New Dover Road, have clusters of B&Bs that are slim on charm but suitable for tired drivers.

$$$ The White House is a classy and elegant B&B. Its seven recently renovated rooms, on a quiet residential lane just two blocks from the bustle of High Street, offer more modern flair than other Canterbury options in this price range (Sb-£55, Db-£75–105 depending on size, 6 St. Peter's Lane, tel. 01227/761-836, www.whitehousecanterbury.co.uk, info@whitehousecanterbury.co.uk, Alison and Gary).

$$$ The Miller's Arms offers 11 comfy rooms adjacent to a cozy pub and restaurant, on a quiet street across from the Stour River (Sb-£65, Db-£80–100, Wi-Fi, parking-£5/day, 2 Mill Lane, tel. 01227/456-057, fax 01227/452-421, www.millerscanterbury.co.uk, millersarms@shepherdneame.co.uk, Declan and Amy).

$$$ Castle House, a 10-minute walk from the cathedral, has 13 spacious, inn-like rooms. It overlooks a major roundabout, but the double-glazed windows keep noise to a minimum (Sb-£75, Db-£81–86, family apartment-£97–110, free Internet access and Wi-Fi, free parking, 28 Castle Street, tel. 01227/761-897, www.castlehousehotel.co.uk, enquiries@castlehousehotel.co.uk).

$$ The Tudor House B&B has eight slanted-floor, older-feeling, Victorian-wallpaper rooms in a 1600s home. Located in Canterbury's center, just two blocks from the cathedral, it has a garden with a river view (S-£32, Sb-£50, D-£59, Db-£69, T-£73–75, 6 Best Lane, tel. & fax 01227/765-650, www.tudorhousecanterbury.co.uk, tudor.house@hotmail.com, Mazi Gerogan and Mamad Arabnia).

$$ Harriet House, a 15-minute walk from the town center, offers five tidy, small rooms. Gracious owners John (a picture framer) and Beryl (a reflexologist) will make you feel right at home. Enjoy the beautiful garden and tiny pond (Sb-£38–45, Db-£55–70, some road noise, parking, 3 Broad Oak Road, tel. 01227/457-363,

Sleep Code

(£1 = about \$1.60, country code: 44, area code: 01227)
S = Single, **D** = Double/Twin, **T** = Triple, **Q** = Quad, **b** = bathroom,
s = shower only. You can assume credit cards are accepted
and breakfast is included unless otherwise noted.

To help you sort easily through these listings, I've divided
the rooms into three categories based on the price for a
standard double room with bath:

\$\$\$ **Higher Priced**—Most rooms £80 or more.
\$\$ **Moderately Priced**—Most rooms between £45-80.
\$ **Lower Priced**—Most rooms £45 or less.

fax 01227/470-507, www.harriethouse.co.uk, merryjb@supanet
.com).

\$ St. John's Court Guest House has an ideal location on a
quiet street in the center of town. No-nonsense Liz Rowe rents
eight basic but bright rooms (all with shared bathrooms down the
hall) in a quaint brick building (S-£25–30, D-£45, T-£65, cash
only, no young children, parking, St. John's Lane, tel. 01227/456-
425, nigelnrw@aol.com).

Eating in Canterbury

As a student town, Canterbury is packed with eateries—especially
along the pedestrianized shopping zone. However, most places
serve only lunch, leaving options pretty thin for dinner. Of these
listings, only Morelli's is closed for dinner.

Old Weavers House serves solid English food in a pleasant,
historic building along the river. Sit inside beneath sunny walls

and creaky beams, or outside
on their riverside garden patio.
This is the most atmospheric
of my listings (£6–7 lunch specials, £9–16 dinner plates, daily
10:30–23:00, 1 St. Peter's Street,
tel. 01227/464-660).

Ask, over a small bridge from
Old Weavers House, is in a renovated home. This chain restaurant
offers decent Italian food at moderate prices. The garden in back,
while pleasant, lacks the Old Weavers House's river view (£8–10
meals, daily 12:00–23:00, big and splittable salads and pasta bowls,
24 High Street, tel. 01227/767-617).

Wagamama, part of the wildly popular British chain known for slinging delicious pan-Asian fare, has a convenient location just off the main shopping street (£6–10 main dishes, daily 12:00–22:00, 7–11 Longmarket Street, tel. 01227/454-307, www.wagamama.com).

Morelli's Restaurant serves typical soups and sandwiches with take-away options. You'll find it above the recommended Wagamama on Longmarket Street, with glassy indoor seating or fine outdoor tables (£4–5 light lunches, daily 9:00–17:00, tel. 01227/784-700).

Pubs: **The Canterbury Tales,** across from the Marlowe Theater, has a relaxed living-room atmosphere, but serves no food (Mon–Wed 17:00–24:00, Thu–Fri 15:00–24:00, Sat 12:00–24:00, closed Sun, 12 The Friars, tel. 01227/768-594).

Canterbury Connections

Remember that Canterbury has two train stations, East and West.

From Canterbury by Train to: London (4/hr direct, 1.5 hrs, trains run between the Canterbury West Station and London's Charing Cross Station and also between the Canterbury East Station and London's Victoria Station), **Dover** (2/hr, 15–30 min, between Canterbury East and Dover Priory), **Rye** (hourly, 1 hr, from Canterbury West, transfer at Ashford International), **Hastings** (hourly, 1 hr, from Canterbury West, transfer at Ashford International), **Brighton** (2/hr, 2.5–3 hrs, 1–3 transfers, complicated but possible—best connections through London's Victoria Station or Ashford International, from Canterbury East or West). Train info: tel. 0845-748-4950, www.nationalrail.co.uk.

By Bus to: London's Victoria Coach Station (hourly, 2–2.5 hrs), **Dover** (hourly, 40 min). Bus info: toll tel. 0870-781-8181, www.nationalexpress.com.

DOVER AND SOUTHEAST ENGLAND

Dover—like much of southern England—sits on a foundation of chalk. Miles of cliffs stand at attention above the beaches; the most famous are the White Cliffs of Dover. Sitting above those cliffs is the impressive Dover Castle, England's primary defensive stronghold from Roman through modern times. From the nearby port, ferries, hydrofoils, and hovercrafts shuttle people and goods back and forth across the English Channel. France is only 23 miles away—on a sunny day, you can see it off in the distance.

Because of its easy access from the Continent, many travelers have a sentimental attachment to Dover as the first place they saw in England. But in recent years—especially since the opening of the English Channel Tunnel in 1994—this workaday town has lost whatever luster it once had. The run-down town center isn't worth a second look. Focus instead on a fun in-and-out visit to Dover's looming castle, standing guard as it has for almost a thousand years. Geologists and romantics may want to take a cruise to get the best view of the famous White Cliffs. (Or, for a more rural and idyllic white cliff experience, visit Beachy Head near Brighton—described on page 230.)

In the southeast English countryside near Dover, you can explore a castle and charming cottage garden at Sissinghurst; stroll the cobbles of the huggable hill town of Rye; and visit the Battle of Hastings site—in the appropriately named town of Battle—where England's future course was charted in 1066.

Planning Your Time

Dover works best as a day trip from Canterbury or London, and is worth a quick visit if you're passing through anyway. Ambitious sightseers can tackle both Dover and Canterbury as a one-day side-trip from London (see page 192).

Orientation to Dover

(area code: 01304)
Gritty, urban-feeling Dover seems bigger than its population of 30,000. The town lies between two cliffs, with Dover Castle on one side and the Western Heights on the other. While the streets stretch longingly toward the water, the core of the town is cut off from the harbor by the rumbling A20 highway (connecting Dover with cities to the west) and a long, eyesore apartment building. Unless you're taking a boat somewhere, or are interested in the goings-on of a busy industrial harbor, there's not much reason to visit the waterfront. Biggin Street is the town's nondescript, mostly pedestrianized shopping area, running between Market Square and Town Hall.

Tourist Information

You'll find the TI in the center of town, attached to the old jail. They sell ferry and bus tickets, and book rooms for a £4 fee (June–Aug daily 9:00–17:30; April–May and Sept Mon–Fri 9:00–17:30, Sat–Sun 10:00–16:00; Oct–March Mon–Fri 9:00–17:30, Sat 10:00–16:00, closed Sun; Old Town Gaol, Biggin Street, tel. 01304/205-108, www.whitecliffscountry.org.uk).

Arrival in Dover

Trains arrive on the west side of town, a five-minute walk from the main pedestrian area and the TI. **Drivers** find that parking is plentiful close to the water—just follow *P* signs. If you arrive by **boat** at the Eastern Docks, walk about 15 minutes along the cliff into town (with the sea on your left), or catch a shuttle bus to the train station (3/hr, daily 7:00–21:00).

Sights in Dover

▲▲Dover Castle

A powerful castle perches grandly atop the White Cliffs of Dover. English troops were garrisoned within the castle's medieval walls for almost 900 years, protecting the coast from European invaders (a record of military service rivaled only by Windsor Castle and the Tower of London). With a medieval Great Keep as its centerpiece and battlements that survey 360 degrees of windswept

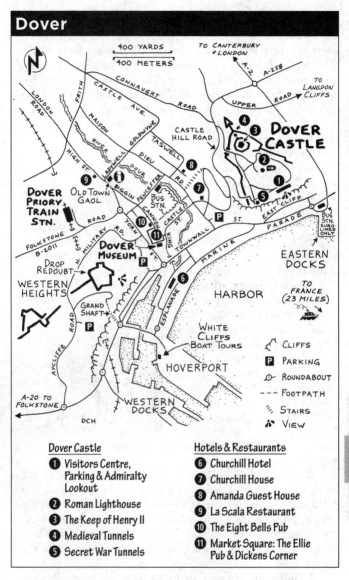

Dover

400 YARDS
400 METERS

Dover Castle
❶ Visitors Centre, Parking & Admiralty Lookout
❷ Roman Lighthouse
❸ The Keep of Henry II
❹ Medieval Tunnels
❺ Secret War Tunnels

Hotels & Restaurants
❻ Churchill Hotel
❼ Churchill House
❽ Amanda Guest House
❾ La Scala Restaurant
❿ The Eight Bells Pub
⓫ Market Square: The Ellie Pub & Dickens Corner

coast, Dover Castle has undeniable majesty. Today, the biggest invading menaces are the throngs of school kids on field trips, so it's best to arrive early. While the historic parts of the castle are unexceptional, the tour of the WWII-era Secret War Tunnels is unique and engaging.

Cost, Hours, Information: £10, £25 family ticket; April–Sept daily 10:00–18:00; Oct daily 10:00–17:00; Nov–Jan Thu–Mon

10:00–16:00, closed Tue–Wed; Feb–March daily 10:00–16:00; tel. 01304/211-067, www.english-heritage.org.uk/dovercastle. Arrive early for the fewest crowds (busiest on summer bank holidays and weekends). When you buy your ticket, ask for an assigned entry time for the included Secret War Tunnels tour—they fill up quickly in high season (generally lasts about 45 min, runs every 10–20 min but can be booked up for hours in advance—or sold out entirely by midday on very busy summer days, 20 people max, last tour departs one hour before closing). Your assigned time will be written on your entry ticket.

Getting There: Once in Dover, getting up to the castle is tricky. Bus #15 departs hourly from the bus station (on Pencester Road) and heads up to the castle. Otherwise, you can take a taxi from downtown (about £5 one-way) or hoof it up the steep hill (30–45 min straight up). By the time you get to the top, you'll know why no invading army ever successfully took the castle. The hike back down is easier, of course—ask for walking directions (using shortcut staircases) at the castle's Visitors Centre before you leave.

Getting Around the Castle: The sporadic and free "land train" does a constant loop around the castle's grounds, shuttling visitors between the Secret War Tunnels, the entrance to the Great Keep, and the Medieval Tunnels (at the lower end of the castle). Though handy for avoiding the ups and downs, the train doesn't run every day. Nothing at the castle is more than a 10-minute walk from anything

else—so you'll likely spend more time waiting for the train than you would walking.

Background: A linchpin for English defense starting in the Middle Ages, Dover Castle was heavily used in the time of Henry VIII and Elizabeth I. After a period of decline, the castle was reinvigorated during the Napoleonic Wars, and became a central command in World War II (when naval headquarters were buried deep in the cliffside). Dover Castle was only retired from active duty in 1984.

❍ Self-Guided Tour: Start your tour of strategically located Dover Castle, considered "the key to England" by potential invaders, near the Visitors Centre where you purchased your ticket. Here you can also pick up a free map describing the sights, including the Battlements Walk—a great addition if time allows. Adjust the order of this tour based on your assigned time for the Secret War Tunnels.

• *Leave the Visitors Centre to the right, and walk around the officers' barracks to find a grassy slope overlooking...*

Admiralty Lookout: The White Cliffs of Dover are directly beneath you. Take in the superb view across the Channel. Can you see France from here? The statue is of British Admiral Sir Bertram Ramsay, who heroically orchestrated the "Miracle of Dunkirk" by rescuing hundreds of thousands of surrounded Allied troops from the French coast during World War II. You'll learn more about him in the Secret War Tunnels.

• *Backtrack past the Visitors Centre, and hike up the path through the guard tower. Emerging on the other side of the guard tower, look up the hill to your right. The round tower behind the flagpole is the oldest structure at the castle, the...*

Roman Lighthouse: The lighthouse *(pharos)* was built during the first century A.D., when Julius Caesar's Roman fleet for the colony of Britannia was based in the harbor below. To guide the boats, they burned wet wood by day (for maximum smoke), and dry wood by night (for maximum light). When the Romans finally left England 400 years later, the *pharos* is said to have burst into flames as the last ship departed. Adjacent to the lighthouse is the unimpressive St. Mary-in-the-Castle Church, built to guard against invading Saxons in the sixth century.

• *Continue to the Great Keep. Pass through the archway and into the courtyard of...*

The Keep of Henry II: The heart of this frontier fortress first

beat in 1066, when a castle was built here after the Battle of Hastings (see sidebar on page 214). In the 12th century, King Henry II (the bad guy in the Thomas Becket story—see page 196 in the Canterbury chapter) added heavy castle fortifications. For centuries, Dover Castle was the most secure fortress in all

of England, and an important symbol of royal might on the coast.

Examine the central building, which was the original keep: The walls are up to 20 feet thick. King Henry II slept on the top floor, surrounded by his best protection against an invading army. Imagine the attempt: As the thundering enemy cavalry makes its advance, the king's defenders throw caltrops (four-starred metal spikes meant to cut through the horses' hooves). His knights unsheathe their swords, and trained crossbow archers ring the keep, sending arrows into foreign armor. Later kings added buildings near the keep (along the inner bailey, which lines the keep yard) to garrison troops during war and provide extra rooms for royal courtiers during peacetime.

Inside the keep, on the second floor, you'll find a sparse, kid-oriented exhibit (with sound effects) that gives a sense of what the castle was like in King Henry VIII's time. Find the well, which helped make the keep even more siege-resistant. Fans of Thomas Becket can look for his chapel, a tiny sacristy called the "upper chapel." If you're feeling energetic, climb all the way to the top of the keep's spiral staircase for a sweeping view of the city and sea beyond. Outside, back at ground level, you'll find the entrance to a somewhat silly 12-minute multimedia show that re-creates a 1216 siege on the castle.

• *After leaving the keep, walk a few paces across the courtyard to the...*

Garrison: This structure surrounding the keep once housed knights and men-at-arms. It's now home to the vaguely interesting Princess of Wales's Royal Regiment and Queen's Regiment Museum, a collection of military memorabilia (sorry, no Princess Diana items).

• *Exit the keep yard at the far end through the King's Gate. You'll cross a stone bridge and then descend a wooden staircase. Under these stairs is the entrance to the...*

Medieval Tunnels: This system of tunnels was originally built in case of a siege. While enjoyable for a kid-in-a-castle experience, there's actually little to see in these tunnels. From here, you can catch the tourist train (if it's running) or do the battlements walk. Much of Dover's success as a defendable castle came from these unique concentric walls—the battlements—which protected the inner keep.

• *There's one more thing to see, and it's the castle's undisputed highlight: the Secret War Tunnels. If the "land train" is running today, you can wait for it; otherwise walk (about 10 min total) along the inside of the castle's outer wall (with the wall on your right) and through the gate. Continue along the wall until you reach the entrance to the...*

Secret War Tunnels: In the 1790s, with the threat of Napoleon  looming, the castle's fortifications were beefed up again. So many troops were stationed here that they needed to tunnel into the chalk to provide sleeping areas for up to 2,000 men. These tunnels were vastly expanded during World War II, when operations for the war effort moved into a bomb-proofed, underground air-raid shelter safe from Hitler's feared Luftwaffe planes. Winston Churchill watched air battles from here, while Allied commanders looked out over a battle zone nicknamed "Hellfire Corner."

To tour the tunnels, show your ticket with the entry time. The 45-minute guided tour—which can be shorter or longer depending on crowds—takes you through the elaborate communications center, an underground hospital, and a command center, while re-creating the wartime atmosphere through sounds and even scents. The original furnishings and equipment have been restored. A 10-minute film at the beginning of the tour gives historical background, and a short film near the end tells you how the evacuation of the battlefield of Dunkirk was coordinated from the tunnels by Admiral Ramsay. Code-named "Operation Dynamo," the mission rescued some 338,000 Allied soldiers from Nazi-occupied France in nine days.

Other Sights in Dover

Dover Museum—This newly refurbished museum, right off the tiny main square, houses a large, impressive, and well-preserved Bronze Age boat unearthed near Dover's shoreline. The boat is displayed on the top floor along with other finds from the site and an exhibit on boat construction techniques (£2.50; April–Sept Mon–Sat 10:00–17:30, Sun 12:00–17:00; Oct–March  Mon–Sat 10:00–17:30, closed Sun; tel. 01304/201-066, www .dovermuseum.co.uk).

The Cliffs of Dover—The cliff called **Western Heights**—opposite Dover Castle, just outside of town—provides a sweeping view of Dover (and occasionally of France). The trail along the cliff weaves around former gun posts originally installed during Napoleonic times, but used most extensively during World War II. It was here that the British military amassed huge decoy forces in an effort to fool the Germans into thinking that a Dover-based attack was imminent. This fake-out maneuver was meant to disguise the plan for the Normandy D-Day invasion. Today, the bunkers are abandoned, but in decent condition. This is the place where you always wished you could play war as a kid...and with a little imagination, you still can. Peaceniks find it an excellent picnic spot. Swimmers launch off from Western Heights to start the swim across the English Channel; give yourself 10 hours to swim to France. To drive to Western Heights, take A20 west past the harbor and turn right at the Aycliffe road.

For a different (and many say better) view of the cliffs, head east of town to **Langdon Cliffs,** with its handy Gateway Visitor Centre (daily March–Oct 10:00–17:00, Nov–Feb 11:00–16:00, tel.

01304/202-756, www.nationaltrust.org.uk). You can walk there from Dover (about 2.5 miles from the train station—just walk under the cliffs with the sea on your right), or you can drive: Head up the Castle Hill Road, pass the castle entrance, then take a sharp right turn onto Upper Road.

Boat Tours—The famous White Cliffs of Dover are almost impossible to appreciate from town. A 50-minute Dover White Cliffs Boat Tour around the harbor will give you all the photo ops you need (£8, £20 family ticket, more expensive bus-and-boat combos available, June–Sept daily at 10:00, 12:00, 14:00, and 16:00; April–May Sat–Sun only, Oct–March by appointment only, mobile 07971/301-379, www.doverwhiteclifftours.com).

Ferries to France—In the mood for a glass of wine and some escargot? A day trip to Calais, France, is only a short boat ride away (walk-on passengers generally £6–8 round trip, about £30 with car, prices double on Sat, 1.25–1.5 hours). Several companies make the journey: P&O Ferries (tel. 08716-646-464, www.po ferries.com), SeaFrance (tel. 0870-571-1711, www.seafrance.com), and Norfolkline (cars only—to Dunkerque, tel. 0870-870-1020, www.norfolkline.com).

Sleeping in Dover

I'd rather sleep in Canterbury, but in a pinch, Dover has a variety of B&Bs spread throughout town (if arriving late at night, take a cab). The guest houses below can recommend another B&B if they're booked up.

$$$ Churchill Hotel is a huge, 81-room, slightly run-down, and formulaic Best Western branch right by the water. It's convenient for travelers arriving at the Eastern Docks (Db-£68–100, sea view for £10 more, "superior" Db for £20 more, Tb-£78–110—sleeps up to 5, breakast-£10, elevator, 15-min walk along the water to the ferry, Dover Waterfront, tel. 01304/203-633, fax 01304/216-320, www.bw-churchillhotel.co.uk, enquiries@churchill-hotel.com).

$$ Churchill House, neatly run by Alastair and Betty Dimech, is comfortable and perfectly located, just at the base of the castle hill. With eight rooms, it's a four-poster-bed type of place (Sb-£25–45, Db-£40–80, cash only, 6 Castle Hill Road, tel. 01304/206-622, www.toastofdover.co.uk, toastofdover @gmail.com).

The homier **$ Amanda Guest House,** on one of the quietest streets in town, works best for drivers (Db-£58–64, Tb-£70–76, cash only but reserve with credit card, easy parking, 20-minute walk from train station to 4 Harold Street, tel. 01304/201-711, http://amandaguesthouse.homestead.com, amandaguesthouse @hotmail.com, Mike and Anne).

Sleep Code

(£1 = about $1.60, country code: 44, area code: 01304)
S = Single, **D** = Double/Twin, **T** = Triple, **Q** = Quad, **b** = bathroom,
s = shower only. You can assume credit cards are accepted
and breakfast is included unless otherwise noted.

To help you sort easily through these listings, I've divided
the rooms into three categories based on the price for a
standard double room with bath:

$$$ **Higher Priced**—Most rooms £80 or more.
$$ **Moderately Priced**—Most rooms between £65–80.
$ **Lower Priced**—Most rooms £65 or less.

Eating in Dover

Your dining options in downtown Dover are few, and not worth
writing home about. Consider having lunch at one of the castle's
cafés or cafeterias.

La Scala is tiny, but in a romantic way, and serves a good
variety of Italian dishes (£7–14 meals, Mon–Sat 12:00–14:00 &
18:00–23:00, closed Sun, 19 High Street, tel. 01304/208-044).

The Eight Bells, smoky and wood-paneled, is a huge pub that
feels like a Vegas lounge. It has good beer and an excellent local
reputation. Along with La Scala, it's one of two dinner options
downtown (£6–9 meals, daily 9:00–24:00, kids allowed before
19:00, 19 Cannon Street, tel. 01304/205-030).

Lunch Eateries on Market Square: Dover's main shopping
square is surrounded by places for a quick lunch. **The Ellie,** a
generic, modern pub at a convenient location (right next door
to the Dover Museum), spills out onto Market Square (£4 sandwiches, £6 main dishes, open daily 10:00–24:00, food served
11:00–15:00 only, inviting outdoor seating on the square, tel.
01304/215-685). Across the square is the more genteel **Dickens
Corner,** a comfy diner with a tearoom upstairs (£3–5 "jacket
potatoes" and soups, Mon–Sat 8:30–17:00, closed Sun, 7 Market
Square, tel. 01304/206-692).

Dover Connections

While the train will get you to most big destinations on the South
Coast, the bus has better connections to smaller towns. Stagecoach offers good one-day (£5.50) or one-week (£18) tickets covering anywhere they go in south England (toll tel. 0870-243-3711,
www.stagecoachbus.com).

DOVER AND SE ENGLAND

The Dover train station is called Dover Priory. Most buses stop at the "bus station" (it's more of a lot) on Pencester Road in the town center. Eurolines buses stop at the Eastern Docks, near the ferries to and from France.

From Dover by Train to: London (3/hr, 2 hrs, some go direct to Victoria Station, others go to Charing Cross Station), **Canterbury** (2/hr, 15–30 min, arrives at Canterbury East Station), **Rye** (hourly, 1.25 hours, transfer at Ashford International), **Hastings** (hourly, 1.5 hrs, transfer at Ashford International), **Brighton** (2/hr, 2.75–3 hrs, transfer at Ashford International or London's Victoria Station). Train info: toll tel. 0845-748-4950, www.nationalrail.co.uk.

By Bus: National Express (toll tel. 0871-781-8181, www.nationalexpress.com) goes to **London** (roughly hourly, about 3 hrs) and **Canterbury** (hourly, 40 min). Stagecoach (toll tel. 0870-243-3711, www.stagecoachbus.com) goes to **Rye** (hourly, 2 hrs) and **Hastings** (hourly, 3 hrs).

Near Dover

Sissinghurst Castle Garden

For a taste of traditional English gardening, this elegant home and well-maintained garden is worth seeking out. Vita Sackville-West, socialite and lover of Virginia Woolf, purchased this castle and land in the early 20th century and transformed the grounds into a beautiful English cottage garden. The gardens are laid out in sections, each with a theme, such as the Herb Garden and the Lime Walk. Every section feels like a small outdoor room. There

is always something blooming here, but the best show is in June, when the famous White Garden bursts with fragrant roses. The castle, formerly a vast and grand affair, has disappeared for the most part, but a tower still stands. Inside are a few small exhibits, and—on the second floor—a series of illustrations that show the development, disintegration, and rebirth of the estate. At the top of the tower, you can survey the garden and orchard from up high. Inside the library wing, a portrait of Vita Sackville-West hangs over the fireplace, along with paintings of other family members, some of whom still live on the property (£9.80, gardens open mid-March–Oct Fri–Tue 11:00–18:30, closed Wed–Thu, shorter hours

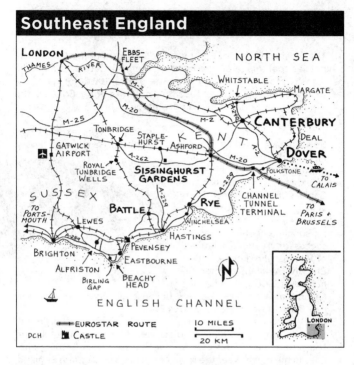

Southeast England

NORTH SEA

LONDON
THAMES
RIVER
EBBS-FLEET
WHITSTABLE
MARGATE
M-2
M-20
M-2
CANTERBURY
M-25
TONBRIDGE
STAPLE-HURST
ASHFORD
K E N T
DEAL
DOVER
GATWICK AIRPORT
ROYAL TUNBRIDGE WELLS
A-262
SISSINGHURST GARDENS
M-20
FOLKSTONE
TO CALAIS
S U S S E X
A-259
CHANNEL TUNNEL TERMINAL
TO PARIS + BRUSSELS
BATTLE
RYE
A-259
TO PORTS-MOUTH
LEWES
WINCHELSEA
A-284
HASTINGS
BRIGHTON
PEVENSEY
ALFRISTON
EASTBOURNE
BIRLING GAP
BEACHY HEAD

E N G L I S H   C H A N N E L

N

LONDON

EUROSTAR ROUTE
CASTLE
DCH
10 MILES
20 KM

for castle and library, café, tel. 01580/710-701, www.nationaltrust.org.uk/sissinghurst). Sissinghurst is about 55 miles west of Dover, off A262, near Cranbrook.

Rye

If you dream of half-timbered pubs and wisteria-covered stone churches, Rye is the photo op you've been looking for. A busy

seaport village for hundreds of years, Rye was frozen in time as silt built up and the sea retreated in the 16th and 17th centuries, leaving only a skinny waterway to remind it of better days. While shipbuilding and smuggling were the mainstays of the economy back then, antique shops and expensive B&Bs drive business these days. Rye is England's version of a hill town, packed with tourists trying to soak up some charm.

Arrival in Rye: As you approach town, notice the canal filled with boats. Follow it along to the old quays. The water line used

DOVER AND SE ENGLAND

The Battle of Hastings

The most epic of all of Europe's medieval *Lord of the Rings*-style battles took place on the most memorable date of the Middle Ages: October 14, 1066. It was the pivotal Battle of Hastings, which came about because the celibate King Edward the Confessor of England had died without an heir, and two nobles claimed the throne.

An Englishman named Harold, Earl of Wessex, said that Edward gave him the throne on his deathbed. He was also chosen king by the traditional council, but support for him was weak. Meanwhile, across the English Channel, French-born William, Duke of Normandy, also claimed that Edward had personally selected *him* as his successor. As the descendant of Vikings who'd once settled England, William claimed he had royal blood. His enemies

called him William the Bastard because his mother was the former Duke of Normandy's mistress.

With the pope's blessing, William patiently gathered and trained a large army and sailed across the Channel. Harold raced south to meet him, his own army exhausted from battling enemies in the north. Near the town of Hastings in southern England, Harold assembled his troops into a wall atop the highest hill and waited for William.

Early in the morning on October 14th, the Norman soldiers

to come up to this area, and the parking lot next to the TI on Strand Quay would have been the wharf. Drivers should ignore the confusing *P* signs, which direct you to parking lots away from the town center—instead, try to squeeze into the small lot next to the TI (by the antique shops) or the larger one across the street.

Tourist Information: The TI has an impressive scale model of the town, presented in a 17-minute sound-and-light show (£3, every 20 min, if it's not running you can peek in at the model for free; TI open daily April–Oct 10:00–17:00, Nov–Dec and March 10:00–16:00, Jan–Feb 10:00–15:00, town audioguide-£3, tel. 01797/226-696, www.visitrye.co.uk).

Sights: Rye's sights try to make too much of this little town, but a stroll along the cobbles is enjoyable. From near the TI, Mermaid Street leads up into the medieval heart of Rye. Along this street (on the left), look for the **Mermaid Inn,** rebuilt in 1420 after the original burned down. Step inside and have a peek into Rye's heyday, or splurge for an expensive lunch (£19–23 trudged up the hill, and the battle was on. First, Norman archers rained arrows on the English. Next, foot soldiers on both sides fought hand-to-hand. William's army began to retreat (a tactical maneuver, say the French). Seeing them flee, the English charged ahead, pursuing them down the hill. Suddenly, the Normans turned and attacked. Riding on horseback, the Norman soldiers were armed with a secret weapon: stirrups, which gave them a foothold to put force behind their lances.

The two sides fought a fierce 14-hour battle, with heavy casualties. Ultimately the Normans decimated the English force. In the battle's climactic finale, Harold was killed (supposedly by an arrow through the eye). William—now "the Conqueror"— marched on to London, where he was crowned King of England in Westminster Abbey on Christmas Day, 1066. William commemorated the dead by building an abbey on the spot of the decisive battle.

The Norman Conquest of England propelled the isolated isle of Britain into the European mainstream. William centralized the government and imported the Romanesque style of architecture— seen at places such as the White Tower at the Tower of London, and Durham Cathedral. The English call this style "Norman." Historians speculate that, were it not for the stirrup, England would have remained on the fringe of Europe (like Scandinavia), French culture and language would have prevailed in the New World...and you'd be reading this book today in French. *Sacré bleu!* William's conquest also muddied the political waters, setting in motion 400 years of conflict between England and France that would not be resolved until the end of the Hundred Years' War, in 1453.

fixed-price lunches, open daily 12:00–14:30 & 19:00–21:30, tel. 01797/223-065). Today, it's a pricey upscale hotel—look for photos of recent celebrity customers just inside the door.

Continuing up Mermaid Street, jog right up West Street to Church Square. The old **Church of St. Mary the Virgin** has a pleasant interior and a tower you can climb for a countryside view (church—free, daily 9:00–17:30, shorter hours in winter; tower— £2.50, same hours as church; tel. 01797/224-935).

Beyond the square, you'll find a miniature castle called the Ypres Tower, housing the **Rye Castle Museum,** with a lookout tower and a modest collection of items from the town's past. Striking up a conversation with the museum's custodian, a lifelong resident, may be the museum's most interesting attraction (£3; April–Oct Thu–Mon 10:30–13:00 & 14:00–17:00, closed Tue–Wed; Nov–March Sat–Sun 10:30–15:30, closed Mon–Fri; tel. 01797/226-728).

Getting There: Rye is about 35 miles southwest of Dover on A259 (the route to Brighton). **Trains** connect to Rye from

London's Charing Cross Station (1–2/hr, 2 hrs, transfer at Ashford International) and Dover (hourly, 1.25 hours, transfer at Ashford International). Stagecoach bus #100 provides a direct connection to Dover (hourly, 2 hrs, toll tel. 0870-243-3711, www.stagecoachbus.com).

Near Rye: Compared to sugary-sweet Rye, modest **Winchelsea** feels like an antacid. Small, inviting, and just far enough away from the maddening crowd, the town makes a good stop for a picnic lunch. The grocery shop on the square sells all you need for a quiet meal on the little village green. Winchelsea is about three miles southwest of Rye on A259, toward Hastings.

Battle

Located about an hour southwest of Dover by car, the town of Battle commemorates a fight no Brit can forget—the Battle of Hastings, which took place on October 14, 1066 (see sidebar on previous page). On that date, a Norman (French) king seized control of England, leading to a string of Norman kings and forever changing the course of English history. The battlefield and adjoining ruined abbey (built soon after the battle to atone for all the spilled blood) are worth ▲▲▲ to British-history buffs, but anyone can appreciate the dramatic story behind the grassy field. Ignore the tourists and take a journey back in time...these fields would have looked almost the same 1,000 years ago. Look across the unassuming little valley and imagine thousands of invading troops. Your visit can last from three minutes to three hours, depending on your imagination.

▲**Battle of Hastings Abbey and Battlefield**—A small museum, battleground overlook, and remaining Battle Abbey buildings illuminate the historical significance of the Battle of Hastings. After buying your ticket and picking up the essential, included audioguide, head to the nearby Visitors Centre to watch an excellent 15-minute film that recounts the story of the battle, with animated scenes from the

famous Bayeux Tapestry and impressive live-action reenactments. Also in the center are replicas of weapons used by the fighters—lift them to appreciate how the Brits invented heavy metal long before Led Zeppelin.

Then head outside, where you have two choices with your audioguide: Follow the short tour along a terrace overlooking the battlefield (about 15 min), or take the longer version out through the woods and actually across the fateful field (about 40 min). With sound effects and a witty but not corny commentary, the audioguide really injects some life into the site. Finally, you'll wind up at the remains of the abbey, where the audioguide relates details of monastic lifestyles. It's interesting and a bit more intact than many other ruined abbeys, but it pales in comparison to the drama of the battle. Walking back to the

entrance, you'll notice that the abbey's former Great Hall now houses another famous English institution—a private school.

Cost and Hours: £6.70, includes audioguide, £16 family ticket, daily April–Sept 10:00–18:00, Oct–March 10:00–16:00, last entry 30 min before closing, children's play area, tel. 01424/775-705, www.english-heritage.org.uk/battleabbey.

Getting There: Battle isn't on a major road, but **drivers** find that it's well-signposted from busy A259, whether you're coming from the east (Dover) or from the west (Brighton). There's a pricey £3 coin-op parking lot next to the abbey. Battle can be reached by **train** from London's Charing Cross or London Bridge stations (2/hr, 1.5 hrs), Hastings (2/hr, 15 min), or Dover (2/hr, 2 hrs, 1–2 transfers). The entrance to Battle Abbey is at the south end of High Street; follow signs from the train station.

Eating in Battle: The **Pilgrims Restaurant,** across the street from the abbey, is an atmospherically crooked half-timbered house serving decent but pricey food with outdoor terrace seating (£7.50 sandwiches, £15–20 main dishes, open daily for lunch and dinner except closed Sun dinner, 1 High Street, tel. 01424/772-314).

DOVER AND SE ENGLAND

BRIGHTON

Brighton—brash and flamboyant, with a carnival flair—is refreshing if you're suffering from an excess of doilies and museums. The city boasts a garish 19th-century Royal Pavilion, a loud and flashy carnival pier, England's most thriving gay community, and a long stretch of cobbled beach. It's no wonder that youthful bohemians and blue-collar Londoners alike make this town their holiday destination of choice.

In the 1790s, with Napoleon's armies running rampant on the Continent, aristocrats could no longer travel abroad on a traditional "Grand Tour" of Europe. King George IV chose the village of Brighthelmstone to build a vacation palace for himself, and royal followers began a frenzy of construction on the seashore. Soon this once-sleepy seaside village was transformed into an elegant resort town. With the rise of train travel, connections to London became quick and cheap, making Brighton an inviting getaway for working-class Londoners.

The countryside near Brighton is packed with tempting sights and worthwhile stopovers for drivers. Go for a walk on the South Downs Way, lick an ice-cream cone in the postcard-pretty village of Alfriston, visit the best white cliffs in England at Beachy Head, and explore the evocative ruins of a Roman fort at Pevensey.

Planning Your Time

Brighton's sights—its Royal Pavilion, Museum and Art Gallery, and pleasure pier—can be seen in just a few hours, making this a doable day trip from London. If you've got a full day and a car, spend the rest of your day heading for Alfriston and Beachy Head.

Debating between Brighton and Portsmouth? Younger, hipper travelers are more likely to be turned on by lively Brighton, while older, more conservative visitors might prefer traditional Portsmouth (see next chapter). Either destination works as an easy day trip from London, but with more time, visiting both is a great plan.

Orientation to Brighton

(area code: 01273)

Brighton is big, with 160,000 people. It feels surprisingly urban for a seaside resort—like the Nice of England. Most tourists focus on the area near the waterfront. The heart of Brighton is the Brighton Pier and, several blocks inland, the Royal Pavilion. Between these two landmarks is the twisty old center of town called The Lanes, with good restaurants and lots of shopping. North of The Lanes and past the Royal Pavilion is the popular, recently revived neighborhood of North Laine, with more shopping and eateries, plus occasional street-music performances. The best accommodations cluster to the east of The Lanes, within a block of the seafront, in the colorful neighborhood called Kemptown.

Tourist Information

The TI is in the Royal Pavilion's gift shop. Pick up the free, good color map of Brighton. They also book rooms (£1.50/person) and sell tickets to various sights and theater productions (daily 10:00–17:00, maybe slightly shorter hours off-season, you'll pay a greedy 50p/min to climb through their phone tree at tel. 0906-711-2255, www.visitbrighton.com).

An walking-tour audioguide of Brighton is available for download to your iPod or other MP3 player (£6, www.coolcity walks.com).

Arrival in Brighton

Trains arrive at Brighton Station, a 15-minute walk from the center. Drivers on A23 enter town on the tree-lined Grand Parade, which goes straight to the water (ending near Brighton Pier). Parking is tricky: Signs will lead you to parking garages near the center, but if you're staying the night, ask your hotelier for the best place to leave your car.

Helpful Hints

Crowd Control: Brighton can overflow with visitors in summer and on weekends. The Brighton Festival (May) and the Summer LGBT Pride Festival (first week of Aug) are the busiest times. Off-season (roughly Oct–March), visitors may find the city quiet, prices slashed, and attractions shuttered.

Laundry: St. James's Laundry is in Kemptown, near my recommended accommodations (self-service open daily 7:30–20:30, or drop-off Mon–Fri 8:30–14:00 for same-day full-service, 53 St. James's Street, tel. 01273/672-395).

Bike Rental: The TI hands out a good, free cycle map listing several rental places. **Planet Cycle Hire,** on the waterfront near the old West Pier between West Street and Montpelier Road, rents bikes by either the hour or the day (£12/day, £20 deposit; April–Sept Thu–Tue 10:00–18:00, closed Wed; Oct–March Fri–Mon 10:00–17:00, closed Tue–Thu; King's Road, tel. 01273/748-881).

Getting Around Brighton

Brighton's well-run bus system is handy, especially if you're staying in one of my recommended guest houses on Kemptown's New Steine Street (£1.50/ride, £3.60 day pass; buy from driver, at TI, or online for slight discount; tel. 01273/886-200, www.buses.co.uk).

Sights in Brighton

▲▲**Brighton Royal Pavilion**—Famous for his scandalous secret marriage to Catholic widow Mrs. Fitzherbert, King George IV was lively, decadent, and trendsetting.

He loved to vacation by the sea and host glamorous dinner parties. George was enamored with Asian cultures, styling his vacation home with exotic decorations from the East. The result is colorful and exuberant...some would say gaudy. Like Brighton itself, the place smacks of faded elegance—but it's fun to tour. It's free to enter the restored Regency gardens surrounding the Pavilion, and the nearby Brighton Museum and Art Gallery (described later).

Cost, Hours, Location: £8.80, includes audioguide, daily April–Sept 9:30–17:45, Oct–March 10:00–17:15, last entry 45 min before closing; head up Pavilion Parade from The Lanes, on Old Steine Road; tel. 03000/290-900, www.royalpavilion.org.uk. If there's a line to buy tickets, dip into the TI (at the gift shop next door) and purchase them for the same price.

❷ Self-Guided Tour: Pick up the free and informative audioguide as you enter. It'll tell you more about these highlights (and other points of interest) along the one-way route.

While George planned the palace as a royal holiday residence, it was used mainly as a party pad to entertain guests.

Brighton

P PARKING

100 YARDS
100 METERS

N

TO A-23,
GATWICK
AIRPORT
& LONDON

TO A-27,
LEWES &
EASTBOURNE

TRAIN STATION

TERMINUS ROAD
CHEAPSIDE
TRAFALGAR STREET
SURREY
GLOUCESTER ROAD
GLOUCESTER PL.
YORK PLACE
RICHMOND PLACE
ALBION HILL

NORTH
LAINE

ROAD
NORTH ROAD
QUEENS ROAD
CHURCH STREET
WINDSOR
PORTLAND
BOND ST.
NEW RD.
MARLBOROUGH PL.
GRAND PARADE
ASHTON RISE
STREET
MORLEY
JOHN
STREET
SUSSEX ST.
KINGSWOOD
CARLTON
BLAKER ST.
STREET

DYKE ROAD

NORTH ST.
POST
HIP PL.
HOUSE LN.
CASTLE ST.
SQ.
EDWARD
HIGH ST.
KEMPTOWN

BRIGHTON MUSEUM & ART GALLERY

ROYAL PAVILION

THE LANES
WEST STREET
DUKE ST.
SHIP ST.
MIDDLE ST.
SOUTH ST.
DUKE
ALBERT ST.
MARKET ST.
ST. BART.
EAST ST.
POOL VALLEY
OLD STEINE
ST. JAMES'S ST.
BROAD
MADEIRA PL.
MARG. ST.
NEW STEINE
ROCK ST.

TO WEST PIER RUINS

KING'S ROAD
GRAND JUNCTION ROAD
MARINE PARADE
MADEIRA DR.
VOLK'S ELECTRIC RAILWAY
DCH

BEACH R

BEACH

BRIGHTON PIER

ENGLISH   CHANNEL

❶ New Steine Street B&Bs
❷ Kempfield House
❸ St. Christopher's Inn
❹ English's of Brighton
❺ Terre à Terre
❻ Market Street Eateries
❼ Bill's Produce Store
❽ Cornish Pasties
❾ Our Cornish Pasty Shop
❿ Wagamama
⓫ Yo! Sushi
⓬ La Capannina
⓭ Launderette
⓮ To Bike Rental

BRIGHTON

They'd be suitably impressed by the grand **Long Gallery.** Here and throughout the Pavilion, examine the fine detail work—such as the "bamboo" stairway decoration that's actually carved from wood.

If guests were impressed by the Long Gallery, they were blown away by the **Banqueting Room.** Imagine England's elite nibbling crumpets under the one-ton chandelier...with its dragons exhaling light through lotus-shaped shades. Notice that the ornate table is permanently set for the dessert course.

The elaborate **Kitchen** was one of the most innovative of its time. Smoke from the fireplace rotated a huge rotisserie that could cook enough meat to feed a hundred hungry diners. The king was so particular about his food that he insisted his kitchen be attached to the dining room (unheard-of at the time). He also had a warming table built to keep food at the optimum temperature.

Head through the gallery and salon into a room dedicated to George's true passion: music. In the massive **Music Room,** the royal band serenaded guests. Take a moment to appreciate the Chinese-inspired decor here and throughout the palace. Known as *chinoiserie,* it was the height of fashion in those days.

The **Private Apartments** were on the ground floor, to more easily accommodate the ailing king (who spent less and less time here near the end of his life). Note that this space is more intimate and cozy than the showpiece halls we've seen elsewhere. (If you're intrigued by all this, dip into the dry but informative 18-minute film about the Pavilion's history.)

Continuing upstairs, you'll stroll through the restored **Yellow Bow Rooms,** then **Queen Victoria's Apartments,** where you'll learn the epilogue to the story of George's party palace. George was a big spender, piling up huge debts. No expense was spared. Prudish Queen Victoria, who took the throne seven years after George's death, wanted more privacy than the Pavilion provided and scorned the excesses in George's court—so she quickly off-loaded the decadent Pavilion to the local town council (which still owns it today). Only recently did Queen Elizabeth II bring the original furniture out of storage and return it to the Pavilion.

Brighton Museum and Art Gallery—This gallery, similar to the Victoria and Albert Museum in London, displays decorative arts with a heavy focus on 20th-century art and design. The modern pseudo-kitsch includes the Dalí-inspired *Mae West Lips Sofa* and Frank Gehry's *Wiggle Chair.* The café above the gallery has a pleasant view of the action (free, Tue 10:00–19:00, Wed–Sat 10:00–17:00, Sun 14:00–17:00, closed Mon except holidays, just north of the Royal Pavilion, tel. 03000/290-900, www.virtual museum.info).

Brighton Pier—Glittering and shiny with amusement rides and carnival games, Brighton Pier is *the* place to go for a fix of "candy

floss" (cotton candy), fortune-tellers, and tacky souvenirs. The pier, opened in 1899 and long known as Palace Pier, has gone in and out of fashion; in recent years, it's come back to life, thanks to a restoration. The main pavilion is a 19th-century gem. If you ignore the fancy video games, you might be able to imagine yourself as a Victorian Londoner out on holiday, seeing brilliant electric lights for the first time (free entry to pier, rides run daily 10:00–21:00, arcade open until 22:00, closing time depends on crowds, tel. 01273/609-361, www.brightonpier.co.uk).

Check out the ruins of the pier to the west. The shorter but once equally festive West Pier disintegrated into the water in the 1970s, due to disrepair. Watch for construction of a new observation tower here. Designed by the architects of the London Eye, the i360 tower's doughnut-like elevator will lift tourists to a bird's-eye view over the town (may be finished sometime in 2010—get details at TI).

Beach—OK, so it isn't Hawaii, but you can walk along the large, flattened cobbles, called "shingles," and get your feet wet.

Sleeping in Brighton

Brighton's bohemian character is fun during the day, but the town can be a little shady at night. The recommended accommodations are in the gay-friendly Kemptown neighborhood, about a block from the beach and within a 10-minute walk of the Brighton Pier and Royal Pavilion.

The best Brighton accommodations are variations on the same theme: a guest house with about a dozen rooms. A guest house offers more professionalism and anonymity than a B&B, and more character(s) than a hotel. As rooms vary in size, one hotel can have four or five different prices for their doubles. ("Sea views" here are unimpressive, and not worth paying extra for.) To complicate matters, in summer, prices skyrocket by £15–30 on weekends, making otherwise good-value places suddenly way overpriced. Summer weekends are also plagued with noisy partygoers roaming the streets until dawn. Avoid sleeping in Brighton on a summer weekend if you can help it—but if you must sleep here, ask for a quieter room away from the road. I've listed the summer ranges; you can assume the lower rates are for weeknights and smaller rooms, while the higher rates are for weekends and fancier and/or

Sleep Code

(£1 = about $1.60, country code: 44, area code: 01273)
S = Single, **D** = Double/Twin, **T** = Triple, **Q** = Quad, **b** = bathroom,
s = shower only. You can assume credit cards are accepted unless otherwise noted.

To help you sort easily through these listings, I've divided the rooms into three categories based on the price for a standard double room with bath:

$$$ Higher Priced—Most rooms £100 or more.
$$ Moderately Priced—Most rooms between £60-100.
$ Lower Priced—Most rooms £60 or less.

seaview rooms. You'll often get a better deal off-season (especially on weeknights).

On New Steine Street

Kemptown's New Steine Street (pronounced "steen")—essentially a long square with a park in the middle—is lined with about a dozen different guest houses. After visiting all of them, these are my favorites. Marine View is more traditional; Sea Spray, New Steine (and its sister hotel, Gulliver's), and Hamptons are mod, stylish, and gay-friendly; and Strawberry Fields is somewhere in between.

Handy bus #7 runs every 10 minutes from just outside the train station to the top of New Steine Street (5-min ride). To return to the center, walk to the bottom of the road and cross the oceanfront street to the bus stand (you'll find schedules there).

$$$ Sea Spray is an innovative concept hotel: Each of the 15 rooms has a different theme, from the Renaissance to Dalí to Elvis. It's a memorable place to spend the night, with art-filled public spaces (Db-£60–135, sea views, some with balconies, pricier suites, free Wi-Fi, sauna, at #26, tel. 01273/680-332, www.sea spraybrighton.co.uk, seaspray@brighton.co.uk).

$$$ New Steine B&B, with 22 coffee-and-cream-colored rooms, combines Old World charm with contemporary chic (S-£49–60, Db-£87–148, Tb-£132–159, Qb-£181–186, check website for discounts, dinner option, free Wi-Fi, bistro, at #10–11, tel. 01273/695-415, www.newsteinehotel.com, reservation@newsteine hotel.com). **$$$ Gulliver's,** their sister hotel two doors down, has similar decor and prices (Sb-£49–54, Db-£87–137, Tb-£132–143, at #12a, tel. 01273/681-546, www.gullivershotel.com, reservation @gullivershotel.com).

$$$ Hamptons Brighton has crisp and stylish nautical decor right out of New England—but with Union Jack accents

(S-£38–48, Sb-£45–55, D-£70–85, Db-£85–130 depending on size, at #3, tel. 01273/675-436).

$$ Strawberry Fields Hotel has 27 rooms with a fun strawberry theme. Sharon and her friendly and competent assistant, Anna, look after you (Ss-£29–45, D-£60–70, Db-£70–98, Wi-Fi on lower floors, at #6–7, tel. 01273/681-576, www.strawberry-fields-hotel.com, strawberryfields@pavilion.co.uk).

$$ Marine View has 11 comfortable rooms (S-£35–40, Db-£65–80, £5 more for sea view, free Wi-Fi, at #24, tel. 01273/603-870, www.mvbrighton.co.uk, info@mvbrighton.co.uk).

Elsewhere in Brighton

Madeira Place, a few blocks closer to the town center than New Steine Street, has its own stretch of guest houses. The best of these is **$$ Kempfield House,** tastefully run in a Georgian townhouse. The 13 rooms are elegantly simple and nicely appointed (Sb-£50–75, Db-£70–110, huge Db-£85–125, check website for discounts, 2-night minimum on weekends, free Wi-Fi, 18 Madeira Place, tel. 01273/777-740, www.kempfieldhouse.co.uk, info@fieldhouse hotels.co.uk).

$ St. Christopher's Inn is your budget hostel option. Smack-dab in the middle of the action, on the main seafront road across from the Brighton Pier, this self-described "party hostel" offers cheap doubles and dorm beds for young people wanting to live it up in Brighton. The ground-floor bar and basement disco can be noisy—light sleepers can try requesting a higher floor (£17–28 for a bunk in 4- to 8-bed dorms, Db-£50–110, prices change dramatically by season—check online for best deals, elevator, 10–12 Grand Junction Road, booking tel. 020/7407-1856, reception tel. 01273/202-035, www.st-christophers.co.uk).

Eating in Brighton

If you haven't filled yourself up with greasy boardwalk fare, you'll find plenty of good, affordable restaurants around town.

In The Lanes

The area known as The Lanes has the best concentration of both trendy and traditional restaurants. My first two listings are pricey, while the Market Street eateries are easier on a tight budget.

English's of Brighton, hiding on the side of the little square on East Street, is a venerable local institution that's been serving seafood specialties for more than 150 years to luminaries such as Charlie Chaplin and Laurence Olivier. The white-tablecloth-classy interior sprawls through several rooms on two floors, and there's seating out on the square (£13–15 fixed-price lunches, £25–30 fixed-price dinners, £17–25 main dishes, Mon–Sat 12:00–22:00, Sun 12:30–21:30, 29–31 East Street, tel. 01273/327-980).

Terre à Terre keeps vegetarians and healthy eaters happy with imaginative dishes and friendly service (£13–15 main dishes, Tue–Fri 12:00–22:30, Sat 12:00–23:00, Sun 12:00–22:00, closed Mon, 71 East Street, tel. 01273/729-051).

On Market Street: This bustling area—more a long, wide square than a "street"—is packed with affordable eateries. Take a spin around to choose your favorite, but check out the following: **Fat Leo** gets high marks from locals for big portions of pasta and the best bang-for-your-pound in a bright, modern interior with seating on two levels. It's not haute cuisine, but it's cheap (£3–9 main dishes, daily 12:00–22:00, at #16–17, tel. 01273/325-135). For a seafront picnic, pick up some pastries and pasties at **Forfars,** baking in Brighton since 1818 (eat at their upstairs café for a few pence more, Mon–Sat 8:00–17:00, closed Sun, at #44, tel. 01273/327-458). **Mai Ped Ped Ped** serves up tasty Thai dishes in a simple, two-story interior (£4–8 light "Thai tapas" lunch dishes, bigger £6–8 dinners, Mon–Sat 11:30–23:00, Sun 11:30–22:00, at #11, tel. 01273/737-373). **The Burger Bar** is a cute little quasi-diner slinging burgers and all-day breakfast fare. As there's no interior seating, you'll have to grab a table on the square (£3–5, cash only, open daily 9:00–18:00, at #11a, tel. 01273/205-979).

In North Laine

Just north of The Lanes and the Royal Pavilion, this former warehouse district is now the cool place to explore, with new restaurants and fun quirky shops popping up all the time.

Bill's Produce Store is a unique café (and yes, produce store) that's immensely popular with locals for its fresh, inventive dishes and smoothies. Get here before the lunch rush to nab a seat and ogle the surroundings—and the fresh-flower-bedecked cakes behind the counter (£3.50–12 lunches, £9–15 dinners, take-away sandwiches, large breakfast menu, Mon–Sat 8:00–22:00, Sun 9:30–16:00, 100 North Road, tel. 01273/692-894, www.bills producestore.co.uk).

Cornish Pasties offers excellent versions of its namesake, including vegetarian varieties, and delicious homemade desserts (Mon–Sat 8:30–19:00, Sun 12:00–18:00, 24 Gardner Street, tel. 01273/688-063). It's lovingly run by Ian and Nese Baldry, who also own **Our Cornish Pasty Shop,** just a block down from the train station (also serves salads, Mon–Fri 6:30–18:00, Sat–Sun 9:00–16:00, 55 Queen's Road, tel. 01273/777-363). Arrive an hour before either store closes to get two pasties for the price of one.

Two reliable Asian chains have branches here (a block apart from each other, off North Road). At **Wagamama,** diners slurp pan-fried, pan-Asian noodles at long, shared tables in a single hall as the harried wait staff scurries around (£6–10 main dishes, Mon–Sat 12:00–23:00, Sun 12:00–22:00, 30 Kensington Street, tel. 01273/688-892, www.wagamama.com). **Yo! Sushi** features a conveyor belt of tasty and creative raw fish (£2–5/plate, Mon–Sat 12:00–23:00, Sun 12:00–22:30, 6–7 Jubilee Street, tel. 01273/689-659).

Near the Recommended Accommodations in Kemptown

To dine closer to home, simply wander the lively streets of Kemptown. St. James's Street, running parallel to the seafront a block inland, is lined with all types of cuisine: cheap burgers and fish-and-chips, Thai, Mediterranean, pub grub, and more. For Italian, try **La Capannina,** a cozy one-room restaurant with a run-by-an-Italian-family feel (£7–10 pizzas and pastas, Tue–Thu 12:00–14:30 & 18:00–23:00, Fri–Sat 12:00–14:30 & 18:00–23:30, Sun 12:00–15:00, Mon 18:00–23:00, just off St. James's Street at 15 Madeira Place, tel. 01273/680-839).

Brighton Connections

Brighton is well-connected to London and most coastal towns.

From Brighton by Train to: London's Gatwick Airport (at least hourly, 25–40 min), **London**'s Victoria Station (1–2/hr direct, 1 hr; also several other connections to different London stations, some requiring transfers), **Portsmouth** (1/hr direct, 1.5 hrs, more with transfer), **Hastings** (2/hr direct, 1–1.25 hrs), **Dover** (2/hr, 2.75–3 hrs, 1–2 transfers), **Canterbury** (2/hr, 2.5–3 hrs, 1–3 transfers). Train info: toll tel. 0845-748-4950, www.nationalrail.co.uk.

By Bus: National Express (toll tel. 0871-781-8181, www.nationalexpress.com) runs buses to **London**'s Gatwick Airport (at least hourly, 45 min), **Heathrow Airport** (almost hourly, 2 hrs), and **London**'s Victoria Coach Station (hourly, 2.5 hrs). Stagecoach buses (toll tel. 0845-121-0170, www.stagecoachbus.com) go to **Portsmouth** (2/hr, 3.5 hrs) and **Arundel** (2/hr, none on Sun, 2.25 hrs, some require transfer).

BRIGHTON

Near Brighton

Stretching east of Brighton is a coastline fringed with broad, rolling green downs, or hills—an area known as the South Downs Way. These hills are an excellent place to practice a favorite sport of the English: walking. Paths, well-tended by local walking clubs, weave through much of the English countryside, attracting weekend and holiday strollers, and anyone looking for fresh air and exercise. On a quick visit, the highlights here are the adorable hamlet of Alfriston and the dramatic chalk cliff of Beachy Head. Just beyond is the ruined Roman fort at Pevensey. I've listed these attractions as you'll reach them traveling eastward from Brighton.

Planning Your Time

These sights can be combined to make a good half-day side trip from Brighton (better in the afternoon; allow more time if you want to squeeze in a South Downs Way walk en route). Drive east on A27, dip down through Alfriston to stroll the cute village center and poke into the clergy house, then continue on to Beachy Head—arriving when the cliffs are gorgeously lit by the late-afternoon sun. Pevensey is skippable but makes for an easy quick visit, as it's just off the main A27/A259 road connecting Brighton to points eastward (Dover or Canterbury).

▲Alfriston

The South Downs Way winds itself inland at Alfriston, set in a peaceful green valley. This tidy, picturesque little one-street

village—half redbrick, half half-timbered, all quaint—is packed with tourists and walkers.

Arrival in Alfriston: Drivers follow *Alfriston* signs south from A27. Park in the giant lot at the north end of town, then stroll up the main drag. Alfriston, while cute, isn't worth the trouble if you don't have a car, but you could take bus #12 or #12A from Brighton south to Seaford, then catch bus #126 to Alfriston (toll tel. 0871-200-2233, www.traveline.org.uk).

Sights: A block behind the main street is the landmark St. Andrew's Church, overlooking an inviting green (the church sometimes hosts concerts—look for the schedule in the entryway). Tucked behind the church (on the right side) is the humble, thatched **Alfriston Clergy House.** This 14th-century house was the

BRIGHTON

Near Brighton

first property ever acquired by the National Trust—for just £10—in 1896. Its small garden is filled with delphiniums and roses, and the interior of the building is well-preserved. This place gives you a look at the lifestyles of the medieval and pious. Docents are sometimes waiting inside to tell you more (£3.90, skimpy £2.50 guidebook; March–Oct Sat–Mon and Wed–Thu 10:30–17:00, closed Tue and Fri; Nov–mid-Dec Sat–Mon and Wed–Thu 11:00–16:00, closed Tue and Fri; last entry 30 min before closing, closed mid-Dec–Feb, tel. 01323/870-001, www.nationaltrust.org.uk/alfriston).

Sleeping near Alfriston: The **$$ Riverdale House B&B,** perched on a ridge with beautiful views over the South Downs, has three recently renovated rooms that tastefully meld traditional character and modern hues. This family-friendly place also features a shared living room with a piano and a cozy sun porch (Db-£80–105 depending on size, family suite-£130, just south of Alfriston on Seaford Road—look for sign on right, tel. 01323/871-038, www.riverdalehouse.co.uk, info@riverdalehouse .co.uk).

Eating in Alfriston: The pubs lining the town's main street— such as Ye Olde Smugglers Inn, The George Inn, and The Star Inn—offer typical pub grub in beautiful half-timbered buildings.

▲▲Beachy Head

The highest chalk sea cliff in England is less well-known but more dramatic and scenic than the White Cliffs of Dover. If you see

one white cliff in England (and one is enough), make it Beachy Head.

The easiest way to appreciate Beachy Head is to drive to the settlement of **Birling Gap,** with easy access to the coastline below the cliff. From Brighton, make your way to the A259 coastal road. (The most scenic approach is to head east on speedy A27, then turn off and head south when you see signs for *Alfriston;* you can visit this picturesque town—described above—on the way to A259, which you'll follow east.)

Once on A259, you can turn off in Friston directly to Birling Gap or—for a slightly longer and more scenic route—continue east on A259 to make a loop of it, passing through the charming village of East Dean (with a good pub, the Tiger Inn, on the village green). Take a spin around the dial of your car's radio—you'll start to hear more French stations than English ones. Shortly after leaving East Dean, you'll see a turnoff on the right for Beachy Head. Follow this road as it rises over the hills, with views over grassy fields on one side and the English Channel on the other. Soon you'll spot the Countryside Centre, with information for walkers and other visitors (May–Oct daily 10:00–16:00, off-season Sat–Sun only 10:00–15:30, tel. 01323/737-273). Then continue on the road, which eventually drops you down into Birling Gap.

Once you arrive in Birling Gap, park at the big, free gravel lot next to the Birling Gap Hotel, and use the staircase to reach the beach. As you stroll under the grand chalky monster, marvel at the otherworldly whiteness of the cliff and the stones underfoot.

South Downs Way

The South Downs Way (often abbreviated SDW) runs for 100 miles along the chalk hills of England's south coast, from Winchester (25 miles inland in Hampshire) to Eastbourne (on the coast of East Sussex). This long, scenic ridge has attracted walkers for thousands of years, and by April 2010 it will officially become England's ninth national park (although it won't be fully operational until 2011). Locals consider these trails a birthright.

The SDW is a bridleway, which means you can walk, bike, or ride a horse. To keep on course, look for the blue arrow signs with a white acorn in the middle or dots of blue paint on posts or trees. It's always a good idea to have a map; the UK Ordnance Survey Explorer maps are excellent and widely available (#125 covers the area around Beachy Head).

Walkers have priority over horses and bicycles, but it's polite to step aside and let them pass. While motorized vehicles are not allowed on the SDW itself, much of the path runs along farm tracks, so you may encounter tractors. Keep a safe distance or you may be plowed under.

It's best to walk east, toward Eastbourne. This will keep the wind behind you and the scenery ahead. While you can

walk along almost the entire southern coast, the best part for a day hike is the three-mile stretch out to Beachy Head from Eastbourne (find the path at the west end of King Edward's Parade, also called B2103; the small car park is often full, so you may need to park elsewhere).

Many people walk the entire 100 miles, staying in B&Bs or hostels in towns along the way, or camping in designated areas. The SDW winds its way through or near many towns and villages, including Exton, Buriton, Arundel, Lewes, and Alfriston. Two good websites are www.southdownsonline.org and www.nationaltrail.co.uk. You can buy a guidebook at most UK bookshops or online through www.amazon.co.uk. Titles include *South Downs Way* by Jim Manthorpe, *South Downs Way National Trail Guide* by Paul Millmore, and *The South Downs Way* by Kev Reynolds.

BRIGHTON

Pick up a chunk of chalk to feel how soft and crumbly it is—the constant sloughing off is why these cliffs are so steep, dramatic, and pearly-white (signs warn you to stay away from the immediate base of the cliffs). Stretching to your right (as you face the sea) are the Seven Sisters cliffs, also offering chalky splendor as far as the eye can see.

If you have time for a **walk,** there are two good routes to consider. For a clifftop walk with great sea views, but not the best vistas of the cliff face itself, hike from the lighthouse called Belletout (you'll see it as you approach the cliffs from the west) to the Countryside Centre. Or, for head-on views of the cliff as you walk, start out in Seaford and hike up the ridge to Hope Gap. Both of these trails are fairly steep, and it's important to watch your step: Long windblown grass fields come to an abrupt end at the cliff edge, with no barrier between you and the sea crashing hundreds of feet below.

If you don't have a car, take bus #12A, which offers good daily service between Brighton and Birling Gap, Seaford, and Beachy Head (2/hr, 1.25 hrs, tel. 01273/886-200, toll tel. 0871-200-2233, www.traveline.org.uk).

Pevensey

This nondescript village, 25 miles east of Brighton (where the A259 coastal route and faster A27 inland route intersect), is a one-street town leading up to a large, brooding Roman fortress. Originally built as a coastal fortifica-  tion in the fourth century, **Pevensey Castle** was also used by the Normans, who landed in 1066 with William the Conqueror at Norman's Bay, just within sight. The moat around the inner castle was probably flushed by the incoming tidewater, although the present coastline has moved farther to the south. The ruins of the castle were also put into action during World War II. While you can pay to go into the castle itself, the best activity—wandering the scenic and grassy field around it—is free (castle entry-£4.30, includes audioguide; April–Sept daily 10:00–18:00; Oct daily 10:00–16:00; Nov–March Sat–Sun only 10:00–16:00, closed Mon–Fri; tel. 01323/762-604, www.english-heritage.org.uk/pevensey). You can also take the train from Brighton to Pevensey (2/hr, 1 hr, tel. 0845-748-4950, www.nationalrail.co.uk).

PORTSMOUTH

Portsmouth, the age-old home of the Royal Navy and Britain's second-busiest ferry port after Dover, is best known for its Historic Dockyard and many nautical sights. For centuries, Britain, a maritime superpower, relied on the fleets in Portsmouth to expand and maintain its vast empire and guard against invaders. When sea power was needed, British leaders—from Henry VIII to Winston Churchill to Tony Blair—called upon Portsmouth to ready the ships.

As a major military target, the city of Portsmouth was flattened by WWII bombs (though ironically, the Historic Dockyard was relatively unscathed). Postwar reconstruction was hasty and poorly planned, and the city became infamous for its bad architecture. But an impressive gentrification is underway here. Efforts to rejuvenate tourism have included refurbishing Old Portsmouth, building a sprawling new waterfront shopping complex, and adding an odd, pointy monolith to the skyline. While Brighton rests on its holiday-making laurels—and is growing a bit shabby—Portsmouth feels hip and modern.

The old nautical sights are as impressive as ever. Visiting landlubbers can tour the HMS *Victory*, which played a key role in Britain's battles with Napoleon's navy, and see artifacts from the *Mary Rose*, a 16th-century warship. But the new spirit of Portsmouth is equally enticing. Portsmouth seems to

expertly balance its dual status as both a city of the past, and one of the future.

Near Portsmouth, on the road to Brighton, are two very different palaces: the ancient remains of Fishbourne Roman Palace, with its striking mosaics; and thriving Arundel Castle, still the proud home of England's top duke.

Planning Your Time

Portsmouth works well as a day trip from London, Bath, or Salisbury. The city's top sights—at the Historic Dockyard—can be seen in a few hours. But thanks to the bustling Gunwharf Quays and Spinnaker Tower, the fine D-Day Museum, and a seaside-holiday atmosphere, you'll have no trouble filling a whole day. Consider spending the night.

Orientation to Portsmouth

(area code: 023)

Portsmouth, situated on a large peninsula, feels smaller than its population of 200,000. Almost all of its visit-worthy sights line up along a two-mile stretch of waterfront, from the Historic Dockyard in the north to the Southsea neighborhood in the south—with its D-Day Museum, beaches, and hovercraft to the Isle of Wight.

Tourist Information

The main TI is located on The Hard, just left of the **Historic Dockyard** gate. On most Saturdays and Sundays, the TI offers guided walks, usually at 14:30 for £3—ask for details (open daily 9:30–17:15, tel. 023/9282-6722, www.visitportsmouth.co.uk, vis @portsmouthcc.gov.uk). A second TI is two miles away, near the D-Day Museum in **Southsea** (March–Oct daily 9:30–17:15; Nov–Feb Mon–Fri 9:30–16:30, closed Sat–Sun; Clarence Esplanade, tel. 023/9282-6722).

At either TI, pick up the free, virtually useless black-and-white map, or shell out £1.50 for a good color one. To tempt you to cross the town and see more of Portsmouth, the main TI sells 10-percent-off tickets for the D-Day Museum (located near the Southsea TI), and the Southsea TI gives out 10 percent discount vouchers for the Historic Dockyard (located near the main TI). If you want to see both sights, you'll save about £2 per person if you go to the main TI upon arrival, buy a discounted D-Day Museum ticket, head out to visit that museum, pick up a Historic Dockyard voucher at the Southsea TI, and then head back to the center to visit the Historic Dockyard.

Bus Tours: With vintage double-decker buses and live guides, **Local Haunts** does a 90-minute tour through Portsmouth (£8,

buy tickets from guide or at TI, April–Sept Wed–Thu and Sun at
14:00, leaves from Stand A at The Hard Interchange Bus Station
near Historic Dockyard, tel. 0800-389-6897, www.localhaunts
.com, info@localhaunts.com).

Arrival in Portsmouth

Portsmouth has two **train** stations. Stay on the train until the final
stop at the Portsmouth Harbour Station, conveniently located one
long block from the TI and the entrance to the Historic Dockyard.
The Hard Interchange Bus Station is just across from the train
station (bus #700 runs from here to Southsea). High-speed, passenger-only catamarans to Ryde on the Isle of Wight depart from
the waterfront in front of the train station (explained later, under
"Portsmouth Connections").

Drivers approach Portsmouth on the M27 motorway.
First take the *Portsmouth (W)* exit, then follow signs for *Historic
Waterfront*. As you get closer, individual parking lots are well-
signposted (the one called "Historic Dockyard" is a garage just two
blocks from the TI).

Getting Around Portsmouth

The walkable core contains the main sights: the Historic Dockyard,
Spinnaker Tower (views), Gunwharf Quays (shopping complex),
Millennium Promenade Walk, and Old Portsmouth. To get to the
D-Day Museum two miles away in Southsea, catch bus #700 from
the Hard Interchange Bus Station, between the main TI and the
train station (90p/ride, £3.50 day pass, 2/hr Mon–Sat, hourly Sun,
10 min).

Sights in Portsmouth

I've listed Portsmouth's sights by neighborhood, from north to
south.

▲▲Historic Dockyard

When Britannia ruled the waves, it did so from Portsmouth's
Historic Dockyard. Britain's great warships, known as the
"Wooden Walls of England," were all that lay between the island
nation and invaders from the Continent. Today, this harbor
is still the base of the Royal Navy. (If you sneak a peek beyond
the guard stations, you can see the British military at work.) The
shipyard offers visitors a glimpse of maritime attractions new and
old. Marvel at the modern-day warships anchored on the docks,
then explore the fantastic collection of historic memorabilia and
preserved ships.

The museum complex has several parts: HMS *Victory,* Royal

Portsmouth

TO LONDON VIA M-3,
SALISBURY,
CHICHESTER,
ARUNDEL &
BRIGHTON

400 YARDS
400 METERS

HMS VICTORY

MARY ROSE (CLOSED UNTIL 2012)

Victory Gallery

Royal Naval Museum

14 13

Action Stations

HISTORIC DOCKYARD

9

QUEEN ST.

15

Mary Rose Museum

HMS WARRIOR

Harbor Cruises

Bus Stn.

PORTSMOUTH HARBOUR STATION

Main Dockyard Entrance

PORTSMOUTH & SOUTHSEA STATION

ALFRED RD.
EDIN. RD.
MARKETWAY
COMMERCIAL ROAD
ARUNDEL
ANGLESEA ROAD

SPINNAKER TOWER & GUNWHARF QUAYS

PARK ROAD

11

CHURCHILL AVE.

OLD PORTS-MOUTH (SPICE ISLAND)

See Detail Map

GEORGE'S ROAD

ST.

CAMBRIDGE ROAD

MUSEUM RD.

KING'S RD.

MIDDLE ST.

Passenger Ferry Dock

7 16

17

8

HIGH

ROUND TOWER

BROAD

GUNWHARF

RD.

PEMBROKE RD.

KING'S TERRACE

ELM GROVE

GROVE RD. S.

SQUARE TOWER

SPUR REDOUBT

KENT

ROAD

DUISBURG WAY

To Isle of Wight

CLARENCE PIER

12

Hoverport

CLARENCE

PARADE

OSBORNE

CLARENCE

AVE. DE CAEN

SOUTHSEA

ESPLANADE

To 10

D-DAY MUSEUM & OVERLORD EMBROIDERY

CASTLE

--- MILLENNIUM PROMENADE
P PARKING
View

OLD PORTSMOUTH

To Isle of Wight

WEST ST.

3 4

5

1

2

6

EAST

TOWER

BROAD ST.

100 YARDS
100 METERS

PORTSMOUTH

DCH

Portsmouth Key

Old Portsmouth Accommodations & Restaurants

❶ Fortitude Cottage

❷ Oyster Cottage

❸ Sailmaker's Loft B&B

❹ The Spice Island Inn

❺ The Still & West Country House Pub

❻ Sallyport Tea Rooms

Other Accommodations & Restaurants

❼ Lombard House

❽ The Duke of Buckingham Pub & Rooms

❾ The Royal Maritime Club

❿ To Portsmouth & Southsea Backpackers Lodge

⓫ Express by Holiday Inn

⓬ Premier Inn Southsea

⓭ Boathouse No. 7 Cafeteria

⓮ Georgian Tearooms

⓯ Costa Coffee & Historic Dockyard Tickets

⓰ Lemon Sole Rest. & Crofts Wine & Beer Cellar

⓱ Good Fortune Restaurant

Naval Museum, *Mary Rose* and *Mary Rose* Museum, HMS *Warrior*, Action Stations, and a harbor cruise. The highlight is the HMS *Victory*, arguably the most important ship in British history. From its deck, Admiral Nelson defeated Napoleon's French fleet at Trafalgar, saving Britain from invasion and escargot. It'll put you in a *Master and Commander* mood—and, in fact, Russell Crowe spent several days here preparing for his role as Captain Jack Aubrey in that 2003 film.

Cost: You can stroll around the shipyard on your own to see the exteriors of the HMS *Victory* and HMS *Warrior* for free (except during special events), but going inside the attractions requires a ticket. You can visit any one sight for £12.50 (HMS *Victory* and Royal Naval Museum count together as a single "sight"), or buy a combo-ticket for £18 that covers everything (good for one year). The Southsea TI hands out 10 percent discount vouchers for this sight (explained earlier, under "Tourist Information").

Hours: The Dockyard is open daily April–Oct 10:00–18:00, Nov–March 10:00–17:30 (last tickets sold 1.5 hours before closing, most boats close 30 min before the Dockyard closes, tel. 023/9272-8060, www.historicdockyard.co.uk). Friendly and knowledgeable docents throughout the complex will happily answer your questions and capably tell tales of the sea.

Crowd-Beating Tips: You might have to wait up to 45 minutes to buy tickets in July and August, when school is out—lines are worst at midday, so try to arrive after lunchtime. In summer, there's usually a second, cash-only ticket desk near the HMS *Victory* (ask the greeter as you enter the Dockyard). You can tour the *Victory* on your own in summer, but in winter (Oct–March),

Nelson's Victory over Napoleon

Admiral Lord Horatio Nelson (1758–1805), a small man who suffered seasickness throughout his career, was a brilliant military strategist. He developed a new plan for taking on Napoleon's fleet: Instead of pulling parallel to the ships and firing broadside, he would drive a line of ships head-on, perpendicular to his opponent's fleet. When the English attacked, they decimated the French, who were unable to return adequate fire. Victory was won, but Nelson, who courageously wore his bright uniform to inspire his men, was lost to a sniper's bullet. While sailors are usually buried at sea, Nelson's body was returned to London, where he was given a grand funeral and then buried in St. Paul's Cathedral. The victory at Trafalgar solidified British dominance of the seas. Although Napoleon would menace Europe for another 10 years, he would never again challenge the British Royal Navy.

you can enter the ship only with a 50-minute tour (you'll get an appointment time for the tour, but as they can fill up by early afternoon, it's best to arrive early in winter).

Because most visitors slowly plod their way back to the *Victory*, the best plan is to do the reverse: Head there first, then work your way back through the other exhibits. This also gets you to the best sights before you get "shipped out." I've listed the attractions in that order.

▲▲▲**HMS Victory**—This grand historic warship changed the course of world history. At the turn of the 19th century, Napoleon's forces were terrorizing the Continent. In 1805, Napoleon amassed a fleet of French and Spanish ships for the purpose of invading England. The Royal Navy managed to blockade the fleets, but some French ships broke through. Admiral Nelson, commander of the British fleet, pursued the ships aboard the HMS *Victory*, cornering them at Cape Trafalgar, off the coast of Spain (see sidebar). Today, the dry-docked HMS *Victory* is so well-preserved that it feels ready to haul anchor and pull out of the harbor at any moment. In fact, it's still a commissioned warship, the world's oldest. For the British, this ship is more a cathedral than a museum.

◐ **Self-Guided Tour:** Visitors follow a one-way route that spirals up and down through the ship's six decks. Here are the highlights.

In the **great cabin,** you'll see Admiral Nelson's quarters. Imagine Nelson and his officers dining at the elegant table—or hunched over maps here to plan an attack. While it looks like an officer's stately quarters, this space is also designed for action:

All of the wood furniture was foldable and could be stored away during battle. The black-and-white checkerboard "tile" flooring—inspired by Nelson's love of southern Italy (and its women)—is actually painted canvas, which could, like the carpets, be rolled up at a moment's notice. It took the crew less than 10 minutes to clear away all the upper-class trappings and turn this space into a fully functional cannon deck. Leaving the Great Cabin, you'll pass Nelson's hanging bunk—even the master of this ship slept on a glorified hammock rather than a bed. (We'll see humbler hammocks soon.)

The **upper gun deck** is filled with original cannons. To prevent the ship from tipping, the lightest were placed higher on the ship, with the heavy ones below. It took a well-trained British sailor two minutes to ready a cannon for firing, compared to the eight minutes French gunners needed to fire their cannons.

Heading up to the **upper deck,** you'll see Captain Hardy's cabin—not quite as posh as his boss Nelson's, but still not bad. Before descending the stairs, notice the small golden plaque on the deck marking the spot where "Nelson fell" during that fateful Battle of Trafalgar—shot by a sniper. From here, the crew rushed him below deck to care for him during his dying hours.

Down in the **middle gundeck,** you can see how the sailors on the ship lived where they worked. When not in battle, they strung hammocks between the guns and ate at tables wedged under their strung-up beds. Sailors ate from square plates to save space. When a man died, his hammock was his burial cloth—his body was sewn up in the hammock, with a last stitch through the nose to ensure the man was really dead. (Since military service was obligatory, faking death was common.)

As you progress deeper into the bowels of the ship, the space becomes smaller and darker (watch your head). It's down here, in the **orlop deck,** that Nelson died, gasping his final words: "Thank God, I have done my duty." The painting next to the spot of his death shows the admiral glowing like a saint as sailors look on in grief. (Whether or not this is an eyewitness account is suspect, however; check the size of the ship—either people were much smaller back then or the painter had never been onboard the *Victory*.) After his death, Nelson was put in a cask filled with brandy to preserve his body. Legend has it that the cask was not quite as full by the time the sailors arrived in London.

Royal Naval Museum—This museum, situated in three buildings, is packed with model ships, paintings, uniforms, and lots more Nelson hero-worship. While interesting, it gets old quickly for all but serious naval history fans. If you dip into only one part, choose the one nearest the *Victory*, called the Victory Gallery. The corny but informative 15-minute "Trafalgar Experience" multimedia show—with movies, mannequins, sound effects, and smoke—offers a blow-by-blow account of the Battle of Trafalgar. It culminates with a viewing of a panoramic painting of the battle.

▲**Mary Rose**—The eerie, melancholy carcass of the *Mary Rose* is closed to the public while it gets a new, £35 million home. This 16th-century warship was Henry VIII's favorite, named after his sister (Mary) and his family emblem (the rose). In July 1545, when a French fleet approached the English coastline, the *Mary Rose* was sent out to engage the enemy. Suddenly, just two miles offshore, a stiff breeze caught the ship and it tipped over. Since all of the gun bays were open, ready for battle, the water overwhelmed the ship and it began to sink. Netting over the hold was intended to keep boarding parties at bay, but instead it trapped 400 sailors as they frantically scrambled to escape. Eventually, the ship and its doomed crew settled, stuck in the mud, in relatively shallow water.

In 1982, about 15 years after the wreck was located, the half of the ship that was encased in mud—and thus preserved—was raised. Today, the *Mary Rose* is still undergoing restoration. Since allowing the ship to dry out too quickly would cause the structure to disintegrate, its remains are being constantly sprayed with a sealing wax solution. Starting in 2011, officials will finally start to let the hull dry out—a process that will take five years.

Inside the wreck were found all sorts of Tudor-era items, such as clothes, dishes, weapons, and even a backgammon board and an oboe-like instrument. These items are shown off in the ***Mary Rose Museum,*** back near the entrance of the Dockyard. A 15-minute film runs every half-hour, telling the story of how they raised the *Rose.* While the museum is a little too kid-oriented and lacks the decorum a shipwreck site deserves, it's still a fascinating look at everyday shipboard life from almost 500 years ago. This museum remains open while the new complex—which will house both the preserved ship and the artifacts—is under construction. Officials hope to get the new museum finished in time for the 2012 Summer Olympics.

HMS Warrior—This ship, while impressive, never saw a day of battle...which explains why it's in such good condition. The *Warrior* was the first ironclad warship, a huge technological advance. Compare this ship, built in 1860, with the *Victory,* which was similar to the common warships at the time. The *Warrior* was unbeatable, and the enemy knew it. Its very existence was sufficient to keep the peace. The late 19th century didn't see many sea battles, however, and by the time warships were needed

again, the *Warrior* was obsolete.

Action Stations—Thinly veiled propaganda for the military, this collection of interactive, high-tech exhibits and simulators is aimed mostly at the young and/or prospective Royal Navy recruits. It's like an Army commercial combined with a noisy video arcade—persuasively fun for kids but irritating to weary adults.

Harbor Cruise—You can scoot around the harbor and back to the Historic Dockyard in about 45 minutes by boat (£5, included in £18 Historic Dockyard combo-ticket, departs about hourly during the summer starting at 11:00, last cruise usually leaves at 16:00 from just inside Dockyard entrance, weather-dependent, tel. 01983/564-602). As it also stops at Gunwharf Quays, taking this cruise at the very end of your Dockyard visit can be a smart way to eliminate the 10–15-minute walk to the Spinnaker Tower and surrounding mall.

Gunwharf Quays and the Spinnaker Tower

Part of the major (and successful) makeover of Portsmouth, the bustling **Gunwharf Quays** (pronounced "keys") is an American-style outdoor shopping-center-on-steroids, with restaurants, shops, and entertainment. You'll find all the top shops here, as well as a casino, a bowling alley, a 14-screen cinema, trendy eateries with good views of the water, and an Express by Holiday Inn (mall open Mon–Fri 10:00–19:00, Sat 9:00–19:00, Sun 10:00–17:00, tel. 023/9283-6700, www.gunwharf-quays.com).

Out at the far end of the shopping zone is the can't-miss-it **Spinnaker Tower.** Like Seattle's vaguely futuristic Space

Needle, the Spinnaker Tower has quickly come to define its city. The 557-foot-tall, £35 million tower is evocative of the billowing ships' sails that have played such a key role in the history of this city and country. Despite massive construction setbacks and cost overruns, the tower finally opened in October 2005. It was not an auspicious beginning: On opening day, the tower's manager became stranded when an elevator broke down. Barring any malfunctions, you can ride to the 330-foot-high view deck for a panorama of the port and sea beyond, or court acrophobia with a stroll across "Europe's biggest glass floor" (£7; daily 10:00–18:00, until 22:00 in Aug; since it can be crowded at midday July–Aug, it's smart to book ahead—and doing so online gets you a 10 percent discount; info tel. 023/9285-7520, booking tel. 023/9285-7521, www.spinnakertower.co.uk).

Getting There: If walking to the mall or Spinnaker Tower from the Historic Dockyard, stay on the mainland past the train station, then go through the modern archway marked *Gunwharf Quays* at the old brick rail bridge.

Old Portsmouth

Portsmouth's historic district—once known as "Spice Island" after the ships' precious cargo—is surprisingly quiet. For a long time, the old sea village was dilapidated and virtually empty. Recently, there's been an effort to revitalize the area, which now has a few inviting pubs and B&Bs. It's a pleasant place to stroll around and imagine how different this district was in the old days, when it was filled with salty fishermen and sailors who told tall tales and sang sea shanties in rough-and-tumble pubs.

Getting There: To get to Old Portsmouth from the Historic Dockyard, walk past the train station, and go through the archway on the right marked *Gunwharf Quays* to cut through the giant shopping complex. Follow signs (or ask anyone to point the way) to exit through the gate on the far end of the complex. Turn right and follow the chain links in the sidewalk to skirt the harbor and reach the old town (the sidewalk markers may be partially obscured by construction).

Old Portsmouth Millennium Promenade Walk—The chain links mark the Millennium Promenade (also called the Renaissance Trail on the TI's map). The chain symbol recalls the great steel chain that once spanned the mouth of the harbor and was raised to block invading warships. For a pleasant hour-long after-dinner stroll, walk the portion of the trail south of Old Portsmouth along the oceanfront. Interpretive panels along the way give you insights into Portsmouth's fascinating history.

• *From the tip of Old Portsmouth, follow the trail around on the ocean side to small* **Capstan Square,** *where the harbor-spanning chain was raised to keep out enemy ships. Pass through a narrow gate and climb up the stairs to the top of the 15th-century* **Round Tower.** *A plaque shows where the wreck of the* Mary Rose *was found. After taking in the view, follow the top of the old stone fortifications down to the Square Tower.*

The 15th-century **Square Tower,** originally the residence of the governor of Portsmouth, was later used to store gunpowder. South of the Square Tower on the left is the small, roofless Royal Garrison Church. Founded in 1212 as a hospice, it was used as a shelter for overseas pilgrims traveling to Canterbury, Chichester, and Winchester. The church was later used by garrisoned troops before the nave lost its roof in a WWII bombing raid.

• *After walking south about a quarter-mile, you'll see a small moat on the left.*

You've reached the **Spur Redoubt,** part of the outer fortifications (see interpretive sign down by moat)—and the end of our walk. To avoid the huge crowds that had gathered in town to see him, Admiral Nelson supposedly passed through this area on September 14, 1805, on his way to the Battle of Trafalgar. From the beach, he was rowed out to the *Victory,* waiting off the Isle of Wight. He didn't return to England alive.

• *Cross the metal bridge over the moat, pass through a tunnel under the earthen fortifications, and immediately turn right and climb up the short path to the top. Walk back along the top of the grassy fortifications. Benches invite you to stop and watch the many passing ferries and other ships or to simply enjoy the sunset. If the weather's clear, you'll see the Isle of Wight from here.*

Southsea

On a sunny day, this appealing seafront neighborhood—with its long, broad, grassy park stretching for miles in front of fine old townhouses—bustles with locals enjoying their city. While it's studded with some humdrum sights and a TI, the main reason to venture to Southsea is for its fine D-Day Museum.

▲**D-Day Museum and Overlord Embroidery**—This museum, worth ▲▲ to history buffs, was built to commemorate the 40th

anniversary of the D-Day invasions. Though it feels a bit dated and faded, it still does an excellent job of re-creating both the atmosphere of WWII England and the planning and execution of the Normandy landing.

The centerpiece of the exhibit is the 272-foot long **Overlord Embroidery** (named for the invasion's code name). The 34 appliquéd panels—stitched together over five years by a team of seamstresses, and originally displayed in a brewery's boardroom—were inspired by the Bayeux Tapestry that recorded William the Conqueror's battles during the Norman invasion of England a thousand years earlier. The panels chronologically trace the years from 1940 to 1944, from the first British men receiving their call-up papers in the mail to the successful implementation of D-Day. It celebrates everyone from famous WWII figures to unsung heroes of the home front. A worthwhile 50p audioguide narrates the whole thing, panel by panel (rent when you buy your ticket).

In the center of the embroidery hall, a movie theater shows a good 15-minute film—a montage of archival wartime footage set to period music (included in entry ticket). Then you'll wander through an exhibit that thoughtfully explains the Battle of Britain and D-Day, including some vehicles that were actually used for the landing. Allow at least 90 minutes for your visit.

Cost, Hours, Location: £6, discounted 10 percent-off tickets sold at main TI—see page 234. Daily April–Sept 10:00–17:30, Oct–March 10:00–17:00, last entry 30 min before closing. A café is on-site. The museum is on the waterfront about two miles south of the Spinnaker Tower (Clarence Esplanade, Southsea, tel. 023/9282-7261, www.ddaymuseum.co.uk). To get from Portsmouth's Hard Interchange Bus Station to the museum, take bus #700 (2/hr Mon–Sat, hourly on Sun, 10 min; ask at the info booth about last return-bus times).

Sleeping in Portsmouth

If you just can't get enough of ships and sea air, Old Portsmouth, just a 15-minute walk from the Historic Dockyard (cutting through the outdoor Gunwharf Quays mall), is charming, fairly quiet, and has several options.

In Old Portsmouth

$$$ Fortitude Cottage, quaint and cozy, rents six modern-feeling rooms and one apartment in two adjoining row houses just a block from the water. Everything is done with care, making these some of the best rooms in Portsmouth. The main building has views, and the top-floor room has its own roof terrace. The new annex rooms are more spacious, with large modern bathrooms (Db-£80–105, Sb pays the Db rate except during slow times, Wi-Fi, 51 Broad Street, tel. 023/9282-3748, www.fortitudecottage.co.uk, info@fortitude cottage.co.uk, Maggie and Mike).

Sleep Code

(£1 = about $1.60, country code: 44, area code: 023)
S = Single, **D** = Double/Twin, **T** = Triple, **Q** = Quad, **b** = bathroom, **s** = shower only. You can assume credit cards are accepted unless otherwise noted.

To help you sort easily through these listings, I've divided the rooms into three categories based on the price for a standard double room with bath:

$$$ **Higher Priced**—Most rooms £75 or more.

$$ **Moderately Priced**—Most rooms between £40–75.

$ **Lower Priced**—Most rooms £40 or less.

$$$ Oyster Cottage is for those who want their B&B to themselves. Witty Carol, who might remind you of Carol Channing, has just one large, light-filled, updated room with a bay-window sitting area, ideal for watching passing boats right up close (Db-£65–80, free parking, 9 Bath Square, tel. 023/9282-3683, www.theoystercottage.co.uk, info@theoystercottage.co.uk).

$$ Sailmaker's Loft B&B, next door, is a straightforward, unpretentious B&B. Originally built as a warehouse, it has one en-suite room and two others that share a bathroom. The two rooms on the ocean side offer front-row seats of the bustling harbor. Owner Bob is an ex-seaman who loves his home port (S-£30, twin D-£60, Db-£70, free parking, 5 Bath Square, tel. 023/9282-3045, www.sailmakersloft.org.uk, sailmakersloft@aol.com).

Between Old Portsmouth and Gunwharf Quays

$$ Lombard House rents two rooms on a quiet residential street next to the cathedral, a five-minute walk from Old Portsmouth. The public areas are tastefully decorated in red and feature original artwork. In 2005, as part of the bicentennial of the Battle of Trafalgar, actor-owners Alex and Finni traveled around Great Britain as Admiral Nelson and his mistress, Lady Emma Hamilton. Alex's museum-quality admiral's costume is on display in their atmospheric breakfast cellar, which also boasts old oak ship beams (Sb-£47, Db-£68, cash only, 9 Lombard Street, tel. 023/9286-2294, mobile 0776-200-1528, finni@victoryfilms.co.uk).

$$ The Duke of Buckingham Pub, a few blocks inland from Old Portsmouth, is likely to have rooms when others are full. While the accommodations take a backseat to the popular pub, the 25 basic rooms—above the bar and in a cottage out back—are clean and new-feeling (S-£45, Sb-£50, D-£50, Db-£65, family room-£75–80, free Wi-Fi, 119 High Street, tel. 023/9282-7067, www.dukeofbuckingham.net, buckingham119@aol.com).

Elsewhere in Portsmouth

$$$ The Royal Maritime Club offers a home away from home to sailors in town who don't want to bunk on the boat. Just two blocks up the road from the Historic Dockyard entrance, it also welcomes tourists, who share its grand public spaces, generous facilities (including a swimming pool, fitness center, game room, self-service laundry, even barbershop) and 120 comfortable, surprisingly newish rooms. The catch: They rent out their ballroom for parties, which can sometimes be noisy into the wee hours—if you're a light sleeper, try requesting a quieter room. It's located two blocks from the Historic Dockyard and four blocks from the train station (Sb-£44, Db-£87, family suites, includes breakfast, elevator, free Wi-Fi, Queen Street, tel. 023/9282-4231, fax 023/9229-3496, www.royalmaritimeclub.co.uk, info@royalmaritimeclub.co.uk).

$ Portsmouth & Southsea Backpackers Lodge is your budget option, with dorm beds and some cheap doubles in a faded old house. This strictly run place is in Southsea, a five-minute walk from the D-Day Museum and about two miles from the central sights (£15 bunks in 4- to 8-bed dorms, D-£34, Db-£38, reception open 7:30–23:00, Internet access, laundry, 4 Florence Road, tel. & fax 023/9283-2495, www.portsmouthbackpackers.co.uk, info @portsmouthbackpackers.co.uk).

Big Chain Hotels

The following hotels (with elevators and 24-hour reception) may have rooms when the other accommodations are full.

$$$ Express by Holiday Inn, located in the shadow of the Spinnaker Tower and within the Gunwharf Quays shopping complex, rents 130 cookie-cutter rooms not far from the Portsmouth Harbour Train Station and Historic Dockyard (£105–120 per room, check website for specials, includes continental breakfast and discounts at some Gunwharf Quays restaurants; free parking for first 24 hours, then £2/day; US reservations tel. 888-465-4329, British reservations tel. 0800-434-040, reception tel. 023/9289-4240, fax 023/9289-4241, www.hiexpress.co.uk, portsmouth @kewgreen.co.uk).

$$ Premier Inn Southsea, a half-mile south of Old Portsmouth along the waterfront, offers 48 modern rooms next to the kitschy, cotton-candy-carnival ambience of Clarence Pier (the noisy pier attractions close down at about 22:30). It's popular with business travelers on weeknights and families on weekends—as the hordes of screaming kids in the family restaurant downstairs can attest (Db for up to two adults and two kids-£65, may be up to £80 during special events, check website for specials, continental breakfast-£5.15, full English breakfast-£7.35, pay Wi-Fi, limited free parking, Long Curtain Road, just off Pier Road, Southsea, tel. 023/9273-4622, fax 023/9273-3048, www.premierinn.com).

Eating in Portsmouth

At the Historic Dockyard

The Historic Dockyard has an acceptable **cafeteria** (called Boathouse No. 7) with a play area that kids enjoy (£4–7 meals, daily 10:00–15:00). The **Georgian Tearooms** are across the pedestrian street in Storehouse #9, with good sandwich and cake offerings (daily 10:00–17:00). The **Costa Coffee** inside the entrance building offers surprisingly good grilled sandwiches, and coffee drinks to go (daily 10:00–17:00).

At Gunwharf Quays

Eating options abound at this bustling mega-mall. Most restaurants line up along the waterfront by the Spinnaker Tower. You'll pay too much in this high-rent district—and many of the places are chains selling mall food—but it's the most convenient one-stop neighborhood for dining.

In and near Old Portsmouth

Dinnertime is the best time to head over to Old Portsmouth, eat at a pub, and then stroll along the Millennium Promenade (described earlier, under "Sights in Portsmouth"). The first two pubs listed here sling overpriced pub grub with gorgeous views, within a french fry's toss of the water—the busy maritime traffic makes for a fascinating backdrop. The next three listings are clustered between Old Portsmouth and Gunwharf Quays, along a quiet, mostly residential street. The last listing is a charming tearoom that closes before dinnertime.

The Spice Island Inn, at the tip of the Old Portsmouth peninsula, has terrific outdoor seating, a family-friendly dining room upstairs, and many vegetarian offerings (£5–9 lunches, £7–12 dinners, food served daily 12:00–21:00, bar open longer, 1 Bath Square, tel. 023/9287-0543).

The Still & West Country House Pub underwent an extensive and expensive renovation a few years ago, and has dining in two appealing zones. Eat from the simpler and cheaper menu on the main floor, or outside on the picnic benches with fantastic views of the harbor (£6 baguette sandwiches and £9 fish and chips). Or head upstairs to the dining room, with higher prices (£9–17 main dishes) but a gorgeous glassed-in conservatory that offers sea views—especially enticing in cold weather (Mon–Sat 11:00–21:00, Sun 11:00–17:00, bar open later, 2 Bath Square, tel. 023/9282-1567).

Lemon Sole is pricey but comes with an innovative "fish counter" concept. After noting your table number, wander back to the fresh fish counter, where you choose your own fillet, pick a sauce, and specify side dishes (figure £18–30, depending on market price). If all this is too much for you—or if you're not into seafood—you can also choose from the à la carte menu (non-fish dishes run about £13–17, fish dishes £18–25). Downstairs and run by the same restaurant is **Crofts,** a cozy 18th-century wine and beer cellar with original brickwork and an old well under the outside stairway. The similar menu focuses more on non-fish dishes (£12–15 main dishes, both open daily 11:30–14:30 & 17:30–22:00, Fri–Sat until 22:30, 123 High Street, tel. 023/9281-1303).

The **Good Fortune**, across the street from Lemon Sole, is a Chinese restaurant favored by locals (21 High Street, tel. 023/9286-3293).

Tearoom: If you're in Old Portsmouth before dinner and could do with a proper afternoon tea, visit the **Sallyport Tea Rooms,** named for a gateway in a fortification—specifically the one in Portsmouth's ramparts that Nelson passed through on his final departure (£4–5 sandwiches, £7 afternoon tea—order in advance, Tue–Sun 10:00–17:00, closed Mon, 35 Broad Street, tel. 023/9281-6265).

Portsmouth Connections

From Portsmouth by Train to: London's **Waterloo Station** (2–3/hr, 1.5–2.25 hrs), **Gatwick Airport** (2/hr, 1.5–1.75 hrs, some require transfer), **Bath** (hourly, 2.25 hrs), **Salisbury** (hourly, 1.25–1.5 hrs), **Brighton** (1/hr direct, 1.5 hrs, more with transfer), **Exeter** (hourly, 3–4 hrs, change in Salisbury). Train info: tel. 0845-748-4950, www.nationalrail.co.uk.

By Bus: For most connections, the train is faster—take the bus only if you're on a tight budget. Stagecoach runs the #700 Coastliner bus to **Brighton** (2/hr, 3–3.75 hrs; tel. 0845-121-0170 or toll tel. 0871-200-2233, www.stagecoachbus.com). National Express buses also go to **Brighton** (1 direct bus/day, 1.75 hrs), **Salisbury** (2/day, 1.5 hrs), and **Bath** (1 direct bus/day, 3 hrs; toll tel. 0871-781-8181, www.nationalexpress.com).

By Ferry to the Isle of Wight: Wightlink Ferries has service to **Fishbourne** (40 min, cars and passengers) and a catamaran to **Ryde** (18 min, passengers only, tel. 0871-376-4342, www.wightlink.co.uk). Hovertravel operates a passenger-only hovercraft from Southsea (2 miles south of Portsmouth) to **Ryde** (2/hr, 10 min, tel. 023/9281-1000, www.hovertravel.co.uk).

If you're interested in visiting Queen Victoria's palatial island retreat, **Osborne House,** ask about a combo-ticket that combines the round-trip boat ride, bus to and from the estate, and admission (£23.20, buy at Hovertravel's Southsea terminal on the day of travel, call ahead for departure days and times, tel. 023/9281-1000).

By International Ferry: P&O Ferries (tel. 08716-645-645, www.poferries.com) sails to **Bilbao,** Spain (2–3/week, 32 hrs). Brittany Ferries (tel. 0871-244-1400, www.brittanyferries.com) sails to France: **Caen** (2–4/day, 3.75 hrs on high-speed boat, 6–7 hrs on slower boat), **Cherbourg** (1–2/day, 3 hrs), and **St. Malo** (night crossing, 1/day, 11 hrs). LD Lines (tel. 0844-576-8836, www.ldlines.co.uk) sails to **Le Havre,** France (1–2/day, 6–8 hrs).

Near Portsmouth

These sights are very near the main A27 road that connects Portsmouth with Brighton. They're worth considering for a stopover if you have time as you pass through.

Fishbourne Roman Palace

In the 1930s, a farmer just outside of Chichester found the remains of a Roman palace on his land. Wary of archaeologists, he didn't  disclose his find until 1960. The ensuing dig revealed a huge Roman-era villa, probably owned by a local tribal chief who was loyal to the Roman Empire. In the main museum building, you'll find the collection's impressive centerpiece: well-preserved floor mosaics, which are on display in their original locations (visitors walk above them on an elevated walkway). Also in the main building is a museum telling the story of the palace and Fishbourne's Roman era. The garden outside was reconstructed to resemble the original Roman plan. Across the parking lot, the new Discovery Centre lets you peek into the offices and warehouses of the archaeologists at work—like a zoo for people in lab coats. You'll learn how the artifacts are handled on their long journey from the ground to the display case. The palace is fairly interesting to most, but likely to fascinate only true fans of Roman history.

Cost and Hours: £7.30, £2 guidebook outlines a very detailed tour, £2.50 illustrated book is good for kids; March–Oct daily 10:00–17:00, until 18:00 in Aug; Nov–mid-Dec and Feb daily 10:00–16:00; mid-Dec–Jan Sat–Sun 10:00–16:00, closed Mon–Fri; café, tel. 01243/785-859, www.sussexpast.co.uk/fishbourne.

Getting There: It's on the southwestern outskirts of the large town of Chichester, well-signed from the main A27 motorway connecting Brighton and Portsmouth. First head for the town of Fishbourne, then follow *Roman Palace* signs through a very residential-feeling neighborhood to the museum. From the Fishbourne train station, the palace is a five-minute walk.

▲Arundel Castle

This impressive castle of Arundel (AHR-uhn-dull) graces the valley below with straight-out-of-a-storybook appeal. The Duke of Norfolk—the top dog among all the English dukes—still lives here, in what amounts to a museum of his own family (the Fitzalan-Howards). Pompous even for a castle, the self-aggrandizing

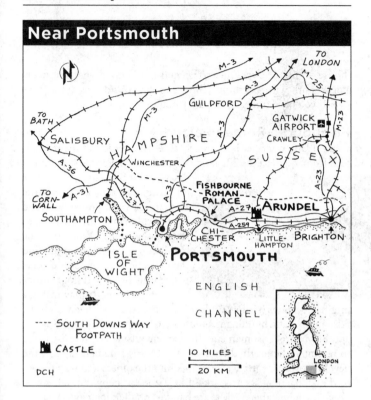

Near Portsmouth

TO LONDON

M-3

TO BATH

GUILDFORD

GATWICK AIRPORT

M-23

CRAWLEY

SALISBURY

HAMPSHIRE

A-3

SUSSEX

A-36

WINCHESTER

M-3

A-3

M-27

FISHBOURNE ROMAN PALACE

A-27

ARUNDEL

TO CORNWALL

A-31

M-27

A-3

A-259

LITTLE-HAMPTON

BRIGHTON

SOUTHAMPTON

CHI-CHESTER

ISLE OF WIGHT

PORTSMOUTH

ENGLISH

CHANNEL

---- SOUTH DOWNS WAY FOOTPATH

CASTLE

10 MILES

20 KM

LONDON

DCH

exhibits, docents who speak in hushed awe of their employers, and opulent interiors offer a somehow off-putting taste of England's affection for its outmoded nobility. Still, castle buffs will find the gorgeous interior worth visiting, and the themed gardens are a delight—check out the Earl's Garden, which is based on 17th-century designs.

Cost and Hours: Castle grounds-£7, grounds and interior-£14. The complex is open April–Oct Tue–Sun, closed Mon (except in Aug) and closed Nov–March. Various parts of the castle are at different times: grounds and Fitzalan Chapel—10:00–17:00; castle keep—11:00–16:30; main castle rooms—12:00–17:00 (the private bedrooms, which cost £1 extra to see, are open only Tue–Fri); last entry at 16:00. Parts of the castle can be unexpectedly closed for private events. Tel. 01903/882-173, www.arundelcastle.org.

Getting There: Arundel Castle is right on A27 between Brighton and Portsmouth—**drivers** just follow signs to the castle, and park at the pay lot across from the castle gate. The town of Arundel is connected by **train** from Portsmouth (1–2/hr, 1–1.5 hrs, 1 transfer) and Brighton (1–2/hr, 1–1.25 hrs, 1–2 transfers);

Stagecoach **buses** also run from Brighton to Arundel (2/hr Mon–Sat, none on Sun, 2.25 hrs, some require transfer).

Background: The castle seems like the perfect medieval fortress. Well, almost...while the castle dates back to the 11th century, most of what you see today is actually a Victorian restoration.

The owners of the castle, the Catholic Dukes of Norfolk, weren't very popular in this Protestant country, and neither was their castle, which endured multiple sieges. The Dukes persevered, however, rebuilding their castle in the 18th and 19th centuries along with a large Catholic church. As you explore the castle, posted explanations fill in the story (such as an English Civil War exhibit with a Catholic spin). For a primer before you begin, consider stopping by the little information room in the gate as you enter the castle grounds (across from the ticket booth).

❷ Self-Guided Tour: The castle is all about its intimidating bulk and opulent interior—so little explanation is necessary. But here are a few tidbits to bring meaning to your visit. Notice that various parts of the castle have different opening times (listed earlier); if you're here in the morning, visit them according to when they open.

Castle Keep: This ancient centerpiece of the castle is a classic motte-and-bailey design, with a stout windowless fortress atop a man-made hill—double defense against attackers. Later, as the castle grew around it, the keep became the last resort in case of an attack. Walking across the bridge to the keep, ponder how easy it would be to keep the keep—it's connected to the outside only by one bridge, and is well defended by strategically placed arrow slits. Inside the keep yard, stairs lead down to a cellar used as both a dungeon and a storehouse for resources in case the keep had to be used for a final stand. If the flag is flying up top, it means the Duke of Norfolk or his heir (the Earl of Arundel) is around.

Main Castle Rooms: This was—and remains—the gorgeously appointed residence of the Duke of Norfolk. As you ogle the decor, docents explain what you're looking at, and they are always eager to tell you about the lineage, heraldry, and personalities of their beloved dukes. You'll pass through a spectacular private **chapel** (19th-century "Catholic Revival") before entering the **Baron's Hall,** with a pair of giant fireplaces and some fine furniture (including a gorgeous inlaid-wood chest). This room is still used for functions...and, occasionally, for filming the British version of *Antiques Roadshow.* Then you'll pass through a **picture gallery**

displaying a *Who's Who* of the Dukes of Norfolk (no, really...who *are* these people?) and enjoy strolling through the formal state dining room, bedrooms, and drawing rooms. Finally, you'll reach the highlight: a wonderful old **library** with rich mahogany woodwork and 10,000 leatherbound books on two levels.

Fitzalan Chapel: This family church—across a tree-filled garden from the main castle—is the final resting place of many of the Dukes of Norfolk. In the nave of the church, notice the grisly double-decker tomb of a 15th-century earl. Called a *memento mori,* or "reminder of death," this was carved during the earl's lifetime—with his virile, healthy self on the top level, and a rotting corpse on the bottom level—to remind him of his own mortality. Flanking the aisle, find the plaques dedicated to the most recent D.'s of N.: Bernard (who died in 1975) and his cousin Miles Francis (died in 2002). Today's Duke—Edward Fitzalan-Howard—is the 18th to hold the title...and you just walked through his house.

Arundel Town: If you have time to kill, check out the adjacent village of Arundel, where you'll find many fine pubs and shops. The **TI** is also happy to suggest nearby boat trips and activities in town (summer Mon–Sat 10:00–17:00, Sun 10:00–16:00; winter daily 10:00–15:00; 1–3 Crown Yard Mews, River Road, tel. 01903/882-268, www.arundel.org.uk).

DARTMOOR

Windswept and desolate, Dartmoor—one of England's best national parks—is one of the few truly wild places you'll find in this densely populated country. Dartmoor's vast medieval commons are still places where all can pass, anyone can graze their sheep, and ponies run wild. Old stone-slab clapper bridges remind hikers that for thousands of years, humans have trod these same paths. In other parts of England, stone circles, stone rows, and standing stones are cause for a tourist frenzy. In Dartmoor, where the terrain is littered with the highest concentration of prehistoric monuments in the UK, they're barely worth a detour.

Locals brag that Dartmoor is England as it was 50 years ago. Maybe that's why it's increasingly a retreat of the rich and famous. You'll find yourself sharing the narrow roads with luxury SUVs, as many retired CEOs and washed-up celebrities have resettled here, in an idyllic and remote countryside far from prying eyes. The area around Chagford has become known as the "Golden Triangle."

All that wealth aside, Dartmoor remains first and foremost the terrain of hikers. Dartmoor gives you a chance to be alone with England's history, jittery sheep, stately wild ponies, and seemingly endless moors. It's also a moody place: At sunset on a clear evening, the gold-tinged heather and rolling hills can be romantic; but on a gray and misty day, it's foreboding—and if you listen hard enough, you might just hear the howl of the hound of the Baskervilles.

Planning Your Time

Dartmoor works well as a stopover between Cornwall (see next chapter) and the rest of England. While you could get a taste of Dartmoor with one overnight (after breakfast, do my self-guided driving tour and/or Scorhill Stone Circle before moving on in the afternoon), it really deserves at least one full day and two overnights to fully appreciate its majesty and mystery. This is one of those places where time slows down...and puts a crimp in an ambitious itinerary.

Getting Around Dartmoor

Drivers have Dartmoor by the tail—but a good map is essential... as is a fair amount of courage. Dartmoor's narrow lanes are the most challenging in England: barely as wide as a single car, and often flanked by tall stone hedges covered in greenery (with an occasional jutting rock near the base that's made to order for slashing tires). As most roads are too narrow for two cars to easily pass, you'll often have to pull up or reverse to the nearest wide spot in the road when encountering another car. Just follow the other driver's lead, pull in your mirrors as needed, and don't be shy to wave a thank you. For driving in Dartmoor, rent the smallest car you can tolerate, and you'll breathe easier.

Dartmoor is tricky for visitors without a car, but there are some **bus** connections. Okehampton and Ivybridge are both on minor rail lines, but the closest major city is Exeter. From the Exeter bus station, the Transmoor Link #82 bus departs twice daily and stops in Moretonhampstead, Postbridge, and Princetown (toll tel. 0871-200-2233, www.traveline.org.uk). Two other bus routes from Exeter also connect to Dartmoor towns (Mon–Fri year-round, no buses Sat–Sun): Bus #173 to Chagford and Moretonhampstead (4/day), and bus #359 to Moretonhampstead (7/day). During the summer (late May–Oct), the **Haytor Hoppa** bus runs on Saturdays from Bovey Tracey up to Haytor and on to Widecombe (£2, 4/day, www.dartmoor-npa.gov.uk). The **Sunday Rover** day pass lets you travel on summer Sundays and Bank Holidays on most buses and trains in Dartmoor (£6.50, buy ticket on bus, late May–mid-Sept, toll tel. 0871-200-2233, www.carfreedaysout.com/dartrover.html).

Orientation to Dartmoor

Dartmoor National Park is vast (368 square miles), but I've focused on the most accessible chunk at the northeastern end of the park, between the A30 and A38 highways.

Throughout Dartmoor, there are more than 10,000 ancient monuments, all accessible to walkers. Princetown, in the center of the moors, has the park's primary information office, with other branches at Postbridge and Haytor (all described later, under "Tourist Information"). The small villages that encroach on the park are charming, and a few (such as Chagford, Moretonhampstead, and Bovey Tracey) are good as home bases for exploring the moors.

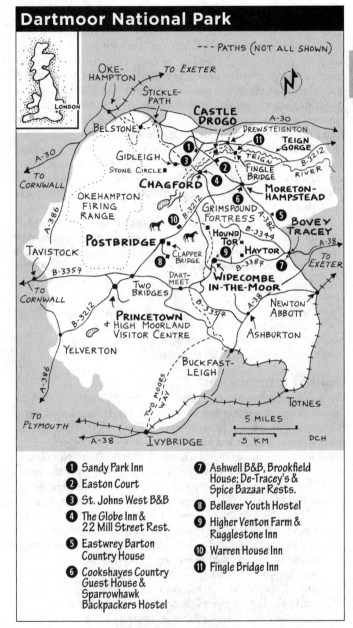

Dartmoor National Park

--- PATHS (NOT ALL SHOWN)

1 Sandy Park Inn

2 Easton Court

3 St. Johns West B&B

4 The Globe Inn &
22 Mill Street Rest.

5 Eastwrey Barton
Country House

6 Cookshayes Country
Guest House &
Sparrowhawk
Backpackers Hostel

7 Ashwell B&B, Brookfield
House; De-Tracey's &
Spice Bazaar Rests.

8 Bellever Youth Hostel

9 Higher Venton Farm &
Rugglestone Inn

10 Warren House Inn

11 Fingle Bridge Inn

Two pieces of gear are essential: good shoes (resistant to mud and "Dartmoor landmines"—wild-horse patties) and an Ordnance Survey map (essential for drivers). You'll need this highly detailed map, not just because the land can be boggy, but also because roads and walking paths are twisty and confusing. (Only two major roads cross the moor, but there are dozens of lesser roads twisting through the countryside—it seems there are five different ways to get between any two points.) The Ordnance Survey produces two good maps of the region. The 1:25,000 Dartmoor map (Explorer #OL28) is ideal for serious hikers, since it shows every ridge, feature, and landmark, but its detail can be overwhelming for drivers. The 1:50,000 map (called "Okehampton & North Dartmoor," Landranger Map #191) is more useful for drivers, and still includes enough detail to use for basic hikes.

Dangers: Parts of the moors are used by the military for target practice. These areas are clearly shown on maps, and marked by red flags when in use—but before going for a hike, always check with a park information office to ensure your route is OK. Other dangers include ticks and adders (a poisonous snake with a black-and-white zigzag stripe). Weather can change quickly here, so wear layers and be prepared for "four seasons in one day" (as locals say). Because Dartmoor is so vast and empty, getting lost is a real threat—a good map and a compass are essential if you're going more than a short distance from your car.

Tourist Information

Most of the bigger villages surrounding Dartmoor have TIs, but the main information center for the park is the **High Moorland Visitor Centre** in Princetown. In addition to hiking info, this office has an interactive exhibit on the history, wildlife, and "countryside code" for walking the moors (daily Easter–Oct 10:00–17:00, Nov–Easter 10:00–16:00, Tavistock Road, tel. 01822/890-414, www.dartmoor -npa.gov.uk). There are also good branches in **Postbridge** (at the big parking lot near the Clapper Bridge, relaxing video upstairs about Dartmoor ponies, Easter–Oct daily 10:00–17:00, Nov–Dec Sat–Sun only 10:00–16:00, closed Jan–Easter, tel. 01822/880-272) and by **Haytor** (Easter–Oct daily 10:00–17:00; Nov–Easter Sat-Sun 10:00–16:00, closed Mon–Fri; tel. 01364/661-520).

At any of these offices, you can buy your Ordnance Survey map and pick up their free information-packed *Dartmoor Guide*, with an insert listing guided walks and events. These offices are the best source of advice on hikes or driving routes, and each one sells an illustrated £1.50 booklet with suggestions for self-guided walks. If you have an iPod or other MP3 player, you can download free, six-mile audio walks starting at the three park information centers (www.dartmoor-npa.gov.uk).

Consider taking a **guided walk** offered by the national park (£3–8 per person, depends on length; get schedule at www .dartmoor-npa.gov.uk or in *Dartmoor Guide*). You can go with your own guide for a hike of your choosing at a similar price—try Tom Soby, who offers a range of walks, including a popular one exploring the places outlined in *The Hound of the Baskervilles* (£7–10/ person to join a scheduled walk, private tours-£36/3 hrs, mobile 0774-856-3096, tomstors@hotmail.com).

Phil Page, a former Dartmoor park manager, offers walks all year on topics from butterflies to literary novels set in Dartmoor (£10/hr for up to 6 people, under 16 free, book in advance, will pick up within a 10-mile limit, tel. 07858/421-148, mobile 07849-840-126, www.dartmoornaturetours.co.uk, enquiries@dartmoor naturetours.co.uk). His wife, Hanneke, rents two rooms at **Yarrow Lodge**, their home in the midst of Yarner Wood, a nature reserve within the national park between Bovey Tracey and Haytor (D-£50, March–Dec only, tel. 01626/836-589, mobile 07849-840-126, www.yarrowlodge.co.uk).

Self-Guided Driving Tour

▲▲▲Pony, Lamb, and Moor Joyride

This all-day driving route is a convenient framework for your

Dartmoor exploration. Linger at the desolate viewpoints you find most appealing, and don't be afraid to venture off this plan for a walk to a secluded stone row or circle. If you have enough time, chase down leads suggested by locals—there are many hidden gems embedded in Dartmoor.

This circular route begins and ends in Chagford, but you can join or leave it wherever you like.

• *Begin in the village of...*

Chagford

Perched on the edge of the moor, this tiny town is not only charming but actually feels like a real, normal slice of English life (www .chagford-parish.co.uk). The small-town ambience here may make you feel like you've stepped into a time warp (or maybe a quaint BBC sitcom). Villages like this one, which was probably established in Saxon times, were built around Dartmoor as tin-mining bases. In 1305, Chagford became one of four Dartmoor stannary towns, a main center for "weighing and paying" the miners. The eight-sided Market House in the village square (known as the "pepper pot") is

DARTMOOR

located on the site of the old stannary court/assayer's office.

St. Michael's Parish Church, at the upper end of town, mostly dates from the 15th century and is built out of the typical stone of the area, gray granite. The hard rock is tough to work, so most buildings here are fairly simple. An incident occurred here that is said to have inspired R. D. Blackmore's *Lorna Doone:* A bride named Mary Whiddon was shot dead by a former suitor as she left the church during her wedding in 1641 (pamphlet available inside). Look among the pews at the needlepoint cushions, a few of which bear a tinner's symbol: three rabbits in a circle that each have two ears, but appear to share only three ears among them. (This motif also shows up in the stained-glass window over the door of the wine store on the town square.)

The little **village square** has all the essentials: bank, post office, small grocery store, pharmacy, butcher, delicatessen, The Big Red Sofa bookstore/coffee shop (local interest books and maps, Mon–Sat 10:00–16:00, closed Sun, tel. 01647/433-883, www.the bigredsofa.co.uk), and a few hardware shops that sell any hiking gear that you might have forgotten (including Ordnance Survey maps). Moorland Dairy, next to the Three Crowns Hotel, sells ice-cream cones, interesting cheeses from the area, and clotted cream by the pound (tel. 01647/432-479). Go gawk inside Bowden's hardware store to see how everything you could possibly ever need can be neatly crammed into one place—don't miss the glassed-in antique-hardware room and the loft full of dozens of Wellington boots (tel. 01647/433-271).

• *Follow* Postbridge *signs directing you to the road south of Chagford, which will take you to busy B3212. Soon after you turn right onto B3212, you'll cross some...*

Cattle Grates

Welcome to wild-pony country. The rumble of your tires over cattle grates—which you'll cross several times on our drive—tells you that you've entered an area without fences, where livestock of all kinds can roam freely. It's also a reminder to slow down and watch the road closely, especially around blind corners—the animals find cars more interesting than scary, and they are often seen sunning themselves in the middle of the road. I've had to lay on my horn several times to

convince a dozing sheep to let me pass. As throughout England, you'll see sheep grazing and fluffy little lambs bounding through the heather. But Dartmoor adds its own unique touch: famously "wild," but remarkably tame, horses. (Actually, the horses are all owned by local farmers, who keep an eye on them as they graze the moors—notice that some horses are branded.) The horses have free rein of Dartmoor, so you may not see them immediately, but eventually you may find a few (or possibly an entire herd). Horses have wandered here for centuries, and the brown ones are probably the most closely related to the ancestral Dartmoor breed. The park discourages people from feeding or even approaching the horses—they get used to mooching, so they often readily come up to people, but may bite or kick without warning.

• *After crossing the cattle grates, you're really into the heart of...*

The Moors

England's green, bucolic landscape is occasionally interrupted by brown, scrubby moorlands like these. It's tricky to define a "moor"—but once you've spent time on one, you'll know them when you see them. A moor is characterized by its relative lack of vegetation, save for high grasses and heather—a dull-brown shrub that thrives here (and briefly turns a brilliant purple when it flowers in late summer). The long, undulating expanses of open land, almost unbroken by trees but scattered with long-forgotten prehistoric stone monuments, makes Dartmoor feel even more evocative and mysterious than other English moors.

• *On the left, you may notice the remains of a hilltop settlement. If you're up for a hike to get a closer look, consider this optional detour: Turn left at the sign to* Widecombe, *and follow the road for a few minutes— keeping an eye on those hilltop ruins above you on the left. Just before the big curve to the right, look for a pullout on the right, and four stone steps on the left. You can park and use these steps to climb up to...*

Grimspound

Dating from 2000 B.C., this Bronze Age fortress was a settlement for 800 years. The outer stone wall was a defense wall, and the inner circles would have been stone huts. Well-populated in ancient times, the moors are thought to have become unlivable in about 1200 B.C. due to climate change, and settlements like these were abandoned.

• *Backtrack to the main road you were on, and continue south. Very soon on the left, just before the little parking lot, look for the worn and weathered stub of a...*

Celtic Cross

All along the road, look for tall stone crosses like this one. These marked the way for villagers to cross the moor, often for funeral processions.

• *Soon after the cross, on the right, you'll see the...*

Warren House Inn

Named for a warrener (rabbit-raiser) who fed bunnies to hungry miners, this pub comes with a fun history. This site has reputedly been occupied by a travelers' rest stop for more than 900 years. In 1845, a pub across the road was falling down from disrepair, so this "new" structure was built. Supposedly embers from the old fire were used to light the fire in the new building—which has burned ever since. While the story is questionable, the food here is good—specializing in (of course) rabbit pie, as well as steak and ale pie. The glorious moorside seating, at picnic benches out front and across the road, make it an enticing stop for a meal or drink (£6–12 main dishes, open Easter–mid-Nov daily for lunch and dinner, mid-Nov–Easter closed Mon–Tue evenings, tel. 01822/880-208, www.warrenhouseinn.co.uk).

• *There's a lot "moor" to see, so let's keep moving. Carry on along the same road into the town of...*

Postbridge

This functional village comes with one of Dartmoor's classic views. As you cross the bridge in the heart of town, on the left you'll see

an ancient bridge parallel to the road. This type of stone bridge, essentially a post and a wide flat stone lintel, is called a clapper bridge. These bridges, which dot the moor, date from the Middle Ages, if not earlier. For a closer look, pull over at the big parking lot on the right soon after the

bridge, near the handy and very helpful national park office. If you have time, consider a hike—Postbridge is a good base for moor walks (pick up their £1.50 booklet for walks from here).

• *Continue down to the village of Two Bridges, where you hit B3357. Our route turns left (east) on this road, but consider detouring to the right (west) to the town of **Princetown** (pronounced "Princeton"), with its High Moorland Visitor Centre (see page 256). Princetown is also home to a high-security prison that held French prisoners during the Napoleonic Wars, and American POWs during the War of 1812. (But if you've already gotten your fill of park info from the Postbridge office, Princetown is skippable.)*

Heading east on B3357, you'll soon have to use some narrower back roads to reach our next stop. You'll feel lost, but use your map and track signs closely: First follow signs down into Dartmeet, then uphill toward Ashburton. After coming back down from the moor, watch for the turnoff on the left to Ponsworthy, then our next stop...

Widecombe-in-the-Moor

Set in the center of the rolling hills, this adorable but shopper-choked village is a scenic stop—and feels crowded after a drive on the empty moor. There's a farmer's market the fourth Saturday of every month (9:30–15:00) and a Thursday craft market during the summer at the 1537 Church House (late May–early Oct 10:00–17:00, www.widecombe-in-the-moor.com). If you're ready for a meal, carry on (turning right at the sign by the Church House) down the country road to the **Rugglestone Inn**—which is more likely to have local farmers drinking a pint than tourists. The prices are surprisingly low, and the quality is good...but watch out for the high-powered local cider (£8–10 main dishes, tel. 01364/621-327, www.rugglestoneinn.co.uk).

• *Leave Widecombe, following signs for* Bovey Tracey *and enjoying the sky-high views. (On a clear day, you can see all the way to the ocean.) Now we'll take a look at two of the better-known "tors" of Dartmoor. If you're tight on time, choose one: Haytor is famous and offers better views, but is more difficult to hike to, while Hound Tor is the more impressive formation.*

On the Bovey Tracey road, you'll spot a turnoff on the left toward M'hampstead, *which we'll take later (or now, if you want to skip Haytor). To see Haytor, continue 1.5 miles farther on—you'll spot it on the hilltop above you on the left. Use the giant parking lot on the right (after a smaller one on the left) and hike up to the grand...*

Haytor

Dartmoor sits up on a granite plateau, and occasionally bare granite "peaks" poke up through the heather. Like lonesome watchtowers looming above the barren landscape, these "tors" are Dartmoor's most distinctive landmarks—and Haytor is the most famous and popular, thanks to its excellent vantage point for panoramic views.

Tors basically look like piles of boulders that you can imagine might have been dragged and dropped on hilltops by prehistoric developers, but they're all natural, caused by weathering. This area is divided into two parts: Haytor itself, and the adjacent Haytor Rocks.

• *If you'd like to detour into the town of* **Bovey Tracey,** *now's the time— it's 10 minutes away on B3387, in the valley beyond the Haytor park information centre (Bovey Tracey described on page 264).*

Or, to continue our loop, backtrack to the Moretonhampstead *turnoff (*M'hampstead *for short), which you'll now follow north* *through the moors. Soon you'll see another tor ahead and on the right. When you get to the little fork, follow the P signs to the right and park to walk up to...*

Hound Tor

Perhaps the most striking tor in Dartmoor, and the inspiration for the Sherlock Holmes story *The Hound of the Baskervilles*, this mighty clump of rocks impresses. According to legend, this stand of stones was once a pack of hunting dogs that had disrupted a witches' coven. As a punishment, the pooches were petrified. (The hunter that owned the dogs

was turned into the nearby tor called Bowerman's Nose, about a mile north of here.) Hike up and scramble over the many levels. In the valley beyond this ridge are faint remains of old Devon longhouses. These were situated at a gentle angle, with animals in the lower part and people in the upper part—liquids and other waste would run downhill, while the heat generated by the livestock would warm its owners above.

• *Our tour is nearly finished. From the Hound Tor parking lot, backtrack a few yards to the little fork and turn right, following signs to* M'hampstead. *You'll drive through the countryside before reaching the larger but still charming town of* **Moretonhampstead**—*a nice place for a stroll, a snack, or to browse the selection of local guidebooks at the TI (daily 9:30–17:00, off-season Fri–Sun only 10:00–16:30; Internet access—first 10 min free, then 50p/30 min; New Street, tel. 01647/440-043, www.moretonhampstead.com).*

If you still have daylight left, consider heading north out of Moretonhampstead on A382 until the turnoff (to the right) for Drewsteignton and the **Fingle Bridge;** *or head back through Chagford and venture to the* **Scorhill stone circle** *(both described under "Sights in Dartmoor," next).*

Sights in Dartmoor

▲**Walks on the Moors**—Pick up your Ordnance Survey map at any local shop or TI and start walking. The Princetown TI also has a map with suggestions for routes through the moors. Postbridge, in the heart of the moorlands, is a fine launch pad for good walks, and has a park information center that can suggest well-outlined routes. Other good walking bases include Belstone in the north (for rugged scenery) and Ivybridge in the south (more forested). You can go almost anywhere—except the firing ranges. These are

---

Letterboxing

The local pastime of letterboxing began as a way to collect tourist postcards. What has evolved is a secret system of logbooks hidden all over Dartmoor—inside metal boxes, squirreled away under rocks, or stuffed in the brush. Your goal: Find the logbook and stamp, and add your name and stamp to as many books as possible (bring your own inkpad just in case). Since this practice is a bit of a secret, you'll need to enlist a local to help you get started. Ask at a local TI or at Bellever Hostel (near Postbridge), or check out www.dartmoorletter boxing.org and www.letterboxingondartmoor.co.uk.

---

technically open for walking when not in use (you'll see red flags if they're closed), but it's probably best to avoid them entirely. For more pointers, read "Orientation to Dartmoor," earlier.

▲▲**Scorhill Stone Circle**—Thousands of Neolithic ruins dot the landscape of Dartmoor, but the Scorhill (SCO-rill) stone circle near Gidleigh may be the best. Stonehenge, *the* iconic stone circle, is much bigger—but it's also packed with crowds and right off a busy road (described in the Near Bath chapter). Tranquil, forgotten Scorhill is yours alone—the way a stone circle should be. As it comes with a scenic stroll across a moor, it's a great sampling of what Dartmoor is all about—as much about the journey as about the destination.

Getting There: The trailhead is about a 15-minute drive west of Chagford. The trailhead is tricky to find—be patient, use your Ordnance Survey map, and solicit help from a local. (I wouldn't attempt it in a heavy fog—but if you do, take along a compass.) From Chagford, follow signs to *Gidleigh*—you'll drive west out of town, bear right (uphill) at the fork, then turn right at the next intersection; from there, cross over the very narrow bridge and go through Murchington, then stay straight, going up and down the hills through Gidleigh. Keep following the same off-the-beaten-path road through the hamlet of Berrydown, until you dead-end at a little parking lot (if in doubt, follow signs for *Scorhill*). Park, then walk through the gate and hike about 15 minutes straight ahead up and over the moor (with a long stone fence on either side of you). After cresting the hill, head down into the gentle valley and look for the circle below (slightly to the left—assuming you've walked straight from the gate). Once there, you'll be alone with the heather, broom, ancient history...and, often, sheep and wild ponies.

▲**Teign Gorge and Fingle Bridge**—Near the town of Drewsteignton, a narrow road leads down into the Teign River Valley. At the end of the road is the **Fingle Bridge Inn,** a pub set along a river and a picturesque old bridge. The food is good and reasonably priced, with daily specials and a hearty ploughman's lunch of open-face sandwiches (£4–8 lunches served from 12:00–15:00, £7–10 dinners; open June–Sept Mon–Sat 11:00–22:00, Sun 11:00–18:00; Oct–May daily 11:00–16:00, sometimes also open for dinner; tel. 01647/281-287). A popular spot for weddings and fly-fishing, the trail across the road makes for an excellent post-meal amble along the river (from B3219, head to Drewsteignton, then look for signs to *Fingle Bridge*).

Up the road, you'll come across **Castle Drogo,** an elaborate country house that has the honor of being the last castle built in England, finished in 1930 (£7.45, mid-March–Oct daily 11:00–17:00, last entry 30 min before closing, generally open weekends only off-season, closed late Dec–mid-Feb, on-site café, tel. 01647/433-306). Some trails on the estate lead down to Fingle Bridge.

Bovey Tracey—This town on the southeastern side of Dartmoor National Park is a good base and offers a few indoor options to explore when the rains chase you off the moors (just 10 minutes' drive west of Haytor on B3387). With about 7,000 people, it's a metropolis by Dartmoor standards. The **TI** is located at the main pay-and-display lot on the right as you drive into town (March–Oct daily 10:00–16:00; Nov–Feb sporadic hours Tue and Fri–Sun—mostly in the afternoons; tel. 01626/832-047, www .boveytracey.gov.uk). You can get online at the library (up to 30 min free, closed Wed, Abbey Road, tel. 01626/832-026, www.devon .gov.uk/library). Accommodations and eateries in Bovey Tracey are suggested later in this chapter.

Bovey Tracey, a pottery town until the 1950s, is becoming known as a center for fine crafts. Clay was quarried nearby, and Josiah Wedgwood even nosed around here when deciding where to locate his china factory (he later chose Staffordshire). The **Devon Guild of Craftsmen** has a gallery/museum and shop in a restored riverside mill downtown (daily 10:00–17:30, until 21:00 Fri mid-June–Aug, Riverside Mill, tel. 01626/832-223, www.crafts.org.uk), and hosts a contemporary arts fair the first weekend in June (www .craftsatboveytracey.co.uk).

The **House of Marbles** sounds goofy enough that you want to visit. It's basically a giant gift shop with some interesting glass-making displays inside. Check out the marble museum displaying antique marbles, ones made of odd materials, and fun, kinetic wire marble mazes in action that always draw a crowd. The place is now the home of Teign Valley Glass Studios, and you can watch artisans at work creating contemporary glassware using traditional skills (in action Tue–Sat 9:00–16:30, Sun 10:00–15:00, lunch and tea breaks posted). Outside in the courtyard are old, circa-1900 "muffle" kilns (signs describe their history). In the gift shop, kids of all ages will love digging through the giant bins of multicolored marbles—they're actually made in Mexico, but big piles of them look really cool (free, Mon–Sat 9:00–17:00, Sun 11:00–17:00, café, at The Old Pottery on Pottery Road, tel. 01626/835-285, www .houseofmarbles.com).

Sleeping in Dartmoor

Befitting such a mysterious destination, accommodations in Dartmoor tend to be quirkier than the English norm, with more character(s) than the staid, hotelesque accommodations in more mainline destinations. Sleeping here really feels like "going local."

Near Chagford

For a description of the handy home-base town of Chagford, see page 257. Most of these accommodations aren't in Chagford itself, but in other villages (or the countryside) nearby. I've provided general directions, but given the confusing spaghetti of back roads here, it's always smart to call ahead for precise arrival instructions.

$$$ Sandy Park Inn, owned by a local bigwig, rents five well-appointed but overpriced rooms above a busy upmarket pub. Although it's in a creaky old 16th-century shell, it comes with modern touches (Sb-£45, Db-£85, cheaper off-season, Wi-Fi, tel. 01647/433-267, www.sandyparkinn.co.uk, sandyparkinn@aol.com). It's on A382 east of Chagford, at the turnoff for the Teign Gorge. For more on the pub, see "Eating in Dartmoor," later.

$$ Easton Court offers five bright, flowery rooms that overlook the gardens where *Brideshead Revisited* was written (decorated with a faux stone circle to ponder). A bit less "colorful" than the other accommodations here (in a good way), it feels like the ideal thatched-roof English guest house (classic Db-£65–70, superior Db-£75–80, Sb for £15 less, free Internet access and Wi-Fi, parking, tel. 01647/433-469, www.easton.co.uk, stay@easton.co.uk, Debra and Paul). It's at the crossroads called Easton, just east of Chagford, right on A382.

$$ St. Johns West is a good-value B&B renting three quiet rooms in a spacious stone farmhouse dating from 1833, and includes a giant yard and gorgeous views over the moors. Colorful, chatty, well-traveled Maureen and John West used to be entertainers on the *QE2*—and they still love to entertain their guests while they

Sleep Code

(£1 = about $1.60, country code: 44, area code: 01364)
S = Single, **D** = Double/Twin, **T** = Triple, **Q** = Quad, **b** = bathroom,
s = shower only. You can assume credit cards are accepted
unless otherwise noted.

To help you sort easily through these listings, I've divided
the rooms into three categories based on the price for a
standard double room with bath:

$$$ **Higher Priced**—Most rooms £80 or more.

$$ **Moderately Priced**—Most rooms between £50–80.

$ **Lower Priced**—Most rooms £50 or less.

cook up breakfast. Maureen's giant personality is as memorable
as her hospitality and good cooking (Sb-£35, Db-£70, cash only,
off-road parking, tel. 01647/432-468, http://stjohnswest.cjb.net,
johnwwest@btinternet.com). It's a mile and a half northwest of
Chagford, above the village of Murchington. Follow the directions to Scorhill Stone Circle on page 263, but as soon as you enter
Murchington, take the right turn uphill (at the sign that says *Way
Down*). Their driveway is near the top of this hill on the left. Ask
them how to get to nearby Spinster's Rock.

$$ Along Chagford's main street, several pubs rent humble
rooms upstairs. The best bet is **The Globe Inn,** with seven decent
rooms (Sb-£38, Db-£75, 9 High Street, pay parking lot nearby,
tel. 01647/433-485, www.globeinnchagford.co.uk, graham@globe
innchagford.co.uk, Graham and Mary). They're also open for
meals (£7–13, daily 11:00–15:00 & 18:00–21:30).

In or near Moretonhampstead

Moretonhampstead—larger and less quaint than Chagford or
Widecombe-in-the-Moor—is a handy home base with its own
share of half-timbered appeal.

$$$ **Eastwrey Barton Country House** is set on a terraced
lawn halfway up the side of the Wray Valley between Moreton-
hampstead and Bovey Tracey. It has five warm and spacious rooms
in a restored Georgian country house (Sb-£68–78, Db-£96–116,
£30 three-course dinners for guests, free Wi-Fi, several nice
lounges, on A382 near Lustleigh, tel. 01647/277-338, www.east
wreybarton.co.uk, info@eastwreybarton.co.uk, friendly Sharon
and Patrick).

$$ **Cookshayes Country Guest House,** on the main B3212
road in the heart of Moretonhampstead, has eight traditional,
homey rooms in a big house. They also serve good dinners for

guests on request (S-£25, Sb-£35–40, D-£45, Db-£50–55, 33 Court Street, tel. 01647/440-374, fax 0167/440-453, www.cookshayes .co.uk, cookshayes@aol.com, gregarious Tracy and chef Barry).

$ Sparrowhawk Backpackers rents cheap beds in the Moretonhampstead town center, in the light-filled loft of a restored stone stable (£15 bunks in coed dorm with curtains, D-£35, £42 family room, bedding provided, kitchen, 45 Ford Street, tel. 01647/440-318, mobile 07870-513-570, www.sparrowhawkback packers.co.uk, ali@sparrowhawkbackpackers.co.uk).

In or near Bovey Tracey

Sleep here if you want to be close to a real town on the edge of the national park, rather than the rustic villages inside Dartmoor. For more on Bovey Tracey, see page 264.

$$ Ashwell B&B is located in the upper part of town. Behind the garden-surrounded house, climb the steep and unique backyard through vegetable gardens, fruit trees, and a small vineyard for nice views of the moors (Sb-£38, Db-£76, 2-night minimum, closed Dec–Feb, off East Street near the church, tel. 01626/830-031, www.ashwell-bb.com, diane.riddell@ukgateway .net, friendly Diane).

$$ Brookfield House offers three bedrooms in a spacious 1906 Edwardian house set on two acres of lawns and gardens (Sb-£50–54, Db-£70–78, no children under 12, closed Dec–Jan, Challabrook Lane, tel. 01626/836-181, www.brookfield-house .com, enquiries@brookfield-house.com, Frances and Laurence).

Near Postbridge

$ Bellever Youth Hostel offers 38 beds in seven rooms on the moors. It's simple and institutional, but it comes with an impressive wildlife area out front to learn about the local terrain (£16/ bunk in 4- to 8-bed rooms, £1 discount per night if arriving by bus, bicycle, or on foot; £3 more for non-members, £6–7 dinners, £1 self-service laundry, members' kitchen, open all year, tel. 0845-371-9622, www.yha.org.uk, bellever@yha.org.uk). It's down a long gravel road in Bellever just south of Postbridge, well-signed from the main road.

Near Widecombe-in-the-Moor

$$ Higher Venton Farm is a simple, middle-of-nowhere 1560 farmhouse renting three basic rooms with eclectic, outmoded decor (S-£30, twin D-£56, Db-£64, tel. 01364/621-235, www .ventonfarm.com, helenhicks@ventonfarm.fsnet.co.uk). It's about a half-mile outside the village of Widecombe-in-the-Moor (follow signs from main intersection to *Rugglestone Inn,* then continue on the same road beyond the inn to the farm).

Eating in Dartmoor

In or near Chagford

Several pubs in Chagford serve microwaved pub grub, but locals recommend venturing into the countryside for a better meal. Also note that many accommodations serve affordable meals to their guests—but always ask in advance so they have time to shop and prepare.

22 Mill Street, pricey but well-regarded, is a cut above the other eateries lining Chagford's main street, both in terms of class and quality (£36–50 fixed-price dinners, open for lunch Wed–Sat and dinner Tue–Sat, reservations smart, tel. 01647/432-244). They also rent two good rooms upstairs with a breakfast and three-course dinner package (Db-£169–209, www.22millst.com).

Sandy Park Inn, which also rents rooms, has a characteristic 16th-century pub and a cozy dining room that serves pricey but good food with great Old World atmosphere (£5–6 sandwiches at lunch, £5–14 main dishes, tel. 01647/433-267). It's a few minutes from Chagford—for location details, see "Sleeping in Dartmoor," earlier.

In Bovey Tracey

De-Tracey's Restaurant offers traditional English fare in the upper part of the town (£6–9 lunches, £10–18 dinners, food served Tue–Sat 12:00–14:00 & 18:30–21:30, Sun–Mon 12:00–14:00, 56 Fore Street, tel. 01626/833-465).

Spice Bazaar offers good Indian food (£7–15 mains, daily 12:00–14:00 & 18:00–23:30, 38 Fore Street, tel. 01626/833-111).

Elsewhere in Dartmoor

Earlier in this chapter, I've described three restaurants that make for good lunch or dinner stops as you explore the moors: **Warren House Inn,** perched atop a moor south of Chagford (see page 260); **Rugglestone Inn,** just outside the village of Widecombe-on-the-Moor (see page 261); and the **Fingle Bridge Inn,** in the Teign Gorge (see page 264).

CORNWALL

Set on a rocky peninsula in the southwest of England, Cornwall has a Celtic vibe. Its rugged scenery and wild, uncultivated appeal make you feel as if you're approaching the end of the world (and many natives would say it's exactly that). Harboring the remnants of an endangered Celtic culture (Cornish), an extinct tin-mining industry, and a gaggle of visit-worthy sights, this is one of England's most popular holiday regions—especially among the English.

Cornwall—part of the "Celtic fringe" of Britain—grew up as a very different place from England, with its own language, called Cornish, which thrived for centuries. Fishing, shipping, and smuggling were the main businesses here for hundreds of years, but in the 18th century, tin-mining became the major industry. The 20th century dealt a double blow to Cornwall: The local pilchard fish became depleted, and cheap Asian and South American tin put an end to mining. Today's predominant trade is tourism, as evidenced by the many tacky tourist traps littering the landscape.

And visitors flock here for good reason. Not only is the area packed with ancient sites, precious villages, and historic monuments, but the climate is also unusually mild. The Gulf Stream often brings warm, almost tropical weather to Cornwall—making it perfect for gardening, walking, basking on the beach, and generally enjoying life.

To see Cornwall, set yourself up in a home base (Penzance or St. Ives) and spend most of your time venturing out on day trips. Romantic St. Ives has an artsy beach-bum ambience and is crowded with holiday-makers in summer. Penzance, on the other hand, is all business—a working-class shipping port with plenty of high-quality accommodations and welcoming eateries. Since Cornwall is best suited for day-tripping, Penzance's relative lack of tourist charm is actually an asset—it's much easier to drive in and out of, and has better public-transportation connections, making it my preferred home base. Sleep in St. Ives only if you're serious about gallery-hopping.

Venture to quaint seaside villages, a dramatic theater, a telegraph museum, a dead tin mine, and a thought-provoking stone circle. Cry "Land Ho!" at Land's End, and consider a chopper or ferry ride to the castaway Isles of Scilly. Farther northeast, the castle of a king named Arthur tickles travelers' imaginations, while unusual gardens thrill green thumbs.

Planning Your Time

Brits spend weeks here on holiday. But for a speedy traveler, two nights based in Penzance or St. Ives, with one solid day rambling around the peninsula, offer a suitable first taste.

Given that it takes so long to get to this edge of the world from the heart of England (figure about a day each way by car or train), it makes sense not to rush your visit. Spending three nights and two days here allows you to slow down, see all the sights, and get a better feel for Cornish culture. Most of the noteworthy sights and villages wrap around the Penwith Peninsula, so you can line them up and see them on a handy circular drive.

The attractions farther east—Tintagel Castle and the gardens—are ideal for breaking up the long journey to or from Cornwall (en route to Bath or Dartmoor).

Getting to Cornwall

By Train: Train travelers arrive in Cornwall at Penzance, the most central and largest city on the coast (see "Penzance Connections," page 280).

By Plane: Cornwall's main airport is Newquay–Cornwall International (www.newquay-airport.co.uk), six miles from Newquay and 35 miles northeast of Penzance. Airlines that serve Newquay include Ryanair (from London–Stansted, www.ryanair.com), Air Southwest (from London–Gatwick, Bath/Bristol, and more; www.airsouthwest.com), and Flybe (from Edinburgh or London–Gatwick, www.flybe.com). Europcar (www.europcar.co.uk) and Hertz (www.hertz.co.uk) rent cars at the airport. Public-transportation connections into Penzance can be tricky—call the Newquay TI for details (tel. 01637/854-020).

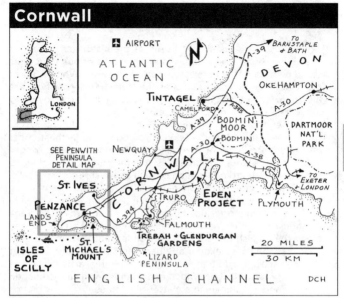

Cornwall

Getting Around Cornwall

This region is most satisfying by car, which allows you to pack a lot into each day. It's challenging but doable by public transportation, in which case you'll have to be more selective. Note that all public-transit routes run less frequently off-season (Oct–April). A tour with guide Harry Safari (see page 276) is an especially useful way to get into the countryside.

By Car: The coastal road—which passes through Penzance and above St. Ives—links together almost all of the best sights. Driving in Cornwall is generally easy, but parking is not, especially in summer—small villages often have tiny parking lots near the water and larger ones outside of town, so it's a good idea to arrive early in the day. Roads can get very congested on bank-holiday weekends and in August, so allow extra time, especially on main routes such as A30 and A38. Narrow, twisty Cornish lanes crisscross the spine of the peninsula, and can save time over the main routes if they're crowded—but you'll need a good map (try the 1:100,000 Ordnance Survey) and, even more importantly, a good navigator. For current traffic conditions, listen to the radio—many rental-car stereos have a setting for automatic traffic updates.

By Bus: It's slow but possible to reach most Cornwall sights by bus, some of which go topless May through September. Most buses are run by First (toll tel. 0871-200-2233, www.firstgroup .com), though Western Greyhound handles the #504 route (tel.

CORNWALL

Cornish History

Cornwall's history is almost as old as the history of humanity. Prehistoric huts, stone circles, and other mysterious structures stand witness to the timeless appeal of Cornwall. While a few of these are easy to reach (such as the Merry Maidens), most are hidden away and best uncovered with a local guide (I enjoy Harry Safari's tours—described on page 276).

When the Romans arrived in Britain in the first century B.C., the native Celtic inhabitants were forced to the farthest, most inhospitable corners of the island. To this day, a "Celtic fringe" still rings England. This includes several groups struggling to keep alive their fading languages, such as Welsh, Scottish Gaelic, Irish Gaelic, Manx (on the Isle of Man)...and Cornish.

This part of Britain—specifically Penzance—was ideally located for shipping, since boats could launch straight into the Atlantic, rather than having to tack from farther east all the way along the English Channel. It's no wonder that Penzance is best known as the namesake for a Gilbert and Sullivan musical about the high seas. In addition to sailors and pirates, artists love this scenic corner of Britain, which can change from sun-drenched to rainy and windblown in a matter of minutes. Dramatic clouds hit Cornwall like a hammer, and the sea here changes color with the sky.

Rich deposits of metals—especially tin—have linked this rugged spit of land to the rest of the world, making Cornwall unexpectedly cosmopolitan. Cornish tin has been found in plumbing as far away as Turkey and Pompeii (Italy). Cornwall wasn't conquered by the Romans—partly because of its remoteness—but also because the Cornish were already Roman trading partners. (You'll find no Roman forts in Cornwall, but you will find Roman goods.) Cornish trading came with an influx of exotic products—Cornish cooking is unique in England for its use of saffron, likely bartered with the Near East for metals.

In the 18th century, Cornwall's tin-mining industry enjoyed a boom (see "Cornish Tin Mining" on page 289). But when the industry went bust in the late 19th century, many miners had to find work elsewhere. Though tin-mining was a back-breaking,

01637/871-871, www.westerngreyhound.com). First has a useful one-day pass called "FirstDay Cornwall" for the region that includes Penzance, St. Ives, Land's End, and the surrounding area (£6.50, buy directly from driver).

You'll find the following bus routes useful:

Buses **#1** and **#1A** connect Penzance with Newlyn and Land's End (Mon–Sat every 1–2 hrs, Sun 2/day, 10 min to Newlyn, 50 min to Land's End); #1A also stops at Porthcurno, near the Telegraph Museum and a steep uphill climb to the Minack Theatre (Mon–Sat 5–6/day, Sun 2/day, 40 min).

menial job, it also required highly skilled miners. Mine owners from around the world began to recruit and relocate unemployed Cornish miners. Throughout the 1860s, 20 percent of Cornish people emigrated, and this "Cornish diaspora" spread the culture from this corner of England across the face of the earth. For example, hundreds of Cornish miners went to California to get in on the Gold Rush. Locals brag, "Anywhere you find a hole in the ground, you'll find a Cornishman at the bottom of it." Likewise, Cornish graveyards read like a geography textbook, as headstones often list the places where the person lived.

The great migration of the late 19th century also left behind many ghost towns, which still dot the Cornish countryside. Today, many of these long-abandoned homes are being bought up by Londoners and converted into holiday villas—driving up prices and forcing out the few remaining locals.

The Cornish language—related to Welsh, and more distantly related to Scottish Gaelic and Irish Gaelic—was widely spoken here through the late 18th century. As the Industrial Revolution shrunk England and the Church refused to offer services in Cornish, the language became obsolete. Cornish survived only among a handful of speakers through the 19th and early 20th centuries. But, remarkably, Cornish held on, and—after a recent EU designation as an official minority language—it's now allowed to be taught in schools again. More people speak Cornish today than two centuries ago, and raising kids to be bilingual is in vogue.

Today, feisty Cornwall, with a half-million residents, is officially and for all practical purposes part of England (unlike Wales or Scotland). But native-born Cornishmen and Cornishwomen still cling to what makes them unique—they're Cornish first, British second. The fledgling Cornish independence movement has never really gotten anywhere, but that doesn't stop locals from displaying the flag of Cornwall: a black field (representing the earth) with a white cross (the tin flowing through the earth). Also look for bumper stickers boasting the Cornish word for "Cornwall": *Kernow*.

Buses **#2** and **#2A** run between Penzance and Marazion near St. Michael's Mount (Mon–Sat 2/hr, Sun every 2 hrs, 10 min).

Bus **#6** connects Penzance with Newlyn (Mon–Sat 3/hr, Sun 2/hr, 10 min) and Mousehole (Mon–Sat 2/hr, Sun 1–2/hr, 20 min).

Buses **#14**, **#17**, **#17A**, and **#17B** connect Penzance and St. Ives (roughly 2/hr, or 1/hr on Sun, 35–50 min trip). Bus **#17B** also stops at Marazion (St. Michael's Mount).

Bus **#300** does a big, made-for-tourists 3.5-hour loop around the Penwith Peninsula (daily, every 2 hrs), connecting Penzance,

St. Ives (40 min), and Land's End (2.5 hrs). Along the way, it stops at Marazion (St. Michael's Mount), the Geevor Tin Mine, Sennen Cove, Porthcurno, and Newlyn.

Bus #504 connects Penzance to some otherwise difficult-to-reach destinations along the southern edge of Penwith (2/day Mon–Sat only, none on Sun): Newlyn (10 min), Mousehole (15 min), Merry Maidens (35 min), Porthcurno (50 min), Minack Theatre (55 min), Land's End (1.25 hrs), and Sennen Cove.

By Train: A scenic (read: slow) rail line connects Penzance and St. Ives, mostly running along the coast (2/day direct, 20 min; at least hourly with transfer in St. Erth, 25–60 min; tel. 0845-748-4950, www.nationalrail.co.uk).

Penzance

Sure enough, Penzance had its share of pirates. Strategically situated near the very tip of Britain, the town was an ideal spot for pirates to hijack and plunder ships returning from the New World with untold treasures. But today's Penzance is less of a rough-and-tumble pirate smuggler's cove and more of a blue-collar transportation hub. Penzance can't compete with the artsy vibe of St. Ives or the precious jewel-box quality of nearby Mousehole, but it's cornered the market on functionality: Well-located B&Bs, good restaurants, train and bus stations, and easy parking make Penzance the most practical home base for exploring the Cornish coast.

Orientation to Penzance

(area code: 01736)
Penzance, with about 20,000 people, is situated on a small peninsula. The eastern part of the peninsula has the TI, harbor, and train and bus stations. The southern part has a broad and inviting promenade, with most of the town's B&Bs nearby. Climbing uphill from the water are various streets, including the bustling Market Jew Street (derived from the Cornish *Marghas Yow,* meaning "Thursday Market") and the more atmospheric, restaurant-lined Chapel Street. The hill is capped by the spire of the Church of St. Mary, and the grandly domed Market House, now a bank.

Tourist Information

The TI, in a kiosk between the bus and train stations, offers tips on the many nearby day-trip options, sells helicopter tickets for the Isles of Scilly, and books rooms for a £3 fee (early July–Aug

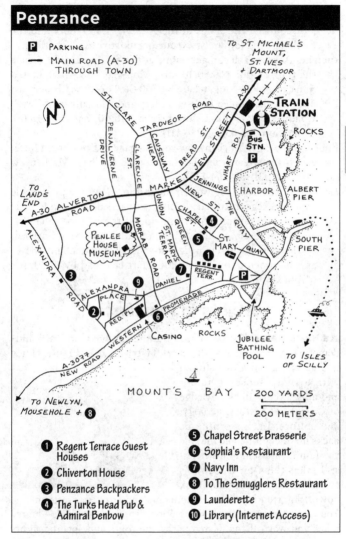

Penzance

P Parking

— Main Road (A-30) through town

To St. Michael's Mount, St. Ives & Dartmoor

TRAIN STATION

ROCKS

Bus Stn.

St. Clare

Tardoveor Road

Penalverne Drive

Clarence St.

Causeway Head

Bread St.

Jew Street

Wharf Rd.

HARBOR

ALBERT PIER

To Lands End
A-30 Alverton Road

Market

Jennings

New St.

The Quay

SOUTH PIER

Penlee House Museum

Morrab Road

St. Mary's Terrace

Union

Queen

Chapel St.

St. Mary

Quay

Alexandra Road

Daniel

Regent Terr.

Alexandra Place

Red. Pl.

Promenade

Casino

Western Road

New Road
A-3077

ROCKS

Jubilee Bathing Pool

To Isles of Scilly

To Newlyn, Mousehole &

MOUNT'S BAY

200 YARDS
200 METERS

1 Regent Terrace Guest Houses
2 Chiverton House
3 Penzance Backpackers
4 The Turks Head Pub & Admiral Benbow
5 Chapel Street Brasserie
6 Sophia's Restaurant
7 Navy Inn
8 To The Smugglers Restaurant
9 Launderette
10 Library (Internet Access)

Mon–Fri 9:00–17:00, Sat 10:00–16:00, Sun 10:00–14:00; Easter–early July and Sept Mon–Sat 9:00–17:00, may close earlier on Sat, closed Sun; Oct–Easter Mon–Fri 9:00–17:00, closed Sat–Sun; tel. 01736/362-207, www.visit-westcornwall.com).

Helpful Hints

Art Pass: Art buffs can consider the £12 Art Pass, which provides unlimited access for seven days to the Penlee House Gallery and Museum in Penzance; the Tate Gallery, Barbara

Hepworth Museum, and Leach Pottery in St. Ives; and a discount at the shops in the Newlyn Art Gallery and the Exchange in Newlyn (www.tate.org.uk/stives/information).

Internet Access: You can get online at the **Station Buffet,** inside the train station (£0.50/10 min, Mon–Sat 7:30–17:30, closed Sun except July–Aug, tel. 01736/360-369) or at the **library,** just up from the Penlee House Gallery and Museum on Morrab Road (£0.90/15 min, Mon–Fri 9:30–18:00, Sat 9:30–16:00, closed Sun, tel. 03001/234-111).

Baggage Storage: You can stow your luggage at **Longboat Hotel,** across the street from the train station (£2/bag, Market Jew Street, tel. 01736/364-137).

Laundry: Penzance's big waterfront **casino,** along the promenade past the Regent Terrace B&Bs, is attached to a handy little launderette (around the right side of the casino; about £4/load for self-service, £2.50 more for full service, same-day full service possible if you bring it soon after the attendant arrives at 9:00, open daily 7:30–20:00, start last load by 18:30, tel. 01736/333-978).

Sights in Penzance

▲▲**Harry Safari Tours**—If you want to explore Cornwall's hidden nooks and crannies with a local, Harry Safari is a must. Harry is a grizzled old Cornishman with a sharp sense of humor and an encyclopedic knowledge of Cornwall's history, geology, and culture. Each morning he packs up to eight people into his van (a mini-museum on wheels) and takes them on Cornwall's twistiest back lanes to track  down forgotten Neolithic monuments and Iron Age settlements. You won't see any of the big attractions listed in this book—Harry takes you way off the beaten path. The route and specific sights covered change based on the weather, the interests of the group, and Harry's whim. If you can handle lots of walking over uneven terrain, and Harry's rapid-fire teasing, this is the single best way to experience the real Cornwall—away from the tourist congestion on the coast. Ask him to demonstrate ley lines, or to explain how paganism gradually evolved into Christianity (£20/person for half-day—4–6 hours depending on route, generally departs Penzance train station daily at 9:30 and St. Ives bus station at 10:00, essential to book ahead since Harry is often out of town, tel. 0845-644-5940, www.harrysafari.com, harrysafariuk@aol.com).

Waterfront Stroll to Newlyn and Mousehole—A broad pedestrian promenade follows the coast around Mount's Bay, from Penzance to Newlyn—perfect for an early-morning or after-dinner stroll (about 30 min one-way). From Newlyn, a coastal footpath extends farther to Mousehole (another 30-min walk; for more on Mousehole, see page 286). Locals say that any fishing that happens these days goes out of Newlyn.

Penlee House Gallery and Museum—Filling a Victorian house in Penlee Park, the gallery hosts a fine collection from painters of the local Newlyn School. These Post-Impressionists, attracted to Cornwall in the late 1800s by the quality of light and the low cost of living, painted seascapes, portraits, and scenes of daily life. The ground floor shows off rotating exhibits from the museum's permanent collection. The upstairs has more paintings and a modest museum about Penzance's prehistoric and more recent history (learn how Penzance, Newlyn, and Mousehole were burned by Spanish raiders in 1595). It's smart to call ahead, as several times a year the museum closes some galleries for a week to rearrange their collection (£3, free on Sat and when rearranging galleries, covered by Art Pass, Easter–Sept Mon–Sat 10:00–17:00, Oct–Easter Mon–Sat 10:30–16:30, closed Sun year-round, last entry 30 min before closing, café, Morrab Road, tel. 01736/363-625, www.penleehouse.org.uk).

Sleeping in Penzance

Guest Houses on Regent Terrace

Set just a block off the seashore, the upmarket guest houses on this street are central and convenient. Rooms in front usually have views of the sea, while those in back overlook a churchyard. Most breakfast rooms are downstairs on the garden level. Though they're all run by friendly proprietors, these places feel more like small hotels than B&Bs. All offer free parking, along with free Wi-Fi and Internet access to guests.

$$$ Camilla House is relaxed and modern, with contemporary class, neutral colors, a sophisticated black-and-white lounge, and lots of luxurious touches throughout. Friendly, helpful Simon and Susan rent eight comfy, sunny rooms, and are a great source for travel tips (Sb-£35, Db-£75–85 depending on size and view, 3-night minimum April–Oct if booking in advance, at #12, tel. & fax 01736/363-771, www.camillahouse.co.uk, enquiries @camillahouse.co.uk).

$$$ Lombard House Hotel offers a chandeliered Georgian townhouse atmosphere. The nine rooms come with slightly older furniture and fixtures than my other listings, but the two top-floor attic rooms are cozy and have fine views (Sb-£40–45, Db-£80–90, Tb-£90–120, large family Qb-£135, at #16, tel. & fax 01736/364-897, www.lombardhousehotel.com, lombardhouse@btconnect.com, Rita and Tom).

$$$ Warwick House has seven fine rooms with a casually posh feel (Sb-£40–42, Db-£76–88, at #17, tel. & fax 01736/363-881, www.warwickhousepenzance.co.uk, enquiry@warwickhouse penzance.co.uk, Chris and Julie). They also rent a two-bedroom cottage in the off-season on the nearby promenade (www.tremor vahcottage.co.uk).

$$$ Chy-an-Mor Hotel has nine rooms done up in a vintage, French-traditional style. The tea is ready for you upon arrival (Sb-£37–40, Db-£70–88, no children under 10, closed for renovations Dec–mid-March, at #15, tel. 01736/363-441, www.chyanmor.co.uk, reception@chyanmor.co.uk, Louise and Richard).

$$$ Blue Seas Hotel has eight sleek, modern rooms (Sb-£38–45, Db-£76–90, check website for special discounts, closed mid-Dec–Jan, at #13, tel. 01736/364-744, www.blueseashotel-penzance.co.uk, info@blueseashotel-penzance.co.uk, Arnaud and Fiona).

Cheaper Options on or near Alexandra Road

Alexandra Road, about a five-minute walk down the promenade from Regent Terrace (and therefore a bit farther from the town center and restaurants), is lined with mid-range accommodations and a hostel.

$$ Chiverton House is a granite Victorian home with six smallish, fine-but-forgettable rooms with modern decor (Sb-£25–30, Db-£50–60, cash only, just off Alexandra Road at 9 Mennaye Road, tel. 01736/332-733, www.chivertonhousebedandbreakfast.co.uk, Alan and Sally).

$ Penzance Backpackers, with 34 beds in seven rooms, is situated in a townhouse on a B&B-studded stretch of Alexandra Road. This is your best bet for budget dorm beds (£15 beds in 6-person dorms, D-£32, tel. 01736/363-836, www.pzbackpack.com, info@pzbackpack.com).

Sleep Code

(£1 = about $1.60, country code: 44, area code: 01736)
S = Single, **D** = Double/Twin, **T** = Triple, **Q** = Quad, **b** = bathroom, **s** = shower only. You can assume credit cards are accepted unless otherwise noted.

To help you sort easily through these listings, I've divided the rooms into three categories based on the price for a standard double room with bath:

  $$$ Higher Priced—Most rooms £75 or more.
    $$ Moderately Priced—Most rooms between £50-75.
     $ Lower Priced—Most rooms less than £50.

CORNWALL

Eating in Penzance

Wherever you eat, check the daily specials lists—most pubs serve fresh local fish and crab, along with the usual options.

On Chapel Street

This historic street, running up into town from the waterfront near Regent Terrace, has several tempting options.

The Turks Head Pub, the oldest pub in Penzance, is a dark, low-beamed gem. It's an all-around pub, serving tasty fish and local ales. This is a popular spot—so be sure to arrive early. There are dining rooms in the back and downstairs, but the pub in front is ideal for rubbing elbows with locals (£5–7 lunches, £8–16 dinners, food served Mon–Sat 11:00–14:30 & 18:00–22:00, Sun 12:00–2:00, on Chapel Street near intersection with Abbey Street, no street number, tel. 01736/363-093).

Chapel Street Brasserie offers a bright, mod interior and food with a French flair—a nice change of pace in stodgy, salty Penzance (£5 breakfast brunch, £7.50–12.50 fixed-price lunches, £15–25 fixed-price dinners, daily 9:30–21:00, 12 Chapel Street, tel. 01736/350-222).

Admiral Benbow is a memorable tourist trap overloaded with over-the-top nautical decor. While hardly local, it's worth poking inside for a lesson on how a theme can be taken to the extreme (£5–8 lunches, £10–13 dinners, food served daily 12:00–14:30 & 17:30–21:30, 46 Chapel Street, tel. 01736/363-448).

Along the Promenade

These two places are on or just off the seaside promenade at the west end of town, toward Newlyn.

Sophia's offers a pleasant contrast to the ship's-hold ambience that predominates in Penzance eateries. This relaxing, light-filled bistro keeps two floors of mostly local eaters happily fed with Cornish cuisine featuring fresh fish and local produce (£6–8 lunches, £11–16 main dishes, check blackboard for daily specials, Easter–Oct Mon–Sat 12:00–14:00, daily from 17:30, closed Nov–Easter, The Promenade, tel. 01736/333-363).

Navy Inn is a friendly, low-key pub that's equal parts traditional/nautical and modern (£5–9 sandwiches, £10–15 main dishes, daily 10:00–22:00, just up Queen Street from The Promenade, tel. 01736/333-232).

Out of Town, in Newlyn

The Smugglers Restaurant is the best option for white-tablecloth dining (dinners only). This is where locals go to celebrate special occasions. Located 1.5 miles southwest of my recommended B&Bs,

it faces the harbor along the main road in Newlyn (£12–20 main dishes; summer daily 19:00–21:30; winter Wed–Sat 19:00–21:30, closed Sun–Tue; 12 Fore Street, tel. 01736/331-501). They also rent out three rooms (Sb-£55, Db-£65–82, www.smugglersnewlyn .co.uk, smugglersnewlyn@btconnect.com).

Penzance Connections

For connections within Cornwall, see page 271.

From Penzance by Train to: London's Paddington Station (about hourly, 5–6 hrs, possible change in Plymouth), **Salisbury** (about hourly, 5–6 hrs, 1–3 transfers), **Edinburgh** (every 1–2 hrs, 11–17 hrs, 1 direct, most transfer in London), **York** (every 1–2 hrs, 8–10 hrs, 1 direct, most transfer in London), **Exeter** (roughly hourly, 3 hrs). Train info: tel. 0845-748-4950, www.nationalrail .co.uk.

By Bus to: Exeter (2/day direct, 4.5 hrs), **Brighton** (4/day, 12 hrs, change at Heathrow), **Portsmouth** (4/day, 10.5–15 hrs, 1 transfer), **London** (5/day direct, 9–9.5 hrs, overnight available, National Express, toll tel. 0871-781-8181, www.nationalexpress.com).

St. Ives

Picturesque St. Ives enjoys three claims to fame: It's a major artists' colony, a top fun-in-the-Cornish-sun holiday destination, and England's surfing mecca. Tourists hit the town like a tidal wave in summer (July–Sept)—when, as a local told me, "You can smell the sweat and suntan oil for miles around." An annual music and arts festival keeps things humming in September (www .stivesseptemberfestival.co.uk). But even in the feeding frenzy of peak season, St. Ives remains mellow. British bohemians and British surfers—two kinds of people you probably didn't expect to meet in England—both abound in St. Ives.

The town's artsy aura is nothing new. With golden light reflecting off the aquamarine waves and twisty lanes, St. Ives began to attract artists in the early 20th century. The potter Bernard Leach practiced his craft here, as did sculptor Barbara Hepworth, and both have galleries in town—along with dozens of other, lesser-known artists. (The TI assured me there are an "untold number" of galleries—and handed me two different brochures suggesting gallery-hopping routes through town.) Museum junkies will seek out St. Ives' branch of the Tate Gallery.

Orientation to St. Ives

(area code: 01736)
About half the size of Penzance, with 11,000 people, St. Ives occupies a few steep bits of land between sandy beaches. The town clusters around its sandy harbor, with a bulbous spit of land just beyond called The Island. From the quaint, waterfront old town, newer development sprawls uphill toward the main road. Thanks to its warren of convoluted lanes, small St. Ives can be difficult to navigate.

Tourist Information

The TI, tucked inside the Guildhall, offers a free walking-tour brochure and a current listing of arts events. They also book rooms for a fee (June–Sept Mon–Fri 9:00–17:00, Sat 10:00–16:00, Sun 10:00–14:00; Oct–May Mon–Fri 9:00–17:00, Sat 10:00–13:00, closed Sun; Street an Pol, tel. 01736/796-297, www.visit-westcornwall.com).

Arrival in St. Ives

St. Ives is a nightmare for **drivers**—parking is scarce, and the streets are congested with slow-moving pedestrians. If you dare—and if it's not too crowded—you can drive right through the heart of St. Ives. Dip down into town, pass along the harbor, then head back up the hill at the far end to reach a pay lot by The Island (near my recommended accommodations).

However, most drivers avoid the tight, pedestrian-clogged lanes by parking at the huge Trenwith parking lot above town, near the Leisure Centre (£5.50 all day), and take the handy £1 shuttle into town. (To find the parking lot, just before you descend into town, follow the signs with a blue bus icon for bus parking.) The bus lets you off in town near the movie theater (take note: this is also where you'll catch the bus for the return trip).

The **train** and **bus** stations are near the waterfront; just exit and walk with the sea on your right into the heart of town. To get here, you can take the cute, historic St. Ives Bay Line that runs above the coast from St. Erth to St. Ives. Catch the train in Penzance, in St. Erth, or at the park-and-ride lot at Lelant Saltings on the way to St. Ives (tel. 01752/233-094 or toll tel. 0845-748-4950, www.nationalrail.co.uk). If you use the train park-and-ride, you get £1 off your Tate Gallery entry fee.

Helpful Hints

Internet Access: You can get online at the **library,** which is just up the street from the TI (£3.60/hr, Tue 9:30–21:30, Wed–Fri 9:30–18:00, Sat 9:30–12:30, closed Sun–Mon, Gabriel Street, tel. 03001/234-111).

Sights in St. Ives

Art-lovers can save money by buying the Art Pass, which includes the first three sights mentioned here, plus others in Cornwall (see page 275).

Tate Gallery—St. Ives very proudly hosts a branch of the prestigious London art museum. The modern building impresses, but the collection—focusing mostly on modern works by relatively obscure local artists—can be a letdown to non-art-lovers (£5.65, £8.55 combo-ticket includes Barbara Hepworth Museum and Sculpture Garden; March–Oct daily 10:00–17:20; Nov–Feb Tue–Sun 10:00–16:20, closed Mon; last entry 20 min before closing, closes periodically to change exhibits, tel. 01736/796-226, www.tate.org.uk/stives).

▲**Barbara Hepworth Museum and Sculpture Garden**—Many visitors find this collection more accessible than the Tate's. Barbara Hepworth was one of the first sculptors to create non-representational art (that is, totally abstract works that didn't attempt to imitate the real world), and she lived most of her life in St. Ives. This modest museum, with a sculpture garden and replica of her studio, shows off Hepworth's curvaceous, undulating forms—inspired by, if not quite resembling, the sea, wind, sand, and light of St. Ives (£4.65, £8.55 combo-ticket includes the Tate, same hours and tel. as the Tate, at the corner of Ayr Lane and Barnoon Hill, www.tate.org.uk/stives/hepworth).

Leach Pottery Studio and Museum—This studio celebrates Bernard Leach, considered one of the founders of the mid-20th-century British studio-pottery movement. New pieces are produced on-site, and a gallery showcases work by leading contemporary potters (£4.50; March–Sept Mon–Sat 10:00–17:00, Sun 11:00–16:00; Oct–Feb Tue–Sat 10:00–16:00, closed Sun–Mon; last entry 30 min before closing, Higher Stennack, tel. 01736/799-703, www.leachpottery.com).

Getting There: The studio is well-marked from the upper outskirts of St. Ives, on the road into town. Park at the Trenwith car park (£5.50 all day—described earlier, under "Arrival in St. Ives"); the studio is a six-minute walk from there (disabled parking only at the studio). During the summer, an hourly shuttle (£1) runs between the studio and the Tate Gallery.

Stroll the Town—Besides gallery-hopping, the best way to enjoy St. Ives is by taking an ice-cream cone on a waterfront stroll. The slate-tile–clad High Street and pleasant waterfront have plenty of shops and ice-cream stands to entertain even the pickiest kids. Boats departing from the harbor can take you on trips around the cliffs and to the coves, a good way to appreciate why the Cornish coast was so popular with bootleggers and pirates.

Hit the Beach—St. Ives is popular with Brits on a "bucket-and-spade" holiday because it's surrounded by sandy beaches. In addition to the sandy, central harbor—home to boats as well as swimmers—you'll find family-friendly Porthminster Beach (west) and surfer-friendly Porthmeor Beach (east). Tiny, secluded Porthgwidden Beach—hiding between the rocks under the high peninsula called The Island—is worth the hike.

Sleeping in St. Ives

(£1 = about $1.60, country code: 44, area code: 01736)
The town's charm wears thin with the hordes of tourists in high season, but the evenings are quiet enough to consider staying over. Both of these options are in tight, twisty old buildings—climbing to your room can feel like spiraling up through a ship's hull.

$$$ Cornerways rents six rooms with lots of grays, blacks, and exposed beams. It's got a smooth nautical-meets-contemporary vibe, with easygoing Tim at the helm (Sb-£30–60, Db-£65–90, cheaper off-season, free Wi-Fi, 1 Bethesda Place, tel. 01736/796-706, www.cornerwaysstives.com, cornerwaysstives@aol.com).

$$$ The Anchorage has four cozy rooms and claustrophobic ceilings (S-£35–80, Db-£70–85, 5 Bunkers Hill, tel. 01736/797-135, www.anchoragestives.co.uk, info@anchoragestives.co.uk, Christopher).

Eating in St. Ives

The opening times for most St. Ives eateries can change from one day to the next, depending on weather and crowds.

Along the Harborfront: The main drag along the harbor has plenty of dining options. Peruse the menus and views, and choose your favorite. I ate well at **Café Coast,** with tasty and well-priced fusion cuisine (English, Asian, and Italian) and a nicely sleek, contemporary seaview ambience. Their £11 early-bird dinner includes an entrée and a glass of wine or beer (£8–12 pizzas, pastas, and main dishes; daily 9:00–22:00, right on the harborfront Wharf Street, tel. 01736/794-925).

Above Porthmeor Beach: Across the street from the Tate Gallery, the **Porthmeor Beach Café** is suspended high above this popular surfing beach (£6–9 sandwiches, salads, and pizzas, £9–13 dinners, daily 9:00–20:30, tel. 01736/793-366).

On Fore Street: Running parallel to the harbor one block inland, Fore Street is lined with tourist shops and some good budget eateries. Near the corner of Salubrious Place, follow the heavenly scent to the **Cornish Bakehouse** for traditional Cornish pasties (tel. 01736/793-632). Just around the corner, **The Dolphin** has good fish-and-chips take-away. Or, for about £1 more, you can eat upstairs, with a sea view—the server will hoist your food up the dumbwaiter for you (tel. 01736/795-701).

And for Dessert: You'll see places hawking "Cornish Ice Cream"—the frozen version of clotted cream, which means it's much creamier than the norm.

St. Ives Connections

The **bus** is more practical than the train for most connections. The most useful lines are #14, #17, and #17A to Penzance; #17B to Penzance via Marazion (St. Michael's Mount); and #300 to Land's End and Penzance (via Geevor Tin Mine, Sennen Cove, Porthcurno, and Marazion). For details, see page 271.

All **train** connections from St. Ives to points eastward go through St. Erth, where you'll switch from the cute little St. Ives Bay Line to the main line to Penzance (see "Penzance Connections" on page 280).

The Penwith Peninsula

The western tip of Cornwall, called the Penwith Peninsula, is a virtual pincushion of worthwhile stops. Literally meaning "Headland," Penwith features rugged, rocky, windblown scenery and the best-preserved bits of traditional Cornish culture. With Penzance or St. Ives as a home base, all of the following destinations are within easy striking distance for a day trip. I've listed them roughly clockwise from Penzance (the first sight, St. Michael's Mount, is east of—and visible from—Penzance). Drivers: Note that B3315 travels west from Penzance, passing the Merry Maidens stone circle and Porthcurno en route to Land's End.

St. Michael's Mount

Similar to France's Mont St. Michel, but on a smaller scale, this dramatic rock island has been inhabited for 1,500 years. Originally a Benedictine monastery, the castle was built up by the St. Aubyn family, who still own it today. If the tide is out, a stone causeway connects the island to the town of Marazion. Otherwise, a short ride in a motorboat (£1.50 each way) will bring you up to

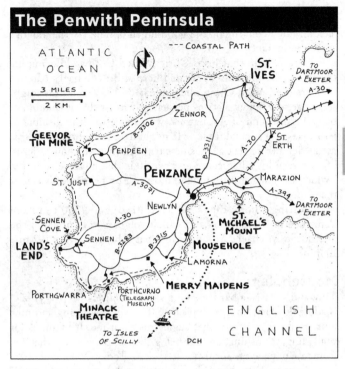

The Penwith Peninsula

the lower gates. A steep and rocky path curves its way up to the castle entrance.

Once inside, the castle is surprisingly petite. The most interesting rooms are the chapel (probably part of the original monastery) and the Chevy Chase room (which will disappoint *Saturday Night Live* fans). Family portraits, some as recent as 1993, adorn the walls. Contrary to popular belief, most of England's castles are now owned by the state or charities. The Great Depression bankrupted many noble English families, who were forced to sell off family estates and heirlooms. This is one of the few open to the public that has remained with the same family since the Middle Ages.

Out on the terrace, views of the Penwith Peninsula are grand, and they get even better when you climb the tower. The windswept gardens below the castle are worth a look for die-hard gardeners (castle and garden-£6.60, garden only-£3; castle open late March–Oct Sun–Fri 10:30–17:00, closed Sat, last entry 45 min before closing; Nov–late March castle tours run "when tides and weather are favourable," usually Tue and Fri at 11:00 and 14:00—call to confirm; garden open May–June Mon–Fri 10:30–17:00, July–Oct Thu–Fri only 10:30–17:00, closed off-season; tel. 01736/710-507,

ferry and tide info tel. 01736/710-265, www.stmichaelsmount
.co.uk). For a convenient and good lunch option, try the mount's
café or restaurant.

Locals claim that Jesus Christ visited Cornwall during his
teen years. Supposedly he landed here at St. Michael's Mount,
then traveled up to Glastonbury (near Bath). While this might
seem patently bogus, natives persuasively insist that it could have
happened: Joseph of Arimathea, who was a wealthy disciple of
Jesus, was also a metal trader. He might have brought Jesus to this
metal-rich peninsula on a business trip. All that we know of Jesus'
life between his adolescence and age 30 is that he traveled in the
"wilderness"...which Britain (and most of Europe) certainly was at
that time.

Getting There: Buses #2, #2A, #17B, and #300 run from
Penzance to Marazion, from which you can walk or catch the
boat to St. Michael's Mount (Mon–Sat 2/hr, Sun every 1–2 hrs,
10 min).

Mousehole

Tiny and salty as a barnacle on a sloop, Mousehole (MOW-zle)
is adorable. Mousehole is typical of the many charming and now
touristy fishing villages that sugar this coastline. It's famous for
smuggling, for fishing, and for being the last place where the pre-
Roman language of Cornish was spoken. Today, Mousehole har-
vests more tourists than fish. The little harbor maintains a small
fleet, but was busier in the past. The tiny passage out of the harbor
is said to be what gave the town its curious name. The best time to
enjoy the simple charm of Mousehole is early in the day, when it's
enhanced by fresh sea air and noisy seagulls. The beachside path
from Newlyn makes an excellent 30-minute stroll (described on
page 277). Drivers might want to skip Mousehole's maddeningly
narrow and twisty lanes.

Getting There: Buses #6 and #504 connect Penzance with
Newlyn (Mon–Sat 3/hr, Sun 2/hr, 10 min) and Mousehole (Mon–
Sat 2/hr, Sun 1–2/hr, 20 min).

Merry Maidens Stone Circle

In ancient times, stone circles
had some sort of significant purpose—probably as a site for religious ceremonies, as a community
meeting place, or, most famously,
as a calendar. This particular stone
circle, far simpler than the famous
ones at Stonehenge and Avebury,
is a reminder that the Penwith

Peninsula was inhabited in the Neolithic Age (roughly 2000 B.C. or earlier). The story behind the name, most likely concocted in the Middle Ages, goes like this: A group of village women decided to go into the fields on the Sabbath for some merriment and dancing. This displeased God, who turned the women to stone to serve as a warning to others.

Getting There: The Merry Maidens are in a grassy field just off B3315 (on the way from Penzance to Land's End). They're easy to miss if you're driving. Coming from Penzance, after passing through Boleigh, look for a pullout on the left near three gates; you'll also see a bus stop and a low-profile stone marker, and, on the right, a green arrow pointing across the road with a faded *Merry Maidens* sign. If you don't have a car, bus #504 takes you from Penzance to the Merry Maidens (2/day Mon–Sat only, none on Sun, 35 min).

Porthcurno

This humdrum hamlet, just off B3315 between Penzance and Land's End, has two worthwhile sights.

▲**Minack Theatre**—For good Cornish theater, try the Minack. This local open-air theater has just about the most spectacular set-

ting of any place—theater or otherwise—in England. This gorgeously landscaped facility can seat up to 750 theatergoers. With seats actually carved into a rocky cliff and a terrace stage perched hundreds of feet over the sea, the Minack is quite a sight. Imagine watching *The Tempest* with only the sunset and crashing waves for scenery. If you aren't a theater buff or don't happen to be here during the theater season, the site is still worth a visit for unbeatable views of the rocky cliffs. The small exhibit on the history of the Minack includes a short video on Rowena Cade, the visionary theater-lover who persevered to build it. There's also a cliff-hanging coffee house.

You can **visit** the theater just to see it (£3.50; Easter–mid-Sept daily 9:30–17:30—except Wed and Fri mid-May–mid-Sept, when it closes at 11:30 for a matinee; mid-Sept–Easter daily 10:00–17:00; last entry 30 min before closing), or you can attend a **performance** during peak season (£7–8.50, £1 booking fee if you use a credit/debit card, performances mid-May–mid-Sept, usually Mon–Fri at 20:00, also Wed and Fri at 14:00, rarely cancelled but dress for the weather, tel. 01736/810-181, www.minack.com).

Getting There: The theater is up an extremely narrow and twisty road above Porthcurno, well-signed from town. From Penzance, bus #504 goes to the theater (2/day Mon–Sat only, none on Sun, 55 min). If you're willing to hike, you can also take buses #1A or #300 from Penzance to the stop in Porthcurno, a steep, quarter-mile uphill climb to the theater (buses run Mon–Sat 5–6/day, Sun 2/day, 40 min). During the summer, the last bus #1A leaves Porthcurno for Penzance after the show, at 23:00 (Mon–Sat only).

Telegraph Museum—In 1870, a telegraph cable was laid from Porthcurno to India. By the time World War II broke out, 14 cables tethered this village to the rest of the world. In 1940, defensive tunnels were built to protect the telegraph station and cables from the Nazis—who were now just 80 miles away in France.

Today, those tunnels house a surprisingly interesting museum, tracing the history of the "Victorian Internet." You'll learn how underwater cables were made possible thanks to a new insulating material (a resin from a Malaysian tree called gutta-percha), how the cables were even more heavily armored in shallower water (where they could be damaged by anchors of passing ships), and how they repaired ruptured cables in the briny deep. About once an hour, a docent gives a history lesson on underwater telegraphy... which, like the museum, is better than it sounds (£5; April–Oct daily 10:00–17:00, Wed until 19:30 late May–mid-Sept; Nov–March Sun–Mon only 10:00–17:00, closed Tue–Sat; last entry one hour before closing, next to main parking lot in Porthcurno on the road up to Minack Theater—look for big white building marked *Museum*, tel. 01736/810-966, www.porthcurno.org.uk).

Getting There: Buses #1A, #300, and #504 from Penzance stop in Porthcurno near the museum (Mon–Sat 5–6/day, Sun 2/day, 40 min).

Land's End

The westernmost point in all of England should seem like a desolate, rugged place. In reality, it's a tacky tourist trap where greedy businesses have chewed up whatever small bit of charm or authenticity this place might once have had. As you approach, you'll see endless signs bragging "the last" (or, in a too-cute spin, "the first and last")... everything: inn, hotel, refreshment stand, postal box, and so on. Come here only if you want to be able to say you've seen it. (Consider lying.)

Cornish Tin Mining

Cornwall's history is tied to its tin-mining industry. While Cornwall has always been known for its metal deposits, a major tin boom began here in the mid-1700s, as new steam-engine-powered pumps allowed tin to be mined below the water table. The industry peaked 200 years ago, when tin was the cutting edge of technology, and Cornwall was the Silicon Valley of Britain.

Mines employed the notorious "company store" system, where workers were paid in tokens that could only be redeemed at the store run by the mine (an obvious conflict of interest—which always worked to the company's advantage). To save money, miners made their own "hardhats." They'd take a felt hat and harden it by dipping it alternately in hot tree resin and soil. Then they'd stick a candle on the brim for light while they worked. Since miners had to buy their own candles (from the company store, of course), they'd extinguish them during their lunch break to make them last longer. Imagine miners huddled underground, munching Cornish pasties in the pitch-blackness.

Miners would climb down into the narrow shafts, and use a hammer and a long bit to slowly drive deep, skinny holes into a vein of tin. Then they'd insert sticks of dynamite. Before safety fuses were invented, quills from bird feathers were used as fuses, so miners setting off gunpowder never knew how much time they had to reach safety before the explosion.

Deadly cave-ins were frequent. These were supposedly caused by mischievous Tommyknockers, Cornish pixies similar to leprechauns. But these mysterious creatures might simply have been a creation of the oxygen-starved imaginations of exhausted miners.

The crumbling smokestacks that dot the Cornish landscape today are the last remnants of this now-dead industry, which couldn't compete with cheap tin from Asia and South America. The ground underfoot is still honeycombed with forgotten tin mines. Older Cornish natives can still remember being in their houses and hearing the miners working underground.

If you do visit, pay the £3 parking fee and walk straight from the parking lot through the low-budget theme park (stop at your own risk) out to the viewpoint. This once was considered the end of the civilized world, the last (or first) thing to be seen by departing (or arriving) ships. After gazing at the sea and guessing how far away from home you are, find out how close you were by checking your hometown at the picture stand on the right. For £10.50, they'll take your photo with a personalized fingerpost and mail it to you.

"Back Door" Approach to Land's End: To appreciate the majesty of this location while avoiding the tourist logjam, consider hiking in from nearby **Sennen Cove.** From the road just north of Land's End, turn off to drive down the steep and narrow road into the village of Sennen, then park at the harbor (where the road dead-ends at the end of town). It's a steep, uphill, but rewarding one-mile hike over the windswept headlands to Land's End, following the South West Coast Path, Britain's longest national trail (for a description, see www.southwestcoastpath.com).

Getting There: Buses #1, #1A, #300, and #504 connect Penzance with Land's End (Mon–Sat every 1–2 hrs, Sun every 2 hrs, 40 min–2.5 hrs depending on bus), while #300 and #504 also stop at Sennen Cove (daily every 2 hrs).

▲Geevor Tin Mine

Once 2,100 feet deep and extending almost a mile under the ocean, the Geevor Mine closed in 1991. Today, it's been converted into a museum, but it retains most of its original buildings and machinery. Exploring the remnants of this recently defunct industry—which for centuries was an integral part of Cornish life—you'll gain an appreciation for the simple, noble life of miners. In late 2008, the mine opened its new, two-story Hard Rock museum in one of its buildings, with exhibits for all ages about mining and the rocks that harbor valuable ores. Even if you're not into heavy metal, this unique look at tin mining is fascinating—and worth ▲▲▲ to those interested in engineering.

Cost and Hours: £8.50, Easter–Oct Sun–Fri 9:00–17:00, Nov–Easter Sun–Fri 9:00–16:00, closed Sat year-round, tours run hourly in summer and at 11:00, 13:00, and 15:00 in winter, last tour one hour before closing, wear good shoes, pick up the free map at entry to follow the route, café, resident cats available for petting, tel. 01736/788-662, www.geevor.com.

Getting There: It's just off the B3306 road along the north coast of Penwith. Or, if you're driving in from the A30 Penzance bypass, take A3071 to St. Just and follow the brown *Historic Mining Area* signs. Take the right fork on B3318 to Pendeen, turn left at the crossroads to drive through Pendeen, and turn right at the Geevor entrance. You can also get here on buses #17 and #300 from Penzance or #300 from St. Ives and Land's End. Show your bus receipt to get a 10 percent discount on admission to the mine.

❸ Self-Guided Tour: Put on your hard hat and wander through the museum. A short film explains the tin-mining process, and a giant model, once used to help engineers keep track of the network of shafts, makes it clear how extensive the mining industry was here.

Then head outside, where you'll walk from shed to shed to see

Cornish Pasties

After working all morning in the tin mines, miners looked forward to their traditional lunch of a Cornish pasty (PASS-tee). Basically a beef stew wrapped in a pastry crust, pasties have a thick, crimped edge that miners could grab with dirty hands without contaminating their food. Because real flour was expensive, early miners skimped by using barley wheat—making for a very tough package. Leftover chunks of dough were often dropped into the mineshaft to appease the Tommyknockers.

Originally a pasty would be filled half with stew, and the rest with dessert, such as jam or apples. Nowadays there's a nice variety of flavors, like lamb and mint, but the full meal deal is rare. The British government is currently seeking trademark protection from the European Union for the Cornish pasty. That means the name could only be applied to those pasties made in Cornwall using traditional techniques and recipes (www.cornishpastyassociation.co.uk).

Look for pasties all over Cornwall. Near the Geevor Tin Mine, you can get hot, authentic, delicious pasties on the main square of the humble town of St. Just, at McFadden and Sons Butchers (Mon–Fri 8:00–17:00, Sat 7:30–16:00—or until 14:00 in winter, closed Sun, 11 Market Square, tel. 01736/788-136).

the various parts of the day-to-day workings of the mine. The most interesting area is "The Dry," where the miners showered, changed, and dried their uniforms between shifts. Though it closed almost two decades ago, it feels as though the miners could show up at any time to clock in. Enjoy the old time-punch clock, the fun stickers on the miners' lockers, and graffiti showing their sense of humor (such as the *Ear Protection Must Be Worn* sign posted next to the toilets). In "The Mill," you'll see how a vast warehouse of "shaking tables"—like giant machines panning for gold—separated the miners' haul into its useable parts.

The finale is a guided half-hour underground tour of an 18th-century mine (which predates the more recent mine that the current buildings supported, and was discovered by modern miners). A docent (often a former mine employee) gives you a coverall and leads you in. The mines—narrow and low (you'll be hunched for most of the tour, and claustrophobes will be miserable)—give you a sense of the difficult life of miners and the perilous conditions under which they worked.

Isles of Scilly

Just off the coast of Cornwall, this group of islands (pronounced "silly") sits right in the path of the Gulf Stream. The warm (or

CORNWALL

at least warmer) climate is perfect for growing a wide variety of exotic plants, so the islands boast plenty of gardens to visit. But half the fun is getting there: A fleet of old, creaky, Penzance-based **helicopters** is ready to whisk you to precarious heights (£96–170 round-trip depending on time, season, and ticket type, 20-min flight, Mon–Sat year-round, no flights Sun or winter holidays, £2 shuttle from Penzance train station to heliport 45 min before each flight, tel. 01736/363-871, www.islesofscillyhelicopter.com). Alternatively, you can take a very slow **boat** called the *Scillonian III* from Penzance (£47.50 one-way, £95 round-trip, 2.75 hrs each way, sporadic schedule but generally departs Mon–Sat at 9:15 in summer, no boats Nov–mid-March, tel. 08457/105-555, www.ios -travel.co.uk). The boat company also runs **planes** out to the islands from the Land's End airport (£64.50 one-way, £129 round-trip, 15-min flight).

East Cornwall

These destinations are a bit farther from Penzance, and closer to Dartmoor National Park (see previous chapter). I've listed them from farthest to nearest to Penzance. Consider visiting them in this order as you approach the tip of Cornwall.

▲▲Tintagel Castle

Wild, rocky, remote, and romantic, Tintagel (tin-TAD-jell) is as dramatic as a castle can be. The real King Arthur—if he actually existed—was supposedly born here and ruled his lands from this rocky point. While the popular tales of Camelot are flights of fantasy, they may be based on a real person. Even though there's no physical record of King Arthur (other than a recently discovered pottery shard), the verbal tradi-  tion is strong enough that experts think a fifth- or sixth-century ruler by that name probably lived in this area, possibly basing himself in modern Camelford (which might be where "Camelot" comes from). Regardless of whether Arthur is fact or fiction, windblown Tintagel Castle is striking. If you can handle lots of steep hiking up and down, this is one of England's most reward-ing ruined-castle experiences. And as a bonus, you get to enjoy a spectacularly scenic stretch of Cornish coastline. Bring a picnic to have lunch with a view.

Cost and Hours: £4.90, daily Easter–Sept 10:00–18:00, Oct 10:00–17:00, Nov–Easter 10:00–16:00, tel. 01840/770-328, www.english-heritage.org.uk.

Getting There: The castle clings to the coast below the tacky town of Tintagel. If you're arriving by car, look for *Tintagel* signs from A39 as it passes through Camelford. Once you enter town, take your pick of parking lots, then hike down the steep road to the main entrance at the rocky bay. Or, if you prefer, take the Land Rover shuttle (£1.20 each way, runs continuously April–Sept). By public transportation, you can take bus #594 from Wadebridge to Tintagel (Mon–Sat hourly, 1/day Sun, 40 min, tel. 01637/871-871, www.westerngreyhound.com).

❍ **Self-Guided Tour:** The main part of the castle is on what's called The Island (actually a rocky peninsula attached by a narrow spit); nearby, on the mainland, is a separate section called the Mainland Courtyard. For the full story, invest in the TI's £4 illustrated guidebook. It's keyed to numbered plaques around the site (which I've also made use of below). Here are the highlights:

After buying your ticket at the main entrance, watch the good seven-minute **film** called *Searching for King Arthur*, which considers the historical and legendary underpinnings of this evocative site.

Head up to the viewpoint overlooking the cove. As you approach the bridge, look for the hole in the cliff below the ruins—supposedly **Merlin's cave.** (If the tide is out, you can climb down to explore the famous wizard's former home...and ponder how he managed to keep the carpet dry and prevent seals from climbing on the furniture.)

Now look up to the top of the giant chunk of rock above Merlin's cave. Appreciate the naturally fortified, easily defendable position of this rock-top castle. Note the narrow and difficult approach to this hunk of land, and you can understand why Tintagel—meaning "fortress with narrow entrance"—is aptly named.

Head up the steps and cross the footbridge, then tackle the very steep climb up to the top of the cliffs, or **The Island.** We'll do a roughly counterclockwise spin around these grounds.

As you enter through the back door, you reach the **Island Courtyard**—castle remnants dating from the Middle Ages (with a *3* plaque). Rather than belonging to Arthur (who would have lived centuries earlier), these structures were built for the brother of a 13th-century king. Notice that the walls are made of stacked sheets of slate, which was mined on this site for many years.

Continue through the ruins and up to the viewpoint platform (marked with a *4* plaque). All around you—including directly below—you'll see the foundations of ruined **Dark Age houses,** which actually date from the time when Arthur most likely lived (the fifth century A.D.). Here archaeologists have found remains of items from as far away as North Africa and the Eastern Mediterranean—evidence of the wealth and status of this castle's owner.

Climb on up to the top of The Island. As you explore, you'll come across several interesting sites. In the walled area called the **garden** (marked *5*), medieval residents could relax and entertain visitors in the summer. The **well** (marked *8*) was the source of water in the Middle Ages, and remains today's last resort in case of fire. The 11th-century **chapel** (marked *10*) is recognizable for the altar at its far end. If you have time, linger up here. The craggy peaks across the tops of the cliffs make a perfect, windblown picnic spot.

After the chapel, you'll head back down the steep steps to the footbridge. From here, for extra credit, consider hiking up the steps across the bridge to the **Mainland Courtyard,** with more medieval remains. If you decide to climb up, you can take a much less steep path behind this courtyard back down to rejoin the main path up the valley.

▲The Eden Project

Set in an abandoned china-clay mine, the Eden Project is an ambitious and futuristic work-in-progress—a theme park of global gardening with an environmental conscience. Exotic plants from all over the world are showcased in two giant biomes, reputedly the largest greenhouses in the world. The displays focus on sustainable farming and ecoconscious planting, but the most interesting thing here is the sheer audacity of the idea. If you're looking for a quaint English cottage garden, this isn't it. Rather than a flowery look at England's past, this "global garden" gives you a sense of how the shrinking of the world will affect us in the future.

After buying your ticket, zigzag down into the pit and work your way through the various exhibits, including the enormous, hot, and hazy Rainforest Biome (where my camera completely fogged up); the smaller and more arid Mediterranean Biome; an eatery-filled walkway connecting them called The Link; The Core, with educational exhibits; and lots of gardens. A land train and an elevator from The Core make it easier to get back up to the visitors center when you're done. Kid-oriented programs, rock and pop concerts, and other special events run throughout the year.

It's an impressive concept, and the biomes are striking. But the educational exhibits are a bit too conceptual to be effective, leaving the whole, expensive experience feeling somehow unmoored.

Cost and Hours: £16; mid-March–Oct daily 9:00–18:00; Nov–mid-March daily 10:00–16:30; last entry 1.5 hrs before closing, cafés, tel. 017626/811-911, www.edenproject.com). The Eden Project is popular and can be crowded, especially on rainy days and weekdays June through August (they told me "wet Wednesdays" are the worst). During peak-of-peak times, you may have to wait up to an hour to get in. Avoid this by arriving after 13:00.

Getting There: Drivers will find the Eden Project well-signposted from both A30 and A39—you'll be directed to A391, and follow signs from there. Park at one of the many outlying lots, then walk down into the Project (or take the park-and-ride shuttle bus). By public transit, first take the train to St. Austell, where you'll meet bus #101 (daily hourly, toll tel. 0871-200-2233, www.firstgroup.com) or #527 (Mon–Sat hourly, Sun 1/day, tel. 01637/871-871, www.westerngreyhound.com). Buses meet most arriving trains for the 20-minute run to the complex (buy combo-ticket for bus and entry fee from driver).

Gardens near Falmouth

Cornwall has many wonderful gardens, some with subtropical varieties of plants that thrive in this mild climate (www.great gardensofcornwall.co.uk). These two gardens are a few miles apart on the same backcountry road, just south of Falmouth.

Getting There: If you're driving, take A39 or A394 into Falmouth until you see brown-and-white *Garden* signs—track these closely through the countryside to the gardens (Glendurgan is the better-signed of the two). If you're without a car, take bus #T4 or #400 from Falmouth, both of which pass near the Penmere train station on their way to the gardens (45 min–2 hrs, www .travelinesw.com).

▲**Trebah Garden**—The "Garden of Dreams" at Trebah (TREE-bah) is a lush and tropical spectacle. Set on 26 acres that bunny-hop down a ravine to the beach below, this tropical garden is an unexpected treat. While most of England suffers from chilly arctic air, the Cornish peninsula is bathed in warmer air from the Gulf Stream—making average temperatures here much milder (the sea here never drops below 50 degrees Fahrenheit). Palms, succulents, bamboo, large azaleas, giant rhubarbs, and the prehistoric-looking gunnera might make you think (or wish) that you're in the tropics rather than Cornwall. The garden's exoticism impresses even non-gardeners (£7.50 March–Oct, £3 Nov–Feb, open daily 10:30–18:30, until dusk in winter, last entry 1.5 hours before closing, colorful year-round but flowers are best late March and April, café, tel. 01326/252-200, www.trebah-garden.co.uk).

While garden-lovers wander in ecstasy, history buffs can ponder the fact that the beach below was used by US troops in World War II to launch the D-Day attack on Omaha Beach.

Glendurgan Garden—Just up the road from Trebah, Glendurgan has a smaller collection of tropical plants mingled with more traditional English garden fare. Similarly set in a broad basin angled to the sea, Glendurgan is bigger but less striking than its neighbor. However, it does come with an extensive, kid-friendly hedge maze (about waist-high—but still entertaining—for an adult), built by the former owner to entertain his 12 children. Gardeners may appreciate its good orchids and its small "Holy Bank" of biblical-themed plants. And down at the seashore, the fishing hamlet of Durgan makes it feel less like just an overblown backyard for aristocrats (£5.75, worthwhile £3 map/guide, mid-Feb–Oct Tue–Sat 10:30–17:30, closed Sun–Mon except Aug when it's open Mon, last entry 30 min before closing, closed Nov–mid-Feb, best in spring, café, tel. 01326/250-906, www.nationaltrust.org.uk).

BATH

The best city to visit within easy striking distance of London is Bath—just a 90-minute train ride away. Two hundred years ago, this city of 85,000 was the trendsetting Hollywood of Britain. If ever a city enjoyed looking in the mirror, Bath's the one. It has more "government-listed" or protected historic buildings per capita than any other town in England. The entire city, built of the creamy warm-tone limestone called "Bath stone," beams in its cover-girl complexion. An architectural chorus line, it's a triumph of the Georgian style. Proud locals remind visitors that the town is routinely banned from the "Britain in Bloom" contest to give other towns a chance to win. Bath's narcissism is justified. Even with its mobs of tourists (2 million per year) and greedy prices, Bath is a joy to visit.

Bath's fame began with the allure of its (supposedly) healing hot springs. Long before the Romans arrived in the first century, Bath was known for its warm waters. Romans named the popular spa town Aquae Sulis, after a local Celtic goddess. The town's importance carried through Saxon times, when it had a huge church on the site of the present-day abbey and was considered the religious capital of Britain. Its influence peaked in 973 with King Edgar's sumptuous coronation in the abbey. Later, Bath prospered as a wool town.

Bath then declined until the mid-1600s, languishing to just a huddle of huts around the abbey, with hot, smelly mud and 3,000 residents, oblivious to the Roman ruins 18 feet below their dirt floors. In fact, with its own walls built upon ancient ones, Bath was no bigger than that Roman town. Then, in 1687, Queen Mary, fighting infertility, bathed here. Within 10 months she gave birth to a son...and a new age of popularity for Bath.

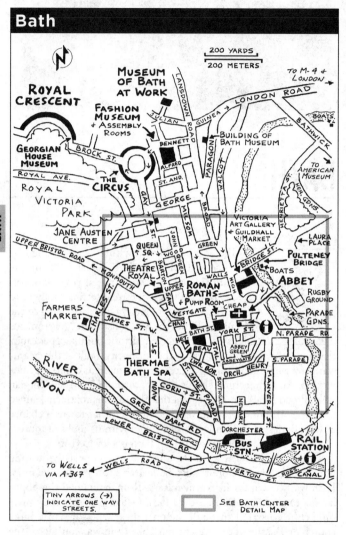

Bath

Royal Crescent

Museum of Bath at Work

Fashion Museum + Assembly Rooms

Georgian House Museum

The Circus

Royal Victoria Park

Jane Austen Centre

Theatre Royal

Farmers' Market

Thermae Bath Spa

River Avon

Building of Bath Museum

Victoria Art Gallery & Guildhall Market

Pulteney Bridge

Roman Baths + Pump Room

Abbey

Parade Gdns

Bus Stn

Rail Station

To M-4 & London

London Road

To American Museum

Laura Place

200 YARDS
200 METERS

To Wells via A-367

Tiny arrows (→) indicate one way streets.

See Bath Center Detail Map

The revitalized town boomed as a spa resort. Ninety percent of the buildings you'll see today are from the 18th century. Local architect John Wood was inspired by the Italian architect Andrea Palladio to build a "new Rome." The town bloomed in the Neoclassical style, and streets were lined not with scrawny sidewalks but with wide "parades," upon which the women in their stylishly wide dresses could spread their fashionable tails.

Beau Nash (1673–1762) was Bath's "master of ceremonies." He organized both the daily regimen of aristocratic visitors and the city, lighting the streets, improving security, banning swords, and opening the Pump Room. Under his fashionable baton, Bath became a city of balls, gaming, and concerts—the place to see and be seen in England. This most civilized place became even more so with the great Neoclassical building spree that followed.

These days, modern tourism has stoked the local economy, as has the fast morning train to London. (A growing number of Bath professionals catch the 7:13 train to Paddington Station every morning.) With renewed access to Bath's soothing hot springs at the Thermae Bath Spa, the venerable waters are in the spotlight again, attracting a new generation of visitors in need of a cure or a soak.

Planning Your Time

Bath deserves two nights even on a quick trip. On a three-week England getaway, spend three nights in Bath, with one day for the city and one day for side-trips (see next chapter). Ideally, use Bath as your jet-lag recovery pillow, and do London at the end of your trip.

Consider starting a three-week English vacation this way:

Day 1: Land at Heathrow. Connect to Bath by National Express bus—the better option—or the less convenient bus/train combination (for details, see page 159). While you don't need or want a car in Bath, and some rental companies have an office there, those who land early and pick up their cars at the airport can visit Windsor Castle (near Heathrow) and/or Stonehenge on their way to Bath. (You can also consider flying into Bristol.) If you have the evening free in Bath, take a walking tour.

Day 2: 9:00–Tour the Roman Baths; 10:30–Catch the free city walking tour; 12:30–Picnic on the open deck of a Bath tour bus; 14:00–Free time in the shopping center of old Bath; 15:30–Tour the Fashion Museum or Museum of Bath at Work. Take the evening walking tour (unless you did last night), enjoy the Bizarre Bath comedy walk, consider seeing a play, or go for a nighttime soak in the Thermae Bath Spa.

Day 3 (and possibly 4): By car, explore nearby sights. Without a car, consider a one-day Avebury/Stonehenge/cute towns minibus tour from Bath (Mad Max tours are best; see "Tours in Bath" later in this chapter).

Orientation to Bath

(area code: 01225)
Bath's town square, three blocks in front of the bus and train station, is a cluster of tourist landmarks, including the abbey, Roman and medieval baths, and the Pump Room.

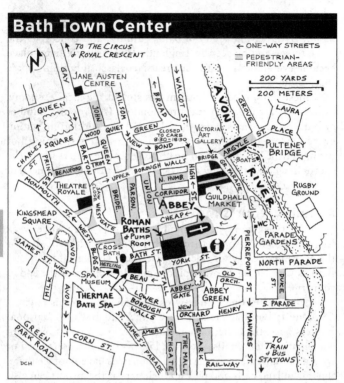

Bath Town Center

Map labels:
TO THE CIRCUS & ROYAL CRESCENT — ← ONE-WAY STREETS — ☐ PEDESTRIAN-FRIENDLY AREAS — 200 YARDS — 200 METERS — JANE AUSTEN CENTRE — VICTORIA ART GALLERY — LAURA PLACE — PULTENEY BRIDGE — QUEEN SQUARE — CHARLES SQUARE — THEATRE ROYALE — KINGSMEAD SQUARE — N. HUMB. CORRIDOR — GUILDHALL MARKET — ABBEY — ROMAN BATHS & PUMP ROOM — CHEAP — RUGBY GROUND — SPA MUSEUM — THERMAE BATH SPA — ABBEY GREEN — NEW ORCHARD — PARADE GARDENS — NORTH PARADE — S. PARADE — GREEN PARK ROAD — RAILWAY — THE MALL — TO TRAIN & BUS STATIONS — AVON — RIVER — BOATS — ARGYLE ST. — GROVE — BRIDGE

Tourist Information

The TI is in the abbey churchyard (Mon–Sat 9:30–18:00, Sun 10:00–16:00, closes one hour early Mon–Sat Oct–May, toll tel. 0870-420-1278, www.visitbath.co.uk, note that their 0906 info number costs 50p/min). The TI sells a chintzy £1 city map. The £1.25 map, available in their shop, is much better—or just use the one included in the free *Bath Visitors' Guide and Map*. While you're at the TI, browse through scads of fliers, books, and maps, or ask them to book you a room (booking tel. 0844-847-5252). They don't bother to print an events flier, so look at the local paper or their daily events board. You can also buy the Great British Heritage Pass here (see page 19).

Arrival in Bath

The Bath Spa **train station** has a national and international tickets desk and a privately run travel agency masquerading as a TI.

Immediately surrounding the train station is a sea of construction, as Bath gets a new mall and underground parking garage (due to be completed in 2011). To get to the TI from the train station, walk two blocks up Manvers Street and turn left at the triangular "square," following the small TI arrow on a signpost.

The **bus station** is west of the train station, just south of Dorchester Street.

My recommended B&Bs are all within a 10- to 15-minute walk or a £4–5 taxi ride from the train station.

Helpful Hints

Festivals: The **Bath Literature Festival** is an open book February 27–March 7 in 2010 (www.bathlitfest.org.uk). The **Bath International Music Festival** bursts into song every spring (classical, folk, jazz, contemporary; May 28–June 12 in 2010, see www.bathmusicfest.org.uk), overlapped by the eclectic **Bath Fringe Festival** (theater, walks, talks, bus trips; May 28–June 13 in 2010, www.bathfringe.co.uk). The **Jane Austen Festival** unfolds genteelly in late September (www.janeausten.co.uk/festival). Bath's festival box office sells tickets for most events and can tell you exactly what's on tonight (2 Church Street, tel. 01225/463-362, www.bath festivals.org.uk). The city's local paper, the *Bath Chronicle*, publishes a "What's On" event listing on Fridays (www .thisisbath.com).

Internet Access: You can get online at the Bath library (£1/20 min with free library membership, Mon–Thu 9:30–19:00, Fri–Sat 9:30–17:00, Sun 13:00–16:00, in The Podium shopping centre on Northgate Street near Pulteney Bridge, tel. 01225/394-041, www.bathnes.gov.uk), or ask your hotel or the TI for recommended Internet cafés.

Laundry: Bring lots of £0.20 and £1 coins, as there are no change machines at these launderettes. **Spruce Goose Launderette** is around the corner from the recommended Brocks Guest House, on the pedestrian lane called Margaret's Buildings (self-service daily 8:00–20:00; full-service Mon, Wed, and Fri 9:00–13:00—but book ahead; tel. 01225/483-309). **Speedy Wash** can pick up your laundry before 11:00 anywhere in town for same-day service (£12/bag, Mon–Fri 7:30–17:30, Sat 8:30–13:00 but no pickup, closed Sun, no self-service, most hotels work with them, 4 Mile End, London Road, tel. 01225/427-616).

Car Rental: Enterprise provides a pickup service for customers to and from their hotels (extra fee for one-way rentals, at Lower Bristol Road outside Bath, tel. 01225/443-311, www .enterprise.com). Others include **Thrifty** (pickup service and one-way rentals available, in the Burnett Business Park in Keynsham—between Bath and Bristol, tel. 01179/867-997,

Bath at a Glance

▲▲▲**Roman and Medieval Baths** Ancient baths that gave the city its name, tourable with good audioguide. **Hours:** Daily July–Aug 9:00–22:00, March–June and Sept–Oct 9:00–18:00, Nov–Feb 9:30–17:30. See page 305.

▲▲▲**Walking Tours** Free top-notch tours, helping you make the most of your visit, led by The Mayor's Corps of Honorary Guides. **Hours:** Sun–Fri at 10:30 and 14:00, Sat at 10:30 only; additional evening walks offered May–Sept Tue and Fri at 19:00. See page 303.

▲▲**Royal Crescent and the Circus** Stately Georgian (Neoclassical) buildings from Bath's late-18th-century glory days. **Hours:** Always viewable. See page 309.

▲▲**Fashion Museum** 400 years of clothing under one roof, plus opulent Assembly Rooms. **Hours:** Daily March–Oct 10:30–18:00, Nov–Feb 10:30–17:00. See page 310.

▲▲**Museum of Bath at Work** Gadget-ridden circa-1900 engineer's shop, foundry, factory, and office, best enjoyed with a live tour. **Hours:** April–Oct daily 10:30–17:00, Nov–March weekends only. See page 311.

▲**Pump Room** Swanky Georgian hall, ideal for a spot of tea or a taste of unforgettably "healthy" spa water. **Hours:** Daily 9:30–12:00 for coffee and breakfast, 12:00–14:30 for lunch, 14:30–16:30 for afternoon tea (open for dinner during Bath International Music Festival, July–Aug, and Christmas holidays only). See page 306.

www.thrifty.co.uk) and **National Europcar** (one-way rentals available, £7 by taxi from the train station, at Brassmill Lane—go west on Upper Bristol Road, tel. 01225/481-982 or 01761/479-205). Skip **Avis**—it's a mile from the Bristol train station; you'd need to rent a car to get there. Most offices close Saturday afternoon and all day Sunday, which complicates weekend pickups. Ideally, take the train or bus from downtown London to Bath, and rent a car as you leave Bath.

Parking: Parking in the city center is difficult—short-term street parking is available but pricey (about £2.50/hr, 2-hour maximum, buy Pay & Display tickets from machine), with cheaper parking in parking lots. For more information, visit www.bathnes.gov.uk/bathnes.

▲**Thermae Bath Spa** Relaxation center that put the bath back in Bath. **Hours:** Daily 9:00–22:00. See page 306.

▲**Abbey** 500-year-old Perpendicular Gothic church, graced with beautiful fan vaulting and stained glass. **Hours:** April–Oct Mon–Sat 9:00–18:00, Sun 13:00–14:30 & 16:30–17:30; Nov–March Mon–Sat 9:00–16:30, Sun 13:00–14:30 & 16:30–17:30. See page 308.

▲**Pulteney Bridge and Parade Gardens** Shop-strewn bridge and relaxing riverside gardens. **Hours:** Bridge—always open; gardens—April–Sept daily 10:00–dusk, shorter hours off-season. See page 308.

▲**Georgian House at No. 1 Royal Crescent** Best opportunity to explore the interior of one of Bath's high-rent Georgian beauties. **Hours:** Mid-Feb–Oct Tue–Sun 10:30–17:00, Nov Tue–Sun 10:30–16:00, closed Mon and Dec–mid-Feb. See page 310.

▲**American Museum** An insightful look primarily at colonial/early-American lifestyles, with 18 furnished rooms and eager-to-talk guides. **Hours:** Mid-March–Oct Tue–Sun 12:00–17:00, closed Mon and Nov–mid-March. See page 312.

Jane Austen Centre Exhibit on 19th-century Bath-based novelist, best for her fans. **Hours:** Mid-March–mid-Nov daily 9:45–17:30, July–Aug Thu–Sat until 19:00; mid-Nov–mid-March Sun–Fri 11:00–16:30, Sat 9:45–17:30. See page 311.

BATH

Tours in Bath

▲▲▲**Walking Tours**—Free two-hour tours are offered by **The Mayor's Corps of Honorary Guides,** led by volunteers who want to share their love of Bath with its many visitors (as the city's mayor first did when he took a group on a guided walk back in the 1930s). Their chatty, historical, and gossip-filled walks are essential for your understanding of this town's amazing Georgian social scene. How else would you learn that the old "chair ho" call for your sedan chair evolved into today's "cheerio" farewell? Tours leave from outside the Pump Room in the abbey churchyard (free, no tips, year-round Sun–Fri at 10:30 and 14:00, Sat at 10:30 only; additional evening walks May–Sept Tue and Fri at 19:00; tel. 01225/477-411, www.thecityofbath.co.uk). Tip for theatergoers: When your guide stops to talk outside the Theatre Royal, skip out for a moment, pop into the box office, and see about snaring a great deal on a play for tonight.

For a **private tour,** call the local guides' bureau (£60/2 hrs, tel. 01225/337-111). For **Ghost Walks** and **Bizarre Bath** tours, see "Nightlife in Bath," later.

▲▲**City Bus Tours**—City Sightseeing's hop-on, hop-off bus tours zip through Bath. Jump on a bus anytime at one of 17 signposted pickup points, pay the driver, climb upstairs, and hear recorded commentary about Bath. City Sightseeing has two 45-minute routes: a city tour (unintelligible audio recording on half the buses, live guides on the other half—choose the latter), and a "Skyline" route outside town (all live guides, stops near the American Museum—15-min walk). On a sunny day, this is a multitasking tourist's dream come true: You can munch a sandwich, work on a tan, snap great photos, and learn a lot, all at the same time. Save money by doing the bus tour first—ticket stubs get you minor discounts at many sights (£11, ticket valid for 2 days and both tour routes, generally 4/hr daily in summer 9:30–18:30, in winter 10:00–15:00, tel. 01225/330-444, www.city-sightseeing.com).

Taxi Tours—Local taxis, driven by good talkers, go where big buses can't. A group of up to four can rent a cab for an hour (about £20) and enjoy a fine, informative, and—with the right cabbie—entertaining private joyride. It's probably cheaper to let the meter run than to pay for an hourly rate, but ask the cabbie for advice.

To Stonehenge, Avebury, and the Cotswolds

Bath is a good launch pad for visiting Wells, Avebury, Stonehenge, and more.

Mad Max Minibus Tours—Operating daily from Bath, Maddy and Paul offer thoughtfully organized, informative tours that run with entertaining guides and a maximum group size of 16 people. Their **Stone Circles** full-day tour covers 110 miles and visits Stonehenge, the Avebury Stone Circles, and two cute villages: Lacock and Castle Combe. Photogenic Lacock is featured in parts of the BBC's *Pride and Prejudice* and the Harry Potter movies, and Castle Combe, the southernmost Cotswold village, is as sweet as they come (£30 plus £6.50 Stonehenge entry, tours run daily 8:45–16:30, arrive 10 min early, leaves early to beat the Stonehenge hordes). Their shorter tour of **Stonehenge and Lacock** leaves daily at 13:15 and returns at 17:15 and, on some days, leaves at 8:45 and returns at 12:45 (£15 plus £6.50 Stonehenge entry).

Mad Max also offers a **Cotswold Discovery** full-day tour, a picturesque romp through the countryside with stops and a cream-tea opportunity in the Cotswolds' quainter villages, including Stow-on-the-Wold, Bibury, Tetbury, the Coln Valley, The Slaughters (optional walk between the two villages), and others (£32.50; runs Sun, Tue, and Thu 8:45–17:15; arrive 10 min early).

If you request it in advance, you can bring your luggage along and use the tour as transportation to Stow or, for £2.50 extra, Moreton-in-Marsh, with easy train connections to Oxford.

All tours depart from Bath at the Glass House shop on the corner of Orange Grove, a one-minute walk from the abbey. Arrive 10 minutes before your departure time and bring cash—credit cards are not accepted. It's better to book ahead—as far ahead as possible in summer—for these popular tours. Online or email reservations are preferable to calling (phone answered daily 8:00–18:00, tel. 07990/505-970, www.madmax.abel.co.uk, maddy@madmax.abel.co.uk). Please honor or cancel your seat reservation.

More Bus Tours—If Mad Max is booked up, don't fret. Plenty of companies in Bath offer tours of varying lengths, prices, and destinations. Note that the cost of admission to sights is usually not included with any tour.

Scarper Tours runs a minibus tour to Stonehenge (£14, 10 percent Rick Steves discount if you book direct, does not include £6.50 Stonehenge entry fee, departs from behind the abbey, daily Easter–Sept at 10:00 and 14:00, Oct–Easter at 13:00 only, tel. 07739/644-155, www.scarpertours.com). The three-hour tour (two hours there and back, an hour at the site) includes driver narration en route.

Celtic Horizons, run by retired teacher Alan Price, offers tours from Bath to a variety of destinations, such as Stonehenge, Avebury, and Wells. He can provide a convenient transfer service (to or from London, Heathrow, Bristol Airport, the Cotswolds, and so on), with or without a tour itinerary en route. Allow about £25/hour for a group (his comfortable minivan seats up to 8 people) and £125 for Heathrow–Bath transfers. It's best to make arrangements and get pricing information by email at alan@celtichorizons.com (cash only, tel. 01373/461-784, http://celtichorizons.com).

Sights in Bath

In the Town Center

▲▲▲**Roman and Medieval Baths**—In ancient Roman times, high society enjoyed the mineral springs at Bath. From

Londinium, Romans traveled so often to Aquae Sulis, as the city was called, to "take a bath" that finally it became known simply as Bath. Today, a fine museum surrounds the ancient bath. It's a one-way system leading you past well-documented displays, Roman artifacts, mosaics, a temple pediment, and the actual mouth of the spring, piled high with Roman pennies. Enjoy some quality time looking into the eyes of Minerva, goddess of the hot springs. The included audioguide makes the visit easy and plenty informative. For those with a big appetite for Roman history, in-depth 40-minute guided tours leave from the end of the museum at the edge of the actual bath (included with ticket, on the hour, a poolside clock is set for the next departure time). The water is greenish because of algae—don't drink it. You can revisit the museum after the tour (£11, £14.50 combo-ticket includes Fashion Museum—a £3.50 savings, family ticket available, daily July–Aug 9:00–22:00, March–June and Sept–Oct 9:00–18:00, Nov–Feb 9:30–17:30, last entry one hour before closing, tel. 01225/477-785, www.roman baths.co.uk). The museum and baths are fun to visit in the evening in summer—romantic, gas-lit, and all yours.

After touring the Roman Baths, stop by the attached Pump Room for a spot of tea, or to gag on the water.

▲**Pump Room**—For centuries, Bath was forgotten as a spa. Then, in 1687, the previously barren Queen Mary bathed here, became pregnant, and bore a male heir to the throne. A few years later, Queen Anne found the water eased her painful gout. Word of its wonder waters spread, and Bath earned its way back on the aristocratic map. High society soon turned the place into one big pleasure palace. The Pump Room, an elegant Georgian hall just above the Roman Baths, offers visitors their best chance to raise a pinky in this Chippendale grandeur. Above the newspaper table and sedan chairs, a statue of Beau Nash himself sniffles down at you. Drop by to sip coffee or tea or to enjoy a light meal (daily 9:30–12:00 for coffee and £6–9 breakfast, 12:00–14:30 for £6–10 lunches, 14:30–16:30 for £17.50 traditional afternoon tea, tea/coffee and pastries also available in the afternoons; open for dinner July–Aug, during Bath International Music Festival, and Christmas holidays only; live music daily—string trio or piano, times vary; tel. 01225/444-477). For just the price of a coffee (£3), you're welcome to drop in anytime—except during lunch—to enjoy the music and atmosphere.

The Spa Water: This is your chance to eat a famous (but forgettable) "Bath bun" and split a drink of the awful curative water (£0.50). The water comes from the King's Spring and is brought to you by an appropriately attired server, who explains that the water is 10,000 years old, pumped up from nearly 100 yards deep, and marinated in 43 wonderful minerals. Convenient public WCs (which use plain old tap water) are in the entry hallway that connects the Pump Room with the baths.

▲**Thermae Bath Spa**—After simmering unused for a quarter-century, Bath's natural thermal springs once again offer R&R for the masses. The state-of-the-art spa is housed in a complex of three

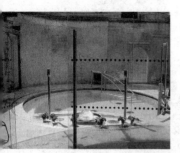

buildings that combine historic structures with controversial (and expensive) new glass-and-steel architecture.

Is the Thermae Bath Spa worth the time and money? The experience is pretty pricey and humble compared to similar German and Hungarian spas. Because you're in a tall, modern building in the city center, it lacks a certain old-time elegance. Jets are very limited, and the only water toys you'll see are big foam noodles. There's no cold plunge—the only way to cool off between steam rooms is to step onto a small, unglamorous balcony. The Royal Bath's two pools are essentially the same, and the water isn't particularly hot in either—in fact, the main attraction is the rooftop view from the top one (best with a partner or as a social experience).

That said, this is the only natural thermal spa in the UK, and a chance to bathe in Bath. If you visit, bring your own swimsuit and come for a couple of hours (Fri night and Sat afternoon are most crowded). Or consider an evening visit, when—on a chilly day—Bath's twilight glows through the steam from the rooftop pool.

Cost: The cheapest spa pass is £22 for two hours, which gains you access to the Royal Bath's large, ground-floor "Minerva Bath"; the four steam rooms and the waterfall shower; and the view-filled, open-air, rooftop thermal pool. If you want to stay longer, it's £32/4 hrs and £52/day (towel, robe, and slippers-£9). The much-hyped £37.50 Twilight Package includes three hours and a meal (one plate, drink, robe, towel, and slippers). This appeal of this package is not the mediocre meal, but being on top of the building at a magical hour (which you can do for less money at the regular rate). Thermae also has all the "pamper thyself" extras: massages, mud wraps, and various healing-type treatments, including "watsu"—water shiatsu (£40–70 extra).

Hours: Daily 9:00–22:00, last entry at 19:30.

Location and Information: It's 100 yards from the Roman and Medieval Baths, on Beau Street. Tel. 01225/331-234, book treatments at www.thermaebathspa.com. There's a salad-and-smoothies café for guests. No kids under 16 allowed.

Cross Bath: This renovated, circular Georgian structure across the street from the main spa provides a simpler and less-expensive bathing option. It has a hot-water fountain that taps directly into the spring, making its water temperature higher than the spa's (£13/90 min, daily 10:00–20:00, last entry at 18:30, changing rooms, no access to Royal Bath, no kids under 12).

Spa Visitor Centre: Also across the street in the Hetling Pump Room, this free, one-room exhibit explains the story of the spa (Mon–Sat 10:00–17:00, Sun 10:00–16:00, £2 audioguide).

▲**Abbey**—The town of Bath wasn't much in the Middle Ages, but an important church has stood on this spot since Anglo-Saxon

times. King Edgar I was crowned here in 973, when the church was much bigger (before the bishop packed up and moved to Wells). Dominating the town center, today's abbey—the last great medieval church of England—is 500 years old and a fine example of Late Perpendicular Gothic, with breezy fan vaulting and enough stained glass to earn it the nickname "Lantern of the West." The glass, red-iron gas-powered lamps, and heating grates on the floor are

all remnants of the 19th century. The window behind the altar shows 52 scenes from the life of Christ. A window to the left of the altar shows Edgar's coronation (worth the £2.50 donation; April–Oct Mon–Sat 9:00–18:00, Sun 13:00–14:30 & 16:30–17:30; Nov–March Mon–Sat 9:00–16:30, Sun 13:00–14:30 & 16:30–17:30; handy flier narrates a self-guided 19-stop tour, tel. 0122/422-462, www.bathabbey.org). Posted on the door is the schedule for concerts, services, and **evensong** (at 16:00 or 17:15, check schedule on website). The facade (c. 1500, but mostly restored) is interesting for some of its carvings. Look for the angels going down the ladder. The statue of Peter (to the left of the door) lost his head to mean iconoclasts; it was re-carved out of his once supersize beard. Take a moment to appreciate the abbey's architecture from the Abbey Green square.

A small but worthwhile exhibit, the abbey's **Heritage Vaults** tell the story of Christianity in Bath since Roman times (free, Mon–Sat 10:00–15:30, closed Sun, entrance just outside church, south side).

▲**Pulteney Bridge, Parade Gardens, and Cruises**—Bath is inclined to compare its shop-lined Pulteney Bridge to Florence's Ponte Vecchio. That's pushing it. But to best enjoy a sunny day, pay about £1 to enter the Parade Gardens below the bridge (April–Sept daily 10:00–dusk, shorter hours off-season, includes deck chairs, ask about concerts held some Sun at 15:00 in summer, www.bathnes.gov.uk). Taking a siesta to relax peacefully at the riverside provides a wonderful break (and memory).

Across the bridge at Pulteney Weir, tour boat companies run

cruises (£8, £4 one-way, up to 7/day if the weather's good, 60 min to Bathampton and back, WCs on board, tel. 01225/312-900). Just take whatever boat is running—all stop in Bathampton (allowing you to hop off and walk back). Boats come with picnic-friendly sundecks.

Guildhall Market—The little shopping mall, located across from Pulteney Bridge, is a frumpy time warp in this affluent town—fun for browsing and picnic shopping. Its cheap Market Café is recommended in "Eating in Bath."

Victoria Art Gallery—This two-story gallery, next to Pulteney Bridge, is filled with paintings from the late 17th century to the present (free, includes audioguide, Tue–Sat 10:00–17:00, Sun 13:30–17:00, closed Mon, WC, tel. 01225/477-233, www.victoriagal.org.uk).

▲▲Royal Crescent and the Circus—If Bath is an architectural cancan, these are its knickers. These first Georgian "condos" by John Wood (the Elder and the Younger) are well-explained

by the city walking tours. "Georgian" is British for "Neoclassical," or dating from the 1770s. As you cruise the Crescent, pretend you're rich. Then pretend you're poor. Notice the "ha ha fence," a drop-off in the front yard that acted as a barrier, invisible from the windows, for keeping out sheep and peasants. The refined and stylish **Royal Crescent Hotel** sits unmarked in the center of the crescent. You're welcome to (politely) drop in to explore its fine ground-floor public spaces and back garden. A gracious and traditional tea is served in the garden out back (£12.50 cream tea, £22.50 afternoon tea, daily 15:00–17:00, sharing is OK, reserve a day in advance in summer, tel. 01225/823-333).

Picture the round Circus as a coliseum turned inside out. Its Doric, Ionic, and Corinthian capital decorations pay homage to its Greco-Roman origin, and are a reminder that Bath (with its seven hills) aspired to be "the Rome of England." The frieze above the first row of columns has hundreds of different panels, each representing the arts, sciences, and crafts. The first floor was high off the ground, to accommodate aristocrats on sedan chairs and women with sky-high hairdos. The tiny round windows on the top floors were the servants' quarters. While the building fronts are uniform, the backs are higgledy-piggledy, infamous for their "hanging loos." Stand in the middle of the Crescent among the grand plane trees, on the capped old well. Imagine the days when there was no indoor plumbing, and the servant girls gathered here to fetch water—this was gossip central. If you stand on the well, your clap echoes three times around the circle (try it).

▲Georgian House at No. 1 Royal Crescent—This museum (corner of Brock Street and Royal Crescent) offers your best look into a period house. Your visit is limited to four roped-off rooms, but if you take your time and talk to the docents stationed in each room, it's worth the £5 admission to get behind one of those classy Georgian facades. The docents are determined to fill you in on all the fascinating details of Georgian life...like how high-class women shaved their eyebrows and pasted on carefully trimmed strips of furry mouse skin in their place. On the bedroom dresser sits a bowl of black beauty marks and a head-scratcher from those pre-shampoo days. Fido spent his days in the kitchen treadmill powering the rotisserie (mid-Feb–Oct Tue–Sun 10:30–17:00, Nov Tue–Sun 10:30–16:00, last entry 30 min before closing, closed Mon and Dec–mid-Feb, £2 guidebook available, no photos, "no stiletto heels, please," tel. 01225/428-126, www.bath-preservation-trust .org.uk). Its WC is accessible from the street (under the entry steps, across from the exit and shop).

▲▲Fashion Museum—Housed underneath Bath's Assembly Rooms, this museum displays four centuries of fashion, organized by theme (bags, shoes, underwear, wedding dresses, and so on). Follow the included audioguide tour, and allow about an hour—unless you pause to lace up a corset and try on a hoop underdress (£7, £14.50 combo-ticket covers Roman Baths—saving you £3.50, family ticket available, daily March–Oct 10:30–18:00, Nov–Feb 10:30–17:00, last entry one hour before closing, on-site self-service café, tel. 01225/477-173, www.fashionmuseum.co.uk).

The **Assembly Rooms,** which you can see for free en route to the museum, are big, grand, empty rooms. Card games, concerts, tea, and dances were held here in the 18th century, before the advent of fancy hotels with grand public spaces made them obsolete. Note the extreme symmetry (pleasing to the aristocratic eye) and the high windows (assuring privacy). After the Allies bombed the historic and well-preserved German city of Lübeck, the Germans picked up a Baedeker guide and chose a similarly lovely city to bomb: Bath. The Assembly Rooms—gutted in this wartime tit-for-tat by WWII bombs—have since been restored to their original splendor. (Only the chandeliers are original.)

Below the Fashion Museum (to the left as you leave, 20 yards away) is one of the few surviving sets of **iron house hardware.** "Link boys" carried torches through the dark streets, lighting the way for big shots in their sedan chairs as they traveled from one affair to the next. The link boys extinguished their torches in the black conical "snuffers." The lamp above was once gas-lit. The crank on the left was used to hoist bulky things to various windows (see the hooks). Few of these sets survived the dark days of the WWII Blitz, when most were collected and melted down, purportedly to make weapons to feed the British war machine. (Not long ago, these well-meaning Brits finally found out that all of their patriotic extra commitment to the national struggle had been for naught, since the metal ended up in junk heaps.)

▲▲**Museum of Bath at Work**—This is the official title for Mr. Bowler's Business, a 1900s engineer's shop, brass foundry, and fizzy-drink factory with a Dickensian office. It's just a pile of meaningless old gadgets—until the included audioguide resurrects Mr. Bowler's creative genius. Featuring other Bath creations through the years, including a 1914 car and the versatile plasticine (proto-Play-Doh), the museum serves as a vivid reminder that there was an industrial side to this spa town. Don't miss the fine "Story of Bath Stone" in the basement (£5, April–Oct daily 10:30–17:00, Nov–March weekends only except closed in Dec, last entry at 16:00, Julian Road, 2 steep blocks up Russell Street from Assembly Rooms, tel. 01225/318-348, www.bath-at-work.org.uk).

Jane Austen Centre—This exhibition focuses on Jane Austen's tumultuous, sometimes-troubled five years in Bath (circa 1800, during which time her father died), and the influence the city had on her writing. There's little of historic substance here; you'll walk through a Georgian townhouse that she didn't live in (one of her real addresses in Bath was a few houses up the road, at 25 Gay Street), and you'll see mostly enlarged reproductions of things associated with her writing. The museum describes various places from two novels set in Bath (*Persuasion* and *Northanger Abbey*). After a live intro (15 min, 2/hr) explaining how this romantic but down-to-earth woman dealt with the silly, shallow, and arrogant aristocrats' world, where "the doing of nothings all day prevents one from doing anything," you'll see a 15-minute video and wander through the rest of the exhibit (£7; mid-March–mid-Nov daily 9:45–17:30, July–Aug Thu–Sat until 19:00; mid-Nov–mid-March Sun–Fri 11:00–16:30, Sat 9:45–17:30; between Queen's Square and the Circus at 40 Gay Street, tel. 01225/443-000, www.janeausten .co.uk). Jane Austen–themed walking tours of the city begin at the TI and end at the Centre (£5, 90 min, Sat–Sun at 11:00, July–Aug also Fri–Sat at 16:00, no reservation necessary).

Outer Bath

Building of Bath Collection—This offers an intriguing behind-the-scenes look at how the Georgian city was actually built (£4, mid-April–Oct Sat–Mon 10:30–17:00, last entry 30 min before closing, closed Tue–Fri and Nov–mid-April, north of the city center on a street called "The Paragon," tel. 01225/333-895, www.bath-preservation-trust.org.uk).

▲**American Museum**—I know, you need this in Bath like you need a Big Mac. The UK's only museum dedicated to American history, this may be the only place that combines Geronimo and Groucho Marx. It has thoughtful exhibits on the history of Native Americans and the Civil War, but the museum's heart is with the decorative arts and cultural artifacts that reveal how Americans lived from colonial times to the mid-19th century. Each of the 18 completely furnished rooms (from a plain 1600s Massachusetts dining/living room to a Rococo Revival explosion in a New Orleans bedroom) is hosted by eager guides, waiting to fill you in on the everyday items that make domestic Yankee history surprisingly interesting. (In the Lee Room, look for the original mouse holes, lovingly backlit, in the floor boards.) One room is a quilter's nirvana. You can easily spend an afternoon here, enjoying the surrounding gardens, arboretum, and trails (£8, mid-March–Oct Tue–Sun 12:00–17:00, last entry one hour before closing, closed Mon and Nov–mid-March, at Claverton Manor, tel. 01225/460-503, www.americanmuseum.org). The museum is outside of town and a headache to reach if you don't have a car (10–15-min walk from bus #18 or the hop-on, hop-off bus stop).

Activities in Bath

Walking—The Bath Skyline Walk is a six-mile wander around the hills surrounding Bath (leaflet at TI). Plenty of other scenic paths are described in the TI's literature. For additional options, get *Country Walks around Bath*, by Tim Mowl (£4.50 at TI or bookstores).

Hiking the Canal to Bathampton—An idyllic towpath leads from the Bath Spa train station, along an old canal to the sleepy village of Bathampton. Immediately behind the station, cross the footbridge and find where the canal hits the river. Turn left, noticing the series of Industrial Age locks, and walk along the towpath, giving thanks that you're not a horse pulling a barge. You'll be in Bathampton in less than an hour, where a classic pub awaits with a nice lunch and cellar-temp beer.

Boating—The Bath Boating Station, in an old Victorian boathouse, rents rowboats, canoes, and punts (£7 per person/first hour, then £3/additional hour, Easter–Sept daily 10:00–18:00, closed off-season, Forester Road, one mile northeast of center, tel. 01225/312-900, www.bathboating.co.uk).

Swimming and Kids' Activities—The Bath Sports and Leisure Centre has a fine pool for laps as well as lots of water slides. Kids have entertaining options in the mini-gym "Active Zone" area, which includes a rock wall and a "Zany Zone" indoor playground (£3.70, Mon–Fri 8:00–22:00, closes earlier Sat–Sun, kids' hours limited, call for open-swim times, just across North Parade Bridge, tel. 01225/486-905, www.aquaterra.org).

Shopping—There's great browsing between the abbey and the Assembly Rooms (Fashion Museum). Shops close at about 17:30, and many are open on Sunday (11:00–16:00). Explore the antique shops lining Bartlett Street, just below the Assembly Rooms.

Nightlife in Bath

For an up-to-date list of events, pick up the local newspaper, the *Bath Chronicle*, on Fridays, when the "What's On" schedule appears (www.thisisbath.com). Younger travelers may enjoy the party-ready bar, club, and nightlife recommendations at www.itchybath.co.uk.

▲▲▲**Bizarre Bath Street Theater**—For an immensely entertaining walking-tour comedy act "with absolutely no history or culture," follow Dom, J. J., or Noel Britten on their creative and entertaining Bizarre Bath walk. This 90-minute "tour," which plays off local passersby as well as tour members, is a belly laugh a minute (£8, or £7 for Rick Steves readers, includes some minor discounts in town, April–Oct nightly at 20:00, smaller groups Mon–Thu, heavy on magic, careful to insult all minorities and sensitivities, just racy enough but still good family fun, leaves from The Huntsman pub near the abbey, confirm at TI or call 01225/335-124, www.bizarrebath.co.uk).

▲**Theatre Royal Performance**—The 18th-century, 800-seat Theatre Royal, newly restored and one of England's loveliest, offers a busy schedule of London West End–type plays, including many "pre-London" dress-rehearsal runs (£15–39, shows generally start at 19:30 or 20:00, matinees at 14:30, box office open Mon–Sat 10:00–20:00, Sun 12:00–20:00, tel. 01225/448-844, www.theatreroyal.org.uk). Forty nosebleed spots on a bench (misnamed "stand-bys") go on sale at noon Monday through Saturday for that day's evening performance (£5, pay cash at box office or—for £3 more—call and book with credit card, 2 tickets maximum). Same-day "standing places" go on sale at 18:00 (12:00 for matinees) for £3 (pay cash at box office, 2 tickets maximum). Or you can snatch up any "last minute" seats for £10–15 a half-hour before "curtain up."

A handy cheap sightseers' tip: During the free Bath walking tour, your guide stops here. Pop into the box office, ask what's playing tonight, and see if there are many seats left. If the play sounds good and plenty of seats remain unsold, you're fairly safe to come back 30 minutes before curtain time to buy a ticket at that cheaper price. Oh...and if you smell jasmine, it's the ghost of Lady Grey, a mistress of Beau Nash.

Evening Walks—Take your choice: comedy (Bizarre Bath, described above), history, or ghost tour. The free city history walks (a daily standard described on page 303) are offered on some summer evenings (2 hours, May–Sept Tue and Fri at 19:00, leave from Pump Room). **Ghost Walks** are a popular way to pass the after-dark hours (£7, cash only, 90 min, year-round Thu–Sat at 20:00, leave from The Garrick's Head pub to the left and behind Theatre Royal as you face it, tel. 01225/350-512, www.ghostwalksofbath.co.uk). The cities of York and Edinburgh—which have houses thought to be actually haunted—are better for these walks.

Pubs—Most pubs in the center are very noisy, catering to a rowdy twentysomething crowd. But on the top end of town, you can still find some classic old places with inviting ambience and live music. These are listed in order from closest to farthest away:

The Old Green Tree, the most convenient of all these pubs, is a rare traditional pub right in the town center (locally brewed real ales, no children, 12 Green Street, tel. 01225/448-259; also recommended under "Eating in Bath" for lunch).

The Star Inn is much appreciated by local beer-lovers for its fine ale and "no machines or music to distract from the chat." It's a "spit 'n' sawdust" place, and its long bench, nicknamed "death row," still comes with a complimentary pinch of snuff from tins on the ledge. Try the Bellringer Ale, made just up the road (Mon–Fri 12:00–14:30 & 17:30–23:00, Sat–Sun 12:00–23:00, no food served, 23 The Vineyards, top of The Paragon/A4 Roman Road, tel. 01225/425-072, generous and friendly welcome from Paul, who runs the place).

The Bell has a jazzy, pierced-and-tattooed, bohemian feel, but with a mellow older crowd. They serve pizza on the large concrete terrace out back in summer, and there's some kind of activity nearly every night, usually involving live music (Mon–Sat 11:00–23:00, Sun 12:00–10:30, sandwiches served all day, 103 Walcot Street, tel. 01225/460-426).

Summer Nights at the Baths—In July and August, you can stretch your sightseeing day at the Roman Baths, open nightly until 22:00 (last entry 21:00), when the gas lamps flame and the baths are far less crowded and more atmospheric. To take a dip yourself, consider popping in to the Thermae Bath Spa (last entry at 19:30).

Sleeping in Bath

Bath is a busy tourist town. Accommodations are expensive, and low-cost alternatives are rare. By far the best budget option is the YMCA—it's central, safe, simple, very well-run, and has plenty of twin rooms available. To get a good B&B, make a telephone reservation in advance. Competition is stiff, and it's worth asking any of these places for a weekday, three-nights-in-a-row, or off-season deal. Friday and Saturday nights are tightest (with many rates going up by about 25 percent)—especially if you're staying only one night, since B&Bs favor those lingering longer. If staying only Saturday night, you're very bad news to a B&B hostess. If you're driving to Bath, stowing your car near the center will cost you (though some less-central B&Bs have parking)—see "Parking" on page 302, or ask your hotelier. Almost every place provides Wi-Fi at no charge to its guests.

BATH

B&Bs near the Royal Crescent

These listings are all a 15-minute uphill walk or an easy £4–5 taxi ride from the train station. Or take any hop-on, hop-off bus tour from the station, get off at the stop nearest your B&B (likely Royal Avenue—confirm with driver), check in, then finish the tour later in the day. The Marlborough Lane places have easier parking, but are less centrally located.

$$$ The Town House, overlooking the Assembly Rooms, is genteel, deluxe, and homey, with three fresh, mod rooms that have a hardwood stylishness. In true B&B style, you'll enjoy a gourmet breakfast at a big family table with the other guests (Db-£95–100 or £115–130 Fri–Sat, 2-night minimum, Wi-Fi, 7 Bennett Street, tel. & fax 01225/422-505, www.thetownhouse bath.co.uk, stay@thetownhousebath.co.uk, Alan and Brenda Willey).

$$ Brocks Guest House has six rooms in a Georgian townhouse built by John Wood in 1765. Located between the prestigious Royal Crescent and the courtly Circus, it was redone in a way that would make the great architect proud (Db-£79–87, Tb-£99, Qb-£115, prices go up about 10 percent Fri–Sat, Wi-Fi, little top-floor library, 32 Brock Street, tel. 01225/338-374, fax 01225/334-245, www.brocksguesthouse.co.uk, brocks@brocksguesthouse .co.uk, run by Sammy and her husband Richard).

$$ Parkside Guest House has five thoughtfully appointed Edwardian rooms—tidy, clean, and homey, with nary a doily in sight—and a spacious back garden (Db-£77, this price is for Rick Steves readers, 11 Marlborough Lane, tel. & fax 01225/429-444, www.parksidebandb.co.uk, post@parksidebandb.co.uk, Erica and Inge Lynall).

Sleep Code

(£1 = about $1.60, country code: 44, area code: 01225)
S = Single, **D** = Double/Twin, **T** = Triple, **Q** = Quad, **b** = bathroom,
s = shower only. Unless otherwise noted, credit cards are
accepted.

To help you sort easily through these listings, I've divided
the rooms into three categories based on the price for a
standard double room with bath:

$$$ **Higher Priced**—Most rooms £100 or more.
  $$ **Moderately Priced**—Most rooms between £60-100.
    $ **Lower Priced**—Most rooms £60 or less.

$$ Elgin Villa rents five comfy, nicely maintained rooms
(Ss-£40, Sb-£55, Ds-£68, Db-£85, Tb-£99, Qb-£120, more expensive for Sat-only stay, discount for 3 nights, includes substantial un-fried breakfast, Wi-Fi, parking, 6 Marlborough Lane, tel. 01225/424-557, www.elginvilla.co.uk, stay@elginvilla.co.uk, Anna).

$$ Cornerways B&B, located on a noisy street, is simple and well-worn, with four rooms and old-fashioned homey touches (Sb-£45–55, Db-£65–75, 15 percent discount with this book and 3-night stay in 2010, Wi-Fi, DVD library, free parking, 47 Crescent Gardens, tel. 01225/422-382, www.cornerwaysbath.co.uk, info @cornerwaysbath.co.uk, Sue Black).

B&Bs East of the River

These listings are a 10-minute walk from the city center. While generally a better value, they are not as conveniently located.

$$$ Villa Magdala rents 18 stately, hotelesque rooms in a freestanding Victorian townhouse opposite a park. In a city that's so insistently Georgian, it's fun to stay in a mansion that's decorated so enthusiastically Victorian (Db-£95–130, less off-season, fancier rooms and family options described on website, inviting lounge, Wi-Fi, free parking, in quiet residential area on Henrietta Street, tel. 01225/466-329, fax 01225/483-207, www.villamagdala .co.uk, enquiries@villamagdala.co.uk; Roy and Lois).

$$$ The Ayrlington, next door to a lawn-bowling green, has 14 attractive rooms with Asian decor, and hints of a more genteel time. Though this well-maintained hotel fronts a busy street, it's quiet and tranquil. Rooms in the back have pleasant views of sports greens and Bath beyond. For the best value, request a standard double with a view of Bath (twin Db-£80–105, standard Db-£100–130, fancy Db-£120–170, big deluxe Db-£130–195, prices spike 30 percent on weekends, see website for specifics, Wi-Fi,

Bath Accommodations

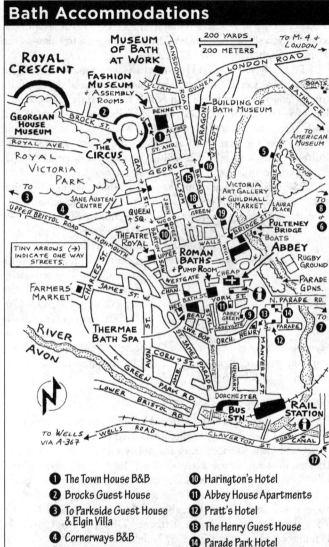

1. The Town House B&B
2. Brocks Guest House
3. To Parkside Guest House & Elgin Villa
4. Cornerways B&B
5. Villa Magdala
6. To The Ayrlington
7. To Holly Villa Guest House
8. To 14 Raby Place
9. Three Abbey Green Guest House
10. Harington's Hotel
11. Abbey House Apartments
12. Pratt's Hotel
13. The Henry Guest House
14. Parade Park Hotel
15. Travelodge Bath Central
16. YMCA
17. White Hart Hostel
18. St. Christopher's Inn
19. Library (Internet Access)

fine garden, easy parking, 24–25 Pulteney Road, tel. 01225/425-495, fax 01225/469-029, www.ayrlington.com, mail@ayrlington.com). If you stay here three weeknights, you get a free pass to the Thermae Bath Spa (worth £22/person).

$$ Holly Villa Guest House, with a cheery garden, six bright rooms, and a cozy TV lounge, is enthusiastically and thoughtfully run by chatty, friendly Jill and Keith McGarrigle (Ds-£60–65, Db-£65–75, Tb-£80–95, cash only, Wi-Fi, free parking; 8-min walk from station and city center—walk over North Parade Bridge, take the first right, and then take the second left to 14 Pulteney Gardens; tel. 01225/310-331, www.hollyvilla.com, jill@hollyvilla.com).

$$ 14 Raby Place is another good value, mixing Georgian glamour with homey warmth and modern, artistic taste within its

five rooms. Muriel Guy—a no-high-tech Luddite—keeps things simple and endearingly friendly. She's a fun-loving live wire who serves organic food for breakfast (S-£35, Db-£70, Tb-£80, cash only; 14 Raby Place—go over bridge on North Parade Road, left on Pulteney Road, cross to church, Raby Place is first row of houses on hill; tel. 01225/465-120).

In the Town Center

$$$ Three Abbey Green Guest House, with seven rooms, is newly renovated, bright, fresh, and located in a quiet, traffic-free courtyard only 50 yards from the abbey and the Roman Baths. Its spacious rooms are a fine value (Db-£85–135, four-poster Db-£145–175, family rooms-£135–195, 2-night minimum on weekends, Internet access and Wi-Fi, tel. 01225/428-558, www.three abbeygreen.com, stay@threeabbeygreen.com, Sue and Derek). They also rent self-catering apartments (Db-£135–155, Qb-£160–195, higher prices are for Fri–Sat, 2-night minimum).

$$$ Harington's Hotel rents 13 fresh, modern, and newly refurbished rooms on a quiet street in the town center. This stylish place feels like a boutique hotel, but with a friendlier, laid-back vibe (Sb-£79–130, standard Db-£88–130, superior Db-£98–140, large superior Db-£108–150, Tb-£138–180, prices vary substantially depending on demand, Wi-Fi, attached restaurant-bar open all day, 10 Queen Street, tel. 01225/461-728, fax 01225/444-804, www.haringtonshotel.co.uk, post@haringtonshotel.co.uk). Melissa and Peter offer a 5 percent discount with this book for three-night stays except on Fridays, Saturdays, and holidays. They also rent several self-catering apartments down the street that can sleep up to three (Db-£130, Tb-£150, much pricier on weekends, includes continental breakfast in the hotel, 2-night minimum) and one apartment with hot tub that sleeps up to eight.

$$$ Abbey House Apartments consist of three flats on Abbey Green and several others scattered around town—all tastefully restored by Laura (who, once upon a time, was a San Francisco Goth rocker). The apartments called Abbey View and Abbey Green (which comes with a washer

and dryer) both have views of the abbey from their nicely equipped kitchens. These are especially practical and economical if you plan on cooking. Laura provides everything you need for simple breakfasts, and it's fun and cheap to stock the fridge or get take-away ethnic cuisine. When Laura meets you to give you the keys, you become a local (Sb-£90, Db-£100–175, 2-night minimum, rooms can sleep four with Murphy and sofa beds, apartments clearly described on website, Wi-Fi, Abbey Green, tel. 01225/464-238, www.laurastownhouseapartments.co.uk, laura@laurastown houseapartments.co.uk).

$$$ Pratt's Hotel is as proper and olde English as you'll find in Bath. Its creaks and frays are aristocratic. Even its public places make you want to sip a brandy, and its 46 rooms are bright and spacious. Since it's in the city center, occasionally it can get noisy—request a quiet room, away from the street (Sb-£90, Db-£90–140, check website for specials, drop-ins after 16:00 may get a better rate if room available, dogs-£7.50 but children under 15 free with 2 adults, attached restaurant-bar, elevator, 4 blocks from station on South Parade, tel. 01225/460-441, fax 01225/448-807, www.forestdale.com, pratts@forestdale.com).

$$ The Henry Guest House is a simple, vertical place, renting eight clean rooms. It's friendly, well-run, and just two blocks in front of the train station (S-£40–45, Sb-£55–65, Db-£85–105, extra bed-£15, family room-£135, 2-night minimum on weekends, Wi-Fi, 6 Henry Street, tel. 01225/424-052, www.thehenry.com, stay@thehenry.com). Steve and Liz also rent two self-catering apartments nearby that sleep up to eight with cots and a sleeper couch—email for group prices.

$$ Parade Park Hotel rents 35 modern, basic rooms in a very central location (S-£49, Sb-£69, D-£69, small Db-£85, large Db-£95–105, Tb-£115, Qb-£110–160, no Wi-Fi, lots of stairs, lively bar downstairs and noisy seagulls, 8-10 North Parade, tel. 01225/463-384, www.paradepark.co.uk, info@paradepark.co.uk).

$$ Travelodge Bath Central, which offers 66 American-style, characterless-yet-comfortable rooms, worries B&Bs with its reasonable prices. As it's located above a nightclub, request a room on the third floor—especially on weekends (Db/Tb/Qb-£70 on weeknights, £85–95 Fri–Sat, prices vary widely—as low as £39 on weeknights if you book online in advance, up to 2 kids sleep free, breakfast extra, Wi-Fi, 1 York Building at George Street, toll tel. 08719-846-219, www.travelodge.co.uk). This is especially economical for families of four (who enjoy the Db price). Another Travelodge is located about a mile from the train station (similar prices, free parking, Rossiter Road, toll tel. 08719-846-407).

Bargain Accommodations

Bath's Best Budget Beds: **$** The **YMCA,** centrally located on a leafy square, has 200 beds in industrial-strength rooms—all with sinks and prison-style furnishings. The place is a godsend for budget travelers—safe, secure, quiet, and efficiently run. With lots of twin rooms and no double beds, this is the only easily accessible budget option in downtown Bath (S-£28, twin D-£44, T-£60, Q-£72, dorm beds-£16, £1/person more Fri–Sat, WCs and showers down the hall, includes continental breakfast, cooked breakfast-£2.20, cheap lunches, linens, lockers, Internet access and Wi-Fi, laundry facilities, down a tiny alley off Broad Street on Broad Street Place, tel. 01225/325-900, fax 01225/462-065, www.bathymca.co.uk, stay@bathymca.co.uk).

Sloppy Backpacker Dorms: **$–$$ White Hart Hostel** is a simple nine-room place offering adults and families good, cheap beds in two- to six-bed dorms (£15/bed, S-£25, D-£40, Db-£50–70, family rooms, kitchen, fine garden out back, 5-min walk behind train station at Widcombe—where Widcombe Hill hits Claverton Street, tel. 01225/313-985, www.whitehartbath.co.uk). The White Hart also has a pub with a reputation for decent food. **$ St. Christopher's Inn,** in a prime, central location, is part of a chain of low-priced, high-energy hubs for backpackers looking for beds and brews. Their beds are so cheap because they know you'll spend money on their beer (46 beds in 4- to 12-bed rooms-£15–21.50, D-£52–58, higher prices on weekends or if you don't book online, check website for specials, Internet access, laundry, lounge with video, lively "Belushi's" pub and bar downstairs, 9 Green Street, tel. 01225/481-444, www.st-christophers.co.uk).

Eating in Bath

Bath is bursting with eateries. There's something for every appetite and budget—just stroll around the center of town. A picnic dinner of deli food or take-out fish-and-chips in the Royal Crescent Park or down by the river is ideal for aristocratic hoboes. The restaurants I recommend are small and popular—reserve a table on Friday and Saturday evenings. Most pricey little bistros offer big savings with their two- and three-course lunches and "pre-theater" specials. In general, you can get two courses for £10 at lunch or £12 in the early evening (compared to £15 for a main course after 18:30 or 19:00). Restaurants advertise their early-bird specials, and as long as you order within the time window, you're in for a cheap meal.

Romantic French and English

Tilleys Bistro, popular with locals, serves healthy French, English, and vegetarian meals with candlelit ambience. Owners Dawn and Dave make you feel as if you are guests at a special dinner party in their elegant living room. Their fun menu lets you build your own meal, and there's an interesting array of £7 starters. If you cap things off with the cheese plate and a glass of the house port, you'll realize that's a passion of Dave's (Mon–Sat 12:00–14:30 & 18:30–22:30, Sun 18:30–22:30 only, reservations smart, 3 North Parade Passage, tel. 01225/484-200).

The Garrick's Head is an elegantly simple gastropub right around the corner from the Theatre Royal, with a pricey restaurant on one side and a bar serving affordable snacks on the other. You're welcome to eat from the bar menu, even if you're in the fancy dining room or outside enjoying some great people-watching (Mon–Sat 11:00–21:00, Sun 12:00–21:00, 8 St. John's Place, tel. 01225/318-368).

The Circus Café and Restaurant is a relaxing little eatery serving rustic European cuisine. They have a romantic interior, with a minimalist modern atmosphere, and four tables on the peaceful street (£7 lunches, £12 dinner plates, open Mon–Sat 12:00–24:00, closed Sun, reservations smart, 34 Brock Street, tel. 01225/466-020).

Casanis French Bistro-Restaurant is a local hit. Chef Laurent, who hails from Nice, cooks "authentic Provençal cuisine" from the south of France, while his wife Jill serves. The decor matches the cuisine—informal, relaxed, simple, and top-quality. The intimate Georgian dining room upstairs is a bit nicer and more spacious than the ground floor (£11.50 two-course lunch specials,

Bath Restaurants

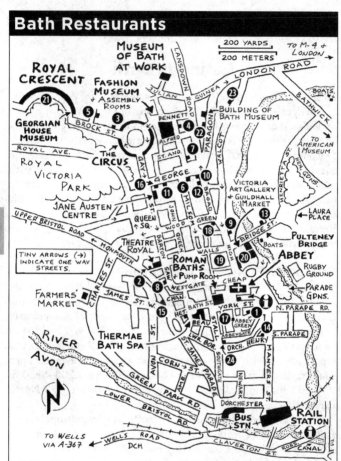

1. Tilleys Bistro & Demuths Vegetarian Rest.
2. The Garrick's Head
3. The Circus Café & Rest.
4. Casanis French Bistro-Rest.
5. Bistro Papillon
6. Loch Fyne Restaurant
7. Yen Sushi
8. Thai Balcony Restaurant
9. Ocean Pearl Oriental Buffet & Waitrose Supermarket
10. Wagamama
11. Martini Restaurant
12. Ask Restaurant
13. Rajpoot Tandoori
14. Yak Yeti Yak
15. Boston Tea Party & Seafoods Fish & Chips
16. Chandos Deli
17. Crystal Palace Pub
18. The Old Green Tree
19. The Cornish Bakehouse
20. Guildhall Market
21. Royal Crescent Hotel (Afternoon Tea)
22. The Star Inn
23. The Bell
24. Marks & Spencer & Café Revive

£20 three-course early dinner from 18:00–19:00, closed Sun–Mon, immediately behind the Assembly Rooms at 4 Saville Row, tel. 01225/780-055).

Bistro Papillon is small, fun, and unpretentious, dishing up "modern-rustic cuisine from the south of France." The cozy, checkered-tablecloth interior has an open kitchen, and the outdoor seating is on a fine pedestrian lane (£8 lunch plates, £13–15 main courses for dinner, Tue–Sat 12:00–14:30 & 18:30–22:00, closed Sun–Mon, reservations smart, 2 Margaret's Buildings, tel. 01225/310-064).

Vegetarian and Seafood

Demuths Vegetarian Restaurant is highly rated and ideal for the well-heeled vegetarian. Its stark, understated interior comes with a vegan vibe (£15 main dishes, daily 10:00–15:30 & 18:00–21:00, 2 North Parade Passage, tel. 01225/446-059).

Loch Fyne Restaurant, a high-energy, Scottish chain restaurant, serves fresh fish at reasonable prices. It fills what was once a lavish bank building with a bright, airy, and youthful atmosphere. The open kitchen adds to the energy (£10–18 meals, £12 two-course special plus wine from lunch until 19:00 on weekdays, daily 12:00–21:30, 24 Milsom Street, tel. 01225/750-120).

Ethnic

Yen Sushi is your basic little sushi bar—stark and sterile, with stools facing a conveyor belt that constantly tempts you with a variety of freshly made delights on color-coded plates. When you're done, they tally your plates and give you the bill (£1.50–3.50 plates, you can fill up for £12 or so, daily 12:00–15:00 & 17:30–22:30, 11 Bartlett Street, tel. 01225/333-313).

Thai Balcony Restaurant's open, spacious interior is so plush, it'll have you wondering, "Where's the Thai wedding?" While locals debate which of Bath's handful of Thai restaurants serves the best food or offers the lowest prices, there's no doubt that Thai Balcony's fun and elegant atmosphere makes for a memorable and enjoyable dinner (£8 two-course lunch special, £8–9 plates, daily 12:00–14:00 & 18:00–22:00, reservations smart on weekends, Saw Close, tel. 01225/444-450).

Ocean Pearl Oriental Buffet is famous for being the restaurant Asian tourists eat at repeatedly. It offers a practical, 40-dish, all-you-can-eat buffet in the modern Podium Shopping Centre and spacious seating in a high, bright dining hall overlooking the river. You'll pay £6.50 for lunch, £13 for dinner, or you can fill up a take-away box for just £4 (daily 12:00–15:00 & 18:00–22:30, in the Podium Shopping Centre on Northgate Street, tel. 01225/331-238).

Wagamama, a stylish, youthful, and modern chain of noodle shops, continues its quest for world domination. There's one in almost every midsize city in the UK, and after you've sampled their udon noodles, fried rice, or curry dishes, you'll know why. Diners enjoy huge portions in a sprawling, loud, and modern hall. Bowls are huge enough for light eaters on a tight budget to share (£7–9 meals, Mon–Sat 12:00–23:00, Sun 12:00–22:00, good vegetarian options, 1 York Buildings, George Street, tel. 01225/337-314, www .wagamama.com).

Martini Restaurant, a hopping, purely Italian place, has class and jovial waiters. It offers a very good eating value (£12–16 entrées, £7–9 pizzas, daily 12:00–14:30 & 18:00–22:30, plenty of veggie options, daily fish specials, extensive wine list, reservations smart on weekends, 9 George Street, tel. 01225/460-818; Mauro, Nunzio, Franco, and chef Luigi).

Ask Restaurant is part of a chain of Italian eateries, serving standard-quality pizza and pasta in a big, 200-seat place with a loud and happy local crowd (£7 pizza and pasta, good salads, daily 12:00–23:00, George Street but entrance on Broad Street, tel. 01225/789-997).

Rajpoot Tandoori serves—by all assessments—the best Indian food in Bath. You'll hike down deep into a cellar, where the plush Indian atmosphere and award-winning cooking make paying the extra pounds palatable. The seating is tight and the ceilings low, but it's air-conditioned (£8 three-course lunch special, £10 plates, £20 dinners, daily 12:00–14:30 & 18:00–23:00, 4 Argyle Street, tel. 01225/466-833, Ali).

Yak Yeti Yak is a fun Nepalese restaurant, with both Western and sit-on-the-floor seating. Sera and his wife Sarah, along with their cheerful, hardworking Nepali team, cook up great traditional food (and plenty of vegetarian plates) at prices a sherpa could handle (£6–7 lunches, £4 veggie plates, £7 meat plates, daily 12:00–14:30 & 17:00–22:30, 5 Pierrepont Street, tel. 01225/442-299).

Simple Options

Light Meals: **Boston Tea Party** feels like a Starbucks—if there were only one. It's fresh and healthy, serving extensive breakfasts, light lunches, and salads. The outdoor seating overlooks a busy square (daily 7:30–19:00, 19 Kingsmead Square, tel. 01225/313-901). **Chandos Deli** has good coffee and tasty £6–7 sandwiches made on artisan breads. This upscale but casual eight-table place serves breakfast and lunch to dedicated foodies who don't want to pay too much (Mon–Sat 9:00–17:00, Sun 11:00–17:00, 12 George Street, tel. 01225/314-418).

Pubs: **Crystal Palace Pub** is an inviting place just a block away from the abbey, facing the delightful little Abbey Green. With a focus on food rather than drink, they serve "pub grub with a Continental flair" in three different spaces, including a picnic-table back patio (£8–10 meals, daily 12:00–20:30, last order by 20:00, no kids after 16:30, Abbey Green, tel. 01225/482-666). **The Old Green Tree,** in the old town center, serves satisfying lunches to locals in a characteristic pub setting. As Bath is not a good pub-grub town, this is likely the best you'll do in the center (real ales on tap, lunch Mon–Sat 12:00–15:00 only, no children, can be crowded on weekend nights, 12 Green Street, tel. 01225/448-259).

Fast Food: **Seafoods Fish & Chips** is respected by lovers of greasy fried fish in Bath. There's diner-style and outdoor seating, or you can get your food to go (£4–5 meals, Mon–Sat 11:30–23:00, takeout until 22:00, Sun 12:00–20:00, 38 Kingsmead Square, tel. 01225/465-190). **The Cornish Bakehouse,** near the Guildhall Market, has freshly baked £2 take-away pasties (open until 17:30, off High Street at 11A The Corridor, tel. 01225/426-635). Munch your picnic enjoying buskers from a bench on the Abbey Square.

Produce Market and Café: **Guildhall Market,** across from Pulteney Bridge, has produce stalls with food for picnickers. At its inexpensive **Market Café,** you can slurp a curry or sip a tea while surrounded by stacks of used books, bananas on the push list, and honest-to-goodness old-time locals (£4 meals including fried breakfasts all day, Mon–Sat 8:00–17:00, closed Sun, tel. 01225/461-593 a block north of the abbey, on High Street).

Supermarkets: **Waitrose,** at the Podium Shopping Centre, is great for picnics, with a good salad bar (Mon–Fri 8:30–20:00, Sat 8:30–19:00, Sun 11:00–17:00, just west of Pulteney Bridge and across from post office on High Street). **Marks & Spencer,** near the train station, has a grocery at the back of its department store, and the pleasant, inexpensive **Café Revive** on the top floor (Mon–Wed and Sat 8:30–18:00, Thu–Fri 8:30–19:00, Sun 11:00–17:00, 16–18 Stall Street).

Bath Connections

Bath's train station is called Bath Spa (toll tel. 0845-748-4950). The National Express bus station is just west of the train station (bus info toll tel. 0871-781-8181, www.nationalexpress.com). For all public bus services in southwestern England, see www.travelinesw.com.

From London to Bath: To get from London to Bath and see Stonehenge to boot, consider an all-day organized **bus tour** from London (and skip out of the return trip; see page 164).

From Bath to London: You can catch a **train** to London's Paddington Station (2/hr, 1.5 hrs, £48 one-way after 9:30, cheaper in advance, www.firstgreatwestern.co.uk), or save money—but not time—by taking the National Express **bus** to Victoria Station (direct buses nearly hourly, a little over 3 hours, one-way-£18, round-trip-£27.50).

From Heathrow to Bath: See page 159. Also consider taking a minibus with Alan Price (see "Celtic Horizons" on page 305).

From Bath to London's Airports: You can reach **Heathrow** directly and easily by National Express bus (10/day, 2–3 hrs, £19 one-way, toll tel. 0871-781-8181, 10p/min, www.nationalexpress .com) or by a train-and-bus combination (take twice-hourly train to Reading, catch twice-hourly airport shuttle bus from there, allow 2.5 hours total, £50–65 depending on time of day, about £10 cheaper when bought in advance, BritRail passholders just pay £15 for bus). Or take the Celtic Horizons minibus to Heathrow.

You can get to **Gatwick** by train (about hourly, 2.5 hrs, £45–60 one-way depending on time of day, £23 in advance, transfer in Reading) or by bus (10/day, 4–5 hrs, £25 one-way, transfer at Heathrow Airport).

Between Bristol Airport and Bath: Located about 20 miles west of Bath, this airport is closer than Heathrow, but they haven't worked out good connections to Bath yet. From Bristol Airport, your most convenient options are to take a taxi (£35) or call Alan Price (see "Celtic Horizons" on page 305). Otherwise, at the airport you can hop aboard the Bristol International Flyer (city bus #330 or #331), which takes you to the Temple Meads train station in Bristol (£9, 2–4/hr, 30 min, buy bus ticket at airport info counter or from driver, tell driver you want the Temple Meads train station). At the Temple Meads Station, check the departure boards for trains going to the Bath Spa train station (4/hr, 15 min, £6). To get from Bath to Bristol Airport, just reverse these directions: Take the train to Temple Meads, then catch the International Flyer bus.

From Bath by Train to: Salisbury (1–2/hr, 1 hr), **Portsmouth** (hourly, 2.25 hrs), **Exeter** (1–2/hr, 1.5–2 hrs, transfer in Bristol or Westbury), **Penzance** (1–2/hr, 4.5–5 hrs, one direct, most 1–2 transfers), **Moreton-in-Marsh** (hourly, 2.5–3 hrs, 2–3 transfers), **York** (2/hr, 4–4.5 hrs, 1–2 transfers in Birmingham, Bristol, and/ or London), **Oxford** (hourly, 1–1.5 hrs, transfer in Didcot), **Cardiff** (hourly, 1–1.5 hrs), **Birmingham** (2/hr, 2 hrs, transfer in Bristol), and **points north** (from Birmingham, a major transportation hub, trains depart for Blackpool, Scotland, and North Wales; use a train/bus combination to reach Ironbridge Gorge and the Lake District).

From Bath by Bus to: Salisbury (hourly, 2.75 hrs, transfer in Warminster; or 1/day direct at 10:35, 1.5 hrs on National Express #300), **Portsmouth** (1/day direct, 3 hrs), **Exeter** (4/day, 3.5–4 hrs, transfer in Bristol), **Penzance** (2/day, 7–8 hrs, transfer in Bristol), **Cheltenham** or **Gloucester** (4/day, 2.5 hrs, transfer in Bristol), **Stratford-upon-Avon** (1/day, 4 hrs, transfer in Bristol), and **Oxford** (1/day direct, 2 hrs, more with transfer). Buses to **Wells** depart nearly hourly, but the last direct bus back leaves before the evensong service is finished (1.25 hrs, last return 17:43, or take 18:15 bus to Bristol, then train to Bath—see page 343). For bus connections to **Avebury** and **Glastonbury,** see the next chapter.

NEAR BATH

Glastonbury, Wells, Avebury, Stonehenge, and Salisbury

Ooooh, mystery, history. Glastonbury is the ancient home of Avalon, King Arthur, and the Holy Grail. Nearby, medieval Wells gathers around its grand cathedral, where you can enjoy an evensong service. Then get Neolithic at every Druid's favorite stone circles, Avebury and Stonehenge. Salisbury is known for its colorful markets and soaring cathedral.

Planning Your Time

Avebury, Glastonbury, and Wells make a wonderful day out from Bath. Splicing in Stonehenge is possible but stretching it. Everybody needs to see Stonehenge, but I'll tell you now, it looks just like it looks. You'll know what I mean when you pay to get in and rub up against the rope fence that keeps tourists at a distance. Avebury is the connoisseur's circle: more subtle and welcoming.

Wells is simply a cute town, much smaller and more medieval than Bath, with a uniquely beautiful cathedral that's best experienced at the 17:15 evensong service (Sun at 15:00). Glastonbury is normally done surgically, in two hours: See the abbey, climb the tor, ponder your hippie past (and where you are now), then scram. Just an hour from Bath, Salisbury makes a pleasant stop, particularly on a market day (Tue, Sat, and every other Wed), though its cathedral looks striking anytime.

Getting Around the Region

By Car: Drivers can do a 133-mile loop, from Bath to Avebury (25 miles) to Stonehenge (30 miles) to Glastonbury (50 miles) to Wells (6 miles) and back to Bath (22 miles).

Sights near Bath

By Bus and Train: Wells and Glastonbury are both easily accessible by bus from Bath. Bus #173 goes direct from Bath to **Wells** (hourly, 1.25 hrs), where you can catch bus #375, #376, or #377 to continue on to **Glastonbury** (4/hr, 20 min). Wells and Glastonbury are also connected to each other by a 9.5-mile foot and bike path.

Many different buses run between Bath and **Avebury,** all requiring one or two transfers (hourly, 1.5 hrs). There is no bus between Avebury and Stonehenge.

A one-hour train trip connects Bath to **Salisbury** (2/hr). With the best public transportation of all these towns, Salisbury is a good jumping-off point for Stonehenge or Avebury by bus or car. The Stonehenge Tour runs buses between Salisbury, Old Sarum, and Stonehenge (see page 353). Buses also run regularly from Salisbury to Avebury (1–2/hr, 1.5–2.5 hrs; Wilts & Dorset bus #2 leaves from St. Paul's Church on Fisherton Street, near the train station, then transfer in Devizes to Stagecoach's bus #49 to Avebury; other combinations possible, some with 2 transfers).

Various bus companies run these routes, including Stagecoach, Bodmans Coaches, the First Bus Company, and Wilts & Dorset.

To find fare information, check with Traveline South West, which combines all the information from these companies into an easy-to-use website that covers all the southwest routes (toll tel. 0871-200-2233, www.travelinesw.com). Buses run much less frequently on Sundays.

By Tour: From Bath, if you don't have a car, the most convenient and quickest way to see Avebury and Stonehenge is to take an all-day bus tour, or a half-day tour just to Stonehenge. Of those tours leaving from Bath, Mad Max is the liveliest (see "Tours in Bath" on page 303).

Glastonbury

Marked by its hill, or "tor," and located on England's most powerful line of prehistoric sites (called a "ley line"), the town of Glastonbury gurgles with history and mystery.

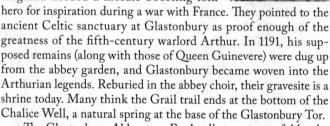

In A.D. 37, Joseph of Arimathea—Jesus' wealthy uncle—brought vessels containing the blood of Jesus to Glastonbury, and, with them, Christianity came to England. (Joseph's visit is plausible—long before Christ, locals traded lead to merchants from the Levant.) While this story is "proven" by fourth-century writings and accepted by the Church, the King-Arthur-and-the-Holy-Grail legends it inspired are not.

Those medieval tales came when England needed a morale-boosting folk hero for inspiration during a war with France. They pointed to the ancient Celtic sanctuary at Glastonbury as proof enough of the greatness of the fifth-century warlord Arthur. In 1191, his supposed remains (along with those of Queen Guinevere) were dug up from the abbey garden, and Glastonbury became woven into the Arthurian legends. Reburied in the abbey choir, their gravesite is a shrine today. Many think the Grail trail ends at the bottom of the Chalice Well, a natural spring at the base of the Glastonbury Tor.

The Glastonbury Abbey was England's most powerful by the 10th century, and was part of a nationwide network of monasteries that by 1500 owned one-sixth of all English land and had four times the income of the Crown. Then Henry VIII dissolved the abbeys in 1536. He was particularly harsh on Glastonbury—he not only destroyed the abbey but also hung and quartered the abbot, sending the parts of his body on four different national tours...at the same time.

But Glastonbury rebounded. In an 18th-century tourism campaign, thousands signed affidavits stating that they'd been healed by water from the Chalice Well, and once again Glastonbury was on the tourist map. Today, Glastonbury and its tor are a center for searchers, too creepy for the mainstream church but just right for those looking for a place to recharge their crystals.

Orientation to Glastonbury

(area code: 01458)

Tourist Information

The TI is on High Street—as are many of the dreadlocked folks who walk it (Mon–Thu 10:00–16:00, Fri–Sat 10:00–16:30, closed Sun, tel. 01458/832-954, www.glastonburytic.co.uk). The TI has several booklets about cycling and walking in the area. The 50p *Glastonbury Town Trail* brochure outlines a good tor-to-town walk (a brisk 10 min). The TI's *Glastonbury Millennium Trail* pamphlet (60p) sends visitors on a historical scavenger hunt, following 20 numbered marble plaques embedded in the pavement throughout the town.

The TI, which occupies a fine 15th-century townhouse, is also home to the **Lake Village Museum**—two humble rooms featuring tools made of stones, bones, and antlers. Preserved in and excavated from the local peat bogs, these tools offer an interesting look at the lives of marshland people in pre-Roman times (£2.50, same hours as TI).

Getting to the Tor

The **Tor Bus** shuttles visitors from the town center and abbey to the base of the tor. If you ask, the bus will stop at the Somerset Rural Life Museum and the Chalice Well (£2.50 round-trip, 2/hr, on the half-hour, daily Easter–Sept 9:30–19:30, Oct–Easter 10:00–15:30, bus does not run during lunchtime, catch bus at St. Dunstan's parking lot in the town center, pick up schedule at TI). A **taxi** to the tor costs £4 one-way—an easier and more economical choice for couples or groups.

Helpful Hints

Market Day: Tuesday is market day for crafts, knickknacks, and produce on the main street. There's also a country market Tuesday mornings in the Town Hall.

Glastonbury Festival: Every summer (June 23–27 in 2010), the gigantic Glastonbury Festival—billing itself as the "largest music and performing arts festival in the world"—brings all manner of postmodern flower children to its notoriously muddy "Healing Fields." Music fans and London's beautiful people make the trek to see the hottest new English and American bands. If you're near Glastonbury during the festival, anticipate increased traffic and crowds (especially on public transportation; more than 135,000 tickets generally sell out), even though the actual music venue is six miles east of town (www.glastonburyfestivals.co.uk).

Sights in Glastonbury

▲▲**Glastonbury Abbey**—The evocative ruins of the first Christian sanctuary in the British Isles stand mysteriously alive in

a lush 36-acre park. Start your visit in the good little museum, where a model shows the abbey in its pre–Henry VIII splendor, and exhibits tell the story of a place "grandly constructed to entice even the dullest of minds to prayer." Then head out to explore the green park, dotted with bits of the ruined abbey.

In the 12th century, because of its legendary connection with Joseph of Arimathea, Glastonbury was the leading Christian pilgrimage site in all of Britain. The popular abbey grew very wealthy and employed a thousand people to serve the needs of the pilgrims. Then, in 1171, Thomas Becket was martyred at Canterbury, and immediately canonized by the pope (who thanked God for the opportunity to rile up the Christian public in England against King Henry II). This was a classic church-state power struggle. The king was excommunicated, and had to crawl through the streets of London on his knees and submit to a whipping from each bishop in England. Religious pilgrims abandoned Glastonbury for Canterbury, leaving Glastonbury suddenly a backwater.

In 1184, there was a devastating fire in the monastery, and in 1191, the abbot here "discovered"—with the help of a divine dream—the tomb and bodies of King Arthur and Queen Guinevere. Of course, this discovery rekindled the pilgrim trade in Glastonbury.

Then, in 1539, King Henry VIII ordered the abbey's destruction. When Glastonbury Abbot Richard Whiting questioned the king's decision, he was branded a traitor, hung at the top of Glastonbury Tor (after carrying up the plank that would support his noose), and his body cut into four pieces. His head was stuck over the gateway to the former abbey precinct. After this

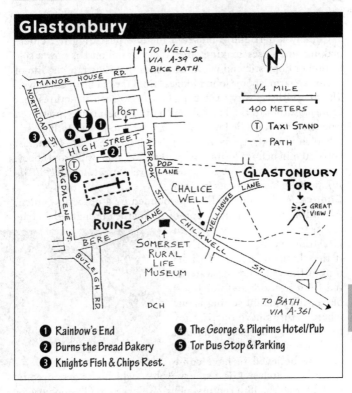

Glastonbury

TO WELLS VIA A-39 OR BIKE PATH

MANOR HOUSE RD.

NORTHLOAD ST.

POST

① **ⓘ** **①**

HIGH STREET

②

③

④

⑤

MAGDALENE ST.

Ⓣ

LAMBROOK ST.

POD LANE

CHALICE WELL

WELLHOUSE LANE

GLASTONBURY TOR

¼ MILE
400 METERS
Ⓣ TAXI STAND
--- PATH

GREAT VIEW!

ABBEY RUINS

BERE LANE

BUTLEIGH RD.

SOMERSET RURAL LIFE MUSEUM

CHILKWELL ST.

DCH

TO BATH VIA A-361

① Rainbow's End
② Burns the Bread Bakery
③ Knights Fish & Chips Rest.

④ The George & Pilgrims Hotel/Pub
⑤ Tor Bus Stop & Parking

harsh example, the other abbots accepted the king's dissolution of England's abbeys. Many returned to monastic centers in France.

Today, the abbey attracts people who find God within. Tie-dyed, starry-eyed pilgrims seem to float through the grounds naturally high. Others lie on the grave of King Arthur, whose burial site is marked off in the center of the abbey ruins.

The only surviving intact building on the grounds is the abbot's conical kitchen. Here, you'll often find Matilda the pilgrim and her monk friend demonstrating life in the abbey kitchen in a kind of medieval cooking show. If you'd like to see the demo, it's best to phone ahead for the schedule, especially off-season. They also offer earnest, costumed "Living History" reenactments (included with your ticket), generally daily March through October at 10:30, 12:00, 14:00, and 16:00—confirm times when you enter.

Cost, Hours, Information: £5, daily June–Aug 9:00–18:00, Sept–May 9:30 or 10:00 to dusk, closing times vary in the winter, last entry 30 min before closing, nearby pay parking, several guided walks offered daily, informative but long-winded 40-min audioguide-£2, as you enter ask about various tour and "show" times, tel. 01458/832-267, www.glastonburyabbey.com.

Somerset Rural Life Museum—Exhibits in this free and extremely kid-friendly museum include peat digging, cider-making, and cheesemaking. The Abbey Farmhouse is now a collection of domestic and work mementos that illustrate the life of Victorian farm laborer John Hodges "from the cradle to the grave." The fine 14th-century tithe barn (one of 30 such structures that funneled tithes to the local abbey), with its beautifully preserved wooden ceiling, is filled with Victorian farm tools and enthusiastic schoolchildren (free, Tue–Sat 10:00–17:00, closed Sun–Mon, last entry 30 min before closing, free parking, 15-min walk from abbey, at intersection of Bere Lane and Chilkwell Street, tel. 01458/831-197, www.somerset.gov.uk/museums).

Chalice Well—The well is surrounded by a peaceful garden. According to tradition, Joseph of Arimathea brought the chal-

ice from the Last Supper to Glastonbury in A.D. 37. Even if the chalice is not in the bottom of the well and the water is red from iron ore and not Jesus' blood, the tranquil setting is one where nature's harmony is a joy to ponder. The stones of the well shaft date from the 12th century, and are believed to have come from the church in Glastonbury Abbey (which was destroyed by fire). During the 18th century, pilgrims flocked to Glastonbury for the well's healing powers. Even today, there's a moment of silence at noon for world peace and healing. Have a drink or take some of the precious water home (£3.50, daily April–Oct 10:00–17:30, Nov–March 10:00–16:00, last entry 30 min before closing, water bottles available for purchase, on Chilkwell Street/A361, drivers can park at Rural Life Museum and walk 5 min, tel. 01458/831-154, www.chalicewell.org.uk).

▲**Glastonbury Tor**—Seen by many as a Mother Goddess symbol, the tor—a natural plug of sandstone on clay—has an undeniable geological charisma.

Climbing the tor is the essential activity on a visit to Glastonbury. A fine Somerset view rewards those who hike to its 520-foot summit. From its top you can survey a former bogland that is still below sea level at high tide. The ribbon-like man-made drainage canals that glisten as they slice through the farmland are the work of Dutch engineers, imported centuries ago to turn the marshy wasteland into something usable.

Looking out, find Glastonbury (at the base of the hill) and Wells (marked by its cathedral) to the right. Above Wells, a TV tower marks the 996-foot high point of the Mendip Hills. It was lead from these hills that attracted the Romans (and, perhaps, Jesus' uncle Joe) so long ago. Stretching to the left, the hills define what was the coastline before those Dutch engineers arrived.

The tor-top tower is the remnant of a chapel dedicated to St. Michael. Early Christians often employed St. Michael, the warrior angel, to combat pagan gods. When a church was built upon a pagan holy ground like this, it was frequently dedicated to Michael. But apparently those pagan gods fought back: St. Michael's Church was destroyed by an earthquake in 1275.

Getting There: The tor is a short bus ride or walk from the town center. Drivers can park at the nearby Rural Life Museum. For details, see "Getting to the Tor" on page 331.

New Age Shopping—Part of the fun of a visit to Glastonbury is just being in a town where every other shop and eatery is a New Age place. If you need spiritual guidance or just a rune reading, wander through the **Glastonbury Experience,** a New Age mall at the bottom of High Street. Locals who are not into this complain that on High Street you can buy any kind of magic crystal or incense, but not a roll of TP. But, as this counterculture is their town's bread and butter, they do their best to sit in their pubs and go "Ommmmm."

Eating in Glastonbury

Glastonbury has no shortage of healthy eateries. The vegetarian **Rainbow's End** is one of several fine lunch cafés for beans, salads, herbal teas, yummy homemade sweets, and New Age people-watching (£8 meals, daily 10:00–16:00, a few doors up from the TI, 17 High Street, tel. 01458/833-896). If you're looking for a midwife or a male-bonding tribal meeting, check their notice board.

Burns the Bread makes hearty pasties (savory meat pies) as well as fresh pies, sandwiches, delicious cookies, and pastries. Ask about the Torsy Moorsy Cake, or try a gingerbread man made with real ginger. Grab a pasty and picnic with the ghosts of Arthur and Guinevere in the abbey ruins (Mon–Sat 6:00–17:00, Sun 11:00–17:00, 14 High Street, tel. 01458/831-532).

Knights Fish and Chips Restaurant has been in business since 1909 because it serves good food (Mon 17:00–21:30, Tue–Sat 12:00–14:15 & 17:00–21:30, closed Sun, eat in or take away, 5 Northload Street, tel. 01458/831-882).

For visitors suffering a New Age overdose, the wonderfully Old World pub in **The George and Pilgrims Hotel** might be exactly what the doctor ordered (1 High Street, also rents rooms for £85–95, tel. 01458/831-146).

Glastonbury Connections

The nearest train station is in Bath. Local buses are run by First Bus Company (toll tel. 0845-606-4446, www.firstgroup.com).

From Glastonbury by Bus to: Wells (4/hr, 20 min, bus #375/#376/#377 runs frequently, bus #29 only 6/day), **Bath** (hourly, allow 2 hours, take bus #375/#376/#377 or #29 to Wells, transfer to bus #173 to Bath, 1.25 hours between Wells and Bath). Buses are sparse on Sundays (generally one bus every hour).

Wells

Because this wonderfully preserved little town has a cathedral, it can be called a city. While it's the biggest town in Somerset, it's England's smallest cathedral city (pop. 9,400), with one of its most interesting cathedrals and a wonderful evensong service. Wells has more medieval buildings still doing what they were originally built to do than any town you'll visit. Market day fills the town square on Wednesday and Saturday.

Tourist Information: The TI, on the main square, has information about the town's sights and nearby cheese factories (April–Oct Mon–Sat 10:00–17:00, Sun 10:00–16:00; Nov–March Mon–Sat 11:00–16:00, closed Sun; tel. 01749/672-552, www.wellstourism.com).

Local Guide: Edie Westmoreland offers town walks in the summer by appointment (£15/group of 2–5 people, £4/person for 8 or more, 1.5-hour tours usually start at Penniless Porch on town square, book three days in advance, tel. 01934/832-350, mobile 07899-836-706, ebwestmoreland@btinternet.com).

Sights in Wells

▲▲Wells Cathedral

England's first completely Gothic cathedral (dating from about 1200) is the highlight of the city. Locals claim this church has the largest collection of medieval statuary north of the Alps.

Cost, Hours, Information: Requested £5.50 donation—not intended to keep you out, daily Easter–Sept 7:00–19:00 or dusk, Oct–Easter 7:00–18:00; 45-min tours Mon–Sat April–Oct

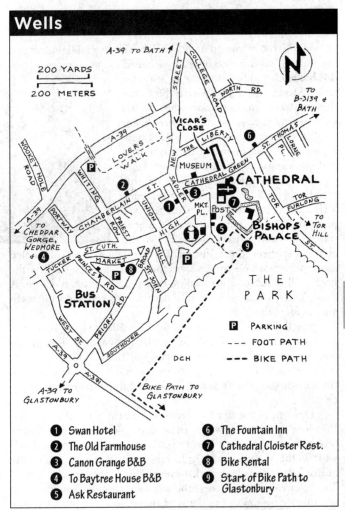

Wells

❶ Swan Hotel	❻ The Fountain Inn
❷ The Old Farmhouse	❼ Cathedral Cloister Rest.
❸ Canon Grange B&B	❽ Bike Rental
❹ To Baytree House B&B	❾ Start of Bike Path to Glastonbury
❺ Ask Restaurant	

at 10:00, 12:00, 13:00, 14:00, and 15:00; pay £3 photography fee at info desk, no flash in choir, good shop, handy Cathedral Cloister Restaurant, tel. 01749/674-483, www.wellscathedral .org.uk.

○ **Self-Guided Tour:** Begin in front of the cathedral. The newly restored west front displays almost 300 original 13th-century carvings of kings and the **Last Judgment.** The bottom row of niches is empty, too easily reached by Cromwell's men, who were hell-bent on destroying "graven images." Stand back and imagine it as a grand Palm Sunday welcome with a cast of hundreds—all gaily painted back then, choristers singing boldly from holes above the doors and trumpets tooting through the holes up by the 12 apostles.

Inside, you're immediately struck by the general lightness and the unique "scissors" or hourglass-shaped **double arch** (added in 1338 to transfer weight from the west—where the foundations were sinking under the tower's weight—to the east, where they were firm). You'll be warmly greeted, reminded how expensive it is to maintain the cathedral, and given a map of its highlights.

The warm tones of the stone interior give the place a modern feel. Until Henry VIII and the Reformation, the interior was painted a gloomy red and green. Later it was whitewashed. Then, in the 1840s, the church experienced the Victorian "great scrape," as locals peeled moldy whitewash off and revealed the bare stone we see today. The floral ceiling painting is based on the original medieval design. A single pattern was discovered under the 17th-century whitewash and repeated throughout.

Small, ornate 15th-century pavilion-like chapels flank the altar, carved in lacy Gothic for wealthy townsmen. The **pulpit** features a post-Reformation, circa-1540 English script—rather than the standard Latin. Since this was not a monastery church, the Reformation didn't destroy it as it did the Glastonbury Abbey church.

Don't miss the fine 14th-century stained glass (the "Golden Window" on the east wall). The medieval **clock,** which depicts the earth at the center of the universe, does a silly but much-loved joust on the quarter-hour (north transept, its face dates from 1390, notice how—like clockwork—every other rider gets clobbered). The outer ring shows hours, the second ring shows minutes, and the inner ring shows the dates of the month and phases of the moon. The fine **crucifix** was carved out of a yew tree by a German prisoner of war during World War II. After the war ended, many of England's German prisoners figured there was little in Germany to go home to, so they stayed, assimilating into English culture.

In the **choir** (the central zone where the daily services are sung), the embroidery work on the cushions is worth a close look. It celebrates the hometowns of important local church leaders.

Head over to the south transept. Notice the **carvings** on the pillars. The figures depict medieval life—a man with a toothache, another man with a thorn in his foot, and, around the top, a ticked-off farmer chasing fruit stealers. Look at the tombstones set in the floor. Notice that there is no brass. After the Reformation in the 1530s, the church was short on cash, so they sold the brass to pay for roof repairs. The **old font** survives from the previous church (A.D. 705) and has been the site of Wells baptisms for almost a thousand years. In the far end of this transept, a little of the muddy green and red that wasn't whitewashed survives.

In the apse, or east end, find the **Lady Chapel** with its fine medieval glass windows. In the 17th century, Puritan troops trashed the precious original glass. Much was repaired, but many of the broken panes were like a puzzle that was never figured out. That's why today many of the windows are simply kaleidoscopes of colored glass.

Well-worn steps lead to the grand fan-vaulted **Chapter House**—an intimate place for the theological equivalent of a huddle among church officials. The cathedral **Reading Room** (£1, Fri–Sat 14:30–16:30 only), with a few old manuscripts, offers a peek into a real 15th-century library.

More Cathedral Sights

▲▲Cathedral Evensong Service—The cathedral choir takes full advantage of heavenly acoustics with a nightly 45-minute evensong service. You will sit right in the old "quire" as you listen to a great pipe organ and boys', girls', and men's voices (Mon–Sat at 17:15, Sun at 15:00, generally no service when school is out July–Aug unless a visiting choir performs, to check call 01749/674-483 or visit www.wellscathedral.org.uk). At 17:05 (Sun at 15:05) the verger ushers visitors to their seats. There's usually plenty of room.

On weekdays and Saturdays, if you need to catch the 17:43 bus to Bath, request a seat on the north side of the presbytery, so you can slip out the side door without disturbing the service (10-min walk to station from cathedral; or go at 18:15 via Bristol—explained under "Wells Connections," later).

The cathedral also hosts several evening **concerts** each month (£10–25, most about £18, generally Thu–Sat at 19:00 or 19:30, box office open Mon–Sat 14:00–16:30, closed Sun, tel. 01749/832-201). Concert tickets are also available at the TI.

Cathedral Green—In the Middle Ages, the cathedral was enclosed within the "Liberty," an area free from civil jurisdiction until the 1800s. The Liberty included the green on the west side of the cathedral, which, from the 13th to the 17th centuries, was a burial place for common folk, including 17th-century plague victims. During the Edwardian period, a local character known as Boney Foster used to dig up the human bones and sell them to tourists. The green later became a cricket pitch, then a field for grazing animals. Today, it's the perfect setting for an impressive cathedral.

Vicar's Close—Lined with perfectly pickled 14th-century houses, this is the oldest continuously occupied complete street in Europe (since 1348, just a block north of the cathedral). It was built to house the vicar's choir, and it still houses church officials.

Bishop's Palace—Next to the cathedral stands the moated Bishop's Palace, built in the 13th century and still in use today as the residence of the Bishop of Bath and Wells. The interior offers a look at elegant furniture and clothing (not worth the £5.50, April–Oct Sun–Fri 10:30–18:00, Sat 10:30–14:00, closed Nov–March some Sat–Sun for events—call to confirm, last entry one hour before closing, £2 guidebook, tel. 01749/678-691, www.bishopspalace.org.uk).

The palace's spring-fed moat, built in the 14th century to protect the bishop during squabbles with the borough, now serves primarily as a pool for swans. The bridge was last drawn in 1831. On the grounds (past the old-timers playing a proper game of croquet—daily after 13:30) is a fine garden, home to the idyllic springs and wells that gave the city its name.

More Sights and Best Views—The mediocre **city museum** is next door to the cathedral (£3; Easter–Oct Mon–Sat 11:00–17:00, Sun 11:00–16:00; Nov–Easter daily 11:00–16:00; 8 Cathedral Green, tel. 01749/673-477, www.wellsmuseum.org.uk). For a fine **cathedral-and-town view** from your own leafy hilltop bench, hike 10 minutes from here up Tor Hill.

Near Wells

Bike Ride from Wells to Glastonbury Tor—This 9.5-mile cycling and foot path is part of the West Country Way Cycle Route (although much of the Wells–Glastonbury segment is on rural highways). Look for the signs that lead you to Glastonbury (small blue metal signs say *Byway*, with a red number *3*).

You can rent a bike in Wells at **Bike City** (£7.50/half-day, £15/ day, Mon–Thu 9:00–17:30, Fri–Sat 9:00–17:00, closed Sun, helmets available, near the bus station on Market Street, tel. 01749/671-711, www.bikecity.biz). They give route advice and handy maps. There is no bike rental in Glastonbury.

Cheddar Cheese—If you're in the mood for a picnic, drop by any local aromatic cheese shop for a great selection of tasty Somerset cheeses. Real farmhouse cheddar puts American cheddar to Velveeta shame. The **Cheddar Gorge Cheese Company,** eight miles west of Wells, is a dairy farm with a guide and viewing area, giving guests a chance to see the cheesemaking process and enjoy a sample (£2, daily 10:00–16:00; take A39, then A371 to Cheddar Gorge; tel. 01934/742-810, www.cheddargorgecheeseco.co.uk).

Scrumpy Farms—Scrumpy is the wonderfully dangerous hard cider brewed in this part of England. You don't find it served in many pubs because of the unruly crowd it attracts. Scrumpy, at 8 percent alcohol, will rot your socks. "Scrumpy Jack," carbonated mass-produced cider, is not real scrumpy. The real stuff is "rough farmhouse cider." This is potent stuff. It's said some farmers throw a side of beef into the vat, and when fermentation is done only the teeth remain.

TIs list local cider farms open to the public, such as **Mr. Wilkins' Land's End Cider Farm,** a great Back Door travel experience (free, Mon–Sat 10:00–20:00, Sun 10:00–13:00; west of Wells in Mudgley, take B3139 from Wells to Wedmore, then B3151 south for 2 miles, farm is a quarter-mile off B3151—tough to find, get close and ask locals; tel. 01934/712-385). Glastonbury's **Somerset Rural Life Museum** also has a cider exhibit.

Apples are pressed from August through December. Hard cider, while not quite scrumpy, is also typical of the West Country, but more fashionable, "decent," and accessible. You can get a pint of hard cider at nearly any pub, drawn straight from the barrel—dry, medium, or sweet.

Castle of Nunney—The centerpiece of the charming village of Nunney (between Bath and Glastonbury, off A361) is a striking 14th-century castle surrounded by a fairy-tale moat. Its rare, French-style design brings to mind the Paris Bastille. The year 1644 was a tumultuous one for Nunney. Its noble family was royalist (and likely closet Catholics). They defied Parliament, so Parliament ordered their castle "slighted" (deliberately destroyed) to ensure that it would threaten the order of the land no more. Looking at this castle, so daunting in the age of bows and arrows, you can see how it was no match for the modern cannon. The pretty Mendip village of Nunney, with its little brook, is worth a wander too.

Sleeping in Wells

Wells is a pleasant overnight stop with a handful of agreeable B&Bs. The first three places listed below are within a short walk of the cathedral.

$$ Swan Hotel, a Best Western facing the cathedral, is a big, comfortable 50-room hotel. Prices for their Tudor-style rooms vary based on whether you want extras like a four-poster bed or a view of the cathedral (Sb-£100, Db-£134, often cheaper if you just show up, ask about weekend deals, Sadler Street, tel. 01749/836-300, fax 01749/836-301, www.swanhotelwells.co.uk, info@swanhotelwells .co.uk).

NEAR BATH

Sleep Code

(£1 = about $1.60, country code: 44, area code: 01749)
S = Single, **D** = Double/Twin, **T** = Triple, **Q** = Quad, **b** = bathroom, **s** = shower only. Unless otherwise indicated, you can assume credit cards are accepted and breakfast is included.

To help you sort easily through these listings, I've divided the rooms into two categories based on the price for a standard double room with bath:

$$ Higher Priced—Most rooms £80 or more.
$ Lower Priced—Most rooms less than £80.

$ The Old Farmhouse, a five-minute walk from the town center, welcomes you with a secluded front garden and two tastefully decorated rooms (Db-£75–80, 2-night minimum, secure parking, 62 Chamberlain Street, tel. 01749/675-058, www.wellsholiday.com, theoldfarmhousewells@hotmail.com, charming owners Felicity and Christopher Wilkes).

$ Canon Grange B&B is a 15th-century watch-your-head beamed house directly in front of the cathedral. It has five homey rooms and a cozy charm (Sb-£50, Db-£68, Db with cathedral view-£74, ask for 10 percent Rick Steves discount with stay of 2 or more nights, family room, on the cathedral green, tel. 01749/671-800, www.canongrange.co.uk, canongrange@email.com, Annette and Ken).

$ Baytree House B&B is a modern and practical home at the edge of town (on a big road, a 10-minute walk to the center), renting five modern, fresh, and comfy rooms (Db-£64, family rooms, Wi-Fi, plush lounge, free parking, near where Strawberry Way hits the A39 road to Cheddar at 85 Portway, tel. 01749/677-933, mobile 07745-287-194, www.baytree-house.co.uk, stay@baytree -house.co.uk, Amanda Bellini).

Eating in Wells

Downtown Wells is tiny. A fine variety of eating options is within a block or two of its market square, including classic pubs, **Ask Restaurant** (a popular Italian chain, £8 pizza and pastas, right on the square in the Market Hall, tel. 01749/677-681), a good pasties-to-go **bakery** (on Sadler Street), and little delis and bakeries serving light meals. **The Fountain Inn** serves good pub grub (50 yards behind the cathedral on St. Thomas Street, tel. 01749/672-317).

For a handy if not heavenly lunch, consider the **Cathedral Cloister Restaurant** in the cathedral, along a lovely stone corridor with leaded windows overlooking cloister tombstones (£4–6 lunches, Mon–Sat 10:00–17:00, Sun 13:00–17:00; closes at 16:30 and occasionally on Sun in winter).

Wells Connections

The nearest train station is in Bath. The bus station in Wells is actually a bus lot, at the intersection of Priory and Princes roads. Local buses are run by First Bus Company (for Wells, toll tel. 0845-606-4446, www.firstgroup.com), while buses to and from London are run by National Express (toll tel. 0871-781-8181, www.nationalexpress.com).

From Wells by Bus to: Bath (hourly, 1.25 hrs, last bus #173 leaves at 17:43), **Glastonbury** (4/hr, 20 min, bus #375/#376/#377 runs frequently, bus #29 only 6/day), **London's Victoria Coach Station** (£28–30, hourly, 4 hrs, change in Bristol, buses run daily 6:10–18:15).

If you miss the 17:43 bus to Bath, you can catch the 18:15 bus to Bristol, then take a 15-minute train ride to Bath, arriving at 19:35.

NEAR BATH

Avebury

Avebury is a prehistoric open-air museum, with a complex of fascinating Neolithic sites all gathered around the great stone henge

(circle). Because the area sports only a thin skin of topsoil over chalk, it is naturally treeless (similar to the area around Stonehenge). Perhaps this unique landscape—where the land connects with the big sky—made it the choice of prehistoric societies for their religious monuments. Whatever the case, Avebury dates to 2800 B.C.—six centuries older than Stonehenge. This complex, the St. Peter's Basilica of Neolithic civilization, makes for a fascinating visit. Many enjoy it more than Stonehenge.

Orientation to Avebury

Avebury, just a little village with a big stone circle, is easy to reach by car, but may not be worth the hassle by public transportation (see "Getting Around the Region," page 328).

Tourist Information

The TI is located within the town chapel. Notice the stone work: It's a mix of bricks and broken stones from the ancient circle (June–Oct Tue–Sun 9:30–17:00, closed Mon, shorter hours Nov–May, Green Street, tel. 01672/539-179, www.visitwiltshire.co.uk). For good information on the Avebury sights, see the websites of the English Heritage (www.english-heritage.org.uk) and the National Trust (www.nationaltrust.org.uk).

Arrival by Car

You must pay to park in Avebury, and your only real option is the flat-fee National Trust parking lot, which is a three-minute walk from the village (£5, £3 after 15:00, summer 9:00–18:00, off-season 9:00–16:00). No other public parking is available in the village.

Sights in Avebury

▲▲**Avebury Stone Circle**—The stone circle at Avebury is bigger (16 times the size), less touristy, and, for many, more interesting than Stonehenge. You're free to wander among 100 stones, ditches, mounds, and curious patterns from the past, as well as the village of Avebury, which grew up in the middle of this fascinating 1,400-foot-wide Neolithic circle.

In the 14th century, in a kind of frenzy of religious paranoia, Avebury villagers buried many of these mysterious pagan stones. Their 18th-century descendants hosted social events in which they broke up the remaining pagan stones (topple, heat up, douse with cold water, and scavenge broken stones as building blocks). In modern times, the buried stones were dug up and re-erected. Concrete markers show where the missing broken-up stones once stood.

To make the roughly half-mile walk around the circle, you'll hike along an impressive earthwork henge—a 30-foot-high outer bank surrounding a ditch 30 feet deep, making a 60-foot-high rampart. This earthen rampart once had stones standing around the perimeter, placed about every 30 feet, and four grand causeway entries. Originally, two smaller circles made of about 200 stones stood within the henge (free, always open).

▲**Ritual Procession Way**—Also known as West Kennet Avenue, this double line of stones provided a ritual procession way leading from Avebury to a long-gone wooden circle dubbed "The

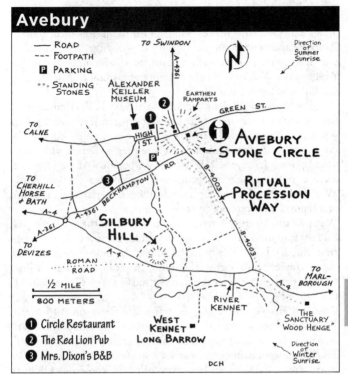

Avebury

— ROAD
--- FOOTPATH
P PARKING
••• STANDING STONES

TO SWINDON

N

Direction of Summer Sunrise

ALEXANDER KEILLER MUSEUM

EARTHEN RAMPARTS

GREEN ST.

TO CALNE

HIGH ST.

AVEBURY STONE CIRCLE

P

RITUAL PROCESSION WAY

TO CHERHILL HORSE & BATH

BECKHAMPTON RD.

B-4003

A-4

A-4361

SILBURY HILL

TO DEVIZES

A-361

ROMAN ROAD

A-4

B-4003

TO MARL-BOROUGH

A-4

½ MILE
800 METERS

RIVER KENNET

THE SANCTUARY "WOOD HENGE"

❶ Circle Restaurant
❷ The Red Lion Pub
❸ Mrs. Dixon's B&B

WEST KENNET LONG BARROW

Direction of Winter Sunrise

DCH

Sanctuary." This "wood henge," thought to have been 1,000 years older than everything else in the area, is considered the genesis of Avebury and its big stone circle. Most of the stones standing along the procession way today were reconstructed in modern times.

▲**Silbury Hill**—This pyramid-shaped hill is a 130-foot-high, yet-to-be-explained mound of chalk just outside of Avebury. More than 4,000 years old, this mound is considered the largest man-made object in prehistoric Europe (with the surface area

of London's Trafalgar Square and the height of the Nelson Column). It's a reminder that we've only just scratched the surface of England's mysterious, ancient, and religious landscape.

Inspired by a legend that the hill hid a gold statue in its cen-

ter, locals tunneled through Silbury Hill in 1830, undermining the structure. Work is currently underway to restore the hill, which remains closed to the public. Archaeologists (who date things like this by carbon-dating snails and other little critters killed in its construction) figure Silbury Hill took only 60 years to build in about 2200 B.C. This makes Silbury Hill the last element built at Avebury and contemporaneous with Stonehenge. Some think it may have been an observation point for all the other bits of the Avebury site. You can still see evidence of a spiral path leading up the hill, and a moat at its base.

The Roman road detoured around Silbury Hill. (Roman engineers often used features of the landscape as visual reference points when building roads. Their roads would commonly kink at the crest of hills or other landmarks, where they realigned with a new visual point.) Later, the hill sported a wooden Saxon fort, which likely acted as a look-out for marauding Vikings. And in World War II, the Royal Observer Corps stationed men up here to count and report Nazi bombers on raids.

West Kennet Long Barrow—A pull-out on the road just past Silbury Hill marks the West Kennet Long Barrow (a 15-min walk from Silbury Hill). This burial chamber, the best-preserved Stone Age chamber tomb in the UK, stands intact on the ridge. It lines up with the rising sun on the summer solstice. You can walk inside the barrow.

Cherhill Horse—Heading west from Avebury on A4 (toward Bath), you'll see an obelisk (a monument to some important earl) above you on the downs, or chalk hills, near the village of Cherhill. You'll also see a white horse carved into the chalk hillside. Above it are the remains of an Iron Age hill fort known as Oldbury Castle—described on an information board at the roadside pull-out. There is one genuinely prehistoric white horse in England (the Uffington White Horse); the Cherhill Horse, like all the others, is just an 18th-century creation. Prehistoric discoveries were all the rage in the 1700s, and it was a fad to make your own fake ones. Throughout southern England, you can cut into the thin layer of topsoil and find chalk. Now, so they don't have to weed, horses like this are cemented and painted white.

Alexander Keiller Museum—This archaeology museum has an interactive exhibit in a 17th-century barn (£5, daily April–Oct 10:00–18:00, Nov–March 10:00–16:00 or dusk, last entry 30 min before closing, tel. 01672/539-250).

Eating and Sleeping in Avebury

The pleasant **Circle Restaurant** serves healthy, hearty à la carte lunches, including vegan and gluten-free dishes, and cream teas on most days (daily April–Oct 10:00–17:30, Nov–March 11:00–15:30, next to National Trust store and the Alexander Keiller museum, tel. 01672/539-514).

The Red Lion has inexpensive, greasy pub grub; a creaky, well-worn, dart-throwing ambience; and a medieval well in its dining room (£6–12 meals, daily 12:00–22:00, tel. 01672/539-266).

Sleeping in Avebury makes lots of sense, since the stones are lonely and wide-open all night. **$ Mrs. Dixon's B&B,** up the road from the public parking lot, rents three cramped and homey rooms. Look for the green-and-white *Bed & Breakfast* sign from the main road (S-£40, D-£60, these prices promised with this book in 2010, cash only, parking available in back, 6 Beckhampton Road, tel. 01672/539-588, run by earthy Mrs. Dixon and crew).

Stonehenge

As old as the pyramids, and older than the Acropolis and the Colosseum, this iconic stone circle amazed medieval Europeans, who figured it was built by a race of giants. And it still impresses visitors today. As one of Europe's most famous sights, Stonehenge does a valiant job of retaining an air of mystery and majesty (partly because cordons, which keep hordes of tourists from trampling all over it, create the illusion that it stands alone in a field). Although some people are underwhelmed by Stonehenge, most of its almost one million annual visitors find that it's worth the trip.

Getting to Stonehenge
By Public Transportation: Catch a train to Salisbury, then go by bus or taxi to Stonehenge (for details, see page 353). Note that there is no public transportation between Avebury and Stonehenge.

By Car: Stonehenge is well-signed just off A303. It's about 15 minutes north of Salisbury, an hour east of Glastonbury, and an hour south of Avebury. From Salisbury, head north on A345 (Castle Road) through Amesbury, go west on A303 for 1.5 miles, veer right onto A344, and it's just ahead on the left, with the parking lot on the right.

By Bus Tour: For tours of Stonehenge from Bath, see page 305 (Mad Max is best); for tours from Salisbury, see page 353.

Orientation to Stonehenge

Cost: £6.50, covered by English Heritage Pass and Great British Heritage Pass (see page 19).

Hours: Daily June–Aug 9:00–19:00, mid-March–May and Sept–mid-Oct 9:30–18:00, mid-Oct–mid-March 9:30–16:00, last entry 30 min before closing.

When to Go: Shorter hours and possible closures June 20–22 due to huge, raucous solstice crowds; £3 parking fee likely in summer—refundable with paid admission.

Information: Entry includes a worthwhile hour-long audio-guide—though they sometimes run out (tel. 01980/623-108 or toll tel. 0870-333-1181, www.english-heritage.org.uk/stone henge).

Reaching the Inner Stones: Special one-hour access to the stones' inner circle—before or after regular visiting hours—costs an extra £14 and must be reserved well in advance. Details can be found on the English Heritage website (look for a link to "Stone Circle Access") or by calling 01722/343-830.

Planned Changes: Future plans for Stonehenge call for the creation of a new visitors center and museum, designed to blend in with the landscape and make the stone circle feel more pristine. Visitors will park farther away and ride a shuttle bus to the site.

Self-Guided Tour

The entrance fee includes a good audioguide, but this commentary will help make your visit even more meaningful.

Walk in from the parking lot, buy your ticket, pick up your included audio-guide, and head through the ugly underpass beneath the road. On the way up the ramp, notice the artist's rendering of what Stonehenge once looked like. As you approach the massive structure, walk right up to the knee-high cordon and let your fellow 21st-century tourists melt away. It's just you and the druids...

England has hundreds of stone circles, but Stonehenge—which literally means "hanging stones"—is unique. It's the only one that has horizontal cross-pieces (called lintels) spanning the vertical monoliths, and the only one with stones that have been made smooth and uniform. What you see here is a bit more than half the original structure—the rest was quarried centuries ago for other buildings.

Now do a slow counterclockwise spin around the monument, and ponder the following points. As you walk, mentally flesh out the missing pieces and re-erect the rubble. Knowledgeable guides posted around the site are happy to answer your questions.

This was a hugely significant location to prehistoric peoples. There are some 500 burial mounds within a three-mile radius of Stonehenge—most likely belonging to kings and chieftains. Built in phases between 3000 and 1000 B.C., Stonehenge's original function may have been simply as a monumental gravestone for a ritual burial site. (So goes one recently popular theory.) But that's not the end of the story, as the monument was expanded over the millennia.

Stonehenge still functions as a remarkably accurate celestial calendar. As the sun rises on the summer solstice (June 21), the "heel stone"—the one set apart from the rest, near the road—lines up with the sun and the altar at the center of the stone circle. A study of more than 300 similar circles in Britain found that each was designed to calculate the movement of the sun, moon, and stars, and to predict eclipses in order to help early societies know when to plant, harvest, and party. Even in modern times, as the summer solstice sun sets in just the right slot at Stonehenge, pagans boogie.

In addition to being a calendar, Stonehenge is built at the precise point where six ley lines intersect. Ley lines are theoretical lines of magnetic or spiritual power that crisscross the globe. Belief in the power of these lines has gone in and out of fashion over time: They are believed to have been very important to prehistoric peoples, but then were largely ignored until the New Age movement of the 20th century. Without realizing it, you follow these ley lines all the time: Many of England's modern highways are built on top of prehistoric paths, and many churches are built on the site of prehistoric monuments where ley lines intersect. If you're a skeptic, ask one of the guides at Stonehenge to demonstrate the ley lines with a pair of L-shaped divining rods...it's creepy and convincing.

Notice that two of the stones (facing the entry passageway) are blemished. At the base of one monolith, it looks like someone has pulled back the stone to reveal a concrete skeleton. This is a clumsy repair job to fix damage done by souvenir-seekers long ago, who actually rented hammers and chisels to take home a piece of Stonehenge. On the stone to the right of the repaired one, notice that the back isn't covered with the same thin layer of protective lichen as the others. The lichen—and some of the stone itself—was sandblasted off to remove graffiti. (No wonder they've got Stonehenge roped off now.)

Stonehenge's builders used two different types of stones. The tall, stout monoliths and lintels are made of sandstone blocks called sarsen stones. Most of the monoliths weigh about 25 tons (the largest is 45 tons), and the lintels are about seven tons apiece. These sarsen stones were brought from "only" 20 miles away. The shorter stones in the middle, called "bluestones," came from the south coast of Wales—240 miles away. (Close if you're taking a train, but far if you're packing a megalith.) Imagine the logistical puzzle of floating six-ton stones up the River Avon, then rolling them on logs about 20 miles to this position...an impressive feat, even in our era of skyscrapers.

Why didn't the builders of Stonehenge use what seem like perfectly adequate stones nearby? This, like many other questions about Stonehenge, remains shrouded in mystery. Think again about the ley lines. Ponder the fact that many experts accept none of the explanations of how these giant stones were transported. Then imagine congregations gathering here 4,000 years ago, raising thought levels, creating a powerful life force transmitted along the ley lines. Maybe a particular kind of stone was essential for maximum energy transmission. Maybe the stones were levitated here. Maybe psychics really do create powerful vibes. Maybe not. It's as unbelievable as electricity used to be.

Salisbury

Salisbury, set in the middle of the expansive Salisbury Plain, is a favorite stop for its striking cathedral and intriguing history. Salisbury was originally settled during the Bronze Age, possibly as early as 600 B.C., and later became a Roman town called Sarum. The modern city of Salisbury developed when the old settlement outgrew its boundaries, prompting the townspeople to move the city from a hill to the river valley below. Most of today's visitors come to  marvel at the famous Salisbury Cathedral, featuring England's tallest spire and largest cathedral green. Collectors, bargain hunters, and foodies will savor Salisbury's colorful market days. And archaeologists will dig the region around Salisbury, with England's highest concentration of ancient sites. The town itself is pleasant and walkable, and is a convenient base camp for visiting the ancient sites of Stonehenge and Avebury, or for exploring the countryside.

Orientation to Salisbury

(area code: 01722)

Salisbury (pop. 45,000) stretches along the River Avon in the shadow of its huge landmark cathedral. The heart of the city clusters around Market Square, which is also a handy parking lot on non-market days. High Street, a block to the west, leads to the medieval North Gate of the Cathedral Close. Shoppers explore the streets south of the square. The area north of Market Square is generally residential, with a few shops and pubs.

Tourist Information

The TI, just off Market Square, hands out free city maps, books rooms for no fee, sells a £1 city guide, sells train tickets with a £1.10 surcharge, and offers free Internet access (May Mon–Sat 9:30–17:00, Sun 10:00–16:00; June–Sept Mon–Sat 9:30–18:00, Sun 10:00–16:00; Oct–April Mon–Sat 9:30–17:00, closed Sun; Fish Row, tel. 01722/334-956, www.visitwiltshire.co.uk).

Ask the TI about 1.5-hour walking tours (£4, April–Oct daily at 11:00, Nov–March Sat–Sun only, depart from TI; other itineraries available, including £4 Ghost Walk May–Sept Fri at 20:00; tel. 01722/320-349, www.salisburycityguides.co.uk).

Arrival in Salisbury

By Train: From the train station, it's a 10-minute walk into the town center. Leave the station to the left, walk about 50 yards down South Western Road, and take the first right (at The Railway Tavern) onto Mill Road, following it around the bend and through the traffic roundabouts. Soon you'll see the Queen Elizabeth Gardens and the cathedral spire on your right. The road becomes Crane Bridge Road, then Crane Street, and finally New Street before intersecting with Catherine/St. John Street. Market Square and the TI are one long block north (left) on Catherine Street, and it's another two short blocks beyond that to the bus station. The Salisbury Cathedral and recommended Exeter Street B&Bs are to the south (right), down St. John Street (which becomes Exeter Street).

By Car: Drivers will find several pay parking lots in Salisbury—simply follow the blue *P* signs. The "Central" lot, behind the giant redbrick Sainsbury's store, is within a 10-minute walk of the TI or cathedral and is best for overnight stays (enter from Churchill Way West or Castle Street, lot open 24 hrs). The "Old George Mall" parking garage is closer to the cathedral and has comparable daytime rates (1 block north of cathedral, enter from New Street; garage open Mon–Sat 7:00–20:00, Sun 10:00–17:00).

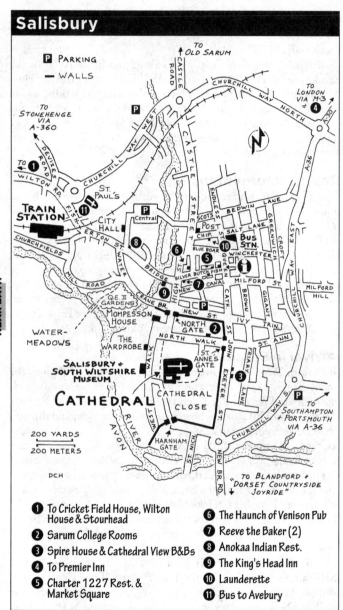

Salisbury

P PARKING
— WALLS

1. To Cricket Field House, Wilton House & Stourhead
2. Sarum College Rooms
3. Spire House & Cathedral View B&Bs
4. To Premier Inn
5. Charter 1227 Rest. & Market Square
6. The Haunch of Venison Pub
7. Reeve the Baker (2)
8. Anokaa Indian Rest.
9. The King's Head Inn
10. Launderette
11. Bus to Avebury

Helpful Hints

Market Days: For centuries, Salisbury has been known for its lively markets. On Tuesdays and Saturdays, Market Square hosts the charter market, with general goods. Every other Wednesday is the farmers market. There are also special markets, such as one with French products. Ask the TI for a current schedule.

Festivals: The Salisbury International Arts Festival runs for just over two weeks at the end of May and beginning of June (likely May 21–June 6 in 2010, www.salisburyfestival.co.uk).

Internet Access: The TI offers a single stand-up Internet terminal at no charge for a quick email check.

Laundry: Washing Well has full-service (£7–13 per load depending on size, 2-hour service, Mon–Sat 8:00–17:30) as well as self-service (Mon–Sat 16:00–21:00, Sun 7:00–20:00, last self-service wash one hour before closing; 28 Chipper Lane, tel. 01722/421-874).

Getting to the Stone Circles: You can get to Stonehenge from Salisbury on **The Stonehenge Tour** bus. Their distinctive red-and-black double-decker buses leave from the Salisbury train station and make a circuit to Stonehenge and Old Sarum (£11, £17.50 with Stonehenge admission, tickets good all day, buy ticket from driver, June–mid-Oct daily 9:30–17:00, 1–2/hr, none on June 21 due to solstice crowds, shorter hours off-season, 30 min from station to Stonehenge, tel. 01722/336-855, check www.thestonehengetour.info for timetable).

A **taxi** from Salisbury to Stonehenge costs about £40 (corral a few fellow tourists and share the cost, call for exact price, includes round-trip from Salisbury to Stonehenge plus an hour at the site, entry fee not included, tel. 01722/339-781 or mobile 07971-255-690, brian@salisburytaxis.co.uk, Brian MacNeillie).

For buses to Avebury's stone circle, see "Salisbury Connections," later.

Sights in Salisbury

▲▲**Salisbury Cathedral**—This magnificent cathedral, visible for miles around because of its huge spire (the tallest in England at 404 feet), is a wonder to behold. The surrounding enormous grassy field (called a "close") makes the Gothic masterpiece look even larger. What's more impressive is that all this was built in a mere 38 years—astonishingly fast for the Middle Ages. When the old hill town of Sarum was moved down to the valley, its cathedral had to be replaced in a hurry. So, in 1220, the townspeople began building, and in 1258 their sparkling-new cathedral was ready for

ribbon-cutting. Since the structure was built in just a few decades, its style is uniform, rather than the patchwork of styles common in cathedrals of the time (which often took centuries to construct).

Cost and Hours: £5 suggested donation; mid-June–Aug Mon–Sat 7:15–19:15, Sun 7:15–18:15; Sept–mid-June daily 7:15–18:15; Chapter House usually opens Mon–Sat at 9:30, Sun at 12:45, and closes 30–45 min before the rest of the cathedral, and closes entirely for special events; choral evensong Mon–Sat at 17:30, Sun at 15:00; excellent cafeteria, tel. 01722/555-120, recorded info tel. 01722/555-113, www.salisburycathedral.org.uk. This working cathedral opens early for services—be respectful if you arrive when one is in session.

Tower Tours: Imagine building a cathedral on this scale before the invention of cranes, bulldozers, or modern scaffolding. An excellent tower tour (1.5–2 hours) helps visitors understand how it was done. You'll climb in between the stone arches and the roof to inspect the vaulting and trussing; see a medieval winch that was used in the construction; and finish with the 330-step climb up the narrow tower for a sweeping view of the Wiltshire countryside (£8; early June–Aug Mon–Sat at 11:15, 14:15, 15:15, and 17:00, Sun at 14:15 and 16:15; May–early June and Sept Mon–Sat at 11:15, 14:15, and 15:15, Sun at 14:15 and 16:15; fewer off-season but usually one at 14:15, no tours in Dec except Christmas week; maximum 12 people, can reserve by calling 01722/555-156).

⊘ Self-Guided Tour: Entering the church, you'll instantly feel the architectural harmony. Volunteer guides posted at the entry are ready to answer your questions. (Free guided tours of the cathedral nave are offered—about twice hourly—when enough people assemble.)

As you look down the nave, notice how the stone columns march identically down the aisle, like a thick gray forest of tree trunks. The arches overhead soar to grand heights, helping church-goers appreciate the vast and amazing heavens.

From the entrance, head to the far wall (the back-left corner). You'll find a model showing how this cathedral was built so quickly in the 13th century. Next to that is the "oldest working clock in existence," dating from the 14th century (the hourly bell has been removed, so as not to interrupt worship services). On the wall by the clock is a bell from the decommissioned ship HMS *Salisbury*. Look closely inside the bell to see the engraved names of crew members' children who were baptized on the ship.

Wander down the aisle past monuments and knights' tombs. When you get to the transept, examine the columns where the arms of the church cross. These posts were supposed to support a more modest bell tower, but when a heavy tower was added 100 years later, the columns bent under the enormous weight, causing the tower to lean sideways. Although the posts were later reinforced, the tower still tilts about 2.5 feet.

Continue down the left side of the choir, and dip into the Morning Chapel. At the back of this chapel, find the spectacular glass prism engraved with images of Salisbury—donated to the church in memory of a soldier who died at the D-Day landing at Normandy.

The oldest part of the church is at the apse (far end), where construction began in 1220: the Trinity Chapel. The giant, modern stained-glass window ponders the theme "prisoners of conscience."

After you leave the nave, pace the cloister and follow signs to the medieval **Chapter House.** All English cathedrals have a chapter house, so called because it's where the daily Bible verse, or chapter, is read. These spaces often served as gathering places for conducting church or town business. Here you can see a modest display of cathedral items plus one must-see display: one of the four original copies of the Magna Carta, a document as important to the English as the Constitution is to Americans. This "Great Charter," dating from 1215, settled a dispute between the slimy King John and some powerful barons. Revolutionary for limiting the monarch's power, the Magna Carta constitutionally guaranteed that the monarch was not above the law. This was one of the first major victories in the long battle between monarchs and nobles.

▲**Cathedral Close**—The enormous green surrounding the cathedral is the largest in England, and one of the loveliest. It's cradled

in the elbow of the River Avon and ringed by row houses, cottages, and grand mansions. The church owns the houses on the green and rents them to lucky people with holy connections. A former prime minister, Edward Heath, lived on the green, not because of his political influence, but because he was once the church organist.

The benches scattered around the green are an excellent place for having a romantic moonlit picnic or for gazing thoughtfully at the leaning spire. Although you may be tempted to linger until it's late, don't—this is still private church property...and the heavy medieval gates of the close shut at about 23:00.

A few houses are open to the public, such as the overpriced Mompesson House and the medieval Wardrobe. The most interesting attraction is the...

▲Salisbury and South Wiltshire Museum—Occupying the building just opposite the cathedral entry, this eclectic and sprawling collection was heralded by travel writer Bill Bryson as one of England's best. While that's a stretch, the museum does offer a little something for everyone, including exhibits on local archaeology and history, a costume gallery, the true-to-its-name "Salisbury Giant" puppet once used by the tailors' guilds during parades, some J. M. W. Turner paintings of the cathedral interior, and a collection of exquisite Wedgwood china and other ceramics. The highlight is the "Stonehenge Gallery," with informative and interactive exhibits explaining the ancient structure. Since there's not yet a good visitors center at the site itself, this makes for a good pre- or post-Stonehenge activity (£6, Mon–Sat 10:00–17:00, July–Aug Sun 12:00–17:00, Sept–June closed Sun, 65 The Close, tel. 01722/332-151, www.salisburymuseum.org.uk).

Sleeping in Salisbury

Salisbury's town center has very few affordable accommodations, and I've listed them below—plus a couple of good choices a little farther out. The town gets particularly crowded during the arts festival (late May through early June).

$$ Cricket Field House, outside of town on A36 toward Wilton, overlooks a cricket pitch and golf course. It has 17 clean, comfortable rooms, a gorgeous garden, and plenty of parking (Sb-£60–68, Db-£70–95, Tb-£105–120, Qb-£100–130, price depends on season, Wilton Road, tel. & fax 01722/322-595, www.cricket fieldhouse.co.uk, cricketfieldcottage@btinternet.com, Brian and Margaret James). While this place works best for drivers, it's just a 15-minute walk from the train station or a five-minute bus ride from the city center.

$$ Sarum College is a theological college that rents 48 rooms in its building right on the peaceful Cathedral Close. Much of the year, it houses visitors to the college, but it usually has rooms for tourists as well—except the week after Christmas, when they close. The slightly institutional but clean rooms share hallways with libraries, bookstores, and offices, and the five attic rooms come with grand cathedral views (S-£45, Sb-£60, D-£70, Db-£95–105 depending on size, meals available at additional cost, elevator, 19 The Close, tel. 01722/424-800, fax 01722/338-508, www.sarum .ac.uk, hospitality@sarum.ac.uk).

$ Spire House B&B, just off the Cathedral Close, is classy and cozy. The four bright, surprisingly quiet rooms come with busy wallpaper, and three have canopied beds (Db-£75, Tb-£85, cash only, no kids under age 8, free Wi-Fi, 84 Exeter Street, tel. 01722/339-213, www.salisbury-bedandbreakfast.com, spire .enquiries@btinternet.com, friendly Lois).

$ Cathedral View B&B, with four rooms next door at #83, is simpler, but still offers a good value in an outstanding location (Db-£75, Tb-£90, cash only, 2-night minimum on weekends, no kids under age 10, free Wi-Fi, 83 Exeter Street, tel. 01722/502-254, www.cathedral-viewbandb.co.uk, enquiries@cathedral-view bandb.co.uk, Wenda and Steve).

$ Premier Inn, just two miles from the city center, offers dozens of prefab and predictable rooms ideal for drivers and families (Db-£65, more during special events, 2 kids ages 15 and under sleep free, breakfast-£5–8, pay Wi-Fi, possible noise from nearby trains, off roundabout at A30 and Pearce Way, toll tel. 08701-977-225, fax 01722/337-889, www.premierinn.com).

Eating in Salisbury

There are plenty of atmospheric pubs all over town. For the best variety of restaurants, head to the Market Square area. Many places offer great "early bird" specials before 20:00.

Charter 1227, an upstairs eatery overlooking Market Square, is a handy place for a nice meal (£10 two-course lunch, £12.27 three-course early-bird dinner before 19:00, open Tue–Sat 12:00–14:30 & 18:00–21:30, closed Sun–Mon, dinner reservations smart, 6 Ox Row, tel. 01722/333-118).

The Haunch of Venison, possibly dating back to 1320, is a Salisbury institution with creaky, crooked floors and the mummified hand of a cheating card player on display (actually a replica; to the left of the fireplace in the House of Lords room). Downstairs, the "occasionally haunted" half-timbered pub serves nouvelle pub grub (£5–8 meals). The restaurant upstairs, while a little pretentious, has a good reputation for its traditional fare (£8–13 main dishes; pub open Mon–Sat 11:00–23:00, Sun 12:00–22:00, food served 12:00–14:30 & 18:00–21:00, reservations smart for dinner, 1 Minster Street, tel. 01722/411-313).

Reeve the Baker, with a branch just up the street from the TI, crafts an array of high-calorie delights and handy pick-me-ups for a fast and affordable lunch. The long cases of pastries and savory treats will make you drool (Mon–Fri 8:00–17:30, Sat 8:00–17:00, Sun 10:00–16:00, cash only; one location is next to the TI at 2 Butcher Row, another is at the corner of Market and Bridge streets at 61 Silver Street, tel. 01722/320-367).

Anokaa is a splurge that's highly acclaimed for its updated Indian cuisine. You won't find the same old chicken *tikka* here, but clever newfangled variations on Indian themes, dished up in a dressy contemporary setting (£9–15 main dishes, £8 lunch buffet, daily 12:00–14:00 & 17:30–22:30, 60 Fisherton Street, tel. 01722/414-142).

The King's Head Inn is a youthful chain pub with a big, open, modern interior and fine outdoor seating overlooking the pretty little River Avon. Its extensive menu has something for everyone (£3–4 sandwiches, £5–8 main dishes, Mon–Fri 7:00–24:00, Sat–Sun 8:00–24:00, kids welcome during the day but they must order meals by 20:30, free Wi-Fi, 1 Bridge Street, tel. 01722/342-050).

Salisbury Connections

From Salisbury by Train to: London's Waterloo Station (1–2/hr, 1.5 hrs), **Bath** (1–2/hr, 1 hr), **Oxford** (2/hr, 2 hrs, 1–2 transfers), **Portsmouth** (hourly, 1.25–1.75 hrs, possible transfers in Southampton and Havant), **Exeter** (1–2/hr, 1.5–3.5 hrs, some require transfers), **Penzance** (roughly hourly, 5–6 hrs, 1–3 transfers). Train info: toll tel. 0845-748-4950, www.nationalrail.co.uk.

By Bus to: Bath (hourly, 2.75 hrs, transfer in Warminster, www.travelinesw.com; or one direct bus/day at 10:35, 1.5 hrs on National Express #300, toll tel. 0871-781-8181, www.national express.com), **Avebury** (1–2/hr, 1.5–2.5 hrs, transfer in Devizes, Pewsey, or Marlborough, www.travelinesw.com). Many of Salisbury's long-distance buses are run by Wilts & Dorset (tel. 01722/336-855, www.wdbus.co.uk). National Express buses go once a day to **Bath** (morning only at 10:35, 1.5 hrs) and **Portsmouth** (at 15:00 or 18:25, 1.5 hrs, possible change at Southampton).

Near Salisbury

Old Sarum

Right here, on a hill overlooking the plain below, is where the original town of Salisbury was founded many centuries ago. While little remains of the old town, the view of the valley is amazing...and a little imagination can transport you back to *very* olde England.

Human settlement in this area stretches back to the Bronze Age, and the Romans, Saxons, and Normans all called this hilltop home. From about 500 B.C. through A.D. 1220, Old Sarum flourished, giving rise to a motte-and-bailey castle, a cathedral, and scores of wooden homes along the town's outer ring. The town grew so quickly that by the Middle Ages, it had outgrown its spot on the hill. In 1220, the local bishop successfully petitioned to move the entire city to the valley below, where space and water was plentiful. So, stone by stone, Old Sarum was packed up and shipped to New Sarum, where builders used nearly all the rubble from the old city to create a brand-new town with a magnificent cathedral.

Old Sarum was eventually abandoned altogether, leaving only a few stone foundations. The grand views of Salisbury from here have "in-spired" painters for ages and provided countless picnickers with a scenic backdrop: Grab a sandwich or snacks from one of the grocery stores in Salisbury or at the excellent Waitrose supermarket on the road between Salisbury and Sarum (Old Sarum entry-£3.50, daily July–Aug 9:00–18:00, April–June and Sept 10:00–17:00, Feb–March and Oct 10:00–16:00, Nov–Jan 11:00–15:00, last entry 30 min before closing, 2 miles north of Salisbury off A345, accessible by Wilts & Dorset bus #5 or #6 or via the Stonehenge Tour Bus—see page 353, tel. 01722/335-398, www.english-heritage.org.uk).

Wilton House

This sprawling estate, with a grand mansion and lush gardens, has been owned by the Earls of Pembroke since King Henry VIII's time. Inside the mansion, you'll find a collection of paintings by Rubens, Rembrandt, Van Dyck, and Brueghel, along with quirky odds-and-ends, such as a lock of Queen Elizabeth I's hair. The perfectly proportioned Double Cube Room has served as everything from a 17th-century state dining room to a secret D-Day planning room during World War II...if only the portraits could talk. The Old Riding School houses a skippable 20-minute film that dramatizes the history of the Pembroke family. Outside, classic English gardens feature a river lazily winding its way through grasses and under Greek-inspired temples. Jane Austen fans particularly enjoy this stately home, where parts of 2005's Oscar-nominated *Pride and Prejudice* were filmed. But, alas, Mr. Darcy has checked out (house and gardens-£12, gardens only-£5; house open Easter weekend and May–Aug Sun–Thu 12:00–17:00, last entry 45 min before closing, closed Sat except holiday weekends; gardens open 2 weeks in mid-April and May–Aug daily 11:00–17:30, Sept Sat–Sun 11:00–17:30, last entry one hour before closing; house and gardens closed Oct–April, except house open Easter weekend and gardens open mid-April; 5 miles west of Salisbury via A36 to Wilton's Minster Street; or bus #60, #60A, or #61 from Salisbury to Wilton; tel. 01722/746-729 or 01722/746-714, www.wiltonhouse.com).

Stourhead

For a serious taste of traditional English landscape, don't miss this 2,650-acre delight. Stourhead, designed by owner Henry Hoare II in the mid-18th century, is a wonderland of rolling hills, meandering paths, placid lakes, and colorful trees, punctuated by classically inspired bridges and monuments. It's what every other English estate aspires to be—like nature, but better (house and garden-£11.60, or £7 to see just one; house open mid-March–Oct Fri–Tue 11:00–17:00, closed Wed–Thu; garden open year-round daily 9:00–18:00, 28 miles west of Salisbury off B3092 in town of Stourton, 3 miles northwest of Mere, tel. 01747/841-152, www.nationaltrust.org.uk).

Drivers or ambitious walkers can visit nearby **King Alfred's Tower** and climb its 205 steps for glorious views of the estate and surrounding countryside (£2.50 to climb tower; April–Aug Fri–Tue 11:00–17:00, closed Wed–Thu; Sept–Oct Sat–Sun only 11:00–17:00; closed Nov–March; 2.5 miles northwest of Stourhead, off Tower Road).

Dorset Countryside Joyride

The region of Dorset, just southwest of Salisbury, is full of rolling fields, winding country lanes, quaint cottages, and villages stuffed with tea shops. Anywhere you go in the area will take you someplace charming, so consider this tour only a suggestion and feel free to get pleasantly lost in the English countryside. You'll be taking some less-traveled roads, so bring along a good map.

Starting in Salisbury, take A354 through Blandford Forum to Winterborne Whitechurch. From here, follow signs and small back roads to the village of Bere Regis, where you'll find some lovely 15th-century buildings, including one with angels carved on the roof. Follow A35 and B3075 to Wareham, where T. E. Lawrence (a.k.a. Lawrence of Arabia) lived; he's buried in nearby Moreton. Continue south on A351 to the dramatic and romantic **Corfe Castle.** This was a favorite residence for medieval kings until it was destroyed by a massive gunpowder blast during a 17th-century siege (£5.50, daily April–Sept 10:00–18:00, March and Oct 10:00–17:00, Nov–Feb 10:00–16:00, tel. 01929/481-294, www.nationaltrust.org.uk). Retrace A351 to Wareham, and then take A352 to Dorchester.

Just northeast of Dorchester on A35, near the village of Stinsford, novelist Thomas Hardy was born in 1840; you'll find his family's cottage nearby in Higher Bockhampton (£3.50, mid-March–Oct Sun–Thu 11:00–17:00, closed Fri–Sat and Nov–mid-March, tel. 01305/262-366, www.nationaltrust.org.uk). While Hardy's heart is buried in Stinsford with his first wife, Emma, the rest of him is in Westminster Abbey's Poets' Corner. Take A35 back to Dorchester. Just west of Dorchester, stay on A35 until it connects to A37; then follow A352 north toward Sherborne.

About eight miles north of Dorchester, on the way to Sherborne, you'll find the little town of **Cerne Abbas,** named for an abbey in the center of town. There are only two streets to

Dorset Joyride

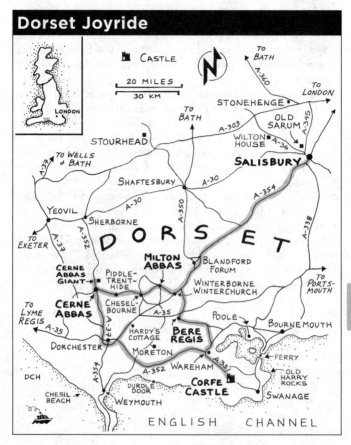

wander down, so take this opportunity to recharge with a cup of tea and a scone. Abbots Tea Room has a nice cream tea (pot of tea, scone, jam, and clotted cream). They also run a B&B (Db-£70–80, less for 2-night stays, cash only, 7 Long St., tel. 01300/341-349, abbots@3Lambs.com). Up the street, you can visit the abbey and its well, reputed to have healing powers.

Just outside of town, a large chalk figure, the **Cerne Abbas Giant,** is carved into the green hillside. Chalk figures such as this one can be found in many parts of the region. Because the soil is only a few inches deep, the overlying grass and dirt can easily be removed to expose the bright white chalk bedrock beneath, creating the outlines. While nobody is sure exactly how old the figures are, or what their original purpose was, they are faithfully maintained by the locals, who mow and clear the fields at least once a year. This particular figure, possibly a fertility god, looks friendly...maybe a little too friendly. Locals claim that if a woman who's having trouble getting pregnant sleeps on the giant for one night, she will soon be able to conceive a child. (A couple of years ago, controversy surrounded this giant, as a 180-foot-tall, donut-hoisting Homer Simpson was painted onto the adjacent hillside. No kidding.)

Leaving Cerne Abbas on country roads toward Piddletrenthide (on the aptly named River Piddle), continue through Cheselbourne to **Milton Abbas.** (This area, by the way, has some of the best town names in the country, such as Droop, Plush, Pleck, and Folly.) The village of Milton Abbas looks overly perfect. In the 18th century, a wealthy man bought up the town's large abbey and estate. His new place was great...except for the neighbors, a bunch of vulgar villagers with houses that cluttered his view from the garden. So, he had the town demolished and rebuilt a mile away. What you see now is probably the first planned community, with identical houses, a pub, and a church. The estate is now a "public school," which is what the English call an expensive private school. From Milton Abbas, signs lead you back to Winterborne Whitechurch, and the A354 to Salisbury.

OXFORD

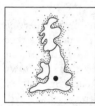

England is home to two world-renowned universities: Oxford and Cambridge. While I prefer the town of Cambridge for its charm (see page 183), Oxford's historic university makes it a heavyweight sight. For centuries, Oxford's stellar graduates have influenced Western civilization—ever since the first homework was assigned here in 1167.

But that doesn't mean that Oxford is stodgy. Although you may see professors in their traditional black robes, this is a fun, young college town, filled with lots of shopping, cheap eats around every corner, and rowdy, rollicking pubs.

While a typical American-style university has one campus, Oxford (like Cambridge) has colleges scattered throughout town. But the sightseers' Oxford is walkable and compact. Many of the streets in the center are pedestrian-only during the day. Stick to the center, and you'll get a feel for workaday Oxford, where knowledge is the town business—and procrastinating over a pint is the students' main hobby. (Local shops sell T-shirts that say, "Don't ask me about my thesis.")

Sample the spirit of Oxford. Step off the busy, urban-feeling High Street into the hushed sanctuary of a grassy college quad. See the dining hall where Harry Potter eats his meals (in the movies, anyway), or the pub where J. R. R. Tolkien first spoke about the Hobbits.

If you haven't yet tried pub grub—or sampled a local British ale—make a point to do so in Oxford, just as its local famous writers did. In Oxford, a town known for traditions, the pubs are where the action is.

To round out your visit, don't miss the excellent Blenheim

Palace—England's best countryside estate, just outside Oxford, and described at the end of this chapter.

Planning Your Time

Oxford is a convenient stop for people visiting the Cotswolds, Blenheim Palace (a five-minute drive away), Stratford-upon-Avon, and Bath. Both Oxford and Cambridge are easy day trips from London...and both are miserable from a budget-accommodations standpoint.

Oxford's colleges are generally open to visitors, but many have set visiting hours or are closed during term times: Michaelmas (Oct–Dec), Hilary (Jan–March), and Trinity (April–June). Most public spaces in the colleges are closed during exams at the end of June.

Orientation to Oxford

(area code: 01865)

Oxford was first built where oxen crossed, or forded, the Cherwell and Isis rivers. (The Isis is another name for the Thames; back then you could row to London from Oxford...in just five days.) The 14th-century Carfax (a.k.a. St. Martin's) Tower marks the town center, at the intersection of Oxford's four main roads: St. Aldate's, Cornmarket Street, High Street, and Queen Street (which leads to the big Westgate Shopping Center and a Marks & Spencer). A pedestrian zone with shops and eateries runs along Broad Street, across Cornmarket (which is essentially an outdoor mall) and parallel to High Street.

Tourist Information

The TI offers walking tours (£7, also ask about Harry Potter and Inklings tours), and the do-it-yourself walking-tour brochure, *Welcome to Oxford* (£1). They also book rooms for a £4 fee, and sell tickets for the City Sightseeing Oxford bus (open Mon–Sat 9:30–17:00, Sun 10:00–16:00, 15–16 Broad Street, tel. 01865/252-200, www.visitoxford.org, tic@oxford.gov.uk). For more on the tours and the bus, see "Tours in Oxford," on the next page.

Arrival in Oxford

From the train station, the city center is a seven-minute walk, a £5 taxi ride, or a quick drive—just follow the signs. Day-trippers can leave their luggage at the recommended Oxford Backpackers Hostel (500 yards from station toward town center, on the right, 9A Hythe Bridge Street, £2/bag, no lockout times). The "travel information desk" in the train station is actually just a sales outlet for City Sightseeing's skippable hop-on, hop-off bus tours. The real TI (described above) is in the city center, several blocks from the Oxford bus station, which is at Gloucester Green.

Drivers day-tripping into Oxford can follow signs to one of the four outlying short-stay parking lots, which are each about a 10-minute walk into town. There's also pay-and-display street parking north of the Ashmolean Museum, on St. Giles Street (carefully monitored, so keep an eye on the time you must return, or you're likely to get ticketed).

Helpful Hints

Bookstore: One of the world's largest bookstores, **Blackwell's,** boasts miles of shelves in its main location (additional satellite shops around town). The huge Norrington Room in the basement holds stacks of books (Sun–Mon 11:00–17:00, Tue 9:30–18:00, Wed–Sat 9:00–18:00, coffee shop upstairs, WC on top floor, 48–51 Broad Street, tel. 01865/792-792, www.blackwell.co.uk). Ask here about literary walking tours (see "Tours in Oxford," next).

Best Views: At the University Church of St. Mary the Virgin, climb the 124 narrow, twisting stairs of the 14th-century bell tower for views of Oxford's many spires and colleges (church free, tower-£3, daily 9:00–17:00, July–Aug until 18:00, tower opens Sun at 11:45, last entry to tower 30 min before closing, coffee shop in vault, High Street, tel. 01865/279-111, www.university-church.ox.ac.uk). For an easier climb, skip up the 99 steps of Carfax Tower (£2.10, daily April–Oct 10:00–17:30, Nov–March 10:00–15:00).

Harry Potter Sights: The look of Hogwarts School was partially based on a few real-life Oxford sights. For details, see page 619, and consider taking a Harry Potter tour (see below).

Tours in Oxford

▲**Walking Tours**—The TI's **city walking tours,** led by Blue Badge guides, explain the history and traditions of the university and take you inside a few of the colleges. Informative and entertaining, they're the best way to experience the city/university mix (£7, Mon–Sat at 11:00 and 14:00, Sun at 14:00, more frequent at busy times, 2 hours, book inside TI, tours depart from sidewalk in front). Some tours include admission to Christ Church College (£7, Fri–Sat at 14:00 only). Also ask about **Harry Potter tours** (£10.50, generally Fri at 15:30, meet at TI) and **literary tours** about C. S. Lewis, J. R. R. Tolkien, and others (£7.50, usually Sat at 15:30, meet at TI).

Blackwell's Walking Tours, led by proper British gentlemen, focus on literary and historic Oxford. Their Inklings tour visits J. R. R. Tolkien's and C. S. Lewis' former haunts. Check

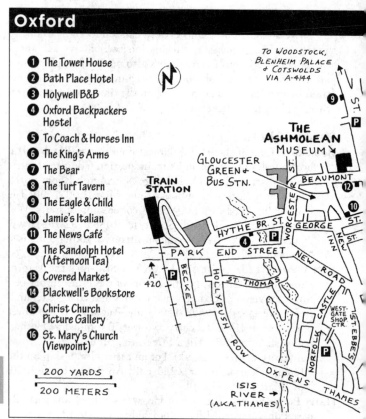

Oxford

1. The Tower House
2. Bath Place Hotel
3. Holywell B&B
4. Oxford Backpackers Hostel
5. To Coach & Horses Inn
6. The King's Arms
7. The Bear
8. The Turf Tavern
9. The Eagle & Child
10. Jamie's Italian
11. The News Café
12. The Randolph Hotel (Afternoon Tea)
13. Covered Market
14. Blackwell's Bookstore
15. Christ Church Picture Gallery
16. St. Mary's Church (Viewpoint)

TO WOODSTOCK, BLENHEIM PALACE & COTSWOLDS VIA A-4144

THE ASHMOLEAN MUSEUM

GLOUCESTER GREEN & BUS STN.

BEAUMONT

TRAIN STATION

HYTHE BR ST.

PARK END STREET

ST. GEORGE

NEW ROAD

A-420

BECKET

ST. THOMAS

HOLLYBUSH ROW

CASTLE

WEST-GATE SHOP. CTR.

NORFOLK

ST EBBES

OXPENS

THAMES

ISIS RIVER → (A.K.A. THAMES)

200 YARDS
200 METERS

Blackwell's bookstore for current tours and times (£7, mid-April–Oct Tue–Fri, 1.5 hours, 48–51 Broad Street, tel. 01865/333-606, http://bookshop.blackwell.co.uk, oxford@blackwell.co.uk).

Hop-on, Hop-off Bus Tours—City Sightseeing Oxford runs bright-red double-decker buses around town, shuttling tourists from one sight to the next. Because Oxford is fairly compact, with colleges that have to be seen on foot, consider this tour only if you've missed a walking tour or have tired feet. If you do go, take a seat up top to see over the college walls (£11.50, can pay driver or buy tickets at TI, 4/hr, daily 9:30–18:30, last bus at 18:00, tel. 01865/790-522, www.citysightseeingoxford.com).

Minivan Tours—Run by Philip Baum, Cotswold Roaming offers a different minivan tour each day with scenic itineraries that include the Cotswolds, Blenheim Palace, Stratford/Warwick Castle, Bath/Castle Combe, and Salisbury/Stonehenge/Avebury (includes admissions for everywhere but Bath and Shakespeare sights). They can also arrange custom tours for small groups on

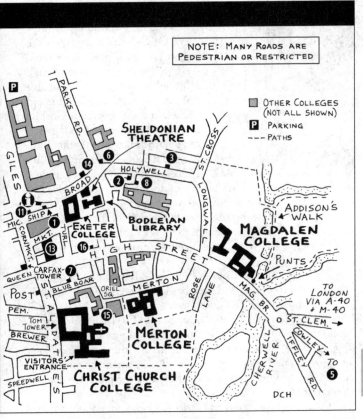

NOTE: MANY ROADS ARE PEDESTRIAN OR RESTRICTED

OTHER COLLEGES (NOT ALL SHOWN)
P PARKING
--- PATHS

request (from £22.50 for half-day tours to Blenheim and the Cotswolds, from £37.50 for full-day tours, tours may not run if there aren't enough people, tel. 01865/308-300, www.cotswold-roaming.co.uk).

Sights in Oxford

The Colleges

Except for the biggies like Christ Church College, most colleges are free and open to visitors in the afternoon. The entrance to each one is easy to spot—just look for a doorway with crests and a flagpole on the top. Each entry has an office with a "custodian" (a live-in caretaker, not a janitor). Inquire there to find out which buildings are open to visitors, and if any plays, music, or lectures are scheduled.

▲**Christ Church College**—This is the alma mater of William Penn (founder of Pennsylvania), John Wesley (influential Methodist

leader), Charles Dodgson (a.k.a. Lewis Carroll), and 13 prime ministers. Of Oxford's colleges, it's the largest and most prestigious (and, some think, most pretentious). Highlights include the impressive staircase, the ornate 800-year-old chapel, and the splendid, Gothic, hammer-beam-roofed hall replicated in the Harry Potter films (£6, Mon–Sat 9:00–17:00, Sun 13:00–17:00, last entry 30 min before closing, tel. 01865/276-492, www.chch.ox.ac.uk). The college is located on St. Aldate's; follow *Vistors' Entrance* signs.

The countryside spreading out to the right of the public entryway is actually part of the college. Simply called The Meadow, this was the setting Lewis Carroll used for croquet scenes in *Alice's Adventures in Wonderland*.

The sleepy **Christ Church Picture Gallery** houses a rotating exhibition of drawings and sketches by Albrecht Dürer, Michelangelo, Leonardo da Vinci, Raphael, and other Old Masters (£3; May–Sept Mon–Sat 10:30–17:00, Sun 14:00–17:00; Oct–April Mon–Sat 10:30–13:00 & 14:00–16:30, Sun 14:00–16:30; tel. 01865/276-172). If you enter from the main visitors' entrance, look for signs to the *Picture Gallery*; if it's April, when the main campus is closed to guests, you can still get to the gallery—enter at Canterbury Gate, off Oriel Square.

Evensong: Every day in Christ Church Cathedral, an excellent choir of students (and fidgety little boys) sings along to the church's pipe organ. This delightful service is open to anyone; linger after the service ends to hear the organist jam (free, daily at 18:00, enter at Tom Tower).

Magdalen College—Sitting on the upper edge of town, this college (pronounced "maudlin") has the largest grounds (big enough to include its own deer park). The best-known path through the college, Addison's Walk, was frequented by C. S. Lewis (£4, daily mid-June–Sept 12:00–18:00, Oct–mid-June 13:00–18:00 or dusk, last entry 30 min before closing; evensong Oct–June Mon and Wed–Sat at 18:00, none July–Sept; High Street next to Magdalen Bridge, tel. 01865/276-000, www.magd.ox.ac.uk).

Merton College—The third-oldest college (at not quite 750 years old), Merton boasts the oldest quad (from the 14th century) and a superb medieval "chained" library, the oldest in Oxford. *The Lord of the Rings* author J. R. R. Tolkien taught here (free, Mon–Fri 14:00–16:00, Sat–Sun 10:00–16:00, Merton Street, tel. 01865/276-310, www.merton.ox.ac.uk). Tours, which are available July–Sept during visiting hours for £2, include the college, chapel, and library (check the Porters' Lodge for tour times).

Exeter College—A smaller college, Exeter is worth a peek to see Sir George Gilbert Scott's jewel-like Neo-Gothic chapel, modeled on Paris' Sainte-Chapelle and featuring *The Adoration of the Magi* tapestry (free, usually open daily 14:00–17:00, Turl Street, tel. 01865/279-600).

Other Sights

The Ashmolean Museum of Art and Archaeology—This eclectic museum reopened in November 2009 after undergoing a £61 million renovation. It now has 39 new galleries, a new education center, conservation studios, and Oxford's first rooftop café. The museum was founded in 1683 by a royal gardener, John Tradescant, who loved to collect interesting items while traveling in search of plants. While it's not as impressive as the big-league museums of London, the new Ashmolean offers lesser-known pieces by Degas, Pissarro, and Van Gogh. It provides this university town a way to see English glass, Chinese porcelain, ancient sculpture, and tapestries without having to ride the train (free, Tue–Sun 10:00–17:00, closed Mon, Beaumont Street, tel. 01865/278-000, www.ashmolean.org).

OXFORD

Sheldonian Theatre—This theater is the first major building project designed by Sir Christopher Wren, who was a physics professor and budding architect at the time. (He later rebuilt St. Paul's Cathedral in London.) The impressive building has an expansive painted ceiling, gold trim, stone columns, pipe organ, and chandeliers (£2, Mon–Sat 10:00–12:30 & 14:00–16:30, until 15:30 in winter, sometimes closed for special events, closed Sun, Broad Street, tel. 01865/277-299).

Bodleian Library—With more than five million books and acres of underground stacks, Bodleian is one of the world's largest and most famous libraries. A copy of every book printed in the UK is sent here. Guided tours, which include the magnificent medieval Duke Humphrey's Library with its "chained" books, leave from the gift shop off the main quad (free to enter, tours-£6; library open Mon–Fri 9:00–17:00, Sat 9:00–16:30, closed Sun; tours

Literary Oxford

Oxford's list of alums is almost laughably impressive. A virtual factory for famous politicians—including a couple dozen prime ministers, Indira Gandhi, and Bill Clinton (who took classes here)—it's also the home of some of the most important scientists of the 20th century. Stephen Hawking (*A Brief History of Time*) went to Oxford, Richard Dawkins (*The Selfish Gene*) teaches at Oxford, and Tim Berners-Lee—inventor of the World Wide Web—got in trouble for hacking into Oxford's computers. But Oxford may be most famous for its literary past.

J. R. R. Tolkien (1892–1973) graduated from the university and was a professor at Oxford, teaching the glories of Anglo-Saxon language and English literature through one of his favorite works, the epic poem *Beowulf*. He spent years in Oxford writing the books he's most famous for: *The Hobbit* and the three books of *The Lord of the Rings* series, beloved by millions of readers.

C. S. Lewis (1898–1963), Tolkien's good friend, was a fellow at Oxford for almost 30 years. Lewis sent generations of children through the back of a wardrobe in his series *The Chronicles of Narnia*. During his time in Oxford, Lewis was also the ringleader of a famous writing society called the Inklings, who met regularly at The Eagle and Child pub (which they called the "bird and baby"—see page 374). Picture these literary geniuses sitting in the pub's familiar confines. Lewis orders another round, while Tolkien tells Frodo's tale—with a pipe probably in hand—for the first time.

The poet **W. H. Auden** (1907–1973) was educated at Oxford, and was a lifelong friend and correspondent of Tolkien's. (He was one of the first critics to publicly praise *The Lord of the Rings*.) Auden may be most familiar to Americans for the line of his poem "Funeral Blues" that was quoted in the film *Four Weddings and a Funeral*: "He was my North, my South, my East and West, / My working week and my Sunday rest, / My noon, my midnight, my talk, my song; / I thought that love would last for ever; I was wrong."

Lewis Carroll (1832–1898), the pen name of Charles Lutwidge

usually Mon–Sat at 10:30, 11:30, 14:00, and 15:00, none on Sun; call to confirm tour times, tel. 01865/277-178).

Punting—Long, flat boats can be rented for punting (pushing with a long pole) along the River Cherwell. Chauffeurs are available, but the do-it-yourself crowd is having more fun, even if they are a little wet (£14/hr, £30 deposit, chauffeured punts-£25/30 min, rowboats and paddle boats available for the less adventurous, cash only, daily March–Oct 9:30–21:00, closed off-season, Magdalen Bridge Boathouse, tel. 01865/202-643, www.oxford punting.co.uk).

Dodgson, was a mathematician who taught at Oxford, where he met young Alice Liddell, the dean's daughter and the real-life inspiration for his most famous book, *Alice's Adventures in Wonderland*. The author lived at Christ Church, and Carroll and Liddell would regularly play croquet—without the Queen of Hearts—in The Meadow.

Aldous Huxley (1894-1963), a prolific novelist and Oxford student, wrote the early science-fiction classic *Brave New World*, about a disturbing, mindless future. His later book, *The Doors of Perception*, was written under the influence of mescaline. (Jim Morrison, another fan of mind-altering experiences, named his band The Doors after the book.)

Literary great **Virginia Woolf** (1882-1941) was banned from using Oxford's library because she was a woman (Oxford didn't begin admitting women until 1920). She later wrote her most important essay, "A Room of One's Own," where she parodied the university she nicknamed "Oxbridge," a combination of Oxford and Cambridge.

Oscar Wilde (1854-1900) did well at Oxford (graduating with the highest grade possible) and went on to become famous for his novels (*The Picture of Dorian Gray*), plays (*The Importance of Being Earnest*), homosexuality (his famous trial sent him to jail), and memorably witty quotes, such as "Men marry because they are tired; women, because they are curious: both are disappointed." Another of his quotes: "I can resist everything except temptation." And another: "We are all in the gutter, but some of us are looking at the stars."

Oxford's other notable literary stars include the poet **Percy Bysshe Shelley, Jonathan Swift** (*Gulliver's Travels*), **T. S. Eliot** (*The Waste Land*), **John le Carré** (*The Spy Who Came in from the Cold*), **Philip Pullman** (*The Golden Compass*, part of his children's book series *His Dark Materials*), **Martin Amis** (*Time's Arrow*), **Helen Fielding** (*Bridget Jones's Diary*), and—maybe most important of all to generations of children's book readers—Theodor Seuss Geisel (a.k.a. **Dr. Seuss**).

Sleeping in Oxford

Sleeping cheaply in Oxford is not easy. The university owns most of the town, so boarding space is at a premium. There are a few high-end hotels in the center, and B&Bs crowd the main roads out of town. Given the easy connections by train to the Cotswolds (Moreton-in-Marsh) and London, I'd make Oxford a day trip, and sleep elsewhere. But if you're spending the night, here are a few reasonable options.

$$$ The Tower House, with tight spaces and low ceilings, has small but sweet rooms, and couldn't be more central. Three of

Sleep Code

(£1 = about $1.60, country code: 44, area code: 01865)
S = Single, **D** = Double/Twin, **T** = Triple, **Q** = Quad, **b** = bathroom,
s = shower only. Unless otherwise noted, credit cards are accepted.

To help you sort easily through these listings, I've divided the rooms into three categories based on the price for a double room with bath:

$$$ Higher Priced—Most rooms £95 or more.
$$ Moderately Priced—Most rooms between £50-95.
$ Lower Priced—Most rooms £50 or less.

the seven rooms share a bathroom with a spacious shower (S-£70, Sb-£90, D-£80, Db-£110, continental breakfast, free Wi-Fi, no parking, request back rooms for quiet in this college town, 15 Ship Street, tel. 01865/246-828, fax 01865/247-508, www.towerhouse oxford.co.uk, reservations@towerhouseoxford.co.uk, managed by kind Ronel).

$$$ Bath Place Hotel has 15 cute, flowery little rooms connected by a maze of impossibly steep and narrow stairways. It's easy to find—just follow the trail of students going to the very popular pub below (Sb-£85–110, Db-£105–140, Tb-£165, Qb-£195, includes buffet breakfast, free Wi-Fi, limited parking-£10/day, 4 Bath Place, tel. 01865/791-812, fax 01865/791-834, www.bathplace .co.uk, info@bathplace.co.uk).

$$ Holywell Bed & Breakfast is hidden away in an ancient row house on quiet Holywell Street, across from New College. Its four twin rooms share two bathrooms (S-£55–60, D-£65–70, cash only, book well in advance, no children under age 16, steep stairs, free Wi-Fi, free parking in adjacent lot, 14 Holywell Street, tel. 01865/721-880, www.holywellbedandbreakfast.com, info@holy wellbedandbreakfast.com, Stuart and Carrie).

$ Oxford Backpackers Hostel, a two-minute walk from the bus and train stations, rents 92 beds in single-sex and mixed dorms. While the ambience is somewhere between grotty and funky, hard-core hostelers appreciate the cheap beds (£16 beds in large dorms, £19 beds in four-person dorms, includes continental breakfast, £2 baggage storage available, pay Internet access, 9A Hythe Bridge Street, tel. 01865/721-761, fax 01865/203-293, www .hostels.co.uk, oxford@hostels.co.uk).

OXFORD

Near Oxford

$$ Coach & Horses Inn, a charming 16th-century inn and pub, is located seven miles southeast of Oxford in Chislehampton, across the street from a bus stop that connects the two towns (Db-£70, free Wi-Fi, tel. 01865/890-255, fax 01865/891-995, www.coachand horsesinn.com, mail@coachandhorsesinn.com).

Eating in Oxford

Pubs

These pubs perfectly conform to what Americans imagine a British pub to be: a rambling series of cozy, well-worn rooms on sloping wooden floors filled with tight clusters of friends enjoying food and ale. The hours listed below are for when food is served—most stay open later to serve drinks.

The King's Arms, across from Blackwell's Bookstore and the Sheldonian Theatre, has an approachable, open atmosphere. They offer good traditional English fare. Have your meal in the pleasant, family-friendly room in the front, or in the terrace seating out back (£7–10 lunches, daily 10:30–24:00, 40 Holywell Street at corner of Parks Road, across from the Sheldonian, tel. 01865/242-369).

The Bear, hidden down a side street and close to the Christ Church Picture Gallery, is one of Oxford's oldest and most charm-

ing pubs. This teensy place proudly sports no right angles (go ahead—check) since 1242. Peruse the framed collections of amputated clothing on the walls and hold on to your tie if you're wearing one. If you're coming for lunch, arrive before 13:00, when they're typically swamped and tables are in short supply (£7–9 meals, food served Mon–Fri 12:00–15:00 & 18:00–20:30, Sat–Sun 12:00–20:30, 6 Alfred Street at corner of Blue Boar Street, tel. 01865/728-164). There are

OXFORD

a few picnic tables out back—leave through the pub's side door to find them, or walk to the left as you're facing the front.

The Turf Tavern—big, boisterous, and tucked into a short pedestrian walkway—is popular for its good food, outdoor beer garden, and warren of cozy rooms nestled against the old city wall (Mon–Sat 11:00–23:00, Sun 12:00–22:30, 4 Bath Place, tel. 01865/243-235). On Holywell Street, listen for the chatter of students enjoying a beer; otherwise, head under the Bridge of Sighs on New College/Queen's Lane.

The Eagle and Child, a long and thin series of rooms, is subdued, smaller, and more intimate than the other pubs listed. A

five-minute walk from the city center, it's more famous for its history and ambience than its food. This was the gathering place of the writers known as the Inklings (see the "Literary Oxford" sidebar, earlier), and a literary vibe still haunts the place. If you're a fan of Middle Earth and Narnia, stop in for a drink under photos of J. R. R. Tolkien and C. S. Lewis (Mon–Sat 11:00–23:00, Sun 12:00–22:00, 49 St. Giles Street, tel. 01865/302-925).

Cafés and Eateries

Jamie's Italian is a new restaurant by British TV's celebrity chef Jamie Oliver. The menu features classic Italian dishes and great prices—main dishes from £10–15 (Mon–Fri 12:00–23:00, Sat 10:00–23:00, Sun 10:00–22:30, 24–26 George Street, tel. 01865/838-383).

The News Café, with a cheerful and bright interior, buzzes with locals, serving hearty main dishes, big salads, and cheaper cream teas than at the large hotels. They serve light food for lunch and dinner, and it's a nice break from the chain eateries on nearby Cornmarket, listed below (£7–10 meals, Sun–Thu 9:00–19:00, Fri–Sat 9:00–22:00, later hours for drinks only, 1 Ship Street, tel. 01865/242-317).

Afternoon Tea: Head to **The Randolph Hotel** for classic English afternoon tea (afternoon tea-£18, traditional cream tea-£11.25, daily 12:00–22:00, Beaumont Street, directly opposite Ashmolean Museum, tel. 0844-879-9132).

Eating Cheap: The **Covered Market,** a farmers-market maze of shops, fruit stands, deli counters, and cafés, has a fine selection for breakfast, lunch, or a picnic (Mon–Sat 9:00–17:30, closed Sun, between Market Street and High Street, near Carfax Tower).

Chain Restaurants on Cornmarket: On Cornmarket, you'll find a slew of chain eateries, including **Pret à Manger** and **West Cornwall Pasty Company.** There's a **Marks & Spencer** nearby on Queen Street, across from Carfax Tower.

Oxford Connections

From Oxford by Train to: London's Paddington Station (2–5/hr, 1–1.5 hrs, may require transfer in Didcot or Reading, cheap £20 "day return" ticket good after 9:30 Mon–Fri or all day Sat–Sun),

Bath (hourly, 1–1.5 hrs, transfer in Didcot), **Moreton-in-Marsh** (hourly, 40 min), **Stratford-upon-Avon** (every 2 hrs, 1.25–2.5 hrs, transfer in Banbury), **Salisbury** (2/hr, 2 hrs, 1–2 transfers), **Portsmouth** (2–4/hr, 2.5–2.75 hrs, 1–2 transfers). Train info: tel. 0845-748-4950, www.nationalrail.co.uk.

By Bus: The Oxford Tube bus runs every 20 minutes to **London**'s Marble Arch and Victoria Coach Station (£13 one-way, £20 round-trip, tel. 01865/772-250, www.oxfordtube.com). The competing Oxford Espress runs every 15 minutes during peak times to the same London stops (otherwise about 2–3/hr; £13 one-way, £20 round-trip, tel. 01865/785-400, www.oxfordbus.co.uk) Both companies depart from the Gloucester Green bus station— just show up and ask which leaves first. An independent bus service called The Airline shuttles students and visitors directly between Oxford and **Heathrow Airport** 24 hours a day (2–3/hr, 1.5 hrs, £20 one-way, £24 round-trip) and to **Gatwick Airport** (hourly, 2–2.5 hrs, £26 one-way, £35 round-trip, tel. 01865/785-400, www .oxfordbus.co.uk). National Express (toll tel. 0871-781-8181, www .nationalexpress.com) runs buses to **Stratford-upon-Avon** (2 direct buses/day, 1 hr). For details on taking a public bus to **Blenheim Palace,** see the next section.

Near Oxford: Blenheim Palace

Just a few minutes' drive from Oxford (and convenient to combine with a drive through the Cotswolds), Blenheim Palace is one of England's best castles—worth ▲▲▲. Too many palaces can send you into a furniture-wax coma. But everyone should see Blenheim.

The Duke of Marlborough's home—the largest in England—is still lived in, which is wonderfully obvious as you prowl through it. Note: Americans who pronounce the place "blen-HEIM" are the butt of jokes. It's "BLEN-em."

Cost, Hours, Information: £17.50, family deals, mid-Feb– Oct daily 10:30–17:30, last tour departs at 16:45, park open but palace closed Nov–mid-Dec Mon–Tue and mid-Dec–mid-Feb, tel. 01993/811-091, recorded info tel. 0870-060-2080, www.blenheim palace.com.

Getting There: Blenheim Palace sits at the edge of the cute cobbled town of Woodstock. The train station nearest the palace (Hanborough, 1.5 miles away) has no taxi or bus service. From Oxford, take a bus to Blenheim (bus #S3 to the palace gate departs from Oxford train station or Oxford's Gloucester Green bus station—a 5-min walk from train station, Mon–Sat 2/hr, less frequent on Sun, 30 min; bus tel. 01865/772-250, www.stagecoachbus.com). If you're coming from the Cotswolds, your easiest train connection is from Moreton-in-Marsh to Oxford, where you can catch the bus to Blenheim.

Background: John Churchill, first duke of Marlborough, beat the French at the Battle of Blenheim in 1704. A thankful Queen Anne built him this nice home, perhaps the finest Baroque building in England (designed by playwright-turned-architect John Vanbrugh). Ten dukes of Marlborough later, it's as impressive as ever. (The current, 11th duke considers the 12th more of an error than an heir, and what to do about him is quite an issue.) The 2,000-acre yard, well designed by Lancelot "Capability" Brown, is as majestic to some as the palace itself. The view just past the outer gate as you enter is a classic.

○ **Self-Guided Tour:** The well-organized palace tour begins with a fine **Churchill exhibit,** centered on the bed in which Sir Winston was born in 1874 (prematurely...begun while his mother was at a Blenheim Palace party). Take your time in the Churchill exhibit. Then catch the 45-minute guided tour (6/hr, included with ticket, last tour at 16:45). When the palace is really busy, they dispense with guided tours and go "free flow," allowing those with an appetite for learning to strike up conversations with docents in each room.

Your ticket also includes the modern, 45-minute, multimedia "visitors' experience"—a tour called **Blenheim Palace: The Untold Story** (6/hr, included with ticket). You're guided through 300 years of history by a maid named Grace Ridley. (If you have limited time to spend at the palace, focus on Churchill instead.)

For a more extensive visit, follow up the general tour with a 30-minute guided walk through the actual **private apartments** of the duke. Tours leave at the top and bottom of each hour (£4.50, generally May–Sept daily 12:00–16:30, tickets are limited, tours don't run if the duke's home, buy from table in library or at Flagstaff info booth outside main gates, enter in corner of courtyard to left of grand palace entry).

Kids enjoy the **pleasure garden** (a tiny train takes you from the palace parking lot to the garden, but if you have a car, it's more efficient simply to drive there). A lush and humid greenhouse flutters with butterflies. A kid zone includes a few second-rate games and the "world's largest symbolic hedge maze." The maze is worth a look if you haven't seen one and could use some exercise.

Churchill fans can visit his **tomb,** just over a mile away in the Bladon town churchyard.

Sleeping near Blenheim Palace

Blenheim nestles up against the two-road town of Woodstock, which offers walkable accommodations and a nice selection of eateries.

$$ Blenheim Guest House, charming and 200 years old, has six rooms in the town center. Literally next door to the palace's green gate, it's a five-minute walk from the palace (Sb-£50, Db-£60–75 depending on size, Wi-Fi, 17 Park Street, tel. 01993/813-814, fax 01993/813-810, www.theblenheim.com, the blenheim@aol.com).

$$ The Townhouse is a refurbished 18th-century stone house with five plush rooms (Sb-£55–70, Db-£75–90, includes breakfast, in town center at 15 High Street, tel. & fax 01993/810-843, www.woodstock-townhouse.com, info@woodstock-townhouse.com).

$$ Wishaw House B&B is grandmotherly and offers two rooms (Sb-£43, D-£56, Tb-£78, 2 Browns Lane, 5-min walk from palace, tel. 01993/811-343, Pat Hillier).

OXFORD

THE COTSWOLDS

The Cotswold Hills, a 25-by-90-mile chunk of Gloucestershire, are dotted with enchanting villages. As with many fairy-tale regions of Europe, the present-day beauty of the Cotswolds was the result of an economic disaster. Wool was a huge industry in medieval England, and Cotswold sheep grew the best wool. A 12th-century saying bragged, "In Europe the best wool is English. In England the best wool is Cotswold." The region prospered. Wool money built fine towns and houses. Local "wool" churches are called "cathedrals" for their scale and wealth. Stained-glass slogans say things like "I thank my God and ever shall, it is the sheep hath paid for all."

With the rise of cotton and the Industrial Revolution, the woolen industry collapsed. Ba-a-a-ad news. The wealthy Cotswold towns fell into a depressed time warp; the homes of impoverished nobility became gracefully dilapidated. Today, visitors enjoy a harmonious blend of man and nature—the most pristine of English countrysides decorated with time-passed villages, rich wool churches, tell-me-a-story stone fences, and "kissing gates" you wouldn't want to experience alone. Appreciated by throngs of 21st-century Romantics, the Cotswolds are enjoying new prosperity.

The north Cotswolds are best. Two of the region's coziest towns, Chipping Campden and Stow-on-the-Wold, are eight and four miles, respectively, from Moreton-in-Marsh, which has the best public transportation connections. Any of these three towns makes a fine home base for your exploration of the thatch-happiest of Cotswold villages and walks.

Planning Your Time

The Cotswolds are an absolute delight by car and, with patience, enjoyable even without a car. On a three-week British trip, I'd spend two nights and a day in the Cotswolds. The Cotswolds' charm has a softening effect on many uptight itineraries. You could enjoy days of walking from a home base here.

Chipping Campden and Stow-on-the-Wold are quaint without being overrun, and both have good accommodations. Stow has a bit more character for an overnight stay, and offers the widest range of choices. The plain town of Moreton is the only one of the three with a train station. With a car, consider really getting away from it all by staying in one of the smaller villages.

If you want to take in some Shakespeare, note that Stow, Chipping Campden, and Moreton are only a 30-minute drive from Stratford, which offers a great evening of world-class entertainment (see Stratford-upon-Avon chapter). And England's greatest countryside palace, Blenheim, is located between Moreton-in-Marsh and Oxford (see Oxford chapter).

One-Day Driver's 100-Mile Cotswold Blitz, Including Blenheim: Use a good map and reshuffle to fit your home base: 9:00–Browse through Chipping Campden, following the self-guided walk; 10:00–Joyride through Snowshill, Stanway, Stanton, the Slaughters, and Bourton-on-the-Water; 13:00–Have lunch at Stow-on-the-Wold, then follow the self-guided walk; 15:00–Drive 30 miles to Blenheim Palace (described in the Oxford chapter) and take the hour-long tour (last tour departs at 16:45); 18:00–Drive home for just the right pub dinner. (If planning on a gourmet countryside pub dinner, reserve in advance by phone.)

Two-Day Plan by Public Transportation: This plan is best for weekdays, when buses run more frequently than on weekends. Make your home base in Moreton-in-Marsh.

Day 1: Take the early bus to Chipping Campden, then bus to Stow (via Moreton). Rent a bike in Stow and explore the countryside, or take a bus to Bourton-on-the-Water and walk to the Slaughters. Have an early dinner in Stow, then return to Moreton at 18:45.

Day 2: Take a day trip to Blenheim Palace via Oxford (train to Oxford, bus to palace—explained in Oxford chapter); or rent a bike and ride to Chastleton House; or take a daylong countryside walk.

Getting Around the Cotswolds

By Bus

The Cotswolds are so well-preserved, in part, because public transportation to and within this area has long been miserable.

To explore the towns, use the bus routes that hop through the region nearly hourly, lacing together main stops and ending at rail stations. In each case, there are about eight buses per day; the entire trip takes about an hour; and on some routes you can get an all-day, unlimited Rover Ticket (£6, individual fares about £2, buy Rover Ticket from driver on participating routes, including #855, #860, and #865). With the help of the TI or the Traveline info line (toll tel. 0871-200-2233),

you can put together a one-way or return trip by public transportation, making for a fine Cotswolds day. Ask the TI for the *Explore the Cotswolds by Public Transport* timetables, which summarize all of the bus routes in the area in separate central, north, and south editions (or download them at www.cotswoldsaonb.org.uk). If you're traveling one-way between two train stations, remember that the Cotswold villages—generally pretty clueless when it comes to the needs of travelers without a car—have no baggage-check services. You'll need to improvise; ask sweetly at the nearest TI or business. Note that bus service is poor on Saturdays and essentially nonexistent on Sundays. For specifics, consult any TI, visit www.traveline.org.uk, or call 0871-200-2233.

While I've based this information on Moreton, you can derive Stow and Chipping Campden bus connections from this same write-up. Here are the bus lines that leave from Moreton:

From Moreton-in-Marsh to Chipping Campden: Buses #21 and #22 run from Moreton-in-Marsh to Chipping Campden to Stratford-upon-Avon. These are the only buses that go all the way through to Chipping Campden. (Bus #H3, which you may see on timetables, connects Stratford and Chipping Campden, but doesn't go all the way to Moreton.)

From Moreton-in-Marsh to Stow-on-the-Wold: Bus #855 goes from Moreton-in-Marsh to Stow-on-the-Wold to Bourton-on-the-Water to Northleach to Cirencester to the Kemble train station. Bus #801 goes from Moreton-in-Marsh to Stow-on-the-Wold to the Slaughters to Bourton-on-the-Water, and ends at Cheltenham.

By Bike

Despite narrow roads and high hedgerows (blocking some views), bikers enjoy the Cotswolds free from the constraints of bus schedules. For each area, TIs have fine route planners that indicate which peaceful, paved lanes are particularly scenic for biking. In summer, it's smart to book your bike a couple of days ahead.

The Cotswolds

TO WORCESTER

A-46

TO M-5

EVESHAM

MICKLETON

TO STRATFORD-UPON-AVON

B-4632

CHIPPING CAMPDEN

BROAD CAMPDEN

TO ILMING-TON

SHIPS-TON

A-34

B-4035

BROADWAY →

A-44

B-4081

STANTON

SNOWS-HILL

BLOCK-LEY

B-4479

MORETON -IN- MARSH

TO TEWKESBURY

STANWAY

A-429

A-44

WINCHE-COMBE

FORD

B-4077

UPPER SWELL

A-424

A-44

B-4632

LOWER SWELL

A-436

TO OXFORD & BLENHEIM PALACE

TO CHELTEN-HAM

B-4068

STOW-ON-THE-WOLD

A-436

UPPER + LOWER SLAUGHTER

BOURTON-ON-THE-WATER

A-429

A-424

TO OXFORD

TO BIBURY, NORTHLEACH & CIRENCESTER

TO BURFORD & OXFORD

5 MILES

5 KM

1 Stanway House
2 Snowshill Lavender
3 Sheepscombe House B&B
4 Hidcote Manor Garden
5 Cotswold Farm Park
6 Chastleton House

—— MAJOR ROAD
— MINOR ROAD
···· COTSWOLD WAY FOOTPATH

LONDON

DCH

THE COTSWOLDS

In **Moreton-in-Marsh,** the nice folks at the Toy Shop rent mountain bikes. You can stop in the shop to rent a bike, or call ahead to pick up or drop off at other times—they're flexible (£15/day with route maps, bike locks, and helmets; shop open Mon and Wed–Fri 9:00–13:00 & 14:00–17:00, Sat 9:00–17:00, closed Sun and Tue, High Street, tel. 01608/650-756).

In **Chipping Campden,** try Cotswold Country Cycles (£15/

day, tandem-£30/day, includes helmets and route maps, delivery for a fee, daily 9:30–dusk, 2 miles north of town at Longlands Farm Cottage, tel. 01386/438-706, mobile 07746-107-728, www .cotswoldcountrycycles.com).

By Foot

Walking guidebooks abound, giving you a world of choices for each of my recommended stops (choose a book with clear maps). Villages are generally no more than three miles apart, and most have pubs that would love to feed and water you. For a list of guided walks, ask at any TI for the free *Cotswold Lion* newspaper. The walks range from 2 to 12 miles, and often involve a stop at a pub or tearoom (April–Sept; *Lion* newspaper also online at www .cotswoldsaonb.org.uk—click on "Publications").

By Car

Distances here are wonderfully short (but only if you invest in the Ordnance Survey map of the Cotswolds, sold locally at TIs and newsstands). Here are distances from Moreton: **Broadway** (10 miles), **Chipping Campden** (8 miles), **Stratford-upon-Avon** (17 miles), **Warwick** (23 miles), **Stow-on-the-Wold** (4 miles), **Blenheim Palace** (20 miles).

Robinson Goss Self Drive, six miles north of Moreton-in-Marsh, offers one-day rentals from £28–47, including everything but gas. They're in the middle of nowhere, but may pick you up for a charge of about £1/mile (Mon–Fri 8:30–17:00, Sat 8:30–12:00, closed Sun, tel. 01608/663-322, www.robgos.co.uk).

Car hiking is great. In this chapter, I cover the postcard-perfect (but discovered) villages. With a car and the local Ordnance Survey map (Tour Map #8, £5), you can easily ramble about and find your own gems. The problem with having a car is that you are less likely to walk. Consider taking a taxi or bus somewhere, so that you can walk back to your car and enjoy the scenery.

By Taxi

Two or three town-to-town taxi trips can make more sense than renting a car. While taking a cab cross-country seems extravagant (about £2.50/mile), the distances are short (Stow to Moreton is 4 miles, Stow to Chipping Campden is 10), and one-way walks are lovely. If you call a cab, confirm that the meter will start only when you are actually picked up. Consider hiring a cab at the hourly "touring rate" (£28–30), rather than the meter rate (e.g., £20 Stow to Chipping Campden). For a few more bucks, you can have a joyride peppered with commentary.

Note that the drivers listed are not typical city taxi services (with many drivers on call), but are mostly individuals—it's smart

Cotswold Appreciation 101

Much history can be read into the names of the area. *Cotswold* could come from the Saxon phrase meaning "hills of sheep's coats." Or it could mean shelter ("cot" like cottage) on the open upland ("wold").

In the Cotswolds, a town's main street (called High Street) needed to be wide to accommodate the sheep and cattle being marched to market (and today, to park tour buses). Some of the most picturesque cottages were once humble row houses of weavers' cottages, usually located along a stream for their waterwheels (good examples in Bibury and Castle Combe). The towns run on slow clocks and yellowed calendars. An entire village might not have a phone booth.

Fields of yellow (rapeseed) and pale blue (linseed) separate pastures dotted with black and white sheep. In just about any B&B, when you open your window in the morning you'll hear sheep baa-ing. The decorative "toadstool" stones dotting front yards throughout the region are medieval staddle stones, which buildings were set upon to keep the rodents out.

Cotswold walls and roofs are made of the local limestone. The limestone roof tiles hang by pegs. To make the weight more bearable, smaller and lighter tiles are higher up. An extremely strict building code keeps towns looking what many locals call "overly quaint."

Towns are small, and everyone seems to know everyone. The area is provincial yet ever-so-polite, and people commonly rescue themselves from a gossipy tangent by saying, "It's all very...mmm...yaaa."

This is walking country. The English love their walks and vigorously defend their age-old right to free passage. Once a year the Rambling Society organizes a "Mass Trespass," when each of the country's 50,000 miles of public footpaths is walked. By assuring that each path is used at least once a year, they stop landlords from putting up fences. Any paths found blocked are unceremoniously unblocked.

Questions to ask locals: Do you think foxhunting should have been banned? Who are the Morris men? What's a kissing gate?

to book ahead if you're arriving in high season, since they can book up in advance on weekends.

To scare up a driver in Moreton, call Richard at **Four Shires** (mobile 07747-802-555) or **Iain's Taxis** (mobile 07789-897-966, £30/hr); in Stow, call Iain (above) or **Tony Knight** (mobile 07887-714-047, £28/hr); and in Chipping Campden, call Iain (above) or **Cotswold Private Hire** (mobile 07980-857-833, £28/hr). Tim Harrison at **Tour the Cotswolds** specializes in tours of the Cotswolds and its gardens (mobile 07779-030-820, www .tourthecotswolds.co.uk; Tim co-runs a recommended B&B in Snowshill—see page 395).

By Tour

Departing from Bath, **Mad Max Minibus Tours** offers a "Cotswold Discovery" full-day tour, and can drop you off in Stow with your luggage if you arrange it in advance (see page 304 of the Bath chapter).

While none of the Cotswold towns offers regularly scheduled walks, many have voluntary warden groups who love to meet visitors and give walks for just a small donation (about £2/person; specific contact information appears below for Chipping Campden).

Chipping Campden

Just touristy enough to be convenient, the north Cotswolds town of Chipping Campden (CAMden) is a ▲▲ sight. This market town, once the home of the richest Cotswold wool merchants, has some incredibly beautiful thatched roofs. Both the great British historian G. M. Trevelyan and I call Chipping Campden's High Street the finest in England.

Orientation to Chipping Campden

(area code: 01386)

Walk the full length of High Street; its width is characteristic of market towns. Go around the block on both ends. On one end, you'll find impressively thatched homes (out Sheep Street, past the public WC and ugly gas station, and right on Westington Street). Walking north on High Street, you'll pass the Market Hall, the wavy roof of the first great wool mansion, a fine and free memorial garden, and, finally, the town's famous 15th-century Perpendicular Gothic "wool" church. (This route is the same as the self-guided town walk described below.)

Tourist Information

Chipping Campden's TI is tucked away in the old police station on High Street. Get the £1 town guide, which includes a map (April–Oct daily 9:30–17:00; Nov–March Mon–Thu 10:00–13:00, Fri–Sun 10:00–16:00; tel. 01386/841-206, www.chippingcampden online.org).

Helpful Hints:

Internet Access: Try the occasionally open **library** (High Street, tel. 01386/840-692, www.gloucestershire.gov.uk/libraries) or **Butty's at The Old Bakehouse**, a casual eatery and Internet café (reasonably priced sandwiches and snacks, free Wi-Fi, pay Internet access-£1.50/15 min, £2.50/30 min, £4/hour, Mon–Sat 7:30–14:30, closed Sun, adjacent to the recommended Old Bakehouse B&B on Lower High Street, tel. 01386/840-401).

Bike Rental: Call **Cotswold Country Cycles**; see "Getting Around the Cotswolds—By Bike" (page 380).

Taxi: Try **Cotswold Private Hire** or **Tour the Cotswolds** (see "Getting Around the Cotswolds—By Taxi," page 382).

Parking: Find a spot anywhere along High Street and park for free with no time limit. There's also a pay-and-display lot (90-min maximum) on High Street (across from TI).

Tours: The local members of the **Cotswold Voluntary Wardens** would be happy to show you around town for a small donation to their conservation society (£2/person, 1-hour walk, walks July–Sept Wed at 14:30, meet at Market Hall). Tour guide and coordinator Ann Colcomb can help arrange for a walk on other days as well (tel. 01386/832-131, www.cotswoldsaonb .com).

Self-Guided Walk

Welcome to Chipping Campden

This 500-yard walk through "Campden" (as locals call their town) takes you from the TI to the church in about 30 minutes.

If it's open, begin at the **Magistrate's Court** (can be closed for meetings, events, and even weddings). This meeting room is in the old police station, located above the TI (free, same hours as TI, ask at TI to go up). Under the open-beamed courtroom, you'll find a humble little exhibit on the town's history.

Campden's most famous monument, the **Market Hall,** stands in front of the TI, marking the town center. It was built in 1627 by the 17th-century Lord of the Manor, Sir Baptist Hicks. (Look for the Hicks family coat of arms in the building's facade.) Back then, it was an elegant—even over-the-top—shopping hall for the townsfolk who'd come here to buy their produce. In the 1940s, it

was almost sold to an American, but the townspeople heroically raised money to buy it first, then gave it to the National Trust for its preservation.

The timbers inside are true to the original. Study the classic Cotswold stone roof, still held together with wooden pegs nailed in from underneath. (Tiles were cut and sold with peg holes, and stacked like waterproof scales.) Buildings all over the region still use these stone shingles. Today, the hall hosts local fairs.

Chipping Campden's **High Street** has changed little architecturally since 1840. (The town's street plan survives from the 12th century.) Notice the harmony of the long rows of buildings. While the street comprises different styles through the centuries, everything you see was made of the same Cotswold stone—the only stone allowed today.

To be level, High Street arcs with the contour of the hillside. Because it's so wide, you know this was a market town. In past centuries, livestock and packhorses laden with piles of freshly shorn fleece would fill the streets. Campden was a sales and distribution center for the wool industry, and merchants from as far as Italy would come here for the prized raw wool.

High Street has no house numbers—people know the houses by their names. In the distance, you can see the town church (where this walk ends).

• *Hike up High Street to just before the first intersection.*

In 1367, William Grevel built what's considered Campden's first stone house: **Grevel House** (on the left). Sheep tycoons had big homes. Imagine back then, when this fine building was surrounded by humble wattle-and-daub huts. It had newfangled chimneys, rather than a crude hole in the roof. (No more rain inside!) Originally a "hall house" with just one big, tall room, it got its upper floor in the 16th century. The finely carved central bay window is a good early example of the Perpendicular Gothic style. The gargoyles scared away bad spirits—and served as rain spouts. The boot scrapers outside each door were fixtures in that muddy age—especially in market towns, where the streets were filled with animal dung.

Chipping Campden

TO HIDCOTE MANOR GARDEN

TO BROADWAY

B-4035

B-4081

TO STRATFORD-UPON-AVON

KINGCOMBE LANE

COTSWOLD WAY FOOTPATH

BACK ENDS

ASTON RD

11

13 **19** **17** **2** **14** **3** **4** **6**

PARK ROAD

HIGH STREET

P

15

16

9 **10** CALF LANE CHURCH ROAD

STATION ROAD

7

TO SNOWSHILL VIA B-4081

SHEEP ST.

WC

12 **20** **18**

5

i **1**

8

WESTINGTON

CATBROOK

GEORGE LANE

NOT TO SCALE

P PARKING

COTSWOLD WAY FOOTPATH

TO MORETON & STOW VIA A-44

Sights

1 Magistrate's Court (above TI)

2 Market Hall

3 Grevel House

4 Ernest Wilson Memorial Garden

5 Baptist Hicks Land & Ruined Mansion

6 Almshouses

7 St. James Church

8 Thatched Houses

Hotels and Restaurants

9 Noel Arms Hotel

10 The Lygon Arms Hotel & Pub

11 Sandalwood House B&B

12 Cornerways B&B

13 The Old Bakehouse & Butty's (Internet Café)

14 Dragon House B&B

15 Eight Bells Rest. & Pub

16 The Volunteer Inn & Maharaja Restaurant

17 Michael's Restaurant

18 Badgers Hall & Bantam Tea Rooms

19 Le Petit Croissant

20 Co-op Grocery

THE COTSWOLDS

• *Continue up High Street for about 100 yards. Go past Church Street (which we'll walk up later). Across the street, you'll find a small Gothic arch leading into a garden.*

The small and secluded **Ernest Wilson Memorial Garden,** once the church's vegetable patch, is a botanist's delight today. It's filled with well-labeled plants that the Victorian botanist Ernest Wilson brought back to England from his extensive travels in Asia. There's a complete history of the garden on the board to the left of the entry (free, open daily until dusk).

• *Backtrack to Church Street. Turn left, walk past the Eight Bells Inn, and head across the street.*

Sprawling adjacent to the town church, the area known as **Baptist Hicks Land** holds Hicks' huge estate and manor house. This influential Lord of the Manor was from "a family of substance," who were merchants of silk and fine clothing as well as moneylenders. Beyond the ornate gate, only a few outbuildings and the charred corner of his mansion survive. The mansion was burned by Royalists in 1645 during the Civil War—notice how Cotswold stone turns red when burned. Hicks housed the poor, making a show of his generosity, adding a long row of almshouses (with his family coat of arms) for neighbors to see as they walked to church. These almshouses (lining Church Street on the left) house pensioners today, as they have since the 17th century.

• *Walk along the wall that lines the Hicks estate to the church, where a scenic, tree-lined lane leads to the front door. On the way, notice the 12 lime trees, one for each of the apostles, that were planted in about 1760 (sorry, no limes).*

One of the finest churches in the Cotswolds, **St. James Church** graces one of its leading towns. Both the town and the church were built by wool wealth. The church is Perpendicular Gothic, with lots of light and strong verticality. Before you leave, notice the fine vestments and altar hangings behind protective blue curtains (near the back of the church). Tombstones pave the floor—memorializing great wool merchants through the ages.

At the altar is a brass relief of William Grevel, the first owner of the Grevel House (see above), and his wife. But it is Sir Baptist Hicks who dominates the church. His huge, canopied tomb is the ornate final resting place for Hicks and his wife, Elizabeth. Study their faces, framed by fancy lace ruffs (trendy in the 1620s). Adjacent—as if in a closet—is a statue of their daughter, Lady Juliana, and her husband, Lutheran Yokels. Juliana commissioned the statue in 1642, when her husband died, but had it closed until *she* died in 1680. Then, the doors were opened, revealing these two people living happily ever after—at least in marble. The hinges were likely used only once.

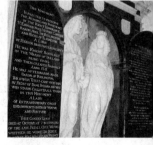

Sleeping in Chipping Campden

In Chipping Campden—as in any town in the Cotswolds—B&Bs offer a better value than hotels. Rooms are generally tight on Saturdays (when many charge a bit more and are reluctant to rent to one-nighters) and in September, which is considered a peak month. Parking is never a problem. Always ask for a discount if staying longer than one or two nights.

$$$ Noel Arms Hotel, the characteristic old hotel on the main square, has welcomed guests for 600 years. Its lobby is decorated with ancient weaponry, and comes with a whiff of the medieval ages. Its 26 rooms are well-furnished with antiques (Sb-£95–115, standard Db-£130, bigger Db-£160, fancier four-poster Db-£180–200, midweek deals, some ground-floor doubles, includes breakfast, attached restaurant/bar, High Street, tel. 01386/840-317, fax 01386/841-136, www.noelarmshotel.com, reception@noelarmshotel.com).

$$ The Lygon Arms Hotel, attached to the popular pub of the same name, has small public areas and 10 cheery, open-beamed rooms (one small older Db-£70–80, huge "superior" Db-£95–120, lovely courtyard Db-£130–160, lower prices are for midweek or multinight stays, family deals, free Wi-Fi, High Street, go through archway and look for hotel reception on the left, tel. 01386/840-318, www.lygonarms.co.uk, sandra@lygonarms.co.uk, Sandra Davenport).

$$ Sandalwood House B&B is a big, comfy home with a pink flowery lounge and a sprawling back garden. Just a five-minute walk from the center of town, it's in a quiet, woodsy, pastoral setting. Its two cheery, pastel rooms are bright and spacious (D/Db-£70–75, T-£90, cheaper if you order a light breakfast instead of full, self-catering apartment sleeps four-£400–500/week, cash only, no kids under age 10, free Wi-Fi, off-street parking, friendly Bobby the cat, tel. & fax 01386/840-091—preferred method of booking, Diana Bendall). To get to Sandalwood House, go west on High Street, and at the church and the Volunteer Inn, turn right and then right again; look for a sign in the hedge on the left, and head up the long driveway.

$$ Cornerways B&B is a fresh, bright, and comfy modern home (not "oldie worldie") a block off High Street. It's run by the delightful Carole Proctor, who can "look out the window and see the church where we were married." The huge, light, airy loft rooms are great for families (Db-£70, Tb-£90, Qb-£110, 2-night minimum, £5 off for 3 or more nights, children's discount, cash only, free Wi-Fi, off-street parking, George Lane, just walk through the arch beside Noel Arms Hotel, tel. 01386/841-307, www.cornerways.info, carole@cornerways.info).

$$ The Old Bakehouse rents five small but pleasant rooms in a 600-year-old home with a plush fireplace lounge. Hardworking Sarah lives just up the road—phone ahead with an arrival time, or call her mobile phone if she's not there when you arrive (Sb-£45, Db-£70, family deals, £5 off for 2 or more nights, cash only, free

---

Sleep Code

(£1 = about $1.60, country code: 44, area code: 01386)
S = Single, **D** = Double/Twin, **T** = Triple, **Q** = Quad, **b** = bathroom,
s = shower only. Unless noted otherwise, you can assume
credit cards are accepted.

To help you sort easily through these listings, I've divided
the rooms into three categories based on the price for a
standard double room with bath:

$$$ Higher Priced—Most rooms £90 or more.
 $$ Moderately Priced—Most rooms between £65-90.
  $ Lower Priced—Most rooms £65 or less.

Wi-Fi, fun attic room that sleeps up to 5 has beams running
through it, Lower High Street, tel. & fax 01386/840-979, mobile
07702-359-530, www.chippingcampden-cotswolds.co.uk, oldbake
house@chippingcampden-cotswolds.co.uk). In addition to the
B&B, Sarah runs **Butty's at the Old Bakehouse,** a casual eatery
and Internet café (see "Helpful Hints," earlier).

$ Dragon House B&B rents two tidy rooms—with medieval
beams and a shared lounge—right on the center of High Street.
They have laundry machines and a sumptuous, stay-awhile garden (Db-£65, £5 off for 3 or more nights, cash only, off-street
parking available, near Market Hall, tel. & fax 01386/840-734,
www.dragonhouse-chipping-campden.com, info@dragonhouse
-chipping-campden.co.uk, Valerie and Graeme the potter). They
also have a cottage that sleeps up to six (Sat–Sat only, £250–750/
week depending on month).

Eating in Chipping Campden

This town—so filled with wealthy residents and tourists—comes
with many choices. Here are some local favorites:

Eight Bells is a charming 14th-century inn on Leysbourne
with a classy and woody restaurant and a more colorful pub (£15–
20 dinners, daily 12:00–14:00 & 18:30–21:00, reservations recommended, tel. 01386/840-371).

The Volunteer Inn serves Indian dishes in their **Maharaja**
restaurant (£6–17 meals, daily 17:00–23:00, grassy courtyard out
back, Lower High Street, tel. 01386/849-281). **The Lygon Arms**
pub also has good food (£8–15 meals, daily).

Michael's, a fun Mediterranean restaurant on High Street,
serves hearty portions and breaks plates at closing every Saturday
night (Tue–Sun 10:30–14:30 & 19:00–22:00, closed Sun nights
and Mon, tel. 01386/840-826).

Picnic: The **Co-op** grocery store is the town's small "super-market" (Mon–Sat 7:00–22:00, Sun 7:00–20:00, across from the market and next to TI on High Street). Munch lunch across the street, on the benches on the little green.

Tearooms

To visit a cute tearoom, try one of these places, located in the town center.

Badgers Hall Tea Room is great for a wide selection of homemade cakes, crumbles, and scones. Along with light lunches, they serve an afternoon tea—a tall and ritualistic tray of dainty sandwiches, pastries, and scones with tea—for half the London price (£25 for 2 people, daily 10:00–16:30; also rents three rooms—Db-£98–110, 2-night minimum, no kids under age 10, Wi-Fi, High Street, tel. 01386/840-839, www.badgershall.com, Karen).

Bantam Tea Rooms, near the Market Hall, is also a good value (Mon–Sat 10:00–17:00, Sun 10:30–17:00, High Street, tel. 01386/840-386).

Le Petit Croissant, a cheery little French deli with a tearoom in the back, serves pastries, quiche, cheese, and wine (Mon–Fri 9:00–17:00, Sat 8:30–17:00, closed Sun, Lower High Street, tel. 01386/841-861).

Near Chipping Campden

Located to the west of Chipping Campden, these are my nominations for the cutest Cotswold villages. Like marshmallows in hot chocolate, Stanway, Stanton, and Snowshill nestle side by side, awaiting your arrival. (Note the Stanway House's limited hours when planning your visit.) Other easy-to-access sights to the west and north of Chipping Campden are also included below.

▲▲Stanway House

The Earl of Wemyss (pronounced "Weemz"), whose family tree charts relatives back to 1202, opens his melancholy home and grounds to visitors just two days a week in the summer. Walking through his house offers a unique glimpse into the lifestyles of England's eccentric and fading nobility.

Cost and Hours: £6, June–Aug Tue and Thu only

THE COTSWOLDS

14:00–17:00, tel. 01386/584-469, www.stanwayfountain.co.uk. His lordship himself narrated the audioguide to his home (£2).

Getting There: By car, leave B4077 at a statue of (the Christian) George slaying the dragon (of pagan superstition); you'll round the corner and see the manor's fine 17th-century Jacobean gatehouse. There's no real public transportation to Stanway.

◐ Self-Guided Tour: Start with the grounds, then head into the house itself.

The Earl recently restored "the tallest fountain in Britain" on the grounds—300 feet tall, gravity-powered, and quite impressive

(fountain spurts for 30 min at 14:45 and 16:00 on opening days).

The bitchin' Tithe Barn (near where you enter the grounds) dates to the 14th century, and predates the manor. It was originally where monks—in the days before money—would accept one-tenth of whatever the peasants produced. Peek inside: This is a great hall for village hoe-downs. While the Tithe Barn is no longer used to greet motley peasants and collect their feudal "rents," the lord still gets rent from his vast landholdings, and hosts community fêtes in his barn.

Stepping into the obviously very lived-in palace, you're free to wander around pretty much as you like, but keep in mind that a family does live here. His lordship is often roaming about as well. The place feels like a time warp. Ask a staff member to demonstrate the spinning rent-collection table. In the great hall, marvel at the one-piece oak shuffleboard table and the 1780 Chippendale exercise chair (half an hour of bouncing on this was considered good for the liver).

The manor dogs have their own cutely painted "family tree," but the Earl admits that his last dog, C. J., was "all character and no breeding." Poke into the office. You can psychoanalyze the lord by the books that fill his library, the videos stacked in front of his bed (with the mink bedspread), and whatever's next to his toilet.

The place has a story to tell. And so do the docents stationed in each room—modern-day peasants who, even without family trees, probably have relatives going back just as far in this village. Really. Talk to these people. Probe. Learn what you can about this side of England.

From Stanway to Stanton: These towns are separated by a row of oak trees and grazing land, with parallel waves echoing the furrows plowed by medieval farmers. Centuries ago, farmers were allotted long strips of land called "furlongs." The idea was to dole out good and bad land equitably. (One square furlong equals an acre.) Over centuries of plowing these, furrows were formed. Let someone else drive, so you can hang out the window under a canopy of oaks, passing stone walls and sheep. Leaving Stanway on the road to Stanton, the first building you'll see (on the left, just outside Stanway) is a thatched cricket pavilion overlooking the village cricket green. Dating only from 1930, it's raised up (as medieval buildings were) on rodent-resistant staddle stones. Stanton's just ahead; follow the signs.

▲Stanton

Pristine Cotswold charm cheers you as you head up the main street of the village of Stanton. Stanton's **Church of St. Michael** betrays a pagan past. It's safe to assume any church dedicated to St. Michael (the archangel who fought the devil) sits upon a sacred pagan site. Stanton is actually at the intersection of two ley lines (geographic lines along which many prehistoric sights are found). You'll see St. Michael's well-worn figure (with a sundial) above the door as you enter. Inside, above the capitals in the nave, find the pagan symbols for the sun and the moon. While the church probably dates back to the ninth century, today's building is mostly from the 15th century, with 13th-century transepts. On the north transept, medieval frescoes show faintly through the 17th-century whitewash. (Once upon a time, medieval frescoes were considered too "papist.") Imagine the church interior colorfully decorated throughout. Original medieval glass is behind the altar. The list of rectors (left side wall) goes back to 1269. Finger the grooves in the back pews, worn away by sheepdog leashes. (A man's sheepdog accompanied him everywhere.)

Horse Rides and Sleeping near Stanton: Anyone can enjoy the Cotswolds from the saddle. Jill Carenza's **Cotswolds Riding Centre,** set just outside Stanton village, is in the most scenic corner of the region. The facility has 50 horses, and takes rank beginners on an hour-long scenic "hack" through the village and into the high country (£27/person for a group hack, £37/person for a semi-private hack, £47 for a private one-person hack; lessons, longer rides, rides for experts, and pub tours available; well-signposted in Stanton, tel. 01386/584-250, www.cotswoldsriding.co.uk).

Jill rents five rooms at her **$$ Vine B&B,** but it takes a backseat to the horses. There's no greeting or check-in, and guests wander around wondering which room is theirs. Still, it's convenient if you want to ride all day (Ds/Db-£69, most rooms with four-poster beds, some stairs, tel. 01386/584-250, fax 01386/584-888, info @cotswoldsriding.co.uk).

Snowshill

Another nearly edible little bundle of cuteness, Snowshill (SNOWS-hill) has a photogenic triangular square with a characteristic pub at its base.

▲**Snowshill Manor**—Dark and mysterious, this old palace is filled with the lifetime collection of Charles Paget Wade. It's one

big, musty celebration of craftsmanship, from finely carved spinning wheels to frightening samurai armor to tiny elaborate figurines carved by prisoners from the bones of meat served at dinner. Taking seriously his family motto, "Let Nothing Perish," Wade dedicated his life and fortune to preserving things finely crafted. The house (whose management made me promise not to promote it as an eccentric collector's pile of curiosities) really shows off Mr. Wade's ability to recognize and acquire fine examples of craftsmanship. It's all very...mmm...yaaa.

This popular sight allows in only 22 people every 10 minutes, and entry times are doled out at the ticket desk (no reservations taken). It can be up to an hour's wait—even more on busy days, especially weekends. A good strategy is to arrive close to the opening time (12:00), and if there's a wait, enjoy the surrounding gardens (it's a 15-min walk up to the manor itself).

Cost and Hours: £8.50, manor house open mid-March–Oct Wed–Sun 12:00–17:00, last entry 50 min before closing, closed Mon–Tue and Nov–March, restaurant, tel. 01386/852-410, www.nationaltrust.org.uk/snowshillmanor.

Getting There: The manor overlooks the town square, but there's no direct access from the square. Park at the shop and follow the walkway through the garden to get to the house. A golf cart–type shuttle to the house is available for those who need assistance.

Snowshill Lavender—In 2000, farmer Charlie Byrd realized

that tourists love lavender. He planted his farm with 250,000 plants, and now visitors come to wander among his 53 acres, which burst with gorgeous lavender blossoms from mid-June through late August. His fragrant fantasy peaks late each July. Farmer Byrd pro-

duces lavender oil (an herbal product valued since ancient times for its healing, calming, and fragrant qualities) and sells it in a delightful shop, along with many other lavender-themed items. Lavender—so famous in France's Provence—is not indigenous to this region, but it fits the climate and soil just fine. A free flier in the shop explains the variations of flowers blooming.

Cost, Hours, Location: £2.50, daily late May–late Aug 10:00–17:00, tel. 01386/854-821, www.snowshill-lavender.co.uk, info@snowshill-lavender.co.uk. It's a half-mile out of Snowshill on Chipping Campden Road (easy parking).

Sleeping near Snowshill: The pretty, one-pub village of Snowshill holds a gem of a B&B. **$$$ Sheepscombe House B&B** is a clean and pristine home on a working sheep farm. It's immersed in the best of Cotswold scenery, with plenty of sheep in the nearby fields. Jacki and Tim Harrison rent three modern, spacious, and thoughtfully appointed rooms (Db-£90–100, Tb-£130–150, folding cots available, free Wi-Fi, just a third of a mile south of Snowshill—look for signs, tel. 01386/853-769, www.broadway-cotswolds.co.uk/sheepscombe.html, reservations @snowshill-broadway.co.uk). Tim, who's happy to give you a local's perspective on this area, also runs Tour the Cotswolds car service (see page 384).

More Sights near Chipping Campden

▲**Hidcote Manor Garden**—If you like gardens, the grounds around this manor house (which has only a few rooms open to the public) are worth a look. Located northeast of Chipping Campden, Hidcote is where garden designers pioneered the notion of creating a series of outdoor "rooms," each with a unique theme (e.g., maple room, red room, and so on) and separated by a yew-tree hedge. Follow your nose through a clever series of small gardens that lead delightfully from one to the next. Among the best in England, Hidcote Gardens are at their fragrant peak from May through July (£9; July–Aug daily 10:00–18:00; mid-March–June and Sept Sat–Wed 10:00–18:00, closed Thu–Fri; Oct Sat–Wed 10:00–17:00, closed Thu–Fri; last entry one hour before closing; closed Nov–mid-March; tearoom, 4 miles northeast of Chipping Campden on B4035, tel. 01386/438-333, www.nationaltrust.org.uk/hidcote).

▲**Cotswold Farm Park**—Here's a delight for young and old alike. This park is the private venture of the Henson family, who are passionate about preserving rare and endangered breeds of local animals. While it feels like a kids' zone (with all the family-friendly facilities you can imagine), it's actually a fascinating chance for anyone to get up close and (very) personal with piles of mostly cute animals, including the sheep that made this region

THE COTSWOLDS

famous—the big and woolly Cotswold Lion. A busy schedule of demonstrations gives you a look at local farm life. Take full advantage of the excellent (and included) audioguide, narrated by founder Joe Henson and filled with his passion for the farm's mission. Buy a bag of seed (50p) upon arrival, or have your map eaten by munchy goats as I did. Check the events board as you enter for times for the milking, shearing, or well-done "sheep show." Tykes love the little

tractor rides, maze, and zip line, but the "touch barn" is where it's at for little kids (£6.75, kids-£5.50, daily mid-March–early Sept 10:30–17:00, last entry 30 min before closing, closed off-season, good £2 guidebook, decent cafeteria, tel. 01451/850-307, www.cotswoldfarmpark.co.uk, well-signposted 15 minutes from Stow just off the Tewkesbury road—B4077).

Broadway—This postcard-pretty town, a couple of miles west of Chipping Campden, is filled with inviting shops and fancy teahouses. Because most big bus tours stop here, I give Broadway a miss. But with a new road that allows traffic to skirt the town, Broadway has gotten cuter than ever. Broadway has good bus connections with Chipping Campden (bus #21, tel. 0871-200-2233—calls are 10p/min, www.traveline.org.uk).

Stow-on-the-Wold

Located 10 miles south of Chipping Campden, Stow-on-the-Wold—with a name that means "meeting place on the uplands"—is the highest point of the Cotswolds. Despite its crowds, it retains its charm, and it merits ▲▲. Most of the tourists are day-trippers, so even summer nights are peaceful. Stow has no real sights other than the town itself, some good pubs, antiques stores, and cute

shops draped seductively around a big town square. Visit the church, with its evocative old door guarded by ancient yew trees and the tombs of wool tycoons. A visit to Stow is not complete until you've locked your partner in the stocks on the green.

Orientation to Stow-on-the-Wold

(area code: 01451)

Tourist Information

At the TI on the main square, get the handy little 50p walking-tour brochure called *Town Trail* and the free *Cotswold Events* guide (TI may move in late 2009 and hours may change; likely open March–Oct Mon and Wed 9:00–16:30, Tue and Thu–Sat 10:00–16:00, closed Sun, Nov–Feb may have shorter hours, tel. 01451/831-082).

Helpful Hints

Internet Access: Try the erratically open **library** in St. Edwards Hall on the main square (tel. 01451/830-352), or the **youth hostel** (17:00–23:00 nightly).

Taxi: See "Getting Around the Cotswolds—By Taxi" (page 382).

Parking: Park anywhere on Market Square free for two hours, or overnight between 16:00 and 11:00 (free 18:00–9:00 plus any 2 hours—they note your license, so you can't just move to another spot; £50 tickets for offenders). One "Long Stay" lot is 400 yards north of the town square at the Tesco supermarket (free, follow the signs).

Self-Guided Walk

Welcome to Stow-on-the-Wold

This little four-stop walk covers about 500 yards and takes about 45 minutes.

Start at the **Stocks on the Market Square.** Imagine this village during the time when people were publicly ridiculed here as

a punishment. Stow was born in pre-Roman times; it's where three trade routes crossed at a high point in the region (altitude: 800 feet). This main square hosted an international fair starting in 1107, and people came from as far away as Italy for the wool fleeces. This grand square was a vast, grassy expanse. Picture it in the Middle Ages (before the buildings in the center were added): a public commons and grazing ground, paths worn through the grass, and no well. Until 1867, Stow had no running water; women fetched water from the "Roman Well" a quarter-mile away.

A thin skin of topsoil covers the Cotswold limestone, from

which these buildings were made. The **Stow Lodge** (next to the church) lies a little lower than the church; the lodge sits on the spot where locals quarried stones for the church. That building, originally the rectory, is now a hotel. The church (where we'll end this little walk) is made of Cotswold stone, and marks the summit of the hill upon which the town was built. The stocks are a great photo op (my kids locked me in for a photo our family used for a Christmas card).

• *Walk past the youth hostel to the market, and cross to the other side of the square. Notice how locals seem to be a part of a tight little community.*

For 500 years, the **Market Cross** stood in the market reminding all Christian merchants to "trade fairly under the sight of God." Notice the stubs of the iron fence in the concrete base—a

reminder of how countless wrought-iron fences were cut down and given to the government to be melted down during World War II. (Recently, it's been disclosed that all that iron ended up in junk heaps—frantic patriotism just wasted.) The plaque on the cross honors the Lord of the Manor, who donated money back to his tenants, allowing the town to finally finance running water in 1878. Scan the square for a tipsy shop that locals call the "wonky house." Because it lists (tilts) so severely, it's a listed building—the facade is protected (but the interior is modern and level). The Kings Arms, with its great gables and scary chimney, was once where travelers parked their horses before spending the night. In the 1600s, this was considered the premium "posting house" between London and Birmingham. Today, the Kings Arms cooks up some of the best food in town, and rents rooms upstairs (see "Sleeping in and Near Stow," later).

During the English Civil War, which pitted Parliamentarians against Royalists, Stow-on-the-Wold remained staunchly loyal to the king. (Charles I is said to have eaten at the Kings Arms before a great battle.) Because of its allegiance, the town has an abundance of pubs with royal names (King's This and Queen's That).

• *Walk past the Kings Arms down Digbeth Street to the little triangular park located in front of the Methodist Church and across from the Royalist Hotel. This hotel—along with about 20 others—claims to be the oldest in England, dating from 947.*

Just beyond the small grassy triangle with benches is the place where—twice a year, in May and October—the Gypsy Horse Fair

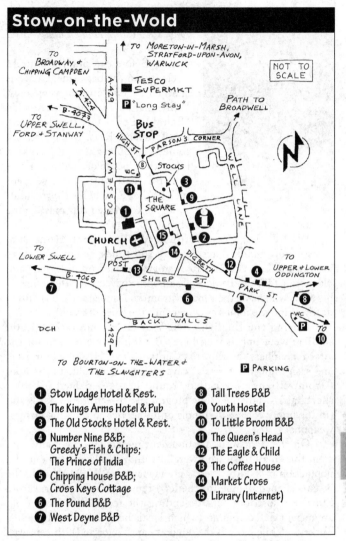

Stow-on-the-Wold

TO MORETON-IN-MARSH, STRATFORD-UPON-AVON, WARWICK

TO BROADWAY & CHIPPING CAMPDEN

TESCO SUPERMKT

P "Long Stay"

PATH TO BROADWELL

TO UPPER SWELL, FORD & STANWAY

B·4077

A·429

Bus Stop

HIGH ST

PARSON'S CORNER

FOSSE WAY

WC

B

Stocks

THE SQUARE

❸ ❾

ELL LANE

N

NOT TO SCALE

❶

❷

i

CHURCH ✠

❶❶

❶❺

TO LOWER SWELL

POST

❶❹

❶❸

DIGBETH

TO UPPER & LOWER ODDINGTON

B·4068

SHEEP ST.

❶❷

❹

❼

❻

PARK ST.

❽

❺

WC

P

TO

BACK WALLS

❿

DCH

A·429

TO BOURTON-ON-THE-WATER & THE SLAUGHTERS

P PARKING

❶ Stow Lodge Hotel & Rest.
❷ The Kings Arms Hotel & Pub
❸ The Old Stocks Hotel & Rest.
❹ Number Nine B&B; Greedy's Fish & Chips; The Prince of India
❺ Chipping House B&B; Cross Keys Cottage
❻ The Pound B&B
❼ West Deyne B&B

❽ Tall Trees B&B
❾ Youth Hostel
❿ To Little Broom B&B
❶❶ The Queen's Head
❶❷ The Eagle & Child
❶❸ The Coffee House
❶❹ Market Cross
❶❺ Library (Internet)

THE COTSWOLDS

attracts Roma (Gypsies) and Travelers (Irish Tinkers) from far and wide. They congregate down the street on the Maugersbury Road. Locals paint a colorful picture of the Roma, Travelers, and horses inundating the town. The young women dress up because the fair also functions as a marriage market.

• Hike up Sheep Street. You'll pass a boutique-filled former brewery yard, Fleece Alley (just wide enough for a single file of sheep to walk on—easier to count them on market days), and a fine antique bookstore.

Turn right on Church Street, which leads past the best coffee shop in town (The Coffee House), and find the church.

Before entering the **church,** circle it. On the back side, a door is flanked by two ancient yew trees. While many view it as the Christian "Behold, I stand at the door and knock" door, J. R. R. Tolkien fans see something quite different. Tolkien hiked the Cotswolds, and had a passion for sketching evocative trees such as this. *Lord of the Rings* enthusiasts are convinced this must be the inspiration for the door into Moria.

While the church (open daily—apart from services—9:00–18:00) dates from Saxon times, today's structure is from the 15th century. Its history is played up in leaflets and plaques just inside the door. The floor is paved with the tombs of big shots who made their money from wool and are still boastful in death. (Find the tombs crowned with the bales of wool.)

During the English Civil War (1615), more than 1,000 soldiers were imprisoned here. The tombstone in front of the altar remembers the Royalist Captain Keyt. His long hair, lace, and sash indicate he was a "cavalier," and true-blue to the king (Cromwellians were called "round heads"—named for their short hair). Study the crude provincial art—childlike skulls and (in the upper corners) symbols of his service to the king (armor, weapons).

On the right wall, a monument remembers the many boys from this small town who were lost in World War I (50 out of a population of 2,000). There were far fewer in World War II. The biscuit-shaped plaque (to the left) remembers an admiral from Stow who lost four sons defending the realm. It's sliced from an ancient fluted column (which locals believe is from Ephesus, Turkey). While most of the windows are Victorian (19th-century), the two sets high up in the clerestory are from the dreamier Pre-Raphaelite school (c. 1920).

Finally, don't miss the kneelers, made by a committed band of women known as "the Kneeler Group." They meet most Tuesday mornings (except sometimes in summer) at 10:30 in the Church Room to needlepoint, sip coffee, and enjoy a good chat. (The vicar assured me that any tourist wanting to join them would be more than welcome. The help would be appreciated and the company would be excellent.)

THE COTSWOLDS

Sleeping in and near Stow

(£1 = about $1.60, country code: 44, area code: 01451)

In Stow

$$$ Stow Lodge Hotel fills the historic church rectory with lots of old English charm. Facing the town square, with its own sprawling and peaceful garden, this lavish old place offers 21 large, thoughtfully appointed rooms with soft beds, stately public spaces, and a cushy-chair lounge (Db-£85–145 depending on season, closed Jan, pay Internet access and free Wi-Fi, off-street parking, The Square, tel. 01451/830-485, fax 01451/831-671, www.stowlodge .com, enquiries@stowlodge.com, helpful Hartley family).

$$$ The Kings Arms, with nine rooms, manages to keep its historic Cotswolds character while still feeling fresh and modern in all the right ways (Sb-£60, Db-£75–110, higher prices are for weekends, steep stairs, off-street parking, Market Square, tel. 01451/830-364, www.thekingsarmsstow.co.uk, info@thekings armsstow.co.uk). Jo, Peter, and Sam run the hotel while Peter's brother Thomas cooks—see "Eating in and Near Stow," later.

$$$ The Old Stocks Hotel, facing the town square, is a good value, even though the building itself is classier than its 18 big, simply furnished rooms. It's friendly and family-run, yet professional as can be. Beware the man-killer beams (Sb-£45–55, standard Db-£90, refurbished "superior" Db-£110, Tb-£120, family deals, ground-floor rooms, attached bar and restaurant, garden patio, off-street parking, The Square, tel. 01451/830-666, fax 01451/870-014, www.oldstockshotel.co.uk, info@oldstockshotel.co.uk).

$$ Number Nine has three large, bright, recently refurbished, and tastefully decorated rooms. This 200-year-old home comes with watch-your-head beamed ceilings and old wooden doors (Db-£60–70, free Internet access and Wi-Fi, 9 Park Street, tel. 01451/870-333, mobile 07779-006-539, www.number-nine.info, enquiries@number-nine.info, James and Carol Brown).

$$ Chipping House B&B is a fine, warm, old place with three rooms and a welcoming lounge—it feels like a visit to auntie's house (Db-£60–70, cash only, Park Street, tel. 01451/831-756, chippinghouse@tesco.net, dog-lovers Merv and Carolyne Oliver).

$$ Cross Keys Cottage offers four smallish but smartly updated rooms with bright floral decor and modern bathrooms. Kindly Margaret and Roger Welton take care of their guests in this 350-year-old beamed cottage (Sb-£55–65, Db-£65–70, cash discount, free Wi-Fi, Park Street, tel. & fax 01451/831-128, rogxmag@hotmail.com).

$ The Pound is the quaint, 500-year-old, slanty, cozy, and low-beamed home of Patricia Whitehead. She offers two bright, inviting, twin-bedded rooms and a classic old fireplace lounge (D-£50–60, T-£85, cash only, downtown on Sheep Street, tel. & fax 01451/830-229, pat-whitehead1@live.co.uk).

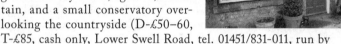

$ West Deyne B&B has two grandmotherly rooms, a garden, a fountain, and a small conservatory overlooking the countryside (D-£50–60, T-£85, cash only, Lower Swell Road, tel. 01451/831-011, run by Joan Cave).

$ Tall Trees B&B, on the Oddington Road 100 yards outside of Stow, comes with horses and chickens on four acres of land. Run by no-nonsense Jennifer, the six contemporary rooms are in an old-style building (Sb-£40–50, Db-£60–70, family room-£100, cash only, two ground-floor rooms, off-street parking, tel. 01451/831-296, fax 01451/870-049, talltreestow@aol.com). She also rents a lovely cottage that sleeps six (£450–900/week, kitchenette, off-street parking).

$ *Hostel:* The **Stow-on-the-Wold Youth Hostel,** on Stow's main square, is the only hostel in the Cotswolds, with 48 beds in nine rooms. It has a friendly atmosphere, good hot meals, and a members' kitchen (dorm bed-£18, non-members-£3 extra, includes sheets, some family rooms with private bathrooms, evening meals, reception closed 10:00–17:00, Internet-£1/15 min, lockers, reserve long in advance, tel. 01451/830-497, fax 01451/870-102, www.yha .org.uk, stow@yha.org.uk, manager Rob). Anyone can eat here: Breakfast is £4.65 and dinner is £9.25.

Near Stow

$ Little Broom B&B hides out in the neighboring hamlet of Maugersbury, which enjoys the peace Stow once had. It rents three cozy rooms that share a fine garden and a pool (S-£30, Sb-£45, D-£50, Db-£55–70, apartment Db-£70 for two people plus £10–15 for each extra person, cash only, tel. & fax 01451/830-510, mobile 07989-832-714). Brenda keeps racehorses just beyond her pool, which hides in a low-lying greenhouse to keep it warm throughout the summer (guests welcome). It's an easy eight-minute walk from Stow: Head east on Park Street, taking the right fork to Maugersbury, then turn right on the road marked *No Through Road.*

Eating in and near Stow

In Stow

These places are all within a five-minute walk of each other, either on the main square or downhill on Queen and Park streets.

Restaurants and Pubs

Stow Lodge is a formal but friendly bar serving fine £8–10 lunches and a popular £24 three-course dinner. This is the choice of the town's proper ladies (daily 12:00–14:00 & 19:00–20:30, smoke-free, veggie options, good wines, also has pricier restaurant, just off main square).

The Old Stocks Hotel Restaurant, which might at first glance seem like a tired and big hotel dining room, is actually a classy place to dine. With attentive service and an interesting menu, they provide tasty and well-presented food. If they're not too busy, you can order more economically from the bar menu, and sit in the fancy dining room enjoying views of the square. In good weather, the garden out back is a hit (£8–15 meals, nightly 18:30–20:30, Fri–Sat until 21:00, reservations recommended on weekends, tel. 01451/830-666).

The Kings Arms has two floors, both serving traditional English fare. Downstairs, you'll find pub food, while upstairs has an "English-with-a-twist" menu in a once-medieval, now-classy ambience (£10–12 pub food, £13–18 meals, daily 12:00–14:30 & 19:00–21:30, sandwiches available all day, reserve for dinner, tel. 01451/830-364).

The Queen's Head faces the Market Square, next to the Stow Lodge. With a classic pub vibe, it's a great place to bring your dog, eat pub grub, and drink the local Cotswold brew, Donnington Ale (£9–19 plates, daily 12:00–14:30 & 18:30–21:00).

The Eagle and Child is more of a hotel restaurant than a pub, with delicious food and indifferent service (meals available daily 12:00–14:30 & 18:00–21:00, afternoon tea available Fri–Sun, Park Street, tel. 01451/830-670).

Eating Cheaply

Head to the grassy triangle where Digbeth hits Sheep Street; there, you'll find take-out fish-and-chips and Indian and Chinese food. You can picnic at the triangle, or on the benches by the stocks on Market Street.

Greedy's Fish and Chips, on Park Street, is a favorite with locals for take-out (Mon–Sat 12:00–14:00 & 16:30–21:00, closed Sun).

The Prince of India offers good Indian food in a delightful setting, to take out or eat in (nightly 18:00–23:30, Park Street, tel. 01451/830-099).

The Coffee House provides a nice break from the horses-and-hounds traditional cuisine found elsewhere, though the service can be slow (£6–10 soups and salads, good coffee, Mon–Sat 9:30–17:00, Sun 10:00–16:00, Church Street, tel. 01451/870-802).

Even Cheaper: Small grocery stores face the main square, and a big **Tesco** supermarket is 200 yards north of town. The youth hostel (see "Sleeping in and near Stow," earlier) welcomes non-hostelers for breakfast (£4.65) or its evening family-style meal (£9.25, drop by early to confirm time and book a spot).

Pub Dinner Hike from Stow

From Stow, consider taking a half-hour scenic countryside walk past the old Roman Well to the village of Broadwell. (At the end of the hike at the road, turn right—downhill—to get to Broadwell.) There, **The Fox Inn** serves good pub dinners and draws traditional ales (food served Mon–Sat 11:30–13:30 & 18:30–21:00, Sun 12:00–14:00 only, on the village green, tel. 01451/870-909).

Great Country Pubs near Stow

These three places—known for their great £10 meals and fine settings—are very popular. Arrive early or phone in a reservation. (If you show up at 20:00, it's unlikely that they'll be able to seat you for dinner if you haven't called first.) These pubs allow "well-behaved children," and are practical only for those with a car. The first two (in Oddington, two miles from Stow) are more trendy and fresh, yet still in a traditional pub setting. The Plough (in Ford, a few miles farther away) is your jolly olde dark pub.

The Horse and Groom Village Inn in Upper Oddington is a smart place with a sea-grass-green carpet in a 16th-century inn, serving modern English and Mediterranean food with a good wine list (32 wines by the glass) and serious beer (daily 12:00–14:00 & 18:30–21:00, tel. 01451/830-584).

The Fox Inn, a different Fox Inn than the one listed above, is old but fresh and famous among locals for its quality cooking (daily 12:00–14:00 & 18:30–22:00, in Lower Oddington, tel. 01451/870-555). They also rent three rooms (Db-£68–95, www.foxinn.net)

The Plough Inn fills a fascinating old building, once an old coaching inn and later a court-house. Ask the bar staff for some fun history—like what "you're barred" means. Eat from the same traditional English menu in the restaurant, bar, or garden. They are serious about both their beer and—judging by the extensive list of homemade temptations—  their desserts (£12–18 meals, food served daily 12:00–14:00 & 18:00–21:00, 4 miles from Stow on Tewkesbury Road in hamlet of Ford, reservations smart, tel. 01386/584-215).

Near Stow-on-the-Wold

These sights are all south of Stow: Some are very close (Bourton-on-the-Water, the Slaughters, and Northleach) and one is 20 miles away (Cirencester).

▲Bourton-on-the-Water

I can't figure out whether they call this "the Venice of the Cotswolds" because of its quaint canals or its frequent miserable crowds. Either way, it's very pretty. This town—four miles south of Stow and a mile from the Slaughters—gets overrun by midday and weekend hordes. Surrounding Bourton's green are sidewalks jammed with disoriented tourists wearing nametags. If you can avoid them, it's worth a drive-through and maybe a short stop. While it can be mobbed with tour groups during the day, it's pleasantly empty in the early evening and after dark.

Parking: Finding a spot here is predictably tough. Even during the busy business day, rather than park in the pay-and-display parking lot a five-minute walk from the center, drive right into town and wait for a spot on High Street just past the village green (there's a long row of free two-hour spots in front of the Edinburgh Woolen Mills Shop).

Tourist Information: The TI is just off Victoria Street (April–Oct Mon–Fri 9:30–17:00, Sat 9:30–17:30, closed Sun, closes one hour earlier Nov–March, tel. 01451/820-211, www.bourtoninfo.com).

Sights: Bourton has three sights worth considering. All are on High Street in the town center. In addition to these, families also enjoy Bourton's kid-perfect **leisure centre** (big pool and sauna, 5-min walk from town center, open daily, call for public hours, tel. 01451/824-024).

▲Motor Museum—This excellent, jumbled museum shows off a lifetime's accumulation of vintage cars, old lacquered signs, threadbare toys, and prewar memorabilia. Wander the car-and-driver displays, from the automobile's early days to the stylish James Bond era. Talk to an elderly Brit who's touring the place for some personal memories (£4, Feb–Nov daily  10:00–18:00, closed Dec–Jan, in the mill facing the town center, tel. 01451/821-255, www.cotswold-motor-museum.com).

Model Railway Exhibition—This exhibit of four model railway layouts is impressive only to train buffs (£2.50, June–Aug daily

THE COTSWOLDS

11:00–17:00, Sept–May weekends only, limited Jan hours, located in the back of a hobby shop, tel. 01451/820-686, www.bourton modelrailway.co.uk).

Model Village—This light but fun display re-creates the town on a 1:9 scale in a tiny park, and has an attached room full of tiny models showing off various bits of British domestic life (£3.25 for the park, £1 more for the model room, daily 10:00–17:45, tel. 01451/820-467).

Lower and Upper Slaughter

Lower Slaughter is a classic village, with ducks, a working water mill, and usually an artist busy at her easel somewhere. Just behind the skippable Old Mill Museum, two kissing gates lead to the path that goes to nearby Upper Slaughter (a 10-minute walk or 2-minute drive away).

In **Upper Slaughter,** walk through the yew trees (sacred in pagan days) down a lane through the raised graveyard (a buildup of centuries of graves) to the peaceful church. In the back of the fine graveyard, the statue of a wistful woman looks over the tomb of an 18th-century rector (sculpted by his son).

By the way, "Slaughter" has nothing to do with lamb chops. It comes from the sloe tree (the one used to make sloe gin). These towns are an easy two-hour round-trip walk from Bourton. You could also walk from Bourton through the Slaughters to Stow. The small roads from Upper Slaughter to Ford and Kineton are some of England's most scenic. Roll your window down and joyride slowly.

▲Northleach

One of the "untouched and untouristed" Cotswold villages, Northleach is worth a short stop. The town's impressive main square and church attest to its position as a major wool center in the Middle Ages. Park in the square called The Green or the adjoining Market Place and pick up a free town map at the **TI**, located on The Green in the black-and-white-striped Fothergills Gallery shop (Tue–Fri 9:30–17:00, Sat 9:30–16:00, closed Sun–Mon, tel. 01451/860-135, www.northleach.gov.uk). If the TI is closed, maps are available at the post office on the Market Place (Mon–Fri 9:00–17:30, Sat 9:00–13:00, closed Sun and for lunch 13:00–14:00) and at other nearby shops. Northleach is nine miles south of Stow, down A429. Bus #855 connects it to Stow and Moreton (tel. 0871-200-2233—calls are 10p/min, www.traveline.org.uk).

▲Keith Harding's World of Mechanical Music—In 1962, Keith Harding, tired of giving ad-lib "living room tours," opened this delightful little one-room place. It offers a unique opportunity to listen to 300 years of amazing self-playing musical instruments.

It's run by people who are passionate about the restoration work they do on these musical marvels. The curators delight in demonstrating about 20 of the museum's machines with each hour-long tour. You'll hear Victorian music boxes and the earliest polyphones (record players) playing cylinders and then discs—all from an age when music was made mechanically, without the help of electricity. The admission fee includes an essential hour-long tour (£8, daily 10:00–17:00, last entry at 15:45, tours go constantly—join one in progress, High Street, Northleach, tel. 01451/860-181, www.mechanicalmusic.co.uk).

Church of Saints Peter and Paul—This fine Perpendicular Gothic church has been called the "cathedral of the Cotswolds." It's one of the Cotswolds' finest two "wool" churches (along with Chipping Campden's), paid for by 15th-century wool tycoons. Find the oldest tombstone. The brass plaques on the floor memorialize big shots, showing sheep and sacks of wool at their long-dead feet, and inscriptions mixing Latin and the old English.

▲Bibury

Six miles northeast of Cirencester, this village is a favorite with British picnickers fond of strolling and fishing. Bibury offers some

relaxing sights, including a row of very old weavers' cottages, a trout farm, a stream teeming with fat fish and proud ducks, and a church surrounded by rosebushes, each tended by a volunteer of the parish. A protected wetlands area on the far side of the stream hosts newts and water voles— walk around to the old weavers' Arlington Row and back on the far side of the marsh, peeking into the rushes for wildlife.

For a closer look at the fish, cross the bridge to the 15-acre Trout Farm, where you can feed them—or catch your own (£3.50, fish food-50p; March–Oct Mon–Sat 9:00–18:00, Sun 10:00–18:00; Nov–Feb daily 10:00–16:00; catch-your-own only available March–Oct weekends and school holidays, tel. 01285/740-215, www.biburytroutfarm.co.uk).

Don't miss the scenic **Coln Valley drive** from A429 to Bibury through the enigmatic villages of Coln St. Dennis, Coln Rogers, Coln Powell, and Winson.

Sleeping in Bibury: If you'd like to spend the night in tiny Bibury, consider **$$ The William Morris B&B,** named for the 19th-century designer and writer (Db-£65–85, cheaper prices are Mon–Thu, cash only, 2 rooms, 200 yards from the bridge at 11 The

THE COTSWOLDS

Street, tel. 01285/740-555, fax 01285/850-648, www.thewilliam
morris.com, info@thewilliammorris.com).

▲▲Cirencester

Almost 2,000 years ago, Cirencester (SIGH-ren-ses-ter) was the
ancient Roman city of Corinium. It's 20 miles from Stow down
A429, which was called Fosse Way in Roman times. In Cirencester,
stop by the **Corinium Museum** to find out why they say, "If you
scratch Gloucestershire, you'll find Rome" (£4.25, Mon–Sat 10:00–
17:00, Sun 14:00–17:00, Park Street, tel. 01285/655-611, www
.cirencester.co.uk/coriniummuseum). Cirencester's church is the
largest of the Cotswolds "wool" churches. The cutesy New Brewery
Arts crafts center entertains visitors with traditional weaving and
potting, workshops, an interesting gallery, and a good coffee shop.
Monday and Friday are general-market days, Friday features an
antiques market, and a crafts market is held on the first and third
Saturdays of the month. The **TI** is in the Corinium Museum
shop (Mon–Sat 10:00–17:00, Sun 14:00–17:00, tel. 01285/654-180,
cirencestervic@cotswold.gov.uk).

Moreton-in-Marsh

This workaday town—worth ▲—is like Stow or Chipping
Campden without the touristy sugar. Rather than gift and antiques
shops, you'll find streets lined with real shops: ironmongers selling
cottage nameplates and carpet shops strewn with the remarkable
patterns that decorate B&B floors. A shin-kickin' traditional market of 100-plus stalls fills High Street each Tuesday, as it has for
the last 400 years (8:00–16:00, handicrafts, farm produce, clothing, great people-watching, best if you go early). The Cotswolds
has an economy aside from tourism, and you'll feel it here.

Orientation to Moreton-in-Marsh

(area code: 01608)
Moreton has a tiny, sleepy train station two blocks from High
Street, lots of bus connections, and the best **TI** in the region (Mon
8:45–16:00, Tue–Thu 8:45–17:15, Fri 8:45–16:45, Sat 10:00–13:00,
closed Sun, good public WC, 50p *Town Trail* leaflet for self-guided
walk, rail and bus schedules, racks of fliers, tel. 01608/650-881).

Helpful Hints

Internet Access: It's free at the **TI** (see above) and at the erratically open **library** (down High Street where it becomes Stow

Moreton-in-Marsh

1 Manor House Hotel
2 Kymalton House
3 Treetops B&B
4 Warwick House
5 The Marshmallow Restaurant
6 The Black Bear Inn
7 Hassan Balti Rest.
8 Tilly's Tea House & Mermaid Fish Shop
9 Ask Restaurant
10 Co-op & Tesco Express
11 Budgens Supermarket
12 Launderette
13 Toy Shop Bike Rental

Road, tel. 01608/650-780).

Laundry: The handy **launderette** is a block in front of the train station on New Road (daily 7:00–19:00, last wash at 18:00, £3.40 self-service wash, £2–3 self-service dry, or drop off Mon–Fri 8:00–17:00 for £2.50 extra and same-day service, tel. 01608/650-888).

Baggage Storage: While there is no formal baggage storage in town, the Black Bear Inn (next to the TI) might let you leave bags there if you buy a drink.

Parking: It's easy—anywhere on High Street is fine any time, as long as you want, for free. On Tuesdays, when the market makes parking tricky, you can park at the Budgens supermarket for £3—refundable if you spend at least £5 in the store.

Bike Rental, Taxis, and Car Rental: See "Getting Around the Cotswolds" (page 379).

Sleeping in Moreton-in-Marsh

(£1 = about $1.60, country code: 44, area code: 01608)

$$$ Manor House Hotel is Moreton's big old hotel, dating from 1545 but sporting such modern amenities as toilets and electricity. Its 35 classy-for-the-Cotswolds rooms and its garden invite relaxation (Sb-£115–155, Db-£145–205, family suite-£210–250, includes breakfast, elevator, pay Wi-Fi, log fire in winter, attached restaurants—no kids under age 8, on far end of High Street away from train station, tel. 01608/650-501, fax 01608/651-481, www.cotswold-inns-hotels.co.uk, info@manor househotel.info).

$ Kymalton House has two bright, tastefully decorated rooms in a gracious modern house. With a pleasant garden, it's set back off of a busy street just outside the town center (Db-£65, cheaper for 3 or more nights, double beds only, cash only, closed Dec–Jan, tel. 01608/650-487, kymalton@uwclub.net, Sylvia and Doug Gould). It's a seven-minute walk from town (walk past Budgens supermarket, turn right on Todenham Road, look for house on the right). They'll happily pick up and drop off train travelers at the station.

$ Treetops B&B is plush, with seven spacious, attractive rooms, a sun lounge, and a three-quarter-acre backyard. Liz and Ben (the family dog) will make you feel right at home—if you meet their two-night minimum (large Db-£65, gigantic Db-£70, ground-floor rooms have patios, free Wi-Fi, set far back from the busy road, London Road, tel. & fax 01608/651-036, www.tree topscotswolds.co.uk, treetops1@talk21.com, Liz and Brian Dean). It's an eight-minute walk from town and the railway station (exit station, keep left, go left on bridge over train tracks, look for sign, then long driveway).

$ Warwick House, just down the road from Treetops, is where "half-American" Charlie Grant rents three rooms in a contemporary, casual house. It's on a noisy road, but the windows are triple-glazed. Charlie will do your laundry if you stay three or more nights (Sb-£38, Db-£60, Tb-£72, cash only, free Wi-Fi and loaner laptop, no kids under age 12, will pick up from train station, London Road, tel. 01608/650-773, www.snoozeandsizzle .com, whbandb@yahoo.com).

Eating in Moreton-in-Marsh

A stroll up and down High Street lets you survey your small-town options.

The Marshmallow is relatively upscale but affordable, with a menu that includes traditional English dishes as well as lasagna and salads (£8–12 entrées, 15 fancy teas, Sun–Mon 10:00–17:00, Tue 10:00–16:00, Wed–Sat 10:00–20:00, reservations advised, shady back garden for summer dining, tel. 01608/651-536).

The Black Bear Inn offers traditional English food. As you enter, choose between the dining room on the left or the pub on the right (£5–10 meals and daily specials, restaurant open daily 12:00–14:00 & 18:30–21:00, pub open daily 11:00–23:00, tel. 01608/652-992).

Hassan Balti, with tasty Bangladeshi food, is a fine value for sit-down or take-out (£7–12 meals, Mon–Fri 18:00–23:30, Sat–Sun 12:00–14:00 & 18:00–23:30, High Street, tel. 01608/650-798).

Tilly's Tea House serves fresh soups, salads, sandwiches, and pastries for lunch in a cheerful spot on High Street across from the TI (£5 light meals, good cream tea-£5, Mon–Sat 9:00–16:30, closed Sun, tel. 01608/650-000).

Ask, a chain restaurant across the street, has decent pastas, pizzas, and salads, and a breezy, family-friendly atmosphere (£8–10 pizzas, daily 12:00–23:00, take-out available, tel. 01608/651-119).

Mermaid fish shop is popular for its take-out fish and tasty selection of traditional pies (Mon–Sat 12:00–14:00 & 17:00–22:30, closed Sun).

Picnic: There's a small **Co-op** grocery on High Street in the town center (Mon–Sat 7:00–20:00, Sun 8:00–20:00), and a **Tesco Express** one door down (Mon–Fri 6:00–23:00, Sat–Sun 7:00–23:00). The big **Budgens** supermarket is indeed super (Mon–Sat 8:00–22:00, Sun 10:00–16:00, far end of High Street). There are picnic tables across the busy street, in pleasant Victoria Park.

Moreton-in-Marsh Connections

Moreton, the only Cotswolds town with a train station, is also the best base to explore the region by bus (see "Getting Around the Cotswolds," page 379).

From Moreton by Train to: London's Paddington Station (one-way-£27–29, round-trip after 8:15-£27, every 1–2 hrs, 1.5–1.75 hrs), **Bath** (hourly, 2–3 hrs, 1–3 transfers), **Oxford** (hourly, 40 min), **Ironbridge Gorge** (hourly, 2.75–3.5 hrs, 2–3 transfers; arrive Telford, then catch bus or cab 7 miles to Ironbridge Gorge—page 436). Train info: tel. 0845-748-4950, www.nationalrail.co.uk.

Near Moreton-in-Marsh

▲Chastleton House

This stately home, located about five miles southeast of Moreton-in-Marsh, was actually lived in by the same family from 1607 until 1991. It offers a rare peek into a Jacobean gentry house. (Jacobean, which comes from the Latin for "James," indicates the style from the time of King James I—the early 1600s.) Built, like most Cotswold palaces, with wool money, it gradually declined with the fortunes of its aristocratic family until, according to the last lady of the house, it  was "held together by cobwebs." It came to the National Trust on condition that they would maintain its musty Jacobean ambience. Wander on creaky floorboards, many of them original, and chat with volunteer guides stationed in each room. It's an uppity place that doesn't encourage spontaneity. The docents are proud to play on one of the best croquet teams in the region (the rules of croquet were formalized in this house in 1868). Page through the early 20th-century family photo albums in the room just off the entry.

Cost, Hours, Location: £8.25; April–Sept Wed–Sat 13:00–17:00, closed Sun–Tue; Oct Wed–Sat 13:00–16:00, closed Sun–Tue; last entry one hour before closing; closed Nov–March; well-signposted, 5-min hike to house from free parking lot, recorded info tel. 01494/755-560, www.nationaltrust.org.uk/chastleton. Only 175 visitors a day are allowed into the home (25 people every 30 min). You can reserve an entry time in advance by phone (tel. 01608/674-981, Mon–Fri 10:00–14:00). Reservations are not possible for same-day visits.

STRATFORD-UPON-AVON

Stratford is Shakespeare's hometown. To see or not to see? Stratford is a must for every big bus tour in England, and probably the single most popular side-trip from London. Sure, it's touristy. But nobody back home would understand if you skipped Shakespeare's house. A walking tour with a play's the thing to bring the Bard to life. And the town's riverside charm, coupled with its hardworking tourist industry, makes it a fun stop.

While you're in the area, explore Warwick, England's finest medieval castle, and stop by Coventry, a blue-collar town with a spirit that the Nazis' bombs couldn't destroy.

Planning Your Time

Stratford, Warwick, and Coventry are a made-to-order day for drivers connecting the Cotswolds with points north (such as Ironbridge Gorge or North Wales). While connections from the Cotswolds to Ironbridge Gorge are tough, Stratford, Warwick, and Coventry are well-served by public transportation.

If you're just passing through Stratford, it's worth a half-day, but to see a play, you'll need to spend the night, or drive in from the nearby Cotswolds (30 min to the south; see previous chapter).

Warwick is England's single most spectacular castle. It's very touristy, but it's also historic and fun (worth three hours of your time). Have lunch in Warwick town. Coventry, the least important stop on a quick trip, is most interesting as a chance to see a real, struggling, Midlands industrial city (with some decent sightseeing).

If you're speedy, you can hit all three sights on a one-day drive-through. If you're more relaxed, see a play and stay in Stratford, then stop by Warwick and Coventry the following morning en route to your next destination.

Orientation to Stratford

(area code: 01789)

Stratford's old town is compact, with the TI and theater along the riverbank, and Shakespeare's birthplace a few blocks inland; you can easily walk to everything except Anne Hathaway's and Mary Arden's places. The river has an idyllic yet playful feel, with a park along both banks, paddleboats, hungry swans, and an old, crank-powered ferry.

Tourist Information

The TI is as central as can be, located where the main street hits the river. While the office has been swallowed whole by gimmicky knickknacks and fliers—and corrupted by a sales-pitch fervor—the people here can still provide a little help. They sell discounted tickets for local and regional sights, including Warwick Castle and Blenheim Palace (April–Sept Mon–Sat 9:00–17:30, Sun 10:00–16:00; Oct–March Mon–Sat 9:00–17:00, Sun 10:00–15:00; free room-finding service, on Bridgefoot, toll tel. 0870-160-7930, www.shakespeare-country.co.uk).

Helpful Hints

Name That Stratford: If you're coming by train or bus, be sure to request a ticket for "Stratford-upon-Avon," not just "Stratford." Another Stratford—also known as Stratford Langthorne, just outside London—is the location for the 2012 Olympics, and is nowhere near where you're trying to go.

Festival: Every year on the weekend following Shakespeare's birthday (traditionally considered to be April 23—also the day he died), Stratford celebrates. The town hosts free events, including activities for children. In 2010, expect tours and hotels to be booked up long in advance surrounding the weekend of April 24–25.

Internet Access: Get online at **Cyber Junction** (£1.50/15 min, £4/hr, daily 10:00–18:00, sometimes later, 28 Greenhill Street, tel. 01789/263-400, www.thecyberjunction.co.uk) or the **library,** on Henley Street just a few doors down from Shakespeare's Birthplace (£5/hr, weekdays generally 9:00–17:30, shorter hours weekends; if computers are all in use, reserve a time at the desk; tel. 01789/292-209, www.warwickshire.gov.uk).

Baggage Storage: Located directly behind the TI, the **Old Barn Shop** stores bags—but be back to pick them up before the store closes, or you're out of luck for the night (£3/bag, Mon–

Sat 10:00–17:00, Sun 10:00–16:00, tel. 01789/269-567).

Laundry: Sparklean, a 10-minute walk from the city center, is near the Grove Road and Broad Walk B&Bs (daily 8:00–21:00, self-serve wash-£8.50, kindly Jane will do it for £10–12 in a few hours if you drop it off by 12:00, 74 Bull Street, tel. 01789/269-075).

Taxis: Try **007 Taxis** (tel. 01789/414-007) or the taxi stand on Woodbridge, near the intersection with High Street. To arrange for a private car and driver, contact **Platinum Cars** (£25/hr, tel. 01789/264-626, www.platinum-cars.co.uk).

Tours in Stratford

Stratford Town Walks—These entertaining, award-winning 90-minute walks introduce you to the town and its famous playwright. Tours run daily year-round, rain or shine. Just show up at the Swan fountain (on the waterfront, opposite Sheep Street) in front of the Royal Shakespeare Theatre and pay the guide (£5, kids-£2, ticket stub offers good discounts to some sights, Mon–Wed at 11:00, Thu–Sun at 14:00, tel. 01789/292-478 or 07855/760-377, www.stratfordtownwalk.co.uk).

They also run an evening ghost walk led by a professional magician (£5, kids-£3, Mon, Thu, and Fri at 19:30, must book in advance).

City Sightseeing Bus Tours—Open-top buses constantly make the rounds, allowing visitors to hop on and hop off at all the Shakespeare sights. Given the far-flung nature of two of the Shakespeare sights, and the value of the fun commentary provided, this tour makes the town more manageable. The full circuit takes about an hour, and comes with a steady and informative commentary (£11, buy tickets on bus or as you board, buses leave from the TI every 20 min in high season from 9:30–17:00, every 30 min off-season; buses alternate between tape-recorded commentary and live guides—for the best tour, wait for a live guide; tel. 01789/412-680, www.citysightseeing-stratford.com).

Sights in Stratford

Shakespearean Sights

Fans of the Bard's work will want to visit at least a few of these sights. Shakespeare's Exhibition and Birthplace has the best historical introduction to the playwright (as well as a disappointing house where he spent his early years). There are four other

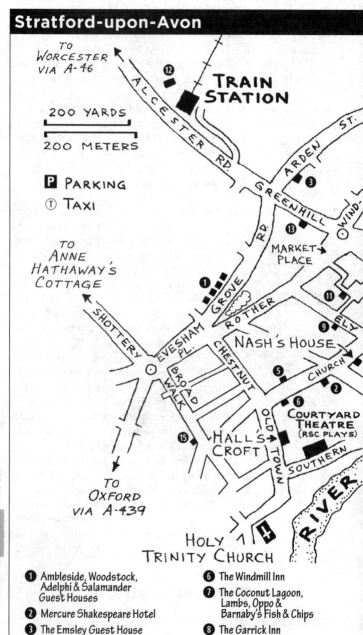

Stratford-upon-Avon

TO WORCESTER VIA A-46

TRAIN STATION

ALCESTER RD.

ARDEN ST.

GREENHILL

200 YARDS
200 METERS

🅿 PARKING
Ⓣ TAXI

TO ANNE HATHAWAY'S COTTAGE

GROVE RD.

ROTHER

MARKET PLACE

SHOTTERY

EVESHAM PL.

BROAD WALK

CHESTNUT

NASH'S HOUSE

CHURCH

ELY

COURTYARD THEATRE (RSC PLAYS)

OLD TOWN

HALL'S CROFT

SOUTHERN

TO OXFORD VIA A-439

HOLY TRINITY CHURCH

RIVER

❶ Ambleside, Woodstock, Adelphi & Salamander Guest Houses

❷ Mercure Shakespeare Hotel

❸ The Emsley Guest House

❹ To Hemmingford House Hostel

❺ Russons Restaurant

❻ The Windmill Inn

❼ The Coconut Lagoon, Lambs, Oppo & Barnaby's Fish & Chips

❽ The Garrick Inn

❾ Kingfisher Fish & Chips

❿ Marks & Spencer

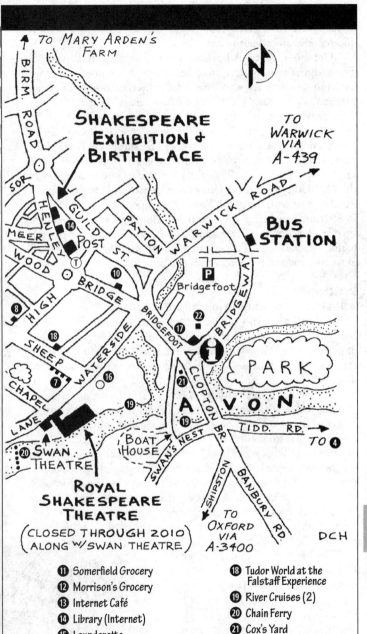

To Mary Arden's Farm

SHAKESPEARE EXHIBITION & BIRTHPLACE

TO WARWICK VIA A-439

BUS STATION

BIRM. ROAD

SOR.

MEER

WOOD

HENLEY

GUILD ST.

Post Office (T)

PAYTON

WARWICK ROAD

BRIDGE

BRIDGEFOOT

Bridgefoot

8

HIGH

18

SHEEP

7

CHAPEL

LANE

WATERSIDE

16

19

BOAT HOUSE

SWAN'S NEST

PARK

AVON

CLOPTON BR.

TIDD. RD.

TO 4

20 Swan Theatre

ROYAL SHAKESPEARE THEATRE
(CLOSED THROUGH 2010 ALONG W/SWAN THEATRE)

SHIPSTON

BANBURY RD.

TO OXFORD VIA A-3400

DCH

- ⑪ Somerfield Grocery
- ⑫ Morrison's Grocery
- ⑬ Internet Café
- ⑭ Library (Internet)
- ⑮ Launderette
- ⑯ Swan Fountain (Town Walks)
- ⑰ City Bus Tours
- ⑱ Tudor World at the Falstaff Experience
- ⑲ River Cruises (2)
- ⑳ Chain Ferry
- ㉑ Cox's Yard
- ㉒ Old Barn Shop (Bag Storage)

Shakespearean properties in and near Stratford, all run by the Shakespeare Birthplace Trust. Each has a garden and helpful docents who love to tell a story.

Combo-Tickets: Admission to the Shakespeare Birthplace Trust sights in town requires one of two combo-tickets; no individual tickets are sold. Individual tickets are sold for Anne Hathaway's Cottage (£6.50) and Mary Arden's Farm (£8), but these make sense only if you visit just these two sights. If you're visiting only the sights in town—Shakespeare's Birthplace, Hall's Croft, and Nash's House—get the £12 **Shakespeare Birthplace combo-ticket.** To add the two sights outside of Stratford—Anne Hathaway's Cottage and Mary Arden's Farm (my favorite)—get the £17 **Shakespeare Five House combo-ticket.** If you've taken a walking tour with Stratford Town Walks (described under "Tours in Stratford," earlier), show your ticket stub to get the Shakespeare Five House combo-ticket for just £12. Tickets are sold at participating sights and the TI, and are good for one year. Shakespeare's grave isn't covered by either combo-ticket.

In Stratford

▲Shakespeare Exhibition and Birthplace—Touring this sight, you'll visit an excellent modern museum before seeing Shakespeare's place of birth (covered by £12 or £17 combo-ticket, daily April–Oct 9:00–17:00, Nov–March 10:00–16:00, in town center on Henley Street, tel. 01789/204-016, www.shakespeare.org.uk).

The **Shakespeare exhibition** provides a fine historical background, with actual historic artifacts. Linger in the museum rather than rushing to the old house, since the meat of your visit is here. It's the best introduction to the life and work of Shakespeare in Stratford, with an original 1623 First Folio of Shakespeare's work. Of the 700 printed, about 150 survive. (Most are in the US, but three are in Stratford.) Western literature owes much to this folio, which collects 36 of the 37 known Shakespeare's plays (*Pericles* missed out). It came with an engraving of the only portrait from living memory of Shakespeare, and likely the most accurate depiction of the great playwright.

The **birthplace,** a half-timbered Elizabethan building furnished as it was when young William was growing up, is filled with bits about his life and work. I found the old house disappointing—only the creaky floorboards feel authentic. After the Shakespeares moved out, the building was used as a pub and a butcher's

The Look of Stratford

There's much more to Stratford than Shakespeare sights. Take time to appreciate the look of the town itself. While the main street goes back to Roman times, the key date for the city was 1196, when the king gave the town "market privileges." Stratford was shaped by its marketplace years. The market's many "departments" were located on logically named streets, whose names still remain: Sheep Street, Corn Street, and so on. Today's street plan—and even the 57' 9" width of the lots—survives from the 12th century. (Some of the modern storefronts in the town center are still that exact width.)

Starting about 1600, three great fires gutted the town, leaving very few buildings older than that era. Since those fires, tinderbox thatch roofs were prohibited—the Old Thatch Tavern on Greenhill Street is the only remaining thatch roof in town, predating the law and grandfathered in.

The town's main drag, Bridge Street, is the oldest street in town, but looks the youngest. It was built in the Regency style—a result of a rough little middle row of wattle-and-daub houses being torn down in the 1820s to double the street's width. Today's Bridge Street buildings retain that early 19th-century style: Regency.

Throughout Stratford, you'll see striking black-and-white, half-timbered buildings, as well as half-timbered structures that were partially plastered over and covered up in the 19th century. During Victorian times, the half-timbered style was considered low-class, but in the 20th century—just as tourists came, preferring the ye olde style—timbers came back into vogue, and the plaster was removed on many old buildings. But any black and white you see is likely to be modern paint. The original coloring was "biscuit yellow" and brown.

shop. Since its restoration in the 1800s, it feels like millions of visitors have rubbed it clean of anything original. While the furnishings seem tacky and modern, they're supposed to be true to 1575, when William was 11. The house becomes interesting only if you talk up the attendants in each room.

While William Shakespeare was born in this house (in 1564), he spent most of his career in London. It was there that he taught his play-going public about human nature, with plots that entertained both the highest and the lowest minds. His tool was an unrivaled mastery of the English language. He retired—rich and famous—back in Stratford, spending his last five years at a house (now long gone) called New Place.

Little is known about Shakespeare the man. The scope of his brilliant work, his humble beginnings, and the fact that no original Shakespeare manuscripts survive raise a few scholarly eyebrows.

While some wonder who penned all these plays, all serious scholars accept his authorship.

Hall's Croft—This former home of Shakespeare's daughter is in the Stratford town center. A fine old Jacobean house, it's the fanciest of the group (she married a doctor). It's worth a quick pop-in if you already have one of the Shakespearean combo-tickets; to make the exhibits on 17th-century medicine interesting, ask the docent for the 15- to 20-minute introduction, which helps bring the plague—and some of the bizarre remedies of the time—to life (covered by £12 or £17 combo-ticket, daily April–Oct 10:00–17:00, Nov–March 11:00–16:00, on-site tearoom, between Church Street and the river on Old Town Street, tel. 01789/292-107).

Nash's House—Built beside New Place (the house where Shakespeare retired), this is the least impressive and least interesting of the Shakespeare-related properties. (Nash was the first husband of Shakespeare's granddaughter.) While Shakespeare's New Place is long gone (notice the foundation in the adjacent garden as you leave), Nash's house has survived. Your visit starts here with a five-minute guided intro in the parlor. The upper level hosts temporary exhibits (covered by £12 or £17 combo-ticket, same hours as Hall's Croft, Chapel Street).

You can get into the neighboring gardens for free, and cheapskates can get a nice view of Nash's House's gardens (included in the entry price to the house) just by walking behind it along Chapel Street.

Shakespeare's Grave—To see his final resting place, head to the riverside Holy Trinity Church (£1.50, not covered by either combo-ticket, free to view for churchgoers, April–Sept Mon–Sat 8:30–18:00, Sun 12:30–17:00, slightly shorter hours Oct–March, 10-min walk past the theater—see its graceful spire as you gaze down the river, tel. 01789/266-316, www.stratford-upon-avon.org). The church marks the ninth-century birthplace of the town, which was once a religious settlement.

Just Outside Stratford
▲▲Mary Arden's Farm and Shakespeare Countryside
Museum—Along with the birthplace museum, this is my favorite of the Shakespearean sights. Famous as the girlhood home of William's mom, this homestead is in Wilmcote (about three miles from Stratford). Built around two historic farmhouses, it's an open-air folk museum depicting 16th-century farm life. It has many more domestic artifacts—and sees far fewer tourists—than the other Shakespeare sights (£8 or covered by £17 combo-ticket, daily April–Oct 10:00–17:00, Nov–March 10:00–16:00).

The first building, **Palmer's farm** (mistaken for Mary Arden's home for hundreds of years, and correctly identified in 2000), is furnished as it would have been in Shakespeare's day.

Mary Arden actually lived in the neighboring **farmhouse,** seemingly less impressive and covered in brick facade. Dorothy Holmes, who lived here until 1979, left it as a 1920s time warp, and that's just what you'll see today. Ask the docent about how they discovered that Palmer's farm was actually built a few years too late to be from Shakespeare's time.

At both buildings, you'll see period interpreters in Tudor costumes. They'll likely be going through the day's chores as people back then would have done—activities such as milking the sheep and cutting wood to do repairs on the house. They're there to answer questions and provide fun, gossipy insight into what life was like at the time.

The grounds also host a 19th-century farming exhibit, as well as enjoyable and informative **falconry demonstrations** with lots of mean-footed birds. Chat with the falconer about their methods for earning the birds' trust. The birds' hunger sets them to flight (a round-trip earns the bird a bit of food; the birds fly when hungry—but don't have the energy if they're *too* hungry). Like Katherine, the wife described as "my falcon" in *The Taming of the Shrew,* these birds are tamed and trained with food as a reward. If things are slow, ask if you can feed one.

Getting to Mary Arden's House: The most convenient way to

Stratford Thanks America

Residents of Stratford are thankful for the many contributions Americans have made to their city and its heritage. Along with pumping up the economy day in and day out with tourist visits, Americans paid for half the rebuilding of the Royal Shakespeare Theatre after it burned down in 1926. The Swan Theatre renovation was funded entirely by American aid. Harvard University inherited—you guessed it—the Harvard House, and it maintains the house today. London's much-loved theater, Shakespeare's Globe, was the dream (and gift) of an American. And there's even an odd but prominent "American Fountain" overlooking Stratford's market square on Rother Street, which was given in 1887 to celebrate the Golden Jubilee of the rule of Queen Victoria.

get here is by car or the hop-on, hop-off bus tour, but it's also possible to reach by train. The Wilmcote train station is directly across the street from Mary Arden's House (£2 round-trip fare, one stop from Stratford-upon-Avon on Birmingham-bound train, 5-min trip, train runs about every hour, call London Midland to confirm departure time—tel. 0844-811-0133, www.londonmidland.com).

▲**Anne Hathaway's Cottage**—Located 1.5 miles out of Stratford (in Shottery), this home is a picturesque, thatch-roofed, 12-room farmhouse where the Bard's wife grew up. William courted Anne here—she was 26, he was only 18—and his tactics proved successful. (Maybe a little too much, as she was several months pregnant at their wedding.) They were married for 34 years, until his death in 1616 at age 52.

Stop in the first room for a fun eight-minute intro talk. (If the place shakes, a tourist has thunked his or her head on the low beams.) The Hathaway family lived here for 400 years, until 1912, and much of the family's 92-acre farm remains part of the sight. While the house has little to do with Shakespeare, it offers an intimate peek at life in Shakespeare's day. Guides in each room do their best to lecture to the stampeding crowds. The garden comes with a prizewinning "traditional cottage garden," a yew maze (planted only in 2001, so not yet a challenge), a great photo-op statue of the British Isles, and a rotating exhibit, generally on a gardening theme (£6.50 or covered by £17 combo-ticket, daily April–Oct 9:00–17:00, Nov–March 10:00–16:00; a 30-min walk, a stop on the hop-on, hop-off tour bus, or a quick taxi ride from Stratford; well-signposted for drivers entering Stratford from any direction, easy and free parking).

Seeing a Shakespeare Play in Stratford

In 2008, the mighty Royal Shakespeare Company (RSC) down-sized, as its historic theater underwent a multiyear renovation (estimated reopening date: late 2010). Most performances are now held in the new Courtyard Theatre, a testing ground for the lights, seats, and structure of the multimillion-dollar renovation of the main theater. (While you're in Stratford, you may also see ads for RSC productions scattered in other smaller theaters around town.)

For the most up-to-date show times, check with the TI or the Royal Shakespeare Company's box office or website (see below).

▲▲Royal Shakespeare Company

The RSC, undoubtedly the best Shakespeare company on earth and a memorable experience, performs year-round in Stratford and in London (see page 122). If you're a Shakespeare fan, see if the RSC schedule fits into your itinerary.

Tickets in Stratford range from £5 (standing) to £50 (Mon–Sat at 19:30, matinees vary, sporadic shows Sun). You'll probably need to buy your tickets ahead of time. Even if there aren't any seats available, you can sometimes buy a returned ticket on the evening of an otherwise sold-out show (box office window open Mon–Sat 9:30–20:00, ticket hotline open 24/7, tel. 0844-800-1100, www .rsc.org.uk). Because the RSC website is so user-friendly, it makes absolutely no sense to pay extra to book tickets through any other source. If you're feeling bold, buy a £5 standing ticket and then slip into an open seat as the lights dim—if there's not something available during the play's first half, chances are there will be plenty of seats after intermission.

Theaters

The Courtyard Theatre—This temporary theater, a two-minute walk down Southern Lane from the original Royal Shakespeare

Theatre, seats 1,000 people, and is a prototype for the new Royal Shakespeare Theatre.

The Royal Shakespeare Theatre—The original theater was built in 1879 to honor the Bard, but burned down in 1926. The big replacement building you see under construction today (facing the riverside park) was erected in 1932. During the design phase, no actors were consulted; as a result, they built the stodgy Edwardian "picture frame"–style stage, even though the more dynamic "thrust"-style stage—which makes it easier for the audience to become engaged—is the actors' choice. (It would also have been closer in design to Shakespeare's Globe stage, which juts into the crowd.) The original ill-conceived design is the reason for the multiyear renovation. When the theater reopens, it will have an updated, thrust-style stage (the kind you'll see in the Courtyard Theatre).

The Swan Theatre—Adjacent to the RSC Theatre is the smaller, Elizabethan-style Swan Theatre, a galleried playhouse that opened in 1986. In the past, the Swan has hosted theater tours, but as part of the renovation of the main theater, the Swan has also shut its doors to visitors.

Non-Shakespearean Sights

Tudor World at the Falstaff Experience—It's a bit gimmicky, but it's about the best non-Shakespeare historical sight in

the town center. (While it's named for a Shakespeare character, the exhibit isn't about the Bard.) Filling Shrieve's House Barn with informative and entertaining exhibits, it sweeps through Tudor history from the plague to Henry VIII's privy chamber to a replica 16th-century tavern. If you're into ghost-spotting, their nightly ghost tours may be your best shot (museum-£5, daily 10:30–17:30; ghost tours-£7.50, daily at 18:00; Sheep Street, toll tel. 0870-350-2770, www.falstaffexperience.co.uk).

Avon Riverfront—The River Avon is a playground of swans and canal boats. The swans have been the mascots of Stratford since 1623, when, seven years after the Bard's death, a poem in his First Folio nicknamed him "the sweet swan of Avon." Join in the bird-scene fun and buy **swan food** (50p) to feed swans and ducks; ask at

the ice-cream stand for details. Don't feed the Canada geese, which locals disdain (according to them, the geese are vicious and have been messing up the eco-balance since they were imported by a king in 1665).

The **canal boats** saw their workhorse days during the short window of time between the start of the Industrial

Stratford, the Birthplace of... Teletubbies

The children's television series *Teletubbies* was first produced at a secret location somewhere around Stratford. Ragdoll, the local TV production company that made *Teletubbies*, became phenomenally successful, also creating the kids' series' *Rosie and Jim, Brum,* and *Boohbah. Teletubbies,* comprising 365 episodes, is no longer in production, but will likely continue to appear in reruns worldwide for years to come. Its creator, Ann Wood, has had quite a ride. Sales of her little stuffed animals went through the roof in Britain, thanks in part to American televangelist Jerry Falwell. Falwell infamously declared that Tinky Winky, the purse-toting purple Teletubby with the triangle above his head, was gay; he issued an alert to parents stating that the Teletubbies were sinisterly promoting deviant lifestyles among preschoolers. At first, Mrs. Wood—a proper and decent English woman—was crushed to hear about his claim. Then sales skyrocketed, and she went on to become Britain's fifth wealthiest woman, the beneficiary of Falwell's homophobic paranoia. Stratford's Ragdoll shop, long a local fixture, closed in 2005, but hopes to eventually reopen in a bigger location (www.ragdoll.co.uk).

Revolution and the establishment of the railways. Today, they're mostly pleasure boats. The boats are long and narrow, so two can pass in the slim canals. There are 2,000 miles of canals in England's Midlands, built to connect centers of industry with seaports and provide vital transportation during the early days of the Industrial Revolution. Stratford was as far inland as you could sail on natural rivers from Bristol; it was the terminus of the man-made Birmingham Canal, built in 1816. Even today, you can motor your canal boat all the way to London from here.

For a little bit of mellow river action, rent a **rowboat** (£4/ hr per person) or, for more of a challenge, pole yourself around on a Cambridge-style **punt** (canal is poleable—only 4 or 5 feet deep; same price and more memories/embarrassment if you do the

punting—don't pay £16/hr for a waterman to do the punting for you). Take a short stop on your lazy tour of the English countryside, and moor your canal boat at Stratford's Canal Basin. You can try a sleepy half-hour **river cruise** (£4, no commentary, Avon Boating, board boat in Bancroft Gardens near the RSC theater or at Swan's Nest Boathouse across the Tramway Bridge, tel. 01789/267-073, www.avon-boating.co.uk), or jump on the oldest surviving **chain ferry** (c. 1937, see photo on previous page) in Britain (50p), which shuttles people across the river just beyond the theater.

Cox's Yard, a riverside timber yard until the 1990s, is a rare physical remnant of the days when Stratford was an industrial port. Today, Cox's is a touristic entertainment center with pubs that have live music most nights (£5–15, schedule at tel. 01789/404-600 or www.coxsyard.co.uk).

Sleeping in Stratford

If you want to spend the night after you catch a show, options abound. Ye olde timbered hotels are scattered through the city center. Most B&Bs are on the fringes of town, right on the busy ring roads that route traffic away from the center. (The recommended places below generally have double-paned windows for rooms in the front.) The weekend after Shakespeare's birthday (April 24–25 in 2010) is particularly tight, but Fridays and Saturdays are busy through the season. This town is so reliant upon the theater for its business that some B&Bs have secondary insurance covering their loss if the Royal Shakespeare Company stops performing in Stratford for any reason.

On Grove Road

These accommodations are at the edge of town on busy Grove Road, across from a grassy park.

$$ Ambleside Guest House is run with quiet efficiency and attentiveness by owners Peter and Ruth. Each of the seven rooms has been completely renovated, including the small but tidy bathrooms. The place has a homey, airy feel, with none of the typical B&B clutter (S-£28–33, Db-£60–75, Tb-£85–105, Qb-£95–125, one ground-floor room, secure parking available, free Wi-Fi, 41 Grove Road, tel. 01789/297-239, fax 01789/295-670, www.amblesideguesthouse.com, ruth@amblesideguesthouse.com—include your phone number in your request, since they prefer to call you back to confirm).

$$ Woodstock Guest House is a friendly, frilly, family-run, and flowery place with five comfortable rooms (Sb-£35–40, Db-£60–70, family room-£75–90, cash only, deals for 2 or more nights, parking, 30 Grove Road, tel. 01789/299-881, www.woodstock-house.co.uk, jackie@woodstock-house.co.uk, owners Denis and bubbly Jackie).

$$ Adelphi Guest House has six rooms—two with four-poster beds—in a newly renovated B&B (S-£35–40, D-£75–80,

Sleep Code

(£1 = about $1.60, country code: 44, area code: 01789)
S = Single, **D** = Double/Twin, **T** = Triple, **Q** = Quad, **b** = bathroom,
s = shower only. Unless noted otherwise, you can assume
credit cards are accepted and breakfast is included.

To help you sort easily through these listings, I've divided
the rooms into three categories based on the price for a
standard double room with bath:

$$$ Higher Priced—Most rooms £90 or more.
$$ Moderately Priced—Most rooms between £60–90.
$ Lower Priced—Most rooms £60 or less.

5 percent surcharge on credit cards, 10 percent discount in
2010—mention this book when you reserve, free Wi-Fi, parking
available if booked in advance, 39 Grove Road, tel. 01789/204-469,
www.adelphi-guesthouse.com, info@adelphi-guesthouse.com,
Martin and Ellen).

$ Salamander Guest House, run by gregarious Frenchman
Pascal and his wife, Anna, rents seven well-priced but basic rooms
(S-£30–35, Db-£50–60, Tb-£60–75, Qb-£80–90, free Wi-Fi, free
on-site parking, 40 Grove Road, tel. & fax 01789/205-728, www
.salamanderguesthouse.co.uk, p.delin@btinternet.com).

Elsewhere in Stratford

$$$ Mercure Shakespeare Hotel, located in a black-and-white
building just up the street from Nash's House, has 74 central, spa-
cious, and elegant rooms. Singles are cheaper on weekends, and
doubles drop in price on Sunday and midweek—check website for
special deals (Sb-£80, standard Db-£130, deluxe Db-£150, prices
soft depending on demand—can be as low as £100 for a double,
parking-£10/day, Wi-Fi in lobby, Chapel Street, tel. 01789/294-
997, fax 01789/415-411, www.mercure.com, h6630-re@accor.com).

$$ The Emsley Guest House holds five bright rooms named
after different counties in England, and has a homey and inviting
atmosphere (Sb-£45–50, Db-£60–80, Tb-£90–120, Q-£120–160,
5-person family room-£150–200, families welcome, off-street
parking, 4 Arden Street, tel. 01789/299-557, www.theemsley.co.uk,
mel@theemsley.co.uk, Melanie and Ray Coulson).

$ *Hostel:* Hemmingford House, with 130 beds in 2- to
10-bed rooms, is a 10-minute bus ride from town (from £25 for
non-members, includes breakfast; take bus #15, #18, or #18A two
miles to Alveston; tel. 01789/297-093 or 0845-371-9661, stratford
@yha.org.uk).

Eating in Stratford

Stratford's numerous eateries vie for your pre- and post-theater business, with special hours and meal deals. (Most offer light two- and three-course menus from 17:30–19:00.) You'll find many hard-working places lined up along Sheep Street and Waterside.

Russons Restaurant, which specializes in fresh fish and seafood, is probably the best place in town. It's cheery and chic, offering international cuisine in a woody and yellow candlelit ambience. Reserve in advance for evening meals (£10–15 plates, Tue–Sat 11:30–14:00 & 17:15–21:00, closed Sun–Mon, 8 Church Street, tel. 01789/268-822).

The Windmill Inn, across from Russons, serves modestly priced but elegant fare in a 17th-century inn. Order drinks and food at the bar, settle into a comfy chair, and wait for your meal to be served (£6–12 plates, Mon–Fri 12:00–19:00, Sat–Sun 12:00–17:00, Church Street, tel. 01789/297-687).

The Coconut Lagoon serves tasty, spicy nouvelle South Indian cuisine and offers pre-theater specials until 19:00: a £10.50 two-course deal or £13.25 for three courses (Tue–Sun 12:00–14:30 & 17:00–23:00, closed Mon, 21 Sheep Street, tel. 01789/293-546).

Lambs is an intimate place serving meat, fish, and veggie dishes with panache (£15 two-course special, £20 three-course special, Mon 17:00–22:00, Tue–Sat 12:00–14:00 & 17:00–22:00, Sun 12:00–14:00 & 18:00–21:00, 12 Sheep Street, tel. 01789/292-554). The related **Oppo Restaurant,** next door, is similar but less formal (Mon–Thu 12:00–14:00 & 17:00–21:30, Fri–Sat 12:00–14:00 & 17:00–23:00, Sun 18:00–21:00, tel. 01789/269-980).

The Garrick Inn bills itself as the oldest pub in town, and comes with a cozy, dimly lit restaurant vibe. They serve pricey but above-average pub cuisine (£11 or less, Mon–Sat 12:00–22:00, Sun 12:00–21:00, 25 High Street, tel. 01789/292-186).

Barnaby's is a greasy fast-food fish-and-chips joint near the waterfront—but it's convenient if you want to get takeout for the riverside park just across the street (daily 11:00–19:30, at Sheep Street and Waterside). For a better set of fish-and-chips, queue up with the locals at **Kingfisher** (Mon–Sat 11:30–13:45 & 17:00–21:30, closed Sun, a long block up at 13 Ely Street, tel. 01789/292-513).

Picnic: For groceries, you'll find **Marks & Spencer** on Bridge Street (Mon–Sat 9:00–18:00, Sun 10:30–16:30, small coffee-and-sandwiches café upstairs, tel. 01789/292-430), **Somerfield** in the Town Centre mall (Mon–Sat 8:00–19:00, Sun 10:00–16:00, tel. 01789/292-604), and a huge **Morrison's** next to the train station, a 10-minute walk from the city center (Mon–Sat 8:00–20:00, Sun 10:00–16:00, pharmacy, tel. 01789/267-675). To picnic, head to the canal and riverfront park between the Royal Shakespeare Theatre and the TI. Choose a bench with views of the river or of vacation houseboats, and munch your fish-and-chips while tossing a few fries into the river to attract swans. It's a fine way to spend a mid-summer night's eve.

Stratford Connections

Remember: When buying tickets or checking schedules, ask for "Stratford-upon-Avon," not just "Stratford" (which is a different town).

From Stratford-upon-Avon by Train to: London (every 2 hrs, 2.25 hrs, direct to Marylebone Station), **Warwick** (every 1–2 hrs, 30 min), **Coventry** (at least hourly, 1.75 hrs, change in Leamington Spa or Birmingham), **Oxford** (every 2 hrs, 1.25–2.5 hrs, change in Banbury). Train info: toll tel. 0845-748-4950, www.nationalrail.co.uk.

By Bus to: Chipping Campden (Mon–Sat 11 buses/day, none on Sun, 35 min, Johnsons Coach & Bus, tel. 01564/797-070, www.johnsonscoaches.co.uk), **Warwick** (hourly by bus, 20 min, tel. 01788/535-555, www.stagecoachbus.com), **Coventry** (hourly, 1.25 hrs, tel. 01788/535-555, www.stagecoachbus.com). Most intercity buses stop on Stratford's Bridge Street (a block up from the TI). For bus info that covers all the region's companies, call Traveline at toll tel. 0871-200-2233 (www.travelinemidlands.co.uk).

By Car: Driving is easy and distances are brief: **Stow-on-the-Wold** (22 miles), **Warwick** (8 miles), **Coventry** (19 miles).

Near Stratford

Warwick

The pleasant town of Warwick—home to England's finest medieval castle—goes about its business almost oblivious to the busloads of tourists passing through. From the castle, a lane leads into the old town center a block away, where you'll find the **TI** (daily 10:00–16:30, tel. 01926/492-212, www.warwick-uk.co.uk), plenty of eateries (including the Ask restaurant chain), and several minor attractions. The TI can also sell same-day tickets to Warwick Castle; there's no discount, but it can save you time in line at the castle.

Sights in Warwick

▲▲Warwick Castle

Almost *too* groomed and organized, this theme park of a castle gives its crowds of visitors a decent value for the stiff £20 entry fee. The cash-poor but enterprising lord hired the folks at Madame Tussauds (now part of Merlin Entertainments, which also owns the London Eye and Legoland) to wring maximum tourist dollars out of his castle. The greedy feel of the place is a little annoying, considering the already-steep admission. But—especially for kids—there just isn't a better medieval castle experience in England.

With a lush, green, grassy moat and fairy-tale fortifications, Warwick will entertain you from dungeon to lookout. Standing inside the castle gate, you can see the mound where the original Norman castle of 1068 stood. Under this "motte," the wooden stockade (or "bailey") defined the courtyard in the way the castle walls do today. The castle is a 14th- and 15th-century fortified shell, holding an 18th- and 19th-century royal residence, surrounded by another one of dandy "Capability" Brown's landscape jobs (like at Blenheim Palace).

Within the castle's mighty walls, there's something for every taste. The Great Hall and six lavish staterooms are the sumptuous

highlights. You'll also find a Madame Tussauds–mastered re-creation of a royal weekend party—an 1898 game of statue-maker (look for a young Winston Churchill). You can ponder the weapons in the fine and educational armory, then see demonstrations outside of a trebuchet (like a catapult) and ballista (a type of giant slingshot). The "King Maker" exhibit (set in 1471, when the townsfolk are getting ready for battle) is highly promoted, but not quite as good as a Disney ride. From the classic ramparts, the tower is a one-way, no-return, 250-step climb, offering a fun perch from which to fire your imaginary longbow. A recently restored mill and engine house come with an attendant who explains how the castle was electrified in 1894. Surrounding everything is a lush, peacock-patrolled, picnic-perfect park, complete with a Victorian rose garden. The

Stratford Area

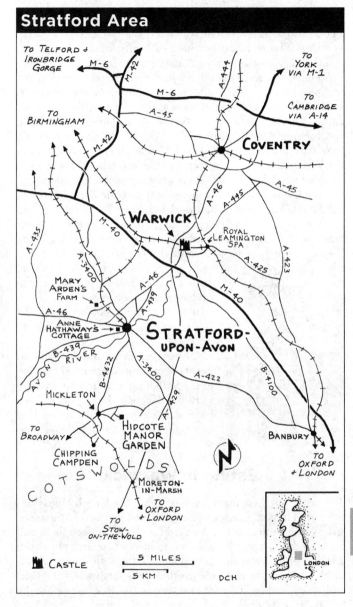

castle grounds are often enlivened by a knight in shining armor on a horse that rotates with a merry band of musical jesters.

Cost, Hours, Location: Steep £20 entry fee (£12 for seniors), includes gardens and nearly all castle attractions—except the gory £7.50 dungeon, crazy pricing scheme varies based on anticipated crowds—may go down to £18 in slow periods, discounted tickets available on the castle's website and at the TI in Stratford. It's open daily April–Oct 10:00–18:00, Nov–March 10:00–17:00. Driving and parking tips are noted under "Warwick Connections—By Car," later. For train travelers, it's a 15-minute, one-mile walk from the Warwick train station to the castle (toll tel. 0870-442-2375, recorded info tel. 0870-442-2000, www.warwick-castle.com).

Audioguide: Three audioguides provide descriptions of the State Apartments, the Royal Weekend Party exhibit, and A Knight's Tale (£3 apiece, or all three for £6, can be combined with online ticket purchase or rented upon arrival). The

£5 guidebook gives you nearly the same script in souvenir-booklet form. Either is worthwhile if you want to understand the various rooms. If you tour the castle without help, pick the brains of the earnest and talkative docents.

Events: During summer, special events (great for kids) are scheduled every half-hour throughout the day (jousting, longbow demo, sword fights, jester acts, and so on). Pick up the daily events flier (which also lists kiosks that sell snacks) and plan accordingly.

Eating in Warwick

The castle has three main lunch options. **The Coach House** has cafeteria fare and grungy seating (located just before the turnstiles). **The Undercroft** offers the best on-site cooked food, and has a sandwich buffet line (located inside, in basement of palace); you can sit under medieval vaults or escape with your food and picnic outside. The **riverside pavilion** sells sandwiches and fish-and-chips, and has fine outdoor seating (in park just before the bridge, behind castle).

Literally a hundred yards from the castle turnstiles—through a tiny gate in the wall—is the workaday commercial district of the town of **Warwick,** with several much more elegant and competitive eateries that serve fine lunches at non-Tussauds prices. It's worth the walk.

Warwick Connections

From Warwick by Train to: London (3/hr, 2 hrs), **Stratford** (every 1–2 hrs, 30 min—buses are better, see below). Warwick's little train station is a 15-minute walk (or £3 taxi) from the castle. It has no official baggage check, but you can ask politely. The castle has a baggage-check facility. Train info: toll tel. 0845-748-4950, www.nationalrail.co.uk.

By Bus to: Stratford (hourly, 20 min, bus #X17, also slower #18), **Coventry** (10/day, 1 hour, bus #X17, www.stagecoachbus .com).

By Car: The main Stratford–Coventry road cuts right through Warwick. Coming from Stratford (8 miles to the south), you'll hit the castle parking lots first (£3.50; if these are full, lurk until a few cars leave and they'll let you in). The four castle lots are expensive, and three of them are a 10- to 15-minute walk from the actual castle; "premium" £6 parking lot next to the entrance, off Castle Lane. Consider continuing into the town center (on the main road). At the TI (near the big square church spire), grab any street-side parking (free for 2 hours). The castle is a block behind the TI.

Coventry

Coventry, a ▲ sight, was bombed to smithereens in 1940 by the Nazi Luftwaffe. From that point on, the German phrase for "to

really blast the heck out of a place" was "to coventrate" it. But Coventry rose from its ashes, and its message to our world is one of forgiveness, reconciliation, and the importance of peace. Browse through Coventry, the closest thing to normal, everyday, urban England that most tourists will ever see. Get a map at the **TI,** located at the cathedral ruins (Mon–Fri 9:30–17:00, Sat–Sun 10:00–16:30, shorter hours off-season, tel. 02476/227-264, www.visitcoventryandwarwickshire .co.uk, tic@cvone.co.uk).

The symbol of Coventry is the bombed-out hulk of its old **cathedral,** with the huge new one adjoining it. The inspirational complex welcomes visitors. Climb the tower (£2.50, daily 9:30–16:00, 180 steps, tel. 02476/225-616, www.coventrycathedral.org.uk).

According to legend, Coventry's most famous hometown girl, Lady Godiva, rode bareback and bare-naked through the town in the 11th century to help lower taxes. You'll see her bronze statue a block from the cathedral (near Broadgate). Just beyond that is the **Coventry Transport Museum,** which features the first, fastest, and most famous cars and motorcycles that came from this "British Detroit" (free, daily 10:00–17:00, tel. 02476/234-270, www.transport-museum.com).

St. Mary's Guildhall has 14th-century tapestries, stained glass, and an ornate ceiling (free, Easter–Sept Sun–Thu 10:00–16:00, closed Fri–Sat, during events, and off-season, www.coventry.gov.uk/stmarys).

Coventry Connections

From Coventry by Train to: Telford Central (near Ironbridge Gorge; 2/hr, 1.5 hrs, change in Birmingham or Wolverhampton), **Warwick** (hourly, 30 min, change in Leamington Spa), **Stratford-upon-Avon** (at least hourly, 1.75 hrs, change in Leamington Spa or Birmingham). Train info: toll tel. 0845-748-4950, www.national rail.co.uk.

Route Tips for Drivers: Stratford to Ironbridge Gorge via Warwick and Coventry

Entering Stratford from the Cotswolds, cross a bridge and pass the TI for the best parking. Veer right (following *Through Traffic, P,* and *Wark* signs), go around the block—turning right and right and right—and enter the multistory Bridgefoot garage (80p/hr, £20/6–24 hrs, you'll find no place easier or cheaper). The TI and City Sightseeing bus stop are a block away. Leaving the garage, circle to the right around the same block, but stay on "the Wark" (Warwick Road, A439). Warwick is eight miles away. The castle is just south of town on the right. (For parking advice, see "Warwick Connections—By Car," earlier.) When you're trying to decide whether to stop in Coventry or not, factor in Birmingham's rush hour—try to avoid driving the section described below between 14:00–20:00, if you can (see next chapter for tips).

If You're Including Coventry: After touring the castle, carry on through the center of Warwick and follow signs to Coventry (still A439, then A46). If you're stopping in Coventry, follow signs painted on the road to the *City Centre,* and then to *Cathedral Parking.* Grab a place in the high-rise parking lot. Leaving Coventry, follow signs to *Nuneaton* and *M6 North* through lots of sprawl, and you're on your way. (See below.)

If You're Skirting Coventry: Take M69 (direction: Leicester) and follow M6 as it threads through giant Birmingham.

Once You're on M6: The highway divides into a free M6 and a toll M6 (designed to help drivers cut through the Birmingham traffic chaos). Take the toll road—£4 is a small price to pay to avoid all the nasty traffic.

When battling through sprawling Birmingham, keep your sights on M6. If you're heading for any points north—Ironbridge Gorge (Telford), North Wales, Liverpool, Blackpool, or the Lakes (Kendal for the South Lake District, Keswick for the North Lake District)—just stay relentlessly on M6 (direction: North West). Each destination is clearly signed directly from M6.

For Ironbridge Gorge, take the T8 exit (don't miss this exit, or you'll have to go all the way to T11 to turn around and back-track). Follow M54 heading toward Telford. Keep an eye out for *Ironbridge* signs and do-si-do through a long series of roundabouts until you're there.

IRONBRIDGE GORGE

The Industrial Revolution was born in the Severn River Valley. In its glory days, this valley (blessed with abundant deposits of iron ore and coal and a river for transport) gave the world its first iron wheels, steam-powered locomotive, and cast-iron bridge (begun in 1779). The museums in Ironbridge Gorge, which capture the flavor of the Victorian Age, take you back into the days when Britain was racing into the modern era, and pulling the rest of the West with her.

Planning Your Time

Without a car, Ironbridge Gorge isn't worth the headache. Drivers can slip it in between the Cotswolds/Stratford/Warwick and points north (such as the Lake District or North Wales). Speed demons zip in for a midday tour of Blists Hill, look at the bridge, and speed out. For an overnight visit, arrive in the early evening to browse the town, and spend the morning and early afternoon touring the sights before driving on (10:00–Museum of the Gorge, which has a nice overview of the entire area; 11:00–Blists Hill Victorian Town for lunch and sightseeing; 15:30–Head to your next destination).

With more time—say, a full month in Britain—I'd spend two nights and a leisurely day: 9:30–Iron Bridge and the town; 10:30–Museum of the Gorge; 11:30–Coalbrookdale Museum of Iron; 14:30–Blists Hill; then dinner at Coalbrookdale Inn.

Orientation to Ironbridge Gorge

(area code: 01952)

The town is just a few blocks gathered around the Iron Bridge, which spans the peaceful, tree-lined Severn River. While the smoke-belching bustle is long gone, knowing that this wooded, sleepy river valley was the "Silicon Valley" of the 19th century makes wandering its brick streets almost a pilgrimage. The actual museum sites are scattered over three miles. The modern cooling towers (for coal, not nuclear energy) that loom ominously over these redbrick remnants seem strangely appropriate.

Tourist Information

The TI is in the tollhouse on the Iron Bridge (Mon–Fri 9:00–17:00, Sat–Sun 10:00–17:00, tel. 01952/884-391). The TI has lots of booklets for sale; hikers like the three booklets of nearby walks (£3–5).

Getting Around Ironbridge Gorge

On weekends from Easter through October, **Gorge Connect** buses link the museum sites (£0.50/ride, £2.50 day ticket, may be free with Museum Passport in 2010—described below, 1–2/hr, April–Oct Sat–Sun 9:00–18:00 only, no buses Mon–Fri, several morning and afternoon runs go to the Telford rail station—schedule on website, tel. 01952/200-005 or 01952/382-121, www.telfordtravelink.co.uk).

Sights in Ironbridge Gorge

▲▲Iron Bridge

While England was at war with her American colonies, this first cast-iron bridge was built in 1779 to show off a wonderful new

building material. Lacking experience with cast iron, the builders erred on the side of sturdiness and constructed it as if it were made out of wood. Notice that the original construction used traditional timber-jointing techniques rather than rivets. (Any rivets are from later repairs.) The valley's centerpiece is free, open all the time, and thought-provoking. Walk across the bridge to the tollhouse/TI/gift shop/museum (free, see "Tourist Information," earlier). Read the fee schedule and notice the subtle slam against royalty. (England was not immune to the revolutionary sentiment brewing in the colonies at this time.) Pedestrians paid half a penny to cross;

Ironbridge Gorge

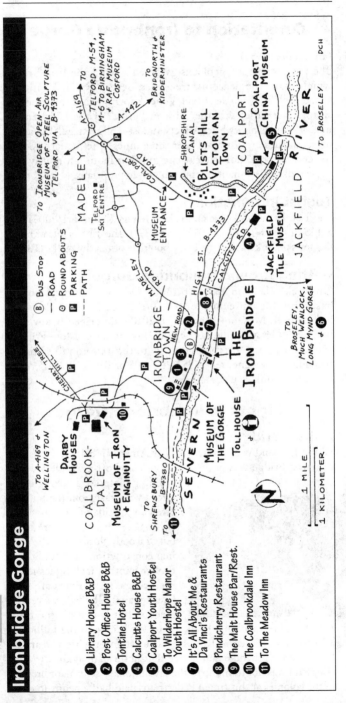

1. Library House B&B
2. Post Office House B&B
3. Tontine Hotel
4. Calcutts House B&B
5. Coalport Youth Hostel
6. To Wilderhope Manor Youth Hostel
7. It's All About Me & Da Vinci's Restaurants
8. Pondicherry Restaurant
9. The Malt House Bar/Rest.
10. The Coalbrookdale Inn
11. To The Meadow Inn

Ⓑ BUS STOP
— ROAD
Ⓞ ROUNDABOUTS
Ⓟ PARKING
--- PATH

DCH

poor people crossed cheaper by coracle—a crude tub-like wood-and-canvas shuttle ferry (you'll see old photos of these upstairs). Cross back to the town and enjoy a pleasant walk downstream along the towpath. Where horses once dragged boats laden with Industrial Age cargo, locals now walk their dogs.

▲▲▲Ironbridge Gorge Industrial Revolution Museums

Locals take pride in the 10 museums located within a few miles of each other, focused on the Iron Bridge and all that it represents. Not all the sights are worth your time. Plan on seeing the Blists Hill Victorian Town, the Museum of the Gorge, and the Coalbrookdale Museum of Iron, using the £20 Museum Passport (described below). The sights share the same opening hours and contact info (daily 10:00–17:00, a few Coalbrookdale sights close Nov–March, tel. 01952/884-391, www.ironbridge.org.uk, tic @ironbridge.org.uk).

Museum Passport: This group of widely scattered sites has varied admission charges (usually £3–7; Blists Hill is £13.25). The £20 Museum Passport (families-£55) covers admission to everything for a year. If you're visiting the area's must-see sights—Blists Hill Victorian Town, the Museum of the Gorge, and the Coalbrookdale Museum of Iron—you'll save a little more than £3 by using the £20 Passport.

Sightseeing Strategies: It helps to see the introductory movie at the Museum of the Gorge first, to help put everything else into context. A few of these museums, located up steep hills from the valley where the Iron Bridge crosses the river, are really only accessible by car. To see the most significant sights in one day by car, you'll park three times: once either in the lot near the TI (across the river from the village) or in the pay lot located at the Museum of the Gorge (the Iron Bridge and Gorge Museum are connected by an easy, flat walk); once at the Blists Hill parking lot; and once outside of the Coalbrookdale Museum of Iron, a former factory, with Enginuity across the lot and the Darby Houses a three-minute uphill hike away.

Museum of the Gorge

Orient yourself to the valley here in the Severn Warehouse (£3.25, daily 10:00–17:00, 500 yards upstream from the bridge, parking-£1). See the excellent 11-minute introductory movie, which lays the groundwork for what you'll see in the other museums. Check out the exhibit and the model of the gorge in its heyday, and buy a Blists Hill guidebook and your Museum Passport. Farther upstream from the museum parking lot is the fine riverside Dale End Park, with picnic areas and a playground.

Blists Hill Victorian Town

Save most of your time and energy for this wonderful town—an immersive, open-air folk museum. You'll wander through 50

acres of Victorian industry, factories, and a re-created community from the 1890s. Pick up the Blists Hill guidebook for a good step-by-step rundown (£13.25, closes at 16:00 in winter, tel. 01952/601-048).

The board by the entry lists which exhibits are staffed with lively docents in Victorian dress. Pop in to say hello to the lonely bankers—when the schoolchildren visit, the bankers lose the popularity contest to the "sweet shop" next door. It's fine to take photos.

Stop by the pharmacy and check out the squirm-inducing setup of the dentist's chair from the time—it'll make you appreciate the marvel of modern dental care. Down the street, kids like watching the candlemaker at work. Check the events in the barn across the path, where hands-on candle-making and other activities take place.

Just as it would've had in Victorian days, the village has a working pub, a greengrocer's shop, a fascinating squatter's cottage, and a snorty, slippery pigsty. Don't miss the explanation of the winding machine at the Blists Hill Mine (demos throughout the day, call for times). Located by the canal, a scale model made for a 2001 television program shows how the Iron Bridge was erected. Walk along the canal to the "inclined plane."

Grab lunch in The New Inn Pub or in the cafeteria near the children's old-time rides.

Coalbrookdale Museum of Iron

This does a fine job of explaining the original iron-smelting process. Compared to the fun and frolicking Blists Hill village, this museum is sleepy (£7.75, includes entry to the Darby Houses, listed later; £1 less in winter—when Darby Houses are closed for lack of light; opposite Darby's furnace).

The Coalbrookdale neighborhood is the birthplace of the Industrial Revolution, where locals like to claim that mass production was invented. Abraham Darby's blast furnace sits like a shrine inside a big glass pyramid (free), surrounded by evocative Industrial Age ruins. It was here that, in 1709, Darby first smelted iron, using coke as fuel. To me, "coke" is a drink, and "smelt" is the past tense of smell...but around here, these words recall the event that kicked off the modern Industrial Age.

All the ingredients of the recipe for big industry were here in abundance—iron ore, top-grade coal, and water for power and shipping. Wander around Abraham Darby's furnace. Before this furnace was built, iron ore was laboriously melted by charcoal. With huge waterwheel-powered bellows, Darby burned top-grade coal at super-hot temperatures (burning off the impurities to make "coke"). Local iron ore was dumped into the furnace and melted. Impurities floated to the top, while the pure iron sank to the bottom of a clay tub in the bottom of the furnace. Twice a day, the plugs were knocked off, allowing the "slag" to drain away on the top and the molten iron to drain out on the bottom. The low-grade slag was used locally on walls and paths. The high-grade iron trickled into molds formed in the sand below the furnace. It cooled into pig iron (named because the molds look like piglets suckling their mother). The pig-iron "planks" were broken off by sledgehammers and shipped away. The Severn River became one of Europe's busiest, shipping pig iron to distant foundries, where it was re-melted and made into cast iron (for projects such as the Iron Bridge), or to forges, where it was worked like toffee into wrought iron.

Enginuity

Located across the parking lot from the Coalbrookdale Museum of Iron, Enginuity is a hands-on funfest for kids. Riffing on Ironbridge's engineering roots, this converted 1709 foundry is full of mesmerizing water contraptions, pumps, magnets, and laser games. Build a dam, try your hand at earthquake-proof construction, navigate a water maze, operate a remote-controlled robot, or power a turbine with your own steam (£7).

Darby Houses

The Darby family, Quakers who were the area's richest neighbors by far, lived in these two homes located just above the Coalbrookdale Museum.

The 18th-century Darby mansion, **Rosehill House,** features a collection of fine china, furniture, and trinkets from various family members. It's decorated in the way the family home would have been in 1850. If the gilt-framed mirrors and fancy china seem a little ostentatious for the normally wealth-shunning Quakers, keep in mind that these folks were rich beyond reason. Docents assure visitors that, in another family's hands, Rosehill would have been completely over the top (included in £7.75 Coalbrookdale Museum of Iron ticket, otherwise £4.15, closed Nov–Easter).

Skip the adjacent **Dale House.** Dating from the 1780s, it's older than Rosehill, but almost completely devoid of interior furniture and exhibits.

Coalport China Museum, Jackfield Tile Museum, and Broseley Pipeworks

Housed in their original factories, these showcase the region's porcelain, decorated tiles, and clay tobacco pipes. These industries were developed to pick up the slack when the iron industry shifted away from the Severn Valley. Each museum features finely decorated pieces, and the china and tile museums offer low-energy workshops.

Ironbridge Open-Air Museum of Steel Sculpture

This park is a striking tribute to the region's industrial heritage. Stroll the 10-acre grounds and spot works by Roy Kitchin and other sculptors stashed in the forest and perched in rolling grasslands (£3, March–Nov Tue–Sun 10:00–17:00, closed Mon except bank holidays, closed Dec–Feb, 2 miles from Iron Bridge, Moss House, Cherry Tree Hill, Coalbrookdale, Telford, tel. 01952/433-152, www.go2.co.uk/steelsculpture).

Near Ironbridge Gorge

Skiing and Swimming—There's a small, brush-covered ski slope with two Poma lifts at Telford Snowboard and Ski Centre in Madeley, two miles from Ironbridge Gorge; you'll see signs for it as you drive into Ironbridge Gorge (£10.20/hr including gear, less for kids, open practice times Mon and Thu 10:00–20:00, Tue and Fri 12:00–22:00, Wed 10:00–19:00, Sat 16:00–18:00, Sun 10:00–16:00, tel. 01952/382-688, www.telford.gov.uk/skicentre). A public swimming pool is up the road on Court Street (Madeley Court Sports Centre, tel. 01952/382-770).

Royal Air Force (RAF) Museum Cosford—This Red Baron magnet displays more than 80 aircraft, from warplanes to rockets. Get the background on ejection seats and a primer on the principles of propulsion (free, daily 10:00–18:00, last entry at 17:00, Shifnal, Shropshire, on A41 near junction with M54, tel. 01902/376-200, www.rafmuseum.org.uk).

More Sights—If you're looking for reasons to linger in Ironbridge Gorge, these sights are all within a short drive: the medieval town of Shrewsbury, the abbey village of Much Wenlock, the scenic Long Mynd gorge at Church Stretton, the castle at Ludlow, and the steam railway at the river town of Bridgnorth. Shoppers like Chester (en route to points north).

Sleeping in Ironbridge Gorge

$$$ Library House is *Better Homes and Gardens* elegant. Located in the town center, a half-block downhill from the bridge, it's a classy, friendly gem that actually used to be a library. The Chaucer room, which includes a small garden, is a delight, but all three of the house's rooms are lovely. The complimentary drink upon arrival is a welcome touch (Sb-£65–75, Db-£75–100, DVD library, Wi-Fi, free parking just up the road or free pass for Ironbridge parking lot, 11 Severn Bank, Ironbridge Gorge, tel. 01952/432-299, www .libraryhouse.com, info@libraryhouse.com). Lizzie Steel—who's joined by her husband and daughters most weekends—will pick you up from the Telford train station if you request it in advance.

Two lesser places, right in the town center, overlook the bridge:

$$ Post Office House B&B is literally above the post office, where the postmaster's wife, Janet Hunter, rents three rooms. It's a shower-in-the-corner, old-fashioned place (Sb-£40–42, Db-£56–60, Tb-£66–90, family room available, discount for two or more nights, cash only, 6 The Square, tel. 01952/433-201, fax 01952/433-582, pohouseironbridge@yahoo.co.uk).

$$ Tontine Hotel is the town's big, 12-room, musty, Industrial Age hotel. Check out the historic photos in the bar (S-£25, Sb-£40, D-£40, Db-£56, en-suite rooms include breakfast—otherwise it's £5 extra, family rooms, 10 percent discount with this book through 2010, The Square, tel. 01952/432-127, fax 01952/432-094, www .tontine-hotel.com, tontinehotel@tiscali.co.uk).

Outside of Town

$$$ Calcutts House rents seven rooms in their 18th-century ironmaster's home and adjacent coach house. Rooms in the main

---

Sleep Code

(£1 = about $1.60, country code: 44, area code: 01952)
S = Single, **D** = Double/Twin, **T** = Triple, **Q** = Quad, **b** = bathroom, **s** = shower only. You can assume credit cards are accepted unless noted otherwise.

To help you sort easily through these listings, I've divided the rooms into three categories based on the price for a standard double room with bath during high season:

$$$ Higher Priced—Most rooms £65 or more.
$$ Moderately Priced—Most rooms between £40-65.
$ Lower Priced—Most rooms £45 or less.

house are elegant, while the coach-house rooms are bright and modern. Ask the owners, Colin and Sarah Williams, how the rooms were named (Db-£52–85, price depends on room size, located on Calcutts Road, Gorge Connect Jackfield bus stop is across street, tel. 01952/882-631, www.calcuttshouse.co.uk, enquiries@calcuttshouse.co.uk).

$ Coalport Youth Hostel, plush for a hostel, fills an old factory at the China Museum in Coalport (£15–20 bunks in mostly 4-bed dorms, bunk-bed Db-£32–48, £3 more for non-members, includes sheets, kitchen, self-service laundry, tel. 01952/588-755, ironbridge@yha.org.uk). Don't confuse this hostel with the area's other hostel, Coalbrookdale, which is only available for groups.

$ Wilderhope Manor Youth Hostel, a beautifully remote 425-year-old manor house, is one of Europe's best hostels. On Wednesday and Sunday afternoons, tourists actually pay to see what hostelers get to sleep in (£19–23 bunks, under 18-£13.50, £3 more for non-members, single-sex dorms, family rooms available, reservations recommended, reception closed 10:00–17:00, restaurant open 17:30–20:00, tel. 01694/771-363, wilderhope@yha.org .uk). It's in Longville-in-the-Dale, six miles from Much Wenlock down B4371 toward Church Stretton.

Eating in Ironbridge Gorge

It's All About Me is an inviting café/bistro/wine bar in a prime location by the river. On a sunny day, sit on their inviting back patio, with peekaboo views of the Iron Bridge. Inside, this two-story place has the same menu upstairs or down: Mediterranean food, including £4 tapas-style small meals called "nibbly bits" (£11 for one course, £16 for two, Tue–Sat 12:00–14:30 & 18:00–21:30, Sun 12:00–16:00 & 18:00–20:45, closed Mon, plenty of indoor/outdoor seating, veggie options, 29 High Street, tel. 01952/432-716).

Pondicherry, in a renovated former police station, serves delicious Indian curries and a few British dishes to keep the less adventurous happy. The mixed vegetarian sampler is popular even with meat-eaters (£12–16 plates, Mon–Sat 17:00–23:00, Sun 17:00–21:30—starts to get hopping after 19:00, 57 Waterloo Street, tel. 01952/433-055).

Da Vinci's serves good, though pricey, Italian food and has a dressy ambience (£15–20 main courses, Tue–Sat 19:00–22:00, closed Sun–Mon, 26 High Street, tel. 01952/432-250).

The Malt House, located in an 18th-century beer house, offers an English menu with a European accent. This is a very popular scene with the local twentysomething gang (£9–15 main courses, bar menu at Jazz Bar, daily 12:00–21:30 except Sun until 22:00, near Museum of the Gorge, 5-min walk from center, The

Wharfage, tel. 01952/433-712). The Malt House is *the* vibrant nightspot in town, with live music and a fun crowd (generally Thu–Sat).

The Coalbrookdale Inn is filled with locals enjoying excellent ales and surprisingly good food. This former "best pub in Britain" has a tradition of offering free samples from a lineup of featured beers. Ask which real ales are available (Mon–Thu 17:00–23:30, Fri–Sun 12:00–23:30, food served 12:00–14:00 & 18:00–21:00, no food Sun evening, reservations unnecessary for the bar but a good idea for the fancier restaurant, lively ladies' loo, across street from Coalbrookdale Museum of Iron, 1 mile from Ironbridge Gorge, 12 Wellington Road, tel. 01952/433-953, www.coalbrookdaleinn .co.uk). Danny and Dawn Wood, the inn's owners, also rent three rooms above the restaurant for about £70.

The Meadow Inn would have appealed to Lawrence Welk. This local favorite serves prizewinning pub grub, and has lovely riverside outdoor seating if the weather cooperates (£8–10 meals, Mon–Fri 12:00–14:30 & 18:00–21:30, Sat–Sun 12:00–21:30, can get crowded, no reservations taken, a pleasant 15-min walk from the center; head upstream, at Dale End Park take the path along the river, the inn is just after railway bridge; tel. 01952/433-193).

Ironbridge Gorge Connections

Ironbridge Gorge is five miles from Telford, which has the nearest train station. To get between Ironbridge Gorge and Telford, take bus #9, #39, #76, #77, or #99 (£3.60 "Day Saver" fare, 1–2/hr, 20–45 min, none on Sun) or a taxi (about £8). Although Telford's train and bus stations are an annoying 15-minute walk apart, you can connect them in five minutes on bus #44 (every 10 min, covered by "Day Saver") or #55 (every 15 min), or with a £3 cab ride. The Telford bus station is part of a large modern mall, an easy place to wait for the bus to Ironbridge Gorge. Buses are run by Arriva (www.arrivabus.co.uk), but you can also call Traveline for departure times and other information (toll tel. 0871-200-2233, www.traveline.org.uk).

The Gorge Connect bus service, which runs among Ironbridge Gorge sights on weekends, makes several morning and afternoon runs between Ironbridge Gorge and the Telford train station. For schedule information on the Gorge Connect, see page 437. If you need a **taxi** while in Ironbridge Gorge, call Central Taxis at tel. 01952/501-050.

By Train from Telford to: Birmingham (2/hr, 40–50 min), **Conwy** in North Wales (9/day, 2.5–3.25 hrs, some change in Chester or Shrewsbury), **Blackpool** (hourly, 2.75–3 hrs, usually 2–3 changes), **Keswick/Lake District** (every 1–2 hrs, 4–4.5

hrs; 3–3.25 hrs to Penrith with 1–2 changes, then catch a bus to Keswick, hourly except Sun 6/day, 40 min, www.stagecoachbus .com), **Edinburgh** (every 1–2 hrs, 4.5–5 hrs, 1–2 changes). Train info: tel. 0845-748-4950, www.nationalrail.co.uk.

By Car to Telford: Driving in from the **Cotswolds** and **Stratford,** take M6 through Birmingham, then exit T8 to M54 to the Telford/Ironbridge exit. Follow the brown *Ironbridge* signs through several roundabouts to Ironbridge Gorge. The traffic north through Birmingham is miserable from 14:00 to 20:00, especially on Fridays. From **Warwick,** consider the M40/M42/ Kidderminster alternative, coming into Ironbridge Gorge on A442 via Bridgnorth to avoid the Birmingham traffic. (Note: On maps, Ironbridge Gorge is often referred to as "Iron Bridge" or "Iron-Bridge.")

BLACKPOOL AND LIVERPOOL

These two bustling cities—wedged between serene North Wales and the even-more-serene Lake District—provide an opportunity to sample the "real" England, both at work (Liverpool) and at play (Blackpool). Scream down roller coasters and eat "candy floss" until you're deliriously queasy at fun-loving Blackpool. In Liverpool, experience industrial England and relive the early mop-top days of some famous Liverpudlians...meet the Beatles.

Blackpool

Blackpool is Britain's tacky, laid-back underbelly. It's one of England's most-visited attractions, the private domain of its working class, a faded and sticky mix of Coney Island, Las Vegas, and Denny's. Juveniles of any age love it. My kids declared it better than Disneyland.

Blackpool grew up with the Industrial Revolution. In the mid-1800s, entire mill towns would close down and take a two-week break here. They came to drink in the fresh air (much needed after a hard year in the mills) and—literally—the seawater. (Back then they figured it was healthy.) Supposedly, Blackpool has fewer rainy days than some other parts of England, because it lies in a rain shadow.

Blackpool's heyday is long past now, as more and more working people can afford the cheap charter flights to sunny Spain. Recently, the resort has become popular for "stag" and "hen"

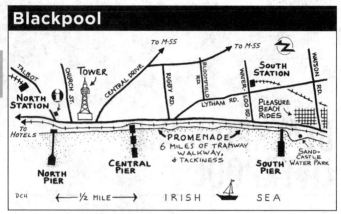

(bachelor and bachelorette) parties—basically a cheap drunk weekend for the twentysomething crowd. Consequently, there are two Blackpools: the daytime Blackpool of kids riding roller coasters and grannies getting early-bird specials; and the drunken, debauched, late-night Blackpool of glass-dance-floor clubs and bars.

But Blackpool is beginning to reinvent itself to draw more visitors. A large overhaul of The Promenade has begun, as well as numerous renovations in the city center. No matter what, the town remains an accessible and affordable fun zone for the Flo and Andy Capps of northern England. People come year after year. They stay for a week, and they love it.

Most Americans don't even consider a stop in Blackpool. Many won't like it. It's an ears-pierced-while-you-wait, tipsy-toupee kind of place. Tacky, yes. Lowbrow, OK. More than a little run-down in parts, sure. But it's as English as can be, and that's what you're here for. An itinerary should feature as many facets of a culture as possible. Blackpool is as English as the queen—and considerably more fun.

Spend the day "muckin' about" the beach promenade of fortune-tellers, fish-and-chips joints, amusement piers, warped mirrors, and Englanders wearing hats with built-in ponytails. A million greedy doors try every trick to get you inside. Huge arcade halls advertise free toilets and broadcast bingo numbers into the streets; the wind machine under a wax Marilyn Monroe blows at a steady gale; and the smell of fries, tobacco, and sugar is everywhere. Milk comes in raspberry or banana in this land where people under incredibly bad wigs look normal. If you're bored in Blackpool, you're just too classy.

Planning Your Time

Ideally, get to Blackpool around lunchtime for a free afternoon and an evening of making bubbles in this cultural mud puddle. For full effect, it's best to visit during peak season: June through early November.

Blackpool's Illuminations, when much of the waterfront is decorated with lights, draws crowds in fall, particularly on weekends (Sept 3–Nov 7 in 2010). The early-evening light is great with the sun setting over the sea. Walk out along the peaceful North Pier at twilight.

Blackpool is easy by car or train. Speed demons with a car can treat it as a midday break (it's just off M6 on M55) and continue north. If you have kids, they'll want more time here (hey, it's cheaper than Disneyland). If you're into nightlife, this town delivers. If you're before or beyond kids and not into kitsch and greasy spoons, skip it. If the weather's great and you love nature, the lakes are just a few hours north. A visit to Blackpool sharpens the wonders of Windermere.

Orientation to Blackpool

(area code: 01253)

Everything clusters along The Promenade, a tacky, glittering six-mile-long beachfront good-time strip mall punctuated by three fun-filled piers reaching out into the sea. The Pleasure Beach rides are near the South Pier. Jutting up near the North Pier is Blackpool's stubby Eiffel-type tower. The most interesting shops, eateries, and theaters are inland from the North Pier. For a break from glitz, walk north along The Promenade or sandy beach— a residential neighborhood stretches for miles. When you've had enough, just hop on the tram or a bus for a quick ride back.

Tourist Information

A spiffy new TI sits about 50 yards inland from the North Pier (Mon–Sat 9:00–17:00, Easter–early Nov Sun 10:00–16:30, closed Sun off-season, 1 Clifton Street, tel. 01253/478-222—the same number gives recorded entertainment info after hours, www.visit blackpool.com). There you'll find a £1 city map, brochures on the amusement centers, and an extremely helpful staff. The free *What's On* booklet lists local events; the TI can book shows for you for a £1.50 fee. If you're going to Sandcastle Waterpark, buy your tickets here to save a few pounds. The TI books rooms for no fee (but collects a 10 percent deposit, which hotels don't recoup; room-finding service closes at 16:30).

Arrival in Blackpool

The main (north) **train** station is three blocks from the town center (no maps given but one is posted, no ATM in station but many in town). There's no luggage storage in town, but if you're desperate, Pleasure Beach has a few lockers big enough for a backpack.

If arriving by **car,** the motorway funnels you down Yeadon Way into a giant parking zone. If you're just spending the day, head for one of the huge £6/day garages. If you're spending the night, drive to the waterfront and head north. My top accommodations are north on The Promenade (easy parking). Leaving Blackpool to go anywhere, follow signs to *M55,* which starts at Blackpool and zips you to M6 (for points north or south).

Helpful Hints

Markets: At the indoor **Abingdon Street Market,** vendors sell baked goods, fruit, bras, jewelry, eggs, and more (Mon–Sat 9:00–17:00, closed Sun). Eight miles north, the **Fleetwood Market** is huge, with two buildings full of produce, clothes, and crafts spilling out onto the street (May–Oct Mon–Tue and Thu–Sat 8:00–17:00, closed Wed and Sun; Nov–April Tue and Fri–Sat only; catch tram marked *Fleetwood,* 30 min, £2.70 one-way).

Tipping: The pubs of Blackpool have a unique tradition of "and (name an amount) your own, luv." Say that here and your bar-maid will add that amount to your bill and drop it into her tip jar. (Say it anywhere else and they won't know what you mean.)

Internet Access: The public library, in the big domed building on Queen Street, lets visitors stand and use its computers for 15 minutes (free, Mon and Fri 9:00–17:00, Tue and Thu 9:00–19:00, Wed and Sat 10:00–17:00, Sun 11:00–14:00, tel. 01253/478-111).

Post Office: The main P.O. is in the basement of the WH Smith store, at 12–16 Bank Hey Street (Mon–Sat 9:00–17:30, closed Sun).

Car Rental: In case you decide to tour the Lake District by car, you'll find plenty of rental agencies in Blackpool (closed Sat afternoon and Sun), including **Avis** (at the airport—just south of the South Pier, tel. 01253/408-003) and **Budget** (434 Waterloo Road—just north of the South Pier, tel. 01253/691-632).

Getting Around Blackpool

Laid-back **tram cars** trundle 13 miles up and down the waterfront, connecting all the sights. Trams come in all shapes and colors (some vintage, some modern, some dressed up like boats), but are all on the same system and take the same tickets. This electric tramway—the first in Europe—dates from 1885 (£1.60–2.70 depending on length of trip, pay conductor, trams come every 10–15 min or so year-round, run 6:00–23:15). Many **buses** also run along The Promenade—make sure you're not standing at a tram stop when you're waiting for a bus (similar prices, pay conductor, tel. 01253/473-001, www.blackpooltransport.com). For £6 you can purchase an all-day pass that covers both trams and buses; buy it on a tram or bus, or at their office on Market Street.

City Sightseeing's one-hour, 16-stop **hop-on, hop-off bus** has a recorded commentary and leaves from the Blackpool Tower every 30 minutes (£7.50, first two weeks of April and June–early Nov daily from 9:00 until last departure at 19:00, mid-April–May Sat–Sun only, none off-season, tel. 01253/473-001, www.city -sightseeing.com).

Taxis are easy to snare in Blackpool, and three to five people travel cheaper by cab than by tram. Hotels can get you a taxi by phone within three minutes (no extra charge).

Sights in Blackpool

▲▲**The Piers**—Blackpool's famous piers were originally built for Victorian landlubbers who wanted to go to sea but were afraid of getting seasick. Each of the three amusement piers has its own personality and is a joy to wander. The sedate **North Pier** is most traditional and refreshingly uncluttered (open first Sat in March to first weekend in Nov, daily 10:00–23:00, £0.50 admission 10:00–17:30 includes discounts on an ice cream or drink and the carousel ride, free admission after 17:30). Dance down its empty planks at twilight to the early English rock playing on its speakers. Its **Carousel Bar** at the end is great for families—with a free kids' DJ nightly from 19:00 to 23:00 (parents drink good beer while the kids bunny-hop and boogie). The something-for-everyone **Central Pier** is lots of fun. Ride its great Ferris wheel for the best view in Blackpool (rich photography at twilight, get the operator to spin you as you bottom out). And check out the sadist running the adjacent Waltzer ride—just watch the miserably ecstatic people spinning. The rollicking **South Pier** is all rides.

From the far end of any pier, look out at the horizon to see the natural-gas drilling platforms in the Irish Sea. In the distance, off the North Shore, a castaway gaggle of wind turbines capture energy.

▲**Blackpool Tower**—This mini–Eiffel Tower is a 100-year-old vertical fun center. You pay £14 to get in (£11 for kids, family tickets available); after that, the fun is free. Work your way up from the bottom through layer after layer of noisy entertainment: a circus

(two to three acts a day, runs Easter–first weekend in Nov), a 3-D cinema, an aquarium, and a wonderful old ballroom with barely live music and golden oldies dancing to golden oldies all day. Enjoy a break at the dance-floor-level pub or on a balcony perch. Kids love this place. With a little marijuana, adults would, too. Ride the glass elevator to the tip of the 500-foot-tall symbol of Blackpool for a smashing view, especially at sunset (Easter–June daily 10:00–17:00; July–early Nov daily 10:00–23:00; early Nov–Easter Wed 10:00–17:00, Sat–Sun 10:00–18:00; may be closed for events, top of tower closed when windy, toll tel. 0844-856-1111, www.theblackpooltower.co.uk). If you want to leave and return, request a hand stamp.

▲**Pleasure Beach**—Rated ▲▲▲ for roller coaster enthusiasts, these 42 acres across The Promenade from the beach attract nearly six million visitors annually, and are lit-

tered with rides galore, an ice show, circus and illusion shows, and varied amusements. Many rides are tame enough for the under-10 set, but the top few offer some of the best thrills in Europe: the Pepsi Max Big One (with a peak of 235 feet and 85 mph, it's one of the world's fastest, highest, and steepest roller coasters), the Infusion (a twisty, loopy speed rush that you ride with feet dangling), and the IceBlast (which rockets you straight up before letting you bungee down). The Bling ride spins gondola riders in three different directions 100 feet above the ground at speeds of more than 60 mph. Also memorable is the Steeplechase—carousel horses stampeding down a roller coaster track (a dream come true for *National Velvet* and *Mary Poppins* fans). The Irn Bru Revolution speeds you over a steep drop and upside-down in a loop, then does it again backward. The Valhalla ride zips you on a Viking boat in watery darkness past scary Nordic things like lutefisk. With two 80-foot drops and lots of hype, first you're scared, then you're soaked, and—finally—you're just glad you survived. The park also offers several old wooden-framed rides full of historic charm—but brittle travelers will want to consider their necks and backs. The tame-looking Wild Mouse, built in 1958, is the jerkiest, and has no doubt kept generations of Blackpool chiropractors in the money.

Admission to Pleasure Beach is £5, which includes a few attractions, then you can pay individually for rides with your £1 tickets (2–7 tickets per ride), or get unlimited rides with a £25–30 armband (price varies with season and day of week, cheaper if purchased in advance on their website). If you haven't pre-purchased your pass, pay the £5 entry fee and have a look around (check to see how long lines are for the top rides)—once you've paid admission to the park, you can upgrade to the armband by paying the difference (daily Easter–early Nov, also open some weekends in winter, opens at about 10:30 and closes as early as 17:00 or as late as 21:30, depending on season, weather, and demand—check website; toll tel. 0871-222-1234, www.pleasurebeachblackpool.com). Note: Pleasure Beach is about two miles (a 45-minute walk) south of the North Pier, so consider taking the tram or bus.

Sandcastle Waterpark—This popular indoor attraction, across the street from Pleasure Beach, has a big pool, long slides, a wave machine, and water, water, everywhere, at a constant temperature of 84 degrees. Featuring the longest tube waterslide in the world, this is a place where most kids could easily spend a day (£11 limited entry/£14 full admission, £9/£11.50 for kids, family passes, discount tickets online and at TI; roughly July–Aug daily 10:00–17:30; April–June and Sept–Oct Sat–Thu 10:00–17:00, Fri 13:30–20:00; Nov–March Sat–Sun only 10:00–16:30—confirm as hours may vary; last admission one hour before closing, tel. 01253/343-602, www.sandcastle-waterpark.co.uk).

▲▲▲People-Watching—Blackpool's top sight is its people. You'll see England here as nowhere else. Grab someone's hand and a big baton of "rock" (candy), and stroll. Grown men walk around with huge teddy bears looking for places to play "bowlingo," a short-lane version of bowling. Ponder the thought of actually retiring here and spending your last years, day after day, wearing plaid pants and a bad toupee, surrounded by Blackpool. This place puts people in a talkative mood. Ask someone to explain the difference between tea and supper. Back at your hotel, join in the chat sessions in the lounge.

▲Illuminations—Blackpool was the first town in England to "go electric" in 1879. Now, every fall, Blackpool stretches its tourist season by illuminating its six miles of waterfront with countless lights, all blinking and twinkling (Sept 3–Nov 7 in 2010). The American in me kept saying, "I've seen bigger, and I've seen better," but I stuffed his mouth with cotton candy and just had some simple fun like everyone else on my specially decorated tram. Look for the animated tableaux on North Shore.

St. Annes-on-Sea—Had enough greasy food and flashing lights? The seaside village of St. Annes is an easy 20-minute bus ride away to the south, and offers a welcome break (buses #7 and #11 run from the Blackpool Tower every 10 minutes, covered by the all-day tram/bus pass). Get off at St. Annes Square, which is the first stop after the bus turns left following the long, dune-side straightaway. The town's promenade and simple Victorian pier feel like a breath of sanity. The broad sand beach is perfect for flying a kite, building a sandcastle, or watching happy dogs play in the surf. Consider strolling the beach northward all the way to the southern edge of The Promenade (about 3 miles); if you max out on sand and sea before that, simply cross the dunes back to the seaside road and find the nearest bus stop.

Nightlife in Blackpool

▲**Showtime**—Blackpool always has a few razzle-dazzle music, dancing-girl, racy-humor, magic, and tumbling shows. Box offices around town can give you a rundown on what's available (£7–30 tickets). Your hotel has the latest. For something more highbrow, try the Opera House for musicals (booking toll tel. 0844-856-1111, info tel. 01253/625-252) and the Grand Theatre for drama and ballet (£15–25, tel. 01253/290-190, www.blackpoolgrand.co.uk). Both are on Church Street, a couple of blocks behind the tower. For the latest in evening entertainment, see the window displays at the TI on The Promenade (www.blackpoollive.com).

▲▲**Funny Girls**—Blackpool's current hot bar is in a dazzling location a couple blocks from the train station. Most nights from 20:00 to 23:30, Funny Girls puts on a "glam bam thank you ma'am" burlesque-in-drag show that delights footballers and grannies alike.

Get your drinks at the bar...unless the transvestites are dancing on it. The show, while racy, is not raunchy. The music is very loud. The crowd is young, old, straight, gay, very down-to-earth, and fun-loving. Go on a weeknight; Friday and Saturday are too jammed. While the area up front can be a mosh pit, there are more sedate tables in back, where service comes with a vampish smile.

There are two tiers of seats: sitting and standing (Sun £4 to stand, £14 to sit; Tue–Thu £3.50 to stand, £11 to sit; Fri £6 to stand, £17.50 to sit; Sat £8 to stand, £19.50 to sit; no shows Mon). Getting dinner here before the show runs about £16 (dinner reservations required, must be 18 to enter, 5 Dickson Road, TI sells tickets; to reserve in advance, call 01253/624-901, or visit box office at 44 Queen Street—open 9:30–17:15, www.funnygirlsshowbar.co.uk).

Other Nightspots—Blackpool's clubs and discos are cheap, with live bands and an interesting crowd (nightly 22:00–2:00 in the morning). With all the stag and hen parties, the late-night streets can be clotted with rude rowdies.

Sleeping in Blackpool

Blackpool's 140,000 people provide 120,000 beds in 3,500 mostly dumpy, cheap, nondescript hotels and B&Bs. Remember, this town's in the business of accommodating the people who can't afford to go to Spain. Most have the same design—minimal character, maximum number of springy beds—and charge £15–25 per person. Empty beds abound except from September through early November, and on summer weekends. It's only really tight on Illuminations weekends (when everyone bumps up prices). I've listed regular high-season prices. With the huge number of hotels in town, prices get really soft in the off-season. There's likely a launderette within a five-minute walk of your hotel; ask your host or hostess.

North of the Tower

These listings are on or near the waterfront in the quiet area they call "the posh end," a mile or two north of Blackpool Tower, with easy parking and easy access to the center by tram or bus. The first two listings have classy extras you wouldn't expect in Blackpool, and aren't too far from the North Pier. The last two are B&Bs with welcoming owners and lots of stairs, a short tram ride or approximately 35-minute walk from the North Pier.

$$$ Barceló Imperial Hotel is where the queen would stay in Blackpool. (They boast that every prime minister since they opened has visited their bar.) With dark-paneled Old World elegance, this splurge has all the comforts at its posh address (standard Db-£115–168 depending on size of room, season, and day of week—Sun and Mon are cheapest; request standard with view—if none available it's £60 extra for "premium" or "deluxe" room with sea view, rates much lower in slow times, check website for deals but call front desk for best standard room available, children stay free, no air-con, parking-£2.50/day, tram stop: Imperial Hotel, North Promenade, tel. 01253/623-971, fax 01253/751-784, www.barcelo-hotels.co.uk, imperialblackpool@barcelo-hotels.co.uk).

$$$ I know, staying at the **Hilton Hotel** in Blackpool is like wearing a tux to eat falafel. But if you need a splurge, this is a grand place with lots of views, a pool, sauna, gym, and comfortable rooms (Db-£110–170, "club deal" Db with lots of extras-£25 more, ask if there are any "special rates" being advertised, best deals online, call front desk to request room with view for no extra charge, air-con, tram stop: Warley Road, North Promenade, tel. 01253/623-434, fax 01253/627-864, www.hilton.com).

$$$ Carlton Hotel, a Best Western, rents business-class rooms at rack rates too high for what you get—check for more reasonable rates online (Sb-£50–70, Db-£80–110, can be a little

Sleep Code

(£1 = about $1.60, country code: 44, area code: 01253)
S = Single, **D** = Double/Twin, **T** = Triple, **Q** = Quad, **b** = bathroom, **s** = shower only. You can assume credit cards are accepted unless otherwise noted.

To help you sort easily through these listings, I've divided the rooms into three categories based on the price for a standard double room with bath:

$$$ Higher Priced—Most rooms £90 or more.
$$ Moderately Priced—Most rooms between £45-90.
$ Lower Priced—Most rooms £45 or less.

higher during Illuminations, sea-view rooms about £10 extra, a long block closer to town from the Imperial, tram stop: Pleasant Street, North Promenade, tel. 01253/628-966, fax 01253/752-587, www.carltonhotelblackpool.co.uk, mail@carltonhotelblackpool .co.uk).

$$ Beechcliffe Private Hotel has seven clean rooms run by a friendly couple, Ken and Carol Selman. The rooms are tight, but this place has a homey touch, and the decor is being nicely updated (Sb-£25, Db-£54–60, kids half-price, home-cooked dinner-£8, tram stop: Cabin; turn left from tram stop, then right at Shaftesbury Avenue, and walk a block away from beach; 16 Shaftesbury Avenue, North Shore, tel. 01253/353-075, www .beechcliffe.co.uk, info@beechcliffe.co.uk). Ken offers rides to or from the train station for no charge.

$$ Robin Hood Hotel is a cheery place with a big, welcoming living room, a family underfoot, and nine spacious rooms with big beds and sea views (especially rooms 1, 5, and 9). Run by nutritionist and therapist Kathy, it also serves as a diet retreat center (Sb-£25–27, Db-£50–54, discount for kids, under 6 free, various facial and massage treatments available, tram stop: St. Stephen's Avenue and walk a block north, 1.5 miles north of tower across from a peaceful stretch of beach, 100 Queens Promenade, North Shore, tel. 01253/351-599, www.robinhoodhotel.co.uk, info @robinhoodhotel.co.uk).

Near the Train Station

$$ Valentine Private Hotel is a handy and adequate 13-room place. It's run with care by on-site owner Anthony and manager Steve, with a plush red bar/sitting room and comfortable rooms. It's just two blocks from the train station and one block from the Funny Girls bar, in a neighborhood that's not exactly upscale, but

Central Blackpool

NOT TO SCALE
NORTH PIER TO CENTRAL PIER
IS ABOUT 1/2 MILE (800 METERS)

++ TROLLEY LINE
P PARKING

BLACKPOOL NORTH TRAIN STN.

To M-55

BUS STN.

KING ST.

CHURCH STREET

MARKET

OPERA HOUSE + WINTER GARDENS

DICKSON RD.

LIBRARY

SPRINGFIELD ROAD

ABINGDON

CHEAPSIDE STREET

QUEEN ST.

CLIFTON ST.

CORONATION STREET

ALBERT RD.

VICTORIA ST.

TO M-55

CENTRAL DRIVE

ABBEY BONNY

CHAPEL

TO SOUTH PIER

TALBOT SQ.

CORPORATION ST.

POST

MARKET ST.

CHURCH ST.

WEST ST.

TOWER

P R O M E N A D E

TO

BEACH

BEACH

NORTH PIER

I R I S H   S E A

CENTRAL PIER

DCH

❶ Valentine Private Hotel
❷ To Hotels North of the Tower
❸ Kwizeen Restaurant
❹ Harry Ramsden's
❺ The Mitre Pub
❻ Abingdon Barbeque
❼ Rocco's Restaurant
❽ Marks & Spencer
❾ Funny Girls (Bar & Show)
❿ Funny Girls (Box Office)

safe and convenient (Sb-£30, Db-£50–60 depending on room, bunk-bed family deals—kids half-price, free Wi-Fi; 2 blocks from station: with back to tracks, exit station far right, go up Springfield 2 blocks to Dickson and turn right, 35 Dickson Road; tel. 01253/622-775, www.valentinehotelblackpool.co.uk, anthony @anthonypalmer.orangehome.co.uk).

Eating in Blackpool

Your hotel may serve a cheap early-evening meal. Generally, food in the tower and along The Promenade is terrible. The following places are all just a few minutes' walk from the Blackpool Tower and the North Pier.

Kwizeen is an elegant bistro away from the beach that serves good Mediterranean and modern English dishes with a focus on local produce. Popular with the natives, they've racked up awards for their locally sourced and creatively prepared food. Don't worry—it's a lot classier inside than it looks from the outside (£13–17 main dishes, £13 two-course and £16 three-course early-bird specials 18:00–19:00, open Mon–Fri 12:00–13:30 & 18:00–21:00, Sat 18:00–21:00, closed Sun, 47–49 King Street, tel. 01253/290-045).

"World Famous" **Harry Ramsden's** will remind you of an English version of Denny's (it's the original location of a now UK-wide chain). This is *the* place for mushy peas, fish-and-chips, and a chance to get goofy with waiters—call the place *Henry* Ramsden's and see what happens (£6–10 meals, order a side of mushy peas, Sun–Thu 11:30–21:00, Fri–Sat 11:30–22:00, off-season until 20:00, 60–63 The Promenade, tel. 01253/294-386).

The Mitre Pub serves light lunches (weekdays 12:00–14:15) and beers in a truly rare, old-time Blackpool ambience. Drop in anytime to survey the fun photos of old Blackpool and for the great people scene (daily 11:00–23:00, Fri–Sat until 24:00, 3 West Street, tel. 01253/623-718).

Abingdon Barbeque, with its expansive deli counter, is mobbed with hungry locals at lunch, munching on cheap roasted  chicken and meat pies. Get a whole chicken and some sides, and you've got lunch for four for less than £10 (daily 7:00–17:00, take-away only, 44 Abingdon Street, tel. 01253/621-817).

Clifton Street: This street is lined with decent ethnic-food eateries, including Indian and Chinese. For Italian, try **Rocco's** (£10 three-course early-bird specials Sun–Thu 17:30–20:00, daily 17:30–23:00, Fri–Sat until 23:30, 36 Clifton Street, tel. 01253/627-440).

Supermarket: **Marks & Spencer** has a big supermarket in its basement (Mon–Wed and Fri 9:00–18:00, Thu 9:00–19:00, Sat 8:30–18:00, Sun 10:30–16:30, near recommended eateries, on Coronation Street and Church Street). Go picnic at the beach.

Blackpool Connections

If you're heading to (or from) Blackpool by train, you'll usually need to transfer at **Preston** (5/hr, 30 min). The following trains leave from Blackpool's main (north) station.

From Blackpool to: Liverpool (hourly, 1.5 hrs), **Keswick/Lake District** (roughly hourly, allow at least 3.5 hrs total for journey: transfer in Preston—30 minutes away, then 1 hr to Penrith, then catch a bus to Keswick, hourly except Sun 8/day, 40 min), **Conwy** in North Wales (roughly hourly, 3–4 hrs, 2–3 transfers), **Edinburgh** (10/day, 3.5 hrs, transfer in Preston), **Glasgow** (1–3/hr,

3 hrs, transfer in Preston), **York** (hourly, 3 hrs, more with change in Manchester), **Moreton-in-Marsh** in the Cotswolds (roughly hourly, 4.5 hrs, 2–3 transfers), **Bath** (hourly, 4.5 hrs, 3 transfers), **London**'s Euston Station (hourly, 3 hrs, 1 transfer). Train info: toll tel. 0845-748-4950, www.nationalrail.co.uk.

Liverpool

Liverpool, a large, bustling city with a downtown full of shopping malls, is a fascinating stop for Beatles fans and those who would

like to look urban England straight in the eye. The city is becoming a favorite holiday spot for Brits, who enjoy its lively atmosphere and cultural and historical sights. In 2008, Liverpool was one of the European Capitals of Culture; to prepare for the honor, the city rode a wave of new construction and architectural face-lifts.

Planning Your Time

If you're a casual Beatles fan, make Liverpool an afternoon pit-stop: Spend most of your time at the Albert Dock, popping in to see The Beatles Story, having lunch at the Tate's lunchtime café (and appreciating the art upstairs), and visiting the Maritime Museum. Consider getting a ticket to ride the ferry across the Mersey, which leaves from the docks north of the Albert Dock.

Beatles Blitz: If the Fab Four are what brought you to Liverpool, arrive the night before and follow this more ambitious, all-day sightseeing plan (which follows the Beatles' lives in roughly chronological order):

9:00–Visit the TI to book a seat on the 10:00 National Trust minibus tour to John and Paul's childhood homes, if you haven't pre-booked a time slot already (see reservations info on page 463). Note that this tour does not run on Mondays and Tuesdays (and not at all Dec–Feb).

9:50–Arrive at the Jurys Inn (just south of the Albert Dock) for the 2.5-hour minibus tour of John and Paul's childhood homes (departs at 10:00 sharp).

12:30–Return to the city center. Walk over to Mathew Street for a quick pop-in to the original (but unimpressive) Cavern Club. (Skip this walk if you're taking the "Magical Mystery" bus tour—explained below—which ends at the club.)

13:00–Walk 15 minutes down to the Albert Dock (or take a bus or taxi). Enjoy lunch in one of my recommended eateries (listed under "Eating in Liverpool").

14:00–Choose between the bus and minivan tours (the "Magical Mystery" bus tour leaves the Albert Dock at 14:30) or The Beatles Story exhibit. Since the tours cover some of the same ground as the National Trust tour, an hour or two at The Beatles Story will satisfy all but the most die-hard fan.

For those who just can't get enough, it's possible to do an afternoon "Magical Mystery" bus tour and also see The Beatles Story (the tour ends at the Cavern Club around 16:15, and The Beatles Story allows a last entry at 17:00).

Orientation to Liverpool

(area code: 0151)

Tourist Information

Liverpool's main TI is on **Whitechapel Street,** a six-minute walk downhill from Lime Street Station. Ignore the pavilion with the information symbol on it—the real TI is a glossy silver storefront on this main shopping street (Mon and Wed–Sat 9:00–18:00, Tue 10:00–18:00, Sun 11:00–16:00, tel. 0151/233-2008, www.visit liverpool.com). Get the free, small map (also available at train station for £1). Walking tours about local history are sometimes offered on Sundays. There's another TI at **Albert Dock** (daily 10:00–17:00, inland from The Beatles Story, tel. 0151/707-0729), and a third at the **airport** (daily 9:00–18:00, tel. 0151/907-1057).

Arrival in Liverpool

From the Lime Street **train** station to the Albert Dock, it's about a 20-minute walk, a short ride on bus #C4 (£1.60 one-way, £3.30 all-day ticket, runs daily every 20 min until 21:00), or a £4 taxi trip. For public-transportation information, visit the Merseytravel center at the main bus center, between Lime Street Station and the TI (Mon–Sat 9:00–17:30, Sun 10:30–16:30, Queen Square, toll tel. 0871-200-2233, www.merseytravel.gov.uk). Regional trains also arrive at the much smaller Central Station, which is essentially a subway stop, located just a few blocks south.

From **Liverpool John Lennon Airport,** take bus #500 to the city center (£2.60, 2/hr).

Drivers approaching Liverpool follow signs to *City Center* and *Albert Dock,* where you'll find a huge car park at the dock.

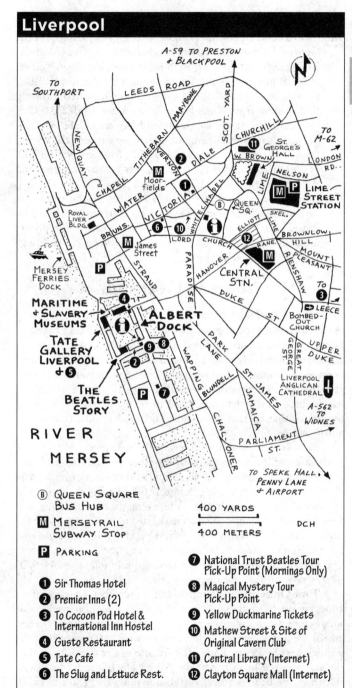

Liverpool

A-59 TO PRESTON + BLACKPOOL

TO SOUTHPORT

LEEDS ROAD

MARYBONE

SCOT. YARD

CHURCHILL

TO M-62

St. George's Hall

W. BROWN

LONDON RD.

NELSON

TITHEBARN

VERNON

DALE

CHAPEL

WATER

VICTORIA

WHITECHAPEL

QUEEN SQ.

NEW QUAY

Moorfields

LIME STREET STATION

ELLIOTT

LIME

SKEL.

BROWNLOW

HILL

Royal Liver Bldg.

BRUNS.

LORD

CHURCH

RENSHAW

MOUNT PLEASANT

James Street

STRAND

PARADISE

HANOVER

CENTRAL STN.

TO

LEECE

Mersey Ferries Dock

MARITIME & SLAVERY MUSEUMS

ALBERT DOCK

DUKE

ST.

BOMBED-OUT CHURCH

UPPER DUKE

TATE GALLERY LIVERPOOL

THE BEATLES STORY

PARK LANE

WAPPING

BLUNDELL

GEORGE ST.

GREAT

LIVERPOOL ANGLICAN CATHEDRAL

ST. JAMES

JAMAICA

A-562 TO WIDNES

RIVER

MERSEY

CHALONER

PARLIAMENT ST.

TO SPEKE HALL, PENNY LANE & AIRPORT

(B) QUEEN SQUARE BUS HUB

M MERSEYRAIL SUBWAY STOP

P PARKING

400 YARDS

400 METERS

DCH

1 Sir Thomas Hotel

2 Premier Inns (2)

3 To Cocoon Pod Hotel & International Inn Hostel

4 Gusto Restaurant

5 Tate Café

6 The Slug and Lettuce Rest.

7 National Trust Beatles Tour Pick-Up Point (Mornings Only)

8 Magical Mystery Tour Pick-Up Point

9 Yellow Duckmarine Tickets

10 Mathew Street & Site of Original Cavern Club

11 Central Library (Internet)

12 Clayton Square Mall (Internet)

Helpful Hints

Internet Access: The Business and Technology department of the **Central Library** lets visitors use computers for free (Mon–Fri 9:00–18:00, Sat 9:00–17:00, Sun 10:00–16:00, boots you off after 30 min but OK to log in again if needed, on William Brown Street, just behind the grand colonnaded building that's across from Lime Street Station, tel. 0151/233-5829). Or get online at the **Le Boulevard Internet Café** (50p-£3/hr, price varies with demand, 20 coin-op terminals, second floor of Clayton Square shopping mall, Mon–Sat 9:00–18:00, Thu until 20:00, Sun 11:00–17:00, between train station and Albert Dock on Ranelagh Street).

Baggage Storage: Look for storage services on the train station's main concourse (£7/item for 24 hrs, open Mon–Thu 7:00–21:00, Fri–Sun 7:00–23:00). Most bus tours and private minivan/car tours are able to accommodate people with luggage (of "reasonable" size).

Tours in Liverpool

Beatles Tours

▲Lennon and McCartney Homes—John and Paul's boyhood homes have both been restored to how they looked during their 1950s childhoods. This isn't Graceland—you won't find an over-the-top rock-and-roll extravaganza here. And if you don't know the difference between John and Paul, you'll likely be bored. But for die-hard Beatles fans who want to get a glimpse into the time and place that created these musical masterminds, this tour is worth ▲▲▲.

Because the houses are in residential neighborhoods—and in both cases, still share walls with neighbors—the National Trust runs only four tours per day in summer (Wed–Sun only) with 14 Beatlemaniacs each, ending before 17:00. Just 7,000 people pass through these doors each year. While some Beatles bus tours stop here for photo ops, only the National Trust tour gets you inside the homes. And don't try to simply show up and stroll right in—you have to be on the tour to be allowed inside.

Cost and Information: £17, recorded info toll tel. 0844-800-4791, www.nationaltrust.org.uk/beatles.

Tour Options: From mid-March to October, tours run four times per day Wed–Sun (no tours Mon–Tue). Plan to arrive 10 minutes before the tour departure time. **Morning tours** (at 10:00 and 10:50) are better, as they follow a more scenic route that includes a quick pass by Penny Lane. They're also easier to reach, as they depart from the Jurys Inn at the Albert Dock (south of and visible from The Beatles Story). **Afternoon tours** (at 14:30 and 15:00) leave from Speke Hall, an out-of-the-way National Trust property located eight miles southeast of Liverpool. Allow 30 minutes to drive from the city center to Speke Hall—follow the brown *Speke Hall* signs through dozens of roundabouts, heading in the general direction of the airport (ample and free parking at the site). If you don't have a car, it takes at least 45 minutes to reach Speke Hall by bus and foot (airport bus #500, 2/hr, 20 min; or slower bus #80A, 4/hr, 40–50 min, direction: Airport; ask driver to let you off at the stop closest to Speke Hall, then walk a well-signed half-mile).

Off-Season: From early to mid-March and in November, tours leave Wed–Sun at 10:00, 12:30, and 15:00, and all depart from the handy Jurys Inn at the Albert Dock. No tours run in winter (Dec–Feb).

Reservations: Because only 14 people are allowed on each tour, it's smart to make a reservation ahead of time, especially for the morning tours. You can reserve online (www.nationaltrust.org .uk/beatles), or by calling 0151/427-7231. If you haven't reserved ahead, you can try to book a same-day tour by calling 0151/707-0729. The afternoon tours generally don't fill up, but remember that it takes 30 minutes (by car) to at least 45 minutes (without a car) to reach the tour's starting point from central Liverpool.

Guides: Each home has a live-in caretaker who will act as your guide. These folks give an entertaining, insightful-to-fans 20- to 30-minute talk, and then leave you time (10–15 minutes) to wander through the house on your own. Ask lots of questions if their spiel peters out early—the docents are a wealth of information. You can take photos of the outside of the house after they give their talk, but not before. They ask you to turn off your mobile phones, and not to bring big bags.

Mendips (John Lennon's Home): Even though he sang about

being a working-class hero, John grew up in the suburbs of Liverpool, surrounded by doctors, lawyers, and—beyond the back fence—Strawberry Field (he added the "s" for the song).

This was the home of John's Aunt Mimi, who raised him in this house from the time he was five years old and once told him, "A guitar's all right, John, but you'll never earn a living by it." John moved out at age 23, but his first wife, Cynthia, bunked here for a while when John made his famous first trip to America. Yoko Ono bought the house in 2002, and gave it as a gift to the National Trust (generating controversy among the neighbors). The stewards, Colin and Sylvia, make this place come to life.

On the surface, it's just a 1930s house carefully restored to how it would have been in the past. But delve deeper. It's been lovingly cared for—restored to be the tidy, well-kept place Mimi would have recognized (down to her apron hanging in the kitchen). It's a lucky quirk of fate that the house's interior remained mostly unchanged after the Lennons left—the bachelor who owned it for the previous decades didn't upgrade much, so even the light switches are true to the time.

If you're a John Lennon fan, it's fun to picture him as a young boy drawing and imagining at his dining room table. It also makes for an interesting comparison to Paul's humbler home, which is the second part of the tour.

20 Forthlin Road (Paul McCartney's Home): In compari-

son to Aunt Mimi's house, the home where Paul grew up is simpler, much less "posh," and even a little ratty around the edges. Michael, Paul's brother, wanted it that way—their mother, Mary (famously mentioned in "Let It Be"), died when the boys were young, and it never had the tidiness of a woman's touch. It's been intentionally scuffed up around the edges to preserve the historical accuracy. Notice the differences—Paul has said that John's house was vastly different and more clearly middle class; at Mendips, there were books on the bookshelves.

More than a hundred Beatles songs were written in this house (including "I Saw Her Standing There") during days Paul and John spent skipping school. The photos from Michael, taken in this house, help make the scene of what's mostly a barren interior much more interesting.

There's no blue plaque identifying the house from the outside—those are only awarded once the person's been dead for 20 years, or when it's been 100 years since their birth, whichever comes first. In fact, Paul hasn't been back inside the house since it was turned into a museum; he knocked on the door twice, but both times the custodian was out...an idea that might give you some comfort if you're not able to get inside yourself.

More Beatles Tours—The "sights" covered by the tours below are basically houses where the Fab Four grew up (exteriors only), places they performed, and spots made famous by the lyrics of their hits ("Penny Lane," "Strawberry Fields," the Eleanor Rigby graveyard, and so on). While boring to anyone not into the Beatles, fans will enjoy the commentary and seeing the shelter on the roundabout, the fire station with the clean machine, and the barber who shaves another customer.

Beatles fans may want to invest a couple of hours taking the **"Magical Mystery" bus tour,** which hits the lads' homes (from the outside), Penny Lane, and so on (£15, 1.75 hours; July–Aug departs daily from the Albert Dock at 12:00 and 14:30; Easter–June and Sept Mon–Fri at 12:00, Sat–Sun at 12:00 and 14:30; Oct–Easter Sat–Sun at 12:00, no tours Mon–Fri; often fills up—book ahead by calling or stopping by any TI, leaves from Gower Street stop at southern end of dock—inland from The Beatles Story, ends at the Cavern Club, tel. 0151/236-9091, www.cavernclub.org).

For something more extensive, fun, and intimate, consider a four-hour minibus Beatles tour from **Phil Hughes.** It's longer because it includes information on historic Liverpool, along with the Beatles stuff. Phil organizes his tour to fit your schedule and will do his best to accommodate you (£15.50/person, £80/private group tour, can coordinate times with National Trust tour of Lennon and McCartney homes, 8-seat minibus, mobile 07961-511-223, tel. 0151/228-4565, www.tourliverpool.co.uk, tourliverpool @hotmail.com).

Jackie Spencer also hits the highlights and does private tours—just say when and where you want to go (up to four people in her minivan-£140, 2.5 hours, longer tours available, will pick you up at hotel or train station, mobile 0799-076-1478, www.beatle guides.com, jackie@beatleguides.com).

Beware of cheaper private-taxi tours promoted by some hotels—kickbacks, not quality, motivate concierges to recommend these tours.

Other Tours

City Bus Tour—The City Sightseeing bus is a hop-on, hop-off bus tour with a canned soundtrack, but considering the size of the city center, it's a quick way to get an overview that links all the major sights in 55 breezy minutes (£8, buy ticket from driver, valid for 24 hours, daily March–Oct 10:00–17:00, Jan–Feb 10:00–16:30, runs every 30 min, tel. 0151/203-3920, www.city-sightseeing.com).

Ferry Cruise—Mersey Ferries offers narrated cruises that depart from Mersey Dock, an easy five-minute walk from the Albert Dock. The 50-minute cruise makes two brief stops on the other side of the river; you can hop off and catch the next boat back (£6.30, year-round, Mon–Fri 10:00–15:00, Sat–Sun 10:00–18:00, leaves at top of hour, café, WCs onboard, tel. 0151/330-1444, www .merseyferries.co.uk).

Harbor and City Tour—The Yellow Duckmarine runs wacky tours of Liverpool's waterfront, city, and docks by land and by sea in its amphibious WWII-era tourist assault vehicles. Be prepared to quack (£12, or £10 midweek and off-peak, family deals, one hour, buy tickets at office on the Albert Dock near The Beatles Story, departs from the Albert Dock every 30 min daily 10:30–17:00, more frequently with demand, tel. 0151/708-7799, www.theyellowduckmarine.co.uk).

Sights in Liverpool

At the Albert Dock

All of these sights are at the Albert Dock. Opened in 1852 by Prince Albert, and enclosing seven acres of water, the Albert Dock is surrounded by five-story brick warehouses. In its day, Liverpool was England's greatest seaport, but at the end of the 19th century, the port wasn't deep enough for the big new ships; trade declined after 1890, and by 1972 it was closed entirely. Like Liverpool itself, the docks have enjoyed a renaissance. Today, they contain the city's main attractions. A half-dozen trendy eateries are lined up here, out of the rain, and padded by lots of shopping mall–type distractions. There's plenty of parking.

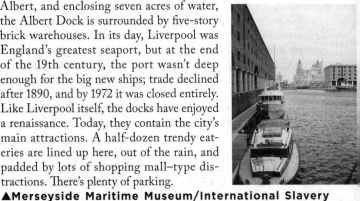

▲**Merseyside Maritime Museum/International Slavery Museum**—These museums tell the story of Liverpool, once the second city of the British Empire. The port prospered in the 18th century as one corner of a commerce triangle with Africa and America. The British shippers profited greatly through exploitation: About 1.5 million enslaved African people passed through Liverpool's docks (if you have African ancestors who arrived in America as slaves, chances are high they came through here). From Liverpool, the British exported manufactured goods to Africa in exchange for enslaved Africans; the slaves were then shipped to the Americas, where they were traded for raw material (cotton, sugar, and tobacco); and the goods were then brought back to Britain. While the merchants on all three sides made money, the big profit came home to England. As Britain's economy boomed, so did Liverpool's. Not all the money made was above-board—a new gallery discusses the profitable business of smuggling.

Three galleries on the third floor make up the International Slavery Museum. They describe life in West Africa, enslavement and the Middle Passage to America, and the legacy of slavery. At the music desk, you can listen to more than 300 songs from many different genres that were influenced by African music.

After participation in the slave trade was outlawed in Britain in the early 1800s, Liverpool kept its port busy as a transfer point for emigrants. If your ancestors came from Scandinavia, Ukraine, or Ireland, they likely left Europe from this port. Between 1830 and 1930, nine million emigrants sailed from Liverpool to find their dreams in the New World. Awe-inspiring steamers such as the *Lusitania* called this port home. One exhibit shows footage and artifacts of three big Liverpool-related shipwrecks: the *Lusitania*, the *Empress of Ireland,* and the *Titanic* (free, daily 10:00–17:00, café, tel. 0151/478-4499, www.liverpoolmuseums.org.uk).

Tate Gallery Liverpool—This prestigious gallery of modern art is near the Maritime Museum. It won't entertain you as well as its London sister, the Tate Modern, but if you're into modern art, any Tate's great (free but £3 suggested donation, £6–8 for special exhibits; Tue–Sun 10:00–17:50, closed Mon except in July–Aug; tel. 0151/702-7400, www.tate.org.uk/liverpool). The Tate has a nice, inexpensive café (recommended later, under "Eating in Liverpool").

▲The Beatles Story—It's sad to think the Beatles are stuck in a museum (and their music turned into a Las Vegas show). Still, while this exhibit is overpriced and not very creative, the story's a fascinating one, and even an avid fan will pick up some new information.

Listen to the included audioguide as you study the knickknacks. Cynthia Lennon, John's first wife, still marvels at the manic power of Beatlemania, while the narrator reminds listeners of all that made the group earth-shattering—and even a little edgy—at the time. For example, performing before the Queen Mother, John Lennon famously quips: "Will the people in the cheaper seats clap your hands? And the rest of you, if you'll just rattle your jewelry." The audioguide captures the Beatles' charm and cheekiness in the way the stuffy wax mannequins can't.

The last few rooms trace the members' solo careers (mostly John and Paul's), and the last few steps are reserved for reverence about John's peace work, including a re-creation of the white room he used while writing "Imagine" (£12.50, includes audioguide, daily 9:00–19:00, last admission two hours before closing, tel. 0151/709-1963, www.beatlesstory.com). The shop has an impressive pile of Beatles buyables.

Sleeping in Liverpool

(£1 = about $1.60, country code: 44, area code: 0151)

B&Bs are a rarity in urban Liverpool. Your best budget options are the boring, predictable, and central chain hotels. Many hotels, including the ones listed below, charge more on weekends, especially when Liverpool's soccer team plays a home game. Rates shoot up even higher two weekends a year: during Beatles Week at the end of August and during the Grand National horse race (April 8–10 in 2010)—avoid these times if you can.

$$ Sir Thomas Hotel is a centrally located hotel that was once a bank, and feels like it. The 39 recently renovated rooms are comfortable, and deluxe rooms are outfitted with stately, heavy decor (Db-£55–70 midweek, £75–100 on non-event weekends, 10-min walk from station, 24 Sir Thomas Street at the corner of Victoria Street, tel. 0151/236-1366, fax 0151/227-1541, www.sirthomashotel.co.uk, reservations@sirthomashotel.co.uk).

$$ Premier Inn, which has pleasant, American-style rooms and a friendly staff, is right on the Albert Dock (Db-£67, mediocre breakfast costs £8 extra—try good cafés nearby instead, next to The Beatles Story, toll tel. 0870-990-6432, www.premierinn.com, liverpool.albert.pti@whitbread.com). There's a second, downtown **$$ Premier Inn** as well. While it's a much less desirable location than the Albert Dock branch, it's just a 10-minute walk from the Lime Street train station (Db-£65, Vernon Street, just off Dale Street, tel. 0151-242-7650).

$$ Cocoon Pod Hotel, in the basement of the hostel (next listing), offers 32 no-nonsense, modern rooms with your choice of two twins or a king. As all the rooms are underground, there are no windows—but at least it's quiet (Sb or Db-£43 Sun–Thu, £53 Fri–Sat, 1- to 3-bedroom apartments from £65, free Wi-Fi, breakfast not included but café next door—with £1/30 min Internet access, laundry, same location and contact info as hostel below, www.cocoonliverpool.co.uk).

$ International Inn Hostel, run by the daughter of the Beatles' first manager, rents 100 budget beds in a former Victorian warehouse. Most nights, the hostel puts on fun, free food-themed events for guests—traditional Liverpudlian stew one night, pancakes the next, and even the occasional chocolate fountain (Db-£36–45, bed in 4- to 10-bed room-£15–20, includes sheets and towels, all rooms have bathrooms, free toast and tea/coffee, £1/30 min Internet access in adjacent café, free Wi-Fi, laundry room, games in lobby, TV lounge, video library, 24-hour reception, café, 4 South Hunter Street, tel. & fax 0151/709-8135, www.internationalinn.co.uk, info@internationalinn.co.uk). From the Lime Street Station, it's an easy 15-minute walk: Follow Lime Street south, which then becomes Renshaw Street, then ends at the bombed-out church. That puts you at the start of Leece Street—walk up three blocks (where it becomes Hardman Street) and hang a left onto South Hunter Street. Or take bus #80A or #86A (3–6/hr, direction: Liverpool Airport or Garston), and get off two stops after the bus veers left at the bombed-out church. If taking a taxi, tell them it's on South Hunter Street near Hardman Street.

Eating in Liverpool

Your best bet is to dine at the Albert Dock (my first two listings, below). Here you'll find a slew of trendy restaurants that come alive with club energy at night, but are sedate and pleasant in the afternoon and early evening.

Gusto, a chain restaurant that doesn't seem like one, serves local businesspeople, travelers, and families alike in its cavernous but classy and fun space (£9 weekday lunch deals, £9 pastas and pizzas, £13–18 meat and fish dishes, children's menu available, daily 11:00–24:00, free Wi-Fi, Albert Dock, tel. 0151/708-6969).

Tate Café, in the Tate Gallery, serves soups, salads, and light lunches in a bright room that feels like one of its galleries (£5–8 lunches, daily 10:00–17:30 except closed Mon Oct–March, Albert Dock, tel. 0151/702-7580).

The Slug and Lettuce, located in the city center, is another chain restaurant/bar. It mostly caters to the after-hours office crowd, who are more interested in drinking than eating, but it'll do in a pinch (£9 plates, Mon–Sat 10:00–22:00, Sun 11:00–22:00, 16 North John Street, tel. 0151/236-8820).

Liverpool Connections

By Train
From Liverpool by Train to: Blackpool (hourly, 1.5 hrs), **Keswick/Lake District** (train to Penrith—roughly hourly with change at Wigan or Preston, 2 hrs; then bus to Keswick—hourly except Sun 8/day, 40 min), **York** (hourly, 2.25 hrs), **Edinburgh** (roughly hourly, 3.5–4 hrs, 1–2 changes), **Glasgow** (about hourly, 3.5 hrs Mon–Fri, 1 transfer), **London**'s Euston Station (hourly, 2 hrs), **Crewe** (2/hr, 45 min), **Chester** (2/hr, 45 min). Train info: toll tel. 0845-748-4950, www.nationalrail.co.uk.

By Ferry
By Ferry to Dublin, Republic of Ireland: It's a seven-hour trip between Liverpool and Dublin by boat. Both ferry companies require you to check in one to two hours before the sailing time—call to confirm the details. Ferries sail daily from both companies

at 22:00, with an additional trip at 10:00 Tue–Sat. P&O Irish Sea Ferries runs a car ferry only—no foot passengers (prices vary, roughly £85–100, 20-min drive north of the city center at Liverpool Freeport—Gladstone dock, toll tel. 0871-664-4777, www.po irishsea.com). On foot or by car, you can use Norfolkline Irish Sea Ferry Services from nearby Birkenhead (£20 for foot passengers on daytime ferries, £20–30 more for overnight ferries, sleeper cabins extra; book online at least one day ahead to avoid £10 phone/in-person booking fee and £20 day-of-sailing fee, Birkenhead Port, toll tel. 0844-499-0007, www.norfolkline-ferries.co.uk). Birkenhead's dock is a 15-minute walk from Hamilton Square Station on Merseyrail's Wirral Line. You can also take a ferry to Dublin via the Isle of Man (www.steam-packet.com).

By Ferry to Belfast, Northern Ireland: Norfolkline Irish Sea Ferry Services sails most mornings (Tue–Sun) at 10:30, and every evening at 22:30 year-round (8 hrs, toll tel. 0844-499-0007, www .norfolkline-ferries.co.uk). You can also take a ferry to Belfast via the Isle of Man (www.steam-packet.com).

Route Tips for Drivers
From Liverpool to Blackpool: Leaving Liverpool, drive north along the waterfront, following signs to *M58* (Preston). Once on M58 (and not before), follow signs to *M6,* and then *M55* into Blackpool.

THE LAKE DISTRICT

In the pristine Lake District, William Wordsworth's poems still shiver in trees and ripple on ponds. This is a land where nature rules, and humanity keeps a wide-eyed but low profile. Relax, recharge, take a cruise or a hike, and maybe even write a poem. Renew your poetic license at Wordsworth's famous Dove Cottage.

The Lake District, about 30 miles long and 30 miles wide, is nature's lush, green playground. Explore it by foot, bike, bus, or car. While not impressive in sheer height (Scafell Pike, the tallest peak in England, is only 3,206 feet), there's a walking-stick charm about the way nature and the culture mix. Locals are fond of declaring that their mountains are older than the Himalayas and were once as tall, but have been worn down by the ages. Walking along a windblown ridge or climbing over a rock fence to look into the eyes of a ragamuffin sheep, even tenderfeet get a chance to feel very outdoorsy. The tradition of staying close to the land remains true—albeit in an updated form—in the 21st century; you'll see restaurants serving organic foods as well as stickers advocating for environmental causes in the windows of local homes.

Dress in layers, and expect rain mixed with brilliant "bright spells" (pubs offer atmospheric shelter at every turn). Drizzly days can be followed by delightful evenings.

Plan to spend the majority of your time in the unspoiled North Lake District. In this chapter, I focus on the town of Keswick, the lake called Derwentwater, and the vast, time-passed Newlands Valley. The North Lake District works great by car or by bus (with easy train access via Penrith), and is manna to nature-lovers, with good accommodations to boot.

The South Lake District—famous primarily for its Wordsworth and Beatrix Potter sights—is closer to London, and gets the promotion, the tour crowds, and the tackiness that comes with them. I strongly recommend that you skip the South Lake District, and enter the region from the north via Penrith. Make your home base in or near Keswick, and side-trip from here into the South Lake District only if you're interested in the Wordsworth and Beatrix Potter sights.

Planning Your Time

On a three-week trip to England, I'd spend two days and two nights in this area. Penrith is the nearest train station, just 40 minutes by bus or car from Keswick. Those without a car will use Keswick as a springboard: Cruise the lake and take one of the many hikes in the Catbells area. Non-hikers can hop on a mini-bus tour. If great scenery is commonplace in your life, the Lake District can be more soothing (and rainy) than exciting. If you're rushed, you could make this area a one-night stand—or even a quick drive-through.

Two-Day Driving Plan: Here's the most exciting way for drivers coming from the south—who'd like to visit South Lake District sights en route to the North Lake District—to pack their day of arrival: On **Day 1,** get an early start, aiming to leave the motorway at Kendal by 10:30; drive along Windermere and through Ambleside; 11:30–Tour Dove Cottage; 12:30–Backtrack to Ambleside, where a small road leads up and over the dramatic Kirkstone Pass (far more scenic northbound than southbound, get out and bite the wind) and down to Glenridding on Lake Ullswater. You could catch the 15:00 boat. Hike six miles (3–4 hours, roughly 15:30–19:00) from Howtown back to Glenridding. Drive to your farmhouse B&B near Keswick, with a stop as the sun sets at Castlerigg Stone Circle. On **Day 2,** make the circular drive from Keswick through the Newlands Valley, Buttermere, Honister Pass, and Borrowdale, and do the Catbells High Ridge Hike. Return to the same farmhouse B&B for the evening.

Getting Around the Lake District

With a Car

Nothing is very far from Keswick and Derwentwater. Pick up a good map, get off the big roads, and leave the car, at least occasionally, for some walking. In summer, the Keswick–Ambleside–Windermere–Bowness corridor (A591) suffers from congestion.

The Lake District

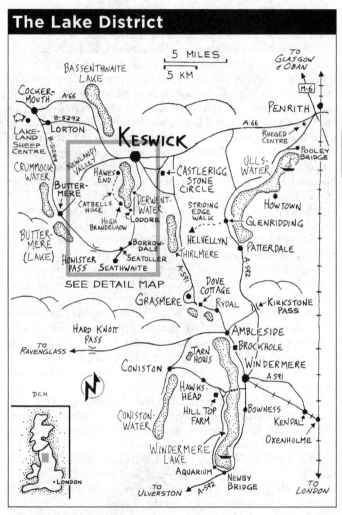

Keswick Motor Company rents cars in Keswick (from £32/day with insurance, Mon–Sat 8:30–17:15, closed Sun, ages 25–70 only, must have an International Driving Permit and passport, Lake Road, a block from Moot Hall in town center, tel. 017687/72064).

Parking is tight throughout the region. It's easiest to just park in the pay-and-display lots (gather small coins, as most machines don't make change). If you're parking free on the roadside, don't block the vital turnouts. Where there are double yellow lines, you must be beyond them.

Without a Car

Those based in Keswick without a car manage fine.

By Bus: Keswick has no real bus station; all buses stop at a turnout in front of the Booths Supermarket. Local buses take you quickly and easily (if not always frequently) to all nearby points of interest. Check the schedule carefully to make sure you can catch the last bus home. The exhaustive *Cumbria & Lakes Rider* bus brochure (50 pages, free, at TI or on any bus) explains the schedules (note that some buses don't run during the winter). Onboard, you can purchase one-day Explorer passes (£10), or get one-day passes for certain routes. A four-day pass is available at the Keswick TI/National Park Visitors Centre. For bus and rail info, call 0871-200-2233 (costs 10p/min), or visit www.traveline.org.uk.

Buses **#X4** and **#X5** connect Penrith train station to Keswick (hourly Mon–Sat, 8/day Sun, 40 min, £5.50).

Bus **#77/#77A,** the Honister Rambler, makes the gorgeous circle from Keswick around Derwentwater, over Honister Pass, through Buttermere, and down the Whinlatter Valley (4/day clockwise, 4/day "anticlockwise," daily Easter–Oct, weekends only in Nov, 1.5-hour loop, £6.50 Honister Dayrider all-day pass).

Bus **#78,** the Borrowdale Rambler, goes topless in the summer, affording a wonderful sightseeing experience in and of itself, heading from Keswick to Lodore Hotel, Grange, Rosthwaite, and Seatoller at the base of Honister Pass (hourly, 2/hr mid-July–Aug, 8/day on Sun, 25 min each way, £5.75 Borrowdale Dayrider all-day pass).

Bus **#108** runs between Penrith and Glenridding, stopping in Pooley Bridge (daily 4–6/day, no Sun service Sept–Easter, 40 min, £14 Ullswater Bus & Boat day pass covers this bus route as well as steamers on Ullswater).

Bus **#208** runs between Keswick and Glenridding (5/day mid-July–Aug, Sat–Sun only late May–mid-July, 45 min).

Bus **#505,** the Coniston Rambler, connects Windermere with Hawkshead (daily Easter–Oct, hourly, 35 min).

Bus **#517,** the Kirkstone Rambler, runs between Windermere and Glenridding (3/day mid-July–Aug, Sat–Sun only Easter–mid-July, 1 hr).

Buses **#555** and **#556** connect Keswick with the south (hourly, 1 hr to Windermere).

Bus **#599,** the open-top Lakes Rider, runs along the main Windermere corridor, connecting the big tourist attractions in the south (3/hr daily Easter–Aug, 50 min each way, £6.50 Central Lakes Dayrider all-day pass, route: Grasmere and Dove Cottage–Rydal Mount–Ambleside–Brockhole–Windermere–Bowness Pier).

By Bike: Several shops rent bikes in Keswick. **Keswick Mountain Bikes** has the largest selection (mountain bikes-

£15–20/day depending on model, includes helmet and toolkit, Mon–Sat 9:00–17:30, Sun 10:00–17:30, can recommend guided bike tours; several locations, including right off the town square, upstairs from the recommended Lakeland Pedlar Restaurant; tel. 017687/75202, www.keswickbikes.co.uk). **Keswick Motor Company** in the town center also rents bikes (£10/4 hours, £15/day, includes helmet). Keswick Mountain Bikes and the TI sell various cycling maps.

By Boat: A circular boat service glides you around Derwentwater, with several hiker-aiding stops along the way (for a cruise/hike option, see the Derwentwater listing, page 479).

By Foot: Hiking information is available everywhere. Consider buying a detailed map (good selection at Keswick TI and at the outdoor gear stores that cram every block; or borrow one from your B&B). For easy hikes, pick up the helpful fliers at TIs and B&Bs that describe routes. The Lake District's TIs advise hikers to check the weather before setting out (for an up-to-date weather report, ask at TI or call toll tel. 0870-055-0575), wear suitable clothing and footwear, and bring a map. Plan for rain. It's wise to watch your footing. Fatalities aren't uncommon—every year, several people die while hiking in the area (some from over-exertion; others are blown off ridges).

By Tour: For organized bus tours that run the roads of the Lake District, see "Tours in Keswick."

Keswick and the North Lake District

As far as touristy Lake District towns go, Keswick (KEZ-ick, population 5,000) is far more enjoyable than Windermere, Bowness, or Ambleside. Many of the place names around Keswick have Norse origins, inherited from the region's 10th-century settlers.

An important mining center for slate, copper, and lead through the Middle Ages, Keswick became a resort in the 19th century. Its fine Victorian buildings recall those Romantic days when city slickers first learned about "communing with nature." Today, the compact town is lined with tearooms, pubs, gift shops, and hiking-gear shops.

Lake Derwentwater is a pleasant 10-minute walk from the town center.

Orientation to Keswick

(area code: 017687)
Keswick is an ideal home base, with plenty of good B&Bs, an easy bus connection to the nearest train station at Penrith, and a prime location near the best lake in the area, Derwentwater. In Keswick, everything is within a 10-minute walk of everything else: the pedestrian town square, the TI, recommended B&Bs, two grocery stores, the municipal pitch-and-putt golf course, the main bus stop, a lakeside boat dock, the post office (with Internet access), and a central parking lot. Thursdays and Saturdays are market days in the town square, but the square is lively every day throughout the summer (no Thu market Jan–Feb).

Keswick town is a delight for wandering. Its centerpiece, Moot Hall (meaning "meeting hall"), was a 16th-century copper warehouse upstairs with an arcade below (closed after World War II). "Keswick" means "cheese farm"—a legacy from the time when the town square was the spot to sell cheese. The town square recently went pedestrians-only, and locals are all abuzz about people tripping over the curbs. (The English, seemingly thrilled by ever-present danger, are endlessly warning visitors to "watch your head," "watch the step," and "mind the gap.")

Keswick and the Lake District are popular with English holiday-makers who prefer to bring their dogs with them on vacation. The town square in Keswick can look like the Westminster Dog Show, and the recommended Dog and Gun pub, where "well-behaved dogs are welcomed," is always full of patient pups. If you are shy about connecting with local people, pal up to an English pooch—you will often find they are happy to introduce you to their owners.

Tourist Information

The TI/National Park Visitors Centre is in Moot Hall, right in the middle of the town square (daily Easter–Oct 9:30–17:30, Nov–Easter 9:30–16:30, tel. 017687/72645, www.lake-district.gov .uk and www.keswick.org). Staffers are pros at advising you about hiking routes. They'll also help you figure out public transportation to outlying sights, and book rooms (you'll pay a £4 booking fee; it's cheaper to call B&Bs direct).

The TI sells the £22 four-day bus pass (but not one-day passes, which you buy onboard), theater tickets, Keswick Launch tickets (at a £1.20 discount), fishing licenses, and brochures and maps that outline nearby hikes (60p–£1.80, including a very simple and

Keswick

LAKE DISTRICT

1 Stanger Street B&Bs
2 Howe Keld; Parkfield & West View Guest Houses
3 Hazeldene Hotel
4 Brundholme Guest House
5 Keswick Youth Hostel
6 To Derwentwater Hostel
7 To Denton House Hostel
8 Morrel's Restaurant
9 The Dog and Gun
10 To The Pheasant
11 Star of Siam

12 Abraham's Tea Room
13 The Lakeland Pedlar & Keswick Mountain Bikes
14 Bryson's Bakery & Tea Room
15 Good Taste Café
16 Maysons Restaurant
17 Keswick Tea Room & Supermarket
18 The Oddfellows Arms
19 Library (Internet Access)
20 Post Office & Internet Café
21 Launderette
22 Theatre by the Lake
23 Keswick Launch Cruises
24 Keswick Motor Co.
25 Cricket Pitch
26 Lawn Bowling; Tennis; Putting Green
27 Photo Fun with Sheep

driver-friendly £1.60 *Lap Map* featuring sights, walks, and a mileage chart). The TI also has books and maps for hikers, cyclists, and drivers (more books are sold at the nearby store that contains the post office).

Check the "What's On Locally" boards (inside the TI's foyer) for information about walks, talks, and entertainment. The daily weather forecast is posted just outside the front door (weather toll tel. 0870-055-0575). Pop upstairs for a series of short videos about the history of Keswick and the Lake District (free). For information about the TI's guided walks, see "Tours in Keswick," later.

Helpful Hints

Book in Advance: Keswick hosts a variety of festivals and conventions, especially during the summer, so it's smart to book ahead. Please honor your bookings—the B&B proprietors here lose out on much-needed business if you don't show up.

A sampling of events for 2010: The Keswick Jazz Festival mellows out the town in mid-May, followed immediately by the new Mountain Festival, then a beer festival in early June (June 4–5 in 2010). The Keswick Religious Convention packs the town with 4,000 evangelical Christians the last three weeks in July.

Several Bank Holiday Mondays in spring and summer (May 3, May 31, and Aug 30 in 2010) draw vacationers from all over the island for three-day weekends.

If you have trouble finding a room (or a B&B that accepts small children), try www.keswick.org to search for available rooms.

Internet Access: Located above the store that contains the post office, **U-Compute** provides Internet access (£2/30 min, £3/hr, unused time valid for 2 weeks, daily May–mid-Sept 8:30–21:00, mid-Sept–April 9:00–17:30, 16 terminals and Wi-Fi—same price, corner of Main and Bank streets, tel. 017687/75127). The **library** has 10 terminals (£2/hr, 50p/15-min minimum charge, Mon and Wed 10:00–19:00, Tue and Fri 10:00–17:00, Thu and Sat 10:00–12:30, closed Sun, tel. 017687/72656). The **launderette** listed next also has Wi-Fi (£2/hr).

Laundry: It's around the corner from the bus station on Main Street, next to the Co-op grocery (self-service Mon–Fri 8:00–19:00, Sat–Sun 9:00–18:00, £6/load wash and dry, change machine and coin-op soap dispenser; £8 full service; tel. 017687/75448).

Tours in Keswick

Guided Walks—Walks of varying levels of difficulty depart from the TI several times a week at 10:00. They're led by local guides, leave regardless of the weather, and sometimes incorporate a bus ride into the outing (£10, Easter–Oct, no tours during religious convention in July, wear suitable clothing and footwear, bring lunch and water, return by 17:00, tel. 017687/72645, www.keswick rambles.org.uk). TIs throughout the region also offer free walks led by "Voluntary Rangers" (generally from Keswick on Sun and Wed in summer, ask for the *National Park Visitor Guide*).

Bus Tours—These are great for people with bucks who'd like to wring maximum experience out of their limited time and see the area without lots of hiking or messing with public transport. For a cheaper alternative, take public buses.

Edwin Jackson of **Helm Wind Tours** can take you around Derwentwater and Buttermere on Fridays (£18, 9:30–12:30) or around Bassenthwaite and Caldbeck on Tuesdays (£16.50, 9:45–12:45; both tours leave from the Keswick bus stop, book at Keswick TI, mobile 07801-928-503). **Show Me Cumbria** runs personalized tours all around the area (£35/first hour, £25/hr after that, charge is per tour—not per person, tel. 01768/866-880, mobile 0780-902-6357, www.showmecumbria.co.uk, andy@showmecumbria.co.uk).

Mountain Goat Tours is the region's dominant tour company. Unfortunately, they run their minibus tours out of Windermere, with pick-ups in Ambleside and Grasmere, but not Keswick—adding about an extra hour of driving, round-trip, for those based in Keswick (£24/half-day, £34/full day, year-round if there are sufficient sign-ups, minimum 4 to a maximum of 16 per hearty bus, book in advance by calling 015394/45161, www.mountain-goat.com).

Sights in Keswick

▲Derwentwater—One of Cumbria's most photographed and popular lakes, Derwentwater has four islands, good circular boat service, plenty of trails, and the pleasant town of Keswick at its

north end. The roadside views aren't much, so hike or cruise. You can walk around the lake (fine trail, floods in heavy rains, 9 miles, 4 hours) or cruise it (1 hour). I suggest a hike/cruise combo. The Lodore Walk and the Catbells High Ridge Hike (both described later, under "Hikes and Drives in the North Lake District") start from Derwentwater docks.

Boating—Keswick Launch runs boats from mid-March to October (2/hr—alternating clockwise and "anticlockwise"—daily 10:00–16:30, July–Aug until 17:30, in winter 5/day weekends only, at end of Lake Road, tel. 017687/72263, www.keswick-launch .co.uk). Boats make seven stops on each one-hour round-trip. The boat trip costs £9 per circle (£1.20 less if you book through TI) with free stopovers, or £1.85 per segment. Stand on the pier Gilligan-style, or the boat may not stop. Keswick Launch also rents pricey **rowboats** for two (£8/30 min, £12/hr).

Keswick Launch's **evening cruise** is a delightful little trip that comes with a glass of wine and a mid-lake stop for a short commentary (£9.50, £21 family ticket, 1 hour, mid-July–Aug at 19:30 every evening—weather permitting and if enough people show up). You're welcome to bring a picnic dinner and munch scenically as you cruise.

▲**Pencil Museum**—Graphite was first discovered centuries ago in Keswick. A hunk of the stuff proved great for marking sheep in the 15th century. In 1832, the first crude Keswick pencil factory opened, and the rest is history (which is what you'll learn about here). While you can't actually tour the 150-year-old factory where the famous Derwent pencils are made, you can enjoy the smell of thousands of pencils getting sharpened for the first time. The adjacent charming and kid-friendly museum is a good way to pass a rainy hour; you may even catch an artist's demonstration. Take a look at the "war pencils" made for WWII bomber crews (filled with tiny maps and compasses) and relax for 10 minutes watching *The Humble Pencil* video in the theater, followed by a sleepy animated-snowman short (£3.25, daily 9:30–17:00, last entry at 16:00, humble café on-site, 3-min walk from the town center, signposted off Main Street, tel. 017687/73626, www.pencilmuseum.co.uk).

Fitz Park—An inviting, grassy park stretches alongside Keswick's tree-lined, duck-filled River Greta. There's plenty of room for kids to burn off energy. Consider an after-dinner stroll on the footpath. You may catch men in white (or frisky schoolboys in uniform) playing a game of cricket. There's the serious bowling green (where you're welcome to watch the experts play), and the public one where tourists are welcome to give lawn bowling a go (£3). You can try tennis on a grass court (£6.50/hr for 2 people, includes rackets) or enjoy the putting green (£2). Find the rental pavilion across the road from the art gallery (open daily 9:30–19:45 or until dusk).

▲**Golf**—A lush nine-hole pitch-and-putt golf course near the gardens in Hope Park separates the town from the lake and offers a classy, cheap, and convenient chance to golf near the birthplace of the sport (£3.50 for 9 holes, £2 for putting, £2.30 for 18 tame holes of "obstacle golf," daily 9:30–19:45 or dusk, may close Nov–Easter, tel. 017687/73445).

Swimming—While the Leisure Centre doesn't have a serious adult pool, it does have an indoor pool kids love, with a huge water slide and wave machine (pool-£4.75, kids-£3.75, family-£14, Mon–Tue 11:00–15:00, Wed 11:00–16:00, Thu 11:00–18:00, Fri 11:00–17:00, Sat–Sun 10:00–17:00, shorter hours off-season, longer during school break, no towels or suits for rent, lockers-£1 deposit, 10-min walk from town center, follow Station Road past Fitz Park and veer left, tel. 017687/72760).

Near Keswick

▲▲Castlerigg Stone Circle—For some reason, 70 percent of England's stone circles are here in Cumbria. This one's the best,

and one of the oldest in Britain. The circle—90 feet across and 5,000 years old—has 38 stones mysteriously laid out on a line between the two tallest peaks on the horizon. They served as a celestial calendar for ritual celebrations. Imagine the ambience here, as ancient people filled this clearing in spring to celebrate fertility, in late summer to commemorate the harvest, and in the winter to celebrate the winter solstice and the coming renewal of light. Festival dates were dictated by how the sun rose and set in relation to the stones. The more that modern academics study this circle, the more meaning they find in the placement of the stones. The two front stones face due north, toward a cut in the mountains. The rare-for-stone-circles "sanctuary" lines up with its center stone to mark where the sun rises on May Day. (Party!) For maximum "goose pimples" (as they say here), show up at sunset (free, open all the time, 3 miles east of Keswick—follow brown signs, 3 min off A66, easy parking).

▲Lakeland Sheep and Wool Centre—If you have a car, this is worth a stop to watch working sheepdogs in action. Catch a demonstration, see the 20 or so different breeds of sheep in Britain, and learn why each is bred. (Kneading the wool of the Merino

sheep, you'll understand why it's so popular for sweaters.) You'll also see the quintessential sheepdog—the border collie—at work. At the end, you can pet whatever is still on stage: dogs, cows, sheep, sometimes a goose... if you can catch one. While

the Visitors Centre and shop are free (daily 9:30–17:30), it's not really worth the trip unless you catch a sheep show (£5 for demo; March–Oct Sun–Thu at 10:30, 12:00, 14:00, and 15:30; no shows Fri–Sat and Nov–Feb, 13 miles west of Keswick on A66, just south of A5086 roundabout in Cockermouth, tel. 01900-822-673, www .sheep-woolcentre.co.uk).

Rheged Centre—This shopping mall, just off a highway round-about (near Penrith, on A66 a mile west of the Keswick exit 40 off M6), has an IMAX theater that shows a rotating schedule of movies throughout the day, including the one-hour *Rheged: The Lost Kingdom*, which tells the story of the region's original Celtic inhabitants (£5 for any movie, £1.50 outdoor playground, daily 10:00–17:30, call ahead to check movie times, the #X4 and #X5 Keswick–Penrith buses stop here, tel. 01768/868-000, www .rheged.com).

Hikes and Drives in the North Lake District

From Keswick

The first four hikes (Lodore, Catbells, Latrigg, and Walla Crag) originate in Keswick; the rest require a car or public transportation to get to the trailhead and/or views.

Lodore Walk—The best hour-long lakeside walk is the 1.5-mile path between the docks at High Brandelhow and Hawes End in Keswick. Continue on foot along the lake back into Keswick or—better yet—go on to Lodore.

Lodore is a good stop for two reasons: Lodore Falls is a 10-minute walk from the dock (behind Lodore Hotel), and Shepherds Crag (a cliff overlooking Lodore) was made famous by pioneer rock climbers. (Their descendants hang from little ridges on its face today.) This is serious climbing (with several fatalities a year).

For a great lunch, or tea and cakes, drop into the much-loved High Lodore Farm Café, where sheep farmer Martin is busy feeding hikers and day-trippers. Eggs come from "the happy hen" (Easter–Oct daily 9:00–17:00, closed Nov–Easter; from the dock, walk up the road, turn right over bridge uphill to café; tel. 017687/77221).

▲▲**Catbells High Ridge Hike**—For a great "king of the mountain" feeling, sweeping views, and a close-up look at the weather blowing over the ridge, hike about two hours from Hawes End in Keswick up along the ridge to Catbells (1,480 feet) and down to High Brandelhow (moderate difficulty). From there, you can catch the boat or take the easy path along the shore of Derwentwater to your Hawes End starting point. (Extending the hike to Lodore

Derwentwater and Newlands Valley

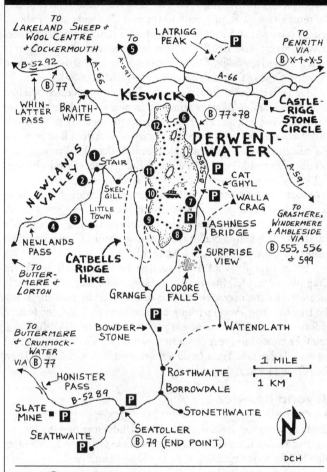

LAKE DISTRICT

Map labels:

TO LAKELAND SHEEP & WOOL CENTRE & COCKERMOUTH

LATRIGG PEAK

TO PENRITH VIA Ⓑ X-4 & X-5

B-5292

Ⓑ 77

WHINLATTER PASS

BRAITHWAITE

KESWICK

A-591

A-66

Ⓑ 77 & 78

CASTLERIGG STONE CIRCLE

Ⓑ 77 & 78

⑫

⑥

DERWENTWATER

NEWLANDS VALLEY

① STAIR

②

SKELGILL

⑪

⑩

P

CAT GHYL

P WALLA CRAG

A-591

LITTLE TOWN

④ ③

⑨

⑦ P

⑧

ASHNESS BRIDGE

TO GRASMERE, WINDERMERE & AMBLESIDE VIA Ⓑ 555, 556 & 599

NEWLANDS PASS

TO BUTTERMERE & LORTON

CATBELLS RIDGE HIKE

SURPRISE VIEW

GRANGE

LODORE FALLS

WATENDLATH

TO BUTTERMERE & CRUMMOCK-WATER VIA Ⓑ 77

BOWDERSTONE

P

1 MILE
1 KM

HONISTER PASS

B-5289

SLATE MINE P

SEATHWAITE P

P

ROSTHWAITE

BORROWDALE

STONETHWAITE

SEATOLLER
Ⓑ 79 (END POINT)

N

DCH

Ⓑ 78 BUS ROUTES
— ROAD
P PARKING
··· BOAT
--- PATH

▲ PEAK
■ POINT OF INTEREST

Newlands Valley

① Uzzicar Farm
② Ellas Crag Guest House
③ Gill Brow Farm B&B
④ Keskadale Farm B&B
⑤ To Dancing Beck B&B

Derwentwater

⑥ Keswick Launch Pier
⑦ Ashness Gate Pier
⑧ Lodore Pier
⑨ High Brandelhow Pier
⑩ Low Brandelhow Pier
⑪ Hawes End Pier
⑫ Nichol End Pier

takes you to a waterfall, rock climbers, a fine café, and another boat dock for a convenient return to Keswick.) Catbells is probably the most dramatic family walk in the area (but wear sturdy shoes, bring a raincoat, and watch your footing). From Keswick, the lake, or your farmhouse B&B, you can see silhouetted stick figures hiking along this ridge. Drivers can park free at Hawes End. The Keswick TI sells a *Catbells* brochure about the hike (60p).

Catbells is just the first of a series of peaks all connected by a fine ridge trail. Hardier hikers continue up to nine miles along this same ridge, enjoying valley and lake views as they arc around the Newlands Valley toward (and even down to) Buttermere. After High Spy, you can descend an easy path into Newlands Valley. An ultimate, very full day-plan would be to take a bus to Buttermere, climb Robinson, and follow the ridge around to Catbells and back to Keswick.

▲▲**More Hikes from Keswick**—The area is riddled with wonderful hikes. B&Bs all have fine advice, but consider these as well:

From downtown Keswick, you can walk the seven-mile **Latrigg** trail, which includes the Castlerigg Stone Circle described earlier (pick up 60p map/guide from TI).

From your Keswick B&B, a fine two-hour walk to **Walla Crag** offers great fell (mountain) walking and a ridge-walk experience without the necessity of a bus or car. Start by strolling along the lake to Great Wood parking lot, and head up Cat Ghyl (where "fell runners"—trail-running enthusiasts—practice) to Walla Crag. You'll be treated to great panoramic views over Derwentwater and surrounding peaks. You can do a shorter version of this walk from the parking lot at Ashness Bridge.

Beyond Keswick

▲▲**Easy Hikes**—For a very short hike and the easiest mountain-climbing sensation around, drive to the **Underscar** parking lot just north of Keswick, and hike 20 minutes to the top of the 1,200-foot-high hill for a commanding view of the town and lake.

From the parking lot at Newlands Pass, at the top of Newlands Valley, an easy one-mile walk to **Knottrigg** from Newlands Pass probably offers more TPCB (thrills per calorie burned) than any

walk in the region.

▲▲**Buttermere Hike**—The ideal little lake with a lovely, circular four-mile stroll offers nonstop, no-sweat Lake District beauty. If you're not a hiker (but kind of wish you were), take this walk. If you're very short on time, at least stop here and get your shoes dirty.

Buttermere is connected with Borrowdale and Derwentwater by a great road that runs over rugged Honister Pass. From Easter through October and on November weekends, bus #77/#77A makes a 1.5-hour round-trip loop between Keswick and Buttermere over Honister Pass. The two-pub hamlet of Buttermere has a pay-and-display parking lot, but many drivers park free along the side of the road. You're welcome to leave your car at the Fish Hotel if you eat in their pub (recommended). There's also a pay parking lot at the Honister Pass end of the lake (at Gatesgarth Farm, £3). The Syke Farm (in the hamlet of Buttermere) is popular for its homemade ice cream (tel. 01768/770-277).

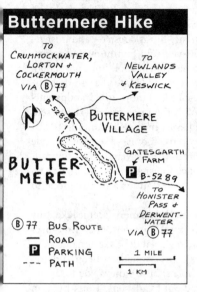

Buttermere Hike

TO CRUMMOCKWATER, LORTON & COCKERMOUTH VIA Ⓑ 77

B-5289

N

BUTTERMERE VILLAGE

TO NEWLANDS VALLEY & KESWICK

BUTTER-MERE

GATESGARTH FARM

P   B-5289

TO HONISTER PASS & DERWENT-WATER VIA Ⓑ 77

Ⓑ 77   BUS ROUTE
—   ROAD
Ⓟ   PARKING
- - -   PATH

1 MILE
1 KM

▲▲**Car Hiking from Keswick**—Distances are short, roads are narrow and have turnouts, and views are rewarding. Get a good map and ask your B&B host for advice. Two miles south of Keswick on the lakeside Borrowdale Valley Road (B5289), take the small road left (signposted *Ashness Bridge, Watendlath*) for a half-mile to the Ashness Packhorse Bridge (a quintessential Lake District scene, parking lot just above on right). A half-mile farther (parking lot on left) and you're startled by the "surprise view" of Derwentwater (great for a lakes photo op). Continuing from here, the road gets extremely narrow en route to the hamlet of Watendlath, which has a tiny lake and lazy farm animals. Return down to Borrowdale Valley Road and back to Keswick, or farther south to scenic Borrowdale and over dramatic Honister Pass to Buttermere.

▲▲**Scenic Circle Drive South of Keswick**—This hour-long drive, which includes Newlands Valley, Buttermere, Honister Pass, and Borrowdale, is demanding. But it's also filled with the best scenery you'll find in the North Lake District. (To do a similar route without a car from Keswick, take loop bus #77/#77A.)

From Keswick, head west on the Cockermouth Road (A66). Take the second Newlands Valley exit (through Braithwaite), and follow signs up the majestic **Newlands Valley.** If the place had a lake, it would be packed with tourists. But it doesn't—and it isn't.

The valley is dotted with 500-year-old family-owned farms. Shearing day is reason to rush home from school. Sons get school out of the way ASAP, and follow their dads into the family business. Neighbor girls marry those sons and move in. Grandparents retire to the cottage next door. With the price of wool depressed, most of the wives supplement the family income by running B&Bs (virtually every farm in the valley rents rooms). The road has one lane, with turnouts for passing. From the Newlands Pass summit, notice the glacial-shaped wilds, once forested, now not. There's an easy hike from your car to a little waterfall (or a thrilling one to Knottrigg, described earlier).

After Newlands Pass, descend to **Buttermere** (scenic lake, tiny hamlet with a pub and ice-cream store), turn left, and climb over rugged **Honister Pass**—strewn with glacial debris, remnants from the old slate mines, and curious, shaggy Swaledale sheep (looking more like goats with their curly horns). The valleys you'll see are textbook examples of those carved out by glaciers. Look high on the hillsides for "hanging valleys"—small glacial-shaped scoops cut off by the huge flow of the biggest glacier, which swept down the main valley. England's last still-functioning **slate mine,** at the summit of Honister Pass, gives tours (£10, 90-min tour; departures daily at 10:30, 12:30, 14:00, and 15:30; Dec–Jan 12:30 tour only, tel. 017687/77230, smart to book ahead, worthwhile slate-filled shop, nice WCs, www.honister.com).

After stark and lonely Honister Pass, drop into sweet and homey **Borrowdale,** with a few lonely hamlets and fine hikes from Seathwaite (get specifics on walks here from your B&B or the TI). Circling back to Keswick past Borrowdale, you pass a number of popular local attractions (climb stairs to the top of the house-size Bowder Stone—signposted, a few minutes walk off the main road), the postcard-pretty Ashness Bridge and "surprise view" (described earlier, turnout signposted), and the rock climbers above Lodore. After that, you're home. A short detour before returning to Keswick takes you to the Castlerigg Stone Circle.

Nightlife in Keswick

▲▲**Theatre by the Lake**—Keswickians brag they enjoy "London theater quality at Keswick prices." Their theater offers events year-round and a wonderful rotation of four to six plays through the summer (plays vary throughout the week, with music concerts on Sun). There are two stages: The main one seats 400, and the smaller "studio" theater seats 100 (and features edgier plays with rough language and nudity, £10–15). Attending a play here is a fine opportunity to do something completely local (£10–23, box office open from 9:30 until curtain time, discounts for old and young, 20:00 shows in summer, usually 19:30 in spring and fall, 19:00 in winter, café, smart to book ahead, parking at the adjacent lot is free after 18:30, tel. 017687/74411, book at TI or www.theatre bythelake.com).

▲▲**Evenings in Keswick**—For a small and remote town, Keswick has many great things to do in the evening. Remember, at this latitude it's light until 22:00 in midsummer. You can **golf** (fine course, pitch-and-putt, goofy golf, or just enjoy the putting green) or **walk** among the grazing sheep in Hope Park as the sun gets ready to set (between the lake and the golf course, access from just above the beach, great photo ops on a balmy eve).

To socialize with locals, head to a pub for one of their special evenings: There's **quiz night** at The Dog and Gun (21:30 on most Thu; £1, proceeds go to Keswick's Mountain Rescue team, which rescues hikers and the occasional sheep). At a quiz night, tourists are more than welcome. Drop in, say you want to join a team, and you're in. If you like trivia, it's a great way to get to know people here. Nearby, The Oddfellows Arms has free **live music** most nights.

Join Bob, the **Town Crier,** when he does his routine many summer Tuesday evenings (£2.50, 90 min, usually starts at 19:30, weekly late May–early July, details at TI). Catch a **movie** at the Alhambra Cinema, a restored old-fashioned movie theater a few minutes' walk from the town center. An **evening lake cruise** is perfect for an extremely scenic and relaxing picnic dinner (mid-July–Aug at 19:30).

Sleeping in Keswick

The Lake District abounds with attractive B&Bs, guest houses, and hostels. It needs them all when summer hordes threaten the serenity of this Romantic mecca.

Reserve your room in advance in high season. From October through April, you should have no trouble finding a room. But to get a particular place (especially on Saturdays), call ahead. If you're using public transportation, you should sleep in Keswick. If you're driving, staying outside Keswick is your best chance for a remote farmhouse experience. Lakeland hostels offer £20 beds and come with an interesting crowd of all ages.

For Keswick, I've featured B&Bs on two streets, each within three blocks of the bus station and town square. Stanger Street, a bit humbler but quiet and handy, has smaller homes and more moderately priced rooms. "The Heads" is a classier area lined with

Sleep Code

(£1 = about $1.60, country code: 44, area code: 017687)
S = Single, **D** = Double/Twin, **T** = Triple, **Q** = Quad, **b** = bathroom,
s = shower only. You can assume credit cards are accepted
unless otherwise noted, and all B&B stays include breakfast.

To help you sort easily through these listings, I've divided
the rooms into three categories based on the price for a
double room with bath:

\$\$\$ Higher Priced—Most rooms £70 or more.
  \$\$ Moderately Priced—Most rooms between £30-70.
    \$ Lower Priced—Most rooms £30 or less.

proud Victorian houses, close to the lake and theater, overlooking
a golf course.

Many of my Keswick listings charge extra for a one-night stay.
Most won't book one-night stays on weekends (but if you show up
and they have a bed free, it's yours) and don't welcome children
under 12 (unless extremely well-behaved). Owners are enthusiastic about offering plenty of advice to get you on the right walking
trail. Most accommodations have inviting lounges with libraries
of books on the region and loaner maps. Take advantage of these
lounges to transform your humble B&B room into a suite.

This is still the countryside—expect huge breakfasts (often
with big selections, including vegetarian options), no phones in the
rooms, and shower systems that might need to be switched on to
get hot water. Parking is pretty easy (park either in congested little
private lots or on the street) except on Saturdays, when you may
need to hunt for a little while.

On Stanger Street

This street, quiet but just a block from Keswick's town center, is
lined with B&Bs situated in Victorian slate townhouses. Each of
these places is small, family-run, and accepts cash only. They are
all good, offering comfortably sized rooms.

\$\$\$ Ellergill Guest House has five spick-and-span rooms
with an airy, contemporary feel—several with views (D-£60,
Db-£70, 2-night minimum, 22 Stanger Street, tel. 017687/73347,
www.ellergill.co.uk, stay@ellergill.co.uk, run by Clare and Robin
Pinkney and dog Tess).

\$\$ Dunsford Guest House rents four rooms decorated
with a Victorian feel, at a good price. Stained glass and wooden
pews give the blue-and-cream breakfast room a country-chapel
vibe (Db-£63, this price promised with this book in 2010, no

children under age 16, free Wi-Fi, parking, 16 Stanger Street, tel. 017687/75059, www.dunsford.net, enquiries@dunsford.net, accommodating Richard and Linda).

$$ Heckberry House's two light, airy rooms are both on the first floor (D with big private bath just outside-£60, Db-£64, 2-night minimum, no children, will pick up from bus station, 12 Stanger Street, tel. 017687/71277, www.heckberry.co.uk, enquiries @heckberry.co.uk, friendly Judith and David).

$$ Badgers Wood B&B, at the top of the street, has six modern, bright, un-frilly view rooms, each named after a different tree (Sb-£36, Db-£68, 2-night minimum, no children under age 12, special diets accommodated, 30 Stanger Street, tel. 017687/72621, www.badgers-wood.co.uk, enquiries@badgers-wood.co.uk, Andrew and Anne).

$$ Abacourt House, with a daisy-fresh breakfast room, has five pleasant doubles (Db-£65, no children, 26 Stanger Street, tel. 017687/72967, www.abacourt.co.uk, abacourt.keswick@btinternet .com, John and Heather).

On The Heads

All of these B&Bs are in an area known as The Heads. Most have good mountain views.

$$$ Howe Keld has the polished feel of a boutique hotel, but offers all the friendliness of a B&B. Completely renovated in 2008, its 14 contemporary-posh rooms are decked out in native woods and slate. It's warm, welcoming, and family-run, with a wide variety of breakfast selections (Sb-£45–50, standard Db-£80, superior Db-£90–102, cash preferred, 2 ground-floor rooms, family deals, free Wi-Fi, toll-free tel. 0800-783-0212 or 017687/72417, www.howekeld.co.uk, david@howekeld.co.uk, run with care by David and Valerie Fisher).

$$$ Parkfield Guest House, thoughtfully run and decorated by John and Susan Berry, is a big Victorian house. Its seven bright and pastel rooms have fine views (Sb-£50, Db-£78 with this book through 2010, Db suite-£98, 2-night minimum, no children under age 16, fresh fruit salads at breakfast, off-street parking available, tel. 017687/72328, www.parkfield-keswick.co.uk, susanberrypark field@hotmail.com).

$$$ West View Guest House, next to the Parkfield, has eight cheery rooms, a relaxing old-school lounge, and a "borrow box" for those desperate for walking gear. Ask Paul or Dawn about the cabinet in the lounge dedicated to pharmaceutical history (Sb-£50, Db-£72, tel. 017687/73638, www.westviewkeswick.co.uk, info @westviewkeswick.co.uk).

$$$ Hazeldene Hotel, on the corner of The Heads, has spacious, bright rooms. The carpeting is dated, but you'll hardly notice, as the views are fantastic (Db-£70–80 depending on view, huge Db suite with grand view-£90–95, Tb-£105, £5 extra for one-night stay, free Wi-Fi, tel. 017687/72106, www.hazeldene-hotel.co.uk, Helen).

$$ Brundholme Guest House has three bright and comfy rooms, all with grand views—especially from the front side—and a friendly and welcoming atmosphere (Db-£62, cash only, tel. 017687/73305, www.brundholme.co.uk, barbara@brundholme.co.uk, Barbara and Paul Motler).

Hostels in and near Keswick

The Lake District's inexpensive hostels, mostly located in great old buildings, are handy sources of information and social fun. The first two hostels—both part of the Youth Hostels Association (www.yha.org.uk)—are former hotels, offering Internet access, laundry machines, and three cheap meals daily; at these, non-members pay about £3 extra a night, or buy a £16 membership.

$ Keswick Youth Hostel, with 85 beds in a converted old mill that overlooks the river, has a great riverside balcony and plenty of handy facilities. Travelers of all ages feel at home here, but book ahead—beds here can be hard to come by from July through September (£20–22 beds, mostly 3- to 4-bed rooms, D-£44, café, bar, center of town just off Station Road before river, tel. 017687/72484, keswick@yha.org.uk).

$ Derwentwater Hostel, in a 200-year-old mansion on the shore of Derwentwater, is two miles south of Keswick and has 88 beds (£16–18 beds in 4- to 22-bed rooms, family rooms, 23:00 curfew, follow B5289 from Keswick, look for sign 100 yards after Ashness exit, tel. 017687/77246, derwentwater@yha.org.uk).

$ Denton House is Keswick's *other* hostel—it's independent (not YHA), spartan, grimy, and institutional, but usually has spaces available (£13–15 beds in 4- to 14-bed dorm rooms, lockers-£1–2, breakfast-£3 extra and offered only when hostel is full—which is most weekends, kitchen, tel. 017687/75351, www.vividevents.co.uk, sales@vividevents.co.uk). From the town square, walk several blocks uphill along Station Street. Just before the bridge over the river, turn right onto Penrith Road; from there, it's a seven-minute riverside walk—the hostel is on the right, not long after the fire station.

West of Keswick, in the Newlands Valley

If you have a car, drive 10 minutes past Keswick down the majestic Newlands Valley (described earlier, under "Scenic Circle Drive South of Keswick"). This valley is studded with 500-year-old farms that have been in the same family for centuries, and now rent rooms to supplement the family income. The rooms are plainer than the B&Bs in town, and come with steep and gravelly roads, plenty of dogs, and an earthy charm. Traditionally, farmhouses lacked central heating, and while they are now heated, you can still request a hot-water bottle to warm up your bed.

Getting to the Newlands Valley: Leave Keswick heading west on the Cockermouth Road (A66). Take the second Newlands Valley exit through Braithwaite, and follow signs through Newlands Valley (drive toward Buttermere). All of my recommended B&Bs are on this road: Uzzicar Farm (under the shale field, which local boys love hiking up to glissade down), Ellas Crag Guest House, then Gill Brow Farm, and finally—the last house before the stark summit—Keskadale Farm (about four miles before Buttermere). The one-lane road has turnouts for passing. Each place offers easy parking, grand views, and perfect tranquility. These are listed in geographical order, the first being a 10-minute drive from Keswick and the last being at the top of the valley (about a 15-min drive from Keswick).

$$$ Uzzicar Farm is a big, rustic place with a comfy B&B in a low-ceilinged, circa-1550 farmhouse—watch out for ducks (S-£45, D or Db-£70, discount for longer stays, family deals, cash only, tel. 017687/78026, www.uzzicarfarm.co.uk, stay@uzzicar farm.co.uk, Helen).

$$ Ellas Crag Guest House, with three rooms—each with a great view—is more of a comfortable stone house than a farm. This homey B&B offers a good mix of modern and traditional decor, including beautifully tiled bathrooms (Ss-£45, Sb-50, Ds-£60, Db-£64, these prices guaranteed with this book through 2010, cash only, 2-night minimum, local free-range meats and eggs for breakfast, sack lunches available, huge DVD library, laundry-£10, tel. 017687/78217, www.ellascrag.co.uk, info@ellascrag.co.uk, Jane and Ed Ma and their children).

$$ Gill Brow Farm is a rough-hewn, working farmhouse where Anne Wilson and her delightful teenage daughter Laura rent two simple but fine rooms (D or Db-£54, 10 percent discount with this book and 3-night stay in 2010, tel. 017687/78270, www .gillbrow-keswick.co.uk, wilson_gillbrow@hotmail.com).

$$ Keskadale Farm is another good farmhouse experience, with Ponderosa hospitality. One of the valley's oldest, the house is made from 500-year-old ship beams. While the two rooms for rent are dark and have dated decor, this working farm is an authentic slice of Lake District life and is your chance to get to know lots of curly-horned sheep and the dogs who herd them. Now that her boys are old enough to help Dad in the fields, Margaret Harryman runs the B&B (Sb-£40, Db-£60–70, £2 extra for one-night stays, cash only, closed Dec–Feb, tel. 017687/78544, fax 017687/78150, www.keskadalefarm.co.uk, info@keskadalefarm.co.uk). They also rent a two-bedroom apartment (£400/week).

LAKE DISTRICT

West and Southwest of Keswick, in Buttermere and Lorton

$$$ Bridge Hotel, just beyond Newlands Valley at Buttermere, offers 21 beautiful rooms—most of them quite spacious—and a classic Old World countryside-hotel experience that includes a fancy dinner (Sb-£89, standard Db-£180–182, superior Db-£198, suite-like Db-£198, £40 less without dinner, free Wi-Fi in lobby, tel. 017687/70252, fax 017687/70215, www.bridge-hotel.com, enquiries@bridge-hotel.com). There are no shops within 10 miles—only peace and quiet a stone's throw from one of the region's most beautiful lakes. The hotel has a dark-wood pub/restaurant on the ground floor.

$$$ The Old Vicarage, with a lovely, genteel feeling, is in what once was the clergyman's house in this tiny village. It has six rooms in the main late-1800s house, and two more in the coach house. The owners, Jane and Peter Smith, offer an optional £21 two-course meal or a £25 three-course meal, with dishes such as rack of lamb (Sb-£75–80, Db-£110–120, one ground-floor room, Church Lane, Lorton, tel. 01900/85656, www.oldvicarage.co.uk, enquiries@oldvicarage.co.uk).

$ Buttermere Hostel, a quarter-mile south of Buttermere village on Honister Pass Road, has good food, 70 beds, family rooms, and a peacefully rural setting (£20 beds in 4- to 6-bed rooms, £2 cheaper mid-week, includes breakfast, inexpensive lunches and dinners, laundry, office open 8:30–10:00 & 17:00–22:30, 23:00 curfew, toll tel. 0845-371-9508, buttermere@yha.org.uk).

North of Keswick, Toward Bassenthwaite Lake

This area has gorgeous views looking down the Newlands Valley, and is still near Keswick.

$$$ Dancing Beck B&B is a newly renovated but very traditional-feeling 1850 house. Its three light-filled rooms come with views and good-size bathrooms. The "Squirrel Room" looks out on nest boxes hung for endangered red squirrels—you may spot some babies (Sb-£35–40, Db-£65–70, cash only; about two miles from Keswick—take A591, turn right at sign for *Millbeck* and *Applethwaite*, second house on the left; tel. 017687/74781, www.dancingbeck.co.uk, lyn.edmondson@btinternet.com, Lynne).

South of Keswick, near Borrowdale

$$$ Seatoller Farm B&B is a rustic 17th-century house in a five-building hamlet where Christine Simpson rents three rooms. The old windows are small, but the abundant flower boxes keep things bright (Db-£70, less for 2 or more nights, tel. 017687/77232, www.seatollerfarm.co.uk, info@seatollerfarm.co.uk). Several restaurants are located about a mile away.

$ Borrowdale Hostel, in secluded Borrowdale Valley just south of Rosthwaite, is a well-run place surrounded by many ways to immerse yourself in nature. The hostel serves cheap dinners, offers sack lunches, and keeps the pantry well-stocked (86 beds, £18–22 beds in 2- to 8-bed dorms, D-£44, £3 more for non-members, family rooms, pay Internet access and Wi-Fi, laundry machines, 3 cheap meals daily, 23:00 curfew, toll tel. 0845-371-9624, borrowdale@yha.org.uk). To reach this hostel from Keswick by bus, take #78, the "Borrowdale Rambler" (hourly, 2/hr mid-July–Aug; last bus from Keswick at 17:40 most of year, at 18:00 mid-July–Aug).

Eating in Keswick

Keswick has a huge variety of eateries catering to its many visitors. Most restaurants stop serving by 21:00. Here's a selection of favorites.

Morrel's Restaurant is the top Keswick choice for a splurge. It's simple yet elegant, serving famously good and creative modern English cuisine (£11–17 meals, £14 two-course meals and £16 three-course meals on Sun, Tue–Sun 17:30–21:00, closed Mon, reservations recommended; tell them if you're going to the theater, otherwise expect a relaxed dinner; all meals cooked to order, 34 Lake Road, tel. 017687/72666).

The Dog and Gun serves good pub food, but mind your head, and tread carefully: Low ceilings and wooden beams loom overhead, while paws poke out from under tables below, as Keswick's canines wait patiently for their masters to finish their beer (£6–10 meals, daily 12:00–21:00, goulash, no chips and proud of it, 2 Lake Road, tel. 017687/73463).

The Pheasant is a bit of a walk outside town, but locals make the trek regularly for the food. The menu offers local pub standards (fish pie, Cumbrian sausage, guinea fowl), as well as lighter, more inventive choices. Check the walls for caricatures of pub regulars, sketched at these tables by a local artist (£9–12 meals, daily 12:00–14:00 & 18:00–21:00, light meals served between lunch and dinner, Crosthwaite Road, tel. 017687/72219). From the town square, it's a 15-minute walk: Follow Main Street past the Pencil Museum, then hang a right onto Crosthwaite Road and walk for 10 minutes; the pub is opposite the Esso station. For a more scenic route, cross the river into Fitz Park, and go left along the riverside path until it ends at the gate to Crosthwaite Road; turn right here and walk for five minutes.

Star of Siam serves authentic Thai dishes in a tasteful dining room (£8–10 plates, daily 12:00–14:30 & 17:30–22:30, 89 Main Street, tel. 017687/71444).

Abraham's Tea Room, popular with locals, may be the best lunch deal in town. It's tucked away on the first floor of the giant George Fisher outdoor store (£4–6 soups and sandwiches, Mon–Fri 10:00–17:00, Sat 9:30–17:00, Sun 10:30–16:30, on the corner where Lake Road turns right).

The Lakeland Pedlar, a wholesome, pleasant café (with a bike shop upstairs), serves freshly baked vegan and vegetarian fare, including soups, organic bread, and daily specials. Their interior is cute. Outside tables face a big parking lot (£7 meals, daily 9:00–17:00, Thu–Sat until 21:00 in summer, Hendersons Yard, find the narrow walkway off Market Street between pink Johnson's sweet shop and The Golden Lion, tel. 017687/74492).

Bryson's Bakery and Tea Room has an enticing ground-floor bakery, with sandwiches and light lunches. The upstairs is a popular tearoom. Order lunch to go from the bakery, or for a few pence more, eat there, either sitting on stools or at a couple of sidewalk tables (£4–8 meals, Mon–Sat 8:30–17:30—tearoom opens at 9:30, Sun 9:30–17:00, 42 Main Street, tel. 017687/72257). Consider their £16 two-person Cumberland Cream Tea, which is like afternoon tea in London, but cheaper, and made with local products. Sandwiches, scones, and little cakes are served on a three-tiered platter with tea.

Good Taste has a small café space but a huge following, and is known for its fresh ingredients and its chef's expertise. Stop by for a light snack of homemade muffins and an espresso, or try a wild-boar burger (Mon–Sat 8:30–16:30, closed Sun, 19 Lake Road, tel. 017687/75973).

Maysons Restaurant, with Californian ambience, is fast and easy, with a buffet line of curry, Cajun, and vegetarian options. The food is cooked fresh on the premises, but it's nothing fancy: You point, and they dish up and microwave (£6–8 plates, cash only; April–Oct daily 11:30–20:45; Nov–March Mon–Thu 11:45–17:00, Fri–Sun 11:45–20:30; family-friendly, also take-out—great for evening cruise picnic, 33 Lake Road, tel. 017687/74104).

Keswick Tea Room, next to Booths supermarket (described next), is popular with locals, and features cheap and cheery regional specialties (Mon–Sat 8:00–18:00, Sun 10:00–16:00).

Picnic: The fine **Booths supermarket** is right where all the buses arrive (Mon–Sat 8:00–21:00, Sun 10:00–16:00, The Headlands). The recommended **Bryson's Bakery** does good sandwiches to go (described earlier). **The Keswickian** serves up old-fashioned fish-and-chips to go (daily 11:00–23:30, on the town square). Just around the corner, **The Cornish Pasty** offers an enticing variety of fresh meat pies to go (£2–3 pies, daily 9:30–17:30 or until the pasties are all gone, across from The Dog and Gun on Borrowdale Road).

In the Newlands Valley

The farmhouse B&Bs of Newlands Valley don't serve dinner, so their guests have two good options: Go into Keswick, or take the lovely 10-minute drive to Buttermere for your evening meal at the **Fish Hotel Pub,** which has fine indoor and outdoor seating, but takes no reservations (£7 meals, daily 12:00–14:00 & 18:00–21:00, family-friendly, good fish and daily specials with fresh vegetables, tel. 017687/70253). The neighboring **Bridge Hotel Pub** is a bit cozier, but less popular (£6–7 meals, daily 12:00–21:30, tel. 017687/70252).

Keswick Connections

The nearest train station to Keswick is in Penrith, with a ticket window (Mon–Sat 5:30–21:00, Sun 11:30–21:00) but no lockers. For train and bus info, check at a local TI, visit www.traveline.org .uk, or call 0845-748-4950 (for train), or 0871-200-2233 (10p/min). Most routes run less frequently on Sundays.

From Keswick by Bus: For connections, see page 474.

From Penrith by Bus to: Keswick (Mon–Sat roughly hourly 7:20–22:45, only 8/day on Sun, 40 min, £5.50, pay driver, Stagecoach buses #X4 and #X5), **Ullswater** and **Glenridding** (6/day, 45 min, bus #108). The Penrith bus stop is just outside the train station (bus schedules posted inside and outside station).

From Penrith by Train to: Blackpool (12/day, 1.75 hrs, change in Preston), **Liverpool** (roughly hourly, 2 hrs, change in Wigan or Preston), **Birmingham**'s New Street Station (roughly hourly, 2.5–3 hrs, some with change in Preston), **Durham** (hourly, 2.5–3.5 hrs, change in Carlisle and Newcastle), **London**'s Euston Station (9/day, 3–3.5 hrs), **Edinburgh** (nearly hourly, 1.75 hrs), **Glasgow** (10/day, 1.5–2 hrs), **Oban** (2/day, morning train 5.75 hrs, evening train 6.75 hrs, both require changing stations in Glasgow, evening train requires additional change in Carlisle).

Route Tips for Drivers

Coming from (or Going to) the West: Only 1,300 feet above sea level, Hard Knott Pass is still a thriller, with a narrow, winding, steeply graded road. Just over the pass are the scant but evocative remains of the Hard Knott Roman fortress. The great views can come with miserable rainstorms, and it can be very slow and frustrating when the one-lane road with turnouts is clogged by traffic. Avoid it on summer weekends.

From Points South (such as Blackpool, Liverpool, or North Wales) to the Lake District: The direct, easy way to Keswick is to leave M6 at Penrith, and take the A66 highway for 16 miles to Keswick. For the scenic sightseeing drive through the south lakes to Keswick, exit M6 on A590/A591 through the towns of Kendal and Windermere to reach Brockhole National Park Visitors Centre. From Brockhole, the A road to Keswick is fastest, but the high road—the tiny road over Kirkstone Pass to Glenridding and lovely Ullswater—is much more dramatic.

Near Keswick: Ullswater

▲▲Ullswater Hike and Boat Ride

Long, narrow Ullswater, which some consider the loveliest lake in the area, offers eight miles of diverse and grand Lake District scenery. While you can drive it or cruise it, I'd ride the boat from the south tip halfway up (to Howtown—which is nothing more than a dock) and hike back. Or walk first, then enjoy an easy ride back. Old-fashioned "steamer" boats (actually diesel-powered) leave **Glenridding** regularly for Howtown (£5.50 one-

way, £9 round-trip, covered by £14 Ullswater Bus & Boat day pass, family rates, June–Aug daily 9/day 9:45–16:45, April–May and Sept 6/day 9:45–15:50, fewer off-season, 35 min one-way, drivers can use safe pay-and-display parking lot—£2/2 hrs, £4/12 hrs; take bus #108 from Penrith, bus #208 from Keswick, or bus #517 from Windermere; café at dock, brochure shows walking route, tel. 017684/82229, www.ullswater-steamers.co.uk).

From Howtown, spend three to four hours hiking and dawdling along the well-marked path by the lake south to Patterdale, and then along the road back to Glenridding. This is a serious seven-mile walk with good views, varied terrain, and a few bridges and farms along the way. For a shorter hike from Howtown Pier, consider a three-mile loop around Hallin Fell. A rainy-day plan is to ride the covered boat up and down the lake to Howtown and back, or to Pooley Bridge at the northern tip of the lake (£12 round-trip, 2–5/day, 2 hrs). Boats don't run in really bad weather—call ahead if it looks iffy.

Helvellyn

Considered by many the best high-mountain hike in the Lake District, this breathtaking round-trip route from Glenridding includes the spectacular Striding Edge—about a half-mile along the ridge. Be careful; do this six-hour hike only in good weather, since the wind can be fierce. While it's not the shortest route, the Glenridding ascent is best. Get advice from the Keswick TI, which has a helpful *Helvellyn from Glenridding* leaflet on the hike (60p).

South Lake District

The South Lake District has a cheesiness similar to other popular English resort destinations, such as Blackpool. Here, piles of low-end vacationers eat ice cream and get candy floss caught in their hair. The area around Windermere is worth a drive-through if you're a fan of Wordsworth or Beatrix Potter; otherwise, spend the majority of your Lake District time (and book your accommodations) up north.

Getting Around

By Car: This is your best option to see the small towns and sights clustered in the South Lake District; consider combining your drive with the bus trip mentioned below.

If you're coming to or leaving the South Lake District from the west, you could take the Hard Knott Pass for a scenic introduction to the area.

By Bus: Buses are a fine way to lace together this gauntlet of sights in the congested Lake Windermere neighborhood. The open-top Lakes Rider bus #599 stops at Bowness Pier (lake cruises), Windermere (train station), Brockhole (National Park Visitors Centre), Ambleside, Rydal Mount, and Grasmere (Dove Cottage). Consider leaving your car at Grasmere and enjoying the breezy and extremely scenic ride, hopping off and on as you like (3/hr daily Easter–Aug, 50 min each way, Central Lakes Dayrider all-day pass-£6.50—buy from driver). Buses #555 and #556 also run between Windermere and Keswick.

Sights in the South Lake District

Wordsworth Sights

William Wordsworth was one of the first writers to reject fast-paced city life. During England's Industrial Age, hearts were muzzled and brains ruled. Science was in, machines were taming nature, and factory hours were taming humans. In reaction to these brainy ideals, a rare few—dubbed Romantics—began to embrace untamed nature and undomesticated emotions.

Back then, nobody climbed a mountain just because it was there—but Wordsworth did. He'd "wander lonely as a cloud" through the countryside, finding inspiration in "plain living and high thinking." He soon attracted a circle of like-minded creative friends.

The emotional highs the Romantics felt weren't all natural. Wordsworth and his poet friends Samuel Taylor Coleridge and Thomas de Quincey got stoned on opium and wrote poetry,

LAKE DISTRICT

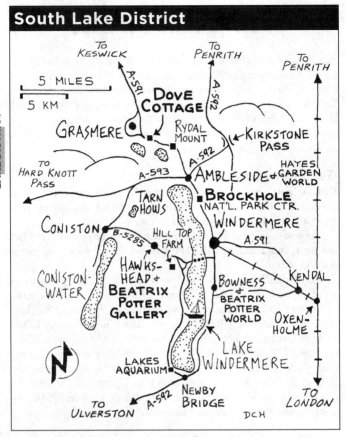

South Lake District

TO KESWICK

TO PENRITH

TO PENRITH

5 MILES

5 KM

A-591

A-592

DOVE COTTAGE

GRASMERE

RYDAL MOUNT

KIRKSTONE PASS

TO HARD KNOTT PASS

A-593

A-592

AMBLESIDE

HAYES GARDEN WORLD

BROCKHOLE NAT'L. PARK CTR.

TARN HOWS

WINDERMERE

CONISTON

B-5285

HILL TOP FARM

A-591

KENDAL

HAWKS-HEAD & BEATRIX POTTER GALLERY

CONISTON-WATER

BOWNESS

BEATRIX POTTER WORLD

OXEN-HOLME

N

LAKES AQUARIUM

LAKE WINDERMERE

TO ULVERSTON

A-592

NEWBY BRIDGE

TO LONDON

DCH

combining their generation's standard painkiller drug with their tree-hugging passions. Today, opium is out of vogue, but the Romantic movement thrives as visitors continue to inundate the region.

▲▲Dove Cottage and Wordsworth Museum—The poet whose appreciation of nature and a back-to-basics lifestyle put this area on the map spent his most productive years (1799–1808) in this well-preserved stone cottage on the edge of Grasmere. After functioning as the Dove and Olive Bow pub for almost 200 years, it was bought by his family. This is where Wordsworth got married, had kids, and wrote much of his best poetry. Still owned by the Wordsworth family, the furniture was his, and the place comes with some amazing artifacts, including the poet's passport and suitcase (he packed light). Even during his lifetime, Wordsworth was famous, and Dove Cottage was turned into a museum in 1891—predating even the National Trust, which protects the house today.

Wordsworth at Dove Cottage

William Wordsworth (1770–1850) was a Lake District home-boy. Born in Cockermouth (in a house now open to the public), he was schooled in Hawkshead. In adulthood, he married a local girl, settled down in Grasmere and Ambleside, and was buried in Grasmere's St. Oswald's churchyard.

But the 30-year-old man who moved into Dove Cottage in 1799 was not the carefree lad who'd roamed the district's lakes and fields. At Cambridge University, he'd been a C student, graduating with no job skills and no interest in a nine-to-five career. Instead, he and a buddy hiked through Europe, where Wordsworth had an epiphany of the "sublime" atop Switzerland's Alps. He lived a year in France, watching the Revolution rage. It stirred his soul. He fell in love with a Frenchwoman who bore his daughter, Caroline. But lack of money forced him to return to England, and the outbreak of war with France kept them apart.

Pining away in London, William hung out in the pubs and coffeehouses with fellow radicals, where he met poet Samuel Taylor Coleridge. They inspired each other to write, edited each other's work, and jointly published a groundbreaking book of poetry.

In 1799, his head buzzing with words and ideas, William and his sister (and soul mate) Dorothy moved into the whitewashed, slate-tiled former inn now known as Dove Cottage. He came into a small inheritance, and dedicated himself to poetry full time. In 1802, with the war over, William returned to France to finally meet his daughter. (He wrote of the rich experience: "It is a beauteous evening, calm and free.../Dear child! Dear Girl! that walkest with me here,/If thou appear untouched by solemn thought,/Thy nature is not therefore less divine.")

Having achieved closure, Wordsworth returned home to marry a former kindergarten classmate, Mary. She moved into Dove Cottage, along with an initially jealous Dorothy. Three of their five children were born here, and the cottage was also home to Mary's sister, the family dog Pepper (a gift from Sir Walter Scott; see Pepper's portrait), and frequent houseguests who bedded down in the pantry: Scott, Coleridge, and Thomas de Quincey, the Timothy Leary of opium.

After almost nine years here, Wordsworth's family and social status had outgrown the humble cottage. They moved first to a house in Grasmere before settling down in Rydal Hall. Wordsworth was changing. After the Dove years, he would write less, settle into a regular government job, quarrel with Coleridge, drift to the right politically, and endure criticism from old friends who branded him a sellout. Still, his poetry—most of it written at Dove—became increasingly famous, and he died honored as England's Poet Laureate.

Wordsworth's Poetry at Dove

At Dove Cottage, Wordsworth was immersed in the beauty of nature and the simple joy of his young, growing family. It was here that he reflected on both his idyllic childhood and his troubled twenties. The following are select lines from two well-known poems from this fertile time.

Ode: Intimations of Immortality

There was a time when meadow, grove, and stream,
The earth, and every common sight, to me did seem
Apparelled in celestial light, the glory and the freshness
    of a dream.
It is not now as it hath been of yore; turn wheresoe'er I
    may, by night or day,
The things which I have seen I now can see no more.
Now while the birds thus sing a joyous song...
To me alone there came a thought of grief...
Whither is fled the visionary gleam?
Where is it now, the glory and the dream?
Our birth is but a sleep and a forgetting:
The Soul...cometh from afar...
Trailing clouds of glory do we come
From God, who is our home.

I Wandered Lonely as a Cloud

I wandered lonely as a cloud
That floats on high o'er vales and hills,
When all at once I saw a crowd,
A host, of golden daffodils;
Beside the lake, beneath the trees,
Fluttering and dancing in the breeze...
For oft, when on my couch I lie
In vacant or in pensive mood,
They flash upon that inward eye
Which is the bliss of solitude;
And then my heart with pleasure fills,
And dances with the daffodils.

Today, Dove Cottage is a must-see for any Wordsworth admirer. Even if you're not a fan, Wordsworth's appreciation of nature, his Romanticism, and the ways his friends unleashed their creative talents with such abandon are appealing. The 30-minute cottage **tour** (departures on the hour and half-hour) and adjoining **museum**—with lots of actual manuscripts hand-written by Wordsworth and his illustrious friends—are both excellent. In dry weather, the garden where the poet was much inspired is worth a wander. (Visit this before leaving the cottage, and pick up the description at the back door.) Allow at least an hour for this two-part attraction (£7.50, daily Feb–Dec 9:30–17:30, last entry at 17:00, last tour at 16:50, closed Jan, bus #555 or #556 from Keswick, tel. 015394/35544, www.wordsworth.org.uk). Parking is free and easy in the Dove Cottage lot facing the main road (A591).

Poetry Readings: On Tuesday evenings in summer, the Wordsworth Trust puts on poetry readings, where national poets read their own works. They're hoping to continue the poetry tradition of the Lake District. Readings are held at the St. Oswald's Church in Grasmere Village (every other Tue at 18:45, runs May–mid-Oct only, two 45-min sessions followed by an optional dinner, £7 at the door or £6 pre-booked, £15 pre-booked dinner, tel. 015394/35544).

Rydal Mount—Wordsworth's final, higher-class home, with a lovely garden and view, lacks the charm of Dove Cottage. It feels

like a B&B. He lived here for 37 years, and his family repurchased it in 1969 (after a 100-year gap). His great-great-great-grand-daughter still calls it home on occasion, as shown by recent family photos sprinkled throughout some rooms. Located just down the road from Dove Cottage, it's worthwhile only for Wordsworth fans (£6; March–Oct daily 9:30–17:00; Nov–Dec and Feb Wed–Sun 11:00–16:00, closed Mon–Tue; closed Jan, 1.5 miles north of Ambleside, well-signed, free and easy parking, bus #555 or #556 from Keswick, tel. 015394/33002, www.rydalmount.co.uk).

Beatrix Potter Sights

Of the many Beatrix Potter commercial ventures in the Lake District, there are two serious Beatrix Potter sights: her farm (Hill Top Farm); and her husband's former office, which is now the Beatrix Potter Gallery, filled with her sketches and paintings. Both sights are in or near Hawkshead, a 20-minute drive south of Ambleside. If you're coming over from Windermere, catch the cute little 15-car ferry (runs constantly except when it's extremely windy, 10-min trip, £3.50 car fare includes all passengers). Note that both of the major sights are closed on Friday.

Hill Top Farm—A hit with Beatrix Potter fans, this farm was left just as it was when she died in 1943. While there's no information here (you'll need to buy the £3.50 guidebook for details on what you see), the dark and intimate cottage, swallowed up in the inspirational and rough nature around it, provides an enjoyable if quick experience (£6.50, tickets often sell out by 14:00, April–Oct

Beatrix Potter
(1866–1943)

As a girl growing up in London, Beatrix Potter vacationed in the Lake District, where she became inspired to write her popular children's books. Unable to get a publisher, she self-published the first two editions of *The Tale of Peter Rabbit* in 1901 and 1902. When she finally  landed a publisher, sales of her books were phenomenal. With the money she made, she bought Hill Top Farm, a 17th-century cottage, and fixed it up, living there from 1905 until she married in 1913. Potter was more than a children's book writer; she was a fine artist, an avid gardener, and a successful farmer. She married a lawyer and put her knack for business to use, amassing a 4,000-acre estate. An early conservationist, she used the garden-cradled cottage as a place to study nature. She willed it—along with the rest of her vast estate—to the National Trust, which she enthusiastically supported. The events of Potter's life were dramatized in the 2007 movie *Miss Potter*, starring Renée Zellweger as Beatrix.

Sat–Thu 10:30–16:30, mid-Feb–March Sat–Thu 11:00–15:30, closed Fri and Nov–mid-Feb, last entry 30 min before closing, in Near Sawrey village, 2 miles south of Hawkshead, bus #525 from Hawkshead, tel. 015394/36269, www.nationaltrust.org.uk/beatrix potter). Drivers can park and buy tickets 150 yards down the road, and walk back to tour the place.

▲▲**Beatrix Potter Gallery**—Located in the cute but extremely touristy town of Hawkshead, this gallery fills her husband's former law office with the wonderful and intimate drawings and water-colors that Potter did to illustrate her books. The best of the Potter sights, the gallery has plenty of explanation about her life and work. Even non-Potter fans find her art surprisingly interesting. Of about 700 works in the gallery's possession, a rotation of about 40 are shown at any one time (£4.50, tiny discount with Hill Top Farm, same hours as Hill Top Farm, bus #505 from Windermere, Main Street, drivers use the nearby pay-and-display lot and walk 200 yards to the town center, tel. 015394/36355, www.national trust.org.uk/beatrixpotter).

Hawkshead—The town of Hawkshead is engulfed in Potter tourism, and the extreme quaintness of it all is off-putting. Just across from the pay-and-display parking lot is the interesting Hawkshead Grammar School Museum, founded in 1585, where William Wordsworth studied from 1779 to 1787. It shows off old school benches and desks whittled with penknife graffiti (£2 includes guided tour; April–Sept Mon–Sat 10:00–13:00 & 14:00–17:00, Sun 13:00–17:00; Oct Mon–Sat 10:00–13:00 & 14:00–15:30, Sun 13:00–15:30; closed Nov–March; bus #505 from Windermere, tel. 015394/36735, www.hawksheadgrammar.org.uk).

The World of Beatrix Potter—This tour, a hit with children, is a gimmicky exhibit with all the history of a Disney ride. The 45-minute experience features a five-minute video trip into the world of Mrs. Tiggywinkle and company, a series of Lake District tableaux starring the same imaginary gang, and an all-about-Beatrix section, with an eight-minute video biography (£7, kids-£3.50, daily Easter–Sept 10:00–18:00, Oct–Easter 10:00–17:00, last entry 30 min before closing, in Bowness near Windermere town, tel. 015394/88444, www.hop-skip-jump.com).

More Sights at Lake Windermere

▲**Brockhole National Park Visitors Centre**—Set in a nicely groomed lakeside park, the center offers a free 15-minute slide show on life in the Lake District (played upon request), an information desk, organized walks (see the park's free *Visitor Guide*), exhibits, a bookshop (excellent selection of maps and guidebooks), a fine cafeteria, gardens, nature walks, and a large parking lot. Check the events board as you enter (free entry but steep £4 parking fee—coins only, or buy ticket at the Visitors Centre 100 yards away from parking lot; mid-Feb–Oct daily 10:00–17:00, closed Nov–mid-Feb, bus #555 from Keswick, buses #505 and #599 from Windermere, tel. 015394/46601, www.lake-district.gov.uk). It's in a stately old lakeside mansion between Ambleside and Windermere on A591. For a joyride around famous Windermere, catch the Brockhole "Green" cruise (£7, hourly April–Oct, more sailings mid-July–Aug, 45-min circle, scant narration).

Lakes Aquarium—This aquarium gives a glimpse of the natural history of Cumbria. Exhibits describe the local wildlife living in lake and coastal environments, including otters, eels, pike, sharks, and the "much maligned brown rat." Experts give various talks throughout the day (£9, kids under 15-£6, family deals, daily 9:00–18:00, until 17:00 in winter, last entry one hour before closing, in Lakeside, by Newby Bridge, at south end of Lake Windermere, tel. 015395/30153, www.lakesaquarium.co.uk).

Hayes Garden World—This extensive gardening center, a popular weekend excursion for locals, offers garden supplies, a bookstore, a playground, and gorgeous grounds. Gardeners could wander this place all afternoon. Upstairs is a fine cafeteria-style restaurant (Mon–Sat 9:00–18:00, Sun 11:00–17:00, at south end of Ambleside on main drag, see *Garden Centre* signs, located at north end of Lake Windermere, tel. 015394/33434, www.hayesgarden world.co.uk).

LAKE DISTRICT

YORK

Historic York is loaded with world-class sights. Marvel at the York Minster, England's finest Gothic church. Ramble The Shambles, York's wonderfully preserved medieval quarter. Enjoy a walking tour led by an old Yorker. Hop a train at Europe's greatest railway museum, travel to the 1800s in the York Castle Museum, and head back a thousand years to Viking York at the Jorvik exhibit.

York has a rich history. In A.D. 71, it was Eboracum, a Roman provincial capital—the northernmost city in the empire. Constantine was actually proclaimed emperor here in A.D. 306. In the fifth century, as Rome was toppling, a Roman emperor sent a letter telling England it was on its own, and York became Eoforwic, the capital of the Anglo-Saxon kingdom of Northumbria.

Locals built a church here in 627, and the town became an early Christian center of learning. The Vikings later took the town, and from the 9th through the 11th centuries, it was a Danish trading center called Jorvik. The invading and conquering Normans destroyed then rebuilt the city, fortifying it with a castle and the walls you see today.

Medieval York, with 9,000 inhabitants, grew rich on the wool trade and became England's second city. Henry VIII used the city's fine Minster as his Anglican Church's northern capital. (In today's Anglican Church, the Archbishop of York is second only to the Archbishop of Canterbury.)

In the Industrial Age, York was the railway hub of northern England. When it was built, York's train station was the world's largest. Today, York's leading industry is tourism.

Planning Your Time

York is the best sightseeing city in England after London. On even a 10-day trip through England, it deserves two nights and a day. For the best 36 hours, follow this plan: Catch the 18:45 free city walking tour on the evening of your arrival (evening tours offered mid-June through Aug). The next morning, be at the Castle Museum when it opens (at 10:00 or 9:30, depending on the day)— it's worth a good two hours. Then browse and sightsee the rest of town. Train buffs love the National Railway Museum, and scholars give the Yorkshire Museum an "A." Tour the Minster at 16:00 before catching the 17:15 evensong service (16:00 on Sun, usually none on Mon). Finish your day with an early-evening stroll along the wall, and perhaps through the abbey gardens. This schedule assumes you're here in the summer (when the evening orientation walk is going) and that there's an evensong on. Confirm your plans with the TI.

Orientation to York

(area code: 01904)

York has about 190,000 people; about 1 in 10 is a student. But despite the city's size, the sightseer's York is small. Virtually everything is within a few minutes' walk: sights, train station, TI, and B&Bs. The longest walk a visitor might take (from a B&B across the old town to the Castle Museum) is 20 minutes.

Bootham Bar, a gate in the medieval town wall, is the hub of your York visit. (In York, a "bar" is a gate and a "gate" is a street. Go ahead—blame the Vikings.) At Bootham Bar and on Exhibition Square you'll find the starting points for most walking tours and bus tours, handy access to the medieval town wall, a public WC, and Bootham Street—which leads to the recommended B&Bs. To find your way around York, use the Minster's towers as a navigational landmark, or follow the strategically placed green signposts, which point out all places of interest to tourists.

Tourist Information

The **Museum Street** TI sells a £1 *York Map and Guide*. Ask for the free monthly *What's On* guide and the *York MiniGuide*, which includes a map and some discounts (April–Oct Mon–Sat 9:00–18:00, Sun 10:00–17:00; Nov–March Mon–Sat 9:00–17:00, Sun 10:00–16:00; 1 Museum Street, tel. 01904/550-099, www.visityork.org). The TI books rooms for a £4 fee. The **train station** TI is smaller but provides all the same information and services (same hours as main TI). Their chalkboard lists "Today's Events in Town."

York and Yorkshire Pass: The TI sells an expensive pass that covers most York sights and a lot of other major sights in the region, and gives you discounts on the City Sightseeing hop-on, hop-off bus tours. You'd have to be a very busy sightseer to make this pass worth it—most will want to skip it (£28/1 day, £38/2 days, £44/3 days, £68/6 days, www.yorkpass.com).

Arrival in York

By Train: The train station is a 10-minute walk from town. Day-trippers can store baggage at platform 1 (£5/24 hrs, Mon–Sat 8:00–20:30, Sun 9:00–20:30). To walk downtown from the station, turn left down Station Road, and follow the crowd toward the Gothic towers of the Minster. After the bridge, a block before the Minster, you'll come upon the TI on your right.

Recommended B&Bs are a 10-minute walk or a £5 taxi ride from the station. To take a shortcut to the B&B area from the train station, exit the station to the left on Station Road. When the road swings right and goes through the old gate, turn left onto the busy street (Leeman Road). Just before that street goes under the rail bridge, turn right and follow the walkway along the tracks. Cross the bridge over the river and continue into the big parking lot. From here, to reach B&Bs on St. Mary's Street, stay to the left as you cross the lot; to reach the Coach House, Hazelwood, or Ardmore, cross the lot to the right. To reach B&Bs on Sycamore, Queen Annes Road, Bootham Terrace, or Grosvenor Terrace, duck through the pedestrian walkway under the tracks (on the left).

By Car: As you near York (and your B&B), you'll hit the A1237 ring road. Follow this to the A19/Thirsk roundabout (next to river on northeast side of town). From the roundabout, follow signs for *York City*, traveling through Clifton into Bootham. All recommended B&Bs are four or five blocks before you hit the medieval city gate (see neighborhood map, page 528). If you're approaching York from the south, take M1 until it becomes A1M, exit at junction 45 onto A64, and follow it for 10 miles until you reach York's ring road (A1237), which allows you to avoid driving through the city center. If you have more time, A19 from Selby is a slower and more scenic route into York.

Helpful Hints

Festivals: The Viking Festival features *lur* horn-blowing, warrior drills, and re-created battles (Feb 17–22 in 2010). The Late Music Festival is in early June...if it starts on time (www.latemusicfestival.org.uk). The Early Music Festival (medieval minstrels, Renaissance dance, and so on) zings its strings in mid-July (July 9–17 in 2010, www.ncem.co.uk/yemf.shtml). And the York Festival of Food and Drink takes a bite out of the last weekend of September (www.yorkfoodfestival.com). The town also fills up on horse-race weekends, especially the Ebor Races in mid-August (check schedules at www.yorkrace course.co.uk). Book a room well in advance during festival times and on weekends any time of year. For a complete list of festivals, see www.yorkfestivals.com.

Internet Access: Evil Eye Lounge, which has 10 terminals, is creaky, hip, and funky (Mon–Sat 10:00–23:00, Sun 11:00–23:00, upstairs at 42 Stonegate, tel. 01904/640-002). **The Basement Internet Café-Bar** overlooks the river (£3/hr, a little cheaper with flyer available at TI, Tue–Sun 11:00–18:00, 9 terminals, basement of City Screens Cinema, at 13 Coney Street, toll tel. 0871-704-2054). The **York Public Library**'s reference desk, on the first floor up, provides Internet access to visitors (£1/hr, Mon–Wed and Fri 9:00–19:45, Thu 9:00–17:15, Sat 9:30–15:45, likely open longer, closed Sun, Museum Street, tel. 01904/552-828).

Laundry: The nearest place is **Haxby Road Launderette,** a long 15-minute walk north of the town center (£8/load self-service, about £1.50 more for drop-off service; start last loads Mon–Fri by 16:30, Sat by 15:45, Sun by 14:45; 124 Haxby Road, tel. 01904/623-379). Some B&Bs will do laundry for a small charge.

Bike Rental: With the exception of the pedestrian center, the town's not great for biking. But there are several fine countryside rides from York, and the riverside New Walk bike path is pleasant. **Bob Trotter Cycles,** just outside Monk Bar, rents bikes and has free cycling maps (£15/day, helmet and map free with this book in 2010, Mon–Sat 9:00–17:30, Sun 10:00–16:00, 13–15 Lord Mayor's Walk, tel. 01904/622-868, www.bobtrottercycles.com). **Europcar** at platform 1 at the train station also rents bikes (£6/5 hrs, £10/day, includes helmet, tel. 01904/656-181).

Taxi: From the train station, taxis zip new arrivals to their B&Bs for £5. Queue up at the taxi stand, or call 01904/623-332 or 01904/638-833; cabbies don't start the meter until you get in.

Car Rental: If you're nearing the end of your trip, consider dropping your car upon arrival in York. The money saved by turning it in early just about pays for the train ticket that whisks you effortlessly to London. In York, you'll find these agencies: **Avis** (Mon–Fri 8:00–18:00, Sat 8:00–13:00, closed Sun, 3 Layerthorpe, tel. 01904/610-460); **Hertz** (Mon–Fri 8:00–18:00, Sat 9:00–13:00, closed Sun, at train station, tel. 01904/612-586); **Budget** (Mon–Fri 8:00–18:00, Sat 8:00–13:00, closed Sun, near the National Railway Museum at 75 Leeman Road, tel. 01904/644-919); and **Europcar** (Mon–Fri

8:00–18:00, Sat until 16:00, closed Sun, train station platform 1, tel. 01904/656-181, central reservations toll tel. 0870-607-5000). Beware: Car-rental agencies close early on Saturday afternoons, and all close on Sundays—when dropping off is OK, but picking up is impossible.

Tours in York

▲▲▲Walking Tours

Free Walks with Volunteer Guides—Charming locals give energetic, entertaining, and free two-hour walks through York (daily at 10:15 all year, plus 14:15 April–Oct, plus 18:45 mid-June–Aug, depart from Exhibition Square in front of the art gallery). These tours often go long because the guides love to teach and tell stories. You're welcome to cut out early—but say so or they'll worry, thinking they lost you.

Yorkwalk Tours—These are more serious 1.5-hour walks with a history focus. They do three different walks: Essential York, Roman York, and York's Snickelways (£5.50 each, Feb–Nov daily at 10:30 and 14:15, Dec–Jan weekends only, depart from Museum Gardens Gate, just show up, tel. 01904/622-303, www.yorkwalk .co.uk—check website, TI, or call for schedule). Tours go rain or shine with as few as two participants.

Haunted Walks—Numerous ghost tours, all offered after dusk, are more fun than informative. "Haunted Walk" relies a bit more on storytelling and history than on masks and surprises (£4, Easter–Oct nightly at 20:00, weekends only Nov–Easter, 1.5 hours, just show up, depart from Exhibition Square in front of the art gallery, end in The Shambles, tel. 01904/621-003).

Local Guide—**Julian Cripps** offers good private walking tours (£25/hr, tel. 01904/709-755, travellersintime@googlemail.com).

▲City Bus Tours

Two companies run hop-on, hop-off bus tours circling York. While you can hop on and off all day, these have no real transportation value because York is so compact. If taking a bus tour, I'd catch either one at Exhibition Square (near Bootham Bar) and ride it for an orientation all the way around. Consider getting off at the National Railway Museum, skipping the last five minutes.

City Sightseeing: This outfit's half-enclosed, bright-red, double-decker buses take tourists past secondary York sights that the city walking tours skip—the mundane perimeter of town. They offer two one-hour routes: Route A sticks more or less to the outline of the town wall; Route B traces the same path, except where it makes a foray out to minor sights south of town. Buses that leave Exhibition Square at the top and bottom of each hour usually have live guides (£10, £12.50 combo-ticket with boat cruise through YorkBoat, pay driver cash, can also buy tickets from TI with credit card; April–Oct buses run 9:15–17:00, Route A every 10 min, Route B 4/day; less frequent off-season; tel. 01904/655-585, www.yorktourbuses.co.uk).

York Pullman Bus Tours: These classic old-time buses are slightly less expensive, with fewer stops, live guides, and two overlapping routes (£8, departs 6/hr from Exhibition Square daily 9:20–17:15, 4/hr Nov–mid-June, 45 min, enclosed bus used when wet, tel. 01904/622-992, www.yorkpullmanbus.co.uk).

Boat Cruise

YorkBoat does a lazy, narrated 45-minute lap along the River Ouse (£7, £12.50 combo-ticket with City Sightseeing bus tours—see above, 4/day Feb–Nov 10:30–17:00 or later; runs every 30 min April–Oct; leaves from Lendal Bridge and King's Staith landing, near Skeldergate Bridge, tel. 01904/628-324, www.yorkboat.co.uk).

Self-Guided Walk

Museum Gardens and Wall

Get a taste of Roman and medieval York on this easy stroll along a segment of York's wall.

• *Start just inside the Museum Gardens Gate (near the river, where Lendal Street hits Museum Street; gate closes at 20:00). About 20 yards to the right of the gate stands...*

Abbey Hospital: The 13th-century facade of the Abbey hospital is interesting mostly because of the ancient Roman tombs stacked just under its vault. These were buried outside the Roman city and discovered recently with the building of a new train line.

• *Continue into the garden. About 50 yards ahead (on the right) is another remnant of ancient Rome, the...*

Multangular Tower: This 12-sided tower (A.D. 300) was likely a catapult station built to protect the town from enemy river traffic. The red ribbon of bricks was a Roman trademark—both structural and decorative. The lower stones are Roman, while the upper, bigger stones are medieval. After Rome fell, York suffered through two centuries of a dark age. Then the Vikings ruled from 780. They built with wood, so almost nothing from that period remains. The Normans came in 1066 and built in stone, generally atop Roman structures (like this wall). The Roman wall which defined the ancient garrison town worked for the Norman town, too. From the 1600s on no such fortified walls were needed in England's interior.

• *Continue about 100 yards (past the Neoclassical building holding the fine Yorkshire Museum on right—likely closed for renovation through Aug 2010, but otherwise worth a visit and described on page 524) to York's ruined...*

St. Mary's Abbey: This abbey dates to the age of William the Conqueror—whose harsh policies of massacres and destruction in this region (called the "Harrowing of the North") made him unpopular. His son Rufus, who tried to improve relations in the 12th century, established a great church here. The church became an abbey that thrived from the 13th century until the Dissolution of the Monasteries in the 16th century. The Dissolution, which came with the Protestant Reformation and break with Rome, was a power play by Henry VIII. He took over the land and riches of the monasteries. Upset with the pope, he wanted his subjects to pay him taxes rather than give the Church tithes. (For more information, see the "England's Anglican Church" sidebar, page 518.)

As you gaze at this ruin, imagine magnificent abbeys like this scattered throughout the realm. Henry VIII destroyed most of them, taking the lead from their roofs and leaving the stones to scavenging townsfolk. Scant as they are today, these ruins still evoke a time of immense monastic power. The one surviving wall was the west half of a very long, skinny nave. The tall arch marked the start of the transept. Stand on the plaque that reads *Crossing beneath central tower,* and look up at the air that now fills the space where a huge tower once stood.

• *Now, backtrack about 50 yards and turn left, walking between the museum and the Roman tower. Continuing between the abbot's palace and the town wall, you're walking along a "snickelway"—a small, characteristic York lane or footpath. The snickelway pops out on...*

Exhibition Square: With the Dissolution, the Abbot's Palace became the **King's Manor** (from the snickelway, make a U-turn to the left and through the gate). Today, it's part of the University of York. Because the northerners were slow to embrace the king's reforms, Henry VIII came here to enforce the Dissolution. He stayed 17 days in this mansion and brought along a thousand troops to make a statement of his determination. You can wander into the grounds and building. The Refectory Café serves cheap cakes, soup, and sandwiches to students, professors, and visitors like you (Mon–Fri 9:30–15:30, closed Sat–Sun).

Exhibition Square is the departure point for various walking and bus tours. You can see the towers of the **Minster** in the distance. (Travelers in the Middle Ages could see the Minster from miles away as they approached the city.) Across the street is a public WC, and **Bootham Bar**—one of the fourth-century Roman gates in York's wall—with access to the best part of the city walls (free, walls open 8:00–dusk).

• *Climb up and...*

York

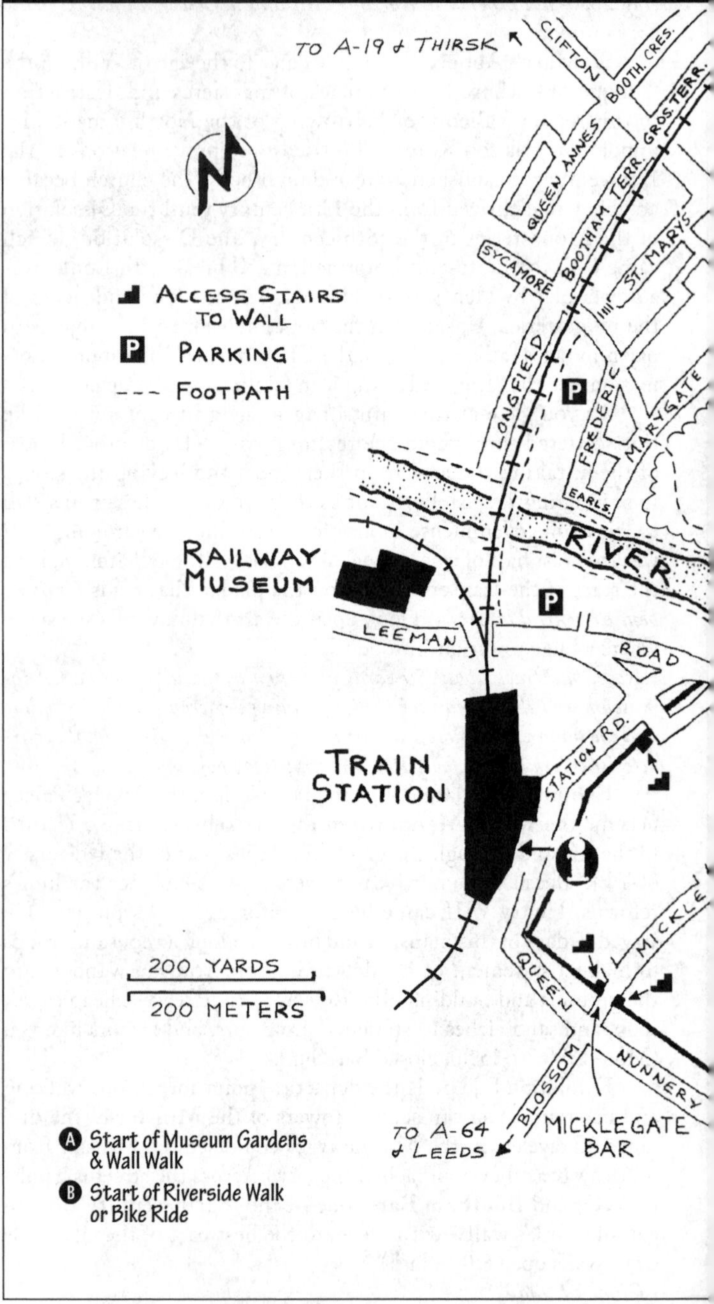

TO A-19 & THIRSK

CLIFTON
BOOTH CRES.
QUEEN ANNES
BOOTHAM TERR.
GROS. TERR.
SYCAMORE
ST. MARYS
LONGFIELD
FREDERIC
MARYGATE
EARLS
RIVER

N

◢ ACCESS STAIRS
TO WALL

P PARKING

--- FOOTPATH

P

RAILWAY
MUSEUM

LEEMAN

P

ROAD

TRAIN
STATION

STATION RD.

ℹ

200 YARDS

200 METERS

QUEEN

L MICKLE

NUNNERY

BLOSSOM

TO A-64
& LEEDS

MICKLEGATE
BAR

🅐 Start of Museum Gardens
& Wall Walk

🅑 Start of Riverside Walk
or Bike Ride

YORK

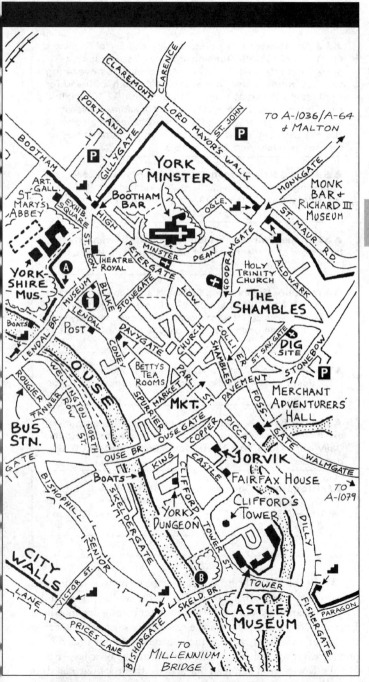

York at a Glance

▲▲▲**York Minster** York's pride and joy, and one of England's finest churches, with stunning stained-glass windows, textbook Decorated Gothic design, and glorious evensong services. **Hours:** Open for worship daily from 7:00 and for sightseeing Mon–Sat from 9:00, Sun from 12:30; flexible closing time (roughly May–Oct at 18:30, earlier off-season); shorter hours for tower and undercroft; evensong services Tue–Sat 17:15, Sun 16:00, occasionally on Mon, sometimes no services mid-July–Aug. See page 515.

▲▲▲**York Castle Museum** Excellent, far-ranging collection displaying everyday objects from Victorian times to the present. **Hours:** Daily 10:00–17:00, often opens at 9:30. See page 521.

▲▲**National Railway Museum** Train buff's nirvana, tracing the history of all manner of rail-bound transport. **Hours:** Daily 10:00–18:00. See page 523.

▲▲**Yorkshire Museum** Sophisticated archaeology museum with York's best Viking exhibit, plus Roman, Saxon, Norman, and Gothic artifacts. **Hours:** Closed for renovation, likely until Aug 2010; when open, probably daily 10:00–17:00. See page 524.

▲**The Shambles** Atmospheric old butchers' quarter, with colorful, tipsy medieval buildings. **Hours:** Always open. See page 521.

▲**Jorvik** Cheesy, crowded, but not-quite-Disney-quality exhibit/ride exploring Viking lifestyles and artifacts. **Hours:** Daily April–Oct 10:00–17:00, Nov–March 10:00–16:00. See page 522.

▲**Fairfax House** Glimpse into an 18th-century Georgian house, with enjoyably chatty docents. **Hours:** Mon–Thu and Sat 11:00–16:30, Sun 13:30–16:30, Fri by tour only at 11:00 and 14:00. See page 524.

Walk the Wall: Hike along the top of the wall behind the Minster to the first corner. York's 12th-century walls are three miles long. Norman kings built the walls to assert control over northern England. Notice the pivots in the crenellations (square notches at the top of a medieval wall), which once held wooden hatches to provide cover for archers. At the corner with the benches—Robin Hood's Tower—you can lean out and see the moat outside. This was originally the Roman ditch that surrounded the fortified garrison town. Continue walking for a fine view of the Minster (better when the scaffolding comes down in 2014), with its truncated main tower and the pointy rooftop of its chapter house.

• *Continue on to the next gate,* **Monk Bar** *(skip the tacky museum in the tower house). Descend the wall at Monk Bar, and step past the portcullis to emerge outside the city's protective wall. Lean against the last bollard and gaze up at the tower, imagining 10 archers behind the arrow slits. Keep an eye on the 12th-century guards, with their stones raised and primed to protect the town. Return through the city wall and go left at the fork in the road to follow Goodramgate a couple of blocks into the old town center. Hiding off Goodramgate on the right is...*

Holy Trinity Church: This church holds rare box pews atop a floor that is sinking as bodies rot and coffins collapse (open Tue–Sun 10:00–16:00, closed Mon). The church is built in the late Perpendicular Gothic style, with lots of clear and precious stained glass from the 13th to 15th centuries. Enjoy the peaceful picnic-friendly gardens.

• *Goodramgate dead ends at...*

King's Square: This lively people-watching zone with its inviting benches is prime real estate for buskers and street performers. Just beyond (crossing the square diagonally) is the most characteristic and touristy street in old York: The Shambles (described on page 521). Our walk ends here, at the midpoint between York's main sights.

Sights in York

▲▲▲York Minster

The pride of York, this largest Gothic church north of the Alps (540 feet long, 200 feet tall) brilliantly shows that the High Middle Ages were far from dark. The word "minster" comes from

the Old English for "monastery," but is now simply used to imply that it's an important church. As it's the seat of a bishop, York Minster is also a cathedral. While Henry VIII destroyed England's great abbeys, this was not part of a monastery and was therefore left standing. It seats 2,000 comfortably; on Christmas and Easter, at least 4,000 worshippers pack the place. Today, more than 250 employees and 300 volunteers work to preserve its heritage and welcome the half-million visitors each year.

Cost, Hours, Tours: The cathedral opens for worship daily at

York Minster

50 YARDS
50 METERS

CHAPTER HOUSE

NAVE

TRANSEPT

CHOIR

SHOP

TOURIST ENTRY

1. West Door & Great West Window
2. Central Tower
3. North Transept
4. South Transept
5. Dragon
6. Choir Screen
7. Choir
8. Chapter House
9. East End
10. Tower & Undercroft

YORK

7:00 and for sightseeing Mon–Sat from 9:00 and Sun from 12:30, when they begin charging £6 admission (you can always worship for free—at the entry simply tell them you're coming for a service). There's no charge for admission after about 17:30—come late to enjoy the quiet church for a free hour or so. Closing time flexes with the season (roughly May–Oct at 18:30, earlier off-season—check the day's closing time posted outside the church, or call for details, tel. 01904/557-216, www.yorkminster.org). The tower and undercroft (£4 apiece) have shorter hours, typically opening a half-hour later and closing at 17:00 (18:00 for the tower). Two combo-ticket options save you money: £8 includes Minster entry and either the tower or the undercroft; £9.50 gets you all three.

After buying your ticket, go directly to the welcome desk, pick up the worthwhile *Welcome to the York Minster* flier, and ask when the next free guided **tour** departs (roughly 2/hr, Mon–Sat 10:30–15:00, one hour, they go even with just one or two people; you can join one in progress, or if none is scheduled, request a departure). The helpful Minster guides, wearing blue armbands, are happy to answer your questions.

Evensong and Church Bells: To experience the cathedral in musical and spiritual action, attend an evensong (Tue–Sat at 17:15, Sun at 16:00, visiting choirs occasionally perform on Mon, 45 min). When the choir is off on school break (mid-July–Aug), visiting choirs usually fill in (confirm at church or TI). Arrive 10 minutes early and wait just outside the choir in the center of the church. You'll be ushered in and can sit in one of the big wooden stalls.

If you're a fan of church bells, you'll experience ding-dong ecstasy daily except Monday (Sun morning about 10:00, Tue practice 19:30–21:30, and Tue–Sat at 16:45 to announce evensong). These performances are especially impressive, as the church now holds a full carillon of 35 bells (it's the only English cathedral to have such a range). Stand in front of the church's west portal and imagine the gang pulling on a dozen ropes (halfway up the right tower—you can actually see the ropes through a little window) while one talented carilloneur plays 22 more bells with a baton-keyboard and foot pedals. On special occasions, you might even catch them playing a Beatles tune.

◔ Self-Guided Tour: Upon entering, head left, to the back (west end) of the church. Stand in front of the grand **west door** (used only on Sundays) on the *Deo Gratias 627–1927* plaque—a place of worship for 1,300 years, thanks to God. Flanking the door, the list of bishops goes unbroken back to the 600s. The statue of Peter with the key and Bible is a reminder that the church is dedicated to St. Peter, and the key to heaven is found through the word of God. While the Minster sits on the remains of a Romanesque church (c. 1100), today's church was begun in 1220 and took 250 years to complete.

Grab a chair and enjoy the nave. Looking down the church, your first impression might be the spaciousness and brightness of the nave (built 1280–1360). The nave—from the middle period of Gothic, called "Decorated Gothic"—is one of the widest Gothic naves in Europe. Rather than risk a stone roof, builders spanned the space with wood. Colorful shields on the arcades are the coats of arms of nobles who helped tall and formidable Edward I, known as "Longshanks," fight the Scots in the 13th century.

The coats of arms in the clerestory (upper-level) glass represent the nobles who helped his son, Edward II, in the same fight. There's more medieval glass in this building than in the rest of England combined. This precious glass survived World War II—hidden in stately homes throughout Yorkshire.

Walk to the very center of the church, under the **central tower.** Look up. Look down. Ask a Minster guide about how gifts and skill saved this tower—which weighs the equivalent of 40 jumbo jets—from collapse. (The first tower collapsed in 1407.) While the tower is 197 feet tall, it was intended to be much taller. Use the neck-saving mirror to marvel at it.

From here, you can survey many impressive features of the church:

England's Anglican Church

The Anglican Church (a.k.a. the Church of England) came into existence in 1534 when Henry VIII declared that he, and not Pope Clement VII, was the head of England's Catholics. The pope had refused to allow Henry to divorce his wife to marry his mistress Anne Boleyn (which Henry did anyway, resulting in the birth of Elizabeth I). Still, Henry regarded himself as a faithful Catholic—just not a *Roman* Catholic—and made relatively few changes in how and what Anglicans worshipped.

Henry's son, Edward VI, instituted many of the changes that Reformation Protestants were bringing about in continental Europe: an emphasis on preaching, people in the pews actually reading the Bible, clergy being allowed to marry, and a more "Protestant" liturgy in English from the revised Book of Common Prayer (1549). The next monarch, Edward's sister Mary I, returned England to the Roman Catholic Church (1553), earning the nickname of "Bloody Mary" for her brutal suppression of Protestant elements. When Elizabeth I succeeded Mary (1558), she soon broke from Rome again. Today, many regard the Anglican Church as a compromise between the Catholic and Protestant traditions.

Is the York Minster the leading Anglican church in England? Yes and no (but mostly no). After a long feud, the archbishops of Canterbury and York agreed that York's bishop would have the title "Primate of England" and Canterbury's would be the "Primate of All England," directing Anglicans on the national level.

In the **north transept,** the grisaille windows—dubbed the "Five Sisters"—are dedicated to British women who died in all wars. Made in 1260 (before colored glass was produced in England), these contain more than 100,000 pieces of glass.

The **south transept** features the tourists' entry, where stairs lead down to the undercroft. The new "bosses" (carved medallions decorating the point where the ribs meet on the ceiling) are a reminder that the roof of this wing of the church was destroyed by fire in 1984. Some believe the fire was God's angry response to a new bishop, David Jenkins, who questioned the literal truth of Jesus' miracles. Others blame an electricity box hit by lightning. Regardless, the entire country came to York's aid. *Blue Peter* (England's top kids' show) conducted a competition among their young viewers to design new bosses. Out of 30,000 entries, there were six winners (the blue ones—e.g., man on the moon, feed the children, save the whales).

Look back at the west end to marvel at the **Great West Window,** especially the stone tracery. While its nickname is the "Heart of Yorkshire," it represents the sacred heart of Christ, meant to remind people of his love for the world.

Find the **dragon** on the right of the nave (two-thirds of the way up). While no one is sure of its purpose, it pivots and has a hole through its neck—so it was likely a mechanism designed to raise a lid on a baptismal font.

The **choir screen** is an ornate wall of carvings separating the nave from the choir. It's lined with all the English kings from

William I (the Conqueror) to Henry VI (during whose reign it was carved, 1461). Numbers indicate the years each reigned. To say "it's slathered in gold leaf" sounds impressive, but the gold is very thin...a nugget the size of a sugar cube is pounded into a sheet the size of a driveway.

Step into the **choir** (or "quire"), where a service is held daily. All the carving was redone after an 1829 fire, but its tradition of glorious evensong services (sung by choristers from the Minster School) goes all the way back to the eighth century.

In the **north transept,** the 18th-century astronomical clock is worth a look (a sign to its left helps you make sense of it). It's dedicated to the heroic Allied aircrews from bases here in northern England who died in World War II (as Britain kept the Nazis from invading in its "darkest hour"). The Book of Remembrance below the clock contains 18,000 names.

A corridor that functions as a small church museum leads to the Gothic, octagonal **Chapter House,** the traditional meet-ing place of the governing body (or chapter) of the Minster. Above the door-way, the Virgin holds Baby Jesus while standing on the devilish serpent. Look for the panel of stained glass that is often on display here (it may also be in the

undercroft). The panel is exquisitely detailed—its minute features would be invisible from the floor of the church and therefore would be "for God's eyes only."

The Chapter House, without an interior support, is remarkable (almost frightening) for its breadth. The fanciful carvings decorat-ing the canopies above the stalls date from 1280 (80 percent are originals) and are some of the Minster's finest. Stroll slowly around the entire room and imagine that the tiny sculpted heads are a 14th-century parade—a fun glimpse of medieval society. Grates still send hot air up robes of attendees on cold winter mornings. A model of the wooden construction illustrates the impressive 1285 engineering.

The Chapter House was the site of an important moment in England's parliamentary history. Fighting the Scots in 1295, Edward I (the "Longshanks" we met earlier) convened the "Model Parliament" here, rather than down south, in London. (The Model Parliament is the name for its early version, back before the legislature was split into the Houses of Commons and Lords.) The government met here through the 20-year reign of Edward II, before moving to London during Edward III's rule in the 14th century.

The church's **east end** is square, lacking a semicircular apse, typical of England's Perpendicular Gothic style (15th century). Monuments (almost no graves) were once strewn throughout the church, but in the Victorian Age, they were gathered into the east end, where you see them today.

The **Great East Window,** the size of a tennis court, is currently behind scaffolding. In the meantime, an interesting display explains the ongoing work. Also, a chart (on the right as you face the window) highlights the core Old Testament scenes in this masterpiece (hard to read from below, even when you can actually see the window). Because of the window's immense size, there's an extra layer of supportive stonework, parts of it wide enough to walk along. In fact, for special occasions, the choir sings from the walkway halfway up the window.

The **tower** and **undercroft** are two extra sights to consider, both accessed from the south transept. One gets you exercise and a view; the other is a basement full of history. You can scale the 275-step tower for the panoramic view (£4, last entry at 18:00 in summer and at 16:00 in winter, not good for kids or acrophobes). The **undercroft** consists of the crypt, treasury, and foundations (£4, last entry at 17:00). The crypt is an actual bit of the Romanesque church, featuring 12th-century Romanesque art, excavated in modern times. The foundations give you a chance to climb down—archaeologically and physically—through the centuries to see the roots of the much smaller, but still huge, Norman (Romanesque) church from 1100 that stood on this spot and, below that, the Roman excavations. Today's Minster stands upon the remains of a Roman fort. Peek also at the modern concrete save-the-church foundations.

Outside the Minster entrance, you'll find the **Roman Column.** Erected in 1971, this column commemorates the 1,900th anniversary of the Roman founding of Eboracum (later renamed York). Across the street is a statue of Constantine, who was in York when his father died. The troops declared him the Roman emperor in A.D. 306 at this site, and six years later, he went to Rome to claim his throne. In A.D. 312, Constantine legalized Christianity, and in A.D. 314, York got its first bishop.

More Sights in York

▲**The Shambles**—This is the most colorful old street in the half-timbered, traffic-free core of town. Walk to the midway point, at

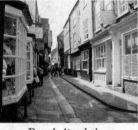

the intersection with Little Shambles. This 100-yard-long street, next to the old market, was once the "street of the butchers" (the name is derived from *shammell*—a butcher's cutting block). In the 16th century, it was busy with red meat. On the hooks under the eaves once hung rabbit, pheasant, beef, lamb, and pigs' heads. Fresh slabs were displayed on the fat sills.

People lived above—as they did even in Roman times. All the garbage was flushed down the street to a mucky pond at the end—a favorite hangout for the town's cats and dogs. Tourist shops now fill the fine 16th-century, half-timbered Tudor buildings. Look above the modern crowds and storefronts to appreciate the classic old English architecture. The soil here wasn't great for building. Notice how things settled in the absence of a good soil engineer.

Little Shambles leads to the frumpy Newgate Market (popular for cheap produce and clothing), created in the 1960s with the demolition of a bunch of lanes as colorful as The Shambles. Return to The Shambles a little farther along, through a covered lane (or "snickelway"). Study the 16th-century oak carpentry—mortise-and-tenon joints with wooden plugs rather than nails.

For a cheap lunch, consider the cute, tiny **St. Crux Parish Hall.** This medieval church is now used by a medley of charities that sell tea, homemade cakes, and light meals. They each book the church for a day, often a year in advance. Chat with the volunteers (Mon–Sat 10:00–16:00, closed Sun, on the left at bottom end of The Shambles, at intersection with Pavement).

▲▲▲**York Castle Museum**—Truly one of Europe's top museums, this is a Victorian home show, the closest thing to a time-tunnel experience England has to offer. Even a speedy museumgoer will want a couple hours here. Stroll down the museum's two re-created streets: Kirkgate, from the Victorian era, with roaming live guides in period dress; and a fun street that re-creates the spirit of the swinging 1960s—"a time when the cultural changes were massive but the cars and skirts were mini."

The "From Cradle to Grave" clothing exhibit and fine costume collection are also impressive. The one-way plan assures that you'll see everything: re-created rooms from the 17th to 20th centuries, prison cells with related exhibits, the domestic side of World War II, giant dollhouses

from 1715 and 1895, Victorian toys, and a century of swimsuit fashions. The museum's £4 guidebook isn't necessary, but it makes a

fine souvenir. The museum proudly offers no audioguides, as its roaming, costumed guides are enthusiastic about talking—engage them (£8, ticket good for one year, £10 combo-ticket with Yorkshire Museum when it re-opens in Aug 2010, daily 10:00–17:00, opens at 9:30 when school's in session, cafeteria midway through museum, tel. 01904/687-687, www.yorkcastle museum.org.uk; at the bottom of the hop-on, hop-off bus route; museum can call you a taxi—worthwhile if you're hurrying to the National Railway Museum).

Clifford's Tower—Located across from the Castle Museum, this ruin is all that's left of York's 13th-century castle, the site of an 1190 massacre of local Jews (read about this at base of hill). If you climb inside, there are fine city views from the top of the ramparts (not worth the £3.50, daily April–Sept 10:00–18:00, Oct 10:00–17:00, Nov–March 10:00–16:00, last entry 30 min before closing).

▲**Jorvik**—Take the "Pirates of the Caribbean," sail them north and back 1,000 years, and you get Jorvik—more a ride than a museum. Innovative 20 years ago, the commercial success of Jorvik (YOR-vik) inspired copycat ride/museums all over England. Some love this attraction, while others call it a gimmicky rip-off. If you're looking for a grown-up museum, skip Jorvik and head instead to the Viking exhibit at the Yorkshire Museum (closed until Aug 2010). If you're thinking Disneyland with a splash of history, Jorvik's fun. To me, Jorvik is a commercial venture designed for kids, with nearly as much square footage devoted to its shop as to the museum. You'll ride a little Disney-type people-mover for 20 minutes through the re-created Viking street of Coppergate. It's the year 975, and you're in the village of Jorvik. Next, your little train takes you through the actual excavation site that inspired the reconstructed village. Everything is true to the dig—even the faces of the models are derived by computer from skulls dug up here. Finally, you'll browse through an impressive gallery of Viking shoes, combs, locks, and other intimate glimpses of that redheaded culture. More than 40,000 artifacts were dug out of the peat bog here in the 1970s. The exhibit on bone archaeology is fascinating (£8.50, £11.50 combo-ticket with Dig—see below, daily April–Oct 10:00–17:00, Nov–March 10:00–16:00, these are last admission times, tel. 01904/615-505, www.vikingjorvik.com).

Dig—This kid-oriented archaeological site gives young visitors an idea of what York looked like during Roman, medieval, Viking, and Victorian eras. Sift through "dirt" (actually shredded tires), reconstruct Roman wall plaster, and have a look at what archaeologists have dug up recently (£5.50, £11.50 combo-ticket with Jorvik, daily 10:00–17:00, last entry one hour before closing, St. Saviour's Church, Saviourgate, tel. 01904/543-402, www.digyork.co.uk).

▲▲**National Railway Museum**—If you like model railways, this is train-car heaven. The thunderous museum shows 200 illustri-

ous years of British railroad history. Fanning out from a grand roundhouse is an array of historic cars and engines, including Queen Victoria's lavish royal car and the very first "stagecoaches on rails," with a crude steam engine from 1830. A working steam engine is sliced open, showing cylinders, driving wheels, and smoke box in action. You'll trace the evolution of steam-powered transportation to the era of the aerodynamic Mallard, famous as the first train to travel at a startling two miles per minute (a marvel back in 1938). There's much more, including exhibits on dining cars, post cars, sleeping cars, train posters, and videos. At the Works section, you can see live train switchboards. And don't miss the English Channel Tunnel video (showing the first handshake at the breakthrough). Purple-shirted "explainers" are everywhere, eager to talk trains. This biggest and best railroad museum anywhere is interesting even to people who think "Pullman" means "don't push" (free, £2.50 audioguide with 60 bits of railroad lore is worthwhile for train buffs, daily 10:00–18:00, tel. 01904/621-261, www.nrm.org.uk).

Getting There: It's about a 15-minute walk from the Minster (southwest of town, behind the train station). A cute little "street train" shuttles you more quickly between the Minster and the Railway Museum (£2 each way, runs daily Easter–Oct, leaves Railway Museum every 30 min 11:00–16:00 at the top and bottom of the hour; leaves the town—from Duncombe Place, 100 yards in front of the Minster—at 15 and 45 min after the hour).

▲▲**Yorkshire Museum**—Located in a lush, picnic-perfect park next to the stately ruins of St. Mary's Abbey, Yorkshire Museum is the city's forgotten, serious "archaeology of York" museum. Unfortunately, it's closed for the first half of 2010 for extensive renovations—but if you're here after it reopens (likely Aug 2010), it's worth a stop.

The museum holds York's best Viking artifacts. While the hordes line up at Jorvik, this museum has no crowds and provides a better historical context. The Roman collection includes slice-of-life exhibits from Roman gods and goddesses and the skull of a man killed by a sword blow to the head. (The latter makes it graphically clear that the struggle between Romans and barbarians was a violent one.) A fine eighth-century Anglo-Saxon helmet shows a bit of barbarian refinement; you'll notice that the Vikings wore some pretty decent shoes and actually combed their hair.

The Middleham Jewel, an exquisitely etched 15th-century pendant, is considered the finest piece of Gothic jewelry in Britain. The noble lady who wore this on a necklace believed that it helped her worship and protected her from illness. The back of the pendant, which rested near her heart, shows the nativity. The front shows the Holy Trinity crowned by a sapphire (which people believed put their prayers at the top of God's to-do list).

The 20-minute video about the creation of the abbey plays continuously, and is worth a look. Kids will enjoy the interactive "Fingerprints of Time" exhibit (prices and times may change post-renovation, but likely: museum entry-£6, ticket good for one year, £10 combo-ticket includes York Castle Museum, daily 10:00–17:00, within Museum Gardens, tel. 01904/687-687, www.yorkshiremuseum.org.uk). Before leaving, enjoy the evocative ruins of St. Mary's Abbey in the park (described on page 511).

▲**Fairfax House**—This well-furnished building is perfectly Georgian inside, with wonderfully pleasant docents eager to talk with you. Built in 1740 and furnished as if it were 1762, the house is compact and bursting with insights into aristocratic life in 18th-century England (£6, Mon–Thu and Sat 11:00–16:30, Sun 13:30–16:30, Fri by tour only at 11:00 and 14:00—the tours are worthwhile, on Castlegate, near Jorvik, tel. 01904/655-543, www.fairfaxhouse.co.uk).

Traditional Tea—York is famous for its elegant teahouses. Drop into one at 16:00 for tea and cakes. Ladies love **Bettys Café Tea Rooms,**

where you pay £8 for a Yorkshire Cream Tea (tea and scones with clotted Yorkshire cream and strawberry jam) or £16 for a full traditional English afternoon tea (tea, delicate sandwiches, scones, and sweets). Your table is so full of doily niceties that the food is served on a little three-tray tower. While you'll pay a little extra here (and the food's nothing special), the ambience and people-watching are hard to beat. If there's a line, it moves quickly (except at dinnertime). Wait for a seat by the windows on the ground level rather than in the much bigger basement (daily 9:00–21:00, piano music nightly 18:00–21:00, tel. 01904/659-142, St. Helen's Square, fine view of street scene from a window seat on the main floor). Near the WC downstairs is a mirror signed by WWII bomber pilots—read the story.

Riverside Walk or Bike Ride—The New Walk is a mile-long, tree-lined riverside lane created in the 1730s as a promenade for York's dandy class to stroll, see, and be seen—and is a fine place for today's visitors to walk or bike. This hour-long walk along a bike path is a great way to enjoy a dose of countryside away from York. It's clearly described in the TI's *New Walk* flier (60p). Start from the riverside under Skeldergate Bridge (near the York Castle Museum), and walk away from town for a mile until you hit the modern Millennium Bridge (check out its thin modern, stainless-steel design). Cross the river, and walk back home, passing through Rowntree Park (a great Edwardian park with lawn bowling for the public, plus family fun including a playground and adventure rides for kids). Energetic bikers can continue past the Millennium Bridge 18 miles to the market town of Selby.

Honorable Mentions

York has a number of other sights and activities (described in TI brochures) that, while interesting, pale in comparison to the biggies.

Merchant Adventurers' Hall—Claiming to be the finest medieval guildhall in Europe (from 1361), it's basically a vast half-timbered building with marvelous exposed beams and 15 minutes' worth of interesting displays about life and commerce back in the days when York was England's second city (£3; April–Sept Mon–Thu 9:00–17:00, Fri–Sat 9:00–15:30, Sun 12:00–16:00; Oct–March Mon–Sat 9:00–15:30, closed Sun; south of The Shambles off Piccadilly, tel. 01904/654-818, www.theyorkcompany.co.uk).

Richard III Museum—This goofy exhibit is like seeing a high school history project. It's interesting only for Richard III enthusiasts (£2.50, daily March–Oct 9:00–17:00, Nov–Feb 9:30–16:00, longer hours possible in summer, filling the top floors of Monk Bar, tel. 01904/634-191, www.richardiiimuseum.co.uk).

York Dungeon—It's gimmicky, but if you insist on papier-mâché gore, it's better than the London Dungeon (£14, daily 10:00–17:30, shorter hours off-season, 12 Clifford Street, tel. 01904/632-599, www.thedungeons.com).

Lawn Bowling Green—Visitors are welcome to watch the action—best in the evenings—at the green on Sycamore Place (near recommended B&Bs). Buy a pint of beer and tell them which B&B you're staying at. Another green is in front of the Coach House Hotel Pub on Marygate.

Near York

Several worthwhile attractions dot the countryside outside York. If you have some extra time here, don't miss the North Yorkshire chapter (next).

Shopping in York

With its medieval lanes lined with classy as well as tacky little shops, York is a hit with shoppers. I find the **antiques malls** interesting. Three places within a few blocks of each other are filled with stalls and cases owned by antiques dealers from the countryside. The malls sell the dealers' bygones on commission. Serious shoppers do better heading for the countryside, but York's shops are a fun browse: The **Antiques Centre York** (Mon–Sat 9:00–17:30, Sun 9:00–16:00, 41 Stonegate, tel. 01904/635-888, www.theantiquescentreyork.co.uk), the **York Antique Centre** (Mon–Fri 10:00–17:00, Sat 10:00–18:00, Sun 10:30–17:00, 2 Lendal, tel. 01904/641-445), and the **Red House Antiques Centre** (Mon–Fri 9:30–17:30, Sat 9:30–18:00, Sun 10:30–17:30, a block from Minster at Duncombe Place, tel. 01904/637-000, www.redhouseyork.co.uk).

You'll find **thrift shops** run by various charity organizations from the beginning of Goodramgate by the wall to just past Deangate. Good deals abound on clothing, purses, accessories, children's toys, books, CDs, and even guitars. If you buy something, you're getting a bargain and at the same time helping the poor, elderly, or even a pet in need of a vet (Mon–Sat 9:30–17:00, Sun 11:00–16:00). On Goodramgate alone you'll find shops run by the British Heart Foundation, Save the Children, and Oxfam (selling donated items as well as free-trade products such as coffee, tea, culinary goods, stationery items, and jewelry made in developing countries and purchased directly from the producers and artisans).

Nightlife in York

Theatre Royal—A full variety of dramas, comedies, and works by Shakespeare entertain the locals in either the main theater or the little 100-seat theater-in-the-round (£10–20, usually Tue–Sat at 19:30, tickets easy to get, on St. Leonard's Place near Bootham Bar and a 5-min walk from recommended B&Bs, booking tel. 01904/623-568, www.yorktheatreroyal.co.uk). Those under 25 and students of any age get tickets for only £5.

Ghost Tours—You'll see flyers, signs, and promoters hawking a variety of not-so-spooky after-dark tours; of these, I'd go for the "Haunted Walks" (for details, see "Tours in York," earlier).

Pubs—Atmospheric, half-timbered pubs abound. Two of my favorites for old-school York ambience are **The Royal Oak** (in the center of town, described under "Eating in York," later) and **The Blue Bell,** a tiny, traditional establishment with a time-warp Edwardian interior. This smallest pub in York serves no food. It has two distinct little rooms—each as cozy as can be—and the owners only recently allowed women to enter (near the east end of town at 53 Fossgate).

Movies—The centrally located City Screens Cinema is right on the river, playing both art-house and mainstream flicks (13 Coney Street, toll tel. 0870-758-3219).

Sleeping in York

I've listed peak-season, book-direct prices. Don't use the TI. Outside of July and August, some prices go soft. B&Bs will often charge £10 more for weekends and sometimes turn away one-night bookings, particularly for peak-season Saturdays. (York is worth two nights anyway.) Prices spike up for horse races and bank holidays (about 20 nights a season). Remember to book ahead during festival times (mid-Feb, early June, early July, mid-Aug, and late Sept—see "Helpful Hints," page 507) and weekends year-round.

B&Bs and Small Hotels

These B&Bs are all small and family-run. They come with plenty of steep stairs (and no elevators) but no traffic noise. For a good selection, call well in advance. B&B owners will generally hold a room with a phone call and work hard to help their guests sightsee and eat smartly. Most have permits to lend for street parking.

Near Bootham Bar

These recommendations are in the handiest B&B neighborhood, a quiet residential area just outside the old town wall's Bootham gate, along the road called Bootham. All are within a 10-minute walk of the Minster and TI, and a 10- to 15-minute walk or taxi ride (£3–5) from the station. If driving, head for the cathedral and follow the medieval wall to the gate called Bootham Bar. The street called Bootham leads away from Bootham Bar.

York Accommodations

1. The Hazelwood
2. Number 23 St. Mary's B&B
3. Crook Lodge B&B
4. Abbey Guest House
5. Abbeyfields Guest House
6. St. Raphael Guesthouse
7. Airden House
8. Arnot House
9. Hedley House Hotel
10. Alcuin Lodge
11. The Coach House Hotel & Rest.
12. Ardmore Guest House
13. The Sycamore
14. Bootham Guest House
15. Number 34 & Amber House
16. Queen Annes Guest House
17. Dean Court Hotel
18. Travelodge York Central
19. Premier Inn
20. Ace Budget Hotel York
21. To Launderette
22. Internet Cafés (2)
23. Library (Internet)
24. Bike Rental

ACCESS STAIRS TO WALL

P PARKING

--- FOOTPATH

200 YARDS

200 METERS

YORK

Sleep Code

(£1 = about $1.60, country code: 44, area code: 01904)
S = Single, **D** = Double/Twin, **T** = Triple, **Q** = Quad, **b** = bathroom,
s = shower only. You can assume credit cards are accepted
unless otherwise noted.

To help you sort easily through these listings, I've divided
the rooms into three categories based on the price for a
standard double room with bath (during high season):

$$$ Higher Priced—Most rooms £90 or more.
$$ Moderately Priced—Most rooms between £60-90.
$ Lower Priced—Most rooms £60 or less.

$$$ The Hazelwood, my most hotelesque listing in this
neighborhood, is plush and more formal than a B&B (there's
always someone at reception). This spacious house has 14
beautifully decorated rooms with modern furnishings and lots
of thoughtful touches (Db-£80/90/110 depending on room size,
two ground-floor rooms, free Internet access and Wi-Fi, laundry
service-£7, free parking, light breakfast option; a fridge, ice, and
travel library in the pleasant basement lounge; 24 Portland Street,
tel. 01904/626-548, www.thehazelwoodyork.com, reservations
@thehazelwoodyork.com, Ian and Carolyn). Ask about their bright
top-floor two-bedroom apartment, great for families and those
with strong legs (continental breakfast only).

$$ Number 23 St. Mary's B&B is extravagantly decorated.
Chris and Julie Simpson have done everything just right and offer
nine spacious and tastefully comfy rooms, a classy lounge, and all
the doily touches (Sb-£48-55, Db-£80-95 depending on room size
and season, discount for longer stays, family room, DVD library
and DVD players, free Wi-Fi, 23 St. Mary's, tel. 01904/622-738,
www.23stmarys.co.uk, stmarys23@hotmail.com).

$$ Crook Lodge B&B, with seven tight but elegantly
charming rooms, serves breakfast in an old Victorian kitchen (Db-
£74-80, cheaper off-season, one ground-floor room, free Wi-Fi,
parking, quiet, 26 St. Mary's, tel. 01904/655-614, www.crooklodge
.co.uk, crooklodge@hotmail.com, Brian and Louise Aiken).

$$ Abbey Guest House is a peaceful refuge overlooking the
River Ouse, with five cheerful, beautifully updated rooms and a
cute little garden (Db-£75-80, four-poster Db with river view-
£80, ask for Rick Steves discount when booking, free Wi-Fi,
free parking, £7 laundry service, 13-14 Earlsborough Terrace,
tel. 01904/627-782, www.abbeyghyork.co.uk, info@abbeygh
york.co.uk, delightful couple Gill—pronounced "Jill"—and Alec

Saville, and a dog aptly named Loofah).

$$ Abbeyfields Guest House has eight comfortable, bright rooms. This doily-free place, which lacks the usual B&B clutter, has been designed with care (Sun–Thu: Sb-£45, Db-£72; Fri–Sat: Sb-£49, Db-£82; doesn't price-gouge during races, free Wi-Fi, 19 Bootham Terrace, tel. 01904/636-471, www.abbeyfields.co.uk, enquire@abbeyfields.co.uk, charming Al and Les).

$$ At St. Raphael Guesthouse, young, creative, and energetic Dom and Zoe understand a traveler's needs. You'll be instant friends. Dom's graphic design training brings a dash of class to their seven comfy rooms, each themed after a different York street, and each lovingly accented with a fresh rose (Db-£76 Sun–Thu, £88 Fri–Sat, free drinks in their guests' fridge, family rooms, free Internet access and Wi-Fi, 44 Queen Annes Road, tel. 01904/645-028, www.straphaelguesthouse.co.uk, info@straphaelguesthouse.co.uk).

$$ Airden House rents nine simple rooms (Db-£70–78, this price with 2-night minimum and this book in 2010, lounge, free parking, 1 St. Mary's, tel. 01904/638-915, www.airdenhouse.co.uk, info@airdenhouse.co.uk).

$$ Arnot House, run by a hardworking daughter-and-mother team, is homey and lushly decorated with Victorian memorabilia. The three well-furnished rooms have little libraries and DVDs (Db-£70–80 depending on size of room, 2-night minimum stay unless it's last-minute, no children, free Wi-Fi, 17 Grosvenor Terrace, tel. 01904/641-966, www.arnothouseyork.co.uk, kim.robbins@virgin.net, Kim).

$$ Hedley House Hotel, well-run by a wonderful family, has 30 clean and spacious rooms. The outdoor hot tub is a fine way to end your day (Sb-£45–70, Db-£70–90, ask for a deal with stay of 2 or more nights, family rooms, 3-course evening meals-£18, free Wi-Fi, parking, 3 Bootham Terrace, tel. 01904/637-404, www.hedleyhouse.com, greg@hedleyhouse.com, Greg and Louise Harrand).

$$ Alcuin Lodge has five relaxing rooms with comfy sofas and solid-wood furnishings (one small top-floor D-£60, Db-£68–74, family room-£80–100, discount for longer stays, laundry-£4–5, free Wi-Fi, free parking, 15 Sycamore Place, tel. 01904/632-222, www.alcuinlodge.com, info@alcuinlodge.com, Pete and Issy).

$$ The Coach House Hotel is a labyrinthine, well-located 17th-century coach house. Facing a bowling green and the abbey walls, it offers 14 huge ceiling-beamed rooms, some with views of the Minster (Sb-£50, Db-£77–81, family room for £130–150 sleeps up to 6, one ground-floor room, free parking, 20 Marygate, tel. 01904/652-780, www.coachhousehotel-york.com, info@coachhousehotel-york.com). This is also a fine place for a cozy pub dinner.

YORK

$$ Ardmore Guest House is a fine little four-room place enthusiastically run by Irishwoman Vera, who's given it a green theme. It's about 15 minutes' walk from the station, but only five minutes from Bootham Bar (Sb-£40, Db-£60–70, Tb-£70, discount for 3 or more nights, cash only, 31 Claremont Terrace, tel. 01904/622-562, mobile 079-3928-3588).

$$ The Sycamore is a fine value, with six homey rooms at the end of a quiet street opposite a fun-to-watch bowling green. A little cramped and funky, it's friendly and well-run (Db-£60–65, Tb-£90–96, Qb-£110, lower price is for weekdays, these are special prices with this book in 2010, may be cheaper off-season, free Wi-Fi, 19 Sycamore Place off Bootham Terrace, tel. 01904/624-712, www.thesycamore.co.uk, mail@thesycamore.co.uk, accommodating Elizabeth and Spiros freely dispense sightseeing advice).

$ Bootham Guest House features gregarious Emma, who welcomes you to her eight simple but cheery and thoughtfully renovated rooms (S-£35, D-£56, £60 Fri–Sat; Db-£60, £70 Fri–Sat; request 5 percent Rick Steves discount with this guidebook in 2010, free Wi-Fi, 56 Bootham Crescent, tel. 01904/672-123, www.boothamguesthouse.com, boothamguesthouse1@hotmail.com).

$ Number 34, run by hardworking Amy and Jason, has four somewhat stark but light, airy rooms at fair prices (May–Oct: Sb-£45, Db-£56, Tb-£78; Nov–April: Sb-£35, Db-£50, Tb-£70, free Wi-Fi, 34 Bootham Crescent, tel. 01904/645-818, www.number34york.co.uk, enquiries@number34york.co.uk).

$ Amber House is a small place with three breezy and well-tended rooms. Their red Oriental Room is worth asking for (Db-£60 Sun–Thu, £68 Fri–Sat; Tb-£80, mention Rick Steves when booking, free Wi-Fi, 36 Bootham Crescent, tel. 01904/620-275, www.amberhouse-york.co.uk, amberhouseyork@hotmail.co.uk, John and Linda).

$ Queen Annes Guest House has six very basic rooms at the best prices in the neighborhood. If you're looking for plush beds and rich decor, look elsewhere. If you'd simply like an affordable, clean place to sleep, this is it (high season: D-£46, Db-£52; off-season: D-£40, Db-£46; prices promised with this book through 2010, family room, ground-floor room, free Wi-Fi, lounge, 24 Queen Annes Road, tel. 01904/629-389, www.queen-annes-guest house.co.uk, info@queen-annes-guesthouse.co.uk, Jason).

Hotels in the Center and Big-Budget Hotel Options

$$$ Dean Court Hotel, a Best Western facing the Minster, is a big, stately hotel with classy lounges and 37 comfortable rooms (Ss/Sb-£104, small Db-£135, standard Db-£160, superior Db-£190, spacious deluxe Db-£210, cheaper midweek and off-season, elevator to most rooms, free Wi-Fi, bistro, restaurant, Duncombe Place, tel. 01904/625-082, fax 01904/620-305, www.deancourt-york .co.uk).

$$ Travelodge York Central offers 93 identical, affordable rooms near the Castle Museum. If you book long in advance on their website, this can be amazingly cheap (last year, as low as £9 for a room). River views make some rooms slightly less boring—after booking online, call the front desk to arrange a view (Db and Tb-£70 Sun–Thu, £85 Fri–Sat, often much lower with Internet deals, kids' bed free, breakfast £4.50 extra, pay Internet access and Wi-Fi, 90 Piccadilly, central reservations toll tel. 08719-848-484, front desk tel. 01904/651-852, www.travelodge.co.uk).

$$ Premier Inn is a 200-room hotel that I hate to recommend, but York has few budget options. This place has no character (you enter through a chain coffee shop) but offers industrial-strength efficiency and straight bargain pricing (Db-£74 Sun–Thu, £79 Fri–Sat, up to 2 kids stay free, breakfast-£8 extra, pay Internet access and Wi-Fi, free parking, 5-min walk to train station, 20 Blossom Street, toll tel. 0870-990-6594, www.premierinn.com, yorkcitycentre.pi@premierinn.com).

Hostel

$ Ace Budget Hotel York is a newly renovated hostel that provides a much-needed option for backpackers. They rent 130 beds in two- to 14-bed rooms, most with great views and all with private bathrooms and thoughtful touches such as reading lights for each bed. They also offer fancier, hotel-quality doubles (£19–30/bed depending on size of dorm, Db-£105, family room, laundry-£3, pay Internet access and Wi-Fi, TV lounge, bar, lockers, 10 minutes' walk from the train station at 88 Mickelgate, tel. 01904/627-720, reception@ace-hotelyork.co.uk, www.ace-hotelyork.co.uk).

Eating in York

York is bursting with inviting eateries. There seems to be a pub serving grub on every corner. And in the last decade or so, the city has become a hot spot for the new British cuisine—every year seems to bring another bistro serving classy dishes made with fresh, local ingredients. I've listed five of my favorites below: Café No. 8, Café Concerto, The Blue Bicycle, J. Baker's, and Melton's Too. These places are each romantic, laid-back, and popular with locals (so reservations are wise for dinner). All have several creative vegetarian options on the menu. Main courses at these places cost about £15–20—not exorbitant by British standards, but not cheap, either.

Fortunately, picnic and light-meals-to-go options abound, and it's easy to find a churchyard, bench, or riverside perch upon which

York Restaurants

1 St. William's Tea Rooms
2 Bettys Café Tea Rooms
3 York Hogroast & Siam House
4 Petergate Fisheries
5 Café Concerto
6 El Piano Restaurant
7 Ask Restaurant
8 The Royal Oak Pub
9 Bengal Brasserie & Caesars
10 The Viceroy of India
11 Little Italy
12 Café No. 8
13 The Coach House
14 Mamma Mia
15 Sainsbury's
16 The Blue Bicycle
17 J. Baker's
18 Melton's Too
19 The Blue Bell

TO A-19 & THIRSK

CLIFTON
BOOTH CRES.
GROS. TERR.
QUEEN ANNE'S
BOOTHAM TERR.
ST. MARY'S
SYCAMORE
MARYGATE
LONGFIELD
FREDERIC
EARLS

P

RAILWAY MUSEUM

RIVER

P

LEEMAN

ROAD

TRAIN STATION

STATION RD.

MICKLE

QUEEN

BLOSSOM

NUNNERY

▪ ACCESS STAIRS TO WALL
P PARKING
--- FOOTPATH

TO A-64 & LEEDS

MICKLEGATE BAR

200 YARDS
200 METERS

to munch cheaply. On a sunny day, perhaps the best picnic spot in town is under the evocative 12th-century ruins of St. Mary's Abbey in the Museum Gardens (near Bootham Bar).

Just Lunch
St. William's Tea Rooms, signed as the "York Minster Tea Rooms," are nestled just behind the Great East Window of the Minster in a wonderful half-timbered 15th-century building (read the history on the menu). They serve quick and tasty lunches. Eat outside (with a scaffolded Minster view), inside (cafeteria under timbers), or in the peaceful cobbled courtyard (tea and pastries served daily 10:30–17:00, £7–8 lunches served daily 12:00–15:00, College Street, tel. 01904/634-830).

Bettys Café Tea Rooms, a favorite among local ladies, is popular for its traditional English afternoon tea (which works as a meal—£16 for tea, delicate sandwiches, scones, and sweets; for details, see page 524).

York Hogroast is a fixture, serving its delicious £3 hearty pork sandwiches with a choice of traditional fillings—try the apple (take-away only, Mon–Fri 11:00–16:00, Sat–Sun 11:00–17:00, 82 Goodramgate). Grab a sandwich and munch in the yard at the nearby Holy Trinity Church (to your left as you exit, peaceful) or in King's Square (to your right as you exit, lively with buskers).

Petergate Fisheries is about the only traditional chippie left in the center (eat in or take out, daily 11:00–18:00, at corner of Goodramgate and Low Petergate at 95 Low Petergate).

Near the Minster
Café Concerto, a casual bistro with a fun menu, wholesome food, and a charming musical theme, has an understandably loyal following (soup, sandwich, and salad meals-£9–10; fancier dinners-£14–20; daily 10:00–22:00, smart to reserve for dinner, also offers take-away, facing the Minster, 21 High Petergate, tel. 01904/610-478).

El Piano Restaurant, a few blocks from the Minster on charming Grape Lane, is a popular veggie option that serves only vegan, gluten-free, and low-sodium dishes in tapas-style portions. The dishes have Indian/Asian/Middle Eastern flavors, and the inside ambience is bubble gum with blinking lights; they also have a pleasant patio out back. If you're eating family-style, three or four plates serve two. Save money at the take-away window (£3–4 to-go "bamboo boats," Mon–Sat 11:00–23:00, Sun 11:00–17:00, between Low Petergate and Swinegate at 15–17 Grape Lane, tel. 01904/610-676).

Ask Restaurant is a cheap and cheery Italian chain, stuffed with happy diners slurping pasta and slicing pizza. Found in historic buildings all over England, York's version lets you dine in the majestic marble-columned yellow hall of its Grand Assembly Rooms. The food may be Italian-chain dull—but the atmosphere is 18th-century deluxe (£8–9 pizza and pastas, daily, Blake Street, tel. 01904/637-254).

Along Goodramgate

Goodramgate is lined with a fun variety of competitive eateries dishing up everything from fish-and-chips and pub grub to tastes of Thailand, India, and Italy. Strolling this lane, you'll find plenty of good options. Working roughly from the center to the medieval gate, Monk Bar, my favorites are:

Siam House serves creative Thai food popular with locals (£7 lunches, £11–13 dinners, Sun–Fri 18:00–22:00, Wed–Fri also 12:00–14:00, Sat 12:00–23:00, 63a Goodramgate, tel. 01904/624-677).

The Royal Oak, a traditional, mellow 16th-century English pub with three cozy rooms, is a York institution. Despite having recently changed owners, the pub should still be serving up hearty dishes and hand-pulled ale—like most of York, they take their ale seriously (a block inside Monk Bar at 18 Goodramgate).

Bengal Brasserie is a local favorite for Indian cuisine (Sun–Fri 18:00–24:00, Sat 12:00–24:00, 21 Goodramgate, tel. 01904/613-131). I also like the **Viceroy of India,** just outside Monk Bar and therefore outside the tourist zone (£6–11 plates, daily 18:00–24:00, out Monk Bar to 26 Monkgate, tel. 01904/622-370).

Two popular (if not quite elegant) Italian places along Goodramgate offer pizzas and pastas for £8: **Little Italy** is a little more intimate (Mon–Fri 11:00–14:30 & 17:00–22:00 except Fri until 22:30, Sat 12:00–23:00, Sun 12:00–21:30, at #12, tel. 01904/623-539), while **Caesars** is bright and boisterous (Mon–Fri 12:00–14:30 & 17:30–23:00, Sat–Sun 12:00–23:00, at #27, tel. 01904/670-914).

Near Bootham Bar and Recommended B&Bs

Café No. 8 is a local favorite and your best bistro choice on Gillygate, serving modern European and veggie options. Grab one of eight tables inside or enjoy a shaded little garden out back if the weather's good. No. 8 feels like Café Concerto (described earlier) but is more romantic, with jazz, modern art, candles, and hardworking Martin bringing it all together. Chef Chris Pragnell uses what's fresh in the market to shape his menu. The food is simple, elegant, and creative—with appetizers such as figs with local bleu cheese (£6–10 lunches, £13–17 dinners, Mon–Fri 11:00–22:00, Sat 10:00–22:00, Sun 10:00–17:00, 8 Gillygate, tel. 01904/653-074).

The **Coach House** serves good-quality fresh food, with veggie options and homemade sweets, in a cozy atmosphere (£8–11, nightly 18:00–21:00, attached to a classic old guest house recommended in "Sleeping in York," 20 Marygate, tel. 01904/652-780).

Mamma Mia is the locals' choice for affordable Italian. The casual eating area features a tempting gelato bar, and in nice weather the back patio is *molto bella* (£8 pizza and pasta, daily 11:30–14:00 & 17:30–23:00, 20 Gillygate, tel. 01904/622-020).

Sainsbury's grocery store is handy and open late (daily 7:00–23:00, 50 yards outside Bootham Bar, on Bootham).

At the East End of Town

This neighborhood is across town from my recommended B&Bs, but still central (and a short walk from the Castle Museum). All three of these places are worth the longer after-dinner stroll.

The Blue Bicycle is no longer a brothel (but if you explore downstairs, you can still imagine when the tiny privacy snugs needed their curtains). Today, it is passionate about fish. The energy of its happy eaters, its charming canalside setting, and its location just beyond the tourist zone make it worth the splurge. Of my recommended York restaurants, this wins the best ambience award. It's a velvety, hardwood scene, a little sultry but fresh...like its fish. Reservations are a must (£10 starters, £20 main dishes, vegetarian and meat options, nightly 18:00–21:30, Thu–Sun also 12:00–14:30, 34 Fossgate, tel. 01904/673-990).

J. Baker's, one of York's newer restaurants, has quickly gained popularity for turning local produce into highbrow versions of classic dishes. At lunchtime, their "grazing menu" makes it affordable to sample several dishes (available à la carte, or £12 for three courses). At dinnertime, the two earth-tone dining rooms—one downstairs, one upstairs—tend to fill up fast, so reservations are smart (£24 two-course meals, £28.50 three-course meals, Tue–Sat 12:00–14:30 & 18:00–22:00, closed Sun–Mon, near the end of The Shambles at 7 Fossgate, tel. 01904/622-688). Across the street is the recommended Blue Bell pub.

Melton's Too is a fun and casual place to eat. This homey, spacious, youthful restaurant serves up elegantly simple meals and a nice selection of tapas, all with a focus on local ingredients (£10–12 main courses, Mon–Sat 10:30–22:30, Sun 10:30–21:30, just past Fossgate at 25 Walmgate, tel. 01904/629-222, Nick).

York Connections

From York by Train to: Durham (3–4/hr, 45 min), **London**'s King's Cross Station (2/hr, 2 hrs), **Bath** (2/hr, 4.5 hrs, 1–2 changes in Birmingham, Bristol, and/or London), **Cambridge** (hourly,

2.5 hrs, change in Peterborough), **Birmingham** (2/hr, 2–2.5 hrs), **Keswick/Lake District** (hourly, with transfers to Penrith then bus, 4.5 hrs), **Edinburgh** (2/hr, 2.5 hrs). Train info: toll tel. 0845-748-4950.

Connections with London's Airports: Heathrow (at least hourly, allow 3 hrs minimum; from airport take Heathrow Express train to London's Paddington Station, transfer by tube to King's Cross, train to York—2/hr, 2 hrs; for details on cheaper but slower tube or bus option from airport to London see page 157), **Gatwick** (at least hourly, allow 3 hrs minimum; from Gatwick, catch First Capital Connect train to London's St. Pancras Station; from there, walk to neighboring King's Cross Station, and catch train to York—2/hr, 2 hrs).

NORTH YORKSHIRE

The countryside to the north of York—dubbed "North Yorkshire"—is speckled with pleasant attractions: the house and office of the "real" rural vet James Herriot, the desolately beautiful North York Moors, an eclectic mansion often used in movies, an engaging folk museum, a quirky World War II museum at a former POW camp, a kitschy scenic steam train, and several looming skeletons of destroyed abbeys. On the Yorkshire coast, you'll find an appealing pair of salty seaside towns—one big and one small. While none of these is a top-tier sight in itself, they complement each other nicely, so a day driving to several is time well spent.

Getting Around North Yorkshire

By Car: Driving is the best option: Distances are short, the towns are small and easy to navigate, and there are plenty of tempting stopovers along the way. Get a good map, and use it thoughtfully to craft an efficient itinerary.

Why Did the Pheasant Cross the Road?: As you drive, watch out for "wild" pheasants absentmindedly crossing the road. These birds are bred and fed by locals, and left to range freely through the woods...until autumn, when hunting season begins, and the fat, tame, and naive pheasants become easy prey.

By Bus and Train: You can reach most of these destinations by public transportation, but it requires patience (and in some cases—such as Rievaulx Abbey—a long walk from where the bus or train drops you off). York serves as a fine hub (buses leave from in front of the railway station), with bus connections to Thirsk, Castle Howard, Eden Camp, Pickering, and Whitby (most run by Coastliner,

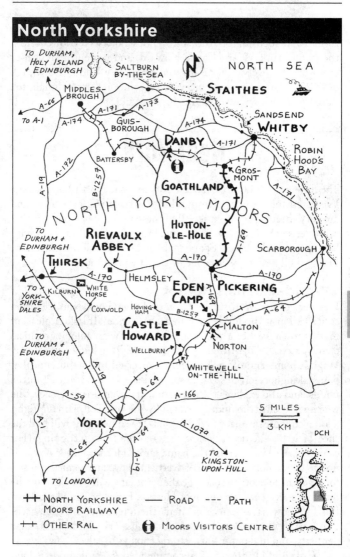

North Yorkshire

Map labels:

TO DURHAM, HOLY ISLAND & EDINBURGH
SALTBURN BY-THE-SEA
NORTH SEA
STAITHES
MIDDLES-BROUGH
A-66
TO A-1
A-171
A-173
A-174
GUIS-BOROUGH
SANDSEND
WHITBY
A-174
DANBY
A-171
A-172
BATTERSBY
GROS-MONT
ROBIN HOOD'S BAY
B-1257
GOATHLAND
NORTH YORK MOORS
A-171
A-19
TO DURHAM & EDINBURGH
RIEVAULX ABBEY
HUTTON-LE-HOLE
THIRSK
A-170
HELMSLEY
A-170
A-169
SCARBOROUGH
TO YORK-SHIRE DALES
KILBURN
WHITE HORSE
EDEN CAMP
PICKERING
A-170
COXWOLD
HOVING-HAM
B-1257
A-164
A-64
CASTLE HOWARD
MALTON
TO DURHAM & EDINBURGH
WELLBURN
NORTON
A-19
WHITEWELL-ON-THE-HILL
A-59
A-64
A-166
5 MILES
3 KM
DCH
A-1
YORK
A-64
A-64
A-19
A-1070
TO KINGSTON-UPON-HULL
TO LONDON

Legend:
╋╋ NORTH YORKSHIRE MOORS RAILWAY
╋╋ OTHER RAIL
— ROAD
--- PATH
ⓘ MOORS VISITORS CENTRE

NORTH YORKSHIRE

tel. 01653/692-556, www.coastliner.co.uk); Hutton-le-Hole and Rievaulx Abbey (via Helmsley) are sparsely connected to York by Moorsbus (tel. 01845/597-000, www.moors.uk.net/moorsbus). A fun old steam train chugs through the middle of the North York Moors, from Pickering to Grosmont, then sometimes on to Whitby. Buses also follow the coastal road north and south of Whitby, including Staithes. I've explained particularly handy connections with each listing below. As specific bus schedules change frequently with the season, always confirm the details at the York TI.

By Tour: Various tour companies offer guided bus excursions from York, focusing on Yorkshire Dales/James Herriot country, the North York Moors, Castle Howard, and more (different tour every day, see website for tours and prices; try Eddie Brown, tel. 01423/321-246, www.eddiebrowntours.com; or York Pullman, tel. 01904/622-992, www.yorkpullmanbus.co.uk).

Near York

The following sights are between York and the North York Moors. I've listed them in order from west to east. If you have a car and are very speedy, you could see all of these in one day—but it makes more sense to pick a few that appeal to you, then link them with lazy countryside drives. Sparse public-transportation connections mean you'll have to choose one or two if you lack a car.

▲World of James Herriot

Devotees of the *All Creatures Great and Small* books and television series can visit the folksy veterinarian's digs in Thirsk, a pleasant market town west of York. James Herriot was an autobiographical character created by Alfred Wight, once the Thirsk town vet. Today Wight's home and office have been converted into a museum that painstakingly re-creates the 1940s Skeldale House featured in the novels, and also explores the development of veterinary science. The worthwhile £2 audioguide, narrated by the vet's son, James Wight, adds even more intimacy to the exhibits. Even non-fans will find the slice-of-1940s-life decor fascinating, and the trivia intriguing. (For example, Alf Wight chose the name James Herriot for his protagonist to avoid violating an anti-advertising law...and named himself for his favorite Scottish soccer goalie.) But fans will be tickled by the museum's reverence for all things Herriot. Even the studio sets from the TV show have been re-created. The interactive children's section is particularly engaging, even for adults: Try your hand at horse dentistry, and find out if you're strong enough to calve a cow.

Cost and Hours: £5.75, recommended £2 audioguide is loud enough to be shared, daily April–Oct 10:00–17:00, Nov–March 11:00–16:00, last entry one hour before closing, 23 Kirkgate, tel. 01845/524-234, www.worldofjamesherriot.org.

Getting There: The museum is just a block up Kirkgate from the main market square in Thirsk. Buses connect York with Thirsk (4/day, none on Sun, 45 min, www.yorkshiretravel.net). The train connection is faster, but deposits you at a station outside of Thirsk, while the bus leaves you at the main square. Drivers can zip there from York on A19 in about 40 minutes.

Nearby: Die-hard Herriot fans might enjoy exploring the **Yorkshire Dales,** westward from and much tamer than the North York Moors. Get details about the region—and information about guided tours—at the TI in York. Approaching Thirsk, keep an eye out on the right side of the road for the **"White Horse"**—a gigantic image in the hillside that overlooks the town of Kilburn. The figure was created by a schoolmaster and his students in 1857, who removed the soil to expose the light-colored bedrock.

▲Rievaulx Abbey

Rievaulx (ree-VOH) is the sprawling ruins of a 12th-century abbey. Since it's not near any major towns, its pre-cut stones were less sus-

ceptible to plunder—so it's been left a bit more intact than many other ruined abbeys. Its beautiful and secluded setting—tucked away in a gentle, sheep-speckled valley—is appealing, but if you've seen other fine old abbeys, this is a rerun. Start with the little museum, then follow the included audioguide through the ruins. You'll learn how monastic life changed during the four centuries between its founding and its destruction by Henry VIII.

Cost and Hours: £5, includes audioguide, generally Easter–Sept daily 10:00–18:00; Oct Thu–Mon 10:00–17:00, closed Tue–Wed; Nov–Easter Thu–Mon 10:00–16:00, closed Tue–Wed; café, tel. 01439/798-228, www.english-heritage.org.uk.

Getting There: Drivers get there in a snap (just a short detour from A170). Bus transportation is trickier. From York, you'd catch a bus to Helmsley (3/day, Mon–Sat, none on Sun, 1.25 hrs). From Helmsley, you can get to the abbey on foot (2 miles), by taxi (call 01439/770-981), or by infrequent bus (#M8, runs daily mid-July–Aug, but only on Sun mid-March–mid-July and Sept–Oct, www.traveline.org.uk).

▲Hutton-le-Hole

This postcard-pretty town, lining up along a river as if posing for

its close-up, is an ideal springboard for a trip into the North York Moors. It has some touristy shops and inviting picnic benches, but Hutton-le-Hole's (pronounced "HOO-ton le hole") biggest attraction is its engaging folk museum. **Ryedale Folk**

Museum illustrates farm life in the moors through reconstructed and furnished 18th-century buildings. At this open-air complex, you'll wander along a line of shops, including a village store—one-stop shopping (the original Costco) to save locals the long trek into the closest market town. Then you'll come to a humble cluster of traditional, lived-in-feeling thatch-roof cottages. If the beds are unmade, notice the "mattress" is made of rope stretched across a frame, which could be tightened for a firmer night's sleep (the origin of the phrase "sleep tight"). The museum is most worthwhile on summer Thursdays and frequent special weekends, when lively costumed docents explain what you're seeing along the way (check online schedule or call ahead).

Cost and Hours: £5.25, daily mid-March–Oct 10:00–17:30, Nov–mid-March 10:00–dusk, last entry at 16:30 in summer, closed late Dec–late Jan, tel. 01751/417-367, www.ryedalefolkmuseum.co.uk.

Getting There: Drivers find it just north of A170. From Hutton-le-Hole, you can plunge northward directly into the North York Moors (which begin suddenly as you leave town). Non-drivers will rely on the sporadic Moorsbus (tel. 01845/597-000, www.moors.uk.net/moorsbus).

▲Castle Howard

Especially popular since the filming of the *Brideshead Revisited* TV miniseries here in 1981, this fine, palatial, 300-year-old home (more a manor than a castle) is a bit overrated but still worth considering. It was commissioned on a whim to John Vanbrugh, a playwright who previously had no architectural training whatsoever—which explains some of his unique flourishes (like the grand, domed entryway that would seem more at home in a Baroque church). Vanbrugh went on to build the even grander Blenheim Palace near Oxford (which is about twice as interesting, if you're choosing between them—see page 375). After being damaged in a 1940 fire, Castle Howard lay in ruins for years before being refurbished in the 1950s and opened to the public. The Howard family, whose precocious daughters are pictured throughout the place, still lives in one wing—and in winter, when the place is closed to the public, they actually use the rooms that are normally on the tour route. The 2008 big-screen version of *Brideshead Revisited,* starring Emma Thompson and Michael Gambon (Albus Dumbledore from the Harry Potter movies), was also filmed here.

The sprawling grounds include several pools, lakes, and fountains, a rose garden, and a quiet wood. As you follow the one-way route through the house, chatty docents posted in key rooms explain what you're seeing. Many of the decorations are "souvenirs" from the Howards' travels—such as replicas of Roman busts and Greek statues, or paintings that attempt to jam several of a Grand Tour city's landmarks onto a single canvas (like today's collage postcards). (Outside, the mini-pyramid on the horizon—behind the big Atlas Fountain—was inspired by a trip to Egypt.) Also watch for the elaborate, multistory, blue Delft porcelain tulip vase—dating from the "Tulip Fever" era of the late 17th century, when a single flower could cost £1,000...so imagine the extravagance of filling the whole vase.

Cost and Hours: £11 for house and grounds, or £5 for grounds only in winter, when the house is closed. The gardens are open daily 10:00–18:30; the house is open daily March–Oct 11:00–16:00, last entry at 16:00; house closed Nov–Feb except late Nov–mid-Dec, when it's decorated for Christmas. Tel. 01653/648-333, www.castlehoward.co.uk.

Getting There: It's in the countryside between Helmsley and Malton. It's ideal by car, but the bus connection eats up the better part of a day, which the castle isn't worth for most travelers (buses #183 and #194 from Malton, Mon–Sat, bus info tel. 0870-608-2608 or 01653/692-556, www.yorkshiretravel.net). York Pullman also offers occasional tours to Castle Howard (tel. 01904/622-992, www.yorkpullmanbus.co.uk).

Eden Camp

Once an internment camp for German and Italian POWs during World War II, this is now a theme museum on Britain's war experience. Sprawling, cluttered, and a bit hokey, the exhibit works best for Brits who want to help their kids (or grandkids) understand the war years. But, even though it's overpromoted, its earnestness will win over WWII buffs, as it energetically tries to convey the spirit of a country Hitler couldn't conquer.

Various barracks detail the rise of Hitler, the fury of the Blitz, and the efforts on the home front—such as rationing and the Local Defense Volunteers, affectionately dubbed "Dads Army." A detailed map and ample posted information are helpful, if a bit overwhelming. Focus your visit on the topics that interest you most. An intense exhibit on the Blitz comes with the sound of bombs, the acrid smell of burning, and quotes such as, "Hitler will send no warning—so always carry your gas mask." Don't miss hut #10, which details the actual purpose of the camp—a prison for captured Nazis and Italians during World War II (think *Hogan's Heroes* in reverse). Enjoy the quirky handmade items—such as a miniature pair of shoes carved out of bread—created by bored POWs who were killing time. Consider the relative delight of being in the care of the gentlemanly English rather than in a Nazi camp. It's no wonder the Germans and Italians settled right in.

Cost, Hours, Information: £5, daily 10:00–17:00, last entry at 16:00, closed late Dec–mid-Jan, cash only, mess-kitchen cafeteria, tel. 01653/697-777, www.edencamp.co.uk.

Getting There: It's near Malton, 18 miles northeast of York. From York, drivers take A169 toward Scarborough, then follow signs to the camp (notice its proximity to Castle Howard—easy to combine these two and more on a day's drive). Or, from York, you can catch Coastliner bus #840 (every 1–2 hrs Mon–Sat, fewer on Sun, 50–60 min, www.yorkshiretravel.net).

Pickering

This functional town is a major crossroads and a proud hub of sorts for this region's meager public transit (TI tel. 01751/473-791). The main reason to visit Pickering is to catch the **North Yorkshire Moors Railway** steam train into the moors (described later). Otherwise, you can browse its Monday market (produce, knick-knacks) and consider its rural-life museum (Hutton-le-Hole's is better)—but don't bother visiting Pickering unless you're passing through anyway.

With more time, consider stopping by Pickering's ruined 13th-century Norman **castle,** built on the site of a wooden castle from William the Conqueror's 11th-century heyday. Appreciate its textbook motte-and-bailey (stone fort on a grassy hilltop) design, and climb to the top to understand its strategic location (£3.50; April–Sept daily 10:00–18:00, closed Oct–March; on the ridge above town, tel. 01751/474-989, www.english-heritage.org.uk).

Getting There: Drivers find Pickering right on A169 north of York (en route to the coast). Or you can catch Coastliner bus #840 from York (every 1–2 hrs Mon–Sat, fewer on Sun, 1.25 hrs, www.yorkshiretravel.net).

North York Moors

In the lonesome North York Moors, sheep seem to outnumber people. In this high, desolate-feeling plateau, with a spongy and inhospitable soil, bleating flocks jockey for position against scrubby heather for control of the terrain. You can almost imagine the mysterious Heathcliff (from *Wuthering Heights,* which was set here) plodding across this terrain. As you pass through this haunt-

ing landscape, crisscrossed by only a few roads, notice how the gloomy brown heather—which blooms briefly with purple flowers at summer's end—is actually burned back by wardens to clear the way for new growth. The vast, undulating expanses of nothingness are punctuated by greener, sparsely populated valleys called dales. Park your car and take a hike across the moors on any small road. You'll come upon a few tidy villages and maybe even old Roman roads.

Drivers can consider The Moors Centre; non-drivers can take the steam train; and anyone might want to stop in Goathland.

The Moors Centre

This visitor facility near Danby provides the best orientation for exploring North York Moors National Park. (Unfortunately, it's at the northern end of the park—not as convenient if you're coming from York.) This grand old lodge, fully renovated in 2007, offers exhibits, shows, nature walks, an information desk, plenty of books and maps, brass rubbing, a cheery cafeteria, and brochures on several good walks that start right outside the front door.

Cost and Hours: Free entry but £2 parking fee; April–Oct daily 10:00–17:00; March and Nov–Dec daily 10:30–15:30; Jan–Feb Sat–Sun 10:30–15:30, closed Mon–Fri; café, tel. 01439/772-737, www.visitnorthyorkshiremoors.co.uk.

Getting There: The Centre is three-fourths of a mile from Danby in Esk Valley, in the northern part of the park (follow signs from Danby, which is a short drive from A171 running along the northern edge of the park).

▲North Yorkshire Moors Railway

This 18-mile, one-hour steam-engine ride between Pickering and Grosmont (GROW-mont) runs almost hourly through some of the best parts of the moors. Sometimes the train continues from Grosmont on to the seaside town of Whitby; otherwise, you might be able to transfer in Grosmont to another, non-steam train to reach Whitby (check schedules before you plan your trip). Once in Whitby, you can use the bus to connect along the coast (such as to Staithes) or go back to York by bus. (For details on getting to Pickering, see previous page.)

Even with the small and dirty windows (try to wipe off the outside of yours before you roll), and with the track situated mostly in a scenic gully, it's a good ride. You can stop along the way for a walk on the moors (or at the appealing village of Goathland—described next) and catch the next train (£15 round-trip to Grosmont, or £20 round-trip to Whitby, includes hop-on, hop-off privileges; runs daily late-March–Oct, and weekends Nov–Dec, no trains Jan–late

March, schedule flexes with the season but generally the first train departs Pickering at 9:00, last train departs Grosmont about 18:20; trip takes about one hour one-way to Grosmont, allow about 2.75 hours round-trip to come back on the same train; tel. 01751/472-508 or 01751/473-799, www.nymr.co.uk). It's not possible to leave luggage at any stop on the steam-train line—pack light if you decide to hike.

Goathland

This tranquil village, huddled along a babbling brook, is worth considering for a sleepy stopover, either on the steam-train trip or for drivers (it's an easy detour from A169, which cuts through the moors). Movie buffs will enjoy Goathland's train station, which was used to film scenes at "Hogwarts Station" for the early Harry Potter movies (for more on Harry Potter sights, see page 619). But Brits know and love Goathland as the setting for the beloved, long-running TV series *Heartbeat,* about a small Yorkshire town in the 1960s. You'll see TV sets intermingled with real buildings, and some shops are even labeled "Aidensfield," for the TV town's fictional name.

The North Yorkshire Coast

Two salty Yorkshire towns—one big (Whitby) and one small (Staithes)—are seaside escapes worth a stop for the seagulls, surf, and Captain Cook lore. If you're not seeing the English coast anywhere else on your trip, and you have an extra day in York, side-tripping here is worthwhile.

Getting to the North Yorkshire Coast

To get from **York** to Whitby, Coastliner bus #840 is best (daily 4–6/day depending on season, 1.75–2.75 hrs, www.yorkshiretravel.net).

To connect Whitby to the **North York Moors,** you can take the historic steam train from Pickering to Grosmont, which often continues into Whitby (otherwise you can sometimes transfer in Grosmont to a Whitby-bound train).

From **Durham,** you can get to Whitby by train via Darlington and Middlesbrough (Durham–Middlesbrough: at least hourly, 1 hr with transfer in Darlington; then Middlesbrough–Whitby: 4/day, 1.5 hrs). The Durham–Middlesbrough train also stops at two towns on the North York Moors (both described earlier): Grosmont (where you can catch the Moors steam train south to Pickering) and Danby (near The Moors Centre).

Getting Around the North Yorkshire Coast

Once in Whitby, Arriva buses #56 and #X56 run at least hourly in each direction up and down the coast, connecting you to Staithes and Sandsend (north); buses #93 and #X93 run at least hourly from Whitby south to Robin Hood's Bay (www.arrivabus.co.uk).

Whitby

An important port since the 12th century, Whitby is today a fun coastal resort town with about 14,000 people and a gaggle of steep

and salty old streets. Its busy harbor is squeezed into a narrow canyon flanked on one side by the stately skeleton of its 11th-century abbey, and on the other by the bluff-topping West Cliff neighborhood. The harborfront zone is a carousel of Coney Island–type amusements and city-dwellers from inland Yorkshire whooping it up. Rounding out Whitby's claim to fame are its connections to Captain Cook and Bram Stoker (whose *Dracula* was partly written here).

Orientation to Whitby

(area code: 01947)

Tourist Information

The TI is on the harbor next to the train and bus stations (daily May–Sept 9:30–17:00, July–Aug until 18:00, Oct–April 10:00–16:30, often closed for lunch in winter, tel. 01723/383-636, www.discoveryorkshirecoast.com).

Arrival in Whitby

If driving, consider first stopping by the hilltop sights (the abbey on one side of town, and West Cliff on the other). Then drive down into the old town center and drop your car across the street from the TI in the pay-and-display parking lot near the train and bus stations. Walk a few steps toward the harbor—and the lone bridge spanning it—to get oriented.

From the bridge, face the sea to consider your options (described in more detail below): On the left is the waterfront promenade called Pier Road/Fish Quay, lined with tacky carnival distractions, as well as the recommended Magpie Café (popular fish-and-chips) and a tacky Dracula exhibit (skip it); above this scene is the West Cliff area, with fine views over town. On the right (across the bridge) is a warren of touristy lanes filled with hard-candy stores, knickknack shops, and the Captain Cook Memorial Museum; overhead is the ruined abbey.

Sights in Whitby

Whitby's main landmark is its ruined **abbey,** set on a bluff overlooking the harbor. Built on the site of a seventh-century monastic settlement, the remains of this 11th-century version echo with the chants of ages past...enough to raise goose bumps even on a vampire (*Dracula* was partly set here). Many of the stones from this formerly grand abbey were used to build houses in the town below (£5.50, includes

audioguide; April–Sept daily 10:00–18:00; Oct–March Thu–Mon 10:00–16:00, closed Tue–Wed; tel. 01947/603-568, www.english -heritage.org.uk).

The abbey is connected to the streets below by a **staircase** of 199 steps. In the olden days, poor people would carry the coffins of the departed up these steps, resting occasionally on broader steps called "coffin rests"...which, for practical reasons, are more frequent near the top.

Down below, the small **Captain Cook Memorial Museum,** in an old shipowner's house where Cook lodged for a few years, offers a dull look at the famous hometown sailor and his exotic voyages. The most interesting bit is the Voyages Room, with a cutaway model of one of Cook's ships, and miniature replicas of everything that went on board (£4, pick up free pamphlet as you enter, daily March–Easter 11:00–15:00, Easter–Oct 9:45–17:00, last entry 30 min before closing, closed Nov–Feb; tucked down little Grape Lane behind the Dolphin Hotel, near the bridge on the abbey side of town; tel. 01947/601-900, www.cookmuseumwhitby.co.uk). Two of Captain Cook's boats (*Resolution* and *Endeavour*) were built in the Whitby shipyards; a full-size replica of the *Endeavour,* which has been used in many swashbuckling films, is often moored in Whitby.

Across the harbor from the abbey is a fun little hilltop park called **West Cliff,** with inviting benches and a lively kids' area. Supposedly it was from this vantage point that Bram Stoker contemplated Whitby's abbey...and inspiration bit him in the neck. In *Dracula,* a boat docks at the long pier, and a black dog—the Count in disguise—jumps off the boat and runs up the 199 steps to the abbey...where he hides out for the next three chapters, until he takes to the sea again. Nearby, the whale bones forming an archway over the path recall Whitby's former status as a major whaling city. When whalers returned to port, they'd prop up bones like these on their ships, as a sign to their wives and mothers (who were anxiously waiting ashore) that the trip had gone safely.

To go for a **walk along the beach,** consider strolling to nearby villages, then walking or catching an Arriva bus back: Sandsend to the north (buses #56 and #X56) is closer than Robin Hood's Bay to the south (buses #93 and #X93, www.arrivabus.co.uk).

Sleeping in Whitby

A collection of inviting B&Bs perches atop the plateau behind West Cliff. Among these, **$$ Crescent Lodge B&B** is a good choice (8 rooms, Sb-£35, Db-£60, just off the main drag as you enter the upper part of town at 27 Crescent Avenue, tel. 01947/820-073, carol@carolyates.wanadoo.co.uk, Carol).

$$ The Dolphin Hotel, in the old-town center at the bridge overlooking the harbor, is a colorful old pub with seven newly renovated rooms upstairs with miniscule yacht-type bathrooms (Db-£60–90, apartment with kitchen-£100, pub closes at 23:00, 3 blocks from train station, Bridge Street, tel. 01947/602-197, www .thedolphinhotel-whitby.co.uk).

$ Whitby's **Abbey House youth hostel** is one of England's most impressive. Right on the abbey grounds above town—and literally built with bits and pieces of that abbey—this 17th-century building has recently undergone an extensive restoration. Now it houses 100 beds in 22 rooms, most of them 4- to 6-bed dormitories with bathrooms. Many rooms have information plaques on the walls explaining the architecture and renovation (£14–27/bed, Db twin-£38–75, price depends on day and season, reception open 7:30–10:00 & 13:00–22:30, no curfew, family rooms, fully wheelchair-accessible rooms, pay Internet access, free Wi-Fi, laundry,

NORTH YORKSHIRE

Sleep Code

(£1 = about $1.60, country code: 44, area code: 01947)
S = Single, **D** = Double/Twin, **T** = Triple, **Q** = Quad, **b** = bathroom, **s** = shower only. You can assume credit cards are accepted unless otherwise noted.

To help you sort easily through these listings, I've divided the rooms into three categories based on the price for a standard double room with bath (during high season):

$$$ Higher Priced—Most rooms £80 or more.
$$ Moderately Priced—Most rooms between £50-80.
$ Lower Priced—Most rooms £50 or less.

kitchen, cafeteria-style restaurant, tel. 01947/602-878, www.yha
.org.uk, whitby@yha.org.uk).

Eating in Whitby

Fish-and-chips are on everybody's mind here. The **Magpie Café** is
a local institution, generally marked by a line of loyal eaters waiting to get in; there's also a carry-out window to the right (£9–11
fish-and-chips, £10–17 fish dinners, daily 11:30–21:00, closed much
of Jan, 14 Pier Road, tel. 01947/602-058). The **Dolphin Hotel**
offers a scenic location with outdoor seating and serviceable food
dead-center in the old town, right at the bridge. They serve £5–10
fish-and-chips and sandwiches for lunch, and an £8–16 grill menu
for dinner (food served daily 12:00–14:30 & 18:00–21:00, from
Oct–May Sat–Sun only, Bridge Street, tel. 01947/602-197).

Staithes

A ragamuffin village where the boy who became Captain James
Cook got his first taste of the sea, Staithes (pronounced "staythz,"
just north of Whitby) is a salty
jumble of cottages bunny-hopping
down a ravine into a tiny harbor.
About a tenth the size of its big
sister down the coast, Staithes is
the yang to Whitby's yin. This
refreshingly unpretentious town
is gloriously stubborn about not
wooing tourists.

    While dead as a doornail
today, in 1816 Staithes was home to 70 boats and the busiest fishing
station in North England. Ten years ago, the town supported 20
fishing boats—today, only three. But fishermen (who pronounce
their town "steers" in the local dialect) still outnumber tourists in
undiscovered Staithes. The town has changed little since Captain
Cook's days. Lots of flies and seagulls seem to have picked the
barren cliffs raw. There's nothing to do but stroll the beach and
nurse a harborside beer or ice cream.

    For a bit more activity, drop by the **lifeboat station,** operated
by the Royal National Lifeboat Institution (RNLI)—Britain's
entirely volunteer answer to the Coast Guard. Entering the big
barn, notice the boards up on the eaves with not-quite-stirring
accounts of the boats being called to duty. As this organization—
England's sole method for responding to maritime emergencies—
is entirely funded by donations, consider supporting the cause with
a coin or two (typically open daily 9:00–18:00 in summer, most

days in winter, shop tel. 01947/840-373, www.staithes-lifeboat
.co.uk).

Getting to Staithes

Staithes is an easy **drive** north of Whitby. Parking is tough—
generally, you can drive in only to unload. Service trucks clog the
windy main (and only) lane much of the day. There's a pay-and-
display lot at the top of the town—an easy downhill walk to the
action (but a more strenuous hike back up). While the **bus** #X56
connection from Whitby to Staithes is fairly straightforward,
there's not much in low-key Staithes to justify the trip (hourly, 30
min; 10-min walk from bus stop into town, www.arrivabus.co.uk).

Sleeping and Eating in Staithes

There are no fancy rooms, and it's a cash-only town with no
ATMs.

$$$ Endeavour Restaurant B&B, tidy and small with four
rooms, is the only place in town that offers parking (Db-£80–95,
serves great food—see below, 1 High Street, tel. 01947/840-825,
www.endeavour-restaurant.co.uk, endeavour.restaurant@virgin
.net, Brian Kay and Charlotte Willoughby).

The **Endeavour Restaurant,** oddly classy for this town, offers
excellent dinners. Reservations are required (£29 two-course meal,
£32 three-course meal, Fri–Sat 12:30–13:30 & 19:00–21:30, closed
Sun–Thu, seafood, vegetarian options—notify in advance, 1 High
Street, tel. 01947/840-825).

A pair of lowbrow pubs serves lunch and dinner daily: **The
Royal George** sits along the main drag. **The Cod and Lobster,**
overlooking the harbor, has scenic outdoor benches and a cozy liv-
ing room warmed by a coal fire. Drop in to see its old-time Staithes
photos.

In nice weather, the best option is to enjoy a drink, snack, or
light meal (i.e., fish-and-chips) sitting at an outdoor table front-
ing the harbor. Try the friendly **Seadrift Café,** which special-
izes in sweets, but also does basic grub (daily 10:00–17:00, tel.
01947/841-345).

DURHAM AND NORTHEAST ENGLAND

Northeast England harbors some of the country's best historical sights. Go for a Roman ramble at Hadrian's Wall, a reminder that Britain was an important Roman colony 2,000 years ago. Make a pilgrimage to Holy Island, where Christianity gained its first toehold in Britain. At Durham, marvel at England's greatest Norman church, and enjoy an evensong service. At the Beamish Museum, travel back in time to the year 1913.

Planning Your Time

For train travelers, Durham is the most convenient overnight stop in this region. If you like Roman ruins, visit Hadrian's Wall (doable with transfers, easiest Easter–Oct). The Beamish Museum is an easy day trip from Durham (25 min by car, one hour by bus). If you're traveling by train, note that it's problematic to visit Durham en route to another destination, since there's no baggage storage in Durham. Either stay overnight or do Durham as a day trip from York.

By car, you can easily visit Beamish Museum, Hadrian's Wall, Bamburgh Castle, and Holy Island. Spend a night in Durham and a night near Hadrian's Wall.

For the best quick visit, arrive in Durham by mid-afternoon in time to tour the cathedral and enjoy the evensong service (Tue–Sat at 17:15, Sun at 15:30). Sleep in Durham. Visit Beamish (25 min north of Durham by car, or 1 hr by bus) the next morning before continuing on to your next destination.

Durham

Without its cathedral, Durham would hardly be noticed. But this magnificently situated cathedral is hard to miss (even if you're zooming by on the train). Seemingly happy to go nowhere, Durham sits along its river, and below its castle and famous cathedral. It has a medieval, cobbled atmosphere and a scraggly peasant's indoor market just off the main square. While Durham is the home to England's third-oldest university, the town feels working-class, surrounded by recently closed coal mines, and filled with tattooed and pierced people in search of job security and a good karaoke bar. Yet Durham has a youthful vibrancy and a small-town warmth that shines—especially on sunny days, when most everyone is licking ice-cream cones.

Orientation to Durham

(area code: 0191)

As it has for a thousand years, tidy little Durham clusters everything safely under its castle, within the protective hairpin bend of the River Wear. The longest walk you'll make will be a 20-minute jaunt from the train station to the cathedral.

Tourist Information

The TI books rooms and local event tickets, and provides train times (Mon–Sat 9:30–17:30, Sun 11:00–16:00, WC, café; 1 block north of Market Place, past St. Nicholas Church, in Gala Theatre building; tel. 0191/384-3720, www.durhamtourism.co.uk, touristinfo@durhamcity.gov.uk).

Arrival in Durham

From the **train station,** follow the road downhill and take the second pedestrian turnoff (within sight of railway bridge), which leads almost immediately over a bridge above the busy road called Alexander Crescent. Then take North Road into town or to the first couple of B&Bs (take Alexander Crescent to the other B&Bs). Or you can just hop on the convenient Cathedral Bus at the train station (described later, under "Getting Around Durham").

Drivers simply surrender to the wonderful 400-space Prince Bishops parking lot (at the roundabout at the base of the old town). It's perfectly safe, and an elevator deposits you right in the heart of Durham (£2/2 hrs, £3.20/4 hrs, a short block from Market Place, tel. 0191/383-9592).

Durham

300 YARDS
300 METERS

TO A·167,
A·691 &
(BEAMISH
& HEXHAM)

(IN GALA THEATRE BUILDING)

TRAIN STATION

PRINCE BISHOPS SHOPPING CENTRE PARKING GARAGE

TO & A·1 (BEAMISH)

BUS STN.

PED. BRIDGE

MILBURNGATE

CLAYPATH

LEAZES ROAD

A·690

Post

MKT. PLACE

SILVER

SADDLER

BOATS

ELVET BRIDGE

PARK

OLD ELVET

FRAMWELLGATE BRIDGE

CASTLE

PALACE GREEN

NORTH BAILEY

SOUTH ST.

CASTLE PATH

WEIR

CATHEDRAL

SOUTH BAILEY

NEW ELVET

CHURCH STREET

HALLGARTH STREET

RIVER WEAR

See Detail Map

TO A·68 (HEXHAM)

MARGERY LANE

GROVE

QUARRY HEADS

PREBENDS BRIDGE

STOCKTON ROAD

TO A·1 MOTORWAY

TO A·167 (YORK)

LANE

P Parking

1 Farnley Tower B&B	9 Café Rouge & Bella Italia
2 Victorian Town House B&B	10 Bimbi's Fish & Chips
3 Castleview Guest House	11 Hide Café
4 Durham Castle Rooms	12 Shaheen's Restaurant
5 Durham Marriott Hotel Royal County	13 The Almshouses
6 Kingslodge Hotel & Rest.	14 The Court Inn Pub
7 To Travelodge Durham	15 To Bistro 21
8 Melanzana Restaurant	16 Marks & Spencer

Helpful Hints

Internet Access: The library, across huge Millennium Place from the TI, has about 40 terminals with free Internet access (Mon–Fri 9:30–19:00, Sat 9:00–17:00, Sun 10:30–16:30, must join for free—bring ID, tel. 0191/386-4003).

Laundry: Durham has none within walking distance; ask at the TI for details if you're willing to drive or take a taxi.

Tours: The TI offers 1.5-hour city walking tours on summer weekends (£4, schedule varies but usually May–Sept Sat–Sun at 14:00—confirm with TI). **David Butler,** the town historian, gives excellent private tours (reasonable prices, tel. 0191/386-1500, dhent@dhent.fsnet.co.uk).

Harry Potter Sights: Durham Cathedral was used in the films, as were other nearby locations. For details, see page 621.

Getting Around Durham

While all my recommended hotels, eateries, and sights are easily walkable in Durham, taxis are available to zip tired tourists to their B&Bs or back to the station (about £4, wait on west side of Framwellgate Bridge on Silver Street).

If you don't feel like walking Durham's hills, hop on the convenient **Cathedral Bus** (also called Service 40) that runs between the train station and the cathedral, with stops near the North Road bus station, Millburngate, Market Place, and some car parks (50p for all-day ticket, 3/hr, leaves train station Mon–Fri 7:55–17:30, Sat 9:10–17:30, Sun 9:50–16:50; last bus leaves cathedral Mon–Sat at 17:40, Sun at 17:00; toll tel. 0871-200-2233).

Self-Guided Walk

Welcome to Durham

• *Begin at Framwellgate Bridge (which connects the train station with the center).*

Framwellgate Bridge was a wonder when it was built in the 12th century—much longer than the river is wide and higher than seemingly necessary. It was well-designed to connect stretches of solid high ground, and to avoid steep descents to the marshy river. Note how elegantly today's Silver Street (which leads toward town) slopes into the Framwellgate Bridge. (Imagine that as late as the 1970s, this people-friendly lane was congested with traffic and buses.)

• *Follow Silver Street up the hill to the town's main square.*

Durham's **Market Place** retains the same plotting the Prince Bishop gave it when he moved villagers here in about 1100. Each plot of land was the same width (about 8 yards). Find today's distinctly narrow buildings (Thomas Cook, Whittard, and the optician shop)—they still fit the 800-year-old plan. The rest of the buildings fronting the square are multiples of that first shop width. Plots were long and skinny, maximizing the number of shops that could have a piece of the Market Place action.

Examine the square's **statues.** Coal has long been the basis of this region's economy. The statue of Neptune was part of an ill-

fated attempt by a coal baron to bribe the townsfolk into embracing a canal project that would make the shipment of his coal more efficient. The statue of the fancy guy on the horse is Charles Stewart Vane, the Third Marquess of Londonderry. A general in Wellington's army, he was an Irish aristocrat who married a local coal heiress. A clever and aggressive businessman, he managed to create a vast business empire controlling every link in the coal business chain—mines, railroads, boats, harbors, and so on.

In the 1850s throughout England, towns were moving their markets off squares and into Industrial Age iron-and-glass market halls. Durham was no exception, and today its **indoor market** (which faces Market Place) is a funky 19th-century delight to explore (Mon–Sat 9:00–17:00). There are also outdoor markets in Market Square (Sat retail market 9:00–16:30, farmer's market third Thu of each month, 8:30–15:30, tel. 0191/384-6153, www.durhammarkets.co.uk).

Do you enjoy the sparse traffic in Durham's old town? It was the first city in England to institute a "congestion fee." Look where traffic enters the old town on the downhill side of the square. The bollard (series of short posts) is up, blocking traffic Monday through Saturday from 10:00 to 16:00. Anyone can drive in...but it costs £2 to get out. This has cut downtown traffic by more than 50 percent. Locals brag that London (which now has a similar congestion fee) was inspired by their success.

• *Head up to the cathedral along Saddler Street. On the left, you'll see a bridge.*

A 12th-century construction, **Elvet Bridge** led to a town market over the river. Like Framwellgate, it was very long (17 arches) to avoid river muck and steep inclines. Even today, Elvet Bridge leads to an unusually wide road—a reminder that it was once swollen to accommodate the market action. Shops lined the right-hand side of Elvet Bridge in the 12th century as they do today. An alley separated the bridge from the buildings on the left. When the bridge was widened, it met the upper stories of the buildings on the left, which became "street level."

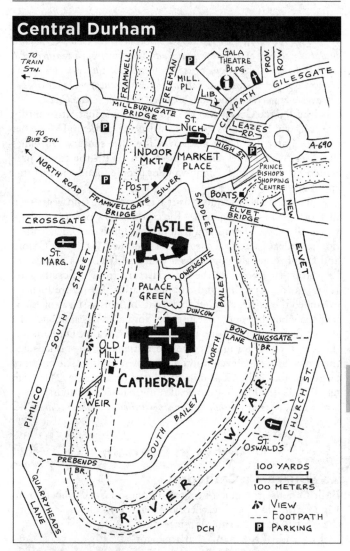

Central Durham

TO TRAIN STN.

GALA THEATRE BLDG.

PROV. ROW

GILESGATE

FRAMWELL

FREEMAN

MILL. PL.

P

LIB.

CLAYPATH

MILLBURNGATE BRIDGE

ST. NICH.

LEAZES RD.

A-690

TO BUS STN.

HIGH ST.

P

NORTH ROAD

P

INDOOR MKT.

MARKET PLACE

FRAMWELLGATE BRIDGE

SILVER

SADDLER

PRINCE BISHOP'S SHOPPING CENTRE

P

POST

BOATS

CROSSGATE

ELVET BRIDGE

ELVET

NEW

SOUTH STREET

CASTLE

OWENGATE

NORTH BAILEY

ST. MARG.

PALACE GREEN

DUNCOW

BOW LANE

KINGSGATE BR.

OLD MILL

CATHEDRAL

PIMLICO

WEIR

SOUTH BAILEY

RIVER WEAR

CHURCH ST.

ST. OSWALD'S

PREBENDS BR.

100 YARDS

100 METERS

QUARRYHEADS LANE

RIVER WEAR

VIEW

FOOTPATH

P PARKING

DCH

DURHAM AND NE ENGLAND

The Scots were on the rampage in the 14th century. After their victory at Bannockburn in 1314, they pushed farther south and actually burned part of Durham. With this new threat, Durham's **city walls** were built. Since people settled within the walls, the population density soared. Soon, open lanes were covered by residences and became tunnels (called "vennels"). A classic vennel leads to Saddlers Yard, a fine little 16th-century courtyard (immediately opposite Elvet Bridge). While these are cute today, centuries ago they were Dickensian nightmares...the filthiest of hovels.

• *Continue up Saddler Street. Between the two* Georgian Window *signs, go through the purple door to see a bit of the medieval wall incorporated into the brickwork of a newer building, and a turret from an earlier wall. Back on Saddler Street, you can see the ghost of the old wall. (It's exactly the width of the building now housing the Salvation Army.) Veer right at Owengate as you continue uphill, until you reach the Palace Green.*

The **Palace Green** was the site of the original 11th-century Saxon town, filling this green between the castle and an earlier church. Later, the town made way for 12th-century Durham's defenses, which now enclose the green. With the threat presented by the Vikings, it's no wonder people found comfort in a spot like this.

The **castle** still stands—as it has for a thousand years—on its motte (man-made mound). The castle is now part of Durham University. Like Oxford and Cambridge, Durham U. is a collection of colleges scattered throughout the town. And, like Oxford and Cambridge, the town has a youthful liveliness because of its university. Look into the old courtyard from the castle gate. It traces the very first and smallest bailey. As future bishops expanded the castle, they left their coats of arms as a way of "signing" the wing they built. Because the Norman kings appointed the Prince Bishops here to rule this part of their realm, Durham was the seat of power for much of northern England. The bishops had their own army and even minted their own coins (castle entrance by guided tour only, £5, 45 min, call ahead for schedule, 24-hr info tel. 0191/334-3800, www.dur.ac.uk/university.college/tours).

• *This walk ends at Durham's stunning* **cathedral,** *which is described next.*

Sights in Durham

▲▲▲Durham's Cathedral

Built to house the much-venerated bones of St. Cuthbert from Lindisfarne, Durham's cathedral offers the best look at Norman architecture in England. ("Norman" is British for "Romanesque.") In addition to touring the cathedral and its attached sights, try to fit in an evensong service.

Cost and Hours: Entry to the cathedral itself is free, though a £4 donation is requested. You must pay to enter its several interior sights: the climbable tower (£4), relic-filled treasury (£2.50), Monk's Dormitory (£1), and boring AV show (£1). It's open mid-July–Aug daily

The History of Durham

Durham's location, tucked inside a tight bend in the River Wear, was ideal for easy fortifications. But it wasn't settled until A.D. 995, with the arrival of St. Cuthbert's body (buried in Durham Cathedral). Shortly after that, a small church and fortification were built upon the site of today's castle and church to house the relic. The castle was a classic "motte-and-bailey" design (with the "motte," or mound, providing a lookout tower for the stockade encircling the protected area, or "bailey"). By 1100, the Prince Bishop's bailey was filled with villagers—and he wanted everyone out. This was *his* place! He provided a wider protective wall, and had the town resettle below, around today's Market Place. But this displaced the townsfolk's cows, so the Prince Bishop constructed a fine stone bridge (today's Framwellgate) connecting the new town to grazing land he established across the river. The bridge had a defensive gate, with a wall circling the peninsula and the river serving as a moat.

9:30–20:00; Sept–mid-July Mon–Sat 9:30–18:00, Sun 12:30–17:30; opens daily at 7:30 for worship and prayer, tel. 0191/386-4266, www.durhamcathedral.co.uk. A bookshop, cafeteria, and WC are tucked away in the cloisters. No photos, videos, or mobile phones are allowed inside the cathedral.

Tours: The cathedral offers regular tours in summer. If one is already in session, you're welcome to join (£4; late July–late Sept Mon–Sat at 10:30, 11:00, and 14:30; tours also possible near Easter and during school vacations in May and Oct, call or check website to confirm schedule, tel. 0191/386-4266).

Evensong: For a thousand years, this cradle of English Christianity has been praising God. To really experience the cathedral, go for an evensong service. Arrive early and ask to be seated in the choir. It's a spiritual Oz, as 40 boys sing psalms—a red-and-white-robed pillow of praise, raised up by the powerful pipe organ. If you're lucky and the service goes well, the organist will run a spiritual musical victory lap as the congregation breaks up (Tue–Sat at 17:15, Sun at 15:30, 1 hour, sometimes sung on Mon; visiting choirs nearly always fill in when choir is off on school break during mid-July–Aug; tel. 0191/386-4266).

Organ Recitals: During July and August on Wednesday evenings, you can catch a recital at the cathedral (£8, 19:30).

⊙ Self-Guided Tour: Begin your visit outside the cathedral. From the Palace Green, notice how this fortress of God stands boldly opposite the Norman keep of Durham's fortress of man.

The **exterior** of this awe-inspiring cathedral—if you look closely—has a serious skin problem. In the 1770s, as the stone was crumbling, they crudely peeled it back a few inches. The scrape marks give the cathedral a bad complexion to this day. For proof of this odd "restoration," study the masonry 10 yards to the right of the door. The L-shaped stones in the corner would normally never be found in a church like this—they only became L-shaped when the surface was cut back.

At the cathedral **door,** the big, bronze, lion-faced knocker (a replica of the 12th-century original—now in the treasury) was used by criminals seeking sanctuary (read the explanation).

Immediately inside, at the **information desk,** church attendants are standing by to happily answer questions. Ideally, follow a church tour. The £1 pamphlet, *A Short Guide to Durham Cathedral,* is informative but dull.

Notice the **modern window** with the novel depiction of the Last Supper (above and to the left of the entry door). It was given to the church by a local department store in 1984. The shapes of the apostles represent worlds and persons of every kind, from the shadowy Judas to the brightness of Jesus. This window is a good reminder that the cathedral remains a living part of the community.

Near the info desk, the **black marble strip** on the floor was as close to the altar as women were allowed in the days when this was a Benedictine church (until 1540). Sit down (ignoring the black line) and let the fine proportions of England's best Norman nave— and arguably Europe's best Romanesque nave—stir you. Any frilly woodwork and stonework were added in later centuries.

The architecture of the **nave** is particularly harmonious because it was built in a mere 40 years (1093–1133). The round arches and zigzag carved decorations are textbook Norman. The church was also proto-Gothic, built by well-traveled French masons and architects who knew the latest innovations from Europe. Its stone and ribbed roof, pointed arches, and flying buttresses were revolutionary in England. Notice the clean lines and simplicity. It's not as cluttered as other churches for several reasons: Out of respect for St. Cuthbert, for centuries no one else was buried here. During Reformation times, sumptuous Catholic decor was cleaned out. And subsequent fires and wars destroyed what Protestants didn't.

Enter the **Galilee Chapel** (late Norman, from 1175) in the back of the nave. The paintings of St. Cuthbert and St. Oswald (seventh-century king of Northumbria) on the side walls of the side altar niche are rare examples of Romanesque (Norman) paintings. Facing this altar, look above to your right to see more faint paintings on the upper walls above the columns. Near the center of the chapel, the upraised tomb topped with a black slab contains

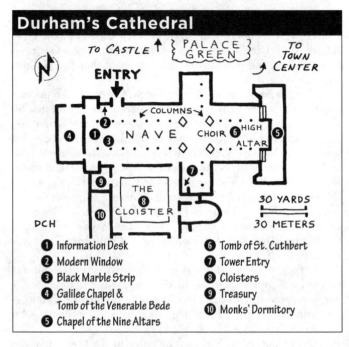

Durham's Cathedral

TO CASTLE ↑ [PALACE GREEN] TO TOWN CENTER

N

ENTRY

← COLUMNS →

NAVE   CHOIR   HIGH ALTAR

THE CLOISTER

DCH

30 YARDS
30 METERS

❶ Information Desk
❷ Modern Window
❸ Black Marble Strip
❹ Galilee Chapel &
   Tomb of the Venerable Bede
❺ Chapel of the Nine Altars

❻ Tomb of St. Cuthbert
❼ Tower Entry
❽ Cloisters
❾ Treasury
❿ Monks' Dormitory

the remains of the Venerable Bede, an eighth-century Christian scholar who wrote the first history of England. The Latin reads, "In this tomb are the bones of the Venerable Bede."

Back in the main church, stroll down the nave to the center, under the highest **bell tower** in Europe (218 feet). Gaze up. The ropes turn wheels upon which bells are mounted. If you're stirred by the cheery ringing of church bells, tune in to the cathedral on Sunday (9:15–10:00 & 14:30–15:30) or Thursday (19:30–21:00 practice, trained bell ringers welcome) when the resounding notes tumble merrily through the entire town.

Continuing east (all medieval churches faced east), you enter the **choir.** Monks worshipped many times a day, and the choir in the center of the church provided a cozy place to gather in this vast, dark, and chilly building. Mass has been said daily here in the heart of the cathedral for 900 years. The fancy wooden chairs are from the 17th century. Behind the altar is the delicately carved Neville Screen from 1380 (made of Normandy stone in London, shipped to Newcastle by sea, then brought here by wagon). Until the Reformation, the niches contained statues of 107 saints. Exit the choir from the far right side (south). Look for the stained-glass window (to your right) that commemorates the church's 1,000th anniversary in 1995. The colorful scenes depict England's history, from coal miners to cows to computers.

Step down behind the high altar into the east end of the church, which contains the 13th-century **Chapel of the Nine Altars.** Built later than the rest of the church, this is Gothic—taller, lighter, and relatively more extravagant than the Norman nave.

Climb a few steps to the **tomb of St. Cuthbert.** An inspirational leader of the early Christian Church in north England, St. Cuthbert lived in the Lindisfarne monastery on Holy Island (100 miles north of Durham). He died in 687. Eleven years later, his body was exhumed and found to be miraculously preserved. This stoked the popularity of his shrine, and pilgrims came in growing numbers. When Vikings raided Lindisfarne in 875, the monks fled with his body (and the famous illuminated *Lindisfarne Gospels,* now in the British Library in London). In 995, after 120 years of roaming, the monks settled in Durham on an easy-to-defend tight bend in the River Wear. This cathedral was built over Cuthbert's tomb.

Throughout the Middle Ages, a shrine stood here and was visited by countless pilgrims. In 1539, during the Reformation—whose proponents advocated focusing on God rather than saints—the shrine was destroyed. But pilgrims still come, especially on St. Cuthbert's feast day—March 20.

Other Cathedral Sights: The entry to the **tower** is in the south transept; the view from the tower will cost you 325 steps and £4 (Mon–Sat 10:00–16:00, closes at 15:00 in winter, last entry 20 min before closing; closed Sun, during events, and in bad weather; must be at least 4'3" tall, no backless shoes). The following sights are within the cloisters: The **treasury,** filled with medieval bits and holy pieces (including Cuthbert's coffin, vestments, and cross), fleshes out this otherwise stark building. The actual relics from St. Cuthbert's tomb are at the far end (treasury well worth the £2.50 admission, Mon–Sat 10:00–16:30, Sun 14:00–16:30). The **Monks' Dormitory,** now a library with an original 14th-century timber roof filled with Anglo-Saxon stones, is worth its £1 admission (likely Mon–Sat 10:00–16:00, Sun 12:30–16:00). Skip the unexceptional **AV show** about St. Cuthbert in the unexceptional undercroft (£1, Mon–Sat 10:00–15:00, no showings Sun, off-season also no showings Fri, closed Nov–early Jan).

Near the treasury, you'll find the **WCs, bookshop** (in the old kitchen), and fine **Undercroft** cafeteria (daily 10:00–16:30, tel. 0191/386-3721).

Activities

Riverside Path—For a 20-minute woodsy escape, walk Durham's riverside path from busy Framwellgate Bridge to sleepy Prebends Bridge.

Boat Cruise and Rental—Hop on the *Prince Bishop* for a relaxing one-hour narrated cruise of the river that nearly surrounds Durham (£6, Easter–Oct, for schedule call 0191/386-9525, check at TI, or go down to dock at Brown's Boat House at Elvet Bridge, just east of old town, www.princebishoprc.co.uk). Sailings vary based on weather and tides. For some exercise with the same scenery, you can rent a rowboat at the same pier (£4/hr per person, £10 deposit, Easter–Sept daily 10:00–18:00, last boat rental one hour before dusk, tel. 0191/386-3779).

Sleeping in Durham

B&Bs

$$$ Farnley Tower, a luxurious B&B, has 13 large rooms with all the comforts. On a quiet street at the top of a hill, it's a 10-minute hike from the town center (Sb-£65, Db-£85, superior Db-£95, family room-£120, some rooms have views, paying with credit card costs 2 percent extra, phones in rooms, easy parking, inviting yard, evening meals at their adjacent, wildly inventive Gourmet Spot restaurant, The Avenue, tel. 0191/375-0011, fax 0191/383-9694, www.farnley-tower.co.uk, enquiries@farnley-tower.co.uk, Raj and Roopal Naik).

$$ Victorian Town House B&B offers three spacious, tastefully updated rooms in an 1853 townhouse in a nice residential area just down the hill from the train station (Sb-£50–60, Db-£80–85, family room-£85–105, cash only, 2 Victoria Terrace, 5-min walk from train or bus station, tel. 05601/459-168, www.durhambedandbreakfast.com, stay@durhambedandbreakfast.com, friendly Jill and Andy).

$$ Castleview Guest House rents six airy, restful rooms in a classy, well-located house close to Silver Street (Sb-£55, Db-£80, cash only, 4 Crossgate, tel. 0191/386-8852, www.castle-view.co.uk, castle_view@hotmail.com, Mike and Anne Williams).

$$ *Student Housing Open to Anyone:* Durham Castle, a student residence actually on the castle grounds facing the cathe-

dral, rents rooms during the summer break (generally end of June–Sept only). Request a room in the stylish main building, or you may get one of the few bomb shelter–style modern dorm rooms (S-£28.50, Sb-£40, D-£51, Db-£70, fancier Db-£180, elegant breakfast hall, parking-£5 on Palace Green or free with voucher from reception, University College, The Castle, Palace Green, tel. 0191/334-4108 or 0191/334-4106, fax 0191/374-7470, www.dur.ac.uk/university.college, durham.castle@durham.ac.uk).

Sleep Code

(£1 = about $1.60, country code: 44, area code: 0191)
S = Single, **D** = Double/Twin, **T** = Triple, **Q** = Quad, **b** = bathroom, **s** = shower only. You can assume credit cards are accepted unless otherwise noted.

To help you sort easily through these listings, I've divided the rooms into three categories based on the price for a standard double room with bath (during high season):

$$$ Higher Priced—Most rooms £85 or more.
$$ Moderately Priced—Most rooms between £50-85.
$ Lower Priced—Most rooms £50 or less.

Hotels

$$$ Durham Marriott Hotel Royal County scatters its 150 posh, four-star rooms among several buildings sprawling along the river near the city center. The Leisure Club has a pool, sauna, Jacuzzi, and fitness equipment (Db-£150, £30 less on weekends, includes breakfast, 2 restaurants, bar, parking, Old Elvet, tel. 0191/386-6821 or toll tel. 0870-400-7286, fax 0191/386-0704, www.marriott.co.uk).

$$ Kingslodge Hotel & Restaurant, a renovated lodge with charming terraces, an attached restaurant, a pub, and a champagne-and-oyster bar, is a cushy option convenient to the train station (Sb-£60, Db-£75, family room-£95, includes breakfast, parking, Waddington Street, Flass Vale, tel. 0191/370-9977, www.kingslodge.info, kingslodgehotel@yahoo.co.uk).

$$ Travelodge Durham's 57 simple rooms are in a converted 1844 train station, with the former waiting room now housing the reception desk (Db-£55–65 but check website for deals, cold breakfast delivered to room—not worth price, half-mile northeast of cathedral, off A690 at Station Lane, Gilesgate, toll tel. 0871-984-6136, fax 0191/386-5461, www.travelodge.co.uk).

Eating in Durham

Durham is a university town with plenty of lively, inexpensive eateries. Stroll down North Road, across Framwellgate Bridge, through Market Place, and up Saddler Street, and consider these places.

Melanzana, just over Elvet Bridge on the other side of town, is a popular Italian restaurant, with £8–11 pizzas and pastas and £11–19 dinners in an inviting setting (Mon–Sat 11:00–22:00, Sun 11:00–21:00, even cheaper during happy hour, 96 Elvet Bridge, tel. 0191/384-0096).

Café Rouge, a chain restaurant with French-bistro food and decor, is just east of Framwellgate Bridge (21 Silver Street, tel. 0191/384-3429). **Bella Italia,** next door and down the stairs, is another chain, with surprisingly good food (20 Silver Street, tel. 0191/386-1060).

Bimbi's, on Market Place, is a standby for fish-and-chips (Mon–Sat 11:00–18:30, Sun 12:00–18:30).

Saddler Street, leading from Market Place up to the cathedral, is lined with eateries. The hip **Hide Café,** with youthful, jazz-filled ambience, serves the best modern continental cuisine in the old town (£6–10 lunches, £8–14 meals, Mon–Sat 12:00–15:00 & 18:00–21:00, Sun 12:00–15:00, reservations smart, 39 Saddler Street, tel. 0191/384-1999).

Shaheen's is the place for good Indian cuisine (£6–10 meals, Tue–Sat 17:00–21:30, closed Sun–Mon, 48 North Bailey Street, just past turnoff to cathedral, tel. 0191/386-0960).

The Almshouses, on the Palace Green across from the cathedral, serves tasty, light meals in a cheap cafeteria setting (£6–7 plates, daily July–Aug 9:00–20:00, Sept–June 9:00–17:00, tel. 0191/386-1054).

The Court Inn, on the outskirts of town, is a local favorite for traditional pub grub (£7–10 meals, daily 11:00–22:20, 5-min walk east of old town over Elvet Bridge, Court Lane, tel. 0191/384-7350).

Bistro 21, with modern French/Mediterranean fare and good seafood, works well for drivers looking for a nontouristy splurge (£15–22 main dishes, £15–18 two- or three-course dinner specials Mon–Thu 18:00–22:00, Fri–Sat 18:00–19:00; open Mon–Sat 12:00–14:00 & 18:00–22:00, Sun 12:00–15:00, 1.5 miles northwest of town, Aykley Heads, tel. 0191/384-4354).

Supermarket: **Marks & Spencer** is in the old town, just off the main square (Mon–Sat 9:00–18:00, Sun 11:00–17:00, 4 Silver Street, across from post office). You can **picnic** in Market Square, sitting around the tiered stone base of the horseman's statue, or on the benches and grass outside the cathedral entrance (but not on the Palace Green, unless the park police have gone home).

Durham Connections

From Durham by Train to: York (3–4/hr, 45 min), **Keswick/Lake District** (train to Penrith—1–2/hr, 2.5–3.5 hrs, change in Carlisle and Newcastle; then bus to Keswick—hourly Mon–Sat, Sun 8/day, 40 min), **London** (2/hr, 3 hrs), **Hadrian's Wall** (take train to Newcastle—1–4/hr, 15 min, then a bus or a train/bus combination to Hadrian's Wall), **Edinburgh** (2/hr, 2 hrs, less frequent in winter), **Bristol** (near Bath, 2/hr, 5 hrs). Train info: toll tel. 0845-748-4950.

DURHAM AND NE ENGLAND

Near Durham: Beamish Museum

This huge 300-acre open-air museum, which re-creates the years 1825 and 1913 in northeast England, takes at least three hours to explore. Vintage trams and cool circa-1910 double-decker buses shuttle visitors to the four stations: Colliery Village, The Town, Pockerley Manor/Waggonway, and Home Farm. Tram routes are more plentiful than bus routes, but attendants on both are helpful and knowledgeable. Signs on the trams advertise a variety of 19th-century products, from "Borax, for washing everything" to "Murton's Reliable Travelling Trunks." This isn't a wax museum. If you touch the exhibits, they may smack you. Attendants at each stop happily explain everything. In fact, the place is only really interesting if you talk to the attendants. In 2008, the "Westoe netty"—a circa 1890 men's public WC—was acquired and rebuilt near the 1913 railway station. The loo became famous in 1972 as the subject in a painting by a local artist.

Cost and Hours: £16, £11 with bus receipt, £6 in winter, choose the Beamish Unlimited Pass at no extra charge for a 2-day visit; Easter–Oct open daily 10:00–17:00; from Nov–Easter only The Town, Colliery Village, and Tramway are open, Tue–Thu and Sat–Sun 10:00–16:00, closed Mon and Fri and most of Dec; check events schedule as you enter, last tickets sold at 15:00 year-round, tel. 0191/370-4000, www.beamish.org.uk, museum @beamish.org.uk.

Getting There: By **car,** the museum is five minutes off the A1/M1 motorway (one exit north of Durham at Chester-le-Street/Junction 63, well signposted, 12 miles and a 25-min drive northwest of Durham). To get to Beamish from Durham by public transportation, catch **bus** #21 or #X1 from the bus station (3–4/hr, 1 hr, £3.30 day pass; transfer at Chester-le-Street to bus #X8, #28, or #28A at central bus kiosk a half-block away, get handy bus schedule at Durham TI, toll tel. 0871-200-2233, www.traveline.org.uk). When you get off the bus at Beamish, the museum is a five-minute walk down the hill. Show your bus receipt for the £5 museum discount. To catch the bus leaving Beamish, the bus stop for bus #X8 is on the side of the street near the pub; the stop for #28 and #28A is on the opposite side of the street.

◆ Self-Guided Tour: Start with the **Colliery Village** (company town around a coal mine), with a school, a church, miners' homes, and a fascinating—if claustrophobic—20-minute tour into the Mahogany drift mine. Your guide will tell you about beams collapsing, gas exploding, and flooding; after that cheerful speech, you'll don a hard hat as you're led into the mine.

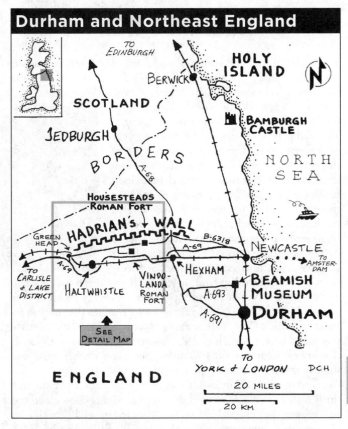

Durham and Northeast England

TO EDINBURGH

BERWICK

HOLY ISLAND

N

SCOTLAND

JEDBURGH

BORDERS

A-68

BAMBURGH CASTLE

NORTH SEA

HOUSESTEADS ROMAN FORT

GREEN HEAD

HADRIAN'S WALL

B-6318

A-69

NEWCASTLE

TO AMSTER-DAM

A-69

TO CARLISLE & LAKE DISTRICT

HALTWHISTLE

VINDO-LANDA ROMAN FORT

HEXHAM

A-693

A-691

BEAMISH MUSEUM

DURHAM

SEE DETAIL MAP

ENGLAND

TO YORK & LONDON

DCH

20 MILES

20 KM

DURHAM AND NE ENGLAND

The Town is a bustling street featuring a 1913 candy shop (the chocolate room in back is worth a stop for chocolate fans), a dentist's office, a Masonic hall, a garage, a working pub (The Sun Inn, Mon–Sat 11:00–16:30, Sun 12:00–16:30), Barclays Bank, and a hardware store featuring a variety of "toilet sets" (not what you think). For lunch, try the Tea Rooms cafeteria (upstairs, daily 10:30–16:30). If the weather is good, picnic in the grassy pavilion next to the tram stop.

Pockerley Manor and the Waggonway has an 1820s manor house whose attendants have plenty to explain. Enjoy the lovely view from the gardens behind the manor, then enter through the kitchen, where bread is baked several times a week. Ask for a sample if you have a taste for tough rye. Adjacent is the re-created first-ever passenger train from 1825, which takes modern-day visitors for a spin on 1825 tracks—a hit with railway buffs. **Home Farm** is the least interesting section.

Hadrian's Wall

This is one of England's most thought-provoking sights. In about A.D. 122, during the reign of Emperor Hadrian, the Romans built this great stone wall. Its actual purpose is still debated. While Rome ruled Britain for 400 years, it never quite ruled its people. The wall may have been used for any number of reasons: to define the northern edge of the empire, to protect Roman Britain from invading Pict tribes from the north (or at least cut down on pesky border raids), to monitor the movement of people, or to simply give an otherwise bored army something to do. (Emperors understood that nothing's more dangerous than a bored army.) Stretching 73 miles coast to coast across the narrowest

stretch of northern England, it was built and defended by some 20,000 troops. Not just a wall, this was a military complex that included forts, ditches, settlements, and a road on the south side. At every mile of the wall, a castle guards a gate, and two turrets stand between each castle. The mile castles are numbered. (Eighty of them cover the 73 miles, because a Roman mile was slightly shorter than our mile.)

Today, several chunks of the wall, ruined forts, and museums thrill history buffs. About a dozen Roman sights cling along the wall's route; the best are Housesteads Roman Fort and Vindolanda. Housesteads shows you where the Romans lived; Vindolanda's museum shows you how they lived.

The Hadrian's Wall National Trail runs 84 miles, following the wall's route from coast to coast (for details, see www.national trail.co.uk/HadriansWall).

Portions of the wall are in Northumberland National Park. The **Once Brewed National Park Visitor Centre** is located along the Hadrian's Wall bus route and has walking guides to the wall and information on the area (Easter–Oct daily 9:30–17:00, Nov–Easter 10:00–15:00 Sat–Sun only, pay parking lot, Military Road, Bardon Mill, tel. 01434/344-396, www.northumberlandnational park.org.uk, tic.oncebrewed@nnpa.org.uk).

Getting to Hadrian's Wall

Hadrian's Wall is anchored by Newcastle on the east and Carlisle on the west. Driving is the most convenient way to see Hadrian's Wall; if you're coming by train, consider renting a car for the day at either Newcastle or Carlisle.

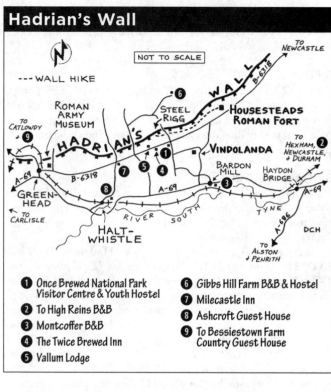

Hadrian's Wall

- ❶ Once Brewed National Park Visitor Centre & Youth Hostel
- ❷ To High Reins B&B
- ❸ Montcoffer B&B
- ❹ The Twice Brewed Inn
- ❺ Vallum Lodge
- ❻ Gibbs Hill Farm B&B & Hostel
- ❼ Milecastle Inn
- ❽ Ashcroft Guest House
- ❾ To Bessiestown Farm Country Guest House

DURHAM AND NE ENGLAND

Public transportation has improved, but the train only gets you *near* the wall. You still need to take a local bus to the Roman sights. If you want to see everything—or even hike part of the wall—stay overnight in a nearby town.

The free "Great Days Out" pamphlet, available at local visitor centers and train stations, has information on how to do the wall, including bus and train timetables, suggested itineraries, and more.

You can also call Haltwhistle's helpful **TI** for schedule information (Easter–Oct Mon–Sat 9:30–13:00 & 14:00–17:00, Sun 13:00–17:00; Nov–Easter Mon–Sat 9:30–12:00 & 13:00–15:30, closed Sun; tel. 01434/322-002, www.hadrians-wall.org).

If you're just passing through for the day on the bus, it's almost impossible to stop and see all the sights—you'll need to study the bus schedule carefully and prioritize. It's also hard to bring your luggage with you. Store your luggage in Newcastle or Carlisle if you're day-tripping (see train information below). If you must travel with luggage, visit Housesteads Roman Fort or Vindolanda, where you can leave baggage at the entrance while exploring.

If you want to walk the wall, **Hadrians Haul** baggage-courier service will send your luggage ahead (£5/bag per pick-up, mobile 07967-564-823, www.hadrianshaul.com).

By Car

Take B6318; it parallels the wall and passes several viewpoints, minor sights, and "severe dips." (If there's a certified nerd or bozo in the car, these road signs add a lot to a photo portrait.) Buy a good local map to help you explore this interesting area more easily and thoroughly.

By Train and Bus

During the peak season, one bus conveniently links all the sights to Newcastle and Carlisle. During the off-season, you will have to take a train and then either a local bus or a taxi to visit the wall.

Between Easter and October, take **Hadrian's Wall bus #AD122** to get to all the Roman sights (£8 day pass, tel. 01434/322-002, www.hadrians-wall.org). The bus runs between Carlisle and Newcastle, stopping at the important Roman sights. Several buses a day have onboard guides on part of the trip (noted on the schedule). For travelers spending the night, this bus also stops near the Once Brewed Youth Hostel, which is about two blocks from The Twice Brewed Inn (both recommended under "Sleeping and Eating near Hadrian's Wall," later).

From Newcastle by Bus #AD122: The bus leaves Newcastle Central Train Station daily at 9:00. If you miss the bus, you will need to take the train to Hexham or Haltwhistle, which has more frequent bus service to the wall.

From Newcastle by Train to: Hexham (Mon–Fri 2/hr, Sat–Sun hourly, 30 min), **Haltwhistle** (Mon–Fri hourly, Sat–Sun almost hourly, 1 hr). Catch bus #AD122 in either town to visit the wall. You can store luggage at the Newcastle train station.

From Carlisle by Bus #AD122: Leaves from English Street outside Carlisle Train Station (Mon–Sat 8/day, Sun 5/day).

From Carlisle by Train to: Hexham (Mon–Sat hourly, Sun 10/day, 45 min), **Haltwhistle** (Mon–Sat hourly, Sun 11/day, 30 min). Catch bus #AD122 in either town to visit the wall. Next to the Carlisle train station, you can store your luggage at **Bar Solo** (£2/bag per day, Mon–Sat 9:00–23:00, opens at 11:00 on Sun, tel. 01228/631-600).

Off-Season Options: If you're traveling off-season (Nov–Easter), you can take a train/bus or a train/taxi combination. For the train/bus option, take a train to Haltwhistle, then bus #185 to the Roman Army Museum, or bus #681 to Vindolanda and Housesteads Roman Fort.

If you're staying near the wall, your B&B host can arrange a taxi (Turnbull tel. 01434/320-105, one-way about £10 from Haltwhistle to Housesteads Roman Fort, arrange for return pickup or have museum staff call a taxi).

Sights at Hadrian's Wall

▲▲**Housesteads Roman Fort**—With its tiny museum, powerful scenery, and the best-preserved segment of the wall, this is your best single stop at Hadrian's Wall. All Roman forts were the same rectangular shape and design, containing a commander's headquarters, barracks, and latrines (lower end); this fort even has a hospital. The fort was built right up to the wall, which is on the far side. From the parking lot and gift shop, it's a half-mile, mostly uphill walk to the entrance of the sprawling fort and minuscule museum (£4.50 for sight and museum—pay up at fort, not at gift shop; daily Easter–Sept 10:00–18:00, Oct–Easter closes at 16:00 or dusk, parking-£3, tel. 01434/344-363, www.english-heritage.org .uk/housesteads). At the car park are WCs, a snack bar, and a gift shop. You can leave your luggage at the gift shop (same hours as fort, tel. 01434/344-525).

▲▲**Hiking the Wall**—From Housesteads, hike west along the wall speaking Latin. For a good, craggy, three-mile walk along the

wall, hike between Housesteads and Steel Rigg (free guides available at Once Brewed Visitor Centre). You'll pass a castle sitting in a nick in a crag (milecastle #39, called Castle Nick). There's a parking lot near Steel Rigg (take the little road up from the Twice Brewed Inn). East of Steel Rigg you'll see the "Robin Hood Tree," a large symmetrical tree (in a little roller-coaster gap) that was featured in the movie *Robin Hood: Prince of Thieves* (with Kevin Costner, 1991).

▲**Vindolanda**—This larger Roman fort (which actually predates the wall by 40 years) and museum are just south of the wall. Although Housesteads has better ruins and the wall, Vindolanda has the better museum, revealing intimate details of Roman life. It's an active dig—from Easter through September, you'll see the work in progress (usually daily, weather permitting). Eight forts were built on this spot. The Romans, by carefully sealing the foundations from each successive fort, left modern-day archaeologists with seven yards of remarkably well-preserved artifacts to excavate: keys, coins, brooches, scales, pottery, glass, tools, leather shoes, bits of cloth, and even a wig. Impressive examples of early

Roman writing were recently discovered here. While the actual letters—written on thin pieces of wood—are in London's British Museum, see the interesting video here and read the translations, including the first known example of a woman writing to a woman (an invitation to a birthday party). These varied letters, about parties held, money owed, and sympathy shared, bring Romans to life in a way that stones alone can't.

From the free parking lot, you'll pay at the entrance, then walk 500 yards of grassy parkland decorated by the foundation stones of the Roman fort and a full-size replica chunk of the wall. At the far side are the museum, gift shop, and cafeteria.

Cost and Hours: £5.20, £8 combo-ticket includes Roman Army Museum, daily April–Sept 10:00–18:00, mid-Feb–March and Oct–mid-Nov 10:00–17:00, mid-Nov–mid-Feb 10:00–16:00, last entry 45 min before closing, can leave luggage at entrance, tel. 01434/344-277, www.vindolanda.com.

Roman Army Museum—This museum, a few miles farther west at Greenhead, is redundant if you've seen Vindolanda. Its film offers a good eagle-eye view of a portion of the wall (£4.20, or buy £8 combo-ticket that includes Vindolanda, same hours as Vindolanda, but closed mid-Nov–mid-Feb, tel. 016977/47485).

Sleeping and Eating near Hadrian's Wall

(£1 = about $1.60, country code: 44)

Near Hexham
(area code: 01434)

$$ High Reins offers four rooms in a stone house built by a shipping tycoon in the 1920s (Sb-£45, Db-£66, cash only, ground-floor bedrooms, lounge, 1 mile west of train station on the western outskirts of Hexham, Leazes Lane, tel. 01434/603-590, www.highreins.co.uk, pwalton@highreins.co.uk, Jan and Peter Walton).

In Bardon Mill
(area code: 01434)

$$ Montcoffer, a restored country home, is decorated with statues, old enameled advertising signs, and other artifacts collected by owner John McGrellis and his wife, Dehlia, whose textile art is displayed in and around your room (Sb-£48, Db-£78, includes hearty breakfasts, ground-floor bedrooms, 2 miles from Vindolanda, Bardon Mill, tel. 01434/344-138, mobile 07912-209-992, www.montcoffer.co.uk, john-dehlia@talk21.com).

$$ The Twice Brewed Inn, two miles west of Housesteads and a half-mile from the wall, rents 14 rooms and serves real ales and decent pub grub all day (pub open daily 11:00–23:00, food served daily 12:00–21:00). It's a friendly pub that serves as the community gathering place (S-£32, D-£55, Db-£70–80, free Internet access for hotel guests, otherwise £1/30 min, Military Road, Bardon Mill, tel. 01434/344-534, www.twicebrewedinn .co.uk, info@twicebrewedinn.co.uk).

$ Once Brewed Youth Hostel is a comfortable place near the Twice Brewed Inn and right next door to the Once Brewed National Park Visitor Centre (£16–19/bed with sheets in 4- to 8-bed room, £3 extra for non-members, breakfast-£4.65, packed lunch-£5, dinner-£9, reception open daily 8:00–10:00 & 16:00–22:00, hostel closed Dec–Jan, Military Road, Bardon Mill, tel. 01434/344-360, fax 01434/344-045, www.yha.org.uk, once brewed@yha.org.uk). The Hadrian's Wall bus #AD122 stops here several times a day.

Other B&Bs include **$$ Vallum Lodge** (Db-£75–80, Military Road, tel. 01434/344-248, www.vallum-lodge.co.uk) and **$$ Gibbs Hill Farm B&B and Hostel** (Db-£60–70, 5-min drive from Housesteads and Vindolanda, tel. 01434/344-030, www .gibbshillfarm.co.uk).

Milecastle Inn cooks up all sorts of exotic game and offers the best dinner around, according to hungry national park rangers (daily 12:00–20:30, smart to reserve, North Road, tel. 01434/321-372).

In Haltwhistle
(area code: 01434)

$$ Ashcroft Guest House, a former vicarage, is 400 yards from the Haltwhistle train station and 200 yards from a Hadrian's Wall bus stop. The family-run B&B has nine rooms, pleasant gardens, and views from the comfy lounge (Sb-£38, Db-£76, four-poster Db-£88, ask about family deals and two-bedroom suite, free Wi-Fi, 1.5 miles from the wall, Lanty's Lonnen, tel. 01434/320-213, www.ashcroftguesthouse.co.uk, info@ashcroftguesthouse .co.uk, Geoff and Christine James).

Near Carlisle
(area code: 01228)

$$$ Bessiestown Farm Country Guest House, located north-west of the Hadrian sights, is convenient for drivers connecting the Lake District and Scotland. It's a quiet and soothing stop in the middle of sheep pastures (Sb-£57, Db-£98, family room-£99–110, fancier suites-£130, discounts for 3-night stays; in Catlowdy, midway between Gretna Green and Hadrian's Wall just north of Carlisle; tel. 01228/577-219, fax 01228/577-019, www.bessiestown .co.uk, info@bessiestown.co.uk, Margaret Sisson).

Holy Island and Bamburgh Castle

This area is worthwhile only for those with a car.

▲Holy Island

Twelve hundred years ago, this "Holy Island" was Christianity's toehold on England. It was the home of St. Cuthbert. We know it today for the *Lindisfarne Gospels*, decorated by monks in the seventh century with some of the finest art from Europe's "Dark Ages" (now in the British Museum). It's a pleasant visit—a quiet town with a striking castle (not worth touring) and an evocative priory.

Lindisfarne Priory: The museum in the priory is tiny but instructive. It's adjacent to the ruined abbey (£4.50; April–Sept daily 9:30–17:00; Oct daily 9:30–16:00; Nov–Jan Mon and Sat–Sun 10:00–14:00, closed Tue–Fri; Feb–March daily 10:00–16:00; tel. 01289/389-200, www.english-heritage.org.uk/LindisfarnePriory). You can wander the abbey grounds and graveyard, and pop in to the church without paying.

Holy Island is reached by a two-mile causeway that's cut off daily by high tides. Tidal charts are posted, warning you when this holy place becomes Holy Island—and you become stranded.

For TI and tide information, check with the **Berwick TI** (generally May–Sept Mon–Sat 10:00–17:00, Sun 11:00–15:00; Oct–April Mon–Sat 10:00–16:00, closed Sun; tel. 01289/330-733, berwicktic@northumberland.gov.uk). Park at the pay-and-display lot and walk five minutes into the town.

▲▲Bamburgh Castle

About 10 miles south of Holy Island, this grand castle dominates the Northumbrian countryside, and overlooks Britain's loveliest beach. The place was bought and passionately refurbished by Lord Armstrong, a Ted Turner–like industrialist and engineer in the 1890s. Its interior, lined with well-described history, feels lived-in because it still is—with Armstrong family portraits and aristocratic-yet-homey knickknacks hanging everywhere. Take advantage of the talkative guides posted throughout the castle. The included **Armstrong Museum** features the inventions of the industrialist family that has owned the castle through modern times (£7.50, daily March–Oct 10:00–17:00, last entry at 16:00, closed Nov–Feb, tel. 01668/214-515, www.bamburghcastle.com). Crisscrossed by walking paths, rolling dunes lead to a vast sandy beach and lots of families on holiday.

BRITISH HISTORY AND CULTURE

Britain was created by force and held together by force. It's really a nation of the 19th century, when this rich Victorian-era empire reached its financial peak. Its traditional industry, buildings, and the popularity of the notion of "Great" Britain are a product of its past wealth.

To best understand the many fascinating guides you'll encounter in your travels, have a basic handle on the sweeping story of this land. (Generally speaking, the nice and bad stories are not true... and the boring ones are.)

What's So Great About Britain?

Regardless of the revolution we had 230-some years ago, many American travelers feel that they "go home" to Britain. This most popular tourist destination has a strange influence and power over us. The more you know of Britain's roots, the better you'll get in touch with your own.

Geographically, the Isle of Britain is small (about the size of Uganda or Idaho)—600 miles long and 300 miles at its widest point. England occupies the southeastern part of Britain (with about 60 percent of its land—similar in size to Louisiana—and 80 percent of its population). England's highest mountain (Scafell Pike in the Lake District) is 3,206 feet, a foothill by our standards. The population is a fifth that of the United States. At its peak in the mid-1800s, Britain owned one-fifth of the world and accounted for more than half the planet's industrial output. Today, the Empire is down to the Isle of Britain itself and a few token, troublesome scraps, such as the Falklands, Gibraltar, and Northern Ireland.

Economically, Great Britain's industrial production is about five percent of the world's total. After emerging from a recession in 1992, Britain's economy enjoyed its longest period of expansion on record. But in 2008, the global economic slowdown, tight credit, and falling home prices pushed Britain back into a recession.

Culturally, Britain is still a world leader. Her heritage, culture, and people cannot be measured in traditional units of power. London is a major exporter of actors, movies, and theater; of rock and classical music; and of writers, painters, and sculptors.

Ethnically, the British Isles are a mix of the descendants of the early Celtic natives (in Scotland, Ireland, Wales, and Cornwall), descendants of the invading Anglo-Saxons who took southeast England in the Dark Ages, and descendants of the conquering Normans of the 11th century...not to mention more recent immigrants from around the world. Cynics call the United Kingdom an English Empire ruled by London, whose dominant Anglo-Saxon English (50 million) far outnumber their Celtic brothers and sisters (10 million).

Politically, Britain is ruled by the House of Commons, with some guidance from the mostly figurehead Queen and House of Lords. Just as the United States Congress is dominated by Democrats and Republicans, Britain's Parliament is dominated by two parties: Labour and Conservative ("Tories"). (A smaller third party, the Liberal Democrats, often sides with Labour.)

The prime minister is the chief executive. He or she is not elected directly by voters; rather, he or she assumes power as the head of the party that wins a majority in Parliamentary elections. Instead of imposing term limits, the Brits allow their prime ministers to choose when to leave office. The ruling party also gets to choose when to hold elections, as long as it's within five years of the previous one—so prime ministers carefully schedule elections for times that (they hope) their party will win.

In the 1980s, Conservatives were in charge under Prime Minister Margaret Thatcher and Prime Minister John Major. As proponents of traditional, Victorian values—community, family, hard work, thrift, and trickle-down economics—they took a Reaganesque approach to Britain's serious social and economic problems.

In 1997, a huge Labour victory brought Tony Blair to the prime ministership. Labour began shoring up a social-service system (health care, education, the minimum wage) undercut by years of Conservative rule. Blair's Labour Party was "New Labour"—akin to Clinton's "New Democrats"—meaning they were fiscally conservative but attentive to the needs of the people. Conservative Party fears of big-spending, bleeding-heart liberalism proved unfounded. The Labour-controlled parliament was also more open to integration with Europe.

Tony Blair started out as a respected and well-liked PM. But after he followed US President George W. Bush into war

Gordon Brown, Prime Minister

Brown, who comes from a humble fishing village in Scotland, was an academic whiz kid who entered the University of Edinburgh at age 16. While he earned a PhD in history there, politics became his overriding passion—enough to ruin a love affair with a Romanian princess. As he rose through the Labour Party ranks, he gained a reputation as a staid and gruff policy wonk. At first accused by the national press of being shifty-eyed (and therefore untrustworthy), Brown later revealed he was actually blind in his left eye from an old rugby injury.

Brown remained a bachelor well into his forties; his wife Sarah (whom he married in 2000) initially preferred to avoid the limelight—which wasn't helping the Browns' popularity. In summer 2009, however, she suddenly came out of hiding, making sure to be photographed at trendy events and posting daily Twitter updates (at this writing, she had 500,000 followers). Of the Browns' three children, one lived only 10 days, and another has been diagnosed with cystic fibrosis—one of the few aspects of Brown's personal life that has garnered him sympathy.

Brown refused to disavow Britain's Iraq involvement, further damaging Labour's popularity. The British media continue to mercilessly lampoon the beleaguered Brown as gloomy, plodding, and boring. As Britain's financial woes continue, it's uncertain how long Brown will hold power. The next general election must be held by June 2010.

with Iraq, his popularity took a nosedive. In May of 2007, Blair announced that he would resign; a few weeks later, his Chancellor of the Exchequer and longtime colleague, Gordon Brown, was sworn in as Britain's new prime minister.

Looking to the future, London is gearing up to host the 2012 Olympic Games.

Challenges Facing Today's Britain

Great as Britain is, the country has its share of challenges. You'll likely hear people talking about some of the following hot-button topics during your visit: the war in Afghanistan, terrorism, immigration, and binge-drinking.

British forces ended combat operations in Iraq in April 2009—but troops remain in Afghanistan, and every new casualty re-invigorates public debate about the merits and possible outcomes of this war.

Like the US, Britain has been coping with its own string of terrorist threats and attacks. On the morning of July 7, 2005, London's commuters were rocked by four different bombs that killed dozens across the city. In the summer of 2006, authorities foiled a plot to carry liquid bombs onto a plane (resulting in the liquid ban air travelers are still experiencing today). On June 29, 2007—just two days after Gordon Brown became prime minister—two car bombs were discovered (and defused) near London's Piccadilly Circus, and the next day, a flaming car drove into the baggage-claim level at Glasgow Airport. Most Brits have accepted that they now live with the possibility of terrorism at home—and that life must go on.

Britain has taken aggressive measures to prevent future attacks, such as installing "CCTV" (closed-circuit) surveillance cameras everywhere, in both public and private places. (You'll frequently see signs warning you that you're being filmed.) These cameras have already proved helpful in piecing together the events leading up to an attack, but as Brits trade their privacy for security, many wonder if they've given up too much.

The terrorist threats have also highlighted issues relating to Britain's large immigrant population (nearly 4 million). Second-generation Muslims—born in Britain, but who strongly identify with other Muslims rather than their British neighbors—were responsible for the July 2005 bombs. Some Brits reacted to the event known as "7/7" as if all the country's Muslims were to blame. At the same time, a handful of radical Islamic clerics began to justify the bombers' violent actions. Unemployment and the economic downturn further stretch the already strained relations between communities within Britain.

The large Muslim population is just one thread in the tapestry of today's Britain. While nine out of ten Brits are white, the country has large minority groups, mainly from Britain's former overseas colonies: India, Pakistan, Bangladesh, Africa, the Caribbean, and many other places. But despite the tensions between some groups, for the most part Britain is well integrated, with minorities represented in most (if not all) walks of life.

Recently another wave of immigration has hit Britain. Throughout the British Isles, you'll see many Eastern Europeans (mostly Poles, Slovaks, and Lithuanians) working in restaurants, cafés, and B&Bs. These transplants—who started arriving after their home countries joined the EU in 2004—can make a lot more money working here than back home. British small-business owners tell me they find these new arrivals to be polite, responsible, and affordable. While a few Brits complain that the new arrivals are taking jobs away from the natives, and others are frustrated that their English is often far from perfect, for the most part Britain has absorbed this new set of immigrants gracefully.

Over the last several years, Britain has seen an epidemic of binge-drinking among young people. A 2007 study revealed that one out of every three British men, and one out of every five British women, routinely drink to excess. It's become commonplace for young adults (typically from their mid-teens to mid-20s) to spend weekend nights drinking at pubs and carousing in the streets. (And they ratchet up the debauchery even more when celebrating a "stag night" or "hen night"—bachelor and bachelorette parties.) While sociologists and politicians scratch their heads about the causes and effects of this phenomenon, tourists are complaining about weekend noise and obnoxious (though generally harmless) young drunks on the streets.

Basic British History for the Traveler

When Julius Caesar landed on the misty and mysterious isle of Britain in 55 B.C., England entered the history books. The primitive Celtic tribes he conquered were themselves invaders (who had earlier conquered the even more mysterious people who built Stonehenge). The Romans built towns and roads, establishing their capital at Londinium. The Celtic natives in Scotland and Wales—consisting of Gaels, Picts, and Scots—were not easily subdued. The Romans built Hadrian's Wall near the Scottish border as protection against their troublesome northern neighbors. Even today, the Celtic language and influence are strongest in these far reaches of Britain.

As Rome fell, so fell Roman Britain, a victim of invaders and internal troubles. Barbarian tribes from Germany and Denmark, called Angles and Saxons, swept through the southern part of the island, establishing Angle-land. These were the days of the real King Arthur, possibly a Christianized Roman general who fought valiantly against invading barbarians, but in vain. In 793, England was hit with the first of two centuries of savage invasions by barbarians from Norway, called the Vikings or Norsemen. The island was plunged into 500 years of Dark Ages—wars, plagues, and poverty—lit only by the dim candle of a few learned Christian monks and missionaries trying to convert the barbarians. The sightseer sees little from this Anglo-Saxon period.

Modern England began with yet another invasion. William the Conqueror and his Norman troops crossed the English Channel from France in 1066. William crowned himself king in Westminster Abbey (where all subsequent coronations would take place) and began building the Tower of London. French-speaking Norman kings ruled the country for two centuries. Then followed two centuries of civil wars, with various noble families vying for the crown. In one of the most bitter feuds, the York and Lancaster families fought the Wars of the Roses, so-called because of the white and red flowers the combatants chose as their symbols. Rife with battles, intrigues, and kings, nobles, and ladies imprisoned and executed in the Tower, it's a wonder the country survived its rulers.

England was finally united by the "third-party" Tudor family. Henry VIII, a Tudor, was England's Renaissance king. He was handsome, athletic, highly sexed, a poet, a scholar, and a musician. He was also arrogant, cruel, gluttonous, and paranoid. He went through six wives in 40 years, divorcing, imprisoning, or beheading them when they no longer suited his needs.

Henry "divorced" England from the Catholic Church, establishing the Protestant Church of England (the Anglican Church) and setting in motion years of religious squabbles. He also "dissolved" the monasteries (circa 1540), left just the shells of many formerly glorious abbeys dotting the countryside, and pocketed their land and wealth for the crown.

Henry's daughter, Queen Elizabeth I, who reigned for 45 years, made England a great trading and naval power (defeating the Spanish Armada) and presided over the Elizabethan era of great writers (such as William Shakespeare) and scientists (such as Francis Bacon).

The longstanding quarrel between England's divine-right kings and Parliament's nobles finally erupted into a civil war (1643). Parliament forces under the Protestant Puritan farmer Oliver Cromwell defeated—and beheaded—King Charles I. This civil war left its mark on much of what you'll see in Britain. Eventually, Parliament invited Charles' son to take the throne. This "restoration of the monarchy" was accompanied by a great colonial expansion and the rebuilding of London (including Christopher Wren's St. Paul's Cathedral), which had been devastated by the Great Fire of 1666.

Britain grew as a naval superpower, colonizing and trading with all parts of the globe. Admiral Horatio Nelson's victory over Napoleon's fleet at the Battle of Trafalgar secured her naval superiority ("Britannia rules the waves"), and 10 years later, the Duke of Wellington stomped Napoleon on land at Waterloo. Nelson and Wellington—both buried in London's St. Paul's Cathedral—are memorialized by many arches, columns, and squares throughout England.

Economically, Britain led the world into the Industrial Age with her mills, factories, coal mines, and trains. By the time of Queen Victoria's reign (1837–1901), Britain was at its zenith of power, with a colonial empire that covered one-fifth of the world.

The 20th century was not kind to Britain. Two world wars devastated the population. The Nazi blitzkrieg reduced much of London to rubble. The colonial empire dwindled to almost nothing, and Britain lost its superpower economic status. The war over the Falkland Islands in 1982 showed how little of the British Empire is left—and how determined the British are to hang on to what remains.

A Typical Castle

A castle is a fortified residence for a medieval noble. Castles come in all shapes and sizes. The simplest "motte-and-bailey" castle consists of a stone tower (a "keep") on a hill (a "motte"), surrounded by a wall that enclosed a yard (or "bailey"). Later castles were much bigger, with more rings of walls, more towers, ingenious booby-traps, and comfy buildings for life during peacetime. Though most castles today are ruins, you can mentally recon-struct them if you know the main features. Be aware that you may see several dif-ferent names for the same thing, depending on the country.

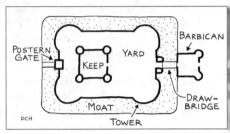

The Keep (or Donjon): The heart of the castle complex was a high, strong stone tower that was the lord's home and refuge of last resort. Inside (or nearby) you'd find the Great Hall—the largest room in the castle, serving as throne room, conference center, and dining hall, hosting epic banquets. Upstairs was the "solar," the lord's sunlit living room.

The Yard (or Bailey or Ward): Safe within the castle walls was an open courtyard dotted with small half-timbered build-ings. In peacetime, knights held jousting tournaments in the yard. During war, when peasants retreated inside the walls for safety, the yard became a mini-village. There was a well and cistern (for crucial water); a kitchen and well-stocked pantry; the chapel; an armory, kennel, and stables; humble cottages for peasants and plusher lodgings for knights; and the garderobe—an outhouse protruding from the wall that emptied into a cesspit.

The Wall: While the main wall surrounded the inner yard and keep, a castle might also have a series of concentric walls offering more lines of defense and enclosing more yards (e.g., the "outer yard" or the "lower bailey").

Walls were made of "ashlar" (stone blocks) and stretched like a "curtain wall" between corner towers. The base of the wall might angle out to make it more difficult for invaders to scale the walls. Narrow slits in the walls, called "loopholes," allowed soldiers to shoot arrows at the enemy while remaining mostly protected.

Towers: Towers on the castle corners helped shore up the walls and served as lookouts. Inside, they housed chapels, living quarters, or the dungeon. Towers could be square or round (e.g., a "drum tower"), with either crenellated tops or conical roofs. A "turret" is a small lookout tower projecting up from the top of the wall and a "bartizan" juts out from a corner.

BRITISH HISTORY

Moat: A ditch circled the wall, often filled with water—but not with crocodiles (despite what you may have seen in cartoons).

Wall Walk (or Allure) and Parapet: Atop the wall was a pathway where guards could patrol and where soldiers stood to fire at the enemy. The soldiers were protected by the parapet, or outer railing of the wall walk. The parapet was studded with stone blocks in a gap-tooth pattern called crenellation. A soldier could hide behind the blocks and shoot through the gaps in between.

Hoardings and Machicolation: Wooden huts called hoardings were built onto the upper parts of the stone walls. They served as watch towers, living quarters, and fighting platforms. A machicolation was a stone ledge jutting out from the wall, fitted with holes in the bottom. If the enemy was scaling the walls, soldiers could drop rocks or boiling oil down through the holes and onto the enemy below.

Gatehouse or Barbican: The castle's main entrance had a variety of ways to control entry. A barbican—a fortified, second gatehouse—might stand outside the castle walls to protect the main gate. In case of attack, a drawbridge could be raised, using counterweights or a chain-and-winch. A heavy iron grill called a portcullis could be lowered across the entrance. If the enemy made it into the gatehouse, soldiers could pour boiling water on them through "murder holes" in the ceiling.

Castles also had a smaller, low-profile "postern gate" around the side. In peacetime, peasants used this unfortified entrance. In wartime, it became the "sally-port" to launch surprise attacks, or to serve as an escape route.

The Besiegers: Before the era of gunpowder, an attacker's main weapon against a big castle was patience—the siege. Armies surrounded the castle, blocked off all supplies, and waited for the enemy to surrender.

They could also attack by undermining ("sapping") the walls, scaling the walls with ladders, or knocking down the gates with a battering ram—a large log suspended with ropes and swung against the door. A siege tower (or belfry) was a wooden tower on wheels that could be rolled to the castle walls and used like a giant fortified ladder. Catapults such as the mighty trebuchet could hurl a one-ton boulder over the walls.

What we don't see: Because most castles are old and ruined, we don't see the half-timbered cottages and wooden structures that once fleshed out the stone castles. Look for square holes in ruined walls that once held the beams supporting the wooden floors. We don't see the whitewashed walls, the frescoes, the tapestries used for insulation, shields with coats-of-arms, or the colorful banners that once flew atop towers. We don't see the knights on horseback, troubadours in tights, ladies in cone-shaped hats, earthy peasants, friars in brown robes, or angry soldiers atop the walls, hurling curses at the enemy.

Royal Families: Past and Present

Royal Lineage

802–1066	Saxon and Danish kings
1066–1154	Norman invasion (William the Conqueror), Norman kings
1154–1399	Plantagenet (kings with French roots)
1399–1461	Lancaster
1462–1485	York
1485–1603	Tudor (Henry VIII, Elizabeth I)
1603–1649	Stuart (civil war and beheading of Charles I)
1649–1653	Commonwealth, no royal head of state
1653–1659	Protectorate, with Cromwell as Lord Protector
1660–1714	Restoration of Stuart monarchy
1714–1901	Hanover (four Georges, Victoria)
1901–1910	Saxe-Coburg (Edward VII)
1910–present	Windsor (George V, Edward VIII, George VI, Elizabeth II)

The Royal Family Today

It seems you can't pick up a British newspaper without some mention of the latest scandal or oddity involving the royal family. Here is the cast of characters:

Queen Elizabeth II wears the traditional crown of her great-great grandmother Victoria. Her husband is Prince Philip, who's not considered king.

Their son, Prince Charles (the Prince of Wales), is next in line to become king. In 1981, Charles married Lady Diana Spencer

BRITISH HISTORY

Another post-Empire hot spot—Northern Ireland, plagued by the "Troubles" between Catholics and Protestants—is cooling off. In the spring of 2007, the unthinkable happened when leaders of the ultra-nationalist party sat down with those of the ultra-unionist party. London returned control of Northern Ireland to the popularly elected Northern Ireland Assembly. Perhaps most important of all, after almost 40 years, the British Army withdrew from Northern Ireland that summer.

The tradition (if not the substance) of greatness continues, presided over by Queen Elizabeth II, her husband, Prince Philip, and their son Prince Charles. With economic problems, the marital turmoil of Charles and the late Princess Diana, and a relentless popular press, the royal family has had a tough time. But the

(Princess Di) who, after their bitter divorce, died in a car crash in 1997. Their two sons, William and Harry, are next in line to the throne after their father. In 2005, Charles married his longtime girlfriend, Camilla Parker Bowles, who is trying to gain respectability with the Queen and the public. But she's not allowed to call herself a princess yet—her current title is Duchess of Cornwall (she'll be Princess Consort—not "Queen"—if and when Charles becomes king).

Prince Charles' siblings are occasionally in the news: Princess Anne, Prince Andrew (who married and divorced Sarah "Fergie" Ferguson), and Prince Edward (who married Di look-alike Sophie Rhys-Jones).

But it's Prince Charles' sons who generate the tabloid buzz these days. Handsome Prince William (b. 1982), a graduate of Scotland's St. Andrews University and an officer in both the Royal Air Force and Royal Navy, serves as the royal family's public face at many charity events, when he's not fulfilling his ongoing military obligations. There's endless speculation about his romantic interests, especially about his long-time, on-again-off-again girlfriend, Kate Middleton (a commoner he met at university). Whomever he marries may eventually become Britain's queen.

Redheaded Prince Harry (b. 1984) made a media splash as a bad boy when he wore a Nazi armband (as an ill-advised joke) to a costume party. Since then, he's proved his mettle as a career soldier. His combat deployment to Iraq was cancelled because of fears his presence would endanger fellow troops, but he served two months in Afghanistan (early 2008). In 2008, he and his regiment did charity work in Africa, and since then he's been training to become a pilot with the Army Air Corps. Harry's love life, like his brother's, is a popular topic for the tabloids.

For more on the monarchy, see www.royal.gov.uk.

queen has stayed above it all, and most British people still jump at an opportunity to see royalty. With the 1997 death of Princess Diana and the historic outpouring of grief, it was clear that the concept of royalty is still alive and well as Britain entered the third millennium.

Queen Elizabeth, who turns 84 in 2010, marked her 57th year on the throne in 2009. While many wonder who will succeed her, the case is fairly straightforward: The queen sees her job as a lifelong position, and legally, Charles (who wants to be king) cannot be skipped over for his son, William. Given the longevity in the family (the queen's mum, born in August of 1900, made it to 101 before she died in 2002), Charles is in for a long wait.

Architecture in Britain

From Stonehenge to Big Ben, travelers are storming castle walls, climbing spiral staircases, and snapping the pictures of 5,000 years of architecture. Let's sort it out.

The oldest ruins—mysterious and prehistoric—date from before Roman times back to 3000 B.C. The earliest sites, such as Stonehenge and Avebury, were built during the Stone and Bronze ages. The remains from these periods are made of huge stones or mounds of earth, even man-made hills, and were created as celestial calendars and for worship or burial. Britain is crisscrossed with lines of these mysterious sights (ley lines). Iron Age people (600 B.C.–A.D. 50) left desolate stone forts. The Romans thrived in Britain from A.D. 50 to 400, building cities, walls, and roads. Evidence of Roman greatness can be seen in lavish villas with ornate mosaic floors, temples uncovered beneath great English churches, and Roman stones in medieval city walls. Roman roads sliced across the island in straight lines. Today, unusually straight rural roads are very likely laid directly on these ancient roads.

As Rome crumbled in the fifth century, so did Roman Britain. Little architecture survives from Dark Ages England, the Saxon period from 500 to 1000. Architecturally, the light was switched on with the Norman Conquest in 1066. As William earned his title "the Conqueror," his French architects built churches and castles in the European Romanesque style.

English Romanesque is called Norman (1066–1200). Norman churches had round arches, thick walls, and small windows; Durham Cathedral and the Chapel of St. John in the Tower of London are prime examples. The Tower of London, with its square keep, small windows, and spiral stone stairways, is a typical Norman castle. You'll see plenty of Norman castles—all built to secure the conquest of these invaders from Normandy.

Gothic architecture (1200–1600) replaced the heavy Norman style with light, vertical buildings, pointed arches, soaring spires, and bigger windows. English Gothic is divided into three stages. Early English (1200–1300) features tall, simple spires; beautifully carved capitals; and elaborate chapter houses (such as the Wells Cathedral). Decorated Gothic (1300–1400) gets fancier, with more elaborate tracery, bigger windows, and ornately carved pinnacles, as you'll see at Westminster Abbey. Finally, the Perpendicular Gothic style (1400–1600, also called "rectilinear") returns to square towers and emphasizes straight, uninterrupted vertical lines from ceiling to floor, with vast windows and exuberant decoration, including fan-vaulted ceilings (King's College Chapel at Cambridge). Through this evolution, the structural ribs (arches meeting at the top of the ceilings) became more and more decorative and fanciful (the most fancy being the star vaulting and fan

Typical Church Architecture

History comes to life when you visit a medieval church. Knowing a few simple terms will enrich your experience. Note that not every church will have every feature, and a "cathedral" isn't a type of church architecture, but rather a governing center for a local bishop.

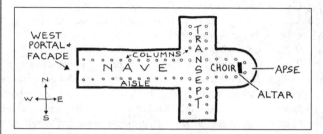

Aisles: The long, generally low-ceilinged arcades that flank the nave.

Altar: The raised area with a ceremonial table (often adorned with candles or a crucifix), where the priest prepares and serves the bread and wine for Communion.

Apse: The space beyond the altar, generally bordered with small chapels.

Choir: A cozy area, often screened off, located within the church nave and near the high altar where services are sung in a more intimate setting.

Cloister: A square-shaped series of hallways surrounding an open-air courtyard, traditionally where monks and nuns got fresh air.

Facade: The outer wall of the church's main (west) entrance, viewable from outside and generally highly decorated.

Groin Vault: An arched ceiling formed where two equal barrel vaults meet at right angles. Less common usage: term for a medieval jock strap.

Narthex: The area (portico or foyer) between the main entry and the nave.

Nave: The long, central section of the church (running west to east, from the entrance to the altar) where the congregation stood through the service.

Transept: The north–south part of the church, which crosses (perpendicularly) the east–west nave. In a traditional Latin cross-shaped floor plan, the transept forms the "arms" of the cross.

West Portal: The main entry to the church (on the west end, opposite the main altar).

vaulting of the Perpendicular style).

As you tour the great medieval churches of Britain, remember that almost everything is symbolic. For instance, on the tombs of knights, if the figure has crossed legs, he was a Crusader. If his feet rest on a dog, he died at home, but if the legs rest on a lion, he died in battle. Local guides and books help us modern pilgrims understand at least a little of what we see.

Gothic houses were a simple mix of woven strips of thin wood, rubble, and plaster called wattle and daub. The famous black-and-white Tudor (or "half-timbered") look came simply from filling in heavy oak frames with wattle and daub.

The Tudor period (1485–1560) was a time of relative peace (the Wars of the Roses were finally over), prosperity, and renaissance. Henry VIII broke with the Catholic Church and "dissolved" (destroyed) the monasteries, leaving scores of Britain's greatest churches as gutted shells. These hauntingly beautiful abbey ruins (Glastonbury, Tintern, Whitby, Rievaulx, Battle, St. Augustine's in Canterbury, St. Mary's in York, and lots more) surrounded by lush lawns are now pleasant city parks.

Although few churches were built during the Tudor period, this was a time of house and mansion construction. Heating a home was becoming popular and affordable, and Tudor buildings featured small square windows and many chimneys. In towns, where land was scarce, many Tudor houses grew up and out, getting wider with each overhanging floor.

The Elizabethan and Jacobean periods (1560–1620) were followed by the English Renaissance style (1620–1720). English architects mixed Gothic and classical styles, then Baroque and classical styles. Although the ornate Baroque never really grabbed Britain, the classical style of the Italian architect Andrea Palladio did. Inigo Jones (1573–1652), Christopher Wren (1632–1723), and those they inspired plastered Britain with enough columns, domes, and symmetry to please a Caesar. The Great Fire of London (1666) cleared the way for an ambitious young Wren to put his mark on London forever with a grand rebuilding scheme, including the great St. Paul's Cathedral and more than 50 other churches.

The celebrants of the Boston Tea Party remember Britain's Georgian period (1720–1840) for its lousy German kings. Georgian architecture was rich and showed off by being very classical. Grand ornamental doorways, fine cast-ironwork on balconies and railings, Chippendale furniture, and white-on-blue Wedgwood ceramics graced rich homes everywhere. John Wood Jr. and Sr. led the way, giving the trendsetting city of Bath its crescents and circles of aristocratic Georgian row houses. "Georgian" is English for "Neoclassical."

The Industrial Revolution shaped the Victorian period (1840–1890) with glass, steel, and iron. Britain had a huge new erector set (so did France's Mr. Eiffel). This was also a Romantic period, reviving the "more Christian" Gothic style. London's Houses of Parliament are Neo-Gothic—just 100 years old but looking 700, except for the telltale modern precision and craftsmanship. Whereas Gothic was stone or concrete, Neo-Gothic was often red brick. These were Britain's glory days, and there was more building in this period than in all previous ages combined.

The architecture of modern times obeys the formula "form follows function"—it worries more about your needs than your eyes. Britain treasures its heritage and takes great pains to build tastefully in historic districts and to preserve its many "listed" buildings. With a booming tourist trade, these quaint reminders of its past—and ours—are becoming a valuable part of the British economy.

British TV

Although it has its share of lowbrow reality programming, much British television is still so good—and so British—that it deserves a mention as a sightseeing treat. After a hard day of castle climbing, watch the telly over tea in the living room of your village B&B.

There are currently five free channels that any television can receive. BBC-1 and BBC-2 are government-regulated and commercial-free. Broadcasting of these two channels (and of the five BBC radio stations) is funded by a mandatory £142-per-year-per-household television and radio license (hmmm, 65 cents per day to escape commercials and public-broadcasting pledge drives). Channels 3, 4, and 5 are privately owned, are a little more lowbrow, and have commercials—but those commercials are often clever and sophisticated, providing a fun look at British life. In addition, about 85 percent of households now receive digital cable or satellite television, which offer dozens of specialty channels, similar to those available in North America.

Like the US, Britain is joining the Digital Age, gradually converting its TV signals to digital-only, which requires a digitally equipped set or a converter. By 2013, the old analog signals will be switched off and only digital signals will be broadcast.

Whereas California "accents" fill our airwaves 24 hours a day, homogenizing the way our country speaks, Britain protects and promotes its regional accents by its choice of TV and radio announcers. See if you can tell where each is from (or ask a local for help).

Commercial-free British TV, while looser than it used to be, is still careful about what it airs and when. But after the 21:00 "watershed" hour, when children are expected to be in bed, some nudity and profanity is allowed, and may cause you to spill your tea.

American programs (such as *Mad Men, Lost, Oprah,* and trash-talk shows) are very popular. The visiting viewer should be sure to tune the TV to a few typical British shows, including a dose of British situation- and political-comedy fun, and the top-notch BBC evening news. British comedies have tickled the American funny bone for years, from sketch comedy *(Monty Python's Flying Circus)* to sitcoms (such as *Are You Being Served?, Fawlty Towers,* and *Absolutely Fabulous*). A more recent cross-the-pond mega-hit, *The Office,* has made its star Ricky Gervais the top name in British comedy today, and has spawned successful adaptations in the US, Germany, France, and French Canada. Quiz shows and reality shows are taken very seriously here (*Who Wants to Be a Millionaire?, American Idol,* and *Dancing with the Stars* are all based on British shows). Jonathan Ross is the David Letterman of Britain for sometimes edgy late-night talk. For a tear-filled, slice-of-life taste of British soaps dealing in all the controversial issues, see the popular *Emmerdale, Coronation Street,* or *EastEnders.*

APPENDIX

Contents

Tourist Information

Tourist Offices

The **Visit Britain** office in the US is a wealth of knowledge. Check it out: tel. 800-462-2748, www.visitbritain.com, travelinfo@visit britain.org. Request free maps of London and Britain and any specific information you may want (such as regional information, a garden-tour map, urban cultural activities brochures, and so on). The phone line is mainly intended as a customer service number for their online shop, and isn't staffed (but they do check their messages). For most questions it's best to enquire by email.

In England, your best first stop in every town is generally the **tourist information office**—abbreviated TI in this book. (The **Britain and London Visitors Centre** in London is particularly good—see page 45.) A TI is a great place to get a city map, advice on public transportation (including bus and train schedules), walking-tour information, information on special events, and recommendations for nightlife. For all the help TIs offer, steer clear of their room-finding services (bloated prices, booking fee up to £4, no opinions, and they take a 10 percent cut from your B&B host). Many TIs have information on the entire country or at least the region, so try to pick up maps for destinations that you'll be visiting later in your trip. If you're arriving in town after the TI closes, call ahead or pick up a map in a neighboring town.

Communicating

Telephones

Smart travelers use the telephone daily to book or reconfirm rooms, get tourist information, reserve restaurants, confirm tour times, or phone home. This section covers dialing instructions, phone cards, and types of phones.

In sum, the cheapest way to go is to buy an international phone card in Britain and make your calls from hotel-room phones or mobile phones, but not pay phones. The handiest—though pricier—way to make calls is by using your mobile phone (brought from home or purchased in Britain).

How to Dial

Calling from the US to Britain, or vice versa, is simple—once you break the code. The European calling chart in this chapter will walk you through it.

Dialing Domestically Within Britain

Britain, like much of the US, uses an area-code dialing system. If you're dialing within an area code, you just dial the local number to be connected; but if you're calling outside your area code, you have to dial both the area code (which starts with a 0) and the local number.

Area codes are listed in this book and by city on phone-booth walls, and are available from directory assistance (dial 118-500, 64p/min). It's most expensive to call within Britain between 8:00 and 13:00, and cheapest between 17:00 and 8:00. Still, a short call across the country is inexpensive; don't hesitate to call long distance.

Dialing Internationally to or from Britain

If you want to make an international call, follow these steps:

1. Dial the international access code (00 if you're calling from Britain, 011 from the US or Canada).

2. Dial the country code of the country you're calling (see European Calling Chart in this chapter).

3. Dial the area code and the local number, keeping in mind

The English Accent

In the olden days, an English person's accent indicated his or her social standing. Eliza Doolittle had the right idea—elocution could make or break you. Wealthier families would send their kids to fancy private schools to learn proper pronunciation. But these days, in a sort of reverse snobbery that has gripped the nation, accents are back. Politicians, newscasters, and movie stars have been favoring deep accents over the Queen's English. While it's hard for American ears to pick out all of the variations, most English can determine where a person is from based on his or her accent...not just the region, but often the village, and even the part of a town.

that if you're calling Britain, drop the initial zero of the area code (the European calling chart lists specifics per country).

Calling from the US to Britain: To call from the US to a recommended London hotel, dial 011 (the US international access code), 44 (Britain's country code), 20 (London's area code without its initial 0), then 7730-8191 (the hotel's number).

Calling from Britain to the US: To call from London to my office in Edmonds, Washington, I dial 00 (Europe's international access code), 1 (the US country code), 425 (Edmonds' area code), and 771-8303.

Note: You might see a + in front of a European number. When dialing the number, replace the + with the international access code of the country you're calling from (00 from Europe, 011 from the US or Canada).

Public Phones

To make calls from public phones, you'll need a lot of coins (Britain doesn't use insertable phone cards, and calls are pricey). Even prepaid international phone cards, described below, are prohibitively expensive on public phones.

Hotel-Room Phones

In-room phones are rare in B&Bs, but if you do have a phone in the room, put it to use for local calls, which are likely cheap (ask for the rates at the front desk first). However, these phones are often a rip-off for long-distance calls, unless you use an international phone card (explained below). Incoming calls are free, making this a cheap way for friends and family to stay in touch (provided they have a good long-distance plan for calls to Europe—and a list of your hotels' phone numbers).

European Calling Chart

Just smile and dial, using this key:
AC = Area Code, LN = Local Number.

European Country	Calling long distance within...	Calling from the US or Canada to...	Calling from a European country to...
Austria	AC + LN	011 + 43 + AC (without the initial zero) + LN	00 + 43 + AC (without the initial zero) + LN
Belgium	LN	011 + 32 + LN (without initial zero)	00 + 32 + LN (without initial zero)
Bosnia-Herzegovina	AC + LN	011 + 387 + AC (without initial zero) + LN	00 + 387 + AC (without initial zero) + LN
Britain	AC + LN	011 + 44 + AC (without initial zero) + LN	00 + 44 + AC (without initial zero) + LN
Croatia	AC + LN	011 + 385 + AC (without initial zero) + LN	00 + 385 + AC (without initial zero) + LN
Czech Republic	LN	011 + 420 + LN	00 + 420 + LN
Denmark	LN	011 + 45 + LN	00 + 45 + LN
Estonia	LN	011 + 372 + LN	00 + 372 + LN
Finland	AC + LN	011 + 358 + AC (without initial zero) + LN	999 + 358 + AC (without initial zero) + LN
France	LN	011 + 33 + LN (without initial zero)	00 + 33 + LN (without initial zero)
Germany	AC + LN	011 + 49 + AC (without initial zero) + LN	00 + 49 + AC (without initial zero) + LN
Gibraltar	LN	011 + 350 + LN	00 + 350 + LN
Greece	LN	011 + 30 + LN	00 + 30 + LN
Hungary	06 + AC + LN	011 + 36 + AC + LN	00 + 36 + AC + LN
Ireland	AC + LN	011 + 353 + AC (without initial zero) + LN	00 + 353 + AC (without initial zero) + LN
Italy	LN	011 + 39 + LN	00 + 39 + LN

European Country	Calling long distance within ...	Calling from the US or Canada to ...	Calling from a European country to ...
Montenegro	AC + LN	011 + 382 + AC (without initial zero) + LN	00 + 382 + AC (without initial zero) + LN
Morocco	LN	011 + 212 + LN (without initial zero)	00 + 212 + LN (without initial zero)
Netherlands	AC + LN	011 + 31 + AC (without initial zero) + LN	00 + 31 + AC (without initial zero) + LN
Norway	LN	011 + 47 + LN	00 + 47 + LN
Poland	LN	011 + 48 + LN (without initial zero)	00 + 48 + LN (without initial zero)
Portugal	LN	011 + 351 + LN	00 + 351 + LN
Slovakia	AC + LN	011 + 421 + AC (without initial zero) + LN	00 + 421 + AC (without initial zero) + LN
Slovenia	AC + LN	011 + 386 + AC (without initial zero) + LN	00 + 386 + AC (without initial zero) + LN
Spain	LN	011 + 34 + LN	00 + 34 + LN
Sweden	AC + LN	011 + 46 + AC (without initial zero) + LN	00 + 46 + AC (without initial zero) + LN
Switzerland	LN	011 + 41 + LN (without initial zero)	00 + 41 + LN (without initial zero)
Turkey	AC (if no initial zero is included, add one) + LN	011 + 90 + AC (without initial zero) + LN	00 + 90 + AC (without initial zero) + LN

- The instructions above apply whether you're calling a land line or mobile phone.
- The international access codes (the first numbers you dial when making an international call) are 011 if you're calling from the US or Canada, or 00 if you're calling from virtually anywhere in Europe (except Finland, where it's 999).
- To call the US or Canada from Europe, dial 00, then 1 (the country code for the US and Canada), then the area code and number. In short, 00 + 1 + AC + LN = Hi, Mom!

Mobile Phones

For most travelers in Britain, a mobile phone is the best option for making calls (if you need more in-depth information than we provide below, see www.ricksteves.com/phones).

Using Your Mobile Phone: Your US mobile phone works in Britain if it's GSM-enabled, tri-band or quad-band, and on a calling plan that includes international calls. For example, with a T-Mobile phone, you'll pay $1 per minute to receive a call, and about $0.35 apiece for text messages.

You can save money if your phone is electronically "unlocked"—then you can simply buy a **SIM card** (a fingernail-size chip that stores the phone's information) in Britain. SIM cards, which give you a British phone number, are sold at mobile-phone stores and some newsstand kiosks for £3–10. When you buy the card, you'll also get some prepaid calling time (£15 gives you about 30 minutes). Simply insert the SIM card in your phone (usually in a slot behind the battery), and it'll work like a British mobile phone. When buying a SIM card, always ask about fees for domestic and international calls, roaming charges, and how to check your credit balance and buy more time. To call home, save money by using an international calling card (described below).

Many **smartphones,** such as the iPhone or BlackBerry, work in Britain—but beware of sky-high fees, especially for data downloading (checking email, browsing the Internet, watching videos, and so on). Ask your provider in advance how to avoid unwittingly "roaming" your way to a huge bill. Some applications allow for cheap or free smartphone calls over a Wi-Fi connection (described under "Calling Over the Internet," below).

Using a British Mobile Phone: Local mobile-phone shops all over Britain sell basic phones for about £30–60 (as low as £10 at Carphone Warehouse chain stores). You'll also need to buy a SIM card (explained above) and prepaid credit for making calls. If you remain in the phone's home country, domestic calls are reasonable, and incoming calls are generally free. You'll pay more if you're "roaming" in another country. If your phone is "unlocked," you can swap out its SIM card for a new one when you travel to other countries.

International Phone Cards

These cards are the cheapest way to make international calls from Britain (less than $0.10 a minute to the US; they also work for local calls). But there's a catch: British Telecom charges a hefty surcharge for using international calling cards from a pay phone (so instead of 100 minutes for a £5 card, you'll get less than 10 minutes—a miserable deal). But they're still a good deal if you use them when calling from a mobile phone or fixed line (e.g., a hotel-room phone; ask at the front desk if they charge any fees for toll-free calls). The cards are sold all over; look for them at newsstand kiosks and hole-in-the-wall long-distance shops. Ask the clerk which of the various brands has the best rates for calls to the US. Because cards are occasionally duds, avoid the more expensive denominations. These cards usually work only in the country where they're purchased (unless otherwise noted on the card).

US Calling Cards: These cards, such as the ones offered by AT&T, Verizon, and Sprint, are the worst option. You'll nearly always save money by using a British international calling card instead.

Calling over the Internet

Some things that seem too good to be true...actually are true. If you're traveling with a laptop, you can make calls using VoIP (Voice over Internet Protocol). With VoIP, two computers act as the phones, and the Internet-based calls are free (or you can pay a few cents to call from your computer to a telephone). The major providers are Skype (www.skype.com) and Google Talk (www.google.com/talk).

Useful Phone Numbers

Understand the various prefixes—numbers starting with 09 are telephone-sex–type expensive. Numbers that begin with 0800 are toll-free, but numbers with prefixes of 0845, 0870, and 0871 cost about 10p per minute. If you have questions about a prefix, call 100 for free help.

Embassies and Consulates

US Consulate and Embassy: tel. 020/7499-9000, passport info tel. 020/7894-0563, passport services available Mon–Fri 8:30–11:30, Mon, Wed, Fri also 14:00–16:00 (24 Grosvenor Square, Tube: Bond Street, www.usembassy.org.uk)

Canadian High Commission: tel. 020/7258-6600, passport services available Mon–Fri 9:30–13:30 (Trafalgar Square, Tube: Charing Cross, www.unitedkingdom.gc.ca)

Emergency Needs

Police and Ambulance: tel. 999

Dialing Assistance

Operator Assistance: tel. 100 (free)

Directory Assistance: tel. 118-500 (64p/min, plus 23p/min connection charge from fixed lines)

International Directory Assistance: tel. 118-505 (£1.99/min, plus 69p connection charge)

Travel Advisories

US Department of State: US tel. 202/647-5225, www.travel
.state.gov

Canadian Department of Foreign Affairs: Canadian tel. 800-
267-6788, www.dfait-maeci.gc.ca

US Centers for Disease Control and Prevention: US tel.
800-CDC-INFO (800-232-4636), www.cdc.gov/travel

Trains and Buses

Train information for trips within England: tel. 0845-748-4950,
overseas tel. 011-44-20-7278-5240 (www.nationalrail.co.uk)

Eurostar (Chunnel Info): tel. 0870-518-6186 (www.eurostar.com)

Trains to all points in Europe: tel. 0870-584-8848 (www.rail
europe.com)

National Express Buses: tel. 0871-781-8181 (www.nationalexpress
.com)

Airports

For online information on the first three airports, check www.baa
.co.uk.

Heathrow (flight info): tel. 0870-000-0123

Gatwick (general info): tel. 0870-000-2468 for all airlines, except
British Airways—tel. 0870-551-1155 (flights) or 0870-850-9850
(booking)

Stansted (general info): tel. 0870-000-0303

Luton (general info): tel. 01582/405-100 (www.london-luton.com)

London City Airport (general info): tel. 020/7646-0088 (www
.londoncityairport.com)

Airlines

Aer Lingus: tel. 0870-876-5000, US tel. 800-474-7424 (www.aer
lingus.com)

Air Canada: tel. 0871-220-1111 (www.aircanada.com)

Alitalia: tel. 0871-424-1424 (www.alitalia.com)

American: tel. 0845-778-9789 (www.aa.com)

bmi: reservations tel. 0870-607-0555, flight info tel. 020/8745-7321
(www.flybmi.com)

British Airways: reservations tel. 0844-493-0787, flight info tel.
0844-493-0777 (www.ba.com)

Brussels Airlines: toll tel. 0905-609-5609, US tel. 516/740 5200,
40p/min (www.brusselsairlines.com)

Continental Airlines: tel. 0845-607-6760 (www.continental.com)

easyJet: tel. 0871-244-2366, 10p/min (www.easyjet.com)

KLM Royal Dutch/Northwest Airlines: tel. 0870-507-4074
(www.klm.com)

Lufthansa: tel. 0871-945-9747 (www.lufthansa.com)

Ryanair: tel. 0871-246-0000 (www.ryanair.com)
Scandinavian Airlines (SAS): tel. 0871-521-2772 (www.flysas
.com)
United Airlines: tel. 0845-844-4777 (www.unitedairlines.co.uk)
US Airways: tel. 0845-600-3300 (www.usair.com)

Heathrow Airport Car-Rental Agencies
Avis: tel. 0844-544-6000 (www.avis.co.uk)
Budget: tel. 0844-544-4600 (www.budget.co.uk)
Enterprise: tel. 020/8897-2100 (www.enterprise.co.uk)
Europcar: tel. 020/8564-3500 (www.europcar.co.uk)
Hertz: tel. 0870-846-0006 (www.hertz.co.uk)

The Internet
The Internet can be an invaluable tool for planning your trip
(researching and booking hotels, checking bus and train sched-

ules, and so on). It's also useful
to get online periodically as
you travel—to reconfirm your
trip plans, check the weather,
catch up on email, blog or post
photos from your trip, or call
folks back home (explained
earlier, under "Calling Over
the Internet").

Some hotels offer a com-
puter in the lobby with Internet access for guests. If you ask politely,
smaller B&Bs may sometimes let you sit at their desk for a few
minutes just to check your email. If you're traveling with a laptop,
see if your hotel has Wi-Fi (wireless Internet access) or a port in
your room where you can plug in a cable to get online. Most hotels
offer Internet access and/or Wi-Fi for free; others charge a fee.

If your hotel doesn't have access, ask your hotelier to direct
you to the nearest place to get online. Most of the towns where I've
listed accommodations in this book also have Internet cafés. Many
libraries offer free access, but they also tend to have limited opening hours, restrict your online time to 30 minutes, and may require
reservations.

Mail
Get stamps at the neighborhood post office, newsstands within
fancy hotels, and some mini-marts and card shops. While you can
arrange for mail delivery to your hotel (allow 10 days for a letter to
arrive), phoning and emailing are so easy that I've dispensed with
mail stops altogether.

Transportation

By Car or Train?

Cars are best for three or more traveling together (especially families with small kids), those packing heavy, and those scouring the countryside. Trains and buses are best for solo travelers, blitz tourists, and city-to-city travelers. While a car gives you the ultimate in mobility and freedom, enables you to search for hotels more easily, and carries your bags for you, the train zips you effortlessly from city to city, usually dropping you in the center and near the tourist office.

England has a great train-and-bus system, and travelers who don't want (or can't afford) to drive a rental car can enjoy an excellent tour using public transportation. England's 100-mph train system is one of Europe's best. Buses pick you up when the trains let you down.

In England, my choice is to connect big cities by train and to explore rural areas (Cornwall, Dartmoor, the Cotswolds, and the Lake District) footloose and fancy-free by rental car. The mix works quite efficiently (e.g., London, Bath, and York by train, with a rental car for the rest). You might consider a BritRail & Drive Pass, which gives you various combinations of rail days and car days to use within two months' time.

Deals on Rails, Wheels, and Wings

Regular tickets on England's great train system (15,000 departures from 2,400 stations daily) are the most expensive per mile in all of Europe. Those who save the biggest are those who book in advance, leave after rush hour (after 9:30), or ride the bus. Now that Britain has privatized its railways, it can be tricky to track down all your options; a single bus or train route can be operated by several companies. However, one British website covers all train lines (www.nationalrail.co.uk), and another covers all bus and train routes in Britain (www.traveline.org.uk). Another good resource, which also has schedules for trains throughout Europe, is German Rail's timetable (http://bahn.hafas.de/bin/query.exe/en).

As with airline tickets, British train tickets can come at many different prices for the same journey. A clerk at any station can figure out the cheapest fare for your trip (or call the helpful National Rail folks at tel. 0845-748-4950, 24 hours daily). Savings can be significant. For a London–York round-trip (standard class), the full fare, with no date stipulated for the return trip, is £112; if you book the day of departure for travel after 9:30, it's £84; and the cheapest fare, booked a couple of months in advance as two one-way tickets, is £29.

While not required on English trains, reservations are free,

Public Transportation Routes in Britain

MAP NOT TO SCALE

London Airports
- **A** Heathrow
- **B** Gatwick
- **C** Luton
- **D** Stansted
- **E** London City

Legend:
- — RAIL
- — EUROSTAR
- --- BUS
- ✈ AIRPORT
- ⋯ FERRY w/ CROSSING TIME

and a good idea for long journeys or any train travel on Sunday. Make them at any train station before 18:00 on the day before you travel.

Buying Train Tickets in Advance: The best fares go to those who book their trips well in advance of their journey. (While only a 7-day minimum advance booking is officially required for the cheapest fares, these go fast—especially in summer—so a 6–8 week advance booking is often necessary.) Keep in mind that when booking in advance, return (round-trip) fares are not always cheaper than buying two single (one-way) tickets. Also note that cheap advance tickets often come with the toughest refund restrictions, so be sure to nail down your travel plans before you reserve. To book ahead, you can go in person to any station, book online at www.nationalrail.co.uk, or call 0845-748-4950 (from the US, call 011-44-20-7278-5240, phone answered 24 hours) to find out the schedule and best fare for your journey; then you'll be referred to the appropriate number to call—depending on the particular rail company—to book your ticket. If you order online, be sure you know what you want; it's tough to reach a person who can change your online reservation. You'll pick up your ticket at the station (unless your order was lost—this service still has some glitches). If you want your ticket mailed to you in the US, you need to allow a couple of weeks and cover the shipping costs. (BritRail passholders, however, cannot use the Web to make reservations.)

Buying Train Tickets en Route: If you'd rather have the flexibility of booking tickets as you go, you can save a few pounds by buying a round-trip ticket, called a "return ticket" (a same-day round-trip, called a "day return," is particularly cheap); buying before 18:00 the day before you depart; traveling after the morning rush hour (this usually means after 9:30 Mon–Fri); and going standard class instead of first class. Preview your options at www.nationalrail.co.uk or www.thetrainline.com.

Senior, Youth, and Family Deals: To get a third off the price of most point-to-point rail tickets, seniors can buy a Senior Railcard (for ages 60 and above) and young people can buy a Young Persons Railcard (for ages 16–25, or for full-time students 26 and above with a valid ISIC card). A Family Railcard allows adults to travel cheaper (about 33 percent) while their kids ages 5 to 15 receive a 60 percent discount for most trips (maximum of 4 adults and 4 kids, www.family-railcard.co.uk). Each card costs £26; see www.railcard.co.uk. Any of these cards are valid for a year on almost all trains except special runs such as the Heathrow Express and Eurostar (fill out application at station, brochures on racks in info center, need to show passport). Youth also need to submit a passport-type photo for the Young Persons Card.

Sample Train Journey

Here is a typical example of a personalized train schedule printed out by England's train stations. At the Salisbury station, I told the clerk that I wanted to leave after 16:30 for Moreton-in-Marsh in the Cotswolds.

Stations	Arrive	Depart	Class
Salisbury	—	16:41	Standard
Bristol	17:48	18:28	1st/Standard
Cheltenham Spa	19:10	19:29	1st/Standard
Worcester	19:52	20:05	1st/Standard
Moreton-in-Marsh	20:42	—	

Even though the trip involved three transfers, this schedule allowed me to easily navigate the rails.

Train departures are listed on overhead boards at the station by their final destination (note that your destination could be an intermediate stop on this route, and not listed on the overhead). It's helpful to ask at the info desk—or any conductor—for the final destination of your next train (such as Oxford), so you'll be able to figure out quickly which platform it's departing from. Upon arrival at Worcester, I looked for *Oxford* on the station's overhead train schedule to determine where to catch my train to Moreton-in-Marsh.

Often the conductor on your previous train can even tell you which platform your next train will depart from, but it's wise to confirm.

Lately, England's train system has experienced a lot of delays, causing more and more travelers to miss their connections. Don't schedule your connections too tight if you need to be at your destination at a specific time.

Railpasses: Consider getting a railpass. The BritRail pass comes in "consecutive day" and "flexi" versions, with price breaks for youths, seniors, off-season travelers, and groups of three of more. Most allow one child under 16 to travel free with a paying adult. If you're exploring England's backcountry with a BritRail pass, standard class is a good choice since many of the smaller train lines don't even offer first-class cars. Choose between England-only BritRail passes and ones that cover Scotland and Wales as well.

More BritRail options include England/Ireland passes, "London Plus" passes (good for travel in most of southeast England but not in London itself), and BritRail & Drive passes (which offer you some rail days and some car-rental days). These BritRail passes, as well as Eurailpasses, get you a discount on the Eurostar train

Railpasses

Prices listed are for 2009 and are subject to change. For the latest prices, details, and train schedules (and easy online ordering), see my comprehensive *Guide to Eurail Passes* at www.ricksteves.com/rail.

"Standard" is the polite British term for "second" class. "Senior" refers to those age 60 and up. No senior discounts for standard class. "Youth" means under age 26. For each adult or senior BritRail or BritRail England pass you buy, one child (5–15) can travel free with you (ask for the **"Family Pass,"** not available with all passes). Additional kids pay the normal half-adult rate. Kids under 5 travel free.

Note: Overnight journeys begun on the final night of your pass can be completed the day after your pass expires—only BritRail allows this trick. A bunk in a twin sleeper costs $75.

BRITRAIL CONSECUTIVE PASS

	Adult 1st Class	Adult Standard	Senior 1st Class	Youth 1st Class	Youth Standard
3 consec. days	$305	$199	$259	$245	$159
4 consec. days	379	249	319	305	199
8 consec. days	535	359	455	425	285
15 consec. days	799	535	679	639	425
22 consec. days	1015	675	859	809	539
1 month	1195	795	1015	955	635

BRITRAIL FLEXIPASS

	Adult 1st Class	Adult Standard	Senior 1st Class	Youth 1st Class	Youth Standard
3 days in 2 months	$375	$255	$319	$299	$205
4 days in 2 months	465	315	399	375	249
8 days in 2 months	679	459	579	545	365
15 days in 2 months	1025	689	869	819	555

BRITRAIL & DRIVE PASS

Any 4 rail days and 2 car days in 2 months.

	1st Class	Standard Class	Extra Car Day
Mini	$546	$382	$44
Economy	553	389	51
Compact	562	398	60
Compact Auto	592	428	90
Intermed. Auto	605	441	103
Minivan Auto	682	518	180

Prices are per person, two traveling together. Third and fourth persons sharing car buy a regular BritRail pass. To order a Rail & Drive pass, call Rail Europe at 800-438-7245. *Not sold by Europe Through the Back Door.*

Map key:

Approximate point-to-point one-way standard-class fares in US dollars by rail (solid line) and bus (dashed line). First class costs 50 percent more. Add up fares for your itinerary to see whether a railpass will save you money.

BRITRAIL ENGLAND CONSECUTIVE PASS

	Adult 1st Class	Adult Standard	Senior 1st Class	Youth 1st Class	Youth Standard
3 consec. days	$239	$159	$205	$195	$129
4 consec. days	$299	$199	$255	$239	$159
8 consec. days	$429	$285	$365	$345	$229
15 consec. days	$645	$429	$549	$515	$345
22 consec. days	$815	$545	$695	$649	$435
1 month	$959	$639	$815	$765	$515

Covers travel only in England, not Scotland, Wales, or Ireland.

BRITRAIL ENGLAND FLEXIPASS

Type of Pass	Adult 1st Class	Adult Standard	Senior 1st Class	Youth 1st Class	Youth Standard
3 days in 2 months	$305	$205	$259	$245	$165
4 days in 2 months	$379	$255	$319	$305	$205
8 days in 2 months	$549	$369	$465	$439	$295
15 days in 2 months	$819	$549	$699	$655	$439

Covers travel only in England, not Scotland, Wales, or Ireland.

BRITRAIL LONDON PLUS PASS

	Adult 1st Class	Adult Standard
2 out of 8 days	$209	$139
4 out of 8 days	289	225
7 out of 15 days	369	269

Covers much of SE England (see London Plus Coverage Map at www.ricksteves.com/rail). Includes vouchers to cover two trips on the Heathrow, Stansted, or Gatwick Express, separate from your counted travel days, which can be used up to 6 months after validating pass. Many trains are standard class only. The 7 p.m. rule for night trains does not apply. Kids 5–15 half price; under 5 free.

BRITRAIL SCOTTISH FREEDOM PASS

4 out of 8 days	$235
8 out of 15 days	315

Valid in Scotland only, standard class only. Not valid on trains that depart before 9:15am, Mon–Fri. Covers Caledonian MacBrayne and Strathclyde ferry service to Scotland's most popular islands. Discounts on some P&O ferries, some Citylink buses & more. Kids 5–15 half fare; under 5 free.

BRITRAIL PASS PLUS IRELAND

	First Class	Standard Class
5 days in 1 month	$699	$469
10 days in 1 month	1245	839

Covers the entire British Isles (England, Wales, Scotland, Northern Ireland, and the Republic of Ireland). No longer covers ferries. Kids 5-15 pay half fare; under 5 free. No Family Pass, Party Pass, Eurail Discount, nor Off-Peak Special. Consider the cost of separate BritRail and Ireland passes.

that zips you to continental Europe under the English Channel. These passes are sold outside of Europe only. For specifics, contact your travel agent or see www.ricksteves.com/rail.

Buses: Although buses are about a third slower than trains, they're also a lot cheaper. Round-trip bus tickets usually cost less than two one-way fares (e.g., London–York one-way costs £26; round-trip costs £36). And buses go many places that trains don't. Budget travelers can save a wad with a bus pass. National Express sells Brit Xplorer bus passes for unlimited travel on consecutive days (£79/7 days, £139/14 days, £219/28 days, sold over the counter, non-UK passport required, tel. 0871-781-8181, www .nationalexpress.com). Check their website to learn about online Funfare deals; senior/youth/family cards and fares; and discounts for advance booking.

If you want to take a bus from your last destination to the nearest airport, you'll find that National Express often offers airport buses. Bus stations are normally at or near train stations (in London, the bus station is a block southwest of Victoria Station). Brits distinguish between "buses" (for in-city travel with lots of stops) and "coaches" (long-distance cross-country runs).

A couple of companies offer **backpackers' bus circuits.** These hop-on, hop-off bus circuits take mostly youth hostelers around the country super-cheap and easy with the assumption that they'll be sleeping in the hostels along the way. For instance, **Backpacker Tours** offers 1–19 day excursions through England and other destinations in Great Britain (from about £65/1 day, £90/3 days, £266/5 days, tel. 0870-745-1046, www.backpackertours.co.uk, sales@back packertours.co.uk).

Renting a Car

To rent a car in England, you must be at least 23 years old and have a valid license. An International Driving Permit is recommended, but not required, if your driver's license has been renewed within the last year ($15 through your local AAA, plus two passport photos, www.aaa.com); however, I've frequently rented cars in Britain and traveled problem-free with just my US license.

Drivers under the age of 25 may incur a young-driver surcharge, and some rental companies do not rent to anyone 75 and over. If you're considered too young or old, look into leasing, which has less-stringent age restrictions (see "Leasing," later).

Research car rentals before you go. It's cheaper to arrange most car rentals from the US. Call several companies and look online to compare rates, or arrange a rental through your hometown travel agent. Two reputable companies among many are Auto Europe (www.autoeurope.com) and Europe by Car (www.ebctravel.com). For the best rental deal, rent by the week with unlimited mileage (but for long trips, consider leasing). If you want to save money on gas, ask for a diesel car.

I normally rent the smallest, least-expensive model with a stick-shift. Almost all rentals are manual by default, so if you need an automatic, you must request one in advance; beware that these cars are usually larger models (not as maneuverable on narrow, winding roads). An automatic transmission adds about 50 percent to the car-rental cost over a manual transmission. But weigh this against the fact that in England you'll be sitting on the right side of the car, and shifting with your left hand...while driving on the left side of the road. The floor pedals are in the same locations as in the US, and the gears are found in the same basic "H" pattern as at home (i.e., first gear, second, etc.).

Expect to pay about $750 per person (based on 2 people sharing the car) for a small economy car for three weeks with unlimited mileage, including gas, parking, and insurance. Consider leasing to save money on insurance and taxes. I normally rent a small, inexpensive model like a Ford Fiesta. For a bigger, roomier, more powerful but inexpensive car, move up to a Ford Focus or VW Polo. Minibuses are a great budget way to go for five to nine people.

Compare pick-up costs (downtown can be cheaper than the airport) and explore drop-off options. If you pick up the car in a smaller city, such as Bath, you'll more likely survive your first day on the English roads. Returning a car at a big-city train station can be tricky; get precise details on the car drop-off location and hours. Note that rental offices usually close from midday Saturday until Monday.

If you drop the car off early or keep it longer, you'll be credited or charged at a fair, prorated price. But keep your receipts in case any questions arise about your billing.

When picking up the car, check it thoroughly and make sure any damage is noted on your rental agreement. Find out how your car's lights, turn signals, wipers, and gas cap function. When you return the car, make sure the agent verifies its condition with you.

Car Insurance Options

When you rent a car, you are liable for a very high deductible, sometimes equal to the entire value of the car. Limit your financial risk by choosing one of these three options: buy Collision Damage Waiver (CDW) coverage from the car-rental company, get coverage through your credit card (free, if your card automatically includes zero-deductible coverage), or buy coverage through Travel Guard.

While each rental company has its own variation, basic **CDW** costs $15–25 a day (figure roughly 25 percent extra) and reduces your liability, but does not eliminate it. When you pick up the car, you'll be offered the chance to "buy down" the basic deductible to zero (for an additional $10–30/day; this is often called "super CDW").

If you opt for credit-card coverage, there's a catch. You'll technically have to decline all coverage offered by the car-rental company, which means they can place a hold on your card (can be up to the full value of the car). In case of damage, it can be time-consuming to resolve the charges with your credit-card company. Before you decide on this option, quiz your credit-card company about how it works.

Finally, you can buy CDW insurance from Travel Guard ($9/day plus a one-time $3 service fee covers you up to $35,000, $250 deductible, tel. 800-826-4919, www.travelguard.com). It's valid everywhere in Europe except the Republic of Ireland, and some Italian car-rental companies refuse to honor it. Oddly, residents of Washington state aren't allowed to buy this coverage.

For more fine print about car-rental insurance, see www.rick steves.com/cdw.

Leasing

For trips of two and a half weeks or more, leasing (which automatically includes zero-deductible collision and theft insurance) is the best way to go. By technically buying and then selling back the car, you save lots of money on tax and insurance. Leasing provides you a brand-new car with unlimited mileage and a 24-hour emergency assistance program. You can lease for as little as 17 days to as long as six months. Car leases must be arranged from the US. One of many reliable companies offering affordable lease packages is Europe by Car (US tel. 800-223-1516, www.ebctravel.com).

Driving in England

Remember to bring your driver's license. Seat belts are required, and kids under age 4 must ride in a child-safety seat. An Automobile Association membership for Britain comes with most rentals (www.theaa.com). Understand its towing and emergency road-service benefits.

Driving in England is basically wonderful—once you remember to stay on the left and after you've mastered the roundabouts. Every year, however, I get a few notes from traveling readers advising me that, for them, trying to drive in England was a nerve-racking and regrettable mistake. If you want to get a little slack on the roads, drop by a gas station or auto shop and buy a green *P* (probationary driver with license) sign to put in your car window (don't get the red *L* sign, which means you're a learner driver without a license and thus prohibited from driving on motorways).

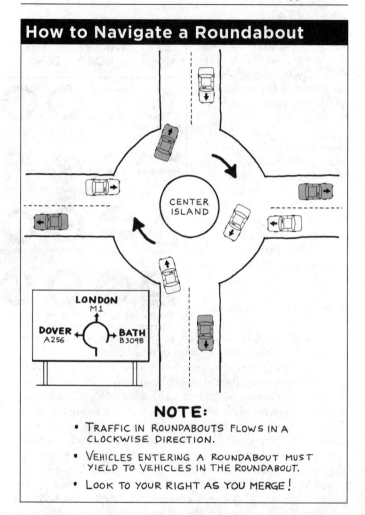

How to Navigate a Roundabout

CENTER ISLAND

LONDON
M1

DOVER
A256

BATH
B3098

NOTE:

• TRAFFIC IN ROUNDABOUTS FLOWS IN A CLOCKWISE DIRECTION.

• VEHICLES ENTERING A ROUNDABOUT MUST YIELD TO VEHICLES IN THE ROUNDABOUT.

• LOOK TO YOUR RIGHT AS YOU MERGE!

Many Yankee drivers find the hardest part isn't driving on the left, but steering from the right. Your instinct is to put yourself on the left side of your lane, which means you may spend your first day or two constantly drifting off the road to the left. It can help to remember that the driver always stays close to the center line.

Roundabouts: Don't let a roundabout spook you. After all, you routinely merge into much faster traffic on American highways back home. Traffic in roundabouts has the right-of-way; entering traffic yields (look to your right as you merge). You'll probably encounter "double-roundabouts"—figure-eights where you'll slingshot from one roundabout directly into another. Just go with the flow and track signs carefully. When approaching an especially complex roundabout, you'll first pass a diagram showing the layout and the various exits. And in many cases, the pavement is painted with which lane you should be in for which road or town.

STOP **AND LEARN THESE ROAD SIGNS**

Speed Limit (mph) — Yield — No Passing — End of No Passing Zone

One Way — Intersection — Main Road — Freeway

Danger — No Entry — No Entry for cars — All Vehicles Prohibited

Parking — No Parking — Customs — Peace

Speed Limits: Speed limits are 30 mph in town, 70 mph on the motorways, and 50 or 60 mph elsewhere. The national sign for 60 mph is a white circle with a black slash. Note that road-surveillance cameras strictly enforce speed limits. Any driver (including foreigners renting cars) photographed speeding will get a nasty bill in the mail. (Cameras—you'll see the foreboding gray boxes—flash on your rear license plate in order not to invade the privacy of anyone sharing the front seat with someone he or she shouldn't be with.)

Freeways: The shortest distance between any two points is usually the motorway. Road signs can be confusing, too few, and too late. Miss a motorway exit and you can lose 30 minutes. Study your map before taking off. Know the cities you'll be lacing together, since road numbers are inconsistent. British road signs are never marked with compass directions (e.g., *A30 West*); instead, you need to know what major town or city you're heading for (*A30 Penzance*). The driving directions in this book are intended to be used with a good local map. An England road atlas, easily purchased at gas stations in England, is money well-spent (see "Maps," page 617).

Fuel: Gas (petrol) costs about $9 per gallon and is self-serve. Diesel rental cars are common; make sure you know what your car takes before you fill up. Unleaded pumps are usually green.

Driving in Cities: Whenever possible, avoid driving in cities. Be warned that London assesses a congestion charge (see page 50). Most cities have modern ring roads to skirt the congestion. Follow signs to the parking lots outside the city core—most are a five- to ten-minute walk to the center—and avoid what can be an unpleasant grid of one-way streets (as in Bath) or roads that are only available to public transportation during the day (as in Oxford).

Driving in Rural Areas: Outside of the big cities and the motorways, British roads tend to be narrow. In towns, you may have to cross over the center line just to get past parked cars. Adjust

England by Car: Mileage and Time

Note: Your times may vary based on traffic, construction, and road conditions.

m = miles
h = hours

your perceptions of personal space: It's not "my side of the road" or "your side of the road," it's just "the road"—and it's shared as a cooperative adventure. If the road's wide enough, both directions of traffic can pass parked cars simultaneously, but frequently you'll have to take turns—follow the locals' lead and drive defensively. Some narrow country lanes are barely wide enough for one car. Go slowly, and if you encounter an oncoming car, look for the nearest pullout (or "passing place")—the driver who's closest to one is expected to use it, even if they have to back up to reach it. If another car pulls over and blinks its headlights, that means, "Go ahead; I'll wait to let you pass." British drivers are quick to offer a friendly wave to thank you for letting them pass (and they appreciate it if you reciprocate). Pull over frequently—to let faster locals pass and to check the map.

Parking: Parking can be confusing. One yellow line marked on the pavement means no parking Monday through Saturday during work hours. Double yellow lines mean no parking at any time. Broken yellow lines mean short stops are OK, but you should always look for explicit signs or ask a passerby. White lines mean you're free to park.

In towns, rather than look for street parking, I generally just pull into the most central and handy "pay and display" parking lot I can find. To "pay and display," feed change into a machine, receive a timed ticket, and display it on the dashboard or stick it to the driver's-side window. Rates are reasonable by US standards, and locals love to share stickers that have time remaining. If you stand by the machine, someone on their way out with time left on their sticker will probably give it to you. Keep a bag of coins in the ashtray or glove box for these machines and for parking meters.

Stock Up: Set your car up for a fun road trip. Establish a cardboard-box munchies pantry. Buy a rack of liter boxes of juice for the trunk, and some Windex and a roll of paper towels (called a "kitchen roll" in Britain) for cleaner sightseeing.

Cheap Flights

If you're visiting one or more cities on a longer European trip, consider intra-European airlines. While trains are still the best way to connect places that are close together, a flight can save both time and money on long journeys.

London is the hub for many cheap, no-frills airlines, which affordably connect the city with other destinations in the British Isles and throughout Europe.

A visit to www.skyscanner.net sorts the numerous options offered by the many airlines, enabling you to see the best schedules for your trip and come up with the best deal. Other good search engines include www.mobissimo.com and www.wegolo.com.

Be aware of the potential drawbacks of flying on the cheap: nonrefundable and nonchangeable tickets, rigid baggage restrictions (and fees if you have more than what's officially allowed), use of airports far outside town, tight schedules that can mean more delays, little in the way of customer assistance if problems arise, and, of course, no frills. To avoid unpleasant surprises, read the small print—especially baggage policies—before you book. If you're traveling with lots of bags, a cheap flight can quickly become a bad deal, due to per-piece baggage fees.

Book in advance. Although you can usually book right up until the flight departs, the cheap seats will often have sold out long before, leaving the most expensive seats for latecomers.

With **bmi,** you can fly inexpensively from London to destinations in the UK and beyond (fares start at about £45 one-way to

Edinburgh, Dublin, Brussels, or Amsterdam). Call toll tel. 0870-607-0555 or US tel. 800-788-0555 or check www.flybmi.com.

Another low-cost airline, **easyJet** flies from Gatwick, Luton, and Stansted. Prices are based on demand, so the least popular routes make for the cheapest fares, especially if you book early (toll tel. 0905-821-0905, calls 65p/min, www.easyjet.com).

Irish-owned **Ryanair** flies from London (mostly Stansted Airport, though also Gatwick and Luton) to often obscure airports near Dublin, Glasgow, Frankfurt, Stockholm, Oslo, Venice, Turin, and many others. Sample fares: London–Dublin—£50 round-trip (sometimes as low as £30), London–Frankfurt—£45 round-trip (Irish toll tel. 0818-303-030, British toll tel. 0871-246-0000, www.ryanair.com). However, be warned that Ryanair charges additional fees for nearly everything. The company requires a mandatory online-only check-in (£5 charge), from 15 days to four hours before your flight (no airport check-in). When checking in, you must also print out your boarding pass; if you show up without it, there's an additional £40 charge. You can carry on only a small day bag; you'll pay a fee for each checked bag (price depends on number of bags; up to three bags allowed per passenger).

Brussels Airlines (formerly Virgin Express) is a Brussels-based company with good rates and hubs in Bristol, Birmingham, Gatwick, Manchester, and Newcastle (book by phone and pick up ticket at airport an hour before your flight, US tel. 516/740-5200, British toll tel. 0905-609-5609—40p/min, www.brusselsairlines.com).

Resources

Resources from Rick Steves

Rick Steves' England 2010 is one of more than 30 titles in a series of **books** on European travel, which includes country guidebooks (such as *Rick Steves' Great Britain*, which includes Scotland and Wales); city and regional guidebooks (including London); and my budget-travel skills handbook, *Rick Steves' Europe Through the Back Door*. My phrase books—for French, Italian, German, Spanish, and Portuguese—are practical and budget-oriented. My other books are *Europe 101* (a crash course on art and history, newly expanded and in full color), *Travel as a Political Act* (a travelogue sprinkled with advice for bringing home a global perspective), *European Christmas* (on

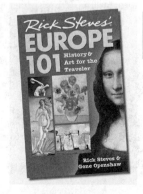

Begin Your Trip at www.ricksteves.com

At our travel website, you'll find a wealth of free information on European destinations, including fresh monthly news and helpful tips from thousands of fellow travelers. You'll also find my latest guidebook updates (www.ricksteves.com/update) and my travel blog.

Our **online Travel Store** offers travel bags and accessories specially designed by Rick Steves to help you travel smarter and lighter. These include my popular carry-on bags (roll-aboard and rucksack versions), money belts, totes, toiletries kits, adapters, other accessories, and a wide selection of guidebooks, planning maps, and DVDs.

Choosing the right **railpass** for your trip—amidst hundreds of options—can drive you nutty. We'll help you choose the best pass for your needs, plus give you a bunch of free extras.

Rick Steves' Europe Through the Back Door travel company offers **tours** with more than three dozen itineraries and about 300 departures reaching the best destinations in this book...and beyond. We offer a 14-day England tour, an 11-day Scotland tour, and a seven-day in-depth London city tour. You'll enjoy great guides, a fun bunch of travel partners (with small groups of about 28), and plenty of room to spread out in a big, comfy bus. You'll find European adventures to fit every vacation length. For all the details, and to get our Tour Catalog and a free Rick Steves Tour Experience DVD (filmed on location during an actual tour), visit www.ricksteves.com or call the Tour Department at 425/608-4217.

traditional and modern-day celebrations), and *Postcards from Europe* (a fun memoir of my travels). For a complete list of my books, see the inside of the last page of this book.

My **TV series**, *Rick Steves' Europe*, covers European destinations in 100 shows, with seven episodes on England (and an additional three on Great Britain at large). My weekly **public radio show**, *Travel with Rick Steves*, features interviews with travel experts from around the world, including several hours on Great Britain and British culture. All the TV scripts and radio shows (which are easy and free to download to an iPod or other MP3 player) are at www.ricksteves.com.

Take advantage of my free, self-guided **audio tours** of the major sights in London. Simply download them from www.ricksteves.com or iTunes (search for "Rick Steves' tours" in the iTunes Store), then transfer them to your iPod or other MP3 player. If your travels take you beyond Britain to France or Italy, download my audio tours of the major sights in Paris, Florence, Rome, and Venice.

Maps

The black-and-white maps in this book, drawn by Dave Hoerlein, are concise and simple. Dave, who is well-traveled in Britain, designed the maps to help you locate recommended places and get to local TIs, where you can pick up more in-depth maps of towns or regions (free or cheap). Better maps are sold at newsstands—before you buy a map, look at it to be sure it has the level of detail you want.

If you'll be lingering in London, buy a city map at a London newsstand; the red *Bensons Mapguide* (£3) is excellent. Even the vending-machine maps sold in Tube stations are good. The *Rough Guide* map to London is well-designed (£5, sold at London bookstores). The *Rick Steves' Britain, Ireland & London City Map* has a good map of London ($6, www.ricksteves.com). Many Londoners, along with obsessive-compulsive tourists, rely on the highly detailed *London A–Z* map book (generally £5–7, called "A to Zed" by locals, available at newsstands).

If you're driving, get a road atlas (1 inch equals 3 miles) covering all of England. Ordnance Survey, AA, and Bartholomew editions are all available for about £7 at tourist information offices, gas stations, and bookstores. Drivers, hikers, and cyclists may want more in-depth maps for the Cotswolds and the Lake District.

Other Guidebooks

If you're like most travelers, this book is all you need. But if you're heading beyond my recommended neighborhoods and destinations, $30 for extra maps and books is money well-spent. Especially for several people traveling by car, the extra weight and expense are negligible.

The following books are worthwhile, though not updated annually; check the publication date before you buy. The *Lonely Planet* and *Let's Go* guidebooks on London and on Britain are fine budget-travel guides. *Lonely Planet*'s guidebooks are more thorough and informative; *Let's Go* books are youth-oriented, with good coverage of nightlife, hostels, and cheap transportation deals. For cultural and sightseeing background, look into Michelin and Cadogan guides to London, England, and Britain. The readable Access guide for London is similarly well-researched. *Secret London* by Andrew Duncan leads the reader on unique walks through a less-touristy London.

If you'll be focusing on London or traveling elsewhere in Britain, consider *Rick Steves' London 2010* or *Rick Steves' Great Britain 2010.*

Recommended Books and Movies

To get a feel for England past and present, check out a few of these books and films.

Nonfiction

For a serious historical overview, wade into *A History of Britain,* a three-volume collection by Simon Schama. *Literary Trails* (Hardyment) reunites famous authors with the environments that inspired them.

In *Notes from a Small Island*, Bill Bryson records his witty notes about every British foible. For more good memoirs, pick up any of the books by Susan Allen Toth on her British travels. If you'll be spending time in the Cotswolds, try *Cider with Rosie,* Laurie Lee's boyhood memoir set just after World War I. Animal-lovers enjoy James Herriot's adventures as a Yorkshire vet, told in *All Creatures Great and Small* and its sequels. And the obsessive world of English soccer is illuminated in Nick Hornby's memoir, *Fever Pitch.*

Fiction

For the classics of British fiction, read anything—and everything—by Charles Dickens, Jane Austen, and the Brontës. Mystery fans can't miss with any of the books by Agatha Christie.

Pillars of the Earth (Follett) traces the building of a fictional 12th-century cathedral in southern England. For a big book on the era of King Richard III, try *The Sunne in Splendour,* one in a series by Sharon Kay Penman. *The Other Boleyn Girl* (Gregory) sets its intrigues in the court of Henry VIII, while *Restoration* (Tremain) returns readers to the time of King Charles II.

Set in the 19th-century Anglican church, *The Warden* (Trollope) dwells on moral dilemmas. *Brideshead Revisited* (Waugh) satirizes the British obsession with class, taking place between the World Wars. A rural village in the 1930s is the social battlefield for E. F. Benson's *Mapp and Lucia.* For evocative Cornish settings, try Daphne du Maurier's *Rebecca* or *The House on the Strand.*

For a more contemporary read, check out *Bridget Jones's Diary* (Fielding), *Behind the Scenes at the Museum* (Atkinson), *White Teeth* (Smith), or *Saturday* (McEwan).

Films

Goodbye, Mr. Chips (1939) is set in a boys' boarding school during Victorian England. If you're in the mood for something completely different, try *Monty Python and the Holy Grail* (1975), a surreal take on the Arthurian legend. *Chariots of Fire* (1981) ran away with the Academy Award for Best Picture.

A Room with a View (1985) and *The Remains of the Day* (1993) include scenes filmed in rural England. Among the many versions of *Pride and Prejudice,* the 1995 BBC miniseries starring Colin Firth is the winner. The all-star *Gosford Park* (2001) is part comedy, part murder mystery, and part critique of England's class stratification in the 1930s. *Hope and Glory* (1987) is a semi-autobiographical story of a boy growing up during WWII's Blitz.

Shadowlands (1993) tells a fictionalized account of author C. S. Lewis' relationship with his future wife. In *The Full Monty* (1997), some working-class Yorkshire lads take it all off to pay the bills. *Calendar Girls* (2003) has a similar setting and premise, if a slightly more noble cause. In *The Duchess* (2008), the 18th-century Duchess of Devonshire glides languidly through life in big skirts and even bigger wigs.

Harry Potter Sights

Harry Potter's story is set in a magical Britain, and all of the places mentioned in the books except London are fictional, but you can visit many real film locations. Some of the locations are closed to visitors, though, or can be an un-magical disappointment in person. But quicker than you can say "Lumos," let's shine a light on where to get your Harry Potter fix if you're a die-hard fan.

Spoiler Warning: Information in this section will ruin surprises for the three of you who haven't yet read or seen any of the Harry Potter books or movies.

London

In the first film, Harry first realizes his wizard powers when talking with a boa constrictor, filmed at the **London Zoo's Reptile House** in Regent's Park (Tube: Great Portland Street).

London bustles along oblivious to the parallel universe of wizards, hidden in the magical Diagon Alley (filmed, like many of the other fictional settings, on a set at Leavesden Studios, north of London). The goblin-run Gringotts Wizarding Bank, though, was filmed in the real-life marble-floored Exhibition Hall of **Australia House** (Tube: Temple), home of the Australian Embassy.

Harry catches the train to Hogwarts at **King's Cross Station.** Inside the glass-roofed train station, on a **pedestrian sky bridge** over the tracks, Hagrid gives Harry a train ticket. Harry heads to platform 9¾. You'll find a fun re-creation—complete with a *Platform 9¾* sign and a luggage cart that appears to be disappearing into the wall—on the way to platform 9. (Walk toward the pedestrian bridge and make a left at the arch.)

In film #3, Harry careens through London's lamp-lit streets on a purple three-decker bus that dumps him at the Leaky Cauldron. In this film, the pub's exterior was shot on rough-looking Stoney Street at the southeast edge of **Borough Street Market,** by The Market Porter pub (Tube: London Bridge).

In film #5, the Order of the Phoenix takes to the sky on broomsticks over London, passing by plenty of identifiable landmarks at night. Far beneath them glow the **London Eye, Big Ben,** and **Buckingham Palace.**

Cinema buffs can visit **Leicester Square** (Tube: Leicester Square), where Daniel Radcliffe and other stars strolled past paparazzi and down red carpets to the Odeon Theater to watch the movies' premieres.

In film #6, the **Millennium Bridge** is attacked and collapses into the Thames.

Near Bath

The mysterious side of Hogwarts is often set in the elaborate, fan-vaulted corridors of the **Gloucester Cathedral** cloisters, 50 miles north of Bath. When Harry and Ron set out to save Hermione, they look down a long, dark Gloucester hallway and spot a 20-foot troll at the far end. And it's here that the walls whisper ominously to Harry, and letters in blood warn: "Enemies of the heir, beware."

The scene showing Harry being chosen for Gryffindor's Quidditch team was shot in the halls of the 13th-century **Lacock Abbey,** 13 miles east of Bath. Harry attends Professor Snape's class in one of the Abbey's bare, peeling-plaster rooms—appropriate to Snape's temperament. (Mad Max tours include Lacock on its day-trip itinerary; for details, see page 304.)

Oxford

Hogwarts, Harry's prestigious wizarding prep school, is a movie creation. But it's made from a number of locations, many of them real places in Oxford. (For information on Harry Potter tours in Oxford, see page 365.)

Christ Church College—with plenty of Harry-related sights that you can tour—inspired two film sets familiar to Potter fans. In the first film, the kids are ferried to Hogwarts, and then ascend a **stone staircase** that leads into the Great Hall. The high-

ceilinged **dining hall** seen throughout the films—tweaked to look much larger in the films—is filled at lunchtime with students at long rows of tables (as it is in the films, minus the weightless candles and flaming braziers).

Later in the first film, Harry sneaks into the restricted book section of Hogwarts Library under a cloak of invisibility. This scene was filmed inside Oxford's **Duke Humfrey's Library.** Hermione reads about the Sorcerer's Stone here, too.

At the end of the first film, Harry awakens from his dark battle into the golden light of the Hogwarts infirmary, filmed in a big-windowed **Divinity School** (downstairs). In film #4 *(Goblet of Fire),* Mad-Eye Moody turns Draco into a ferret on the grounds of **Bodleian Library.**

Durham and Northeast England

In the first film, Harry walks with his white owl, Hedwig, through a snowy cloister courtyard located in **Durham's Cathedral** (see listing on page 560). The bird soars up and over the church's twin 13th-century towers.

Harry first learns to fly a broomstick on the green grass of Hogwarts school grounds, filmed inside the walls of **Alnwick Castle,** located 30 miles from Newcastle. In film #2, this is where the Weasleys' flying car crashes into the Whomping Willow.

Holidays and Festivals

This list includes many—but not all—major festivals in major cities, plus national holidays observed throughout Great Britain. Some dates have yet to be set. Before planning a trip around a festival, make sure you verify the festival dates by checking the festival's website or contacting the Visit Britain office (listed at the beginning of this chapter). Many sights and banks close down on national holidays—keep this in mind when planning your itinerary.

Many British towns have holiday festivals in late November and early December, with markets, music, and entertainment in the Christmas spirit. Two of these include York's St. Nicholas Fayre (www.yuletideyork.com) and Keswick's Victorian Fayre.

For specifics and a more comprehensive list of festivals, contact the Visit Britain office (listed at the beginning of the appendix).

Jan 1	New Year's Day
Feb (one week)	London Fashion Week (www.london fashionweek.co.uk)
Feb 17–22	Jorvik Viking Festival, York (costumed warriors, battles; www.jorvik-viking -centre.co.uk)
Feb 27–March 7	Literature Festival, Bath (www.bathlit fest.org.uk)
April 2	Good Friday
April 4–5	Easter Sunday and Monday
May 3	Early May Bank Holiday
Mid-May	Jazz Festival, Keswick
May 25–29	Chelsea Flower Show, London (book tickets ahead for this popular event at www.rhs.org.uk/chelsea)
May 28–June 12	International Music Festival, Bath (www.bathmusicfest.org.uk)
May 28–June 13	Fringe Festival, Bath (alternative music, dance, and theater; www.bathfringe .co.uk)
May 31	Spring Bank Holiday
Early June	Late Music Festival, York (www.late musicfestival.org.uk)
June 4–5	Beer Festival, Keswick (music, shows; www.keswickbeerfestival.co.uk)
June 13	Trooping the Colour, London (military bands and pageantry, Queen's birthday parade)

2010

JANUARY						
S	M	T	W	T	F	S
					1	2
3	4	5	6	7	8	9
10	11	12	13	14	15	16
17	18	19	20	21	22	23
24/31	25	26	27	28	29	30

FEBRUARY						
S	M	T	W	T	F	S
	1	2	3	4	5	6
7	8	9	10	11	12	13
14	15	16	17	18	19	20
21	22	23	24	25	26	27
28						

MARCH						
S	M	T	W	T	F	S
	1	2	3	4	5	6
7	8	9	10	11	12	13
14	15	16	17	18	19	20
21	22	23	24	25	26	27
28	29	30	31			

APRIL						
S	M	T	W	T	F	S
				1	2	3
4	5	6	7	8	9	10
11	12	13	14	15	16	17
18	19	20	21	22	23	24
25	26	27	28	29	30	

MAY						
S	M	T	W	T	F	S
						1
2	3	4	5	6	7	8
9	10	11	12	13	14	15
16	17	18	19	20	21	22
23/30	24/31	25	26	27	28	29

JUNE						
S	M	T	W	T	F	S
		1	2	3	4	5
6	7	8	9	10	11	12
13	14	15	16	17	18	19
20	21	22	23	24	25	26
27	28	29	30			

JULY						
S	M	T	W	T	F	S
				1	2	3
4	5	6	7	8	9	10
11	12	13	14	15	16	17
18	19	20	21	22	23	24
25	26	27	28	29	30	31

AUGUST						
S	M	T	W	T	F	S
1	2	3	4	5	6	7
8	9	10	11	12	13	14
15	16	17	18	19	20	21
22	23	24	25	26	27	28
29	30	31				

SEPTEMBER						
S	M	T	W	T	F	S
			1	2	3	4
5	6	7	8	9	10	11
12	13	14	15	16	17	18
19	20	21	22	23	24	25
26	27	28	29	30		

OCTOBER						
S	M	T	W	T	F	S
					1	2
3	4	5	6	7	8	9
10	11	12	13	14	15	16
17	18	19	20	21	22	23
24/31	25	26	27	28	29	30

NOVEMBER						
S	M	T	W	T	F	S
	1	2	3	4	5	6
7	8	9	10	11	12	13
14	15	16	17	18	19	20
21	22	23	24	25	26	27
28	29	30				

DECEMBER						
S	M	T	W	T	F	S
		1	2	3	4	
5	6	7	8	9	10	11
12	13	14	15	16	17	18
19	20	21	22	23	24	25
26	27	28	29	30	31	

June 15–19	Royal Ascot Horse Race, Ascot (near Windsor; www.ascot.co.uk)
June 21–July 4	Wimbledon Tennis Championship, London (www.wimbledon.org)
July 9–17	Early Music Festival, York (www.ncem .co.uk/yemf.shtml)
July 29–Aug 1	Cambridge Folk Festival (buy tickets early at www.cambridgefolkfestival .co.uk)
Sept 3–Nov 7	Illuminations, Blackpool (waterfront light festival)
Aug 29–30	Notting Hill Carnival, London (costumes, Caribbean music)
Aug 30	Summer Bank Holiday (England and Wales only, not Scotland)
Sept (one week)	London Fashion Week (www.london fashionweek.co.uk)

Late Sept	York Festival of Food and Drink (www .yorkfoodfestival.com)
Late Sept	Jane Austen Festival (www.janeausten .co.uk), Bath
Nov 5	Bonfire Night, or Guy Fawkes Night, Britain (fireworks, bonfires, effigy-burning of 1605 traitor Guy Fawkes)
Dec 24–26	Christmas holidays

Conversions and Climate

Numbers and Stumblers

- In Europe, dates appear as day/month/year, so Christmas is 25/12/10.
- What Americans call the second floor of a building is the first floor in Britain.
- On escalators and moving sidewalks, Brits keep the left "lane" open for passing. Keep to the right.
- When pointing, use your whole hand, palm down.
- When counting with fingers, start with your thumb. If you hold up your first finger to request one item, you'll probably get two.
- To avoid the British version of giving someone "the finger," don't hold up the first two fingers of your hand with your palm facing you. (It looks like a reversed victory sign.)
- And please...don't call your waist pack a "fanny pack."

Metric Conversions (approximate)

Britain uses the metric system for everything but driving measurements. Weight and volume are typically calculated in metric: A kilogram is 2.2 pounds, and a liter is about a quart. The weight of a person is measured by "stone" (one stone equals 14 pounds). Temperatures are generally given in both Celsius and Fahrenheit.

On the road, Britain uses miles and posts speed limits in miles per hour.

1 foot = 0.3 meter	1 square yard = 0.8 square meter
1 yard = 0.9 meter	1 square mile = 2.6 square kilometers
1 mile = 1.6 kilometers	1 ounce = 28 grams
1 centimeter = 0.4 inch	1 quart = 0.95 liter
1 meter = 39.4 inches	1 kilogram = 2.2 pounds
1 kilometer = 0.62 mile	32°F = 0°C

Weights and Measures
1 British pint = 1.2 US pints
1 imperial gallon = 1.2 US gallons or about 4.5 liters
1 stone = 14 pounds (a 168-pound person weighs 12 stone)

Clothing Sizes
When shopping for clothing, use these US-to-Britain comparisons as general guidelines (but note that no conversion is perfect).
- Women's dresses and blouses: Add 4 (US women's size 10 = UK size 14)
- Men's suits and jackets: US and UK use the same sizing
- Men's shirts: US and UK use the same sizing
- Women's shoes: Subtract 2½ (US size 8 = UK size 5½)
- Men's shoes: Subtract about ½ (US size 9 = UK size 8½)

Climate
First line, average daily high temperature; second line, average daily low; third line, days without rain. For more detailed weather statistics for destinations in this book (as well as the rest of the world), check www.worldclimate.com.

J	F	M	A	M	J	J	A	S	O	N	D
LONDON											
43°	44°	50°	56°	62°	69°	71°	71°	65°	58°	50°	45°
36°	36°	38°	42°	47°	53°	56°	56°	52°	46°	42°	38°
16	15	20	18	19	19	19	20	17	18	15	16
YORK											
43°	44°	49°	55°	61°	67°	70°	69°	64°	57°	49°	45°
33°	34°	36°	40°	44°	50°	54°	53°	50°	44°	39°	36°
14	13	18	17	18	16	16	17	16	16	13	14

Temperature Conversion: Fahrenheit and Celsius

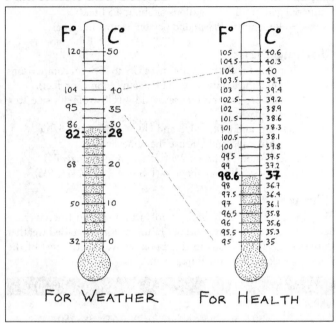

Britain uses both Celsius and Fahrenheit to take its temperature. For a rough conversion from Celsius to Fahrenheit, double the number and add 30. For weather, remember that 28°C is 82°F—perfect. For health, 37°C is just right.

Essential Packing Checklist

Whether you're traveling for five days or five weeks, here's what you'll need to bring. Remember to pack light to enjoy the sweet freedom of true mobility. Happy travels!

- ❏ 5 shirts
- ❏ 1 sweater or lightweight fleece jacket
- ❏ 2 pairs pants
- ❏ 1 pair shorts
- ❏ 1 swimsuit (women only—men can use shorts)
- ❏ 5 pairs underwear and socks
- ❏ 1 pair shoes
- ❏ 1 rainproof jacket
- ❏ Tie or scarf
- ❏ Money belt
- ❏ Money—your mix of:
  - ❏ Debit card for ATM withdrawals
  - ❏ Credit card
  - ❏ Hard cash in US dollars ($20 bills)
- ❏ Documents (and back-up photocopies)
- ❏ Passport
- ❏ Printout of airline e-ticket
- ❏ Driver's license
- ❏ Student ID and hostel card
- ❏ Railpass/car rental voucher
- ❏ Insurance details
- ❏ Daypack
- ❏ Sealable plastic baggies
- ❏ Camera and related gear
- ❏ Empty water bottle
- ❏ Wristwatch and alarm clock
- ❏ Earplugs
- ❏ First-aid kit
- ❏ Medicine (labeled)
- ❏ Extra glasses/contacts and prescriptions
- ❏ Sunscreen and sunglasses
- ❏ Toiletries kit
- ❏ Soap
- ❏ Laundry soap
- ❏ Clothesline
- ❏ Small towel
- ❏ Sewing kit
- ❏ Travel information
- ❏ Necessary map(s)
- ❏ Address list (email and mailing addresses)
- ❏ Postcards and photos from home
- ❏ Notepad and pen
- ❏ Journal

If you plan to carry on your luggage, note that all liquids must be in three-ounce or smaller containers and fit within a single quart-size baggie. For details, see www.tsa.gov/travelers.

Hotel Reservation

To: _____   _____
        hotel   *email or fax*

From: _____   _____
        name   *email or fax*

Today's date: _____ / _____ / _____
              day   *month* *year*

Dear Hotel _____ ,

Please make this reservation for me:

Name: _____

Total # of people: _____   # of rooms: _____   # of nights: _____

Arriving: _____ / _____ / _____   My time of arrival (24-hr clock): _____
          day *month* *year*   (I will telephone if I will be late)

Departing: ____ / ____ / ____
           day *month* *year*

Room(s): Single____   Double ____   Twin ____   Triple ____   Quad____

With: Toilet ____   Shower____   Bath ____   Sink only____

Special needs: View____   Quiet____   Cheapest ____   Ground Floor____

Please email or fax confirmation of my reservation, along with the type of room reserved and the price. Please also inform me of your cancellation policy. After I hear from you, I will quickly send my credit-card information as a deposit to hold the room. Thank you.

_____
Name

_____
Address

_____
City   *State*   *Zip Code*   *Country*

Before hoteliers can make your reservation, they want to know the information listed above. You can use this form as the basis for your email, or you can photocopy this page, fill in the information, and send it as a fax (also available online at www.ricksteves.com/reservation).

British–Yankee Vocabulary

For a longer list, plus a dry-witted primer on British culture, see *The Septic's Companion* (Chris Rae).

advert–advertisement

afters–dessert

anticlockwise–counterclockwise

aubergine–eggplant

banger–sausage

bangers and mash–sausage and mashed potatoes

Bank Holiday–legal holiday

bap–small roll

bespoke–custom-made

billion–a thousand of our billions (a million million)

biro–ballpoint pen

biscuit–cookie

black pudding–sausage made from dried blood

bloody–damn

blow off–fart

bobby–policeman ("the Bill" is more common)

Bob's your uncle–there you go (with a shrug), naturally

boffin–nerd, geek

bollocks–testicles; also used as an exclamation of strong disbelief or disagreement

bolshy–argumentative

bomb–success or failure

bonnet–car hood

boot–car trunk

braces–suspenders

bridle way–path for walkers, bikers, and horse riders

brilliant–cool

brolly–umbrella

bubble and squeak–cabbage and potatoes fried together

bum–butt

candy floss–cotton candy

caravan–trailer

car-boot sale–temporary flea market, often for charity

car park–parking lot

casualty–emergency room

cat's eyes–road reflectors

ceilidh (KAY-lee)–informal evening of song and folk fun (Scottish and Irish)

cheap and cheerful–budget but adequate

cheap and nasty–cheap and bad quality

cheers–good-bye or thanks; also a toast

chemist–pharmacist

chicory–endive

chippie–fish-and-chips shop; carpenter

chips–French fries

chock-a-block–jam-packed

chuffed–pleased

cider–alcoholic apple cider

clearway–road where you can't stop

coach–long-distance bus

concession–discounted admission

concs (pronounced "conks")– short for "concession"

cos–romaine lettuce

cotton buds–Q-tips

courgette–zucchini

craic (pronounced "crack")– fun, good conversation (Irish/Scottish and spreading to England)

crisps–potato chips

cuppa–cup of tea

dear–expensive

dicey–iffy, risky

digestives–round graham cookies

dinner–lunch or dinner

diversion–detour

donkey's years–ages, long time

draughts–checkers

draw–marijuana

dual carriageway–divided highway (four lanes)

dummy–pacifier

elevenses–coffee-and-biscuits break before lunch

elvers–baby eels

face flannel–washcloth

fag–cigarette

fagged–exhausted

faggot–sausage

fancy–to like, to be attracted to (a person)

fanny–vagina

fell–hill or high plain (Lake District)

first floor–second floor

fizzy drink–pop or soda

flutter–a bet

football–soccer

force–waterfall (Lake District)

fortnight–two weeks (shortened from "fourteen nights")

fringe–hair bangs

Frogs–French people

fruit machine–slot machine

full Monty–whole shebang, everything

gallery–balcony

gammon–ham

gangway–aisle

gaol–jail (same pronunciation)

gateau (or gateaux)–cake

gear lever–stick shift

geezer–"dude"

give way–yield

glen–narrow valley (Scotland)

goods wagon–freight truck

green fingers–green thumbs

half eight–8:30 (not 7:30)

heath–open treeless land

hen night–bachelorette party

holiday–vacation

homely–homey or cozy

hoover–vacuum cleaner

ice lolly–Popsicle

interval–intermission

ironmonger–hardware store

ish–more or less

jacket potato–baked potato

jelly–Jell-O

Joe Bloggs–John Q. Public

jumble sale–rummage sale

jumper–sweater

just a tick–just a second

kipper–smoked herring

knackered–exhausted (Cockney: cream crackered)

knickers–ladies' panties

knocking shop–brothel

knock up–wake up or visit (old-fashioned)

ladybird–ladybug

lady fingers–flat, spongy cookie

lady's finger–okra

lager–light, fizzy beer

left luggage–baggage check

lemonade–lemon-lime pop like 7-Up, fizzy

lemon squash–lemonade, not fizzy

let–rent

licenced–restaurant authorized to sell alcohol

lift–elevator

listed–protected historic building

loo–toilet or bathroom

lorry–truck

mac–mackintosh raincoat

mangetout–snow peas

marrow–summer squash

mate–buddy (boy or girl)

mean–stingy

mental–wild, memorable

mews–former stables converted to two-story rowhouses

mobile (MOH-bile)–cell phone

moggie–cat
motorway–freeway
naff–tacky or trashy
nappy–diaper
natter–talk on and on
neep–Scottish for turnip
newsagent–corner store
nought–zero
noughts & crosses–tic-tac-toe
off-licence–liquor store
on offer–for sale
panto, pantomime–fairy-tale play performed at Christmas (silly but fun)
pants–underwear, briefs
pasty (PASS-tee)–crusted savory (usually meat) pie from Cornwall
pavement–sidewalk
pear-shaped–messed up, gone wrong
petrol–gas
pillar box–mailbox
pissed (rude), **paralytic, bevvied, wellied, popped up, merry, trollied, ratted, rat-arsed, pissed as a newt**–drunk
pitch–playing field
plaster–Band-Aid
publican–pub owner
public school–private "prep" school (e.g., Eton)
pudding–dessert in general
pull, to be on the–on the prowl
punter–customer, especially in gambling
put a sock in it–shut up
queue–line
queue up–line up
quid–pound (£1)
randy–horny
rasher–slice of bacon
redundant, made–laid off
Remembrance Day–Veterans' Day

return ticket–round trip
ring up–call (telephone)
roundabout–traffic circle
rubber–eraser
rubbish–bad
sausage roll–sausage wrapped in a flaky pastry
Scotch egg–hard-boiled egg wrapped in sausage meat
self-catering–accommodation with kitchen
Sellotape–Scotch tape
services–freeway rest area
serviette–napkin
setee–couch
shag–intercourse (cruder than in the US)
shandy–lager and 7-Up
silencer–car muffler
single ticket–one-way ticket
skip–Dumpster
sleeping policeman–speed bumps
smalls–underwear
snogging–kissing, making out
sod–mildly offensive insult
sod it, sod off–screw it, screw off
soda–soda water (not pop)
solicitor–lawyer
spanner–wrench
spend a penny–urinate
stag night–bachelor party
starkers–buck naked
starters–appetizers
state school–public school
sticking plaster–Band-Aid
sticky tape–Scotch tape
stone–14 pounds (weight)
stroppy–bad-tempered
subway–underground walkway
suet–fat from animal rendering (sometimes used in cooking)
sultanas–golden raisins
surgical spirit–rubbing alcohol

suspenders–garters
suss out–figure out
swede–rutabaga
ta–thank you
take the mickey/take the piss–tease
tatty–worn out or tacky
taxi rank–taxi stand
telly–TV
tenement–stone apartment house (not necessarily a slum)
tenner–£10 bill
theatre–live stage
tick–a check mark
tight as a fish's bum–cheapskate (watertight)
tights–panty hose
tin–can
tip–public dump
tipper lorry–dump truck
top hole–first rate
top up–refill (a drink, mobile-phone credit, petrol tank, etc.)

torch–flashlight
towel, press-on–panty liner
towpath–path along a river
trainers–sneakers
Tube–subway
twee–quaint, cutesy
twitcher–bird-watcher
Underground–subway
verge–grassy edge of road
verger–church official
way out–exit
wee (adj)–small (Scottish)
wee (verb)–urinate
Wellingtons, wellies–rubber boots
whacked–exhausted
whinge (rhymes with hinge)–whine
wind up–tease, irritate
witter on–gab and gab
yob–hooligan
zebra crossing–crosswalk
zed–the letter Z

INDEX

INDEX

MAP INDEX

Free information and great gear t[o

▶ Plan Your Trip

Browse thousands of articles and a wealth of money-saving tips for planning your dream trip. You'll find up-to-date information on Europe's best destinations, packing smart, getting around, finding rooms, staying healthy, avoiding scams and more.

▶ Eurail Passes

Find out, step-by-step, if a rail pass makes sense for your trip—and how to avoid buying more than you need. Get a bunch of free extras!

▶ Graffiti Wall & Travelers' Helpline

Learn, ask, share—our online community of savvy travelers is a great resource for first-time travelers to Europe, as well as seasoned pros.

Rick Steves' Europe Through the Back Door, Inc.

NOW AVAILABLE

RICK STEVES APPS FOR THE iPHONE OR iPOD TOUCH

With these apps you can:

► Spin the compass icon to switch views between sights, hotels, and restaurant selections—and get details on cost, hours, address, and phone number.

► Tap any point on the screen to read Rick's detailed information, including history and suggested viewpoints.

► Get a deeper view into Rick's tours with audio and video segments.

Go to iTunes to download the following apps:

Rick Steves' Louvre Tour

Rick Steves' Historic Paris Walk

Rick Steves' Orsay Museum Tour

Rick Steves' Versailles

Rick Steves' Ancient Rome Tour

Rick Steves' St. Peter's Basilica Tour

Once downloaded, these apps are completely self-contained on your iPhone or iPod Touch, so you will not incur pricey roaming charges during use overseas.

Rick Steves books and DVDs are available at bookstores and through online booksellers.
Rick Steves guidebooks are published by Avalon Travel, a member of the Perseus Books Group.
Rick Steves apps are produced by Übermind, a boutique Seattle-based software consultancy firm.

Credits

Researchers
To help update this book, Rick relied on...

Gretchen Strauch

Gretchen lived in St. Andrews, Scotland, for one year, where she studied philosophy and medieval history; her subsequent addictions to Scrumpy Jack and British Kit Kats have kept her coming back ever since. Raised in rural California, she now lives in Seattle and edits Rick Steves guidebooks.

Lauren Mills

Lauren, a map editor and in-house search engine at Rick Steves, was an ardent Anglophile even before bringing home her British husband as a souvenir. They live in Seattle with their cat Keswick.

Tom Griffin

Tom fell in love with England thanks to Monty Python, William Shakespeare, and a crazy summer living in London's Earls Court neighborhood. Before joining the book department at Rick Steves, he was a magazine editor, newspaper reporter, and Berlitz teacher. He lives in Seattle with his wife.

Cathy McDonald

Cathy, an editor and researcher for Rick Steves, enjoys England's natural history and how it affects its people. She lives in Seattle, where she has written about the Pacific Northwest for more than 15 years as a free-lancer for *The Seattle Times*.

Contributor
Gene Openshaw

Gene is the co-author of seven Rick Steves books. For this book, he wrote material on Europe's art, history, and contemporary culture. When not traveling, Gene enjoys composing music, recovering from his 1973 trip to Europe with Rick, and living everyday life with his daughter.

Images

Location	Photographer
Front color matter: British Museum	Rick Steves
Front color matter: York Minster	Rick Steves
Introduction: Whitby	Cameron Hewitt
England: Salisbury Cathedral	Cameron Hewitt
London: Houses of Parliament	Rick Steves
Greenwich, Windsor, and Cambridge:	
Windsor's Changing of the Guard	Lauren Mills
Canterbury: Canterbury	Sarah Murdoch
Dover: White Cliffs of Dover	David C. Hoerlein
Brighton: Brighton Pier	Sarah Murdoch
Portsmouth:	
View from the Spinnaker Tower	Cameron Hewitt
Dartmoor: Dartmoor Ponies	Cameron Hewitt
Cornwall: Mousehole	Sarah Murdoch
Bath: Pulteney Bridge	Lauren Mills
Near Bath: Avebury Stone Circle	David C. Hoerlein
Oxford: Spires of Old Souls	Melanie Jeschke
The Cotswolds: Typical Cotswold Scene	Dominic Bonuccelli
Stratford-Upon-Avon:	
Anne Hathaway's Cottage	Rick Steves
Ironbridge Gorge: The Iron Bridge	Lauren Mills
Blackpool and Liverpool: Blackpool	Rick Steves
Lake District: Derwentwater	Rick Steves
York: York Minster	Rick Steves
North Yorkshire: Whitby Abbey	Cameron Hewitt
Durham and Northeast England:	
Durham Cathedral	David C. Hoerlein

Acknowledgements

Thanks to Roy and Jodi Nicholls for their research help, to Sarah Murdoch for writing the original version of the southern England chapters, to Melanie Jeschke for the original version of the Oxford chapter, and to friends listed in this book, who put the "Great" in Great Britain.

Rick Steves' Guidebook Series

Country Guides

Rick Steves' Best of Europe
Rick Steves' Croatia & Slovenia
Rick Steves' Eastern Europe
Rick Steves' England
Rick Steves' France
Rick Steves' Germany
Rick Steves' Great Britain
Rick Steves' Ireland
Rick Steves' Italy
Rick Steves' Portugal
Rick Steves' Scandinavia
Rick Steves' Spain
Rick Steves' Switzerland

City and Regional Guides

Rick Steves' Amsterdam, Bruges & Brussels
Rick Steves' Athens & the Peloponnese
Rick Steves' Budapest
Rick Steves' Florence & Tuscany
Rick Steves' Istanbul
Rick Steves' London
Rick Steves' Paris
Rick Steves' Prague & the Czech Republic
Rick Steves' Provence & the French Riviera
Rick Steves' Rome
Rick Steves' Venice
Rick Steves' Vienna, Salzburg & Tirol

Rick Steves' Phrase Books

French
French/Italian/German
German
Italian
Portuguese
Spanish

Other Books

Rick Steves' Europe 101: History and Art for the Traveler
Rick Steves' Europe Through the Back Door
Rick Steves' European Christmas
Rick Steves' Postcards from Europe
Rick Steves' Travel as a Political Act

Avalon Travel
a member of the Perseus Books Group
1700 Fourth Street
Berkeley, CA 94710

Text © 2009 by Rick Steves
Portions of this book appeared in *Rick Steves' Great Britain* © 2009, 2008, 2007, 2006, 2005, 2004, 2003, 2002, 2001
Maps © 2009 by Europe Through the Back Door. All rights reserved.

Printed in the U.S.A. by Worzalla
First printing November 2009

ISBN 978-1-59880-292-4
ISSN 1930-4617

For the latest on Rick's lectures, guidebooks, tours, public radio show, and public television series, contact Europe Through the Back Door, Box 2009, Edmonds, WA 98020, 425/771-8303, fax 425/771-0833, www.ricksteves.com, rick@ricksteves.com.

Europe Through the Back Door Reviewing Editors: Cameron Hewitt, Jennifer Madison Davis
ETBD Editors: Gretchen Strauch, Tom Griffin, Cathy McDonald, Sarah McCormic, Cathy Lu
ETBD Managing Editor: Risa Laib
Research Assistance: Gretchen Strauch, Lauren Mills, Tom Griffin, Cathy McDonald
Avalon Travel Senior Editor and Series Manager: Madhu Prasher
Avalon Travel Project Editor: Kelly Lydick
Copy Editor: Matthew Reed Baker
Proofreader: Jennifer Malnick
Indexer: Carl Wikander
Production and Layout: McGuire Barber Design
Cover Design: Kimberly Glyder Design
Graphic Content Director: Laura VanDeventer
Maps and Graphics: David C. Hoerlein, Laura VanDeventer, Brice Ticen, Lauren Mills, Barb Geisler, Pat O'Connor, Mike Morgenfeld
Front Matter Color Photos: British Museum, London © Rick Steves; York Minster, York © Rick Steves; London Eye © Dominic Bonuccelli; Bibury © Lauren Mills; Beachy Head © Cameron Hewitt; London Guards © Dominic Bonuccelli; Castlerigg © Rick Steves
Front Cover Photo: Arundel Castle © Cameron Hewitt
Additional Photography: Rick Steves, Cameron Hewitt, Sarah Murdoch, Gene Openshaw, Lauren Mills, Bruce VanDeventer, Melanie Jeschke, David C. Hoerlein, Jennifer Hauseman, Darbi Macy, Patrick Luscri